CLASSICS
IN
CHINESE PHILOSOPHY

CLASSICS IN CHINESE PHILOSOPHY

Edited by

WADE BASKIN
Southeastern State College

1974

LITTLEFIELD, ADAMS & CO.
Totowa, New Jersey

Published 1974 by
LITTLEFIELD, ADAMS & CO.

by arrangement with Philosophical Library, Inc.

Library of Congress Cataloging in Publication Data

Baskin, Wade, comp.
  Classics in Chinese Philosophy

  (A Littlefield, Adams Quality Paperback No. 274)
  Includes bibliographical references.
  1. Philosophy, Chinese—Collected works.   I. Title.
B125.B34   1974   181'.11   74-3244
ISBN 0-8226-0274-1

Printed in the United States of America

PREFACE

During the last century China has undergone more change than during any other period in its long and often turbulent history. Roughly a quarter of the world's population has been directly affected by the radical transformation that culminated in the establishment of the present Communist state — one which claims to have translated into reality the Confucian ideal of securing the equality of all men. In underdeveloped regions throughout the world, wherever the quest for social justice has been checked, millions of people have been indirectly affected by these changes. Western scholars, somewhat perplexed by what has already happened, are trying to determine the causes underlying the whole succession of events.

Believing that recent developments are best understood when viewed from a historical perspective, the editor of this work has tried to present in one volume a conspectus of the brilliant and many-sided development of Chinese philosophy.

The study of Chinese philosophy has been severely restricted by the difficulties of the classical literary style and, until recently, by the absence of reliable translations. Problems of terminology abound because the same Chinese term is translated differently in the works of different philosophers. I have endeavored in the introductory statement preceding each selection to help the reader to cope with these lexical problems. By adopting a chronological arrangement of the materials and calling attention to interlinking developments, I hope to have provided the reader with a practical means of familiarizing himself with the most important documents of the cultural heritage of China, the cradle of the world's oldest civilization, from the Confucian *Analects* to the theoretical statements of Mao Tse-tung.

W. B.

Thanks are due to Professor Jung Young Lee, of
the University of North Dakota, for kindly assisting
in checking proofs and text.

CONTENTS

Confucius

CONFUCIUS (551-478 B.C.). Though legend obscures his life, it is known that Confucius (K'ung Fu-tse) was born in Lu, was married at an early age, served as a public official, was eminently successful as a teacher, and continued throughout his lifetime to advocate social reform. He had at least one son and one daughter. His mother died when he was twenty-four, and he followed the ancient Chinese custom of retiring from active life to mourn her death for a period of three years. He devoted much time to meditation and to the study of history in order to become a statesman as well as a philosopher and devote himself to the task of reconstructing the moral and material welfare of the people. He began his teaching career at the age of thirty and soon attracted a large following. He also rose in the ranks of the administrative hierarchy, finally receiving an appointment as Minister of Crime and Chief Judge in his native province of Lu. He became a national hero, for it was said that his very appointment was equivalent to putting an end to crime; there were no cases to try. Eventually, however, he was ousted from his judicial position by jealous rivals. Somewhat disillusioned, he spent the rest of his life traveling from state to state with a few disciples, lecturing, and teaching. He devoted the last five years of his life to literary pursuits and died in 478 B.C., at the age of 73.

A traditionalist, he tried to reform society by educating people in what he thought to be the right traditions.

Central to his teachings is the ethical principle of the maintenance of *jen* (humanity, sympathy, human-heartedness, benevolence, reciprocity, or forbearance) between men. The bond of sympathy is preserved by the rectification of names (*cheng ming*). Every person should discharge the duties befitting his position in society: the ruler should rule, the minister should minister, a father should be a father, a son should be a son, etc. Each person should treat his subordinates as he would be treated by those holding positions superior to his own. Thus he was a reformer, but the reforms he championed were based on tradition.

The Tảo (way, course of nature, cosmic order, etc.), common to all Chinese philosophies, was to him a way of conduct leading to universal happiness. Divorced from religion or a clear concept of Heaven, his ethics was based on his observation of men in society. The right way is not rigid but allows the individual to choose his conduct according to his circumstances. Wisdom is to know man, virtue to love man. Virtue consists not only in the negative avoidance of extremes but also in the positive act of bringing these extremes into harmony.

For more than two thousand years after his death, his legacy exerted a dominant influence over the intellectual and political life of the Chinese people. Eventually the Confucian scriptures became the required texts in all education and the basis for selecting government officials through competitive examinations. Confucius claimed that he did not write the six classics (*Liu I*) but simply collected the legacy of the past. The six classics (*I Ching; Shih,* or the *Book of Odes; Shu,* or the *Book of History; Li,* or *Rituals; Yüeh,* or *Music;* and *Chun Chiu,* or *Spring and Autumn Annals*) were supplemented by Confucius' *Analects* and by the *Book of Mencius,* a collection of the teachings of his most illustrious follower. Confucius must be reckoned as the most important thinker in Chinese history and one of the most influential men in world history.

The Teachings of the Master

From *The Confucian Analects*, translated by William Jennings, London, George Routledge & Sons Limited, 1895.

ADVANTAGE, DESTINY AND DUTY

(5)

1. TOPICS on which the Master rarely spoke were — Advantage, and Destiny, and Duty of man to man.

2. A man of the village of Tah-hiang exclaimed of him, 'A great man is Confucius! — a man of extensive learning, and yet in nothing has he quite made himself a name!'

The Master heard of this, and mentioning it to his disciples he said, 'What then shall I take in hand? Shall I become a carriage-driver, or an archer? Let me be a driver!'

3. 'The (sacrificial) cap,' he once said, 'should, according to the Rules, be of linen; but in these days it is of pure silk. However, as it is economical, I do as all do.

'The Rule says, "Make your bow when at the lower end of the hall"; but nowadays the bowing is done at the upper part. This is great freedom; and I, though I go in *opposition* to the crowd, bow when at the lower end.'

4. The Master barred four (words); — he would have no 'shall's, no 'must's, no 'certainly's, no 'I's[1].

---

1. I believe I am alone in this method of interpretation, but think I am right. The teaching is against arbitrariness, obstinacy, and self-assertion. The last expression is literally 'no I's. There is nothing in the Chinese language equivalent to our inverted commas. See also next paragraph.

5. Once, in the town of K'wang, fearing (that his life was going to be taken), the Master exclaimed, 'King Wăn is dead and gone; but is not "*wăn*[1]" with you here? If Heaven be about to allow this "*wăn*" to perish, then they who survive *its* decease will get no benefit from it. But so long as Heaven does not allow it to perish, what can the men of K'wang do to me?'

6. A high State official, after questioning Tsz-kung, said 'Your Master is a sage, then? How many and what varied abilities must be his!'

The disciple replied, 'Certainly Heaven is allowing him full opportunities of becoming a sage, in addition to the fact that his abilities *are* many and varied.'

When the Master heard of this he remarked, 'Does that high official know me? In my early years my position in life was low, and *hence* my ability in many ways, though exercised in trifling matters. In the *gentleman* is there indeed such variety (of ability)? No.'

(From this, the disciple) Lau used to say, ' 'Twas a saying of the Master: "At a time when I was not called upon to use them, I acquired my proficiency in the polite arts." '

7. 'Am *I*, indeed,' said the Master, 'possessed of knowledge? I know nothing. Let a vulgar fellow come to me with a question, — a man with an emptyish head, — I may thrash out with him the matter to end, and exhaust myself in doing it.'

1. 'Wăn' was the honorary appellation of the great sage and ruler, whose praise is in the *Shi-King* as one of the founders of the Chow dynasty, and the term represented civic talent and virtues, as distinct from Wu, the martial talent — the latter being the honorary title of his son and successor. 'Wăn' also often stands for literature, polite accomplishments, *literae humaniores*. Here Confucius simply means, 'If you kill me, you kill a sage,' etc.

4

8. 'Ah!' exclaimed he once, 'the phoenix does not come! and no symbols issue from the river[1]! May I not as well give up?'

9. Whenever the Master met with a person in mourning, or with one in full-dress cap and kirtle, or with a blind person, although they might be *young* persons, he would make a point of rising on their appearance, or, if crossing their path, would do so with quickened step[2]!

10. Once Yen Yŭen[3] exclaimed with a sigh, (with reference to the Master's doctrines), 'If I look up to them, they are ever the higher; if I try to penetrate them, they are ever the harder; if I gaze at them as if before my eyes, lo, they are behind me! — Gradually and gently the Master with skill lures men on. By literary lore he gave me breadth; by the Rules of Propriety he narrowed me down. — When I desire a respite, I find it impossible; and after I have exhausted my powers, there seems to be something standing straight up in front of me, and though I have the mind to make towards it I make no advance at all.'

1. These birds, in Chinese fable and poetry, were supposed to appear as the harbingers of good, when virtuous men were numerous, and when the empire was about to become prosperous.

The 'symbols from the river' have reference also to an ancient fable, in which a dragon-horse emerged from the water with symbolic outlines on his back—lines which first suggested to the Emperor Fuh Hsi the eight mystic diagrams, afterwards the subject of the obscure Classic — the *I Ching*, or *Book of Changes*. No such omens of good, no such revelations from the spirit-world, *now!* Confucius does not neccessarily show that he believed in such fables.

2. This, in each case, to show his respect or sympathy. The 'mourning' should be, more strictly, *half-mourning*, or mourning attire long worn. The 'cap and kirtle' should also be cap, robe, and skirt, denoting a person of honourable position.

3. Hwúi.

11. Once when the Master was seriously ill, Tsz-lu induced the other disciples to feign they were high officials acting in his service. — During a respite from his malady the Master exclaimed, 'Ah! how long has Tsz-lu's conduct been false? Whom should *I* delude, if I were to pretend to have officials under me, having none? Should I deceive Heaven? Besides, were I to die, I would rather die in the hands of yourselves, my disciples, than in the hands of officials. And though I should fail to have a grand funeral over me, I should hardly be left on my death on the public highway, should I?'

12. Tsz-kung once said to him, 'Here is a fine gem. Would you guard it carefully in a casket and store it away, or seek a good price for it and sell it?' 'Sell it, indeed,' said the Master, — 'that would I; but I should wait for the bidder[1].'

13. The Master protested he would 'go and live among the nine wild tribes.[2]'

'A rude life,' said some one; — 'how could you put up with it?'

'What rudeness would there be,' he replied 'if a "superior man" was living in their midst?'

14. Once he remarked, 'After I came back from Wei to Lu the music was put right, and each of the Festal Odes and Hymns was given its appropriate place and use.'

---

1. By the 'fine gem' is said to have been meant the Master's own high qualification for official employment, which he seemed to set too little store upon. He sees the point in the question, and answers, 'I will wait till I am asked.'

2. By way of expressing his regret that his influence was so little among civilized folk.

6

15. 'Ah! which one of these following,' he asked on one occasion, 'are to be found (exemplified) in me,[1] — (proper) service rendered to superiors when abroad; duty to father and elder brother when at home; duty that shrinks from no exertion when dear ones die; and keeping free from the confusing effects of wine?'

16. Standing once on the bank of a mountain-stream, he said (musingly), 'Like this are those that pass away — no cessation, day or night[2]!'
Other sayings: —

17. 'I have not yet met with the man who loves Virtue as he loves Beauty.

18. 'Take an illustration from the making of a hill. A simple basketful is wanting to complete it, and the work stops. So I stop short.
'Take an illustration from the *levelling* of the ground. Suppose again just one basketful (is left), when the work has so progressed. There *I* desist[3]!

19. 'Ah! it was Hwúi, was it not? who, when I had given him his lesson, was the unflagging one!

20. 'Alas for Hwúi! I saw him (ever) making progress. I never saw him stopping short.

21. 'Blade, but no bloom, — or else bloom, but no produce; — ay, that is the way with some!

---

1. Chinese commentators think the question, as in 3.2, too self-depreciatory and make it mean, 'What is there in me *besides* these?'

2. I give the ordinary meaning of the words; some native commentators make them allude to changes in mundane matters, or things of time, or of the 'times'; and others take them as a hint to the disciples about unremitting study.

3. Admonition to his students to persevere with their learning to its completion.

7

22. 'Reverent regard is due to youth[1]. How know we what difference there may be in them in the future from what they are now? Yet when they have reached the age of forty or fifty, and are still unknown in the world, then indeed they are no more worthy of such regard.

23. 'Can any do otherwise than assent to words said to them by way of correction? Only let them reform by such advice, and it will then be reckoned valuable. Can any be other than pleased with words of gentle suasion? Only let them comply with them fully, and such will be accounted valuable. With those who are pleased without so complying, and those who assent but do not reform, I can do nothing at all.

24. (1) 'Give prominent place to loyalty and sincerity.
    (2) 'Have no associates (in study) who are not (advanced) somewhat like yourself.
    (3) 'When you have erred, be not afraid to correct yourself.

25. 'It may be possible to seize and carry off the chief commander of a large army,[2] but not possible so to rob one poor fellow of his will.

26. 'One who stands, — clad in hempen robe, the worse for wear, — among others clad in furs of fox and badger, and yet unabashed; — 'tis Tsz-lu, that, is it not?'

Tsz-lu used always to be humming over the lines —
    'From envy and enmity free,
    What deed doth he other than good[3]?

'How should such a rule of life,' asked the Master, 'be *sufficient* to make any one good?'

---

1. Almost exactly the *maxima debetur puero reverentia* of Juvenal.
2. Lit. three forces — each of 12,500 men.
3. *Shi-King*, I. iii. 8.

8

27. 'When the year grows chilly, we know the pine and cypress are the last to fade.'[1]

28. 'The wise escape doubt; the good-hearted, trouble; the bold, apprehension.

29. 'Some may study side by side, and yet be asunder when they come to the logic of things. Some may go on together in this latter course, but be wide apart in the standards they reach in it. Some, again, may together reach the same standard, and yet be diverse in weight (of character).'

30. 'The blossom is out on the cherry tree,
    With a flutter on every spray.
Dost think that my thoughts go not out to thee?
Ah, why art thou far away[2]!'

(Commenting on these lines) the Master said 'There can hardly have been much "though going out." What does distance signify?'

PROPRIETY, VIRTUE, AND FRIENDSHIP
(8)

1. Yen Yüen was asking about man's proper regard for his fellow-man. The Master said to him, 'Self-control, and a habit of falling back upon propriety, (virtually) effect it. Let these conditions be fulfilled for one day, and every one round will betake himself to the duty. Is it to begin in oneself, or think you, indeed; it is to begin in others?'

---

1. Good men are like the evergreens.
2. From a spring-song — one of the pieces expurgated by Confucius from the collection out of which he compiled the *Shi-King*. The point of his little comment is not very clear.

9

'I wanted you to be good enough,' said Yen Yüen, 'to give me a brief synopsis of it.'

Then said the Master, 'Without propriety use not your eyes; without it use not your ears, nor your tongue, nor a limb of your body.'

'I may be lacking in diligence,' said Yen Yuen, 'but with your favour I will endeavour to carry out this advice.'

2. Chung-kung asked about man's proper regard for his fellows.

To him the Master replied thus: — 'When you go forth from your door, be as if you were meeting some guest of importance. When you are making use of the common people (for State purposes), be as if you were taking part in a great religious function. Do not set before others what you do not desire yourself. Let there be no resentful feelings against you when you are away in the country, and none when at home.'

'I may lack diligence,' said Chung-kung, 'but with your favour I will endeavour to carry out this advice.'

3. Sz-ma Niu[1] asked the like question. The answer he received was this: — 'The words of the man who has a proper regard for his fellows are uttered with difficulty.'

' "His words — uttered with difficulty"?' he echoed (in surprise). 'Is that what is meant by proper regard for one's fellow-creatures?'

'Where there is difficulty in *doing*,' the Master replied, 'will there not be some difficulty in *utterance*?'

4. The same disciple put a question about the 'superior man.' — 'Superior men,' he replied, 'are free from trouble and apprehension.'

' "Free from trouble and apprehension!" ' said he. 'Does *that* make them "superior men"?'

---

1. Another disciple. Each seems to have been answered according to his ability or character.

10

The Master added, 'Where there is found, upon intro-spection, to be no chronic disease, how shall there be any trouble? how shall there be any apprehension?'

5. The same disciple, being in trouble, remarked, 'I am alone in having no brother, while all else have theirs — younger or elder.'

Tsz-hiá said to him, 'I have heard this[1]: "Death and life have destined times; wealth and honours rest with Heaven. Let the superior man keep watch over himself without ceas-ing, showing deference to others, with propriety of man-ners, — and all within the four seas[2] will be his brethren. How should he be distressed for lack of brothers!"'

6. Tsz-chang asked what (sort of man) might be termed 'enlightened.'

The Master replied, 'That man, with whom drenching slander and cutting calumny gain no currency, may well be called enlightened. Ay, he with whom such things make no way may well be called enlightened in the extreme[3].'

7. Tsz-kung put a question relative to government. — In reply the Master mentioned (three essentials): — sufficient food, sufficient armament, and the people's confidence.

'But,' said the disciple, 'if you cannot really have all three, and one has to be given up, which would you give up first?'

'The armament,' he replied.

'And if you are obliged to give up one of the remaining two, which would it be?'

'The food,' said he. 'Death has been the portion of all men from of old. Without the people's trust nothing can stand.'

---

1. From Confucius, it is generally thought.

2. The supposed boundaries of the earth; but evidently, as in the *Shi-King*, IV. v. 3, a *meiosis* for the empire.

3. This is no proper answer, but it had doubtless reference to some circumstances unmentioned.

11. Duke King of Ts'i consulted Confucius about government. — His answer was, 'Let a prince be a prince, and ministers be ministers; let fathers be fathers, and sons be sons.'

'Good!' exclaimed the duke; 'truly if a prince fail to be a prince, and ministers to be ministers, and if fathers be not fathers, and sons not sons, then, even though I may have my allowances of grain[1], should I ever be able to relish it?'

13. 'In *hearing* causes, I am like other men,' said the Master. 'The great point is — to *prevent* litigation.'

14. Tsz-chang having raised some question about government, the Master said to him, 'In the settlement of its (principles) be unwearied; in its administration — see to that loyally.'

15. 'The man of wide research,' said he, 'who also restrains himself by the Rules of Propriety, is not likely to transgress.'

16. Again, 'The noble-minded man makes the most of others' good qualities, not the worst of their bad ones. Men of small mind do the reverse of this.'

18. Ki K'ang, being much troubled on account of robbers abroad, consulted Confucius on the matter. He received this reply: 'If you, sir, were not covetous, neither would they steal, even were you to bribe them to do so.'

19. Ki K'ang, when consulting Confucius about the government, said, 'Suppose I were to put to death the disorderly for the better encouragement of the orderly; — what say you to that?'

'Sir,' replied Confucius, 'in the administration of government why resort to capital punishment? Covet what is good,

---

1. I.e. revenue, or personal allowance from the State.

and the people will be good. The virtue of the noble-minded man is as the wind, and that of inferior men as grass; the grass must bend, when the wind blows upon it.'

20. Tsz-chang asked how (otherwise) he would describe the learned official who might be termed influential.

'What, I wonder, do you mean by one who is influential?' said the Master.

'I mean,' replied the disciple, 'one who is sure to have a reputation throughout the country, as well as at home.'

'That,' said the Master, 'is reputation, not influence. The influential man, then, if he be one who is genuinely straight-forward and loves what is just and right, a discriminator of men's words, and an observer of their looks, and in honour careful to prefer others to himself — will certainly have in-fluence, both throughout the country and at home. — The man of (mere) reputation, on the other hand, who spe-ciously affects philanthropy, though in his way of proce-dure he acts contrary to it, while yet quite evidently en-grossed with that virtue, — will certainly have reputation, both in the country and at home.'

21. Fan Ch'i, strolling with him over the ground below the place of the rain-dance, said to him, 'I venture to ask how to raise the standard of virtue, how to reform dissolute habits, and how to discern what is illusory?'

'Ah! a good question indeed!' he exclaimed. 'Well, is not putting duty first, and success second, a way of raising the standard of virtue? And is not attacking the evil in one-self, and not the evil which is in others, a way of reform-ing dissolute habits? And as to illusions, is not one morning's fit of anger, causing a man to forget himself, and even in-volving in the consequences those who are near and dear to him, — is not that an illusion?'

22. The same disciple asked him what was meant by 'a right regard for one's fellow-creatures.' He replied, 'It is love to man.'

13

Asked by him again what was meant by wisdom, he replied, 'It is knowledge of man.'

Fan Ch'i did not quite grasp his meaning.

The Master went on to say, 'Lift up the straight, set aside the crooked, so can you make the crooked straight.'

Fan Ch'i left him, and meeting with Tsz-Hiá he said, 'I had an interview just now with the Master, and I asked him what wisdom was. In his answer he said, "Lift up the straight, set aside the crooked, and so can you make the crooked straight." What was his meaning?'

'Ah! words rich in meaning, those,' said the other. 'When Shun was emperor, and was selecting his men from among the multitude, he "lifted up" Káu-yáu; and men devoid of right feelings towards their kind went far away. And when T'ang was emperor, and chose out his men from the crowd, he "lifted up" I-yin, — with the same result.[1]

23. Tsz-kung was consulting him about a friend. 'Speak to him frankly, and respectfully,' said the Master, 'and gently lead him on. If you do not succeed, then stop; do not submit yourself to indignity.'

24. The learned Tsang observed, 'In the society of books the "superior man" collects his friends; in the society of his friends he is furthering goodwill among men.'

THE ART OF GOVERNING
(9)

1. Tsz-lu was asking about government. 'Lead the way in it,' said the Master, 'and work hard at it.'

Requested to say more, he added, 'And do not tire of it.'

---

1. The former was made Minister of Crime and Controller of the frontier tribes, and it is chiefly to him that the glories of Shun's reign are attributed. The latter was T'ang's prime minister, and he is spoken of as the destroyer of the Hiá dynasty and founder of the Shang (or Yin).

2. Chung-kung, on being made first minister to the Chief of the Ki family, consulted the Master about government, and to him he said, 'Let the heads of offices *be* heads. Excuse small faults. Promote men of sagacity and talent.'

'But,' he asked, 'how am I to know the sagacious and talented, before promoting them?'

'Promote those whom you do know,' said the Master. 'As to those of whom you are uncertain, will *others* omit to notice them?'

3. Tsz-lu said to the Master, 'As the prince of Wei, sir, has been waiting for you to act for him in his government, what is it your intention to take in hand first?'

'One thing of necessity,' he answered, — 'the rectification of terms[1].'

'That!' exclaimed Tsz-lu. 'How far away you are, sir! Why such rectification?'

'What a rustic you are, Tsz-lu!' rejoined the Master. 'A gentleman would be a little reserved and reticent in matters which he does not understand. — If terms be incorrect, language will be incongruous; and if language be incongruous, deeds will be imperfect. — So, again, when deeds are imperfect, propriety and harmony cannot prevail, and when this is the case laws relating to crime will fail in their aim; if these last so fail, the people will not know where to set hand or foot. — Hence, a man of superior mind, certain first of his terms, is fitted to speak; and being certain of what he says can proceed upon it. In the language of such a person there is nothing *heedlessly irregular,* — and that is the sum of the matter.'

4. Fan Ch'i requested that he might learn something of husbandry. '(For *that*)' said the Master, 'I am not equal to an old husbandman.' Might he then learn something of

1. See 8. 11: 'Let a prince be a prince,' etc.

gardening?' he asked. 'I am not equal to an old gardener[1],' was the reply.

'A man of little mind, that!' said the Master, when Fan Ch'i had gone out. 'Let a man who is set over the people love propriety, and they will not presume to be disrespectful. Let him be a lover of righteousness, and they will not presume to be aught but submissive. Let him love faithfulness and truth, and they will not presume not to lend him their hearty assistance. Ah, if all this only *were* so, the people from all sides would come to such a one, carrying their children on their backs. What need to turn his hand to husbandry?'

5. 'Though a man,' said he, 'could hum through the *Odes* — the three hundred — yet should show himself unskilled when given some administrative work to do for his country; though he might know *much* (of that other lore), yet if, when sent on a mission to any quarter, he could answer no question personally and unaided, what after all is he good for?'

6. 'Let (a leader),' said he, 'show rectitude in his own personal character, and even without directions from him things will go well. If he be not personally upright, his directions will not be complied with.'

7. Once he made the remark, 'The governments of Lu and of Wei are in brotherhood.[2]'

8. Of King, a son of the duke of Wei, he observed that 'he managed his household matters well. On his coming into possession, he thought, "What a strange conglomeration!" — Coming to possess a little more, it was, "Strange, such a

---

1. A commentator (Yen Ts'an) gives the proverb, 'About ploughing ask the labourer, about weaving ask the maid.'
2. The States had been held at the beginning of the dynasty by two brothers, and they had now fared much in the same way for centuries.

result!" And when he became wealthy, "Strange, such elegance.[1]"'

9. The Master was on a journey to Wei, and Yen Yu was driving him. — 'What multitudes of people!' he exclaimed. Yen Yu asked him, 'Seeing they are so numerous, what more would you do for them?'

'Enrich them,' replied the Master[2].

'And after enriching them, what more would you do for them?'

'Instruct them.'

10. 'Were any one (of our princes) to employ me,' he said, 'after a twelvemonth I might have made some tolerable progress; but give me three years, and my work should be done.'

11. Again, 'How true is that saying, "Let good men have the management of a country for a century, and they would be adequate to cope with evildoers, and thus do away with capital punishments."'

12. Again, 'Suppose (the ruler) to possess true kingly qualities, then surely after one generation[3] there would be good-will among men.'

13. Again, 'Let a ruler but see to his own rectitude, and what trouble will he then have in the work before him? If he be unable to rectify himself, how is he to rectify others?'

1. His excellent management is to be seen in his gradual prosperity, but his indifference about wealth is noted at the various stages of it.

2. We find Mencius inculcating the same ideas. How true they are! The first thing is to raise the material welfare of a people; they will then, says Mencius, 'have a fixed heart;' and it will be easier to raise their morals. 'Wealth,' says Mr. Danson (*Wealth of Households*, Clarendon Press), 'is not virtue; but it tends to make virtue easy.... To use it well is to elevate in the scale of being all over whom we have influence.... We must needs think of "the Good Samaritan" as of one who had pence to spare.'

3. The Chinese reckon a generation at 30 years.

14. Once when Yen Yu was leaving the Court, the Master accosted him. 'Why so late?' he asked. 'Busy with legislation,' Yen replied. 'The details[1] of it,' suggested the Master; 'had it been legislation, I should have been there to hear it, even though I am not in office.'

15. Duke Ting asked if there were one sentence which (if acted upon) might have the effect of making a country prosperous.

Confucius answered, 'A sentence could hardly be supposed to do so much as that. But there is a proverb people use which says, "To play the prince is hard, to play the minister not easy." Assuming that it is *understood* that "to play the prince is hard," would it not be *probable* that with that one sentence the country should be made to prosper?'

'Is there, then,' he asked, 'one sentence which (if acted upon) would have the effect of ruining a country?'

Confucius again replied, 'A sentence could hardly be supposed to do so much as that. But there is a proverb men have which says, "Not gladly would I play the prince, unless my words were ne'er withstood." Assuming that the (words) were good, and that none withstood them, would not that also be good? But assuming that they were *not* good, and yet none withstood them, would it not be probable that with one saying he would work his country's ruin?'

19. Fan Ch'i was asking him about duty to one's fellow-men. 'Be courteous,' he replied, 'in your private sphere; be serious in any duty you take in hand to do; be leal-hearted in your intercourse with others. Even though you were to go amongst the wild tribes, it would not be right for you to neglect these duties.'

1. Yen Yu was in the service of the ambitious Chief of the Ki family. The Master thought that business there should be executive rather than legislative. The commentators, however, suppose he meant the family affairs.

20. In answer to Tsz-kung, who asked 'how he would characterize one who could fitly be called "learned official"?' the Master said, 'He may be so called who in his private life is affected with a sense of his own unworthiness, and who, when sent on a mission to any quarter of the empire, would not disgrace his prince's commands.'

'May I presume,' said his questioner, 'to ask what sort you would put next to such?'

'Him who is spoken of by his kinsmen as a dutiful son, and whom the folks of his neighbourhood call "good brother."'

'May I venture to ask whom you would place next in order?'

'Such as are sure to be true to their word, and effective in their work. . . .

23. 'The nobler-minded man,' he remarked, 'will be agreeable even when he disagrees; the small minded man will agree and be disagreeable.'

24. Tsz-kung was consulting him, and asked, 'What say you of a person who was liked by all in his village?'

'That will scarcely do,' he answered.

'What, then, if they all *dis*liked him?'

'That, too,' said he, 'is scarcely enough. Better if he were liked by the *good* folk in the village, and disliked by the *bad*.'

25. 'The superior man,' he once observed, 'is easy to serve, but difficult to please. Try to please him by the adoption of wrong principles, and you will fail. Also, when such a one employs others, he uses them according to their capacity. — The inferior man is, on the other hand, difficult to serve, but easy to please. Try to please *him* by the adoption of wrong principles, and you will succeed. And when *he* employs others he requires them to be fully prepared (for everything).'

19

26. Again, 'The superior man can be high without being haughty. The inferior man can be haughty if not high.'

27. 'The firm, the unflinching, the plain and simple, the slow to speak,' said he once, 'are approximating towards their duty to their fellowmen.'

28. Tsz-lu asked how he would characterize one who might fitly be called an educated gentleman. The Master replied, 'He who can properly be so called will have in him a seriousness of purpose, a habit of controlling himself, and an agreeableness of manner: among his friends and associates the seriousness and the self-control, and among his brethren the agreeableness of manner[1].'

PRACTICAL WISDOM

(11)

Other sayings of the Master: —

11. 'They who care not for the morrow will the sooner have their sorrow.

12. 'Ah, 'tis hopeless! I have not yet met with the man who loves Virtue as he loves Beauty.

13. 'Was not Tsang Wăn like one who surreptitiously came by the post he held? He knew the worth of Hwúi of Liu-hiá[2], and could not stand in his presence.

14. 'Be generous yourself, and exact little from others; then you banish complaints.

---

1. Poor Tsz-lu was wanting in all these qualifications, and the reply was, as usual, limited to what *he* had yet to learn.
2. A high official in Lu about fifty years before Confucius.

15. 'With one who does not come to me inquiring "What of this?" and "What of that?" I never can ask "What of this?" and give him up.

16. 'If a number (of students) are all day together, and in their conversation never approach the subject of righteousness, but are fond merely of giving currency to smart little sayings, they are difficult indeed (to manage).

17. 'When the "superior man" regards righteousness as the thing material, gives operation to it according to the rules of propriety, lets it issue in humility, and become complete in sincerity, — there indeed is your superior man!

18. 'The trouble of the superior man will be his own want of ability: it will be no trouble to him that others do not know him.

19. 'Such a man thinks it hard to end his days and leave a name to be no longer named.

20. 'The superior man is exacting of himself; the common man is exacting of others.

21. 'A superior man has self-respect, and does not strive; is sociable, yet no party man.

22. 'He does not promote a man because of his words, nor pass over the words because of the man.'

23. Tsz-kung put to him the question, 'Is there one word upon which the whole life may proceed?'
The Master replied, 'Is not RECIPROCITY such a word?[1] — what you do not yourself desire, do not put before others.'

---

1. I render the word as Dr. Legge has done, but with a little hesitation. The dictionaries give the meaning as benevolence, forbearance, considerateness, sympathy, to excuse, to bear patiently, etc.

26. 'Artful speech is the confusion of Virtue. Impatience over little things introduces confusion into great schemes.

27. 'What is disliked by the masses needs inquiring into; so also does that which they have a preference for.

28. 'A man may give breadth to his principles: it is not principles (in themselves) that give breadth to the man.

29. 'Not to retract after committing an error may itself be called error.

30. 'If I have passed the whole day without food and the whole night without sleep, occupied with my thoughts, it profits me nothing: I were better engaged in learning.

31. 'The superior man deliberates upon how he may walk in truth, not upon what he may eat. The farmer may plough, and be on the way to want: the student learns, and on his way to emolument. To live a right life is the concern of men of nobler minds: poverty gives them none.

'If there be intellectual attainments, and the humanity within *is* powerful enough to keep guard over them, yet, unless (in a ruler) there be dignity in his rule, the people will fail to show him respect.

'Again, given the intellectual attainments, and humanity sufficient to keep watch over them, and also dignity in ruling, yet if his movements be not in accordance with the Rules of Propriety, he is not yet fully qualified.

33. 'The superior man may not be conversant with petty details, and yet may have important matters put into his hands. The inferior man may not be charged with important matters, yet may be conversant with the petty details.

34. 'Good-fellowship is more to men than fire and water. I have seen men stepping into fire and into water, and meeting with death thereby; I have not yet seen a man die from planting his steps in the path of good-fellowship.

35. 'Rely upon good-nature. 'Twill not allow precedence (even) to a teacher.

36. 'The superior man is inflexibly upright, and takes not things upon trust.

37. 'In serving your prince, make your service the serious concern, and let salary be a secondary matter.

38. 'Where instruction is to given, there must be no distinction of persons[1].

39. 'Where men's methods are not identical, there can be no planning by one on behalf of another.

40. 'In speaking, perspicuity is all that is needed.'

AUTHORITY, KNOWLEDGE, AND THE SUPERIOR MAN
(12)

2. 'When the empire is well ordered,' said Confucius, 'it is from the emperor[2] that edicts regarding ceremonial, music, and expeditions to quell (rebellion) go forth. When it is being ill governed, such edicts emanate from the feudal lords; and when the latter is the case, it will be strange if in ten generations there is not a collapse. If they emanate (merely) from the high officials, it will be strange if the collapse do not come in five generations. When the State-edicts are in the hands of the subsidiary ministers, it will be strange if in *three* generations there is no collapse.

'When the empire is well ordered, government is not (left) in the hands of high officials.

'When the empire is well ordered, the common people will cease to discuss (public matters).'

1. He made none in the case of his own son, and note thereon.
2. Lit. the Son of Heaven.

23

4. 'There are,' said he, 'three kinds of friendships which are profitable, and three which are detrimental. To make friends with the upright, with the trustworthy, with the experienced[1], is to gain benefit; to make friends with the subtly perverse, with the artfully pliant, with the subtle in speech, is detrimental.'

5. Again, 'There are three kinds of pleasure which are profitable, and three which are detrimental. To take pleasure in going regularly through the various branches of Ceremonial and Music[2], in speaking of others' goodness, in having many worthy wise friends, is profitable. To take pleasure in wild *bold* pleasures, in idling carelessly about, in the (too) jovial accompaniments of feasting, is detrimental.'

6. Again, 'Three errors there be, into which they who wait upon their superior may fall: — (1) to speak before the opportunity comes to them to speak, which I call heedless haste; (2) refraining from speaking when the opportunity has come, which I call concealment; and (3) speaking, regardless of the mood he is in[3], which I call blindness.'

7. Again, 'Three things a superior should guard against: — (1) against the lusts of the flesh in his earlier years while the vital powers[4] are not fully developed and fixed, (2) against the spirit of combativeness when he has come to the age of robust manhood and when the vital powers are matured and strong, and (3) against ambitiousness when old age has come on and the vital powers have become weak and decayed.

1. Lit. those who have heard much, or learnt much.
2. The first as leading to propriety, the second as tending to general *bon accord*.
3. Lit. without noticing the expression on his face.
4. Lit. blood and breath. This age is put down by one commentator as that below 29.

8. 'Three things also such a man greatly reveres: — (1) the ordinances of Heaven, (2) great men, (3) words of sages. — The inferior man knows not the ordinances of Heaven and therefore reveres them not, is unduly familiar in the presence of great men, and scoffs at the words of sages.

9. 'They whose knowledge comes by birth are of all men the first (in understanding); they to whom it comes by study are next; men of poor intellectual capacity, who yet study, may be added as a yet inferior class; and lowest of all are they who are poor in intellect and never learn.

10. 'Nine things there are of which the superior man should be mindful: — to be clear in vision, quick in hearing, genial in expression, respectful in demeanour, true in word, serious in duty, inquiring in doubt, firmly self-controlled in anger, just and fair when way to success opens out before him.'

I CHING (BOOK OF CHANGES) is one of the Confucian classics. Though some of the commentaries now included in *I Ching* (also called *Yî King*) have been ascribed to him, Confucius claimed that he had simply collected the materials that make up this work and the five other works representing the Chinese legacy. Legend ascribes the eight trigrams from which the whole system of *I Ching* was developed to Fu Hsi (2953-2838 B.C.), the first of the Five Emperors, the sixty-four hexagrams to King Wắn (r. 1171-1122 B.C.), and the explanatory texts to Duke Kâu (d. 1094 B.C.). Fu Hsi is said to have constructed his trigrams from the markings on the back of a tortoise. The seven commentaries that follow the hexagrams and the explanatory texts, though attributed to Confucius, are probably the work of many hands over a considerable period of time, from as early as the sixth century B.C. to the third century B.C. *I Ching* has the distinction of being a work cherished not only by Confucianists but also by Taoists.

Each of the sixty-four hexagrams has a name and is formed by two trigrams, each consisting of three lines, divided or undivided. These hexagrams relate to the ancient practice of divination based on the markings on burned tortoise shells, and in later, more simplified procedures, on prescribed arrangements of milfoil stalks. The cryptic texts that follow each hexagram yield no definite philosophical conclusions but enabled commentators to trace the outline of a rational approach to a dynamic universe. A divided line represents the weak principle of the universe (*yin*), an undivided line, the strong principle (*yang*).

I Ching had a powerful impact on Neo-Confucians, who quoted it frequently and wrote commentaries on it. The ancient work is said to have intrigued Confucius and to have exerted more influence on philosophy than any other Confucian classic. C. G. Jung and Hermann Hesse, like many other twentieth-century thinkers, testify to its enduring appeal.

27

I Ching (Book of Changes)

From *I Ching*, translated by James Legge. Published in a second edition in 1899 by Clarendon Press as Volume XVI of "The Sacred Books of the East."

I THE *KH*IEN HEXAGRAM

CH'IEN

Explanation of the entire figure by King Wăn

KHIEN (represents) what is great and originating, penetrating, advantageous, correct and firm.

Explanation of the separate lines by the duke of Kâu

1. In the first (or lowest) NINE, undivided, (we see its subject as) the dragon lying hid (in the deep). It is not the time for active doing.

2. In the second NINE, *undivided*, (we see its subject as) the dragon appearing in the field. It will be advantageous to meet with the great man.

3. In the third NINE, undivided, (we see its subject as) the superior man active and vigilant all the day, and in the evening still careful and apprehensive. (The position is) dangerous, but there will be no mistake.

4. In the fourth NINE, undivided, (we see its subject as the dragon looking) as if he were leaping up, but still in the deep. There will be no mistake.

5. In the fifth NINE, undivided (we see its subject as) the dragon on the wing in the sky. It will be advantageous to meet with the great man.

6. In the sixth (or topmost) NINE, undivided, (we see its subject as) the dragon exceeding the proper limits. There will be occasion for repentance.

7. (The lines of this hexagram are all strong and undivided, as appears from) the use of the number NINE. If the host of dragons (thus) appearing were to divest themselves of their heads, there would be good fortune.

The Text under each hexagram consists of one paragraph by king Wăn, explaining the figure as a whole, and of six (in the case of hexagrams 1 and 2, of seven) paragraphs by the duke of Kâu, explaining the individual lines. The explanatory notices introduced above to this effect will not be repeated. A double space will be used to mark off the portion of king Wăn from that of his son.

Each hexagram consists of two of the trigrams of Fû-hsî, the lower being called 'the inner,' and the one above 'the outer.' The lines, however, are numbered from one to six, commencing with the lowest. To denote the number of it and of the sixth line, the terms for 'commencing' and 'topmost' are used. The intermediate lines are simply 'second,' 'third,' etc. As the lines must be either whole or divided, technically called strong and weak, yang and yin, this distinction is indicated by the application to them of the numbers nine and six. All whole lines are nine, all divided lines, six.

Two explanations have been proposed of this application of these numbers. The Khien trigram, it is said, contains 3 strokes (☰), and the Khwăn 6 (☷). But the yang contains the yin in itself, and its representative number will be $3+6=9$, while the yin, not containing the yang, will only have its own number or 6. This explanation, entirely arbitrary, is now deservedly abandoned. The other is based on the use of the 'four Hsiang,' or emblematic figures (⚌ the great or old yang, ⚍ the young yang, ⚎ the old yin, and ⚏ the young yin). To these are assigned (by what process is unimportant for our present purpose) the numbers 9, 8, 7, 6. They were 'the old yang,' represented by 9, and 'the old yin,' represented by 6, that, in the manipulation of the stalks to form new diagrams, determined the changes of figure; and so 9 and 6 came to be used as the names of a yang line and a yin line respectively. This explanation is now universally acquiesced in. The nomenclature of first nine, nine two, etc., or first six, six two, etc., however, is merely a jargon; and I have preferred to use, instead of it, in the translation, in order to describe the lines, the names 'undivided' and 'divided.'

29

K h w ă n (represents) what is great and originating, penetrating, advantageous, correct and having the firmness of a mare. When the superior man (here intended) has to make any movement, if he take the initiative, he will go astray; if he follow, he will find his (proper) lord. The advantageousness will be seen in his getting friends in the south-west, and losing friends in the north-east. If he rest in correctness and firmness, there will be good fortune.

1. In the first six, divided, (we see its subject) treading on hoarfrost. The strong ice will come (by and by).

2. The second six, divided, (shows the attribute of) being straight, square, and great. (Its operation), without repeated efforts, will be in every respect advantageous.

3. The third six, divided, (shows its subject) keeping his excellence under restraint, but firmly maintaining it. If he should have occasion to engage in the king's service, though he will not claim the success (for himself), he will bring affairs to a good issue.

4. The fourth six, divided, (shows the symbol of) a sack tied up. There will be no ground for blame or for praise.

5. The fifth six, divided, (shows) the yellow lower garment. There will be great good fortune.

6. The sixth six, divided (shows) dragons fighting in the wild. Their blood is purple and yellow.

7. (The lines of this hexagram are all weak and divided, as appears from) the use of the number six. If those (who are thus represented) be perpetually correct and firm, advantage will arise.

APPENDIX I

SECTION I

I. 1. Vast is the 'great and originating (power)' indicated by Khien! All things owe to it their beginning: — it contains all the meaning belonging to (the name) heaven.

2. The clouds move and the rain is distributed; the various things appear in their developed forms.

3. (The sages) grandly understand (the connexion between) the end and the beginning, and how (the indications of) the six lines (in the hexagram) are accomplished, (each) in its season. (Accordingly) they mount (the carriage) drawn by those six dragons at the proper times, and drive through the sky.

4. The method of Khien is to change and transform, so that everything obtains its correct nature as appointed (by the mind of Heaven); and (there-after the conditions of) great harmony are preserved in union. The result is 'what is advantageous, and correct and firm.'

5. (The sage) appears aloft, high above all things, and the myriad states all enjoy repose.

II. 1. Complete is the 'great and originating (capacity)' indicated by K h w ă n ! All things owe to it their birth; — it receives obediently the influences of Heaven.

2. K h w ă n, in its largeness, supports and contains all things. Its excellent capacity matches the unlimited power (of Khien). Its comprehension is wide, and its brightness great. The various things obtain (by it) their full development.

3. The mare is a creature of earthly kind. Its (power of) moving on the earth is without limit; it is mild and docile, advantageous and firm: — such is the course of the superior man.

31

4. 'If he take the initiative, he goes astray:' — he misses, that is, his proper course. 'If he follow,' he is docile, and gets into his regular (course). 'In the south-west he will get friends:' — he will be walking with those of his own class. 'In the north-east he will lose friends:' — but in the end there will be ground for congratulation.

5. 'The good fortune arising from resting in firmness' corresponds to the unlimited capacity of the earth.

APPENDIX II

Treatise on the Symbolism of the Hexagrams, and of the duke of Kâu's Explanations of the several Lines.

Like the Text under each hexagram, what is said under each in this treatise on its symbolism is divided into two portions. The first is called 'the Great Symbolism,' and is occupied with the trigrammatic composition of the hexagram, to the statement of which is always subjoined an exhibition of the use which should, or has been, made of the lesson suggested by the meaning of the whole figure in the administration of affairs, or in self-government. If the treatise be rightly ascribed to Confucius, this practical application of the teaching of the symbols is eminently characteristic of his method in inculcating truth and duty; though we often find it difficult to trace the connexion between his premiss and conclusion. This portion of the treatise will be separated by a double space from what follows, — 'the Lesser Symbolism,' in the explanations of the several lines.

I. *Khi*en is formed by redoubling the trigram of the same name. In the case of other hexagrams of similar formation, the repetition of the trigram is pointed out. That is not done here, according to Fû Hsî, 'because there is but one heaven.' But the motion of heaven is a complete revolution every day, resumed again the next; so moves 'the unwearied sun from day to day,' making it a good symbol of renewed, untiring effort.

II. Khwăn is formed by redoubling the trigram of the same name and having 'the earth for its symbol.' As in the former hexagram, the repetition is emphatic, not otherwise affecting the meaning of the hexagram. 'As there is but one heaven,' says Fû Hsî, 'so there is but one earth.' The first part of 'the Great Symbolism' appears in Canon McClatchie's version as — 'Khwăn is the generative part of earth.' By 'generative part' he probably means 'the productive or prolific faculty.' If he mean anything else, there comes out a conclusion antagonistic to his own view of the 'mythology' of the Yî. The character Shî, which he translates by 'generative part,' is defined in Dr. Williams' dictionary as 'the virility of males.' Such is the special significance of it. If it were so used here, the earth would be masculine.

SECTION I

I. Heaven, in its motion, (gives the idea of) strength. The superior man, in accordance with this, nerves himself to ceaseless activity.

1. 'The dragon lies hid in the deep; — it is not the time for active doing:' — (this appears from) the strong and undivided line's being in the lowest place.

2. 'The dragon appears in the field:' — the diffusion of virtuous influence has been wide.

3. 'Active and vigilant all the day:' — (this refers to) the treading of the (proper) path over and over again.

4. 'He seems to be leaping up, but is still in the deep:' — if he advance, there will be no error.

5. 'The dragon is on the wing in the sky:' — the great man rouses himself to his work.

6. 'The dragon exceeds the proper limits; — there will be occasion for repentance:' — a state of fulness, that is, should not be indulged in long.

7. 'The same NINE (undivided) used' (in all the places of this hexagram), but the attribute of heaven (thereby denoted) should not (always) take the foremost place.

II. The (capacity and sustaining) power of the earth is what is denoted by K h w ă n. The superior man, in accordance with this, with his large virtue supports (men and) things.

1. 'He is treading on hoarfrost; — the strong ice will come (by and by):' — the cold (air) has begun to take form. Allow it to go on quietly according to its nature, and (the hoarfrost) will come to strong ice.

2. The movements indicated by the second SIX, (divided), is 'from the straight (line) to the square.' '(Its opera-

tion), without repeated effort, in every way advantageous,' shows the brilliant result of the way of earth.

3. 'He keeps his excellence under restraint, but firmly maintains it:' — at the proper time he will manifest it. 'He may have occasion to engage in the king's service:' — great is the glory of his wisdom.

4. 'A sack tied up; — there will be no error:' — this shows how, through carefulness, no injury will be received.

5. 'The yellow lower-garment; — there will be great good fortune:' — this follows from that ornamental (colour's) being in the right and central place.

6. 'The dragons fight in the wild:' — the (onward) course (indicated by K h w ǎ n) is pursued to extremity.

7. ('The lines are all weak and divided, as appears from) the use of the number six:' — but (those who are thus represented) becoming perpetually correct and firm, there will thereby be a great consummation.

APPENDIX III

The Great Appendix   Section . I

Chapter I. 1. Heaven is lofty and honourable; earth is low. (Their symbols), K h i e n and K h w ǎ n, (with their respective meanings), were determined (in accordance with this).

Chapter I is an attempt to show the correspondency between the phenomena of external nature ever changing, and the figures of the Yî King ever varying. The first four paragraphs, it is said, show, from the phenomena of production and transformation in external nature, the principles on which the figures of the Yî were made. The fifth and sixth paragraphs show, particularly, how the attributes represented by the figures Khien and Khwǎn are to be found in (the operations of) heaven and earth. The last two paragraphs show both those attributes embodied or realised in man. The realisation takes place, indeed, fully only in the sage or the ideal man, who thus becomes the pattern for all men.

Things low and high appear displayed in a similar relation. The (upper and lower trigrams, and the relative position of individual lines, as) noble and mean, had their places assigned accordingly.

Movement and rest are the regular qualities (of their respective subjects). Hence comes the definite distinction (of the several lines) as the strong and the weak.

(Affairs) are arranged together according to their tendencies, and things are divided according to their classes. Hence were produced (the interpretations in the Yî, concerning) what is good [or lucky] and evil [or unlucky].

In the heavens there are the (different) figures there completed, and on the earth there are the (different) bodies there formed. (Corresponding to them) were the changes and transformations exhibited (in the Yî).

2. After this fashion a strong and a weak line were manipulated together (till there were the eight trigrams), and those eight trigrams were added, each to itself and to all the others, (till the sixty-four hexagrams were formed).

3. We have the exciting forces of thunder and lightning; the fertilising influences of wind and rain; and the revolutions of the sun and moon, which give rise to cold and warmth.

4. The attributes expressed by *Kh*ien constitute the male; those expressed by Khwăn constitute the female.

5. *Kh*ien (symbolises Heaven, which) directs the great beginnings of things; Khwăn (symbolises Earth, which) gives to them their completion.

6. It is by the ease with which it proceeds that *Kh*ien directs (as it does), and by its unhesitating response that Khwăn exhibits such ability.

7. (He who attains to this) ease (of Heaven) will be easily understood, and (he who attains to this) freedom from

laborious effort (of the Earth) will be easily followed. He who is easily understood will have adherents, and he who is easily followed will achieve success. He who has adherents can continue long, and he who achieves success can become great. To be able to continue long shows the virtue of the wise and able man; to be able to become great is the heritage he will acquire.

8. With the attainment of such ease and such freedom from laborious effort, the mastery is got of all principles under the sky. With the attainment of that mastery, (the sage) makes good his position in the middle (between heaven and earth).

Chapter II. 9. The sages set forth the diagrams, inspected the emblems contained in them, and appended their explanations; — in this way the good fortune and bad (indicated by them) were made clear.

10. The strong and the weak (lines) displace each other, and produce the changes and transformations (in the figures).

11. Therefore the good fortune and evil (mentioned in the explanations) are the indications of the right and wrong (in men's conduct of affairs), and the repentance and regret (similarly mentioned) are the indications of their sorrow and anxiety.

12. The changes and transformations (of the lines) are the emblems of the advance and retrogression (of the vital force in nature). Thus what we call the strong and the weak (lines) become the emblems of day and night. The movements which take place in the six places (of the hexagram) show the course of the three extremes (i.e. of the three Powers in their perfect operation).

13. Therefore what the superior man rests in, in whatever position he is placed, is the order shown in the Yi;

and the study which gives him the greatest pleasure is that of the explanations of the several lines.

14. Therefore the superior man, when living quietly, contemplates the emblems and studies the explanations of them; when initiating any movement, he contemplates the changes (that are made in divining), and studies the prognostications from them. Thus 'is help extended to him from Heaven; there will be good fortune, and advantage in every movement.'

Chapter III. 15. The T h w a n speak of the emblematic figures (of the complete diagrams). The Y â o speak of the changes (taking place in the several lines).

16. The expressions about good fortune or bad are used with reference to (the figures and lines, as) being right or wrong (according to the conditions of time and place): those about repentance or regret refer to small faults (in the satisfying those conditions); when it is said 'there will be no error,' or 'no blame,' there is reference to (the subject) repairing an error by what is good.

17. Therefore the distinction of (the upper and lower trigrams and of the individual lines) as noble or mean is decided by the (relative) position (of the lines); the regulations of small and great are found in the diagrams, and the discriminations of good and bad fortune appear in the (subjoined) explanations.

18. Anxiety against (having occasion for) repentance or regret should be felt at the boundary line (between good and evil). The stirring up the thought of (securing that there shall be) no blame arises from (the feeling of) repentance.

19. Thus of the diagrams some are small, and some are great; and of the explanations some are startling, and some are unexciting. Every one of those explanations has reference to the tendencies (indicated by symbols).

Chapter IV. 20. The Yî was made on a principle of accordance with heaven and earth, and shows us therefore, without rent or confusion, the course (of things) in heaven and earth.

21. (The sage), in accordance with (the Yî), looking up, contemplates the brilliant phenomena of the heavens, and, looking down, examines the definite arrangements of the earth; — thus he knows the causes of darkness (or, what is obscure) and light (or, what is bright). He traces things to their beginning, and follows them to their end; — thus he knows what can be said about death and life. (He perceives how the union of) essence and breath form things, and the (disappearance or) wandering away of the soul produces the change (of their constitution); — thus he knows the characteristics of the anima and animus.

22. There is a similarity between him and heaven and earth, and hence there is no contrariety in him to them. His knowledge embraces all things, and his course is (intended to be) helpful to all under the sky; — and hence he falls into no error. He acts according to the exigency of circumstances without being carried away by their current; he rejoices in Heaven and knows its ordinations; — and hence he has no anxieties. He rests in his own (present) position, and cherishes (the spirit of) generous benevolence; — and hence he can love (without reserve).

23. (Through the Yî), he comprehends as in a mould or enclosure the transformations of heaven and earth without any error; by an ever-varying adaptation he completes (the nature of) all things without exception; he penetrates to a knowledge of the course of day and night (and all other connected phenomena); — it is thus that his operation is spirit-like, unconditioned by place, while the changes which he produces are not restricted to any form.

Chapter V. 24. The successive movement of the inactive

and active operations constitutes what is called the course (of things).

25. That which ensues as the result (of their movement) is goodness; that which shows it in its completeness is the nature (of men and things).

26. The benevolent see it and call it benevolence. The wise see it and call it wisdom. The common people, acting daily according to it, yet have no knowledge of it. Thus it is that the course (of things), as seen by the superior man, is seen by few.

27. It is manifested in the benevolence (of its operations), and (then again) it conceals and stores up its resources. It gives their stimulus to all things, without having the same anxieties that possess the sage. Complete is its abundant virtue and the greatness of its stores!

28. Its rich possessions is what is intended by 'the greatness of its stores;' the daily renovation which it produces is what is meant by 'the abundance of its virtue.'

29. Production and reproduction is what is called (the process of) change.

30. The formation of the semblance (shadowy forms of things) is what we attribute to *K h i e n*; the giving to them their specific forms is what we attribute to *K h w ǎ n*.

31. The exhaustive use of the numbers (that turn up in manipulating the stalks), and (thereby) knowing (the character of) coming events, is what we call prognosticating; the comprehension of the changes (indicated leads us to) what we call the business (to be done).

32. That which is unfathomable in (the movement of) the inactive and active operations is (the presence of a) spiritual (power).

Chapter VI. 33. Yes, wide is the Yî and great! If we speak

of it in its farthest reaching, no limit çan be set to it; if we speak of it with reference to what is near at hand, (its lessons are) still and correct; if we speak of it in connexion with all between heaven and earth, it embraces all.

34. There is *K h* i e n. In its (individual) stillness it is self-absorbed; when exerting its motive power it goes straight forward; and thus it is that its productive action is on a grand scale. There is K h w ǎ n. In its (individual) stillness, it is self-collected and capacious; when exerting its motive power, it develops its resources, and thus its productive action is on a wide scale.

35. In its breadth and greatness (the Yî) corresponds to heaven and earth; in its ever-recurring changes, it corresponds to the four seasons; in its mention of the bright or active, and the dark or inactive operation, it corresponds to the sun and moon; and the excellence seen in the ease and ready response (of its various operations) corresponds to the perfect operations (presented to us in the phenomena of nature).

Chapter VII. 36. The Master said: — 'Is not the Yî a perfect book?' It was by the Yî that the sages exalted their

In paragraph 30 the names *Kh*ien and Khwǎn take the place of yin and yang, as used in paragraphs 24 and 32. In *Kh*ien, the symbol of heaven, every one of its lines is undivided; it is the concentration of the yang faculty; so Khwǎn, the symbol of the earth, is the concentration of the yin. The critics themselves call attention to the equivalence of the symbolic names here given to yin and yang. The connexion of the two is necessary to the production of any one substantial thing. The yang originates a shadowy outline which the yin fills up with a definite substance. So actually in nature Heaven (*Kh*ien) and Earth (Khwǎn) operate together in the production of all material things and beings.

The 'numbers,' mentioned in paragraph 31, are not all or any numbers generally, but 7, 8, 9, 6, those assigned to the four 'emblematic figures,' that grow out of the undivided and divided lines, and by means of which the hexagrams are made up in divination. The 'future or coming events' which are prognosticated are not particular events, which the diviner has not already forecast, but the character of events or courses of actions already contemplated, as good or evil, lucky or unlucky, in their issue.

virtue, and enlarged their sphere of occupation. Their wisdom was high, and their rules of conduct were solid. That loftiness was after the pattern of heaven; that solidity, after the pattern of earth.

37. Heaven and earth having their positions as assigned to them, the changes (of nature) take place between them. The nature (of man) having been completed and being continually preserved it is the gate of all good courses and righteousness.

Chapter VIII. 38. The sage was able to survey all the complex phenomena under the sky. He then considered in his mind how they could be figured, and (by means of the diagrams) represented their material forms and their character. Hence these (diagrams) are denominated Semblances (or emblematic figures, the H s i a n g).

39. A (later) sage was able to survey the motive influences working all under the sky. He contemplated them in their common action and special nature, in order to bring out the standard and proper tendency of each. He then appended his explanation (to each line of the diagrams), to determine the good or evil indicated by it. Hence those (lines with their explanations) are denominated Imitations (the Y â o).

40. (The diagrams) speak of the most complex phenomena under the sky, and yet there is nothing in them that need awaken dislike; the explanations of the lines speak of the subtlest movements under the sky, and yet there is nothing in them to produce confusion.

41. (A learner) will consider what is said (under the diagrams), then speak; he will deliberate on what is said (in the explanations of the lines), and then move. By such consideration and deliberations he will be able to make all the changes which he undertakes successful. . . .

77. May we not say that *K h i e n* and *K h w ǎ n* [= the y a n g and y i n, or the undivided and divided lines] are the secret and substance of the Yî? *K h i e n* and *K h w ǎ n* being established in their several places, the system of changes was thereby constituted. If *K h i e n* and *K h w ǎ n* were taken away, there would be no means of seeing that system; and if that system were not seen, *K h i e n* and *K h w ǎ n* would almost cease to act.

78. Hence that which is antecedent to the material form exists, we say, as an ideal method, and that which is subsequent to the material form exists, we say, as a definite thing.

Transformation and shaping is what we call change; carrying this out and operating with it is what we call generalising the method; taking the result and setting it forth for all the people under heaven is, we say, (securing the success of) the business of life.

79. Hence, to speak of the emblematic figures: — (The sage) was able to survey all the complex phenomena under the sky. He then considered in his mind how they could be figured, and (by means of the diagrams) represented their material forms and their character. Hence those (diagrams) are denominated Semblances. A (later) sage was able to survey the motive influences working all under the sky. He contemplated them in their common action and special nature, in order to bring out the standard and proper tendency of each. He then appended his explanation (to each line), to determine the good or evil indicated by it. Hence those (lines with their explanations) are denominated Imitations (the Yâo).

80. The most thorough mastery of all complex phenomena under the sky is obtained from the diagrams. The greatest stimulus to movement in adaptation to all affairs under the sky is obtained from the explanations.

81. The transformations and shaping that take place are obtained from the changes (of the lines); the carrying this out and operating with it is obtained from the general method (that has been established). The seeing their spirit-like intimations and understanding them depended on their being the proper men; and the completing (the study of) them by silent meditation, and securing the faith of others without the use of words depended on their virtuous conduct.

Section II

Chapter I. 1. The eight trigrams having been completed in their proper order, there were in each the (three) emblematic lines. They were then multiplied by a process of addition till the (six) component lines appeared.

2. The strong line and the weak push themselves each into the place of the other and hence the changes (of the diagrams) take place. The appended explanations attach to every form of them in character (of good or ill), and hence the movements (suggested by divination) are determined accordingly.

3. Good fortune and ill, occasion for repentance or regret, all arise from these movements.

4. The strong and the weak (lines) have their fixed and proper places (in the diagrams); their changes, however varied, are according to the requirements of the time (when they take place).

5. Good fortune and ill are continually prevailing each against the other by an exact rule.

6. By the same rule, heaven and earth, in their course continually give forth (their lessons); the sun and moon

continually emit their light; all the movements under the sky are constantly subject to this one and the same rule.

7. *K h* ie n, (the symbol of heaven, and) conveying the idea of strength, shows to men its easy (and natural) action. *K h* w ǎ n, (the symbol of earth, and) conveying the idea of docility, shows to men its compendious (receptivity and operation).

8. The Y â o (or lines) are imitative representations of this. The H s i a n g, or emblematic figures, are pictorial representations of the same.

9. The movements of the lines and figures take place (at the hand of the operator), and are unseen; the good fortune or ill is seen openly and is beyond. The work to be done appears by the changes; the sympathies of the sages are seen in their explanations.

10. The great attribute of heaven and earth is the giving and maintaining life. What is most precious for the sage is to get (highest) place — (in which he can be the human representative of heaven and earth). What will guard this position for him? Men. How shall he collect a large population round him? By the power of his wealth. The right administration of that wealth, correct instructions to the people, and prohibitions against wrong-doing; — these constitute his righteousness.

Chapter III. 24. Therefore what we call the Yî is (a collection of) emblematic lines. They are styled emblematic as being resemblances.

25. What we call the T h w a n (or king Wǎn's explanations) are based on the significance (of each hexagram as a whole).

26. We call the lines (of the figures) Y â o from their being according to the movements taking place all under the sky.

27. In this way (we see) the rise of good fortune and evil, and the manifestation of repentance and regret.

Chapter IV. 28. In the Y a n g trigrams (or those of the undivided line) there are more of the Y i n lines, and in the Y i n trigrams (or those of the divided line) there are more of the Y a n g lines.

29. What is the cause of this? It is because the Y a n g lines are odd (or made by one stroke), and the Y i n lines are even (or made by two strokes).

30. What (method of) virtuous conduct is thus intimated? In the Y a n g trigrams we have one ruler, and two subjects, — suggesting the way of the superior man. In the Y i n trigrams we have two rulers, and one subject, — suggesting the way of the small man.

Chapter VI. 45. The Master said: — '(The trigrams) *Kh*i e n and K h w ă n may be regarded as the gate of the Yî.' *Kh*i e n represents what is of the y a n g nature (bright and active); K h w ă n what is of the yin nature (shaded and inactive). These two unite according to their qualities, and there comes the embodiment of the result by the strong and weak (lines). In this way we have the phenomena of heaven and earth visibly exhibited, and can comprehend the operation of the spiritual intelligence.

46. The appellations and names (of the diagrams and lines) are various, but do not go beyond (what is to be ascribed to the operation of these two conditions). When we examine the nature and style (of the appended explanations), they seem to express the ideas of a decaying age.

Chapter III, paragraphs 24-27, treats of the Yî as made up of figurative diagrams, which again are composed of lines ever changing, in accordance with the phenomena of nature and human experience, while to the resulting figures their moral character and providential issues are appended by the sages.

47. The Y î exhibits the past, and (teaches us to) discriminate (the issues of) the future; it makes manifest what is minute, and brings to light what is obscure. (Then king Wăn) opened (its symbols), and distinguished things in accordance with its names, so that all his words were correct and his explanations decisive; — (the book) was now complete.

48. The appellations and names (of the diagrams and lines) are but small matters, but the classes of things comprehended under them are large. Their scope reaches far, and the explanations attached to them are elegant. The words are indirect, but to the point; the matters seem plainly set forth, but there is a secret principle in them. Their object is, in cases that are doubtful, to help the people in their conduct, and to make plain the recompenses of good and evil.

Chapter XII. 66. (The hexagram) *K h* i e n represents the strongest of all under the sky. Through this quality its operations are always manifested with ease, for it knows where there would be peril and embarrassment. (The hexagram) K h w ă n represents the most docile of all under the sky. Through this quality its operations are always manifested with the promptest decision, for it knows where there would be obstruction.

67. (The sages, who are thus represented, and who made the Y î,) were able to rejoice in heart (in the absolute truth of things), and were able (also) to weigh carefully matters

The principal object, it is said, of chapter VI, paragraphs 45-48, is to set forth the views of king Wăn and his son in the explanation which they appended to the diagrams and lines; and in doing this the writer begins in 45, with Fû-hsî's starting, in the formation of his eight trigrams, from the devising of the whole and divided lines, to represent the two primitive forms in nature. The two 'pure' trigrams formed of these lines, unmixed, give rise to all the others, or rather the lines of which they are formed do so; and are thus compared to a gate by which the various diagrams enter to complete the system that is intended to represent the changing phenomena of nature and experience.

46

that could occasion anxiety; (thus) they fixed the good and bad fortune (of all things) under the sky, and could accomplish the things requiring strenuous efforts.

68. Therefore amid the changes and transformations (taking place in heaven and earth), and the words and deeds of men, events that are to be fortunate have their happy omens. (The sages) knew the definite principles underlying the prognostications of the former class, and the future of those of the latter, (now to be) ascertained by divination.

69. The places of heaven and earth (in the diagrams) having been determined, the sages were able (by means of the Yî) to carry out and complete their ability. (In this way even) the common people were able to share with them in (deciding about) the counsels of men and counsels of spiritual beings.

70. The eight trigrams communicate their information by their emblematic figures. The explanations appended to the lines and the completed figures tell how the contemplation of them affected (the makers). The strong and the weak lines appear mixed in them, and (thus) the good and the evil (which they indicate) can be seen.

71. The changes and movements (which take place in the manipulation of the stalks and the formation of the diagrams) speak as from the standpoint of what is advantageous. The (intimations of) good and evil vary according to the place and nature (of the lines). Thus they may indicate a mutual influence (in any two of them) of love or hatred, and good or evil is the result; or that mutual influence may be affected by the nearness of the lines to, or their distance from, each other, and then repentance or regret is the result; or the influence may be that of truth or of hypocrisy, and then the result is what is advantageous, or what is injurious. In all these relations of the (lines in the) Yî, if two are near and do not blend harmoniously, there may be (all these results), — evil, or what is injurious, or occasion for repentance and regret.

47

72. The language of him who is meditating a revolt (from the right) betrays his inward shame; that of him whose inward heart doubts about it diverges to other topics. The words of a good man are few; those of a coarse man are many. The words of one who slanders what is good are unsubstantial; those of him who is losing what he ought to keep are crooked.

APPENDIX IV

Supplementary to the Thwan and Yâo on the first and second Hexagrams, and showing how they may be interpreted of man's nature and doings.

Section I *Khien*

Chapter I. 1. What is called (under *Khien*) 'the great and originating' is (in man) the first and chief quality of goodness; what is called 'the penetrating' is the assemblage of excellences; what is called 'the advantageous' is the harmony of all that is right; and what is called 'the correct and firm' is the faculty of action.

2. The superior man, embodying benevolence, is fit to preside over men; presenting the assemblage of excellences, he is fit to show in himself the union of all propriety; benefiting (all) creatures, he is fit to exhibit the harmony of all that is right; correct and firm, he is fit to manage (all) affairs.

3. The fact that the superior man practises these four virtues justifies the application to him of the words —'*Khien* represents what is great and orginating, penetrating, advantageous, correct and firm.'

48

Section II   K h w ǎ n

Chapter I. 1. (What is indicated by) K h w a n is most gentle and weak, but, when put in motion, is hard and strong; it is most still, but is able to give every definite form.

2. 'By following, it obtains its (proper) lord,' and pursues its regular (course).

3. It contains all things in itself, and its transforming (power) is glorious.

4. Yes, what docility marks the way of K h w ǎ n! It receives the influences of heaven, and acts at the proper time.

Chapter II. 5. The family that accumulates goodness is sure to have superabundant happiness, and the family that accumulates evil is sure to have superabundant misery. The murder of a ruler by his minister, or of his father by a son, is not the result of the events of one morning or one evening. The causes of it have gradually accumulated, — through the absence of early discrimination. The words of the Y î, 'He treads on the hoar-frost; the strong ice will come (by and by),' show the natural (issue and growth of things).

6. 'Straight' indicates the correctness (of the internal principle), and 'square', the righteousness (of the external act). The superior man, (thus represented), by his self-reverence maintains the inward (correctness), and in righteousness adjusts his external acts. His reverence and righteousness being (thus) established, his virtues are not solitary instances or of a single class. 'Straight, square, and great, working his operations, without repeated efforts, in every respect advantageous:' — this shows how (such a one) has no doubts as to what he does.

7. Although (the subject of) this divided line has excellent qualities, he (does not display them, but) keeps them under restraint. 'If he engage with them in the service of

49

the king, and be successful, he will not claim that success for himself:' — this is the way of the earth, of a wife, of a minister. The way of the earth is — 'not to claim the merit of achievement,' but on behalf (of heaven) to bring things to their proper issue.

8. Through the changes and transformations produced by heaven and earth, plants and trees grow luxuriantly. If (the reciprocal influence of) heaven and earth were shut up and restrained, we should have (a state that might suggest to us) the case of men of virtue and ability lying in obscurity. The words of the Yî, 'A sack tied up: — there will be no ground for blame or for praise,' are in reality a lesson of caution.

9. The superior man (emblemed here) by the 'yellow' and correct (colour), is possessed of comprehension and discrimination. He occupies the correct position (of supremacy), but (that emblem) is on (the lower part of) his person. His excellence is in the centre (of his being), but it diffuses a complacency over his four limbs, and is manifested in his (conduct of) affairs: — this is the perfection of excellence.

10. (The subject of) the yin (or divided line) thinking himself equal to the (subject of the) y a n g, or undivided line, there is sure to be 'a contest.' As if indignant at there being no acknowledgment of the (superiority of the subject of the) y a n g line, (the text uses the term 'dragons.' But still the (subject of neither line) can leave his class, and hence we have 'the blood' mentioned. The mention of that as being (both) 'azure and yellow' indicates the mixture of heaven and earth. Heaven's (colour) is azure and earth's is yellow.

APPENDIX V

Treatise of Remarks on the Trigrams

Chapter I. 1. Anciently, when the sages made the Yî, in order to give mysterious assistance to the spiritual Intelligences, they produced (the rules for the use of) the divining plant.

2. The number 3 was assigned to heaven, 2 to earth, and from these came the (other) numbers.

3. They contemplated the changes in the divided and undivided lines (by the process of manipulating the stalks), and formed the trigrams; from the movements that took place in the strong and weak lines, they produced (their teaching about) the separate lines. There ensued a harmonious conformity to the course (of duty) and to virtue, with a discrimination of what was right (in each particular case). They (thus) made an exhaustive discrimination of what was right, and effected the complete development of (every) nature, till they arrived (in the Yî) at what was appointed for it (by Heaven).

Chapter II. 4. Anciently, when the sages made the Yî, it was with the design that (its figures) should be in conformity with the principles underlying the natures (of men and things), and the ordinances (for them) appointed (by Heaven). With this view they exhibited (in them) the way of heaven, calling (the lines) y i n and y a n g; the way of earth, calling (them) the weak (or soft) and the strong (or hard); and the way of men, under the names of benevolence and righteousness. Each (trigram) embraced (those) three Powers; and, being repeated, its full form consisted of six lines. A distinction was made of (the places assigned) to the y i n and y a n g lines, which were variously occupied, now by the strong and now by the weak forms, and thus the figure (of each hexagram) was completed.

Chapter III. 5. (The symbols of) heaven and earth received their determinate positions; (those for) mountains and collections of water interchanged their influences; (those for) thunder and wind excited each other the more; and (those for) water and fire did each other no harm. (Then) among these eight symbols there was a mutual communication.

6. The numbering of the past is a natural process; the knowledge of the coming is anticipation. Therefore in the Yî we have (both) anticipation (and the natural process).

Lao Tzŭ

LAO TZŬ (c. 480-390 B.C.). The life of Lao Tzŭ
(Lao-tse or Lao-tze) is shrouded in mystery. Whether
he was the same as Li Ehr and Li An, whether he actually talked with Confucius, and whether he was a
priest-teacher and custodian of documents in Ch'u, are
controversial. In all probability the spiritual movement
later called Tåoism started long before the birth of the
man who condensed and recorded its basic beliefs.
Though tradition assigns the most famous of the Tåoists
to 570 B.C., modern scholars place him variously between 600 and 200 B.C., or regard him as a legendary
figure. He became a popular object of worship, and
was considered the founder of the religion of Tåoism
after the ancient *fang shih* or priest-magicians movement was incorporated into Chang Ling's "Way of the
Five Bushels of Rice" in the first century A.D. Later
Tåoist tradition conferred on him the title Lao Chün
(Lord Lao) and made him a member of the Tåoist
Triad, and regarded Buddha as his incarnation. He was
honored by Imperial order in 666 A.D. as the Most High
Emperor of Mystic Origin and in 1013 as the Most
High Lord Lao.

In the writings attributed to him, known at first as
the *Lao-tzŭ* and later as *Tåo Te Ching* (*Doctrine of the
Power of the Way*), the shadowy philosopher develops
a plan of life based on simplicity and purity. Tåo
(the Way) is spontaneous, beyond good and evil; it is
nature, the all-embracing First Principle. Only by practicing virtue (*te*) and inaction (*wei-wu*), shunning the

53

artificialities of civilization, abjuring high ambitions and aspirations, and taking things as they come can man live according to the Tâo. Modeling one's own life on the Tâo is more important than anything else, including the ideals of *jen* (sympathy or human-heartedness), *i* (righteousness), and *li* (rituals). "Master Lao's" doctrine of reality, different from that perceptible by the senses and similar to that assumed by Plato, still survives. Though Tâoism later incorporated ideas of various origin, it has retained its mystical faith in the unity of Pure Being. Probably no one except Confucius has exerted a more far-reaching influence on Chinese minds than Lao Tzŭ.

Tâo Te Ching contains some five thousand words and is the most hallowed work in the Tâoist canon. It has been translated into English more often than any other work of Chinese literature. Uneven and epigrammatic, it deals unsystematically with ethics, psychology, and metaphysics. For centuries its very obscurity has challenged the imagination of scholars. Its prodigious influence has extended beyond philosophy to art and literature.

Tâo Te Ching

Chapters 1-30, translated by Dagobert D. Runes; chapters 31-81, translated by James Legge (published in 1891 by Oxford University Press as Volume XXXIX of "The Sacred Books of the East").

THE spirit one can talk about is not the eternal spirit, and what you can name is not the eternal name.

Nameless — Tâo is the beginning of the heavens and the Earth.

If you name it — it is no more than Matter.

Therefore: he who conceives of nature freely grasps this Spirit and he who strives for material things is left with only the shell.

Spirit and matter are both one in their origin, yet different in appearance.

This unity is a mystery — truly the mystery of all mysteries, the gate to all spirituality. [1]

Only when man recognizes beauty as such does ugliness become reality. Only when man recognizes goodness as such does evil become reality.

Because: being and nothingness began as one. Weight and weightlessness cannot exist alone. Distance and brevity prove each other and so do height and depth. Tune and voice abound together and past and present flow into one.

Therefore the Sage remains in serenity whatever happens and silently does his teaching.

As matters proceed, the Sage is not irritated.

He works but wants no possessions. He acts but does not linger at single things. He creates but does not hang on a single word and because he is not tied to It, he will never miss It. [2]

Not to give preference to the high and mighty will deter the envy of the people. Not to show greed for wealth will keep the people in order.

To demonstrate no desire will give them peace in their hearts.

Therefore, when the Sage governs, he frees his people of passionate wishes and offers serenity to their souls.

The Sage weakens greedy curiosity and strengthens the backbone of the upright. So does he master true serenity in good government. [3]

The Spirit is free of things yet inexhaustible in its impact.

The Spirit is like the creator of all being. He dulls the sharp meanness that clarifies all confusion. He unifies in kindness. He knows the oneness of man with all dust. The Spirit is eternal. I know not when It began. It almost seemed to have preceded the Lord Itself. [4]

Heaven and earth know no preference. They look upon all beings as upon wooden animals. The sage knows no preference. He looks upon people as if they were made of wood. The space between heaven and earth is like an ocean of wind and the emptiness of which creation follows creation. Words cannot describe It. It must be perceived by one's inmost self. [5]

The Spirit of the deep never dies.
It is the eternal mother:
The gateway through which wind
The ever-protecting roots of Heaven and earth.
It is eternal becoming, effortless creation. [6]

Heaven and earth endure forever.
Why do Heaven and earth endure eternally?

Because they live not for themselves
But for eternity.
So does the Sage withdraw
In order that his inner Self may advance.
He loses his Self to preserve his Self.
Is it not that he fulfills his Being by giving up his being? [7]

Generosity is like the Waters.
It is a balm to all beings and rejects none.
It dwells in places shunned by the masses, and therefore
                close to the Spirit.
Generosity seeks out in dwellings the humble,
in thinking depth,
in giving love,
in speaking truth,
in ruling justice,
in work knowledge
in all our deeds the proper time.
Generosity does not reject and therefore will not be
                rejected. [8]

The full decanter if carried will spill over,
The knife in use will lose its edge.
Treasures of gold and gems are difficult to protect.
Wealth and rank when joined by arrogance will now perish.
To fulfill one's tasks, to find acceptance and then to retire
                to loneliness, is the true spiritual way. [9]

Who finds union of mind and heart will reach immortality.
Who masters his passions and turns them to deeds of kind-
                ness, is greater than a King.
Who cleanses and clears his soul becomes free of vice.
Who governs in love and justice is a benefactor even in
                mere contemplation.
He is fearless should even the heavens come down.

Who has insight in the depths of Times, may have not
              knowledge, yet supreme wisdom.
To work and conserve, to work without greed for possessions,
To work and let others use the produce,
To encourage and not dominate,
That I call deep virtue. [10]

Thirty spikes run into one hub: yet in the emptiness of the
Wheel lies its essence.
From clay a jar is formed: yet in its emptiness lies the es-
sence of the container.
Rooms are made by cutting windows and doors into the
walls, yet in its emptiness lies the essence of the room.
The visual matter can be observed but it is the Invisible
that constitutes its true being. [11]

Fine colors blind eyes to true reality
Fine Tones shut out the other sounds.
Fine spices deaden the taste.
Races and hunts disturb a gentle soul.
Gems and gold seduce the heart.
The Sage follows not the eyes but the soul,
Not the senses but the essence. [12]

Forgiveness is to be shunned like a disgrace.
Ambition for honors is a burden like the body.
Forgiveness denigrates; one lives in hope to obtain, in
              fear of losing it.
Ambition for honors is a burden like the body.
The body is burdensome.
If I had no body
I would be burdenfree.
Who honors the community as himself is worthy of her.
Who loves the community as himself makes her his own. [13]

We search for it yet see it not;

58

it is the invisible.
We listen for it, yet hear it not;
it is the inaudible.
We grasp for it, yet touch it not;
it is the untouchable.
Its trinity is inseparable.
We recognize it only as *one*, innerbound.
Its distance is incomprehensible,
Its depth can not be fathomed.
Eternally creative, it can not be defined.
It goes back to Nothingness.
It can be called: The form of the formless, the face of the
faceless.
It can be called: The incomprehensible Mysterious.
You walk towards it and find not even its Beginning.
You follow it and there is no End.
Who understands the Spirit of the old Sages masters his
own time, and thru them the very root of all
time.
Such is the continuum of the Spirit. [14]

The great sages of *antiquity* were wise and intuitive.
It is difficult to comprehend their depth.
They were cautious like men who are crossing an ice-
covered river,
Cautious like people wary of certain neighbors.
Reserved as only guests are.
Relenting like melting ice, plain as uncut timber, open like
a valley.
Dark as deep water.
Who can as they interpret the turbulent thru serenity?
Who can as they thru their own lives revive the dead souls?
Who is filled with serene thoughts desires no other ful-
fillment,
Who desires no other fulfillment is not attacked by novelties
of the day.
Such man can be of simple status yet reach perfection. [15]

Who ascends the peak of Emptiness
Will reach serenity.
All Beings do I see arise and then return whence they came.
To return to one's origin means to acquiesce.
To acquiesce means to have fulfilled one's destiny.
To fulfill one's destiny means to have comprehended eternity.
To comprehend eternity means to be enlightened.
Not to comprehend eternity means to be subject of passions, and that is evil.
Comprehending eternity makes one magnanimous.
Magnanimity makes one just.
To be just is Kingly.
The Kingly is Heavenly.
The Heavenly is the Spiritual.
The Spirit is Immortal.
And thus the ephemerality of the body can not harm us. [16]

When a ruler is truly great the people hardly notice his existence.
Some of their successors were admired, some were feared, some were despised,
Rulers without faith in the people lost the people's confidence.
The great rulers did not grandize themselves,
They performed their tasks and the people felt: We are among ourselves. [17]

Where the great Spirit is in decline, there is much talk of love and liberty.
Where the great Spirit is in decline, there is much talk of prudence and equality.
Where peace is absent in the family, there is much talk of family devotion.
When suppression darkens the lands, everywhere there is talk of loyalty and obedience. [18]

Pretend not to saintliness, nor to smartness and the people
will prosper!
Talk not of Humanity nor of absolute Justice and the peo-
ple will return to family devotion.
Give up the great profits as well as your Luxuries and there
will be fewer thieves and robbers.
In all these things the pretense is harmful.
Therefore one must retain the lasting virtues:
To retain Simple goodness, humility and moderation. [19]

Give up the Booklearning and you may win serenity.
The difference between yes and certainty, how meaningless
— but that between good and evil, how im-
measurably great.
The world venerates Booklearning, I can not participate.
Perhaps this is limitless delusion.
The people glory in their festivals, as if on top of a great
tower.
I alone am silent, as no message had reached me of these
events, like a child that yet can not smile, de-
serted, homeless.
They all overflow, I alone seem empty.
O my foolish heart; I am confused.
They appear unperturbed, I alone step in the dark.
They appear exuberant, I alone am sad, sad as the sea.
Torn apart like a vagrant.
They are imbued with usefulness,
Only I am clumsy like a peasant,
I am different from them,
Yet I am on my knees before Creative Nature. [20]

True Virtue is born of Reason,
The essence of reason is unfathomable and incomprehen-
sible.
The faces of reason can not be discerned,
The world that appears in reason, no one knows how.

Impenetrable is the darkness where the heart of Being
dwells,
This Being is Truth itself and Faith itself.
From eternity to eternity, they will never perish.
Who saw the beginning of All.
The beginning of All, one knows only thru the perennial
Spirit. [21]

What is half will become perfect.
What is crooked will become straight.
What is empty will be filled.
What is old will be rejuvenated.
Who has little, will receive in plenty.
Who has much, will be deprived.
The Sage embraces the All and becomes the Idol of the
World.
He does not look out for himself, and thus he glories.
He does not please himself, and thus the world possesses
him.
He does not flaunt his accomplishments, and thus the world
venerates him.
He strives not to be on top, thus he will be elevated.
He does not attack, and the world around him is still.
Truly: Everything flows freely into the seeker of perfec-
tion. [22]

To speak sparingly is the natural course.
A whirlwind lasts not throughout the morning.
A spray rain lasts not the day.
Such it is between heaven and earth.
And such it is with man.
Who dedicates himself to reason will become one with
reason.
Who dedicates himself to virtue, will become one with
virtue.
Who gives to evil will become one with evil.

Who is one with reason, will be embraced by reason.
Who is one with virtue, will be embraced by virtue.
Who joins evil will be one with evil.
Who has no faith, will never inspire faith. [23]

No one can stand solid when on his toes.
No one can run with spread legs.
Who admires himself will not be venerated.
Who is pleased with oneself, the world will not praise.
Who praises himself, merits little appreciation.
Who pushes for the top, will not be elevated.
For the Spirit he is a leftover, an odd growth on the body.
The people will look upon him in disdain,
And those who live by reason will not emulate his like. [24]

There is a Being of Perfection, incomprehensible.
It ever was, still and formless, before they came, stars and
        earth.
Unchangeable and alone, unencumbered, whirling thru
        Time,
I name it, Creative Nature.
It has no name, shall I call it Tâo, the Spirit?
Or the substance, the infinite?
The infinite in unlimited attributes?
The great Distant, that forever returns!
Tâo is great, the Heavens are great.
The Universe is great.
May the ruler be in tune with the Spirit.
Four things are great in the world,
May the ruler be one of them.
Man is under the law of the earth, the earth under the law
        of the Universe,
The Universe under the law of Tâo and Tâo is the Law
        itself. [25]

Serenity is wiser than superficiality, dignity is master of
        turbulence.

The Sage does not step off the path of serenity.
He is not distracted by *unruly* passions, angered in contemplation nothing can perturb him.
Woe, if the ruler of the land considers himself more important than the realm.
His follower loses, who succumbs to frivolity,
His dominance loses, who is driven by passions. [26]

An experienced wanderer needs neither guideposts nor paths.
A good mathematician needs no counting board.
A good orator needs no false arguments.
A good locksmith needs no key.
The Sage is a good helper of man and never despairs.
Such is his enlightenment.
The Sage is the teacher of the confused, and values his pupil.
Who does not honor his teacher,
Who does not value his pupil, lacks wisdom in spite of his knowledge.
Such is true Spirituality. [27]

Whoever is manly and strong, yet gentle of deeds, becomes the stream of the world, remains in steadfast virtue and returns to nature like a child.
Whoever feels in himself the Light and fights Darkness becomes a symbol for the World.
Whoever becomes a symbol for the world, steadfast in virtue, returns to the very substance of Being.
Whoever feels his own Height still lives in humility, becomes like a fertile valley.
Whoever becomes a valley of the world, is of eternal virtue and returns to the very substance of Being.
Man is like uncut timber, only intuitive insight brings about perfection.
The Sage in his virtue is the first in his community.
A true ruler has no need of aggression. [28]

Whoever wishes to rise by conquest will fail.
The true goal in life is spiritual and can not be conquered
by force.
The aggressor destroys it,
The conqueror loses it.
Mankind is forever in change,
Some run ahead, soon they fall back.
Some are powerful, soon they weaken.
Some are fiery, soon they are cold.
Some are victorious, soon defeated.
The Sage is not moved by earthly ambitions,
he avoids self aggrandizement,
he avoids self elevation. [29]

Whoever advises the ruler in the spirit of Tâo will avoid
rule by force of arms; force begets force.
Where armies are arrayed against each other, grow thistle
and thorn.
Wars are the parents of hunger and misery.
The Sage wants peace, nothing else, he aspires never for
conquest.
He is victorious in restraint, victorious without arrogance,
victorious without presumption, victorious
without demonstration and offense.
Whoever seeks military adventures will perish in them.
Such is the fate of rapaciousness.
Such is the fate of materialism. [30]

Now arms, however beautiful, are instruments of evil
omen, hateful, it may be said, to all creatures. Therefore
they who have the Tâo do not like to employ them.

The superior man ordinarily considers the left hand the
most honourable place, but in time of war the right hand.
Those sharp weapons are instruments of evil omen, and
not the instruments of the superior man; — he uses them
only on the compulsion of necessity. Calm and repose are

what he prizes; victory (by force of arms) is to him un-desirable. To consider this desirable would be to delight in the slaughter of men; and he who delights in the slaughter of men cannot get his will in the kingdom.

On occasions of festivity to be on the left hand is the prized position; on occasions of mourning, the right hand. The second in command of the army has his place on the left; the general commanding in chief has his on the right; — his place, that is, is assigned to him as in the rites of mourning. He who has killed multitudes of men should weep for them with the bitterest grief; and the victor in battle has his place (rightly) according to those rites. [31]

The Tâo, considered as unchanging, has no name.

Though in its primordial simplicity it may be small, the whole world dares not deal with (one embodying) it as a minister. If a feudal prince or the king could guard and hold it, all would spontaneously submit themselves to him.

Heaven and Earth (under its guidance) unite together and send down the sweet dew, which, without the direc-tions of men, reaches equally everywhere as of its own accord.

As soon as it proceeds to action, it has a name. When it once has that name, (men) can know to rest in it. When they know to rest in it, they can be free from all risk of failure and error.

The relation of the Tâo to all the world is like that of the great rivers and seas to the streams from the valleys. [32]

He who knows other men is discerning; he who knows himself is intelligent. He who overcomes others is strong; he who overcomes himself is mighty. He who is satisfied with his lot is rich; he who goes on acting with energy has a (firm) will.

He who does not fail in the requirements of his position, continues long; he who dies and yet does not perish, has longevity. [33]

All-pervading is the Great Tâo! It may be found on the left hand and on the right.

All things depend on it for their production, which it gives to them, not one refusing obedience to it. When its work is accomplished, it does not claim the name of having done it. It clothes all things as with a garment, and makes no assumption of being their lord; — it may be named in the smallest things. All things return (to their root and disappear), and do not know that it is it which presides over their doing so; — it may be named in the greatest things.

Hence the sage is able (in the same way) to accomplish his great achievements. It is through his not making himself great that he can accomplish them. [34]

To him who holds in his hands the Great Image (of the invisible Tâo), the whole world repairs. Men resort to him, and receive no hurt, but (find) rest, peace, and the feeling of ease.

Music and dainties will make the passing guest stop (for a time). But though the Tâo as it comes from the mouth, seems insipid and has no flavour, though it seems not worth being looked at or listened to, the use of it is inexhaustible. [35]

When one is about to take an inspiration, he is sure to make a (previous) expiration; when he is going to weaken another, he will first strengthen him; when he is going to overthrow another, he will first have raised him up; when he is going to despoil another, he will first have made gifts to him: — this is called 'Hiding the light (of his procedure).'

The soft overcomes the hard; and the weak the strong.

Fishes should not be taken from the deep; instruments for the profit of a state should not be shown to the people. [36]

The Tâo in its regular course does nothing (for the sake of doing it), and so there is nothing which it does not do.

If princes and kings were able to maintain it, all things would of themselves be transformed by them.

If this transformation became to me an object of desire, I would express the desire by the nameless simplicity.

Simplicity without a name
Is free from all external aim.
With no desire, at rest and still,
All things go right as of their will. [37]

(Those who) possessed in highest degree the attributes (of the Tâo) did not (seek) to show them, and therefore they possessed them (in fullest measure). (Those who) possessed in a lower degree those attributes (sought how) not to lose them, and therefore they did not possess them (in fullest measure).

(Those who) possessed in the highest degree those attributes did nothing (with a purpose), and had no need to do anything. (Those who) possessed them in a lower degree were (always) doing, and had need to be so doing.

(Those who) possessed the highest benevolence were (always seeking) to carry it out, and had no need to be doing so. (Those who) possessed the highest righteousness were (always seeking) to carry it out, and had need to be so doing.

(Those who) possessed the highest (sense of) propriety were (always seeking) to show it, and when men did not respond to it, they bared the arm and marched up to them.

Thus it was that when the Tâo was lost, its attributes appeared; when its attributes were lost, benevolence appeared; when benevolence was lost, righteousness appeared; and when righteousness was lost, the proprieties appeared.

Now propriety is the attenuated form of leal-heartedness and good faith, and is also the commencement of disorder; swift apprehension is (only) a flower of the Tâo, and is the beginning of stupidity.

Thus it is that the Great man abides by what is solid and eschews what is flimsy; dwells with the fruit and not with the flower. It is thus that he puts away the one and makes choice of the other. [38]

The things which from of old have got the One (the Tâo) are —

Heaven which by it is bright and pure;
Earth rendered thereby firm and sure;
Spirits with powers by it supplied;
Valleys kept full throughout their void;
All creatures which through it do live;
Princes and kings who from it get
The model which to all they give.

All these are the results of the One (Tâo).
If heaven were not thus pure, it soon would
    rend;
If earth were not thus sure, 'twould break and
    bend;

Without these powers, the spirits soon would fail;
If not so filled, the drought would parch each vale;
Without that life, creatures would pass away;
Princes and kings, without that moral sway,
However grand and high, would all decay.

Thus it is that dignity finds its (firm) root in its (previous) meanness, and what is lofty finds its stability in the lowness (from which it rises). Hence princes and kings call themselves 'Orphans,' 'Men of small virtue,' and as 'Carriages without a nave.' Is not this an acknowledgment that in their considering themselves mean they see the foundation of their dignity? So it is that in the enumeration of the different parts of a carriage we do not come on what makes it answer the ends of a carriage. They do not wish to show themselves elegant-looking as jade, but (prefer) to be coarse-looking as an (ordinary) stone. [39]

The movement of the Tâo
By contraries proceeds;
And weakness marks the course
of Tâo's mighty deeds.

All things under heaven sprang from It as existing (and named); that existence sprang from It as non-existent (and not named). [40]

Scholars of the highest class, when they hear about the Tâo, earnestly carry it into practice. Scholars of the middle class, when they have heard about it, seem now to keep it and now to lose it. Scholars of the lowest class, when they have heard about it, laugh greatly at it. If it were not (thus) laughed at, it would not be fit to be the T â o.

Therefore the sentence-makers have thus expressed themselves: —

'The T â o, when brightest seen, seems light to lack;
Who progress in it makes, seems drawing back;
Its even way is like a rugged track.
Its highest virtue from the vale doth rise;
Its greatest beauty seems to offend the eyes;
And he has most whose lot the least supplies.
Its firmest virtue seems but poor and low;
Its solid truth seems change to undergo;
Its largest square doth yet no corner show;
A vessel great, it is the slowest made;
Loud is its sound, but never word it said;
A semblance great, the shadow of a shade.'

The T â o is hidden, and has no name; but it is the T â o which is skilful at imparting (to all things what they need) and making them complete. [41]

The T â o produced One; One produced Two; Two produced Three; Three produced All things. All things leave behind them the obscurity (out of which they have come), and go forward to embrace the Brightness (into which they

70

have emerged), while they are harmonised by the Breath of Vacancy.

What men dislike is to be orphans, to have little virtue, to be as carriages without naves; and yet these are the designations which kings and princes use for themselves. So it is that some things are increased by being diminished, and others are diminished by being increased.

What other men (thus) teach, I also teach. The violent and strong do not die their natural death. I will make this the basis of my teaching. [42]

The softest thing in the world dashes against and overcomes the hardest; that which has no (substantial) existence enters where there is no crevice. I know hereby what advantage belongs to doing nothing (with a purpose).

There are few in the world who attain to the teaching without words, and the advantage arising from non-action. [43]

Or fame or life,
  Which do you hold more dear?
Or life or wealth,
  To which would you adhere?
Keep life and lose those other things;
Keep them and lose your life: — which
      brings
  Sorrow and pain more near?
Thus we may see,
  Who cleaves to fame
  Rejects what is more great;
Who loves large stores
  Gives up the richer state.
      Who is content
      Needs fear no shame.
      Who knows to stop
      Incurs no blame.

From danger free
Long live shall he. [44]

Who thinks his great achievements poor
Shall find his vigour long endure.
Of greatest fulness, deemed a void,
Exhaustion ne'er shall stem the tide.
Do thou what's straight still crooked deem;
Thy greatest art still stupid seem,
And eloquence a stammering scream.

Constant action overcomes cold; being still overcomes heat. Purity and stillness give the correct law to all under heaven. [45]

When the T â o prevails in the world, they send back their swift horses to (draw) the dung-carts. When the T â o is disregarded in the world, the warhorses breed in the border lands.

There is no guilt greater than to sanction ambition; no calamity greater than to be discontented with one's lot; no fault greater than the wish to be getting. Therefore the sufficiency of contentment is an enduring and unchanging sufficiency. [46]

Without going outside his door, one understands (all that takes place) under the sky; without looking out from his window, one sees the T â o of Heaven. The farther that one goes out (from himself), the less he knows.

Therefore the sages got their knowledge without travelling; gave their (right) names to things without seeing them; and accomplished their ends without any purpose of doing so. [47]

He who devotes himself to learning (seeks) from day to day to increase (his knowledge); he who devotes himself to the T â o (seeks) from day to day to diminish (his doing).

He diminishes it and again diminishes it, till he arrives at doing nothing (on purpose). Having arrived at this point of non-action, there is nothing which he does not do.

He who gets as his own all under heaven does so by giving himself no trouble (with that end). If one take trouble (with that end), he is not equal to getting as his all under heaven. [48]

The sage has no invariable mind of his own; he makes the mind of the people his mind.

To those who are good (to me), I am good; and to those who are not (to me), I am also good; — and thus (all) get to be good. To those who are sincere (with me), I am sincere; and to those who are not sincere (with me), I am also sincere; — and thus (all) get to be sincere.

The sage has in the world an appearance of indecision, and keeps his mind in a state of indifference to all. The people all keep their eyes and ears directed to him, and he deals with them all as his children. [49]

Men come forth and live; they enter (again) and die.

Of every ten three are ministers of life (to themselves); and three are ministers of death.

There are also three in every ten whose aim is to live, but whose movements tend to the land (or place) of death. And for what reason? Because of their excessive endeavours to perpetuate life.

But I have heard that he who is skilful in managing the life entrusted to him for a time travels on the land without having to shun rhinoceros or tiger, and enters a host without having to avoid buff coat or sharp weapon. The rhinoceros finds no place in him into which to thrust its horn, nor the tiger a place in which to fix its claws, nor the weapon a place to admit its point. And for what reason? Because there is in him no place of death. [50]

All things are produced by the T â o, and nourished by its outflowing operation. They receive their forms according to the nature of each, and are completed according to the circumstances of their condition. Therefore all things without exception honour the T â o, and exalt its outflowing operation.

This honouring of the T â o and exalting of its operation is not the result of any ordination, but always a spontaneous tribute.

Thus it is that the T â o produces (all things), nourishes them, brings them to their full growth, nurses them, completes them, matures them, maintains them, and overspreads them.

It produces them and makes no claim to the possession of them; it carries them though their processes and does not vaunt its ability in doing so; it brings them to maturity and exercises no control over them; — this is called its mysterious operation. [51]

(The T â o) which originated all under the sky is to be considered as the mother of them all.

When the mother is founded, we know what her children should be. When one knows that he is his mother's child, and proceeds to guard (the qualities of) the mother that belong to him, to the end of his life he will be free from all peril.

Let him keep his mouth closed, and shut up the portals (of his nostrils), and all his life he will be exempt from laborious exertion. Let him keep his mouth open, and (spend his breath) in the promotion of his affairs, and all his life there will be no safety for him.

The perception of what is small is (the secret of) clearsightedness; the guarding of what is soft and tender is (the secret of) strength.

Who uses well his light,
Reverting to its (source so) bright,
Will from his body ward all blight,
And hides the unchanging from men's sight. [52]

If I were suddenly to become known, and (put into a position to) conduct (a government) according to the Great T â o, what I should be most afraid of would be a boastful display.

The great T â o (or way) is very level and easy; but people love the by-ways.

Their court(-yards and buildings) shall be well kept, but their fields shall be ill-cultivated, and their granaries very empty. They shall wear elegant and ornamented robes, carry a sharp sword at their girdle, pamper themselves in eating and drinking, and have a superabundance of property and wealth; — such (princes) may be called robbers and boasters. This is contrary to the T â o surely! [53]

What (T â o's) skilful planter plants
    Can never be uptorn;
What his skilful arms enfold,
    From him can ne'er be borne.
Sons shall bring in lengthening line,
    Sacrifices to his shrine.
T â o when nursed within one's self,
    His vigour will make true;
And where the family it rules
    What riches will accrue!
The neighbourhood where it prevails
    In thriving will abound;
And when 'tis seen throughout the state,
Good fortune will be found.
    Employ it the kingdom o'er,
    And men thrive all around.

In this way the effect will be seen in the person, by the observation of different cases; in the family; in the neighbourhood; in the state; and in the kingdom.

How do I know that this effect is sure to hold thus all under the sky? By this (method of observation). [54]

He who has in himself abundantly the attributes (of the Tâo) is like an infant. Poisonous insects will not sting him; fierce beasts will not seize him; birds of prey will not strike him.

(The infant's) bones are weak and its sinews soft, but yet its grasp is firm. It knows not yet the union of male and female, and yet its virile member may be excited;— showing the perfection of its physical essence. All day long it will cry without its throat becoming hoarse; — showing the harmony (in its constitution).

To him by whom this harmony is known,
(The secret of) the unchanging (Tâo) is shown,
And in the knowledge wisdom finds its throne.
All life-increasing arts to evil turn;
Where the mind makes the vital breath to burn,
(False) is the strength, (and o'er it we should mourn.)

When things have become strong, they (then) become old, which may be said to be contrary to the Tâo. Whatever is contrary to the Tâo soon ends. [55]

He who knows (the Tâo) does not (care to) speak (about it); he who is (ever ready to) speak about it does not know it.

He (who knows it) will keep his mouth shut and close the portals (of his nostrils). He will blunt his sharp points and unravel the complications of things; he will temper his brightness, and bring himself into agreement with the obscurity (of others). This is called 'the Mysterious Agreement.'

76

(Such an one) cannot be treated familiarly or distantly; he is beyond all consideration of profit or injury; of nobility or meanness: — he is the noblest man under heaven. [56]

A state may be ruled by (measures of) correction; weapons of war may be used with crafty dexterity; (but) the kingdom is made one's own (only) by freedom from action and purpose.

How do I know that it is so? By these facts: — In the kingdom the multiplication of prohibitive enactments increases the poverty of the people; the more implements to add to their profit that the people have, the greater disorder is there in the state and clan; the more acts of crafty dexterity that men possess, the more do strange contrivances appear; the more display there is of legislation, the more thieves and robbers there are.

Therefore a sage has said, 'I will do nothing (of purpose), and the people will be transformed of themselves; I will be fond of keeping still, and the people will of themselves become correct. I will take no trouble about it, and the people will of themselves become rich; I will manifest no ambition, and the people will of themselves attain to the primitive simplicity.' [57]

> The government that seems the most unwise,
> Oft goodness to the people best supplies;
> That which is meddling, touching everything,
> Will work but ill, and disappointment bring.

Misery! — happiness is to be found by its side! Happiness! — misery lurks beneath it! Who knows what either will come to in the end?

Shall we then dispense with correction? The (method of) correction shall by a turn become distortion, and the good in it shall by a turn become evil. The delusion of the people (on this point) has indeed subsisted for a long time.

Therefore the sage is (like) a square which cuts no one (with its angles); (like) a corner which injures no one (with its sharpness). He is straightforward, but allows himself no license; he is bright, but does not dazzle. [58]

For regulating the human (in our constitution) and rendering the (proper) service to the heavenly, there is nothing like moderation.

It is only by this moderation that there is effected an early return (to man's normal state). That early return is what I call the repeated accumulation of the attributes (of the T â o). With that repeated accumulation of those attributes, there comes the subjugation (of every obstacle to such return). Of this subjugation we know not what shall be the limit; and when one knows not what the limit shall be, he may be the ruler of a state.

He who possesses the mother of the state may continue long. His case is like that (of the plant) of which we say that its roots are deep and its flower stalks firm: — this is the way to secure that its enduring life shall long be seen. [59]

Governing a great state is like cooking small fish.

Let the kingdom be governed according to the T â o, and the manes of the departed will not manifest their spiritual energy. It is not that those manes have not that spiritual energy, but it will not be employed to hurt men. It is not that it could not hurt men, but neither does the ruling sage hurt them.

When these two do not injuriously affect each other, their good influences converge in the virtue (of the T â o). [60]

What makes a great state is its being (like) a low-lying, down-flowing (stream); — it becomes the centre to which tend (all the small states) under heaven.

(To illustrate from) the case of all females: — the female always overcomes the male by her stillness. Stillness may be considered (a sort of) abasement.

Thus it is that a great state, by condescending to small states, gains them for itself; and that small states, by abasing themselves to a great state, win it over to them. In the one case the abasement leads to gaining adherents, in the other case to procuring favour.

The great state only wishes to unite men together and nourish them; a small state only wishes to be received by, and to serve, the other. Each gets what it desires, but the great state must learn to abase itself. [61]

T â o has of all things the most honoured place.
   No treasures give good men so rich a grace;
   Bad men it guards, and doth their ill efface.
(Its) admirable words can purchase honour; (its) admirable deeds can raise their performer above others. Even men who are not good are not abandoned by it.

Therefore when the sovereign occupies his place as the Son of Heaven, and he has appointed his three ducal ministers though (a prince) were to send in a round symbol-of-rank large enough to fill both the hands, and that as the precursor of the team of horses (in the court-yard), such an offering would not be equal to (a lesson of) this T â o, which one might present on his knees.

Why was it that the ancients prized this T â o so much? Was it not because it could be got by seeking for it, and the guilty could escape (from the stain of their guilt) by it? This is the reason why all under heaven consider it the most valuable thing. [62]

(It is the way of the T â o) to act without (thinking of) acting; to conduct affairs without (feeling the) trouble of them; to taste without discerning any flavour; to consider what is small as great, and a few as many; and to recompense injury with kindness.

(The master of it) anticipates things that are difficult while they are easy, and does things that would become great while they are small. All difficult things in the world are sure to arise from a previous state in which they were easy, and all great things from one in which they were small. Therefore the sage, while he never does what is great, is able on that account to accomplish the greatest things.

He who lightly promises is sure to keep but little faith; he who is continually thinking things easy is sure to find them difficult. Therefore the sage sees difficulty even in what seems easy, and so never has any difficulties. [63]

That which is at rest is easily kept hold of; before a thing has given indications of its presence, it is easy to take measures against it; that which is brittle is easily broken; that which is very small is easily dispersed. Action should be taken before a thing has made its appearance; order should be secured before disorder has begun.

The tree which fills the arms grew from the tiniest sprout; the tower of nine storeys rose from a (small) heap of earth; the journey of a thousand l î commenced with a single step.

He who acts (with an ulterior purpose) does harm; he who takes hold of a thing (in the same way) loses his hold. The sage does not act (so), and therefore does no harm; he does not lay hold (so), and therefore does not lose his hold. (But) people in their conduct of affairs are constantly ruining them when they are on the eve of success. If they were careful at the end, as (they should be) at the beginning, they would not so ruin them.

Therefore the sage desires what (other men) do not desire, and does not prize things difficult to get; he learns what (other men) do not learn, and turns back to what the multitude of men have passed by. Thus he helps the natural development of all things, and does not dare to act (with an ulterior purpose of his own). [64]

The ancients who showed their skill in practising the T â o did so, not to enlighten the people, but rather to make them simple and ignorant.

The difficulty in governing the people arises from their having much knowledge. He who (tries to) govern a state by his wisdom is a scourge to it; while he who does not (try to) do so is a blessing.

He who knows these two things finds in them also his model and rule. Ability to know this model and rule constitutes what we call the mysterious excellence (of a governor). Deep and farreaching is such mysterious excellence, showing indeed its possessor as opposite to others, but leading them to a great conformity to him. [65]

That whereby the rivers and seas are able to receive the homage and tribute of all the valley streams, is their skill in being lower than they; — it is thus that they are the kings of them all. So it is that the sage (ruler), wishing to be above men, puts himself by his words below them, and, wishing to be before them, places his person behind them.

In this way though he has his place above them, men do not feel his weight, nor though he has his place before them, do they feel it an injury to them.

Therefore all in the world delight to exalt him and do not weary of him. Because he does not strive, no one finds it possible to strive with him. [66]

All the world says that, while my T â o is great, it yet appears to be inferior (to other systems of teaching). Now it is just its greatness that makes it seem to be inferior. If it were like any other (system), for long would its smallness have been known!

But I have three precious things which I prize and hold fast. The first is gentleness; the second is economy; and the third is shrinking from taking precedence of others.

With that gentleness I can be bold; with that economy I can be liberal; shrinking from taking precedence of others, I can become a vessel of the highest honour. Now-a-days they give up gentleness and are all for being bold; economy,

and are all for being liberal; the hindmost place, and seek
only to be foremost; — (of all which the end is) death.

Gentleness is sure to be victorious even in battle, and
firmly to maintain its ground. Heaven will save its possessor,
by his (very) gentleness protecting him. [67]

> He who in (Tâo's) wars has skill
>   Assumes no martial port;
> He who fights with most good will
>   To rage makes no resort.
> He who vanquishes yet still
>   Keeps from his foes apart;
> He whose hests men most fulfil
>   Yet humbly plies his art.
> Thus we say, 'He ne'er contends,
>   And therein is his might.'
> Thus we say, 'Men's wills he bends,
>   That they with him unite.'
> Thus we say, 'Like Heaven's his ends,
>   No sage of old more bright.' [68]

A master of the art of war has said, 'I do not dare to be
the host (to commence the war); I prefer to be the guest
(to act on the defensive). I do not dare to advance an inch;
I prefer to retire a foot.' This is called marshalling the ranks
where there are no ranks; baring the arms (to fight) where
there are no arms to bare; grasping the weapon where there
is no weapon to grasp; advancing against the enemy where
there is no enemy.

There is no calamity greater than lightly engaging in war.
To do that is near losing (the gentleness) which is so precious. Thus it is that when opposing weapons are (actually)
crossed, he who deplores (the situation) conquers. [69]

My words are very easy to know, and very easy to practise; but there is no one in the world who is able to know
and able to practise them.

There is an originating and all-comprehending (principle) in my words, and an authoritative law for the things (which I enforce). It is because they do not know these, that men do not know me.

They who know me are few, and I am on that account —(the more) to be prized. It is thus that the sage wears (a poor garb of) hair cloth, while he carries his (signet of) jade in his bosom. [70]

To know and yet (think) we do not know is the highest (attainment); not to know (and yet think) we do know is a disease.

It is simply by being pained at (the thought of) having this disease that we are preserved from it. The sage has not the disease. He knows the pain that would be inseparable from it, and therefore he does not have it. [71]

When the people do not fear what they ought to fear, that which is their great dread will come on them.

Let them not thoughtlessly indulge themselves in their ordinary life; let them not act as if weary of what that life depends on.

It is by avoiding such indulgence that such weariness does not arise.

Therefore the sage knows (these things) of himself, but does not parade (his knowledge); loves, but does not (appear to set a) value on, himself. And thus he puts the latter alternative away and makes choice of the former. [72]

He whose boldness appears in his daring (to do wrong, in defiance of the laws) is put to death; he whose boldness appears in this not daring (to do so) lives on. Of these two cases the one appears to be advantageous, and the other to be injurious. But

When Heaven's anger smites a man,
Who the cause shall truly scan?

On this account the sage feels a difficulty (as to what to do in the former case).

It is the way of Heaven not to strive, and yet it skilfully overcomes; not to speak, and yet it is skilful in (obtaining) a reply, does not call, and yet men come to it of themselves. Its demonstrations are quiet, and yet its plans are skilful and effective. The meshes of the net of Heaven are large; far apart, but letting nothing escape. [73]

The people do not fear death; to what purpose is it to (try to) frighten them with death? If the people were always in awe of death, and I could always seize those who do wrong, and put them to death, who would dare to do wrong?

There is always One who presides over the infliction of death. He who would inflict death in the room of him who so presides over it may be described as hewing wood instead of a great carpenter. Seldom is it that who undertakes the hewing, instead of the great carpenter, does not cut his own hands! [74]

The people suffer from famine because of the multitude of taxes consumed by their superiors. It is through this that they suffer famine.

The people are difficult to govern because of the (excessive) agency of their superiors (in governing them). It is through this that they are difficult to govern.

The people make light of dying because of the greatness of their labours in seeking for the means of living. It is this which makes them think light of dying. Thus it is that to leave the subject of living altogether out of view is better than to set a high value on it. [75]

Man at his birth is supple and weak; at his death, firm and strong. (So it is with) all things. Trees and plants, in their early growth, are soft and brittle; at their death, dry and withered.

Thus it is that firmness and strength are the concomitants of death; softness and weakness, the concomitants of life.

Hence he who (relies on) the strength of his forces does not conquer; and a tree which is strong will fill the out-stretched arms, (and thereby invites the feller.)

Therefore the place of what is firm and strong is below, and that of what is soft and weak is above. [76]

May not the Way (or T â o) of Heaven be compared to the (method of) bending a bow? The (part of the bow) which was high is brought low, and what was low is raised up. (So Heaven) diminishes where there is superabundance, and supplements where there is deficiency.

It is the Way of Heaven to diminish superabundance, and to supplement deficiency. It is not so with the way of man. He takes away from those who have not enough to add to his own superabundance.

Who can take his own superabundance and therewith serve all under heaven? Only he who is in possession of the T â o!

Therefore the (ruling) sage acts without claiming the results as his; he achieves his merit and does not rest (arrogantly) in it: — he does not wish to display his superiority. [77]

There is nothing in the world more soft and weak than water, and yet for attacking things that are firm and strong there is nothing that can take precedence of it; — for there is nothing (so effectual) for which it can be changed.

Every one in the world knows that the soft overcomes the hard, and the weak the strong, but no one is able to carry it out in practice.

> Therefore a sage has said,
> 'He who accepts his state's reproach,
>   Is hailed therefore its altars' lord;
> To him who bears men's direful woes
>   They all the name of King accord.'

Words that are strictly true seem to be paradoxical. [78]

When a reconciliation is effected (between two parties) after a great animosity, there is sure to be a grudge remaining (in the mind of the one who was wrong). And how can this be beneficial (to the other)?

Therefore (to guard against this), the sage keeps the left-hand portion of the record of the engagement, and does not insist on the (speedy) fulfilment of it by the other party. (So), he who has the attributes (of the Tâo) regards (only) the conditions of the engagement, while he who has not those attributes regards only the conditions favourable to himself.

In the Way of Heaven, there is no partiality of love; it is always on the side of the good man. [79]

In a little state with a small population, I would so order it, that, though there were individuals with the abilities of ten or a hundred men, there should be no employment of them; I would make the people, while looking on death as a grievous thing, yet not remove elsewhere (to avoid it).

Though they had boats and carriages, they should have no occasion to ride in them; though they had buff coats and sharp weapons, they should have no occasion to don or use them.

I would make the people return to the use of knotted cords (instead of the written characters).

They should think their (coarse) food sweet; their (plain) clothes beautiful; their (poor) dwellings places of rest; and their common (simple) ways sources of enjoyment.

There should be a neighbouring state within sight, and the voices of the fowls and dogs should be heard all the way from it to us, but I would make the people to old age, even to death, not have any intercourse with it. [80]

Sincere words are not fine; fine words are not sincere.

Those who are skilled (in the T â o) do not dispute (about it); the disputatious are not skilled in it. Those who know (the T â o) are not extensively learned; the extensively learned do not know it.

The sage does not accumulate (for himsef). The more that he expends for others, the more does he possess of his own; the more that he gives to others, the more does he have himself.

With all the sharpness of the Way of Heaven, it injures not; with all the doing in the way of the sage he does not strive. [81]

Mo Tzŭ

MO TZŬ (*c.* 470-396 B.C.). The apostle of universal love and founder of the philosophical school of Mohism was a contemporary of Socrates. Mo Tzŭ (born Mo Ti and known also as Me Ti as well as by the Latinized name of Mocius) is believed to have been a native of Sung or Lu, a capable civil servant, and a victorious general. Born a few years after Socrates' death, he is said to have accepted Confusianism at first, only to reject it later because of its burdensome code of rituals and its silence concerning the positive side of religion. He had a place of special importance among the "hundred philosophers" of ancient China. His philosophical system, singled out by Mencius as being one of the most dangerous rivals of Confucianism, combines religious spirituality and utilitarian nationalism. A skilled logician and an experienced dialectician, he is credited with having used his talents to avert several wars. He spent most of his life traveling in search of a sympathetic prince who would use his teachings to right the wrongs of the world. Moism and Confucianism were eminent rivals for two centuries.

The practice of universal love and altruism, according to Mo Tzŭ, can bring peace to the world and happiness to man. His compassion for the people led him to castigate unjust rulers. His doctrine comes very close to proclaiming the equality of all men. In his system *jen* (sympathy, human-heartedness) and *î* (righteousness) are combined in a universal love that can lead to the best form of government and a state blessed with five goods: increase of population, good order, elimination of war, enrichment, and life under benevolent spirits. What he called the principle of identification with the superior requires the ruler to identify his will with that of Heaven, his subordinates with his own will, and so on. Heaven not only desires righteousness but also wills that all men practice brotherly love.

Mo Tzŭ's doctrine of universal love and obedience to the will of Heaven made him the most active promulgator of religion. After his most famous and original doctrine was embodied in an organized church, as many as 170 of his followers were said to be ready to die at his command. Two centuries later, however, Mohism was eclipsed by the more popular doctrines of Confucianism and Tâoism.

The *Mo Tzŭ*, a collection of writings that bears his name and records his teachings (some of the fifteen chapters that make up the collection are thought to represent the views of his followers, and eighteen of the seventy-five original sections have been lost), was neglected until it was rediscovered and reappraised in the twentieth century. The nobility of soul revealed in his life of service to others, his doctrine of universal brotherhood and mutual profit, and his devotion to the cause of peace accounts for the recent resurgence of interest in the writings of the "Altruist."

The Mo Tzŭ Book

From *Chinese Philosophy in Classical Times*, edited by E. H. Hughes, London, J. M. Dent & Sons Ltd.

ON STANDARD PATTERNS

OUR Master Mo Said: Any one in the Great Society who takes any business in hand, cannot dispense with a standard pattern. For there to be no standard and the business to succeed, this just does not happen. Even the best experts who act as generals and councillors-of-state, all have standards (of action); and so also even with the best craftsmen. They use a carpenter's square for making squares and compasses for making circles: a piece of string for making straight lines and a plumb line for getting the perpendicular. It makes no difference whether a craftsman is skilled or not: all alike use these five (devices) as standards, only the skilled are accurate. But, although the unskilled fail to be accurate, they nevertheless get much better results if they follow these standards in the work which they do. Thus it is that craftsmen in their work have the measurements which these standards give.

Now take the great ones who rule our Great Society, and the less great ones who rule the different states, but who have no standards of measurement (for their actions). In this they are less critically minded than the craftsman. That being so, what standard may be taken as suitable for ruling? Will it do if everybody imitates his father and mother? The number of fathers and mothers in the Great Society is large, but the number of human-hearted [*jen*] ones is small. If everybody were to imitate his father and mother, this standard would not be a human-hearted one. For a standard, however, to be not human-hearted makes it impossible for it to be a standard. Will it do then if everybody imitates his teacher?[1] The number of teachers is large, but the number of human-hearted ones is small. If everybody were to imitate his teacher . . . this standard would not be a human-hearted one. Will it do then if everybody imitates his sovereign? The number of princes is large, but the number of human-hearted ones is small. If everybody imitated his sovereign, this standard would not be a human-hearted one. Hence, fathers and mothers, teachers and sovereigns cannot be taken as standards for ruling.

That being so, what standard may be taken as suitable for ruling? The answer is that nothing is equal to imitating Heaven. Heaven's actions are all-inclusive and not private-minded, its[2] blessings substantial and unceasing, its revelations abiding and incorruptible. Thus it was that the Sage-kings imitated it. Having taken Heaven as their standard, their every movement and every action was bound to be measured in relation to Heaven. What Heaven wanted, that they did: what Heaven did not want, that they stopped doing.

The question now is, what does Heaven want and what does it hate? Heaven wants men to love[3] and be profitable to each other, and does not want men to hate and maltreat

1. It is a distinctive feature of Mo Ti's reasoning that he was not afraid of repetition. The argument is given in exactly the same words in relation to different sets of people, etc. Where this becomes boring to the reader it will be omitted.

2. It seems best to translate by 'it' and 'its.' Yet, as modern Chinese philosophers generally affirm, Mo Ti's 'Heaven' is equivalent to a Being or even a Person with a Will. Cp. below where Heaven is described as 'embracing all men in its love of them.'

3. Mo Ti seldom used Confucius's word *jen* (man-to-man-ness, human-heartedness). His word *ai* is one expressing rather the feeling of love. On the other hand, his utilitarian mind made him construe love in terms of doing good, being useful to your fellow men.

each other. How do we know that Heaven wants men to love and be profitable to each other? Because it embraces all in its love of them, embraces all in its benefits to them. How do we know that Heaven embraces all . . . ? Because it embraces all in its possession of them and in its gifts of food.

Take then the Great Society. There are no large or small states: all are Heaven's townships. Take men. There are no young men or old, no patricians or plebeians: all are Heaven's subjects. This is so, for there is no one who does not fatten oxen and sheep and dogs and pigs and make pure wine and sacrificial cakes with which to do reverence and service to Heaven. Can this be anything else than Heaven owning all and giving food to all? Assuming then that Heaven embraces all and gives food to all, how could it be said that it does not want men to love and benefit each other?

Hence I say that Heaven is sure to give happiness to those who love and benefit other men, and is sure to bring calamities on those who hate and maltreat other men. I maintain that the man who murders an innocent person will meet with misfortune. What other explanation is there of the fact that when men murder each other, Heaven brings calamity on them? This is the way in which we know that Heaven wants men to love and benefit each other and does not want them to hate and maltreat each other.

ON THE WILL OF HEAVEN

The word of our Master Mo:[1] What is the explanation of the disorder everywhere? It is that our leaders in society are clear about less important matters and not clear about more important matters. How do we know that they are clear about less important matters and not clear about more

1. This introductory expression occurs frequently, and makes one wonder whether these writings may not have been written for liturgical purposes.

important? Because they are not clear about Heaven's purposes. How do we know that they are not clear about Heaven's purposes? By taking family life we know it. Take the case of a man who has offended the head of his family. He can still find another family in which to take refuge. None the less fathers and elder brothers are constantly warning the young, bidding them be careful in the family. . . . And then take the case of a man who misconducts himself in his country. He can still find another country in which to take refuge. None the less fathers and elder brothers are constantly warning the young. . . . Now, however, take the case of all men living under the sky and serving Heaven. If they offend against Heaven, there is no place where they can take refuge. And yet people have not the knowledge to warn each other. By this I[1] know that if a matter is supremely important no one knows about it.

Thus it is that our Master Mo has the word: Be careful! You must do what Heaven wants and avoid what Heaven hates. He (then) said: What does Heaven want and what does it hate? Heaven wants righteousness and hates what is to it unrighteous. How do we know that this is so? The answer is that righteousness is rectifying.[2] (Then) how is it known that righteousness is making right? (By the fact that) if the Great Society possesses righteousness it is well ordered, and if it does not possess righteousness it is in confusion. By this means we know that righteousness is rectifying, but, on the other hand, that there is no rectifying

1. The actual character for 'I' seldom occurs in classical writings. It does occur from time to time in the *Mo Tzŭ Book*. I take *wu* to mean 'I,' and *wo* to mean 'we,' but there are contexts where this does not work.

2. In the argument which follows it becomes clear that *cheng* (making right) refers both to making the individual right and making the whole community right. The second of the synoptic records (c. 27) here makes Mo Ti mean 'rectifying the government of the country,' and that was a current Confucian definition of government, but the evidence of c. 26 as of this c. 28 points to Mo Ti very much having the individual in mind. Dr. Mei Yi-pao's translation 'righteousness is the standard' does not seem warranted, well as it fits in with Mo Ti's emphasis on uniformity and the necessity for having a standard.

of those above (socially) by those below. Rectification must be from above downwards.

This being so, the fact is that the common people are unsuccessful if they follow their own inclinations in making right.[1] There are the minor officials who make them right. Also the minor officials are unsuccessful if they follow their own inclinations in making right. There are the high officials who make them right. Also the high officials are unsuccessful. . . . There are the feudal lords who make them right. Also the feudal lords are unsuccessful. . . . There are the Three Dukes who make them right. The Three Dukes are unsuccessful. . . . There is the Son of Heaven who makes them right. The Son of Heaven is unsuccessful if he follows his own inclinations in making right. There is Heaven which makes him right.

Take the leaders in society who want to act righteously. It follows (logically) that they must not fail to obey the Will of Heaven. The question then is: what is the Will of Heaven like? The answer is: to love all men everywhere alike. How is this known? By the fact that Heaven gives food to all men alike. How is this known? (By the fact that) from ancient times to the present day there has been no remote, isolated, barbarian country but has fattened oxen and sheep and dogs and pigs and prepared sacrificial cakes and wine in order to sacrifice to the High Ruler [*Shang Ti*] and the mountains and river and the spirits. By this means it is known that (Heaven) gives food to all alike. Assuming that it gives food to all alike, it follows that it must love all alike. . . . Further, that Heaven loves the hundred clans is proved not merely by this. Take all the countries with their grain-eating people. For every innocent man murdered there is bound to be some calamity. Who

1. All the evidence points to Mo Ti having a profound love of the common man; but in his political opinions he was the very reverse of democratic.

does the murdering? The answer is, man. Who sends the calamity? The answer is, Heaven. If it be not exactly true that Heaven loves these people, for what reason does Heaven send calamities for the murder of innocent men?[1]

I maintain that a wise and good man is sure to reward good and punish wickedness. How do I know this? I know it by means of the Sage-kings of the Three Eras, because in those past days Yao, Shun, Yü, T'ang, Wen, and Wu loved all alike in the Great Society and followed this up by benefiting their hundred clans, changing their purposes, taking the lead in worshipping the High Ruler, the mountains and streams, and the spirits. Heaven saw this as loving and benefiting what it loved, so it loved and benefited these (Sage-kings). Thus it rewarded these kings, setting them up in the supreme position of Son of Heaven in order that they might be a pattern to all. They are named 'sage men,' and by this is learnt the proof[2] of goodness and its reward. . . .

What is it like to have government by force? The answer is: the big logically will attack the small, the strong will plunder the weak, the majority will maltreat the minority, the clever will deceive the simple, the patricians will despise the plebeians, the rich will disdain the poor, and the young will rob the old. Thus all the states in our Great Society will injure each other grievously, precisely by the use of water, fire, poison, and lethal weapons. In this way there will be no profit to heaven above or to the spirits in the middle sphere or to men below — three no-profits making no profit anyway, a state of affairs to be described as armed violence against Heaven.

1. The use of the rhetorical question came to play a great part in Chinese prose. Confucius clearly was an adept at using it, but it was Mo Ti who gave this literary device its sharply logical force, using it to make a *reductio ad absurdum*.

2. *Cheng* (evidence) occurs only once in the *Analects*, and then with the meaning of giving evidence about a crime. Here we find it in an argument used as proof. We cannot be sure that Mo Ti started this use, but it is clear that sooner or later his followers had it.

The subsequent paragraphs do not add materially to our understanding of Mo Ti's belief in Heaven. They are concerned with proving the illogicality of the 'leaders in society.' On the one hand, they denounce those who rob on a small scale, whilst, on the other, they claim as righteous something which is 'several million times worse,' namely the attacking of a weak country by a strong. There occurs here a characteristic example of Mo Ti's power of sarcasm.

This is something which confuses us. According to this, what is the difference between confusing the distinction between black and white and (confusing that between) sweet and bitter? Take the case of a man who when he is shown a few black objects calls them black, but when he is shown a large number of black objects calls them white. He would have to admit that his eyesight was in disorder and that he did not know the difference between black and white. Take also the case of a man given a few sweet things to taste. . . .

AGAINST FATALISM

It is very necessary that the statements of these believers in fate should be clearly differentiated. Nevertheless how this theory is to be clearly differentiated is a difficult question.

The word of our Master Mo: A standard must be set up. A statement without a standard (of reference) is like fixing the quarters in which the sun will rise and set by means of a revolving potter's wheel. Since that is not the way to attain a clear knowledge of the distinctions between what is right and wrong and beneficial and injurious, therefore a statement must pass three tests. What is meant by 'three tests'? In the words of our Master Mo, there is the test of a solid foundation (to a statement), the test of its verifiability, and the test of its applicability. In what way can a foundation be given? By building the statement on the facts about the ancient Sage-kings. In what way can it be verified? By ascertaining the facts about what people generally have heard with their own ears and seen with their own eyes. In what way can a statement be applied? By adopting it for the purposes of disciplinary government and observing what there is of profit to the state and to the people.

ON ALL-EMBRACING LOVE

The sage man who takes in hand the ordering of the Great Society must know what it is that gives rise to disorder: only so can he put it in order. If he does not know what gives rise to disorder, then he cannot make order. This is illustrated by the physician and his attack on men's diseases. He must know what it is that gives rise to disease. Only so can he attack it. If he does not know this, then he cannot attack it.

Why should the ordering of disorder in the state be unique in not being like this? . . . The sage man who has the ordering of the Great Society cannot but examine into what gives rise to disorder. When this examination is made, the rise of disorder is (found to be) people not loving each other, ministers of state and sons not being filial to their sovereigns and fathers: that is what is called disorder. Sons love themselves and not their fathers: and the result is that they injure their fathers in profiting themselves. Younger brothers love themselves and not their elder brothers; and the result is . . . Ministers love themselves and not their sovereigns: and the result is . . . So in the case of fathers who have no compassion for their sons, and elder brothers for their younger brothers, and sovereigns for their ministers. This also is universally described as disorder. Fathers love themselves and not their sons: and the result is they injure their sons in profiting themselves. . . .

If we go to the robbers all over the country, it is just the same. Robbers love their households and do not love the households of different kinds of people. The result is that they rob these other households in order to profit their own. And the same applies to the great officers who throw each other's clans into confusion and the feudal lords who attack each other's countries. . . . Examine all this as to its origin: it all comes from failure to love one another. . . . If the whole of society had mutual love without discrimination, country would not attack country, clan would not throw clan into confusion: there would be no robbers: sovereigns and ministers, fathers and sons, all would be compassionate and filial. In this state of affairs it follows that the Great Society would be well ordered. . . . Thus it was that our Master Mo said that he could not but urge that men should be loved. This is his word. . . .

The knights and gentlemen everywhere to-day, however, say that although in theory this kind of all-embracingness is very good, none the less it is very difficult for universal application. The word of our Master Mo is: The leaders in society simply do not understand what is to their profit, nor do they distinguish the facts.[1] Take the case of besieging a city. To fight in the fields, to achieve fame at the cost of one's life: this is what all men everywhere find very difficult. Yet if their sovereign calls for it, then the whole body of knights are able to do it. How very different from this is mutual all-embracing love and the mutual exchange of profit. To love and benefit another is to have him follow on and love and benefit you. To hate and injure another is to have him follow on and hate and injure you. What is there difficult in this? The fact is simply that no ruler has em-

---

1. Emending *pien* (to argue) to *pien* (to distinguish). The text in any case requires emendation. Another question is whether *ch'i ku*, translated as 'their facts,' is not rather 'their reasons,' in which case Mo Ti, or his early disciples, had reached that pitch of abstract analysis which enables a logician to say 'this is a cause' and 'that is an effect.'

bodied it in his government and no knight has embodied it in his conduct.

Formerly Duke Ling of Ch'u State liked his knights to have small waists. Thus it was that his court officers all limited themselves to one meal a day. Having exhaled their breath they tightened their belts. It was only by leaning against a wall that they could stand up. Within a year the whole court was black in the face. There is the fact: the sovereign called for it, and the ministers were able to do it. . . . This is the kind of thing which people find to be difficult. . . .

None the less, the knights and gentlemen everywhere say that it [i.e. all-embracing love] cannot be put into practice. To illustrate this they say it would be like picking up Mount T'ai and stepping over the river Ch'i. The word of our Master Mo denounces this as an illustration. He said that picking up Mount T'ai and stepping over the river Ch'i should be described as beyond the limit of human strength, and from antiquity down to the present day there never had been a man who could do this. How different is mutual all-embracing love and the mutual exchange of benefits! In the old days the Sage-kings put it into practice. As to how it is known that this was so,[1] in the old days when Yü[2] brought the Great Society into order, he dug out the West River and Yu Tou River in order to drain off the waters of the Ch'ü, Sun, and Huang Rivers. In the north he dammed the Yuan and Ku Rivers in order to fill up the Hou Chih Ti and Hu Chih basins. He made a watershed of the Ti Chu (range) and made a tunnel through Mount Nung Men. He did this to benefit the people of the Yui, Tai, Hu, and Ho tribes together with the people west of the Yellow River.

1. In c. 16 there is an interesting variant of this: 'We are not contemporaries of theirs: we have not heard their voices nor seen their faces. We know by means of what is written on bamboo and silk (strips) and what is engraved in metal and stone and handed down to later generations.'
2. He was the patron saint, so to speak, of the Mohists, as Yao and Shun were of the Confucianists.

. . . This expresses what Yü did. I, to-day, can practise all-embracingness.

Our Master Mo said that the man who criticizes others must have something as an alternative. To criticize without an alternative is like using fire to put out a fire. The (idea) the man expresses is logically indefensible.

I regard all-embracingness as exactly right. In this way quick ears and clear eyes co-operate in hearing and seeing, arms and legs are immeasurably strengthened to co-operate in movement and action, whilst those who possess the Way co-operate untiringly in teaching it. In this way those who are old and without wife and child have their bodily needs served so that they complete their tale of years, whilst the helpless young, children who are fatherless and motherless, have something they can trust so that their bodies can grow big and strong. . . .

It is incomprehensible what it is that makes the knights on hearing about all-inclusiveness oppose it. What are the facts of the case? As it is, the words of these knightly opponents do not stop at denunciation. They say, It is excellent, but none the less it is unusable.

The word of our Master Mo: If it is unusable, even I will oppose it. How can it be both good and unusable? Let us go forward along two lines. Suppose there are two knights, one of them holding fast to discrimination (in love), the other to all-embracingness. The result will be that the one who discriminates will make the following statement: It would be absurd for me to regard my friend's body as I regard my own, to regard his parents as I do my own. The result would be that when he observed his friend to be hungry and cold, he would not feed him or clothe him: when his friend was ill, he would not tend him: when his friend died, he would not bury him. These would be the words of the man who discriminates, and also his deeds. The knight who is all-embracing would not speak or act like that. He would say: I have heard that the high-minded knight in the Great Society must regard his friend's body as his own, his friend's parents as his own: only then can he be regarded as a high-minded knight. The result would be that when he observed his friend to be hungry and cold, he would feed and clothe him. . . .

Now if we come to the point that the words of the two knights contradict each other and their actions are diametrically opposed, we have to assume that both speak the truth and both act accordingly, so that each man's words and actions agree like the two halves of a tally: not a word is spoken which is not put into practice. In that case the question may well be put: Suppose a great stretch of country here and a man putting on his harness for going out on a campaign in which the scale of life and death cannot be known. . . . Do you know or do you not know to whom he would entrust his household and his parents and the care of his wife and children? Would it be to the friend who was all-embracing or the friend who discriminated? I think that on such an occasion as this there are no fools anywhere, whether men or women. Even though he were opposed to the all-embracing man, he would still put him in charge.

IN CONDEMNATION OF AGGRESSIVE WARFARE

There is an old proverb: If your plans fail, learn the future from the past, learn the invisible from the visible. With plans of this nature one may be both successful and wise.

Take the case of a country about to go to war. In winter the cold is to be feared, in summer the heat. This means that neither winter nor summer is the time for such action. But if in the spring, then the people miss their sowing and planting: if in the autumn, then they miss reaping and harvesting. If they miss only one season, then the number of people who will die of cold and hunger is incalculable.

Now let us reckon the army's equipment, the arrows, standards, tents, armour, shields, and sword hilts: the number of these which will break and perish and not come back is beyond reckoning. So also with the spears, lances, swords, daggers, war chariots, and baggage wagons: the number of those which will get smashed and ruined and never come back is beyond reckoning. So also with oxen and horses who go out fat and come back lean, or die there and do not come back at all: a number beyond reckoning. So also with people: the incalculable number who die, owing to the food supply being cut off or failing through the distance of transport; the number who, living under bad conditions with irregular meals and excesses of hunger and repletion, fall sick by the road and die. The army casualties also are incalculably large, perhaps whole armies perishing. Hence the spirits lose their worshippers, again to an incalculable extent, whilst the state robs the people of their incomes and diminishes their sources of profit.

All this is so: and why? The answer in defence of it is: we covet the fame and the profit of being victors in war. That is why it takes place. And the word of our Master Mo in reply is: Reckon up what they win for themselves; it is nothing of any use. Reckon up what they gain: it is the exact opposite of profit; far less than the loss. Take the case of an attack on a town with its inner wall one mile, its outer two miles, in circumference. To capture this without the thrust of a spear or the death of a man would be an empty achievement. As it is, however, the deaths at most must be reckoned by the ten thousand, at least by the thousand, and all that can be obtained is one or two miles of township. And all the time the great states have empty [i.e. half-populated] townships to be reckoned by the thousand — waiting to be occupied peacefully — and uncultivated lands to be reckoned by the ten thousand — waiting to be opened up peacefully. Thus then the amount of land waiting to be possessed is in excess, the population waiting to be ruled in true kingly fashion insufficient. Now then: to bring the people to death and to aggravate the troubles of high and low in order to quarrel over a half-populated township, this logically is to throw away that of which you have too little and to double that of which you have too much. To put the affairs of state right in this fashion is directly counter to the interest of the state.

ON MODERATION IN THE RITES OF MOURNING

The word of our Master Mo . . . When in the past ages of the Three Dynasties the Sage-kings were no more, the Great Society lost hold of righteousness, and some later leaders in society regarded elaborate funerals and prolonged mourning periods as signs of human-hearted righteousness and the duty of filial sons. Others regarded the elaborate funerals and prolonged mourning periods as not human-heartedness, not righteousness, and not the duty of filial sons. . . .

Since there are doubts arising from the contentions of both sides, let us look into the matter from the angle of the rectification of the state, the family, and the people in them. Reckon up whether elaborate funerals and prolonged mourning fits in with these three benefits. It is my opinion that if by the application of these principles the poor can really be enriched, the population be increased, social instability be changed to stability, and disorder be made good order, then elaborate funerals and prolonged mourning periods will be signs of human-heartedness [jen], righteousness, and the duty of filial sons, and those who plan on behalf of man must on no account refrain from advocating these practices. A jen sovereign will promote them throughout society, making them into institutions which the people must believe and observe from the cradle to the grave. My opinion, however, also is that if by applying these principles the poor cannot really be enriched, nor the population increased . . . then elaborate funerals will not be . . . the duty of filial sons, and those who plan on behalf of men must on no account refrain from prohibiting these practices. A *jen* sovereign will seek to eradicate them from society. . . . For the fact is that the promotion of profit and the eradication of injury throughout society as a means to bring state and people into confusion, this has never happened in the history of man. . . .

If the country be stricken with poverty, the sacrificial cakes and wine will be adulterated. If the population drop, there will be few to worship the High Ruler and the spirits. If the country be in disorder, sacrifices will not be made at the proper time. Not only so: there are cases of the worship of the High Ruler and the spirits being forbidden by the Government. In these circumstances the High Ruler and the spirits will begin to follow on by taking control of the matter. They will ask whether it is better to have men or not to have them. Then logically the High Ruler and the spirits will send down judgment on their crimes, will visit them with calamities, will punish them and cast them out. Is not this logically the situation which arises?

ON MODERATION IN SPENDING

. . . In ancient times the regulations of the Sage-kings made standards of moderation to the effect that all the artisans in the Great Society, the wheelwrights, tanners, potters, carpenters, should take in hand what they best could do, and that when they had met the needs of the common people they should stop. Whatever meant extra expense without extra profit to the people, that the Sage-kings refused to have made. . . . Thus with regard to standards for eating and drinking, the regulations were that no one should go beyond what satisfied hunger and prolonged the power of breathing, what strengthened legs and arms and made keen the powers of hearing and seeing. People were not to go to the length of blending the five flavours and harmonizing the different perfumes, or to procure rare delicacies from distant countries. How we come to know that this was so is through Yao. He ruled from Chiao Tu in the south to Yu Tu in the north, from where the sun rose in the east to where it set in the west. There were none who did not come and do homage to him. Turning to the meals he most liked to have, they were those without two kinds of millet and soup with a second course of meat. He ate out of an earthen bowl and drank from an earthen cup. . . . The Sage-king did not practise the strict observance of the social code with its bowing and scraping and passing the wine cup round.

. . . So with the regulations about clothes, the standard was not to go beyond dark purple silks in the winter, seeing that they are both light and warm, or in the summer beyond linen clothes, seeing that they are both light and cool. Thus whatever added to the expense but did not add to profit, the Sage-kings refused to have made.

THE EXALTATION OF MEN OF WORTH

The word of our Master Mo: To-day kings, dukes, and the big men in society, in making systems of government in their states, all want the country to be rich, the population big, and the administration of justice such as to produce order. But instead of getting wealth they get poverty, instead of a big population a small one, instead of order disorder. This then is basically to miss what they want and get what they hate. What are the facts about this matter?

The word of our Master Mo: Disorder consists in the failure of the kings, dukes, and big men . . . to promote men of worth and use the services of able men in administration. The facts are that if a country has plenty of worthy officers, then the order provided by the state is an unbreakable one, but if it has few such officers, then its order is easily broken. Thus it is that the business of the big men consists primarily in increasing the number of men of worth; and the question then is what is the (right) method for doing this.

The word of our Master Mo: To illustrate, if you want to increase the number of expert archers and drivers in the country, you will certainly have to enrich them, elevate their social status, honour them, and praise them before you can obtain a full complement of them.[1] How much more this applies to worthy officers, to men of solid virtue, with a command of language, learned in the method of the Way! These, to be sure, are the treasures of the state, the assistants of its guardian deities. These also must be enriched, have their social status enhanced, should be honoured and praised before a country's full complement of worthy officers can be reached.

When the Sage-kings of antiquity began to govern their word was: The unrighteous shall not be enriched, the unrighteous shall not be ennobled, the unrighteous shall not have court favour, the unrighteous shall not stand near the royal person. The rich and noble, when they heard this, all retired and consulted to this effect: We originally depended on our wealth and station, and now our lord promotes the righteous regardless of whether they are poor and base-born. That being so, it follows that we must on no account be unrighteous. . . .

In those days, therefore, there was a hierarchy of virtue and rewards on the basis of work done. . . . Officials were not permanently ennobled and the rank and file endlessly at the bottom of the social scale. The man of ability was elevated, the man of no ability put below him: public spirit was encouraged, and personal grudges put away. . . .

They cannot make their own clothes, so they are sure to employ expert tailors. . . . They have not learnt to exalt worth and employ ability in the work of government. . . . Accordingly relatives of the men who with cause are rich

1. The *a fortiori* device of dialectic is of common occurrence in these essays. This is the first time it appears in Chinese literature.

and of high station, and handsome engaging fellows, these are employed. Is there any guarantee that they will be wise and prudent? This is to employ the unwise and imprudent to order the state.

Lieh Tzŭ

LIEH TZŬ (*c.* 450-375 B.C.). Tradition ascribes the third most important document of Tâoism to a half-legendary sage who was probably a contemporary of Socrates. Lieh Tzŭ (Lieh Tse, Lieh Yü Ku, Lieh Yü-k'ao, or Licius) is known to us only through the writings of others. Revered by the Tâoist school from the period of its ascendancy in the third century B.C., he is known mainly through the book that purports to set forth his teachings.

The *Lieh tzŭ* ranks third in importance, after the *Tâo Te Ching* and the *Chuang Tzŭ*, but it is by far the most readable of the classics of Tâoism. It contains material from an earlier period, but scholarly opinion now is that it was written as late as the fourth century A.D., the second great creative period of Tâoism. It is a collection of stories, sayings, and brief essays. Each of its eight chapters deals with a single theme. The *Yang Chu* chapter, strangely out of keeping with the other chapters, preaches a hedonistic doctrine. The other chapters serve as a good introduction to Tâoist thought and to the ideal of heightened perceptiveness and re-sponsiveness in a world marked by novelty and irrationality.

The theme of the first chapter of the book ("Heaven's Gifts") is reconciliation with death. The metaphysical premise is that only the Tâo can escape change; all things originate in the Tâo and return to it. The chapter offers a number of reasons for accepting death as well as the final destruction of heaven and earth.

Heaven's Gifts

From *The Book of Lieh-tzŭ*, translated by A. C. Graham, London, John Murray, 1960. Copyright 1960 by A. C. Graham.

LIEH-TZŬ was living in Pu-t'ien, the game preserve of the state of Cheng. For forty years no one noticed him, and the prince, the nobles and the high officials of the state regarded him as one of the common people. There was famine in Cheng, and he decided to move to Wei. His disciples said to him:

'Master, you are going away, and have set no time for your return. Your disciples presume to make a request. What are you going to teach us before you go? Did not your master Hu-tzŭ tell you anything?'

'What did Hu-tzŭ ever say?' Lieh-tzŭ answered smiling. 'However, I did once overhear him talking to Po-hun Wu-jen; I will try to tell you what he said. These were his words:

' "There are the born and the Unborn, the changing and the Unchanging. The Unborn can give birth to the born, the Unchanging can change the changing. The born cannot escape birth, the changing cannot escape change; therefore birth and change are the norm. Things for which birth and change are the norm are at all times being born and changing. They simply follow the alternations of the Yin and Yang and the four seasons.

> The Unborn is by our side yet alone,
> The Unchanging goes forth and returns.
> Going forth and returning, its successions are endless;
> By our side and alone, its Way is boundless.

"The *Book of the Yellow Emperor* says:

The Valley Spirit never dies:
It is called the dark doe.
The gate of the dark doe
Is called the root of heaven and earth.
It goes on and on, something which almost exists;
Use it, it never runs out.

"Therefore that which gives birth to things is unborn, that which changes things is unchanging." '

Lieh-tzŭ said:
'Formerly the sages reduced heaven and earth to a system by means of the Yin and Yang. But if all that has shape was born from the Shapeless, from what were heaven and earth born? I answer: There was a Primal Simplicity, there was a Primal Commencement, there were Primal Beginnings, there was a Primal Material. The Primal simplicity preceded the appearance of the breath. The Primal Commencement was the beginning of the breath. The Primal Beginnings were the breath beginning to assume shape. The Primal Material was the breath when it began to assume substance. Breath, shape and substance were complete, but things were not yet separated from each other; hence the name "Confusion". "Confusion" means that the myriad things were confounded and not yet separated from each other.

'Looking you do not see it, listening you do not hear it, groping you do not touch it; hence the name "Simple". The Simple had no shape nor bounds, the Simple altered and became one, and from one altered to sevenfold, from sevenfold to ninefold. Becoming ninefold is the last of the alterations of the breath. Then it reverted to unity; unity is the beginning of the alterations of shape. The pure and light rose to become heaven, the muddy and heavy fell to become earth, the breath which harmoniously blend both became man. Hence the essences contained by heaven and

111

earth, and the birth and changing of the myriad things.'
Lieh-tzŭ said:

'Heaven and earth cannot achieve everything;
The sage is not capable of everything;
None of the myriad things can be used for everything.

For this reason

It is the office of heaven to beget and to shelter,
The office of earth to shape and to support,
The office of the sage to teach and reform,
The office of each thing to perform its function.

Consequently, there are ways in which earth excels heaven, and ways which each thing is more intelligent than the sage. Why is this? Heaven which begets and shelters cannot shape and support, earth which shapes and supports cannot teach and reform, the sage who teaches and reforms cannot make things act counter to their functions, things with set functions cannot leave their places. Hence Way of heaven and earth must be either Yin or Yang, the teaching of the sage must be either kindness or justice, and the myriad things, whatever their functions, must be either hard or soft. All these observe their functions and cannot leave their places.

'Hence there are the begotten and the Begetter of the begotten, shapes and the Shaper of shapes, sound and the Sounder of sounds, colours and the Colourer of colours, flavours and the Flavourer of flavours. What begetting begets dies, but the Begetter of the begotten never ends. What shaping shapes is real, but the Shaper of shapes has never existed. What sounding sounds is heard, but the Sounder of sounds has never issued forth. What colouring colours is visible, but the Colourer of colours never appears. What flavouring flavours is tasted, but the Flavourer of flavours is never disclosed. All are the offices of That Which Does Nothing. It is able to

Make sweet or bitter, make foul or fragrant.
Shorten or lengthen, round off or square,
Kill or beget, warm or cool.
Float or sink, sound the *kung* note or the *shang*,
Bring forth or submerge, blacken or yellow,
Make sweet or bitter, make foul or fragrant.

It knows nothing and is capable of nothing; yet there is nothing which it does not know, nothing of which it is incapable.'

When Lieh-tzǔ was eating at the roadside on a journey to Wei, he saw a skull a hundred years old. He picked a stalk, pointed at it, and said, turning to his disciple Pai-feng:

'Only he and I know that you were never born and will never die. Is it he who is truly miserable, is it we who are truly happy?

'Within the seeds of things there are germs. When they find water they develop in successive stages. Reaching water on the edge of land, they become a scum. Breeding on the bank, they become the plantain. When the plantain reaches dung, it becomes the crowfoot. The root of the crowfoot becomes woodlice, the leaves become butterflies. The butterfly suddenly changes into an insect which breeds under the stove and looks as though it has shed its skin, named the *ch'ü-to*. After a thousand days the *ch'ü-to* changes into a bird named the *kan-yü-ku*. The saliva of the *kan-yü-ku* becomes the *ssu-mi*, which becomes the vinegar animalcula *yi-lu*, which begets the animalcula *huang-k'uang*, which begets the *chiu-yu*, which begets the gnat, which begets the firefly.

'The *yang-hsi*, combining with an old bamboo which has not put forth shoots, begets the *ch'ing-ning*. This begets the leopard which begets the horse, which begets man. Man in due course returns to the germs. All the myriad things come out of germs and go back to germs.'

The Book of the Yellow Emperor says:

'When a shape stirs, it begets not a shape but a shadow. When a sound stirs, it begets not a sound but an echo.

When Nothing stirs, it begets not nothing but something.'

That which has shape is that which must come to an end. Will heaven and earth end? They will end together with me. Will there ever be no more ending? I do not know. Will the Way end? At bottom it has had no beginning. Will there ever be no more of it? At bottom it does not exist.

Whatever is born reverts to being unborn, whatever has shape reverts to being shapeless. But unborn it is not the basically Unborn, shapeless it is not the basically Shapeless. That which is born is that which in principle must come to an end. Whatever ends cannot escape its end, just as whatever is born cannot escape birth; and to wish to live forever, and have no more of ending, is to be deluded about our lot.

The spirit is the possession of heaven, the bones are the possession of earth. What belongs to heaven is pure and disperses, what belongs to earth is dense and sticks together. When spirit parts from body, each returns to its true state. That is why ghosts are called *kuei*; *kuei* means 'one who has gone home', they have gone back to their true home. The Yellow Emperor said:

'When my spirit goes through its door,
And my bones return to the root form which they grew,
What will remain of me?'

From his birth to his end, man passes through four great changes: infancy, youth, old age, death. In infancy his energies are concentrated and his inclinations are one — the ultimate of harmony. Other things do not harm him, nothing can add to the virtue in him. In youth, the energies in his blood are in turmoil and overwhelm him, desires and cares rise up and fill him. Others attack him, therefore the virtue wanes in him. When he is old, desires and cares weaken, his body is about to rest. Nothing contends to get ahead of him, and although he has not reached the perfection of infancy, compared with his youth there is a great difference for the better. When he dies, he goes to his rest, rises again to his zenith.

114

Yang Chu

YANG CHU (*c.* 440-260 B.C.). The most important document of Chinese hedonism is the *Yang Chu*
chapter of the *Lieh-tzŭ*. Some of the ideas presented in
this famous chapter and attributed to a wise-man recluse about whom little is known, recall the teachings
of Epicurus, who probably preceded him, as well as
those of Lao Tzŭ.

Yang Chu (Yang Tschu, Yang-Tse, or Yang-Sheng)
may have been the first promulgator of a simpler form
of the mystical doctrine of Tâoism, but tradition makes
him the successor of Lao Tzŭ. Critics objected to his
teachings, particularly on hedonism and egotism, yet
he seems to have shared a strong sense of naturalism
with Lao Tzŭ and Chuang Tzŭ. Urging avoidance of
material pleasure and purity of conduct, he talked of
"letting life run its course freely," of "not injuring our
material existence with things," and of "ignoring not
only riches and fame but also life and death." Heaven
and men are the twin sources of our social world. The
artificial part of the world, that made by man and
called civilization, is to be shunned in favor of life according to pure nature, Heaven's creation.

The teachings of Yang Chu, together with those of
Mo Tzŭ, strongly rivaled Confucianism at the time of
Mencius (372-289 B.C.). His main doctrine of fol-
lowing nature and preserving life was distorted by his

successors. "Each man for himself" was misconstrued as the rankest form of egotism, and through the centuries he has been labeled the "Egotist," the man who "would not give up a single hair for the benefit of the whole world." He actually believed that one should never allow the slightest injury for the sake of material benefits, and that "the only way to treat life is to let it have its own way, neither hindering it nor obstructing it."

The book bearing the name of Lieh Tzŭ is a collection of sayings and stories. Partially borrowed from older sources, it was probably written around 300 A.D. The famous *Yang Chu* chapter of the *Lieh-tzŭ* (Chapter 7) sets forth in a few brief passages a refreshingly unorthodox philosophy based on the principle of making the most of life by "following the desires of one's heart and refraining from contradicting the inclinations of nature."

The Yang Chu Chapter
of the Lieh-tzŭ

From *The Book of Lieh-tzŭ*, translated by A. C. Graham, London, John Murray, 1960. Copyright 1960 by A. C. Graham.

Y ANG Chu travelled in Lu, and lodged with Mr. Meng. Mr. Meng asked him a question.

'We are simply the men we are. What use is reputation?'

—'A reputation helps us to get rich.'

'Once rich, why not be done with it?'

—'It helps us to win high rank.'

'Once we have high rank, why not be done with it?'

—'It will help when we are dead.'

'Once dead, what good will it do us?'

—'It will help our descendants.'

'What use will our reputations be to our descendants?'

—'Caring for reputation vexes the body and withers the heart; but the man who takes advantage of his reputation can prosper his whole clan and benefit his whole district, not to speak of his own descendants.'

'But whoever cares for reputation must be honest, and if honest he will be poor. He must be humble, and if humble he will not rise in rank.'

—'When Kuan Chung was chief minister in Ch'i, he was lewd when his ruler was lewd, extravagant when his ruler was extravagant. He accorded with his ruler in thought and in speech, and by the practice of his Way the state won hegemony; but after his death, the Kuan family was still only the Kuan family. When T'ien Heng was chief minister in Ch'i, he behaved unassumingly when his ruler was

117

arrogant, behaved generously when his ruler was grasping. The people all went over to him, and in this way he won 'So if you really live up to your reputation, you will be poor; if your reputation is pretence, you will be rich.'

—'Reality has nothing to do with reputation, reputation has nothing to do with reality. Reputation is nothing but pretence. Formerly Yao and Shun pretended to resign the Empire to Hsü Yu and Shan Chüan but did not give it up, and were blessed with its possession for a hundred years. Po Yi and Shu Ch'i, who really resigned the fief of Ku-chu, did end by losing this state, and died of starvation on Mount Shou-yang. The difference between the reality and the pretence could not be put more plainly.'

Yang Chu said:

'A hundred years is the term of the longest life, but not one man in a thousand lives so long. Should there be one who lives out his span, infancy and senility take nearly half of it. The nights lost in sleep, the days wasted even when we are awake, take nearly half the rest. Pain and sickness, sorrow and toil, ruin and loss, anxiety and fear, take nearly half of the rest. Of the dozen or so years which remain, if we reckon how long we are at ease and content, without the least care, it does not amount to the space of an hour.

'Then what is a man to live for? Where is he to find happiness? Only in fine clothes and good food, music and beautiful women. But we cannot always have enough good clothes and food to satisfy us, cannot always be playing with women and listening to music. Then again, we are checked by punishments and seduced by rewards, led forward by the hope of reputation, driven back by fear of the law. Busily we compete for an hour's empty praise, and scheme for glory which will outlast our deaths; even in our solitude we comply with what we see others do, hear others say, and repent of what our own thoughts approve and reject. In vain we lose the utmost enjoyment of the prime of life, we cannot give ourselves up to the hour. How are we different from prisoners weighted with chains and fetters?

'The men of the distant past knew that in life we are here for a moment and in death we are gone for a moment. Therefore they acted as their hearts prompted, and did not rebel against their spontaneous desires; while life lasted they did not refuse its pleasures, and so they were not seduced by the hope of reputation. They roamed as their nature prompted, and did not rebel against the desires common to all things; they did not prefer a reputation after death, and so punishment did not affect them. Whether they were reputed and praised more or less than others, whether their destined years were many or few, they did not take into account.'

Yang Chu said:

'It is in life that the myriad things of the world are different; in death they are all the same. In life, there are clever and foolish, noble and vile; these are the differences. In death, there are stench and rot, decay and extinction; in this we are all the same.

'*However, whether we are clever or foolish, noble or vile, is not our own doing, and neither are stench and rot, decay and extinction. Hence we do not bring about our own life or death, cleverness or foolishness, nobility or vileness. However, the myriad things all equally live and die, are equally clever and foolish, noble and vile.*

'Some in ten years, some in a hundred, we all die; saints and sages die, the wicked and foolish die. In life they were Yao and Shun, in death they are rotten bones; in life they were Chieh and Chou, in death they are rotten bones. Rotten bones are all the same, who can tell them apart? Make haste to enjoy your life while you have it; why care what happens when you are dead?'

Yang Chu said:

'It is not that Po Yi had no desires, his was the worst sort possession of the state of Ch'i, and his descendants have enjoyed it without interruption down to the present day.'

of pride in one's own purity, and because of it he starved to death. It is not that Chan Ch'in had no passions, his was the worst sort of pride in one's own correctness, and because of it he weakened his clan. They went to these extremes in treating mistaken "purity" and "correctness" as virtues.'

Yang Chu said:

'Yüan Hsien grew poor in Lu, Tzŭ-kung grew rich in Wei.[1] Yüan Hsien's poverty injured his life, Tzŭ-kung's wealth involved him in trouble.'

'If that is so, wealth and poverty are both bad; where is the right course to be found?'

'It is to be found in enjoying life, in freeing ourselves from care. Hence those who are good at enjoying life are not poor, and those who are good at freeing themselves from care do not get rich.'

Yang Chu said:

'There is an old saying that each of us should pity the living and abandon the dead. This saying puts it exactly. The way to pity others is not simply to feel for them. When they are toiling we can give them ease, hungry we can feed them, cold we can warm them, in trouble we can help them to get through. The way to abandon the dead is not to refuse to feel sorry for them. But we should not put pearls or jade in their mouths, dress them in brocades, lay out sacrifical victims, prepare funeral vessels.'

Yen-tzŭ asked Kuan Chung about 'tending life'. Kuan Chung answered:

'It is simply living without restraint; do not suppress, do not restrict.'

'Tell me the details.'

'Give yourself up to whatever your ears wish to listen to, your eyes to look on, your nostrils to turn to, your mouth to say, your body to find ease in, your will to achieve. What the ears wish to hear is music and song, and if these are denied them, I say that the sense of hearing is restricted. What the

---

1. Two disciples of Confucius.

eyes wish to see is the beauty of women, and if this is denied them, I say that the sense of sight is restricted. What the nostrils wish to turn to is orchids and spices, and if these are denied them, I say that the sense of smell is restricted. What the mouth wishes to discuss is truth and falsehood, and if this is denied it, I say that the intelligence is restricted. What the body wishes to find ease in is fine clothes and good food, and if these are denied it, I say that its comfort is restricted. What the will wishes to achieve is freedom and leisure, and if it is denied these, I say that man's nature is restricted.

'All these restrictions are oppressive masters. If you can rid yourself of these oppressive masters, and wait serenely for death, whether you last a day, a month, a year, ten years, it will be what I call "tending life". If you are bound to these oppressive masters, and cannot escape their ban, though you were to survive miserably for a hundred years, a thousand, ten thousand, I would not call it "tending life".'

Then Kuan Chung in his turn questioned Yen-tzŭ:

'I have told you about "tending life". What can you tell me about taking leave of the dead?'

'It does not matter how we take leave of the dead. What is there to say about it?'

'I insist on hearing.'

'Once I am dead, what concern is it of mine? It is the same to me whether you burn me or sink me in a river, bury me or leave me in the open, throw me in a ditch wrapped in grass or put me in a stone coffin dressed in a dragon-blazoned jacket and embroidered skirt. I leave it to chance.'

Kuan Chung turned to Pao Shu-ya and Huang-tzŭ, and said:

1. The phrase *yang-sheng* ('tending life', 'tending the living') had different meanings for different schools. For individualists of the 4th century B.C. (deriving from the historical Yang Chu himself) it meant the satisfaction of personal needs without injuring health and life. For Confucians, 'tending the living' and 'taking leave of the dead' were the filial duties of supporting and decently burying one's parents. The present passage gives the Confucian terms a hedonist reinterpretation.

'Between the two of us, we have said all that there is to say about the Way to live and to die.'

Tzŭ-ch'an was chief minister in Cheng. Within three years of his taking sole charge of the government, the good had submitted to his reforms and the wicked dreaded his prohibitions; the state of Cheng was in good order and the other states were afraid of it. But he had an elder brother called Kung-sun Chao who was fond of wine, and a younger brother called Kung-sun Mu who was fond of women. Chao had collected in his house a thousand jars of wine and a whole hillock of yeast for brewing; and for a hundred paces outside his door the smell of the dregs came to meet men's nostrils. When he was carried away by wine, he did not know whether there was peace or war in the world, he did not notice mistakes which he had time to repent, he forgot the possessions in his own house, the degrees of affinity of his kinsmen, and that it is better to live than to die. Even if he had stood in water or fire with sword blades clashing before him, he would not have known it.

In the back courtyard of Mu's house there was a row of several dozen rooms, and he picked young and lovely girls to fill them. When he was excited by lust, he shut the door on his kinsmen and stopped meeting and going out with his friends; he fled into his harem, where the nights were too short to satisfy him, and left thwarted if he had to come out once in three months. Any beautiful virgin in the district he was sure to tempt with gifts and invite through go-betweens, giving up only if he could not catch her.

Tzŭ-ch'an, who worried about them night and day, went privately to consult Teng Hsi.

'I have heard,' he said, 'that a man should influence his family by setting his own life in order, influence the state by setting his own family in order — meaning that the example you set to those nearest to you extends to those further away. My administration has set the state in order, yet my family is in anarchy. Have I been doing things the wrong

122

way round? Tell me a method of helping these two men.'

'I have long marvelled at it,' said Teng Hsi, 'but did not wish to be the first to raise the question. Why not look out for an opportunity to set their lives in order, make them understand the importance of keeping their health, appeal to their respect for propriety and duty?'

Tzŭ-ch'an took his advice. He found an opportunity to visit his brothers, and told them:

'It is knowledge and foresight which make man nobler than the beasts and birds. Knowledge and foresight lead us to propriety and duty. Learn to live properly and dutifully, and reputation and office will be yours. But if you act on the promptings of your passions, and excite yourselves with pleasure and lust, you will endanger health and life. Should you listen to what I say, you can repent in a morning and draw your salaries by the evening.'

Chao and Mu answered:

'We have long known it, and long since made our choice. Why should we need your advice to make us see it? Always life is precious and death comes too soon. We must never forget that we are living this precious life, waiting for death which comes too soon; and to wish to impress others with your respect for propriety and duty, distorting your natural passions to call up a good name, in our judgement is worse than death. We wish to enjoy this single life to the full, draining the utmost pleasure from its best years. For us the only misfortune is a belly too weak to drink without restraint, potency which fails before our lust is satisfied. We have no time to worry that our reputation is ugly and our health in danger.

'Besides, is it not mean and pitiable that you, whom success in ruling the state has made proud, should wish to disturb our hearts with sophistries, and flatter our thoughts with hopes of glory and salary? We in turn would like to dispute the issue with you. The man who is good at ordering the lives of others does not necessarily succeed, but overworks himself trying. The man who is good at ordering his own life gives scope to his nature without needing to disorder the lives of others. Your method of ruling other may be realised temporarily in a single state, but it is out of accord with men's hearts. Our method of ruling ourselves may be extended to the whole world, until the Way of ruler and subject is brought to an end. We have long wanted to make you understand our way of life, but on the contrary it is you who come to teach us yours!'

Tzŭ-ch'an was bewildered and had no answer to give. On another day he told Teng Hsi, who said:

'You have been living with True Men without knowing it. Who says you are a wise man? The good government of the state of Cheng is mere chance, you cannot take the credit for it.'

Tuan-mu Shu of Wei was a descendant of Tzŭ-kung.[1] He lived on his inheritance, a family property worth ten thousand pieces of gold. He did not bother with the issue of his time, but followed his impulse and did as he pleased. The things which all men desire to do, with which our inclinations desire to be amused, he did them all, amused himself with them all. His walls and rooms, terraces and pavilions, parks and gardens, lakes and ponds, his food and drink, carriages and dress, singers and musicians, wife and concubines, bore comparison with those of the rulers of Ch'i and Ch'u. Whatever his passions inclined him to enjoy, whatever his ear wished to hear, his eye to see and his mouth to taste, he would send for without fail, even if it came from a different region or a border country and was not a product of the Middle Kingdom, as though it were something from just across his wall or his hedge. When he travelled he always went wherever he pleased, however perilous the mountains and rivers, however long and distant the roads, as other men walk a few paces. Every day the guests in his court were counted in hundreds, and down

1. A disciple of Confucius.

124

in his kitchen the fire never went out, up in his hall and chambers the musicians never stopped playing. The leftovers of his banquets he scattered far and wide, first in his own clan, next in the town and the villages around, finally all over the country.

When he reached the age of sixty, and his vitality and health were beginning to wane, he let go of his family affairs, and gave away all the precious things in his treasuries and storehouses, all his carriages and robes and concubines, finishing them all within a year, keeping nothing for his own children and grandchildren. When he fell ill, he had no medicine or needle in store; and when he died, lacked the price of his own burial. The people throughout the whole country who had enjoyed his bounty made a collection among themselves to bury him, and restored the property of his children and grandchildren.

When Ch'in Ku-li heard of it, he said:

'Tuan-mu Shu was a madman. He disgraced the disciple of Confucius who was his ancestor.'

When Tuan-kan Mu heard of it, he said:

'Tuan-mu Shu was a man who understood; his qualities surpassed those of his ancestor. All his actions, everything he did, astonished commonplace minds, but truly reason approves them. Most of the gentlemen in Wei live by the manners they have been taught; naturally they are incapable of grasping what was in this man's mind.'

Meng Sun-yang asked Yang Chu:

'Suppose that a man values his life and takes care of his body; may he hope by such means to live for ever?'

'It is impossible to live for ever.'

'May he hope to prolong his life?'

'It is impossible to prolong life. Valuing life cannot preserve it, taking care of the body cannot do it good. Besides, what is the point of prolonging life? Our five passions, our likes and dislikes, are the same now as they were of old. The safety and danger of our four limbs, the joy and bitterness of worldly affairs, changes of fortune, good government and discord, are the same now as they were of old. We have heard it already, seen it already, experienced it already. Even a hundred years is enough to satiate us; could we endure the bitterness of still longer life?'

'If it is so, and swift destruction is better than prolonged life, you can get what you want by treading on blades and spear-points, rushing into fire and boiling water.'

'No. While you are alive, resign yourself and let life run its course; satisfy all your desires and wait for death. When it is time to die, resign yourself and let death run its course; go right to your destination, which is extinction. Be resigned to everything, let everything run its course; why need you delay it or speed it on its way?'

Yang Chu said:

'*Po-ch'eng Tzŭ-kao would not benefit others at the cost of one hair; he renounced his state and retired to plough the fields. The Great Yü did not keep even his body for his own benefit; he worked to drain the Flood until one side of him was paralysed. A man of ancient times, if he could have benefited the Empire by the loss of one hair, would not have given it; and if everything in the Empire had been offered to him alone, would not have taken it. When no one would lose a hair and no one would benefit the Empire, the Empire was in good order.*'[1]

1. This passage (with the succeeding dialogue) does not come from the hedonist author; it is a garbled account of the doctrines of the historical Yang Chu from a much older source, probably a document of the rival school of Mo-tzŭ, the advocate of universal love. The original doctrine of Yang Chu is still visible behind the passage, which makes much better sense when its distortion is corrected:

'Po-ch'eng Tzŭ-kao would not *accept any external benefit* at the cost of one hair; he renounced his state and retired to plough the field ... When no one would lose a hair, and no one would *take* the Empire, the Empire was in good order.'

In the dialogue which follows, it is clear that Yang Chu and his disciple are arguing against the sacrifice of a hair to '*gain* a kingdom', while Ch'in Ku-li (a disciple of Mo-tzŭ) interprets this as refusing to 'help the world'. This is why it embarrasses Ch'in Ku-li to admit that he would not cripple himself to gain a kingdom; it amounts to admitting that he would refuse the opportunity to benefit its people by good government.

Ch'in Ku-li asked Yang Chu:

'If you could help the whole world by sacrificing one hair of your body, would you do it?'

'The world certainly will not be helped by one hair.'

'But supposing it did help, would you do it?'

Yang Chu did not answer him. When Ch'in Ku-li came out he told Meng Sun-yang, who said:

'You do not understand what is in my Master's mind. Let me explain. If you could win ten thousand pieces of gold by injuring your skin and flesh, would you do it?'

'I would.'

'If you could gain a kingdom by cutting off one limb at the joint, would you do it?'

Ch'in Ku-li was silent for a while. Meng Sun-yang continued:

'It is clear that one hair is a trifle compared with skin and flesh, and skin and flesh compared with one joint. However, enough hairs are worth as much as skin and flesh, enough skin and flesh as much as one joint. You cannot deny that one hair has its place among the myriad parts of the body; how can one treat it lightly?'

Ch'in Ku-li said:

'I do not know how to answer you. I can only say that if you were to question Lao-tzŭ and Kuan-yin about your opinion they would agree with you, and if I were to question the Great Yü and Mo-tzŭ about mine they would agree with me.'

Meng Sun-yang thereupon turned to his disciples and changed the subject.

Yang-Chu said:

'The men whom the world admires are Shun, Yü, the Duke of Chou and Confucius. The men whom the world condemns are Chieh and Chou. Yet Shun ploughed at Ho-yang, and made pots at Lei-tse; his four limbs did not find a moment's ease, his mouth and stomach did not get good and sufficient food; he was a man unloved by his parents, treated as a stranger by his younger brothers and sisters. He was thirty before he married, and then without telling his parents. When Yao abdicated the throne to him, he was already old and his wits had deteriorated. Since his eldest son Shang-chün was incompetent, he had to abdicate the throne to Yü, and died at the end of a miserable life. He was the most wretched and afflicted man under the sky.

'When Kun, the father of Yü, was in charge of draining the earth during the Flood, and failed to complete the work, Shun executed him in Yü-shan. Yü inherited the work and served the enemy who had killed his father, thinking of nothing but his duty to the land. His children and estate were uncared for, he passed his door too busy to go in, half his body became paralysed, his hands and feet calloused. When Shun abdicated the throne to him, he made his palace humble but his ceremonial sash and cap beautiful, and died at the end of a miserable life. He was the most careworn and overdriven man under the sky.

'After the death of King Wu, in the childhood of King Ch'eng, the Duke of Chou controlled the administration of the Empire, to the displeasure of the Duke of Shao. Rumors slandering the Duke of Chou circulated through the country, forcing him to retire to the East for three years. He executed his elder brothers and banished his younger brothers, himself barely escaping with his life. He died at the end of a miserable life, in more danger and fear than any man under the sky.

'Confucius understood the Way of the Five Emperors and Three Kings, and accepted the invitations of the rulers of his time. They chopped down a tree over his head in Sung, he had to scrape away his footprints in Wei, he was at the end of his resources in Sung and Chou, he was trapped by his enemies in Ch'en and Ts'ai, he was humiliated by the Chi family and insulted by Yang Hu, and died at the end of a miserable life. He was the most harried and distraught man under the sky.

'All those four sages lived without a day's joy, and died

leaving a reputation which will last ten thousand generations. Truly the reality was not what their reputation should have earned them. Though we praise them they do not know it; though we value them they do not know it. It matters no more to them than to stumps of trees and clods of earth.

'Chieh inherited the wealth of successive reigns, and sat facing South on the Imperial throne. He had enough wit to hold down his subjects, enough authority to make all tremble within the four seas. He gave himself up to all that amused his ears and eyes, did all that his thought and inclination suggested to him, and died at the end of a merry life. He was the freest, most boisterous man under the sky.

'Chou also inherited the wealth of successive reigns, and sat facing South on the Imperial throne. His authority prevailed everywhere, his will was obeyed everywhere. He vented his passions in a palace a hundred acres square, and let loose his desire in a night four months long.[1] He did not vex himself about propriety and duty, and was executed at the end of a merry life. He was the most carefree, the least constrained man under the sky.

'Those two villains lived in the joy of following their desires, and dying incurred the reputation of fools and tyrants. Truly the reality was not what their reputation deserved. Whether we revile or praise them they do not know it; does it mean any more to them than to stumps of trees and clods of earth?

'The four sages, although the world admires them, suffered to the end of their lives, and death was the last home of all of them. The two villains, although the world condemns them, were happy to the end of their lives, and again death was their last home.'

---

1. A banquet lasting a hundred and twenty days, called the 'Drinking Bout of the Long Night'.

Yang Chu visited the King of Liang, and told him that ruling the Empire was like rolling it in the palm of your hand. The King said:

'You have one wife and one concubine, whom you cannot control, and a garden of three acres, which you cannot weed. Are you the person to tell me that it is so easy to rule the Empire?'

'Have you seen a shepherd with his flock? Send a boy four foot high with a stick on his shoulder to follow a flock of a hundred sheep, and it will go East or West as he wishes. Make Yao lead one sheep, with Shun following behind with a stick on his shoulder, and they couldn't make the sheep budge. Besides, I have heard that the fish which can swallow a boat does not swim in side streams, the high-flying hawk and swan do not settle in ponds and puddles. Why? Because their aims are set very high. The Huang-chung and Ta-lü music cannot accompany the dance in common entertainments. Why? Because its sound is too far above the ordinary. It is this that is meant by the saying: "One who sets out on a great enterprise does not concern himself with trifles; one who achieves great successes does not achieve small ones".'

Yang Chu said:

'The events of the distant past have vanished; who has recorded them? The actions of the Three Highnesses are as nearly lost as surviving; the actions of the Five Emperors are as near dream as waking; the actions of the Three Kings hover in and out of sight. Out of a hundred thousand we do not remember one. Of the events of our own time, we have seen some and heard of some, but we do not remember one in ten thousand. Of events happening this very moment, we notice some and ignore some, and we shall not remember one in a thousand. From the distant past to the present day the years are indeed too many to count; but during the three hundred thousand years and more since Fu-hsi, the memory of worth and folly, beauty and ugliness, success and failure, right and wrong, has always without exception faded and vanished . . . swiftly or slowly, that is the only difference.

'If we presume on the praise or slander of an hour, so that we wither the spirit and vex the body, seeking a reputation which will survive our deaths by a few hundred years, how will this suffice to moisten our dry bones, and renew the joy of life?'

Yang Chu said:

'*Man resembles the other species between heaven and earth, and like them owes his nature to the Five Elements. He is the most intelligent of living things. But in man, nails and teeth are not strong enough to provide defence, skin and flesh are too soft for protection; he cannot run fast enough to escape danger, and he lacks fur and feathers to ward off heat and cold. He must depend on other things in order to tend his nature, must trust in knowledge and not rely on force. Hence the most valuable use of knowledge is for self-preservation, while the most ignoble use of force is to attack others.*

'*However, my body is not my possession; yet once born, I have no choice but to keep it intact. Other things are not my possessions; yet once I exist, I cannot dispense with them. Certainly, it is by the body that we live; but it is by means of other things that we tend it.*

'*Although I keep life and body intact, I cannot possess this body; although I may not dispense with things, I cannot possess these things. To possess these things, possess this body, would be violently to reserve for oneself body and things which belong to the world. Is it not only the sage, only the highest man, who treats as common possessions the body and the things which belong to the world? It is this which is meant by "highest of the highest".*'[1]

1. This passage is clearly not the work of the hedonist author; nor, since it values knowledge, does it seem to be characteristically Tâoist. It discusses the relative importance of external possessions and the preserva-

131

Yang Chu said:

'People find no rest because of four aims — long life, re-putation, office, possessions. Whoever has these four aims dreads spirits, dreads other men, dreads authority, dreads punishment. I call him "a man in flight from things".

> He can be killed, he can be given life;
> The destiny which decides is outside him.

If you do not go against destiny, why should you yearn for long life? If you are not conceited about honours, why should you yearn for reputation? If you do not want power, why should you yearn for office? If you are not greedy for wealth, why should you yearn for possessions? One who sees this I call "a man in accord with things".

> Nothing in the world counters him;
> The destiny which decides is within him.

'Hence the saying,

> "Without office and marriage
> Men's satisfactions would be halved.
> If they did not eat and wear clothes
> The Way of ruler and subject would cease." '[1]

A Chou proverb says that 'You can kill a peasant by let-ting him sit down'. He thinks it natural and normal to work from morning to night; he thinks that nothing tastes better than a dinner of beans. His skin and flesh are thick and

tion of one's body, the problem which engaged the historical Yang Chu, and perhaps comes from some offshoot of his school. The extreme doctrine, ascribed to Yang Chu himself, that the body should always be preferred, is rejected on the grounds that (1) Men, unlike animals, cannot exists without external possessions, (2) We cannot possess even the body, since we cannot prevent it undergoing the processes of growth and decay common to all things.

1. It is likely that the next saying of Yang Chu should follow straight on here, the intervening passage being an interpolation by the editor of *Lieh-tzŭ*.

coarse, his joints and muscles supple and vigorous. If one morning you were to put him on soft furs behind silken curtains, and offer him good millet and meat and fragrant oranges, it would unsettle his mind and injure his health, and he would fall ill with fever. On the other hand if the ruler of Sung or Lu were to change places with the peasant, he would be worn out before he had worked an hour. Therefore when the rustic is satisfied and pleased with anything, he says there is nothing better in the world.

There was once a peasant in Sung, whose ordinary coat was of tangled hemp and barely kept him alive through the winter. When the spring sun rose in the East, he warmed his body in the sunshine. He did not know that there were such things in the world as wide halls and secluded chambers, floss silk and fox furs. He turned to his wife and said:

'No one knows how warm it is to bare one's back to the sun. I shall make a present of this knowledge to our ruler, and he will richly reward me.'

But a rich man of the village told him:

'Once there was a man who had a taste for broad beans, nettle-hemp seeds, celery and southernwood shoots, and recommended them to some important people of the district. When they tried the dish, it stung their mouths and pained their stomachs. They all smiled coldly and put the blame on him, and he was very embarrassed. You are just like him.'

Yang Chu said:

'A grand house, fine clothes, good food, beautiful women — if you have these four, what more do you need from outside yourself? One who has them yet seeks more from outside himself has an insatiable nature. An insatiable nature is a grub eating away one's vital forces.'

Being loyal is not enough to make the ruler safe; all it can do is endanger oneself. Being dutiful is not enough to benefit others; all it can do is interfere with one's life. When it is seen that loyalty is not the way to make the ruler safe, the good reputation of the loyal will disappear; when it is seen that duty is not the way to benefit others, the good reputation of the dutiful will come to an end. It was the Way of ancient times that both ruler and subject should be safe, both others and oneself should be benefited.

Yü Hsiung said that 'The man who dispenses with reputation is free from care'. Lao-tzŭ said that 'Reputation is the guest who comes and goes, reality is the host who stays', yet fretful people never stop running after a good reputation. Is a reputation really indispensable, is it really impossible to treat it as a passing guest?

Now a good reputation brings honour and glory, a bad one humiliation and disgrace. Honour and glory bring ease and joy, humiliation and disgrace bring care and vexation. It is care and vexation which go against our nature, ease and joy which accord with it. Then a real gain is attached to reputation. How can we dispense with it, how can we treat it as a passing guest? The one thing we should dislike is getting involved in real difficulties by clinging to reputation. If you involve yourself in real difficulties by clinging to it, you will have irremediable ruin to worry about, not only the choice between ease and care, joy and vexation!

Shang Yang

SHANG YANG (*c.* 400-338 B.C.). A leading advocate of political realism as taught by the Legalist School of the fourth century B.C., Shang Yang (Kung-sun Yang or Wei Yang), reformed the government of Tsin. He abolished serfdom, organized a bureaucratic government, and put into effect a strict legal code that applied uniformly to all classes. A native of the state of Wei, he had to move to the westernmost Chinese state, one of the most backward, to put his ideas into practice. Although he came to a bad end, within a century the system which he had initiated brought the state of Ch'in to supremacy over all the other states.

Shang Yang was a realist of realists, devoting himself completely to the material strength of the state. He was the first to see clearly that the coming of the bureaucratic state heralded the systematic development of law. Thus he is justly credited with the founding of the Fa Chia, or Legalist School. His philosophy puts the law (*fa*) above all else, whereas Shen Pu-hai's Legalism stresses autocratic power (*shih*), and Han Fei's, statecraft (*shu*).

How much of the *Book of Lord Shang* was written by Shang Yang is controversial. Some of the surviving essays are plainly the contributions of later thinkers.

135

The Book of Lord Shang

From *Chinese Philosophy in Classical Times*, edited by E. H. Hughes. London, M. M. Dent & Sons Ltd.

THE REFORM OF THE LAW

DUKE Hsiao discussed his policy. The three Great Officers, Lord Shang, Kan Lung, and Tu Chih, were in attendance on the prince. Their thoughts dwelt on the vicissitudes of the world's affairs; and they discussed the principles of rectifying the law, seeking for a way of directing the people. The prince said, 'I intend now to alter the laws, so as to obtain orderly government, and to reform the rites so as to teach the people; but I am afraid the empire will criticize me.' Lord Shang said, 'I have heard it said that he who hesitates in action does not accomplish anything, and he who hesitates in affairs gains no merit. Let Your Highness settle your thoughts quickly about altering the laws and perhaps not heed the criticism of the empire.'

Lord Shang said, '. . . There is more than one way to govern the world, and there is no necessity to imitate antiquity, in order to take appropriate measures for the state. T'ang and Wu succeeded in attaining supremacy without following antiquity, and, as for the downfall of Yin and Hsia, they were ruined without rites having been altered. Consequently, those who act counter to antiquity, do not necessarily deserve blame, nor do those who follow established rites merit much praise. Let Your Highness not hesitate.' Duke Hsiao said, '. . . One should, in one's plans, be directed by the needs of the times — I have no doubts about it.' Thereupon, in consequence, he issued the order to bring waste lands under cultivation.

AN ORDER TO CULTIVATE WASTE LANDS

[There are twenty arguments adduced, of which the following are selected.]

3. If dignities are not conferred nor offices given according to deviating standards, then the people will not prize learning, nor besides will they hold agriculture cheap. If they do not prize learning, they will be stupid, and being stupid, they will have no interest in outside things. When they have no interest in outside things, the country will exert itself in agriculture and not neglect it; and when the people do not hold agriculture cheap, the country will be peaceful and free from peril. If the country is peaceful and free from peril, exerts itself in agriculture and does not neglect it, then it is certain waste lands will be brought under cultivation.

4. If government salaries are liberal and consequently taxes numerous, then the large number of persons who live on others involves ruin for agriculture; but if they are assessed according to a calculated [i.e. very limited] number of persons who live on others, and if people are made to work hard, then the wicked and licentious, the idle and lazy will have nothing on which to live and they will take up agriculture. When they take up agriculture, then it is certain waste lands will be brought under cultivation.

5. Do not allow merchants to buy grain or farmers to sell grain. If farmers may not sell their grain, then the lazy and inactive ones will exert themselves and be energetic; and if merchants may not buy grain, then they will have no particular joy over abundant years. Having no particular joy over abundant years, they do not make copious profits in years of famine; and making no copious profits, merchants are fearful, and being fearful, they desire to turn farmers. If lazy and inactive farmers exert themselves and become energetic, and if merchants desire to turn farmer,

then it is certain waste lands will be brought under cultivation.

7. If it is impossible to hire servants, great prefects and heads of families are not supported, and beloved sons cannot eat in laziness. . . . Then it is certain waste lands will be brought under cultivation.

9. If mountains and moors are brought into one hand [under one control], then the people who hate agriculture, the tardy and lazy, and those who desire double profits,[1] will have no means of subsistence. This being so, they will certainly become farmers, and so it is certain waste lands will be brought under cultivation.

10. If the prices of wine and meat are made high and the taxes on them so heavy that they amount to ten times the cost of production, then merchants and retailers will be few, farmers will not be able to enjoy drinking bouts, and officials will not over-eat. . . . Then it is certain waste lands will be brought under cultivation.

16. If the administration of all the districts is of one pattern, then (people) will be obedient; eccentric men will not be able to be ostentatious, and successive officials will not dare to make changes; and if they act wrongly and abolish (the existing administration), it will be impossible to keep their actions hidden. . . . Then the official appurtenances will be few,[2] and the people will not be harassed . . . taxes will not be troublesome. . . . Then it is certain waste lands will be brought under cultivation.

AGRICULTURE AND WAR

The means whereby a ruler of men encourages the people are office and rank: the means whereby a country is made prosperous are agriculture and war.

The people say, 'We till diligently, first to fill the public

---

1. i.e., are averse to working unless there is prospect of double profit.
2. The official class will be a small one.

granaries, and then to keep the rest for the nourishment of our parents. For the sake of our superiors we forget our love of life and fight for the honour of the ruler and for the peace of the country. But if the granaries are empty, the ruler debased, and the family poor, then it is best to seek office. Let us then combine relatives and friends and think of other plans.' Eminent men will then apply themselves to the study of the *Odes* and *History* and pursue these improper standards: insignificant individuals will occupy themselves with trade and practise arts and crafts, all in order to avoid farming and fighting. Where the people are given to such teachings, how can the grain be anything but scarce and the soldiers anything but weak?

If, in a country, there are the following ten things: the *Odes* and *History*, rites and music, virtue and the cultivation thereof, benevolence and integrity, and sophistry and intelligence, then the ruler has no one whom he can employ for defence and warfare. If a country be governed by means of these ten things, it will be dismembered as soon as an enemy approaches, and even if no enemy approaches, it will be poor. But if a country banish these ten things, enemies will not dare to approach, and even if they should, they would be driven back. When it mobilizes its army and attacks, it will gain victories; when it holds the army in reserve and does not attack, it will be rich. . . . Therefore sages and intelligent princes are what they are, not because they are able to get to the bottom of everything, but because they understand what is essential[1] in everything.

If (the people's) attention is devoted to agriculture, then they will be simple, and being simple, they may be made correct. . . . Being single-minded,[2] their careers may be made dependent on rewards and penalties: being single-minded, they may be used abroad.

1. From a purely utilitarian point of view.
2. i.e. thinking only of profit and loss.

THE ELIMINATION OF STRENGTH

Thirteen kinds of statistics[1] are known in a strong country: the number of granaries within its borders, the number of able-bodied men and women, the number of old and weak people, the number of officials and officers, the number of those making a livelihood by talking, the number of useful people, the number of horses and oxen, the quantity of fodder and straw.

THE CALCULATION OF LAND

It is the nature of the people, when they are hungry, to strive for food: when they are tired, to strive for rest: when they suffer hardship, to seek enjoyment: when they are in a state of humiliation, to strive for honour. . . . Therefore it is said, 'Where fame and profit meet, that is the way the people will follow.' . . . It the profit comes from the soil, the people will use their strength to the full; if fame results from war, then they will fight to the death.

ON UNIFICATION

Now, a true sage, in establishing laws, alters old customs and causes the people to be engaged in agriculture night and day. It is necessary to understand this.

A true sage, in administering a country, is able to consolidate its strength and to reduce it. . . . Therefore, for one who administers a country, the way in which he consolidates its strength is by making the country rich and its soldiers strong: the way in which he reduces the people's force is by attacking the country's enemies, and so encouraging the people to die for their country. . . . So an intelligent ruler who knows how to combine these two principles will be strong.

1. In c. 6 reference is made to 'the statistical method of administering a country.'

but the country of the one who does not know how to combine these two will come to be dismembered.

THE EMPLOYMENT OF LAWS

I have heard that when the intelligent princes of antiquity established laws,[1] the people ceased to be wicked: when they undertook an enterprise, the required ability was spontaneously forthcoming: when they distributed rewards, the army became strong. These three principles were the root of government. Indeed, the reason why people were not wicked when laws were established was that the laws were clear and the people generally profited by them: the reason why the required ability was forthcoming spontaneously when an enterprise was undertaken was that the desired achievement was clearly defined; and because this was so, the people exerted their strength. . . .

For a prince there exists the fact that people have likes and dislikes; and therefore, for it to be possible to govern the people, it is necessary that the prince should examine these likes and dislikes. Likes and dislikes are the basis of rewards and punishments. Now the nature of man is to like titles and emoluments and to dislike punishments and penalties. A prince institutes these two in order to guide men's wills; and so he establishes what they desire. Now if titles follow upon the people's exertion of strength, if rewards follow upon their acquisition of merit, and if the prince succeeds in making people believe in this as firmly as they do in the shining of sun and moon, then his army will have no equal.

Further, if the law has neither measures nor figures,[2] then

1. Laws (fa) in the sense of this book are not old inherited customs with the force of law, but a carefully arranged system of rewards and punishments for specifically defined acts. This system an intelligent ruler should think out and publish abroad and put into force without fear or favour.

2. i.e., an exact grading of merits and demerits, with a clear statement as to how much the reward or punishment will be.

affairs will daily become more complicated, and, although laws have been established, yet the result will be that the administration will be in disorder. Therefore an intelligent prince, in directing his people, will so direct them that they will exert their strength to the utmost, in order to strive for a particular merit; and if, when they have acquired merit, riches and honour follow upon it, there will be no bravery in private causes. . . . Therefore, in general, an intelligent prince in his administration relies on force and not on virtue. . . . Laws are the means whereby success (in administration) is obtained.

MAKING ORDERS STRICT

In applying punishments, light offences should be punished heavily: if light offences do not appear, heavy offences will not come. This is said to be abolishing penalties by means of penalties; and if penalties are abolished affairs succeed. If crimes are serious and penalties light, penalties will appear and trouble will arise. This is said to be bringing about penalties by means of penalties, and such a state will surely come to be dismembered.

THE CULTIVATION OF FIXED STANDARDS

Orderly government is brought about in a state by three things. The first is law, the second good faith, and the third fixed standards. Law is administered in common by the prince and his ministers. Good faith is established in common by the prince and his ministers. The right standard is fixed by the prince alone. If a ruler of men fail to observe, there will be danger: if prince and ministers neglect the law and act according to their own self-interest, disorder will be the inevitable result. Therefore, if law is established, rights and duties are made clear, and self-interest does not harm the law: then there is orderly government. If the fixing of the right standard is decided by the prince alone, there is prestige. If the people have faith in his rewards, then their activities will achieve results, and if they have faith in his penalties, then wickedness will have no starting-point. Only an intelligent ruler loves fixed standards and values good faith, and will not, for the sake of self-interest, harm the law. For if a ruler speaks many liberal words but cuts down his rewards, then his subjects will not be of service to him, and if he issues one severe order after another, but does not apply the penalties, people will despise the death penalty.

Those who are engaged in governing in the world are for the most part lax in regard to law, and place reliance on private appraisal,[1] and this is what brings disorder in a state. The early kings hung up scales with standard weights, and fixed the length of feet and inches, and to the present day these are followed as models because their divisions were clear. Now suppose the standard scale were abolished but a decision had to be made on the weight of something, and suppose feet and inches were abolished but a decision had to be made about length, even an intelligent merchant would not apply this system, because it lacked definiteness. Now, if the back be turned on models and measures, and reliance be placed on private appraisal, in all those cases there will be a lack of definiteness. Only a Yao would be able to judge knowledge and ability, worth or unworth, without a model. But the world does not consist exclusively of Yaos! Therefore the ancient kings understood that no reliance should be placed on individual opinions or biased approval, so they set up models and made the distinctions clear. Those who fulfilled the standard were rewarded, those who harmed the public interest were punished. The standards for rewards and punishments were not wrong in their appraisals, and therefore people did not dispute them. But if the bestowal of office and the granting of rank are not carried out according to the labour borne, then loyal ministers have no ad-

1. This is an attack on the Confucianists and their emphasis on moral influence exercised by the prince and his officials.

vancement; and if in awarding rewards and giving emoluments the respective merits are not weighed, then fighting soldiers will not serve their prince.

PRINCE AND MINISTER

I have heard that the gate through which the people are guided depends on where their superiors lead. Therefore, whether one succeeds in making people farm or fight, or in making them into travelling politicians, or in making them into scholars, depends on what their superiors encourage. If their superiors encourage merit and labour, people will fight; if they encourage the *Odes* and the *History*, people will become scholars. For people's attitude towards profit is just like the tendency of water to flow downwards, without preference for any of the four sides. The people are only interested in obtaining profit, and what they will do depends on what their superiors encourage. If men with angry eyes, who clench their fists and call themselves brave, are successful; if men in flowing robes, who idly talk, are successful; if men who waste their time and spend their days in idleness, and save their efforts for obtaining benefit through private channels, are successful — if these three kinds of people, though they have no merit, all obtain respectful treatment, then people will leave off farming and fighting and do this: either they will extort it by practising flattery or they will struggle for it by acts of bravery. Thus farmers and fighters will dwindle daily, and itinerant officeseekers will increase more and more, with the result that the country will fall into disorder, the land will be dismembered, the army will be weak, and the ruler debased. This would be the result of relaxing laws and regulations and placing reliance on men of fame and reputation. Therefore an intelligent ruler is cautious with regard to laws and regulations: he does not hearken to words which are not in accordance with the laws (which he has promulgated): he does not exalt actions which are not in accordance with the laws: he (himself)

144

does not perform deeds which are not in accordance with the laws. But he hearkens to words which are in accordance with the law: he exalts actions which are in accordance with the law: performs deeds which are in accordance with the law. Thus the state will enjoy order, the land will be wide, the army will be strong, and the ruler will be honoured. This is the climax of good government, and it is imperative for a ruler of men to examine it.

ATTENTION TO LAW

A country of a thousand chariots is able to preserve itself by defence, and a country of ten thousand chariots is able to round itself off by fighting [i.e. wars of aggression] — even (a bad ruler like) Chieh, unwilling (as he would be) to whittle down a word of this statement, would yet be able to subdue his enemies. And if abroad one is incapable of waging war and at home one is incapable of defence, then even (a good ruler like) Yao could not pacify for any misbehaviour a country that (normally) would be no match for him. Looking at it from this point of view, that through which the country is important and that through which the ruler is honoured is force. Force being the basis of both, how is it then that no ruler on earth succeeds in developing force? Bring about a condition where people find it bitter not to till the soil, and where they find it dangerous not to fight. These are two things which filial sons, though they dislike them, do for their fathers' sake, and loyal ministers, though they dislike them, do for their sovereign's sake. Nowadays, if you wish to stimulate the multitude of people, to make them do what even filial sons and loyal ministers dislike doing, I think it is useless, unless you compel them by means of punishments and stimulate them by means of rewards. . . . Therefore my teaching is to issue such orders that people, if they are desirous of profit, can attain their aim only by agriculture, and if they want to avoid harm, can escape it only by war.

Hui Shih

HUI SHIH (*c.* 380-305 B.C.). The School of Names (Ming-chia) produced two famous dialecticians, Kung-wun Lung and Hui Shih (Hui-tse or Hui Shi). Always sensitive to the element of unceasing change in nature, Hui Shih stressed the relativity of all things, universal love, and improvement of society by the rectification of names. His teachings are preserved only in the book of the brilliant precursor of Tâoism, Chuang Tzǔ, who acclaimed him as the worthiest of his adversaries and evidently placed him above Confucius. Hui Shih probably was older than Chuang Tzǔ and died before the latter had finished his book *Chuang Tzǔ*. He appears to have been a disciple of Tzǔ Ssu, the grandson of Confucius. Like the Mohists, he was a pacifist. Some of the aphorisms attributed to him by Chuang Tzǔ are highly paradoxical.

The Aphorisms

From *Chinese Philosophy in Classical Times*, edited by E. H. Hughes, Everyman's Library, New York, E. P. Dutton.

HUI Shih explored the significance of things . . . and said:

1. That beyond which there is nothing greater should be called the great unit. That beyond which there is nothing smaller should be called the small unit.

2. That which has no thickness cannot be increased in thickness, (but) its size can be a thousand miles (long).

3. The heavens are as low as the earth, mountains on the same level as marshes.

4. The sun exactly at noon is exactly (beginning to) go down. And a creature exactly when he is born is exactly (beginning to) die.

5. A great similarity compared with a small similarity is very different. This state of affairs should be described as a small similarity-in-dissimilarity. The myriad things in Nature are both completely similar and completely dissimilar. This state of affairs should be described as a great similarity-in-dissimilarity.

6. The Southern region (beyond the borders of China and not fully explored) has no limit and yet has a limit.

7. To-day I go to Yueh State and I arrive there in the past.

8. Linked rings can be sundered.

9. I know that the hub of the world is north of Yen State and south of Yueh State.

10. Love all things equally: the heavens and the earth are one composite body.

Chuang Tzŭ

CHUANG TZŬ (between 399 and 286 B.C.). Modern scholars consider Chuang Tzŭ (Tschuang-tse, Chuang Chou, or Kwang-tze) as among the most brilliant of all the Chinese philosophers. Ranked, after Lao Tzŭ, as the second greatest Tâoist, he went beyond his predecessor, sharpening differences between Confucinism and Tâoism and placing greater stress not only on following one's nature but also on nourishing it and adapting it to environment.

He was a scholar, a poet, and a master of dialectic and logic. Once a petty officer in his native state (now Honan) in the revolutionary and romantic south, he lived most of his life as a recluse. He is said to have refused the office of prime minister under King Wei because his duties would have made it impossible for him to follow his natural inclinations (*te*). Almost indifferent to human society, he sought neither to change things nor to preserve them, but only to rise above them. His ideal was to achieve a state of absolute freedom, in which the distinctions between "I" and "thou," happiness and wretchedness, good and evil, life and death, are forgotten or equated, and man has become one with the infinite. Deeply aware of the unity concealed by the constant flux and incessant transformation produced by the dynamic, ever-changing sweep of nature, he longed for the "transcendental bliss" that would bring peace of mind and enable man to live harmoniously in his surroundings, "letting nature take its course, without being conscious of the fact."

The book which bears his name is one of the wittiest,

most imaginative works of Chinese literature and has never ceased to fascinate Chinese minds. The most important sections of this collection of essays set down some of the earliest Tâoist beliefs, leading some scholars to the conclusion that Chuang Tzŭ, if he was not the founder of the doctrine subsequently called Taoism, was its precursor. The extent of his soaring imagination and the power of his style were never matched by later Tâoists. One of the most important philosophical works ever written, it contains many profound insights and a number of aphorisms which even the uneducated are fond of quoting.

Many of the characters in the *Chuang Tzŭ* are recluses. Farmers or fishermen, they live close to nature, shunning political and social institutions, Parable, allegory, paradox, and fanciful imagery abound. A favorite device is to use a historical figure like Confucius to illustrate a Tâoist idea. The whole work is suffused by an almost naive delight in the wondrous manifestations of nature, conceived as a cosmic balance of actions and reactions. *Tâo* (universal nature) and *te* (individual nature) must be harmonized. Man must renounce the artificialities of civilization and live according to his inner nature. Withdrawal from the world is effected in three stages: forgetting each worldly thing, then the world as a whole, and finally one's existence. Union with the Tâo brings sudden enlightenment. Upon achieving the highest knowledge, the sage becomes immortal.

The Writings of Chuang Tzŭ

From *The Texts of Tâoism*, translated by James Legge. Published in 1891 by Oxford University Press as Volume XXIX of "The Sacred Books of the East."

ENJOYMENT IN UNTROUBLED EASE

1. IN the Northern Ocean there is a fish, the name of which is K h w ă n[1] — I do not know how many l î in size. It changes into a bird with the name of P h ă n g, the back of which is (also) — I do not know how many l î in extent. When this bird rouses itself and flies, its wings are like clouds all round the sky. When the sea is moved (so as to bear it along), it prepares to remove to the Southern Ocean. The Southern Ocean is the Pool of Heaven.

There is the (book called) *K h î H s i e h*,[2] — a record of marvels. We have in it these words: — 'When the p h ă n g is removing to the Southern Ocean it flaps (its wings) on the water for 3000 l î. Then it ascends on a whirlwind 90,000 l î, and it rests only at the end of six months.' (But similar to this is the movement of the breezes which we call) the

---

1. The k h w ă n and the p h ă n g are both fabulous creatures, far transcending in size the dimensions ascribed by the wildest fancy of the West to the k r a k e n and the r o c. Chuang Tzŭ represents them as so huge by way of contrast to the small creatures which he is intending to introduce; — to show that size has nothing to do with the T â o, and the perfect enjoyment which the possession of it affords. The passage is a good specimen of the Y ü Y e n, metaphorical or parabolical narratives or stories, which are the chief characteristic of our author's writings; but the reader must keep in mind that the idea or lesson in its 'lodging' is generally of a Tâoistic nature.

2. There may have been a book with this title, to which Chuang Tzŭ appeals, as if feeling that what he had said needed to be substantiated.

horses of the fields, of the dust (which quivers in the sunbeams), and of living things as they are blown against one another by the air.[1] Is its azure the proper colour of the sky? Or is it occasioned by its distance and illimitable extent? If one were looking down (from above), the very same appearance would just meet his view.

2. And moreover, (to speak of) the accumulation of water; — if it be not great, it will not have strength to support a large boat. Upset a cup of water in a cavity, and a straw will float on it as if it were a boat. Place a cup in it, and it will stick fast; — the water is shallow and the boat is large. (So it is with) the accumulation of wind; if it be not great, it will not have strength to support great wings. Therefore (the p h ǎ n g ascended to) the height of 90,000 lî, and there was such a mass of wind beneath it; thenceforth the accumulation of wind was sufficient. As it seemed to bear the blue sky on its back, and there was nothing to obstruct or arrest its course, it could pursue its way to the South.

A cicada and a little dove laughed at it, saying, 'We make an effort and fly towards an elm or sapanwood tree; and sometimes before we reach it, we can do no more but drop to the ground. Of what use is it for this (creature) to rise 90,000 lî, and make for the South?' He who goes to the grassy suburbs,[2] returning to the third meal (of the day), will have his belly as full as when he set out; he who goes to a distance of 100 lî will have to pound his grain where he stops for the night; he who goes a thousand lî, will have to carry with him provisions for three months. What should these two small creatures know about the matter? The knowledge of that which is small does not

1. This seems to be interjected as an afterthought, suggesting to the reader that the p h ǎ n g, soaring along at such a height, was only an exaggerated form of the common phenomena with which he was familiar.

2. In Chinese, Mang Chang; but this is not the name of any particular place. The phrase denotes the grassy suburbs (from their green colour), not far from any city or town.

reach to that which is great; (the experience of) a few years does not reach to that of many. How do we know that it is so? The mushroom of a morning does not know (what takes place between) the beginning and end of a month; the short-lived cicada does not know (what takes place between) the spring and autumn. These are instances of a short term of life. In the south of *Khû*[1] there is the (tree) called M i n g-l i n g'[2] whose spring is 500 years, and its autumn the same; in high antiquity there was that called T â-*k h* u n,[3] whose spring was 8000 years, and its autumn the same. And P h ǎ ng T z û[4] is the one man renowned to the present day for his length of life: — if all men were (to wish) to match him, would they not be miserable?

3. In the questions put by Thang[5] to *Kî* we have similar statements: — 'In the bare and barren north there is the dark vast ocean, — the Pool of Heaven. In it there is a fish, several thousand l î in breadth, while no one knows its length. Its name is the k h w ǎ n. There is (also) a bird named the p h ǎ n g; its back is like the Thâi mountain, while its wings are like clouds all round the sky. On a whirlwind it mounts upwards as on the whorls of a goat's horn for 90,000 l î, till, far removed from the cloudy vapours, it bears on its back the blue sky, and then it shapes its course for

1. The great state of the South, having its capital Ying in the present Hû-pei, and afterwards the chief competitor with *Kh*in for the sovereignty of the kingdom.

2. Taken by some as the name of a tortoise.

3. This and the Ming-ling tree, as well as the mushroom mentioned above, together with the k w h a n and p h ǎ n g, are all mentioned in the fifth Book of the writings of Lieh-Tze, referred to in the next paragraph.

4. Or 'the patriarch Phǎng.' Confucius compared himself to him (Analects, VII, I); — 'our old Phǎng;' and Kû Hsî thinks he was a worthy officer of the Shang dynasty. Whoever he was, the legends about him are a mass of Tâoistic fables. At the end of the Shang dynasty (B.C. 1123) he was more than 767 years old, and still in unabated vigour. We read of his losing 49 wives and 54 sons; and that he still left two sons, Wû and I, who died in Fû-*k*ien, and gave their names to the Wû-î or Bô-î hills, from which we get our Bohea tea! See Mayers' 'Chinese Reader's Manual,' p. 175.

5. The founder of the Shang dynasty (B.C. 1766-1754). In Lieh-tze his interlocutor is called Hsiâ Ko, and Tze-kî.

153

the South, and proceeds to the ocean there.' A quail by the side of a marsh laughed at it, and said, 'Where is it going to? I spring up with a bound, and come down again when I have reached but a few fathoms, and then fly about among the brushwood and bushes; and this is the perfection of flying. Where is that creature going to?' This shows the difference between the small and the great.

Thus it is that men, whose wisdom is sufficient for the duties of some one office, or whose conduct will secure harmony in some one district, or whose virtue is befitting a ruler so that they could efficiently govern some one state, are sure to look on themselves in this manner (like the quail), and yet Yung-tze of Sung[1] would have smiled and laughed at them. (This Yung-tze), though the whole world should have praised him, would not for that have stimulated himself to greater endeavour, and though the whole world should have condemned him, would not have exercised any more repression of his course; so fixed was he in the difference between the internal (judgment of himself) and the external (judgment of others), so distinctly had he marked out the bounding limit of glory and disgrace. Here, however, he stopped. His place in the world indeed had become indifferent to him, but still he had not planted himself firmly (in the right position).

There was Lieh-tze[2], who rode on the wind and pursued his way, with an admirable indifference (to all external things), returning, however, after fifteen days, (to his place). In regard to the things that (are supposed to) contribute

1. We can hardly tell who this Yung-tze was. Sung was a duchy, comprehending portions of the present provinces of Honan, An-hui, and Kiang-sû.

2. Whether there ever was a personage called Lieh-tze or Lieh Yü-khâu, and what is the real character of the writings that go under his name, are questions that cannot be more than thus alluded to in a note. He is often introduced by Chuang Tzŭ, and many narratives are common to their books. Here he comes before us, not as a thinker and writer, but as a semi-supernatural being, who has only not yet attained to the highest consummations of the Tâo.

to happiness, he was free from all endeavours to obtain them; but though he had not to walk, there was still something for which he had to wait. But suppose one who mounts on (the ether of) heaven and earth in its normal operation, and drives along the six elemental energies of the changing (seasons), thus enjoying himself in the illimitable, — what has he to wait for[1]? Therefore it is said, 'The Perfect man has no (thought of) self; the Spirit-like man, none of merit; the Sagely-minded man, none of fame[1].'

4. Yâo[2], proposing to resign the throne to Hsü Yû[3], said, 'When the sun and moon have come forth, if the torches have not been put out, would it not be difficult for them to give light? When the seasonal rains are coming down, if we still keep watering the ground, will not our toil be labour lost for all the good it will do? Do you, Master, stand forth (as sovereign), and the kingdom will (at once) be well governed. If I still (continue to) preside over it I must look on myself as vainly occupying the place; — I beg to resign the throne to you.' Hsü Yû said, 'You, Sir, govern the kingdom, and the kingdom is well governed. If I in these circumstances take your place, shall I not be doing so for the sake of the name? But the name is but the guest of the reality; — shall I be playing the part of the guest? The tailor-bird makes its nest in the deep forest, but only uses a single branch; the mole[4] drinks from the Ho, but only takes what fills its belly. Return and rest in being ruler, — I will have

1. The description of a master of the Tâo, exalted by it, unless the predicates about him be nothing but the ravings of a wild extravagance, above mere mortal man. In the conclusion, however, he is presented under three different phrases, which the reader will do well to keep in mind.

2. The great sovereign with whom the documents of the Shû King commence: — B.C. 2357-2257.

3. A counsellor of Yâo, who is once mentioned by Sze-mâ Khien in his account of Po-î, — in the first Book of his Biographies. Hsü Yû is here the instance of 'the Sagely man,' with whom the desire of a name or fame has no influence.

4. Some say the tapir.

155

nothing to do with the throne. Though the cook were not attending to his kitchen, the representative of the dead and the officer of prayer would not leave their cups and stands to take his place.'

5. Kien Wû[1] asked Lien Shû,[1] saying, 'I heard Khieh-yü[2] talking words which were great, but had nothing corresponding to them (in reality); — once gone, they could not be brought back. I was frightened by them; — they were like the Milky Way[3] which cannot be traced to its beginning or end. They had no connexion with one another, and were not akin to the experience of men.' 'What were his words?' asked Lien Shû, and the other replied, (He said) that 'Far away on the hill of Kû-shih there dwelt a Spirit-like man whose flesh and skin were (smooth) as ice and (white) as snow; that his manner was elegant and delicate as that of a virgin; that he did not eat any of the five grains, but inhaled the wind and drank the dew; that he mounted on the clouds, drove along the flying dragons, rambling and enjoying himself beyond the four seas; that by the concentration of his spirit-like powers he could save men from disease and pestilence, and secure every year a plentiful harvest.' These words appeared to me wild and incoherent and I did not believe them. 'So it is,' said Lien Shû. 'The blind have no perception of the beauty of elegant figures, nor the deaf of the sound of bells and drums. But is it only the bodily senses of which deafness and blindness can be predicated? There is also a similar defect in the intelligence; and of this your words supply an illustration in yourself. That man, with those attributes, though all things were one mass of confusion, and he heard in that

1. Known to us only through Chuang Tzŭ.

2. 'The madman of Khû' of the Analects, XVIII, 5, who eschews intercourse with Confucius. See Hwang-fû Mî's account of him, under the surname and name of Lû Thung, in his Notices of Eminent Tâoists, I. 25.

3. Literally, 'the Ho and the Han;' but the name of those rivers combined was used to denote 'the Milky Way.'

condition the whole world crying out to him to be rectified, would not have to address himself laboriously to the task, as if it were his business to rectify the world. Nothing could hurt that man; the greatest floods, reaching to the sky, could not drown him, nor would he feel the fervour of the greatest heats melting metals and stones till they flowed, and scorching all the ground and hills. From the dust and chaff of himself, he could still mould and fashion Yâos and Shuns[1]; — how should he be willing to occupy himself with things[2]?'

6. A man of Sung, who dealt in the ceremonial caps (of Yin),[3] went with them to Yüeh,[4] the peope of which cut off their hair and tattooed their bodies, so that they had no use for them. Yâo ruled the people of the kingdom, and maintained a perfect government within the four seas. Having gone to see the four (Perfect) Ones[5] on the distant hill of Kû-shih, when (he returned to his capital) on the south of the Fan water,[6] his throne appeared no more to his deep-sunk oblivious eyes.[7]

7. Hui-tze[8] told Chuang Tzŭ, *saying*, 'The king of Wei[9]

1. Shun was the successor of Yâo in the ancient kingdom.
2. All this description is to give us an idea of the 'Spirit-like man.' We have in it the results of the Tâo in its fullest embodiment.
3. See the Lî Kî, IX, iii, 3.
4. A state, part of the present province of Kieh-kiang.
5. Said to have been Hsü Yû mentioned above, with Nieh Khüeh, Wang I, and Phî-î, who will by and by come before us.
6. A river in Shan-hsî, on which was the capital of Yâo; — a tributary of the Ho.
7. This paragraph is intended to give us an idea of 'the Perfect man,' who has no thought of himself. The description, however, is brief and tame, compared with the accounts of Hsü Yû and of 'the Spirit-like man.'
8. Or Hui Shih, the chief minister of 'King Hui of Liang (or Wei), (B.C. 370-333),' with an interview between whom and Mencius the works of that philosopher commence. He was a friend of Chuang Tzŭ, and an eccentric thinker; and in Book XXXIII there is a long account of several of his views. I do not think that the conversations about 'the great calabash' and 'the great tree' really took place; Chuang Tzŭ probably invented them, to illustrate his point that size had nothing to do with Tâo, and that things which seemed useless were not really so when rightly used.
9. Called also Liang from the name of its capital. Wei was one of the three states (subsequently kingdoms), into which the great fief of Zin was divided about B.C. 400.

157

sent me some seeds of a large calabash, which I sowed. The fruit, when fully grown, could contain five piculs (of anything). I used it to contain water, but it was so heavy that I could not lift it by myself. I cut it in two to make the parts into drinking vessels; but the dried shells were too wide and unstable and would not hold (the liquor); nothing but large useless things! Because of their uselessness I knocked them to pieces.' Chuang Tzŭ replied, 'You were indeed stupid, my master, in the use of what was large. There was a man of sung who was skilful at making a salve which kept the hands from getting chapped; and (his family) for generations had made the bleaching of cocoon-silk their business. A stranger heard of it, and proposed to buy the art of the preparation for a hundred ounces of silver. The kindred all came together, and considered the proposal. "We have," said they, "been bleaching cocoon-silk for generations, and have only gained a little money. Now in one morning we can sell to this man our art for a hundred ounces; — let him have it." The stranger accordingly got it and went away with it to give counsel to the king of Wû[1], who was then engaged in hostilities with Yüeh. The king gave him the command of his fleet, and in the winter he had an engagement with that of Yüeh, on which he inflicted a great defeat[2], and was invested with a portion of territory taken from Yüeh. The keeping the hands from getting chapped was the same in both cases; but in the one case it led to the investiture (of the possessor of the salve), and in the other it had only enabled its owners to continue their bleaching. The difference of result was owing to the different use made of the art. Now you, Sir, had calabashes large enough to hold five piculs; — why did you not think of making large bottle-gourds of them, by means of which you could have floated over rivers and lakes, instead of giving yourself the sorrow of finding that they were useless for holding anything. Your

1. A great and ancient state on the sea-board, north of Yüeh. The name remains in the district of Wû-kiang in the prefecture of Sû-kâu.
2. The salve gave the troops of Wû a great advantage in a war on the Kiang, especially in winter.

mind, my master, would seem to have been closed against all intelligence!'

Hui-tze said to Chuang Tzŭ, 'I have a large tree, which men call the Ailantus[1]. Its trunk swells out to a large size, but is not fit for a carpenter to apply his line to it; its smaller branches are knotted and crooked, so that disk and square cannot be used on them. Though planted on the wayside, a builder would not turn his head to look at it. Now your words, Sir, are great, but of no use;— all unite in putting them away from them.' Chuang Tzŭ replied, 'Have you never seen a wild cat or a weasel? There it lies, crouching and low, till the wanderer approaches; east and west it leaps about, avoiding neither what is high nor what is low, till it is caught in a trap, or dies in a net. Again there is the Yak[2], so large that it is like a cloud hanging in the sky. It is large indeed, but it cannot catch mice. You, Sir, have a large tree and are troubled because it is of no use; — why do you not plant it in a tract where there is nothing else, or in a wide and barren wild? There you might saunter idly by its side, or in the enjoyment of untroubled ease sleep beneath it. Neither bill nor axe would shorten its existence; there would be nothing to injure it. What is there in its uselessness to cause you distress? [Book I, Part I, Section I.]

THE ADJUSTMENT OF CONTROVERSIES

1. Nan-kwo Tze-*khî*[3] was seated, leaning forward on his stool. He was looking up to heaven and breathed gently, seeming to be in a trance, and to have lost all consciousness

1. The Ailantus glandulosa, common in the north of China, called 'the fetid tree,' from the odour of its leaves.
2. The bos grunniens of Tibet, the long tail of which is in great demand for making standards and chowries.
3. Nan-kwo, 'the southern suburb,' had probably been the quarter where Tze-*khî* had resided, and is used as his surname. He is introduced several times by Chuang Tzŭ in his writings: — Books IV, 7; XXVII, 4, and perhaps elsewhere.

of any companion. (His disciple), Yen *Kh*ang Tze-yû,[1] who was in attendance and standing before him, said, 'What is this? Can the body be made to become thus like a withered tree, and the mind to become like slaked lime? His appearance as he leans forward on the stool to-day is such as I never saw him have before in the same position.' Tze-*kh*î said, 'Yen, you do well to ask such a question, I had just now lost myself[2]; but how should you understand it? You may have heard the notes[3] of Man, but have not heard those of Earth; you may have heard the notes of Earth, but have not heard those of Heaven.'

Tze-yû said, 'I venture to ask from you a description of all these.' The reply was, 'When the breath of the Great Mass (of nature) comes strongly, it is called Wind. Sometimes it does not come so; but when it does, then from a myriad apertures there issues its excited noise; — have you not heard it in a prolonged gale? Take the projecting bluff of a mountain forest; — in the great trees, a hundred spans round, the apertures and cavities are like the nostrils, or the mouth, or the ears; now square, now round like a cup or a mortar; here like a wet footprint, and there like a large puddle. (The sounds issuing from them are like) those of fretted water, of the arrowy whizz, of the stern command, of the inhaling of the breath, of the shout, of the gruff note, of the deep wail, of the sad and piping note. The first notes are slight, and those that follow deeper, but in harmony

1. We have the surname of this disciple, Y e n; his name, Y e n; his honorary or posthumous epithet (*K h* a n g); and his ordinary appellation, Tze-yû. The use of the epithet shows that he and his master had lived before our author.

2. 'He had lost himself;' that is, he had become unconscious of all around him, and even of himself, as if he were about to enter into the state of 'an Immortal,' a mild form of the Buddhistic s a m â d h i. But his attitude and appearance were intended by Chuang Tzŭ to indicate what should be the mental condition in reference to the inquiry pursued in the Book; — a condition, it appears to me, of a g n o s t i c i s m.

3. The Chinese term here (l â i) denotes a reed or pipe, with three holes, by a combination of which there was formed the rudimentary or reed organ. Our author uses it for the sounds or notes heard in nature various as the various opinions of men in their discussions about things.

160

with them. Gentle winds produce a small response; violent winds a great one. When the fierce gusts have passed away, all the apertures are empty (and still); — have you not seen this in the bending and quivering of the branches and leaves?'

Tze-yû said, 'The notes of Earth then are simply those which come from its myriad apertures; and the notes of Man may just be compared to those which (are brought from the tubes of) bamboo; — allow me to ask about the notes of Heaven[1].' Tze-khî replied, 'When (the wind) blows, (the sounds from) the myriad apertures are different, and (its cessation) makes them stop of themselves. Both of these things arise from (the wind and the apertures) themselves: — should there be any other agency that excites them?'

2. Great knowledge is wide and comprehensive; small knowledge is partial and restricted. Great speech is exact and complete; small speech is (merely) so much talk[2]. When we sleep, the soul communicates with (what is external to us); when we awake, the body is set free. Our intercourse with others then leads to various activity, and daily there is the striving of mind with mind. There are hesitancies; deep difficulties; reservations; small apprehensions causing restless distress, and great apprehensions producing endless fears. Where their utterances are like arrows from a bow, we have those who feel it their charge to pronounce what is right and what is wrong; where they are given out like the the conditions of a covenant, we have those who maintain their views, determined to overcome. (The weakness of

1. The sounds of Earth have been described fully and graphically. Of the sounds of Man very little is said, but they form the subject of the next paragraph. Nothing is said in answer to the disciple's inquiry about the notes of Heaven. It is intimated, however, that there is no necessity to introduce any foreign Influence or Power like Heaven in connexion with the notes of Earth. The term Heaven, indeed, is about to pass with our author into a mere synonym of Tâo, the natural 'c o u r s e' of the phenomena of men and things.

2. Words are the 'sounds' of Man; and knowledge is the 'wind' by which they are excited.

their arguments), like the decay (of things) in autumn and winter, shows the failing (of the minds of some) from day to day; or it is like their water which, once voided, cannot be gathered up again. Then their ideas seem as if fast bound with cords, showing that the mind is become like an old and dry moat, and that it is nigh to death, and cannot be restored to vigour and brightness.

Joy and anger, sadness and pleasure, anticipation and regret, fickleness and fixedness, vehemence and indolence, eagerness and tardiness; — (all these moods), like music from an empty tube, or mushrooms from the warm moisture, day and night succeed to one another and come before us, and we do not know whence they sprout. Let us stop! Let us stop! Can we expect to find out suddenly how they are produced?

If there were not (the views of) another, I should not have mine; if there were not I (with my views), his would be uncalled for: — this is nearly a true statement of the case, but we do not know what it is that makes it be so. It might seem as if there would be a true Governor[1] concerned in it, but we do not find any trace (of his presence and acting). That such an One could act so I believe; but we do not see His form. He has affections, but He has no form.

Given the body, with its hundred parts, its nine openings, and its six viscera, all complete in their places, which do I love the most? Do you love them all equally? or do you love some more than others? Is it not the case that they all perform the part of your servants and waiting women? All of them being such, are they not incompetent to rule one another? or do they take it in turns to be now ruler and now servants? There must be a true Ruler (among

1. 'A true Governor' would be a good enough translation for 'the true God.' But Chuang Tzŭ did not admit any supernatural Power or Being as working in man. His true Governor was the T â o; and this will be increasingly evident as we proceed with the study of his Books.

them)[1] whether by searching you can find out His character or not, there is neither advantage nor hurt, so far as the truth of His operation is concerned. When once we have received the bodily form complete, its parts do not fail to perform their functions till the end comes. In conflict with things or in harmony with them, they pursue their course to the end, with the speed of a galloping horse which cannot be stopped; — is it not sad? To be constantly toiling all one's lifetime, without seeing the fruit of one's labour, and to be weary and worn out with his labour, without knowing where he is going to: — is it not a deplorable case? Men may say, 'But it is not death;' yet of what advantage is this? When the body is decomposed, the mind will be the same along with it: — must not the case be pronounced very deplorable[2]? Is the life of man indeed enveloped in such darkness? Is it I alone to whom it appears so? And does it not appear to be so to other men?

3. If we were to follow the judgments of the predetermined mind, who would be left alone and without a teacher[3]? Not only woud it be so with those who know the sequences (of knowledge and feeling) and make their own selection among them, but it would be so as well with the stupid and unthinking. For one who has not this determined mind, to have his affirmations and negations is like the case described in the saying, 'He went to Yüeh today, and arrived at it yesterday.'[4] It would be making what was not a fact to be a fact. But even the spirit-like Yû[5]

1. The name 'Ruler' is different from 'Governor' above; but they both indicate the same concept in the author's mind.
2. The proper reply to this would be that the mind is not dissolved with the body; and Chuang Tzŭ's real opinion, as we shall find, was that life and death were but phases in the phenomenal development. But the course of his argument suggests to us the question here, 'Is life worth living?'
3. This 'teacher' is 'the T â o.'
4. Expressing the absurdity of the case. This is one of the sayings of Hui-tze.
5. The successor and counsellor of Shun, who coped with and remedied the flood of Yâo.

163

could not have known how to do this and how should one like me be able to do it?

But speech is not like the blowing (of the wind); the speaker has (a meaning in) his words. If, however, what he says, be indeterminate (as from a mind not made up), does he then really speak or not? He thinks that his words are different from the chirpings of fledgelings; but is there any distinction between them or not? But how can the T â o be so obscured, that there should be 'a True' and 'a False' in it? How can speech be so obscured that there should be 'the Right' and 'the Wrong' about them? Where shall the T â o go to that it will not be found? Where shall speech be found that it will be inappropriate? T â o becomes obscured through the small comprehension (of the mind), and speech comes to be obscure through the vaingloriousness (of the speaker). So it is that we have the contentions between the Literati[1] and the Mohists[2], the one side affirming what the other denies, and vice versa. If we would decide on their several affirmations and denials, no plan is like bringing the (proper) light (of the mind)[3] to bear on them.

All subjects may be looked at from (two points of view), — from that and from this. If I look at a thing from another's point of view, I do not see it; only as I know it. Hence it is said, 'That view comes from this; and this view is a consequence of that:' — which is the theory that that view and this — (the opposite views) — produce each the other[4]. Although it be so, there is affirmed now life and now death; now death and now life; now the admissibility of a thing and now its inadmissibility; now its inadmissibil-

1. The followers of Confucius.
2. The disciples of Mih-tze, or Mih Tî, the heresiarch, whom Mencius attacked so fiercely; — see Mencius, V, 1, 5, et al. His era must be assigned between Confucius and Mencius.
3. That is, the perfect mind, the principle of the T â o.
4. As taught by Hui-tze; — see XXXIII, 7; but it is doubtful if the quotation from Hui's teaching be complete.

ity and now its admissibility. (The disputants) now affirm and now deny; now deny and now affirm. Therefore the sagely man does not pursue this method, but views things in the light of (his) Heaven[1] (-ly nature), and hence forms his judgment of what is right.

This view is the same as that, and that view is the same as this. But that view involves both a right and a wrong; and this view involves also a right and a wrong: — are there indeed, or are there not the two views, that and this? They have not found their point of correspondency which is called the pivot of the Tâo. As soon as one finds this pivot, he stands in the centre of the ring (of thought), where he can respond without end to the changing views; — without end to those affirming, and without end to those denying. Therefore I said, 'There is nothing like the proper light (of the mind).'

4. By means of a finger (of my own) to illustrate that the finger (of another) is not a finger is not so good a plan as to illustrate that it is not so by means of what is (acknowledged to be) not a finger; and by means of (what I call) a horse to illustrate that (what another calls) a horse is not so, is not so good a plan as to illustrate that it is not a horse, by means of what is (acknowledged to be) not a horse.[2] (All things in) heaven and earth may be (dealt with as) a finger; (each of) their myriads may be (dealt with as) a horse. Does a thing seem so to me? (I say that) it is so. Does it seem not so to me? (I say that) it is not so. A path is formed by (constant) treading on the ground. A thing is called by its

1. Equivalent to the Tâo.
2. The language of our authors here is understood to have reference to the views of Kung-sun Lung, a contemporary of Hui-tze, and a sophist like him. One of his treatises or arguments had the title of 'The White Horse,' and another that of 'Pointing to Things.' If these had been preserved, we might have seen more clearly the appropriateness of the text here. But the illustration of the monkeys and their actions shows us the scope of the whole paragraph to be that controversialists, whose views are substantially the same, may yet differ, and that with heat, in words.

165

name through the (constant) application of the name to it. How is it so? It is so because it is so. How is it not so? It is not so, because it is not so. Everything has its inherent character and its proper capability. There is nothing which has not these. Therefore, this being so, if we take a stalk of grain [1] and a (large) pillar, a loathsome (leper) and (a beauty like) Hsî Shih[2], things large and things insecure, things crafty and things strange; — they may in the light of the T â o all be reduced to the same category (of opinion about them).

It was separation that led to completion; from completion ensued dissolution. But all things, without regard to their completion and dissolution, may again be comprehended in their unity; — it is only the far reaching in thought who know how to comprehend them in this unity. This being so, let us give up our devotion to our own views, and occupy ourselves with the ordinary views. These ordinary views are grounded on the use of things. (The study of that) use leads to the comprehensive judgment, and that judgment secures the success (of the inquiry). That success gained, we are near (to the object of our search), and there we stop. When we stop, and yet we do not know how it is so, we have what is called the T âo.

When we toil our spirits and intelligence, obstinately determined (to establish our own view), and do not know the agreement (which underlies it and the views of others), we have what is called 'In the morning three.' What is meant by that 'In the morning three?' A keeper of monkeys, in giving them out their acorns, (once) said, 'In the morning I will give you three (measures) and in the evening four.' This made them all angry, and he said. 'Very well. In the morning I will give you four and in the evening three.'

1. The character in the text means both 'a stalk of grain' 'a horizontal beam.' Each meaning has its advocates here.
2. A famous beauty, a courtesan presented by the king of Yüeh to his enemy, the king of Wû, and who hastened on his progress to ruin and death; she herself perishing at the same time.

His two proposals were substantially the same, but the result of the one was to make the creatures angry, and of the other to make them pleased: — an illustration of the point I am insisting on. Therefore the sagely man brings together a dispute in its affirmations and denials, and rests in the equal fashioning of Heaven[1]. Both sides of the question are admissible.

5. Among the men of old their knowledge reached the extreme point. What was that extreme point? Some held that at first there was not anything. This is the extreme point, the utmost point to which nothing can be added. A second class held that there was something, but without any responsive recognition[2] of it (on the part of men).

A third class held that there was such recognition, but there had not begun to be any expression of different opinions about it.

It was through the definite expression of different opinions about it that there ensued injury to (the doctrine of) the Tâo. It was this injury to the (doctrine of the) Tâo which led to the formation of (partial) preferences. Was it indeed after such preferences were formed that the injury came? or did the injury precede the rise of such preferences? If the injury arose after their formation, Kâo's method of playing on the lute was natural. If the injury arose before their formation, there would have been no such playing on the lute as Kâo's.[3]

Kâo Wan's playing on the lute, Shih Kwang's indicating time with his staff, and Hui-tze's (giving his views), while

1. Literally, 'the Heaven-Mould or Moulder,' — another name for the T â o, by which all things are fashioned.

2. The ordinary reading here is f a n g, 'a boundary' or 'distinctive limit.' Lin Hsî-kung adopts the reading, 'a response,' and I have followed him.

3. Kâo Wan and Shih Kwang were both musicians of the state of Tzin. Shih, which appears as Kwang's surname, was his denomination as 'music-master.' It is difficult to understand the reason why Chuang Tzŭ introduces these men and their ways, or how it helps his argument.

leaning against a dryandra tree (were all extraordinary). The knowledge of the three men (in their several arts) was nearly perfect, and therefore they practised them to the end of their lives. They loved them because they were different from those of others. They loved them and wished to make them known to others. But as they could not be made clear, though they tried to make them so, they ended with the obscure (discussions) about 'the hard' and 'the white.' And their sons,[1] moreover, with all the threads of their fathers' compositions, yet to the end of their lives accomplished nothing. If they, proceeding in this way, could be said to have succeeded, then am I also successful; if they cannot be pronounced successful, neither I nor any other can succeed.

Therefore the scintillations of light from the midst of confusion and perplexity are indeed valued by the sagely man; but not to use one's own views and to take his position on the ordinary views is what is called using the (proper) light.

6. But here now are some other sayings.[2] — I do not know whether they are of the same character as those which I have already given, or of a different character. Whether they be of the same character or not when looked at along with them, they have a character of their own, which cannot be distinguished from the others. But though this be the case, let me try to explain myself.

There was a beginning. There was a beginning before that beginning.[3] There was a beginning previous to that beginning before there was the beginning.

There was existence; there had been no existence. There was no existence before the beginning of that no existence[2].

1. Perhaps we should read here 'son,' with special reference to the son of Hui-tze.

2. Referring, I think, to those below commencing 'There was a beginning.'

3. That is, looking at things from the standpoint of an original non-existence, and discarding all considerations of space and time.

There was no existence previous to the no existence before the beginning of the no existence. If suddenly there was non-existence, we do not know whether it was really anything existing, or really not existing. Now I have said what I have said, but I do not know whether what I have said be really anything to the point or not.

Under heaven there is nothing greater than the tip of an autumn down, and the Thâi mountain is small. There is no one more long-lived than a child which dies prematurely, and Phang Tzŭ did not live out his time. Heaven, Earth, and I were produced together, and all things and I are one. Since they are one, can there be speech about them? But since they are spoken of as one, must there not be room for speech? One and Speech are two; two and one are three. Going on from this (in our enumeration), the most skilful reckoner cannot reach (the end of the necessary numbers), and how much less can ordinary people do so! Therefore from non-existence we proceed to existence till we arrive at three; proceeding from existence to existence, to how many should we reach? Let us abjure such procedure, and simply rest here[1].

7. The Tâo at first met with no responsive recognition. Speech at first had no constant forms of expression. Because of this there came the demarcations (of different views). Let me describe those demarcations: — they are the Left and the Right[2]; the Relations and their Obligations[3]; Classifications[4] and their Distinctions; Emulations and Contentions. These are what are called 'the Eight Qualities.' Outside the limits of the world of men,[5] the sage occupies his

1. On this concluding clause, Tiâo Hung says: — 'Avoiding such procedure, there will be no affirmations and denials' (no contraries).
2. That is, direct opposites.
3. Literally, 'righteousnesses;' the proper way of dealing with the relations.
4. Literally, 'separations.'
5. Literally, 'the six conjunctions,' meaning the four cardinal points of space, with the zenith and nadir; sometimes a name for the universe of space. Here we must restrict the meaning as I have done.

thoughts, but does not discuss about anything; inside those limits he occupies his thoughts, but does not pass any judgments. In the *Khun Khiû*,[1] which embraces the history of the former kings, the sage indicates his judgments, but does not argue (in vindication of them). Thus it is that he separates his characters from one another without appearing to do so, and argues without the form of argument. How does he do so? The sage cherishes his views in his own breast, while men generally state theirs argumentatively, to show them to others. Hence we have the saying, 'Disputation is a proof of not seeing clearly.'

The Great Tâo[2] does not admit of being praised. The Great Argument does not require words. Great Benevolence is not (officiously) benevolent. Great Disinterestedness does not vaunt its humility. Great Courage is not seen in stubborn bravery.

The T â o that is displayed is not the T â o. Words that are argumentative do not reach the point. Benevolence that is constantly exercised does not accomplish its object. Disinterestedness that vaunts its purity is not genuine. Courage that is most stubborn is ineffectual. These five seem to be round (and complete), but they tend to become square (and immovable). Therefore the knowledge that stops at what it does not know is the greatest. Who knows the argument that needs no words, and the Way that is not to be trodden?

He who is able to know this has what is called 'The Heavenly Treasure-house.'[3] He may pour into it without its being filled; he may pour from it without its being exhausted; and all the while he does not know whence (the supply) comes. This is what is called 'The Store of Light.'

Therefore of old Yâo asked Shun, saying, 'I wish to smite

1. 'The Spring and Autumn;' — Confucius's Annals of Lû, here complimented by Chuang Tzŭ. See in Mencius, IV, ii, 21.
2. Compare the Tâo Teh King, ch. 25, et al.
3. Names for the T â o.

(the rulers of) Tung, Kwei, and Hsü-âo.[1] Even when stand-ing in my court, I cannot get them out of my mind. How is it so?' Shun replied, 'Those three rulers live (in their little states) as if they were among the mugwort and other brushwood; —how is it that you cannot get them out of your mind? Formerly, ten suns came out together, and all things were illuminated by them; — how much should (your) virtue exceed (all) suns!'

8. Nieh Khüeh asked Wang I,[2] saying, 'Do you know, Sir, what all creatures agree in approving and affirming?' 'How should I know it?' was the reply. 'Do you know what it is that you do not know?' asked the other again, and he got the same reply. He asked a third time, — 'Then are all crea-tures thus without knowledge?' and Wang I answered as before, (adding however), 'Notwithstanding, I will try and explain my meaning. How do you know that when I say "I know it," I really (am showing that) I do not know it, and that when I say "I do not know it," I really am showing that I do know it. And let me ask you some questions: — 'If a man sleep in a damp place, he will have a pain in his loins, and half his body will be as if it were dead; but will it be so with an eel? If he be living in a tree, he will be frightened and all in a tremble; but will it be so with a monkey? And does any one of the three know his right place? Men eat animals that have been fed on grain and grass; deer feed on the thickset grass; centipedes enjoy small snakes; owls and crows delight in mice; but does any one of the four know the right taste? The dog-headed monkey finds its mate in the female gibbon; the elk and the axis deer cohabit; and

1. Three small states. Is Yâo's wish to smite an instance of the 'quality' of 'emulation' or jealousy?

2. Both Tâoistic worthies of the time of Yâo, supposed to have been two of the Perfect Ones whom Yâo visited on the distant hill of Kû-shih (I, par. 6). According to Hwang Mî, Wang I was the teacher of Nieh Khüeh, and he again of Hsü Yû.

the eel enjoys itself with other fishes. Mâo Thiang[1] and Lî Kî[1] were accounted by men to be most beautiful, but when fishes saw them, they dived deep in the water from them; when birds, they flew from them aloft; and when deer saw them, they separated and fled away.[2] But did any of these four know which in the world is the right female attraction? As I look at the matter, the first principles of benevolence and righteousness and the paths of approval and disapproval are inextricably mixed and confused together: — how is it possible that I should know how to discriminate among them?'

Nieh Khüeh said (further), 'Since you, Sir, do not know what is advantageous and what is hurtful, is the P e r f e c t man also in the same way without the knowledge of them?' Wang I replied, 'The Perfect man is spirit-like. Great lakes might be boiling about him, and he would not feel their heat; the Ho and the Han might be frozen up, and he would not feel the cold; the hurrying thunderbolts might split the mountains, and the wind shake the ocean, without being able to make him afraid. Being such, he mounts on the clouds of the air, rides on the sun and moon, and rambles at ease beyond the four seas. Neither death nor life makes any change in him, and how much less should the considerations of advantage and injury do so!'[3]

9. Khü Thiâo-tze[4] asked Khang-wû Tze,[4] saying, 'I heard

1. Two famous beauties; — the former, a contemporary of Hsî Shih (par. 4, note 2), and like her also, of the state of Yüeh; the latter, the daughter of a barbarian chief among the Western Jung. She was captured by duke Hsien of Tzin, in B.C. 672. He subsequently made her his wife, — to the great injury of his family and state.
2. Not thinking them beautiful, as men did, but frightened and repelled by them.
3. Compare Book I, pars. 3 and 5.
4. We know nothing of the former of these men, but what is mentioned here; the other appears also in Book XXV, 6. If 'the master' that immediately follows be Confucius they must have been contemporary with him. The Khiû in Khang-wû's reply would seem to make it certain 'the master' was Confucius, but the oldest critics, and some modern ones as well, think that Khang-wû's name was also Khiû. But this view is

172

the Master (speaking of such language as the following):
— "The sagely man does not occupy himself with worldly
affairs. He does not put himself in the way of what is profitable, nor try to avoid what is hurtful; he has no pleasure in
seeking (for anything from any one); he does not care to
be found in (any established) Way; he speaks without
speaking; he does not speak when he speaks; thus finding
his enjoyment outside the dust and dirt (of the world)."
The Master considered all this to be a shoreless flow of
mere words, and I consider it to describe the course of the
Mysterious Way. — What do you, Sir, think of it?' *Khang-
wû* Tze replied, 'The hearing of such words would have
perplexed even Hwang-Tî, and how should *Khiû* be competent to understand them? And you, moreover, are too
hasty in forming your estimate (of their meaning). You see
the egg, and (immediately) look out for the cock (that is
to be hatched from it); you see the bow, and (immediately) look out for the dove (that is to be brought down
by it) being roasted. I will try to explain the thing to you
in a rough way; do you in the same way listen to me.

'How could any one stand by the side of the sun and
moon, and hold under his arm all space and all time? (Such
language only means that the sagely man) keeps his mouth
shut, and puts aside questions that are uncertain and dark;
making his inferior capacities unite with him in honouring
(the One Lord). Men in general bustle about and toil; the
sagely man seems stupid and to know nothing[1]. He blends
ten thousand years together in the one (conception of time);
the myriad things all pursue their spontaneous course, and
they are all before him as doing so.

'How do I know that the love of life is not a delusion? and
that the dislike of death is not like a young person's losing

attended with more difficulties than the other. By the clause interjected
in the translation after the first 'Master,' I have avoided the incongruity of
ascribing the long description of Tâoism to Confucius.
1. Compare Lao-tze's account of himself in his Work, ch. 20.

173

his way, and not knowing that he is (really) going home? Lî Kî[1] was a daughter of the border Warden of Ai. When (the ruler of) the state of Tin first got possession of her, she wept till the tears wetted all the front of her dress. But when she came to the place of the king,[2] shared with him his luxurious couch, and ate his grain-and-grass-fed meat, then she regretted that she had wept. How do I know that the dead do not repent of their former craving for life?

'Those who dream of (the pleasures of) drinking may in the morning wail and weep; those who dream of wailing and weeping may in the morning be going out to hunt. When they were dreaming they did not know it was a dream; in their dream they may even have tried to interpret it[3]; but when they awoke they knew that it was a dream. And there is the great awaking, after which we shall know that this life was a great dream. All the while, the stupid think they are awake, and with nice discrimination insist on their knowledge; now playing the part of rulers, and now of grooms. Bigoted was that *Khiû*! He and you are both dreaming. I who say that you are dreaming am dreaming myself. These words seem very strange; but if after ten thousand ages we once meet with a great sage who knows how to explain them, it will be as if we met him (unexpectedly) some morning or evening.

10. 'Since you made me enter into this discussion with you, if you have got the better of me and not I of you, are you indeed right, and I indeed wrong? If I have got the better of you and not you of me, am I indeed right and you indeed wrong? Is the one of us right and the other wrong?

---

1. See note to # 8. The lady is there said to have been the daughter of a barbarian chief; here she appears as the child of the border Warden of Ai. But her maiden surname of *Kî* shows her father must have been a scion of the royal family of *Kâu*. Had he forsaken his warden-ship, and joined one of the Tî tribes, which had adopted him as its chief?

2. Tzin was only a marquisate. How does Chuang Tzŭ speak of its ruler as 'a king?'

3. This could not be; a man does not come to himself in his dream, and in that state try to interpret it.

174

are we both right or both wrong? Since we cannot come to a mutual and common understanding, men will certainly continue in darkness on the subject.

'Whom shall I employ to adjudicate in the matter? If I employ one who agrees with you, how can he, agreeing with you, do so correctly? And the same may be said if I employ one who agrees with me. It will be the same if I employ one who differs from us both or one who agrees with us both. In this way I and you and those others would all not be able to come to a mutual understanding; and shall we then wait for that (great sage)? (We need not do so.) To wait on others to learn how conflicting opinions are changed is simply like not so waiting at all. The harmonising of them is to be found in the invisible operation of Heaven, and by following this on into the unlimited past. It is by this method that we can complete our years (without our minds being disturbed)[1].

'What is meant by harmonising (conflicting opinions) in the invisible operations of Heaven? There is the affirmation and the denial of it; and there is the assertion of an opinion and the rejection of it. If the affirmation be according to the reality of the fact, it is certainly different from the denial of it: — there can be no dispute about that. If the assertion of an opinion be correct, it is certainly different from its rejection: — neither can there be any dispute about that. Let us forget the lapse of time; let us forget the conflict of opinions. Let us make our appeal to the Infinite, and take up our position there[2].'

11. The Penumbra asked the Shadow[3], saying, 'Formerly

1. In Book XXVII, par. 1, the phrase which I have called here 'the invisible operation of Heaven,' is said to be the same as 'the Heavenly Mould or Moulder,' that is, the Heavenly Fashioner, one of the Tâoistic names for the T â o.
2. That is, all things being traced up to the unity of the T â o, we have found the pivot to which all conflicting opinions, all affirmations, all denials, all positions and negatives converge, and bring to bear on them the proper light of the mind. Compare paragraph 3.
3. A story to the same effect as this here, with some textual variations, occurs in Book XXVII, immediately after par. 1 referred to above.

you were walking on, and now you have stopped; formerly you were sitting, and now you have risen up: — how is it that you are so without stability?' The Shadow replied, 'I wait for the movements of something else to do what I do, and that something else on which I wait waits further on another to do as it does[1]. My waiting, — is it for the scales of a snake, or the wings of a cicada[2]? How should I know why I do one thing, or do not do another[3]?

'Formerly, I, Kwăng Kâu, dreamt that I was a butterfly, a butterfly flying about, feeling that it was enjoying itself. I did not know that it was Kâu. Suddenly I awoke, and was myself again, the veritable Kâu. I did not know whether it had formery been Kâu dreaming that he was a butterfly, or it was now a butterfly dreaming that it was Kâu. But between Kâu and a butterfly there must be a difference.[4] This is a case of what is called the Transformation of Things[4].'
[Book II, Part I, Section II.]

---

1. The mind cannot rest in second causes, and the first cause, if there be one, is inscrutable.
2. Even these must wait for the will of the creature; but the case of the shadow is still more remarkable.
3. I have put this interrogatively, as being more graphic.
4. Hsüan Ying, in his remarks on these two sentences, brings out the force of the story very successfully: — 'Looking at them in their ordinary appearance, there was necessarily a difference between them, but in the delusion of the dream each of them appeared the other, and they could not distinguish themselves! Kâu could be a butterfly, and the butterfly could be Kâu; — we may see that in the world all traces of that and this may pass away, as they come under the influence of transformations.' But the Tâoism here can hardly be distinguished from the Buddhism that holds that all human experience is merely so much m â y a or illusion.

Mencius

MENCIUS (372-289 B.C.). Known to his successors as the greatest Confucian in the history of Chinese philosophy, Mencius (Meng Tzŭ, or "Master Meng") studied with a disciple of Tzŭ Ssu, who was the grandson of Confucius and himself an influential philosopher. Like Confucius, whom he called the greatest sage of all time, Mencius based his teachings upon the principle of *jen* (humanity), supplemented by the concept of *i* (righteousness). These two principles are considered, respectively, man's mind and man's path. It behooves man to "develop his nature to the fullest" and to "exercise his mind to the limit."

Mencius was a native of the ancient feudal state of Lu (now Shantung Province), a member of the governing class, and a contemporary of Hsün Tzŭ, Chuang Tzŭ, and Plato. His most significant work was done as a teacher. Like Confucius he spent most of his life visiting the court of one feudal lord after another, trying in vain to persuade some ruler to put his teachings into practice. His filial devotion is attested by his actions. When his mother died, he left his public office in Ch'i and entered upon a three-year period of mourning (312-309 B.C.). Toward the end of his life he went into seclusion and devoted his remaining years to perfecting and teaching his philosophy. He vigorously opposed the doctrines of Yang Chu and Mo Tzŭ, who tried to discredit the cult and doctrine of Confucianism, and he advanced the moralism and humanism of his predecessor.

177

He taught that everyone has in him the "four beginnings" of humanity, righteousness, propriety, and wisdom; that man is a microcosm ("all things are complete within us"); and that one who knows completely his own nature, knows Heaven. Above all, he taught that human nature is originally and essentially good, and he made this tenet the foundation of his philosophy. He was the first to make righteousness the highest of moral values and to introduce meditation into the teachings of Confucius.

Since all men are equally good and have an equal opportunity to become sages, he insisted, the aim of government should be the welfare of the people. In keeping with the general orientation of Chinese thought, he stressed the responsibility of rulers to their people, holding that a ruler who allowed his subjects to live in ignorance and misery should be deposed, and believed that the practice of love or humanity (*jen*) must start with the family. "Between father and son," he cautioned, "there should be affection; between sovereign and ministers, there should be righteousness; between husband and wife, attention to their separate functions; between old and young, a proper order; and between friends, good faith."

It was Mencius who restored the authority of Confucius and recorded in a book which bears his name, and which was canonized during the Sung era (960-1279), thoughts gleaned from a lifetime of extensive travels and keen observations of people of all classes. Extracts from his book became favorite reading in Europe early in the eighteenth century and have continued in their popularity. Voltaire and Rousseau quoted his thoughts. In this way he influenced, at least indirectly, leaders of the French Revolution.

The Sayings of Mencius

From *The Sayings of Mencius,* translated by James Legge, New York, The Colonial Press, 1900.

MENCIUS went to see King Hwuy of Lëang. The king said, "Venerable Sir, since you have not counted a distance of a thousand li too far to come here may I presume that you are likewise provided with counsels to profit my kingdom?" Mencius replied, "Why must your Majesty use that word 'profit'? What I am likewise provided with are counsels to benevolence and righteousness; and these are my only topics.

"If your Majesty say, 'What is to be done to profit my kingdom?' the great officers will say, 'What is to be done to profit our families?' and the inferior officers and the common people will say, 'What is to be done to profit our persons?' Superiors and inferiors will try to take the profit the one from the other, and the kingdom will be endangered. In the kingdom of ten thousand chariots, the murderer of his ruler will be the chief of a family of a thousand chariots. In the State of a thousand chariots, the murderer of his ruler will be the chief of a family of a hundred chariots. To have a thousand in ten thousand, and a hundred in a thousand, cannot be regarded as not a large allowance; but if righteousness be put last and profit first, they will not be satisfied without snatching all.

"There never was a man trained to benevolence who neglected his parents. There never was a man trained to righteousness who made his ruler an after consideration. Let your majesty likewise make benevolence and righteousness

179

your only themes — Why must you speak of profit?"

When Mencius, another day, was seeing King Hwuy of Lëang, the King went and stood with him by a pond, and, looking round on the wild geese and deer, large and small said, "Do wise and good princes also take pleasure in these things?" Mencius replied, "Being wise and good, they then have pleasure in these things. If they are not wise and good, though they have these things, they do not find pleasure. It is said in the 'Book of Poetry': —

'When he planned the commencement of the Marvellous tower,
He planned it, and defined it,
And the people in crowds undertook the work,
And in no time completed it.
When he planned the commencement, he said,
"Be not in a hurry."
But the people came as if they were his children.
The king was in the Marvellous park,
Where the does were lying down —
The does so sleek and fat;
With the white birds glistening.
The king was by the Marvellous pond; —
How full was it of fishes leaping about!'

King Wan used the strength of the people to make his tower and pond, and the people rejoiced to do the work, calling the tower 'the Marvellous Tower,' and the pond 'the Marvellous Pond,' and being glad that he had his deer, his fishes and turtles. The ancients caused their people to have pleasure as well as themselves, and therefore they could enjoy it.

"In the Declaration of T'ang it is said, 'O Sun, when wilt thou expire? We will die together with thee.' The people wished for Këeh's death, though they should die with him. Although he had his tower, his pond, birds and animals, how could he have pleasure alone?"

180

King Hwuy of Lëang said, "Small as my virtue is, in the government of my kingdom, I do indeed exert my mind to the utmost. If the year be bad inside the Ho, I remove as many of the people as I can to the east of it, and convey grain to the country inside. If the year be bad on the east of the river, I act on the same plan. On examining the governmental methods of the neighboring kingdoms, I do not find there is any ruler who exerts his mind as I do. And yet the people of the neighboring kings do not decrease, nor do my people increase — how is this?"

Mencius replied, "Your Majesty loves war; allow me to take an illustration from war. The soldiers move forward at the sound of the drum; and when the edges of their weapons have been crossed, on one side, they throw away their buff coats, trail their weapons behind them, and run. Some run a hundred paces and then stop; some run fifty paces and stop. What would you think if these, because they had run but fifty paces, should laugh at those who ran a hundred paces?" The king said, "They cannot do so. They only did not run a hundred paces; but they also ran." Mencius said, "Since your Majesty knows this you have no ground to expect that your people will become more numerous than those of the neighboring kingdoms.

"If the seasons of husbandry be not interfered with, the grain will be more than can be eaten. If close nets are not allowed to enter the pools and ponds, the fish and turtles will be more than can be consumed. If the axes and bills enter the hillforests only at the proper times, the wood will be more than can be used. When the grain and fish and turtles are more than can be eaten, and there is more wood than can be used, this enables the people to nourish their living and do all offices for their dead, without any feeling against any. But this condition, in which the people nourish their living, and do all offices to their dead without having any feeling against any, is the first step in the Royal way.

"Let mulberry trees be planted about the homesteads with their five acres, and persons of fifty years will be able to wear silk. In keeping fowls, pigs, dogs, and swine, let not their time of breeding be neglected, and persons of seventy years will be able to eat flesh. Let there not be taken away the time that is proper for the cultivation of the field allotment of a hundred acres, and the family of several mouths will not suffer from hunger. Let careful attention be paid to the teaching in the various schools, with repeated inculcation of the filial and fraternal duties, and gray-haired men will not be seen upon the roads, carrying burdens on their backs or on their heads. It has never been that the ruler of a State where these results were seen, persons of seventy wearing silk and eating flesh, and the black-haired people suffering neither from hunger nor cold, did not attain to the Royal dignity.

"Your dogs and swine eat the food of men, and you do not know to store up of the abundance. There are people dying from famine on the roads, and you do not know to issue your stores for their relief. When men die, you say, 'It is not owing to me; it is owing to the year.' In what does this differ from stabbing a man and killing him, and then saying, 'It was not I; it was the weapon'? Let your Majesty cease to lay the blame on the year and instantly the people, all under the sky, will come to you."

King Hwuy of Lëang said, "I wish quietly to receive your instructions." Mencius replied, "Is there any difference between killing a man with a stick and with a sword?" "There is no difference," was the answer.

Mencius continued, "Is there any difference between doing it with a sword and with governmental measures?" "There is not," was the answer again.

Mencius then said, "In your stalls there are fat beasts; in in your stables there are fat horses. But your people have the look of hunger, and in the fields there are those who have died of famine. This is leading on beasts to devour men. Beasts devour one another, and men hate them for doing so. When he who is called the parent of the people conducts his government so as to be chargeable with leading on beasts to devour men, where is that parental relation to the people? Chung-ne said, 'Was he not without posterity who first made wooden images to bury with the dead?' So he said, because that man made the semblances of men and used them for that purpose; what shall be thought of him who causes his people to die of hunger?"

King Hwuy of Lëang said, "There was not in the kingdom a stronger State than Ts'in, as you, venerable Sir, know. But since it descended to me, on the east we were defeated by Ts'e, and then my eldest son perished; on the west we lost seven hundred li of territory to Ts'in; and on the south we have sustained disgrace at the hands of Ts'oo. I have brought shame on my departed predecessors, and wish on their account to wipe it away once for all. What course is to be pursued to accomplish this?"

Mencius replied, "With a territory only a hundred li square it has been possible to obtain the Royal dignity. If your Majesty will indeed dispense a benevolent government to the people, being sparing in the use of punishments and fines, and making the taxes and levies of produce light, so causing that the fields shall be ploughed deep, and the weeding well attended to, and that the able-bodied, during their days of leisure, shall cultivate their filial piety, fraternal duty, faithfulness, and truth, serving thereby, at home, their fathers and elder brothers, and, abroad, their elders and superiors, you will then have a people who can be employed with sticks which they have prepared to oppose the strong buff-coats and sharp weapons of the troops of Ts'in and Ts'oo.

"The rulers of those States, rob their people of their time, so that they cannot plough and weed their fields in order to support their parents. Parents suffer from cold and hunger; elder and younger brothers, wives and children, are separated and scattered abroad. Those rulers drive their people into pitfalls or into the water; and your Majesty will go to punish them. In such a case, who will oppose your Majesty?

In accordance with this is the saying, 'The benevolent has no enemy!' I beg your Majesty not to doubt what I said."

Mencius had an interview with King Sëang[1] of Lëang. When he came out he said to some persons, "When I looked at him from a distance, he did not appear like a ruler; when I drew near to him, I saw nothing venerable about him. Abruptly he asked me, 'How can the kingdom, all under the sky, be settled?' I replied, 'It will be settled by being united under one sway.'

" 'Who can so unite it?' he asked.

"I replied, 'He who has no pleasure in killing men can so unite it.'

" 'Who can give it to him?' he asked.

"I replied, 'All under heaven will give it to him. Does your Majesty know the way of the growing grain? During the seventh and eighth months, when drought prevails, the plants become dry. Then the clouds collect densely in the heavens, and send down torrents of rain, so that the grain erects itself as if by a shoot. When it does so, who can keep it back? Now among those who are shepherds of men throughout the kingdom, there is not one who does not find pleasure in killing men. If there were one who did not find pleasure in killing men, all the people under the sky would be looking towards him with outstretched necks. Such being indeed the case, the people would go to him as water flows downwards with a rush, which no one can repress."

King Seuen of Ts'e asked, saying "May I be informed by you of the transactions of Hwan of Ts'e and Wan of Ts'in?"

Mencius replied, "There were none of the disciples of Chung-ne who spoke about the affairs of Hwan and Wan,

1. Sëang was the son of King Hwuy. The first year of his reign is supposed to be B.C. 317. Sëang's name was Hih. As a posthumous epithet, Sëang has various meanings: "Land-enlarger and Virtuous"; Successful in Arms." The interview here recorded seems to have taken place immediately after Hih's accession, and Mencius, it is said, was so disappointed by it that he soon after left the country.

and therefore they have not been transmitted to these after-ages; your servant has not heard of them. If you will have me speak, let it be about the principles of attaining to the Royal sway."

The king said, "Of what kind must his virtue be who can attain to the Royal sway?" Mencius said, "If he loves and protects the people, it is impossible to prevent him from attaining it."

The king said, "Is such an one as poor I competent to love and protect the people?" "Yes," was the reply. "From what do you know that I am competent to that?" "I have heard," said Mencius, "from Hoo Heih the following incident: — 'The king,' said he, "was sitting aloft in the hall, when some people appeared leading a bull past below it. The king saw it, and asked where the bull was going, and being answered that they were going to consecrate a bell with its blood, he said, "Let it go, I cannot bear its frightened appearance — as if it were an innocent person going to the place of death." They asked in reply whether, if they did so, they should omit the consecration of the bell, but the king said, "How can that be omitted? Change it for a sheep." I do not know whether this incident occurred."

"It did," said the king, and Mencius replied, "The heart seen in this is sufficient to carry you to the Royal sway. The people all supposed that your Majesty grudged the animal, but your servant knows surely that it was your Majesty's not being able to bear the sight of the creature's distress which made you do as you did."

The king said, "You are right yet there really was an appearance of what the people imagined. But though Ts'e be narrow and small, how should I grudge a bull? Indeed it was because I could not bear its frightened appearance, as if it were an innocent person going to the place of death, that therefore I changed it for a sheep."

Mencius said, "Let not your Majesty deem it strange that the people should think you grudged the animal. When you changed a large one for a small, how should they know the true reason? If you felt pained by its being led without any guilt to the place of death, what was there to choose between a bull and a sheep?" The king laughed and said, "What really was my mind in the matter? I did not grudge the value of the bull, and yet I changed it for a sheep! There was reason in the people's saying that I grudged the creature."

Mencius said, "There is no harm in their saying so. It was an artifice of benevolence. You saw the bull, and had not seen the sheep. So is the superior man affected towards animals, that, having seen them alive, he cannot bear to see them die, and, having heard their dying cries, he cannot bear to eat their flesh. On this account he keeps away from his stalls and kitchen."

The king was pleased and said, "The Ode says,

'What other men have in their minds,
I can measure by reflection.'

This might be spoken of you, my Master. I indeed did the thing, but when I turned my thoughts inward and sought for it, I could not discover my own mind. When you, Master, spoke those words, the movements of compassion began to work in my mind. But how is it that heart has in it what is equal to the attainment of the Royal sway?"

Mencius said, "Suppose a man were to make this statement to your Majesty, 'My strength is sufficient to lift three thousand catties, but not sufficient to lift one feather; my eyesight is sharp enough to examine the point of an autumn hair, but I do not see a wagon-load of fagots,' would your Majesty allow what he said?" "No," was the king's remark, and Mencius proceeded, "Now here is kindness sufficient to reach to animals, and yet no benefits are extended from it to the people — how is this? is an exception to be made here? The truth is, the feather's not being lifted is because the strength was not used; the wagon-load of firewood's not being seen is because the eyesight was not used; and the people's not being loved and protected is because the kindness is not used. Therefore your Majesty's not attaining to the Royal sway is because you do not do it, and not because you are not able to do it."

The king asked, "How may the difference between him who does not do a thing and him who is not able to do it be graphically set forth?" Mencius replied, "In such a thing as taking the T'ae mountain under your arm, and leaping with it over the North Sea, if you say to people, 'I am not able to do it,' that is a real case of not being able. In such a matter as breaking off a branch from a tree at the order of a superior, if you say to people, 'I am not able to do it,' it is not a case of not being able to do it. And so your Majesty's not attaining to the Royal sway is not such a case as that of taking the T'ae mountain under your arm and leaping over the North Sea with it; but it is a case like that of breaking off a branch from a tree.

"Treat with reverence due to age the elders in your own family, so that those in the families of others shall be similarly treated; treat with the kindness due to youth the young in your own family, so that those in the families of others shall be similarly treated — do this and the kingdom may be made to go round in your palm. It is said in the 'Book of Poetry,'

> 'His example acted on his wife,
> Extended to his brethren,
> And was felt by all the clans and States;'

telling us how King Wan simply took this kindly heart, and exercised it towards those parties. Therefore the carrying out of the feeling of kindness by a ruler will suffice for the love and protection of all within the four seas; and if he do not carry it out, he will not be able to protect his wife and children. The way in which the ancients came greatly to surpass other men was no other than this, that they carried out well what they did, so as to affect others. Now your kindness is sufficient to reach to animals, and yet no benefits are extended from it to the people. How is this? Is an exception to be made here?

"By weighing we know what things are light, and what heavy. By measuring we know what things are long, and what short. All things are so dealt with, and the mind requires specially to be so. I beg your Majesty to measure it.

"Your Majesty collects your equipments of war, endangers your soldiers and officers and excites the resentment of the various princes — do these things cause you pleasure in your mind?"

The king said, "No. How should I derive pleasure from these things? My object in them is to seek for what I greatly desire."

Mencius said, "May I hear from you what it is that your Majesty greatly desires?" The king laughed, and did not speak. Mencius resumed, "Are you led to desire it because you have not enough of rich and sweet food for your mouth? or because you have not enough of light and warm clothing for your body? or because you have not enough of beautifully colored objects to satisfy your eyes? or because there are not voices and sounds enough to fill your ears? or because you have not enough of attendants and favorites to stand before you and receive your orders? Your Majesty's various officers are sufficient to supply you with all these things. How can your Majesty have such a desire on account of them?" "No," said the king, "my desire is not on account of them." Mencius observed, "Then what your Majesty greatly desires can be known. You desire to enlarge your territories, to have Ts'in and Ts'oo coming to your court, to rule the Middle States, and to attract to you the barbarous tribes that surround them. But to do what you do in order to seek for what you desire is like climbing a tree to seek for fish."

"Is it so bad as that?" said the king. "I apprehend it is worse," was the reply. "If you climb a tree to seek a fish, although you do not get the fish, you have no subsequent calamity. But if you do what you do in order to seek for what you desire, doing it even with all your heart, you will assuredly afterwards meet with calamities." The king said, "May I hear what they will be?" Mencius replied, "If the people of Tsow were fighting with the people of Ts'oo, which of them does your Majesty think would conquer?" "The people of Ts'oo would conquer," was the answer, and Mencius pursued, "So then, a small State cannot contend with a great, few cannot contend with many, nor can the weak contend with the strong. The territory within the seas would embrace nine divisions, each of a thousand li square. All Ts'e together is one of them. If with one part you try to subdue the other eight, what is the difference between that and Tsow's contending with Ts'oo? With the desire which you have, you must turn back to the proper course for its attainment.

"Now, if your Majesty will institute a government whose actions shall all be benevolent, this will cause all the officers in the kingdom to wish to stand in your Majesty's court, the farmers all to wish to plough in your Majesty's fields, the merchants, both travelling and stationary, all to wish to store their goods in your Majesty's market-places, travellers and visitors all to wish to travel on your Majesty's roads, and all under heaven who feel aggrieved by their rulers to wish to come and complain to your Majesty. When they are so bent, who will be able to keep them back?"

The king said, "I am stupid and cannot advance to this. But I wish you, my Master, to assist my intentions. Teach me clearly, and although I am deficient in intelligence and vigor, I should like to try at least to institute such a government."

Mencius replied, "They are only men of education, who, without a certain livelihood, are able to maintain a fixed heart. As to the people, if they have not a certain livelihood, they will be found not to have a fixed heart. And if they have not a fixed heart, there is nothing which they will not do in the way of self-abandonment, of moral deflection, of depravity, and of wild license. When they have thus been involved in crime, to follow them up and punish them, is to entrap the people. How can such a thing as entrapping the people be done under the rule of a benevolent man?

"Therefore, an intelligent ruler will regulate the livelihood of the people, so as to make sure that, above, they shall have sufficient wherewith to serve their parents, and below, sufficient wherewith to support their wives and children; that in good years they shall always be abundantly satisfied, and that in bad years they shall not be in danger of perishing. After this he may urge them, and they will proceed to what is good, for in this case the people will follow after that with readiness.

"But now the livelihood of the people is so regulated, that, above, they have not sufficient wherewith to serve their parents, and, below, they have not sufficient wherewith to support their wives and children; even in good years their lives are always embittered, and in bad years they are in danger of perishing. In such circumstances their only object is to escape from death, and they are afraid they will not succeed in doing so — what leisure have they to cultivate propriety and righteousness?

"If your Majesty wishes to carry out a benevolent government, why not turn back to what is the essential step to its attainment?

"Let mulberry trees be planted about the homesteads with their five acres, and persons of fifty years will be able to wear silk. In keeping fowls, pigs, dogs, and swine, let not their times of breeding be neglected, and persons of seventy years will be able to eat flesh. Let there not be taken away the time that is proper for the cultivation of the field-allotment of a hundred acres, and the family of eight mouths will not suffer from hunger. Let careful attention be paid to the teaching in the various schools, with repeated inculcation of the filial and fraternal duties, and gray-haired men will not be seen upon the roads, carrying burdens on their backs or on their heads. It has never been that the ruler of a State, where these results were seen, the old wearing and eating flesh, and the black-haired people suffering neither from hunger nor cold, did not attain to the Royal dignity." [Book I]

Wan Chang[1] asked Mencius, saying, "When Shun went into the fields, he cried out and wept towards the pitying heavens. Why did he cry out and weep?" Mencius replied, "He was dissatisfied and full of earnest desire."

Wan Chang said, "When his parents love him, a son rejoices and forgets them not; and when they hate him, though they punish him, he does not allow himself to be dissatisfied. Was Shun then dissatisfied with his parents?" Mencius said, "Ch'ang Seih asked Kung-ming Kaou, saying, 'As to Shun's going into the fields, I have received your instructions; but I do not understand about his weeping and crying out to the pitying heavens, and to his parents.' Kung-ming Kaou answered him, 'You do not understand that matter.' Now Kung-ming Kaou thought that the heart of a filial son like Shun could not be so free from sorrow as Seih seemed to imagine he might have been. Shun would be saying, 'I exert my strength to cultivate the fields, but I am thereby only discharging my duty as a son. What is there wrong in me that my parents do not love me?'

"The emperor caused his own children — nine sons and two daughters — the various officers, oxen and sheep, storehouses and granaries, all to be prepared for the service of Shun amid the channeled fields. Most of the officers in the empire repaired to him. The emperor designed that he should superintend the empire along with himself, and then to transfer it to him. But because his parents were not in accord with him, he felt like a poor man who has nowhere to turn to.

1. The tradition is that it was in company with Wan's disciples that Mencius, baffled in all his hopes of doing public service, and having retired into privacy, composed the Seven Books which constitute his works. The part which follows is all occupied with discussions in vindication of Shun and other ancient worthies.

"To be an object of complacency to the officers of the empire is what men desire; but it was not sufficient to remove the sorrow of Shun. The possession of beauty is what men desire: but though Shun had for his wives the two daughters of the emperor, it was not sufficient to remove his sorrow. Riches are what men desire, but though the empire was the rich property of Shun, it was not enough to remove his sorrow. Honors are what men desire, but though Shun had the dignity of being the son of Heaven, it was not sufficient to remove his sorrow. The reason why his being the object of men's complacency, the possession of beauty, riches, and honors, could not remove his sorrow was because it could be removed only by his being in entire accord with his parents.

"The desire of a child is towards his father and mother. When he becomes conscious of the attractions of beauty, his desire is towards young and beautiful women. When he comes to have a wife and children, his desire is towards them. When he obtains office, his desire is towards his ruler; and if he cannot get the regard of his ruler, he burns within. But the man of great filial piety, all his life, has his desire towards his parents. In the great Shun I see the case of one whose desire was towards them when he was fifty years old."

Wan Chang asked Mencius, saying, "It is said in the 'Book of Poetry,'

'How do we proceed in taking a wife?
Announcement must first be made to our parents.'

If the rule be indeed as thus expressed, no one ought to have illustrated it so well as Shun — how was it that Shun's marriage took place without his informing his parents?" Mencius replied, "If he had informed them, he would not have been able to marry. That male and female dwell together is the greatest of human relations. If Shun had informed his parents, he must have made void this greatest of human relations, and incurred thereby their resentment. It was on this account that he did not inform them."

Wan Chang said, "As to Shun's marrying without making announcement to his parents, I have heard your instructions. But how was it that the emperor gave him his daughters as wives without informing his parents?" Mencius said, "The emperor also knew that, if he informed his parents, he could not have given him his daughters as wives."

Wan Chang said, "His parents set Shun to repair a granary, and then removed the ladder by which he had ascended; after which Koo-sow set fire to it. They sent him to dig a well, from which he managed to get out; but they, not knowing this, proceeded to cover it up. His brother, Sëang, said, 'Of this scheme to cover up the city-farming gentleman the merit is all mine. Let my parents have his oxen and sheep; let them have his granaries and storehouses. His shield and spear shall be mine; his lute shall be mine; his carved bow shall be mine; and I will make his two wives attend for me to my bed.' Sëang then went away and entered Shun's house, and there was Shun upon a couch with his lute. Sëang said, 'I am come simply because I was thinking anxiously about you,' and at the same time he looked ashamed. Shun said to him, 'There are all my officers; do you take the management of them for me.' I do not know whether Shun was ignorant of Sëang's wishing to kill him." Mencius replied, "How could he be ignorant of it? But when Sëang was sorrowful, he was also sorrowful, and when Sëang was joyful, he was also joyful."

Wan Chang continued, "Then was Shun one who rejoiced hypocritically?" "No," was the reply. "Formerly some one sent a present of a live fish to Tsze-ch'an of Ch'ing. Tsze-ch'an ordered his pond-keeper to feed it in the pond; but the man cooked it and reported the execution of his commission, saying, 'When I first let it go, it looked embarrassed. In a little while it seemed to be somewhat at ease, and then it swam away as if delighted.' 'It had got into its element!' said Tsze-ch'an. The pond-keeper went out and said, 'Who calls Tsze-ch'an wise? When I had cooked and eaten the fish, he said, "It has got into its element! It has got into its element!"' Thus a superior man may be imposed on by what seems to be as it ought to be, but it is difficult to entrap him by what is contrary to right principle. Sëang came in the way in which the love of his elder brother would have made him come, and therefore Shun truly believed him, and rejoiced at it. What hypocrisy was there?"

Wan Chang said, "Sëang made it his daily business to kill Shun; why was it that, when the latter was raised to be the son of Heaven, he only banished him?" Mencius replied, "He invested him with a State, and some have said that it was banishing him." Wan Chang said, 'Shun banished the Superintendent of Works to Yew-chow, sent away Hwan-tow to Mount Ts'ung, slew the Prince of San Mëaou in San-wei, and imprisoned K'wan on Mount Yu. When those four criminals were thus dealt with, all under heaven submitted to him; it was a cutting off of men who were destitute of benevolence. But Sëang was of all men the most destitute of benevolence, and Shun invested him with the State of Pe; of what crime had the people of Pe been guilty? Does a benevolent man really act thus? In the case of other men, he cut them off; in the case of his brother, he invested him with a State." Mencius replied, "A benevolent man does not lay up anger, nor cherish resentment against his brother, but only regards him with affection and love. Regarding him with affection, he wishes him to enjoy honor; loving him, he wishes him to be rich. The investing him with Pe was to enrich and ennoble him. If while Shun himself was emperor, his brother had been a common man, could he have been said to regard him with affection and love?"

Wan Chang said, "I venture to ask what is meant by some saying that it was a banishing of Sëang." Mencius replied, "Sëang could do nothing of himself in his State. The emperor appointed an officer to manage its government, and to pay over its revenues to him; and therefore it was said that it was a banishing of him? How indeed could he be allowed the means of oppressing the people there? Nevertheless, Shun wished to be continually seeing him, and therefore he came unceasingly to court, as is signified in that expression, 'He did not wait for the rendering of tribute, or affairs of government to receive the prince of Pe.'"

Hëen-k'ëw Mung asked Mencius, saying, "There is the old saying, 'An officer of complete virtue cannot be employed as a minister by his ruler, nor treated as a son by his father.' Shun stood with his face to the south, and Yaou, at the end of all the feudal princes, appeared in his court with his face to the north. Koo-sow also appeared at Shun's court with his face to the north; and when Shun saw him, his countenance assumed a look of distress. Confucius said, 'At this time the empire was in a perilous condition indeed! How unsettled was its state!' I do not know whether what is thus said really took place." Mencius said, "No. These are not the words of a superior man, but the sayings of an uncultivated person of the east of Ts'e. When Yaou was old, Shun took the management of affairs for him. It is said in the Canon of Yaou, 'After twenty-eight years, Fang-heun demised, and the people mourned for him as for a parent three years. All within the four seas, the eight instruments of music were stopped and hushed.' Confucius said, 'There are not two suns in the sky, nor two sovereigns over the people. If Shun had already been in the position of the son of Heaven, and had moreover led on all the feudal princes of the empire to observe the three years' mourning for Yaou, there must in that case have been two sons of Heaven.'"

Hëen-k'ëw Mung said, "On the point of Shun's not employing Yaou as a minister, I have received your instructions. But it is said in the 'Book of Poetry,'

> 'Under the wide heaven,
> All is the king's land;

195

> Within the sea-boundaries of the land,
> All are the king's servants.'

When Shun became emperor, I venture to ask how it was that Koo-sow was not one of his servants." Mencius replied, "That Ode is not to be understood in that way; it speaks of being laboriously engaged in the king's business, and not being able to nourish one's parents, as if the subject of it said, 'This is all the king's business, but I alone am supposed to have ability, and made to toil in it.' Therefore those who explain the Odes must not insist on one term so as to do violence to a sentence, nor on a sentence so as to do violence to the general scope. They must try with their thoughts to meet that scope, and then they will apprehend it. If we simply take single sentences, there is that in the Ode called the 'Yun Han,'

> 'Of the remnant of Chow, among the black-
> haired people,
> There will not be half a man left.'

If it had really been thus expressed, then not an individual of the people of Chow would have been left.

"Of all that a filial son can attain to, there is nothing greater than his honoring his parents. Of what can be attained to in honoring one's parents, there is nothing greater than the nourishing them with the empire. To be the father of the son of Heaven is the height of honor. To be nourished with the empire is the height of nourishment. In this was verified the sentiment in the 'Book of Poetry,'

> 'Ever thinking how to be filial,
> His filial mind was the model which he
> supplied.'

"In the 'Book of History' it is said, 'With respectful service he appeared before Koo-sow, looking grave and awe-struck, till Koo-sow also was transformed by his example.' This is the true case of the scholar of complete virtue not being treated as a son by his father."

Wan Chang said, "It is said that Yaou gave the empire to Shun; was it so?" Mencius replied, "No; the emperor cannot give the empire to another." "Yes; but Shun possessed the empire. Who gave it to him?" "Heaven gave it to him," was the reply.

" 'Heaven gave it to him'; did Heaven confer the appointment on him with specific injunctions?" Mencius said, "No; Heaven does not speak. It simply showed its will by his personal conduct, and by his conduct of affairs."

" 'It showed its will by his personal conduct, and by his conduct of affairs,' " returned the other; "how was this?" Mencius said, "The emperor can present a man to Heaven, but he cannot make Heaven give that man the empire. A feudal prince can present a man to the emperor to take his place, but he cannot make the emperor give the princedom to that man. A great officer can present a man to his prince, but he cannot cause the prince to make that man a great officer in his own room. Anciently Yaou presented Shun to Heaven, and Heaven accepted him; he displayed him to the people, and the people accepted him. Therefore I say, 'Heaven does not speak. It simply indicated its will by his personal conduct, and by his conduct of affairs.' "

Chang said, "I presume to ask how it was that Yaou presented Shun to Heaven, and Heaven accepted him, and displayed him to the people, and the people accepted him." The reply was, "He caused him to preside over the sacrifices, and all the Spirits were well pleased with them; thus it was that Heaven accepted him. He caused him to preside over the conduct of affairs, and affairs were well administered, so that all the people reposed under him; thus it was that the people accepted him. Heaven gave the empire to him, and the people gave it to him. Therefore I said, 'The emperor cannot give the empire to another.'

"Shun assisted Yaou in the government for twenty and

eight years; this was more than man could have done, and was from Heaven. When the three years' mourning consequent on the death of Yaou were accomplished, Shun withdrew from the son of Yaou to the south of the southern Ho. The princes of the empire, however, repairing to court, went not to the son of Yaou, but to Shun. Litigants went not to the son of Yaou, but to Shun. Singers sang not the son of Yaou, but Shun. Therefore I said that it was Heaven that gave him the empire. It was after this that he went to the Middle State, and occupied the seat of the son of Heaven. If he had before these things taken up his residence in the palace of Yaou, and applied pressure to his son, it would have been an act of usurpation, and not the gift of Heaven.

"This view of Shun's obtaining the empire is in accordance with what is said in The Great Declaration — 'Heaven sees as my people see, Heaven hears as my people hear.'"

Wan Chang said, "People say, 'When the disposal of the empire came to Yu, his virtue was inferior to that of Yaou and Shun, and he did not transmit it to the worthiest, but to his son.' Was it so?" Mencius replied, "No; it was not so. When Heaven gave the empire to the worthiest, it was given to the worthiest; when Heaven gave it to the son of the preceding emperor, it was given to that son. Formerly Shun presented Yu to Heaven for a period of seventeen years; and when the three years' mourning, consequent on the death of Shun, were accomplished, Yu withdrew from the son of Yu to Yang-shing. The people of the empire followed him as, after the death of Yaou, they had not followed his son, but followed Shun. Yu presented Yih to Heaven for a period of seven years; and when the three years' mourning consequent on the death of Yu were accomplished, Yih withdrew from the son of Yu to the north of Mount K'e. The princes repairing to court, and litigants, went not to Yih, but to K'e, saying, 'He is the son of our ruler.' Singers did not sing Yih, but they sang K'e, saying, 'He is the son of our ruler.'

"That Tan-choo was not equal to his father, and Shun's son also not equal to his; that Shun assisted Yaou, and Yu assisted Shun, for a period of many years, conferring benefits on the people for a long time; that K'e was virtuous and able, and could reverently enter into and continue the ways of Yu; that Yih assisted Yu for a period of a few years, conferring benefits on the people not for a long time; that the length of time that Shun, Yu, and Yih, assisted in the government was so different; and that the sons of the emperors were one a man of talents and virtue, and the other two inferior to their fathers: — all these things were from Heaven, and what could not be produced by man. That which is done without any one's seeming to do it is from Heaven. That which comes to pass without any one's seeming to bring it about is from Heaven.

"In the case of a private man's obtaining the empire, there must be in him virtue equal to that of Shun and Yu, and moreover there must be the presenting him to Heaven by the preceding emperor. It was on this latter account that Chung-ne did not obtain the kingdom.

"When the throne descends by natural succession, he who is displaced by Heaven must be like Këeh or Chow. It was on this account that Yih, E Yin, and the duke of Chow did not obtain the kingdom.

"E Yin assisted T'ang so that he became sovereign of the kingdom. After the demise of T'ang, T'ae-ting having died without being appointed in his place, Wae-ping reigned two years, and Chung-jin four. T'ae-Këah then was turning upside down the canons and examples of T'ang, and E Yin placed him in T'ung for three years. There he repented of his errors, was contrite, and reformed himself. In T'ung he came to dwell in benevolence and moved towards righteousness, during those three years listening to the lessons given to him by E Yin, after which that minister again returned with him to Poh.

"The duke of Chow's not getting the kingdom was like

that of Yih's not getting the throne of Hëa, or E Yin's that of Yin.

"Confucius said, 'T'ang and Yu resigned the throne to the worthiest; the founders of the Hëa, Yin, and Chow dynasties transmitted it to their sons. The principle of righteousness was the same in all the cases.'"

Wan Chang asked Mencius, saying, "People say that E Yin sought an introduction to T'ang by his knowledge of cookery; was it so?" Mencius replied, "No, it was not so. E Yin was farming in the lands of the State of Sin, delighting in the principles of Yaou and Shun. In any matter contrary to the righteousness which they prescribed, or to the course which they enjoined, though he had been salaried with the empire, he would not have regarded it; though there had been yoked for him a thousand teams, he would not have looked at them. In any matter contrary to the righteousness which they prescribed, or to the course which they enjoined, he would not have given nor taken even a single straw.

"T'ang sent persons with presents of silk to ask him to enter his service. With an air of indifference and self-satisfaction, he said, 'What can I do with these silks with which T'ang invites me? Is it not best for me to abide in these channeled fields, and therein delight myself with the principles of Yaou and Shun?'

"T'ang thrice sent persons thus to invite him. After this, with the change of purpose displayed in his countenance, he spoke in a different style, saying, 'Instead of abiding in the channeled fields, and therein delighting myself with the principles of Yaou and Shun, had I not better make this ruler one after the style of Yaou and Shun? had I not better make this people like the people of Yaou and Shun? had I not better in my own person see these things for myself? Heaven's plan in the production of this people is this: — That they who are first informed, should instruct those who are later in being informed, and those who first

200

to do so. I am the one of Heaven's people who have first apprehended; I will take these principles and instruct this people in them. If I do not instruct them, who will do so?'

"He thought that among all the people of the kingdom, apprehend principles should instruct those who are slower even the private men and women, if there were any that did not enjoy such benefits as Yaou and Shun conferred, it was as if he himself pushed them into a ditch. He took upon himself the heavy charge of all under Heaven in this way, and therefore he went to T'ang, and pressed upon him the duty of attacking Hëa, and saving the people.

"I have not heard of one who bent himself and at the same time made others straight; how much less could one disgrace himself, and thereby rectify the whole kingdom? The actions of the sages have been different. Some have kept far away from office, and others have drawn near to it; some have left their offices, and others have not done so; that in which these different courses all meet, is simply the keeping of their persons pure.

"I have heard that E Yin sought an introduction to T'ang by the principles of Yaou and Shun; I have not heard he did so by his knowledge of cookery.

"In the 'instructions of E', it is said, 'Heaven, destroying Këeh, commenced attacking him in the palace of Muh; we commenced in Poh.'"

Wan Chang asked Mencius, saying, "Some say that Confucius in Wei lived with an ulcer-doctor, and in Ts'e with Tseih Hwan, the chief of the eunuchs; was it so?" Mencius said, "No, it was not so. Those are the inventions of men fond of strange things.

"In Wei he lived in the house of Yen Ch'ow-yëw. The wife of the officer Mei and the wife of Tsze-lu were sisters. Mei-tsze spoke to Tsze-lu, saying, 'If Confucius will lodge with me, he may get to be a high noble of Wei.' Tsze-lu reported this to Confucius, who said, 'That is as ordered by Heaven.' Confucius advanced according to propriety, and retired according to righteousness. In regard to his obtaining office and honor or not obtaining them, he said, 'That is as ordered.' But if he had lodged with an ulcer-doctor and with Tseih Hwan, the chief of the eunuchs, that would neither have been according to righteousness nor any ordering of Heaven.

"When Confucius, being dissatisfied in Lu and Wei, had left those states, he met with the attempt of Hwan, the master of the Horse, in Sung, to intercept and kill him, so that he had to pass through Sung in the dress of a private man. At that time, though he was in circumstances of distress, he lodged in the house of Ching-tsze, the minister of works, who was then a minister of Chow, the marquis of Ch'in.

"I have heard that ministers in the service of a court may be known from those to whom they are hosts, and that ministers coming from a distance may be known from those with whom they lodge. If Confucius had lodged with an ulcer-doctor and with Tseih Hwan, the chief of the eunuchs, how could he have been Confucius?"

Wan Chang asked Mencius, saying, "Some say that Pih-le He sold himself to a cattle-keeper of Ts'in for five sheep-skins, and fed his cattle for him, to seek an introduction to Duke Muh of Ts'in; is this true?" Mencius said, "No, it was not so. This is the invention of some one fond of strange things.

"Pih-le He was a man of Yu. The people of Ts'in by the inducement of a *peih* of Ch'uy-Keih and a team of Këuh-ch'an horses were asking liberty to march through Yu to attack Kwoh. Kung Che-k'e remonstrated with the duke of Yu, asking him not to grant their request, but Pih-le He did not remonstrate.

"When he knew that the duke of Yu was not to be remonstrated with, and went in consequence from that State to Ts'in, he had reached the age of seventy. If by that time he did not know that it would be a disgraceful thing to seek for an introduction to Duke Muh of Ts'in by feeding cattle, could he be called wise? But not remonstrating where it was of no use to remonstrate, could he be said not to be wise? Knowing that the duke of Yu would be ruined, and leaving his State before that event, he could not be said to be not wise. As soon as he was advanced in Ts'in, he knew that Duke Muh was one with whom he could have a field for action, and became chief minister to him; could he be said to be not wise? Acting as chief minister in Ts'in, he made his ruler distinguished throughout the kingdom, and worthy to be handed down to future ages; if he had been a man of talents and virtue, could he have done this? As to selling himself in order to bring about the destruction of his ruler, even a villager who had a regard for himself, would not do such a thing; and shall we say that a man of talents and virtue did it?"

Tzŭ Ssu

TZŬ SSU (*c*. 335-288 B.C.). Tzŭ Ssu was a grandson of Confucius. Often he evoked his ancestor's authority; but he also expressed thoughts of his own. Confucius had begun to distinguish between true and supposed knowledge, while Tzŭ Ssu proceeded to meditations on the relativity of human knowledge of the Universe. He tried to analyze as many types of action as possible, and believed that the reality of the universe can be copied in the character of any wise man who is conscious of his moral and intellectual duties. Though *The Way of The Mean (Chung Yung)* is traditionally ascribed to Tzŭ Ssu, it may be of later origin.

The Way of the Mean

From *Chinese Philosophy in Classical Times*, edited by E. H. Hughes, Everyman's Library, New York, E. P. Dutton.

CHUNG-NI [Confucius] said, "The man of true breeding is the mean in action. The man of no breeding is the reverse. The relation of the man of true breeding to the mean in action is that, being a man of true breeding, he consistently holds to the Mean. The reverse relationship of the man of no breeding is that, being what he is, he has no sense of moral caution."

The Master said, "Perfect is the mean in action, and for a long time now very few people have had the capacity for it."

The Master said, "I know why the Way is not pursued. (It is because) the learned run to excess and the ignorant fall short. I know why the Way is not understood. The good run to excess and the bad fall short. . . ."

The Master said, "Alas, this failure to pursue the Way!"

The Master said, "Consider Shun, the man of great wisdom. He loved to ask advice and to examine plain speech. He never referred to what was evil, and publicly praised what was good. By grasping these two extremes he put into effect the Mean among his people. In this way he was Shun [i.e. a sage-emperor], was he not?"

The Master said, "All men say 'I know,' but they are driven into nets, caught in traps, fall into pitfalls, and not one knows how to avoid this. All men say 'I know,' but, should they choose the mean in action, they could not persist in it for a round month."

The Master said, "Hui, a real man! He chose the mean in action, and, if he succeeded in one element of good, he grasped it firmly, cherished it in his bosom, and never let it go."

The Master said, "The states and families of the Great Society might have equal divisions of land: men might refuse noble station and the wealth that goes with it: they might trample the naked sword under foot; but the mean in action, it is impossible for them to achieve that."

Tzŭ Lu inquired about strong men, and the Master said, "It is strong men of the southern kind, or strong men of the northern kind, or, maybe, making yourself strong (that you have in mind)? The (typical) strong man of the north lives under arms and dies without a murmur: it is the habit of a man of true force to be like this. Hence the man of true breeding, how steadfast he is in his strength, having a spirit of concord and not giving way to pressure. He takes up a central position, and does not waver one way or another. How steadfast his strength, for, when there is good government, he does not change his original principles, and, when there is vile government, he does not change, even though his life be at stake."

The Way of the enlightened man is widely apparent and yet hidden. Thus the ordinary man and woman, ignorant though they are, can yet have some knowledge of it; and yet in its perfection even a sage finds that there is something there which he does not know. Take the vast size of heaven and earth; men can still find room for criticism of it. Hence, when the enlightened man speaks of supreme bigness, it cannot be contained within the world of our experience; nor, when he speaks of supreme smallness, can it be split up in the world of our experience into nothing. As is said in the *Odes*: "The hawk beats its way up to the height of heaven, the fish dives down into the abyss." That refers to things being examined from above and from below. Thus the Way of the enlightened man, its early shoots coming into existence in the ordinary man and woman, but in its ultimate extent to be examined in the light of heaven and earth.

The Master said, "The Way is not far removed from men. If a man pursues a way which removes him from men, he cannot be in the Way. In the *Odes* there is the word, 'When hewing an axe handle, hew an axe handle. The pattern of it is close at hand.' You grasp an axe handle to hew an axe handle, although, when you look from the one to the other [i.e from the axe in your hand to the block of wood], they are very different." Therefore the right kind of ruler uses men to control men and attempts nothing beyond their correction; and fidelity and mutual service (these two human qualities) cannot be outside the scope of the Way. The treatment which you do not like for yourself you must not hand out to others. . . .

The acts of the enlightened man agree with the station in life in which he finds himself, and he is not concerned with matters outside that station. If he is a man of wealth and high position, he acts as such. If he is a poor man and low in the social scale, he acts accordingly. So also if he is among barbarians, or if he meets trouble. In fact, there is no situation into which he comes in which he is not himself.

Hsun Tzŭ

HSUN TZŬ (between 335 and 238 B.C.). Little is
known of the life of Hsün Tzŭ (Hsün-tze, Hsün Ch'ing,
Ch'ing-tzŭ, or Hsün K'uang) except that he was a high
official in the states of Ch'i and Ch'u at the end of the
Chou period, that he was the teacher of Hans Fei Tzŭ
and of Li Ssu, the prime minister who helped the first
Ch'in ruler to unify the empire, and that he lost his
post when his master, Lord Ch'un shen, was assassinated in 238 B.C. The third great Confucian thinker,
after Confucius and Mencius, he occupies the same
position in the Chinese triumvirate as the third member of the Greek triumvirate consisting of Socrates,
Plato, and Aristotle. More prolific and more erudite
than his predecessors, he was the first to set down his
ideas in well-organized essays and to provide a complete, systematic statement of Confucianism.

Hsün Tzŭ examined critically the views of his predecessors and adopted a thoroughly rationalistic set of
principles. He countered Mencius' doctrine of the innate goodness of man with the argument that all men
are born equally evil and require strict discipline if they
are to become good. He criticized Chuang Tzŭ for
slighting human problems, legalists for thinking that
laws can replace virtue in a ruler, and Moism for its
stress on frugality, social conformity, and meager burial
rites. He rejected supernaturalism but not divination
based on tortoise shells and milfoil stalks. His argument in favor of a philosophy of culture embracing the
study of the classics and observance of rituals includes

209

these points: no single pattern of conduct is inborn since customs differ throughout the world; basic human nature and moral principles do not change; every man is by nature desirous of gain, sensuous, envious of others; only by rigorous training can man be made to create order rather than disorder in society. Thus he remained Confucian in his insistence on traditional morality as the rational basis for human society.

He made important contributions to dialectic, psychology, and epistemology. The influence of his book, in thirty-two chapters, did not wane until the rise of Neo-Confucianism in the ninth century. The triumph of Mencius was formalized in the twelfth century, when the *Mencius* was included among the Confucian classics.

Self-Cultivation

From *The Works of Hsüntze*, translated by Homer H. Dubs, London, Probsthain, 1928.

WHEN you see the good, you should be respectful and investigate yourself to see if you have this virtue or not; when you see evil, you should be anxious and examine yourself to see if you have it. If you possess this goodness, you should be firm in it and prize it. If you possess this evil, you should feel it as a calamity and hate yourself. Hence he who criticizes me and does so correctly is my teacher; he who tells me that I am right and does so correctly is my friend; he who flatters me mistreats me. Therefore the superior man exalts his teacher, clings to his friend, and greatly hates the man who mistreats him. If a man prizes and seeks for the good without ever being self-satisfied, and if he receives the admonitions of others and is able to be warned thereby, even though he did not desire to make progress, could he fail to do so?

The small-minded man is just the opposite of this. He is extremely disorderly, but hates that others should criticize him; he is extremely unworthy, but desires that others should consider him a Worthy; his heart is like a tiger or wolf, his actions are bestial, but yet he hates that others should consider him a public injury. He associates closely with those who flatter him, and is distant from those who would reprove or differ from him. The correction of error is for him a laughing matter, and great faithfulness is mistreatment. Although he does not desire to be ruined, can he avoid it? The ode says:

"Now they agree, now they slander one another;
   Things are in a very sad plight.
If they are given good counsel,
   They all oppose it;
If they are given bad counsel,
   They all accord with it."

This is what I mean.

The man who controls his feelings and cultivates his character by the method of everywhere and always doing right, although he may not live as long as Peng, yet if he is strong in cultivating himself, his fame will equal that of Yao and Yu. That which enables a person to act appropriately to the occasion, that which enables him to be successful when in office, and to bear poverty when out of office, is the rules of proper conduct (*Li*) and faithfulness. Whenever a person deals with flesh and blood, purposes and plans, when it is according to the rules of proper conduct (*Li*), then his government will be successful. If he does not act according to the rules of proper conduct (*Li*), he is either wrong and confused, or careless and negligent. Food and drink, clothing, dwelling places, and movements, if in accordance with the rules of proper conduct (*Li*), will accord to the situation; if not in accordance with the rules of proper conduct (*Li*), they will meet with ruin and calamity. A person's appearance, his bearing, his advancing and retiring when he hastens or walks slowly, if according to the rules of proper conduct (*Li*), is beautiful; if not according to the rules of proper conduct (*Li*), then he will be haughty, intractable, depraved, banal, and rude. Hence a man who has no sense of what is proper (*Li*) is without a means of livelihood; a matter which is not proper (*Li*) will not be brought to accomplishment; a government without *Li* will not be peaceful. The ode says:

"Every rite (*Li*) is according to rule,
Every smile and word is as it should be"—

this is what I mean.

To lead the people according to the right is to give them teaching; to follow the right is obedience. To lead people according to the wrong is to mislead them; to follow the wrong is sycophancy. To know that the right is right and that the wrong is wrong is wisdom; to think that the right is wrong and that the wrong is right is stupidity. To injure the virtuous is slander; to maltreat the virtuous is oppression. To say that the right is right and the wrong is wrong is uprightness. To steal goods is theft. Hidden actions are deceit. Easy talk is boasting. By turns showing alacrity in doing things and neglecting them is inconstancy. To hold fast to the motive of gain and to discard justice (Yi) is to be the most injurious possible kind of person. To have heard much is to have a wide knowledge; to have heard little is to be shallow; to have seen little is to be ignorant. To progress with difficulty is to be slow-going; to forget easily is to be leaky. A little and ordered is to be well-controlled; much and in confusion is to be disorderly.

If a person's animal feelings are strong and severe, then let him weaken them so that he may harmonize himself. If his thoughts are crafty and secretive, then let him unify them so that they may be easily good. If he is bold and violent, then let him guide his feelings, so as to control them. If he is hasty, talkative, and seeking for gain, then let him moderate himself so as to be large-minded. If he is inferior, tardy in important matters, and avaricious, then let him raise himself to a high purpose. If his talents are ordinary or inferior, then let him be importunate to make friends with a teacher. If he is impertinent and proud, then let him reflect on the calamities that will ensue. If he is simple, sincere, upright, and ingenuous, then let him make himself harmonious by the rules of proper conduct (Li) and music. Of all the methods of controlling the body and nourishing the mind, there is none more direct than proper conduct (Li), none more important than getting a teacher, none more divine than to have but one desire. These are what I mean by the methods of controlling the body and nourishing the mind.

If a person's will is cultivated, then he can be prouder than the rich and the honourable; if he has emphasized the right Way (*Tâo*) and justice (*Yi*), then he can despise kings and dukes; he can contemplate that which is within him and despise outer things. It is said: the superior man employs things; the small-minded man is the servant of things — this expresses what I mean. To work hard but to have his mind peaceful — do that! To have small gain but much justice (*Yi*) — do that! To serve an unjust (*Yi*) prince and obtain high position is not as good as serving a poor prince and being able to follow the right. The good farmer will not refuse to plough because there is no rain: the good merchant will not refuse to trade because he loses money. The scholar or superior man is not remiss concerning the right Way (*Tâo*) because of poverty.

If a man's deportment is respectful, his heart loyal and faithful, his methods according to the rules of proper conduct (*Li*) and justice (*Yi*), and his ruling passions love and benevolence (*Jen*), were he to rule over the empire, although he were harassed by the four barbarian tribes, people would not fail to honour him. If he presses forward to perform an arduous undertaking, but is willing to yield to others an affair that is readily done or pleasant to do, if he is upright and sincere, if he holds to his undertakings and is careful of details, were he to rule over the empire, although he were harassed by the four barbarian tribes, the people would not fail to keep him in office. If his deportment is haughty and prejudiced, his heart scheming and deceitful, his methods those of Shentze and Micius and his ruling passions unregulated and vile, were he to rule over the country, although he were successful in all directions, the people would not fail to despise him. If he is careless, timid, and if, when there is an arduous undertaking, he turns it over to another, if he is persuasive and keen for it and if, when there is an affair readily done and pleasant, he shows no indirection in seeking it, if he is depraved and not upright, if he becomes careless when he has to do difficult things, were he to rule over the whole country, although he were successful in all directions, he would not fail to be rejected.

In walking be reverend and upright and do not get stained by mud. In walking do not bend your head as though you were going to hit something. If you meet a companion, bow first; do not be afraid. For if a gentleman only wishes to cultivate himself, he is not offended at meeting a commoner.

The bay Chi could go a thousand *li* in a day; an old broken-down horse can make that distance in ten days too. If you wish to exhaust the inexhaustible, to pursue the illimitable, even if you go so far as to break your bones and utterly destroy your sinews, to the end of your days you will not be able to reach your goal. But if there is a limit, then, although a thousand *li* are a great distance, whether slowly or quickly, whether first or last, how could you fail to arrive at your goal? But the person who does not know the Way (*Tâo*), can he exhaust the inexhaustible or pursue the illimitable? Can his purpose ever see its fulfilment? Hence there is no reason why the problems of "hardness and whiteness", "likeness and unlikeness," "whether there is thickness or no thickness" should not be investigated, but the superior man does not discuss them; he stops at the limit of profitable discussion. Wonderful and gigantic conduct is certainly difficult, but the conduct of the superior man stops at the limit of what is profitable. For the scholar says, "Wait," and he stops and waits for me; I go on and catch up with him. Then how can it be that either slowly or quickly, either first or last, he cannot reach the goal together with him? For a lame tortoise can go a thousand *li* by not resting a half step; by heaping up earth not stopping, a mound or hill can be made high. By stopping its source and opening its channel, a large or small river can be dried up; by alternately advancing and retreating, going to the left and the right, the six noble steeds could not arrive at the goal. The ability of two men may be greatly different; how could it be that a lame tortoise could be equal to the six noble steeds? Yet the lame tortoise arrives at the goal and the six noble steeds do not. There is no other reason for it than that the one keeps on and the other does not.

Though the road (*Tâo*) be short, if a person does not travel on it, he will never get there; though a matter be small, if he does not do it, it will never be accomplished; if a man takes many days of leisure, he will not show much progress. He who loves to follow the Way and carries it out is a scholar. He who has a firm purpose and treads the Way is a superior man. He who is inexhaustibly wise and illustrious in virtue is the sage.[1]

A man who is without a rule for action is bewildered; if he has a rule, but does not understand it, he is timid; if he relies upon the rule and knows of what kind it is, then only is he calm.

The rules of proper conduct (*Li*) is that whereby a person's character is corrected; a teacher is that whereby the rules of proper conduct (*Li*) are corrected. Without rules for proper conduct (*Li*) how can I correct myself? Without a teacher how can I know what particular action is according to the rules of proper conduct? If a person is to live according to the rules of proper conduct (*Li*), then his emotions must be naturally those that go with the rules of proper conduct (*Li*); if he is to speak like his teacher, then his knowledge must be equal to that of his teacher. When a person's emotions are naturally in accordance with the rules of proper conduct (*Li*), and his knowledge is equal to that of his teacher, then he is a sage. For to go contrary to the rules for proper action (*Li*) is the same as to be without a

---

1. These are the three grades of virtue and wisdom regularly mentioned by Hsün-Tzŭ.

rule for action; to go contrary to one's teacher is the same as to be without a teacher. Not to hold as right the ways of one's teacher and to prefer one's own ways, is like a blind man distinguishing colours or a deaf man distinguishing sounds; there is no way of getting rid of confusion and error. Hence the student follows the rules of proper conduct (*Li*) and the ways of his teacher. But the teacher considers himself to be the correct measure of all things and honours that which nature has implanted within him. The Ode says:

> "He has not learned, he did not know,
> But he followed the laws of God"—

this expresses what I mean.[1]

Upright, honest, obedient, and reverent to elders — such an one can be said to be a good young man. Add to that a love of study, respectfulness, brilliancy, and not feeling himself superior to his equals — such an one can become a superior man. Weak, stupid, afraid to work, without humility or a sense of shame, but fond of eating and drinking — such an one can be called a bad young man. Add to that the qualities of being dissolute, overbearing, disobedient, dangerous, injurious, and disrespectful — such an one can be called an unfortunate young man, who, when led into wrong, may suffer capital punishment.

If a person treats the aged and honourable as they should be treated, men in middle life will give him their allegiance. If he treats leniently the unworthy, then those who are wise will gather to him. If in his actions he does not pay attention whether others know of them or not, and gives without seeking for a return, then the worthy and unworthy will unite in honouring him. If a man has these three

---

1. *Book of Odes,* III, 1, vii, 7. The meaning of this passage is that the way of the teacher secretly agrees with the way of Heaven, as King Wen unconsciously followed the laws of Heaven, although he had not studied them.

characteristics, although he had great misfortunes, would Heaven fail to do as he wished?[1]

The superior man only slightly seeks for profit; he is quick to keep away from evil. He is timorous in fleeing shame and courageous in doing the right (*Tâo*).

The superior man, when poor, has a profound purpose; when rich or honourable, he is respectful; when retired, he does not become lazy; when working hard or fatigued, his bearing is not careless. When angry, he does not go to the extreme and snatch things away; when happy, he does not go to the extreme and give things away. The superior man, when poor, has a profound purpose, because he stresses benevolence (*Jen*). When rich or honourable, he is respectful, because he humbles himself. When retired, he does not become lazy, because he carefully selects the principles of his life. When working hard or fatigued, his bearing is not careless, because he esteems the beautiful.[2] When angry he does not go to extremes and snatch things away; when happy, he does not go to extremes and give things away, because in this way he overcomes selfishness. The *History* says—

> "Without any selfish likings
> Reverence the Way (*Tâo*) of the Kings;
> Without any selfish dislikes,
> Reverence the path of the Kings."

This speaks of the superior man's ability to make public spirit overcome selfish desires.

1. The Chinese implies the answer, No.
2. Not the beauty of painting, sculpture, or music, but the beauty of perfect action.

Kung-sun Lung

KUNG-SUN LUNG (c. 320-250 B.C.). Pure philosophy dominated the life of Kung-sun Lung, a disciple of Hui Shih, but did not prevent him from taking an active role in the affairs of his time. Dissatisfied with existing conditions, he advocated the study of the relation between names and actualities in an attempt to provide a better life for all people. Thus he carried further the inquiry urged by Confucius, trying to discover not only whether a person was discharging the duties designated by his title but also the nature of the relation of names to things. His study of the absoluteness of concepts and names led him to a conclusion resembling the Platonic theory of universals.

Like Hui Shih and the Moists, he was a pacifist. He preached universal love and tried to establish its truth dialectically, by the rectification of names. Only concepts or universals, which he calls, *chih,* are real. Truth lies beyond particulars (*wu*) and is one; therefore, men should practice universal love and hate none.

His delight in discovering paradoxes matched that of other dialecticians of the School of Names. He insisted that he could prove the smallest to be the greatest, the similar to be dissimilar, and the moving to be at rest. By casting his arguments in the form of a dialogue, he was able to present both opposing and supporting facts. In this respect he represents the highest achievement of classical Chinese philosophy.

One famous episode in his life demonstrates the effectiveness of his arguments. Told that he could not cross the frontier into another city because horses were not allowed to enter the city, he argued that a white horse was not white, and that his horse should be allowed to cross the frontier since it was white. The bewildered guards did not detain him.

219

A Discussion on White Horses

From *Chinese Philosophy in Classical Times,* edited by E. H. Hughes, Everyman's Library, New York, E. P. Dutton.

A. (You say that) a white horse is not a horse: is this (logically[1]) admissible?

B. It is.

A. How can that be so?

B. The term 'horse' is the means by which a bodily form is named. The term 'white' is the means by which a colour is named. The naming of a colour is not the naming of a form. Therefore I say that a white horse is not a horse.

A. Since there are white horses in existence, it is not admissible[2] to say that there are no horses in existence, (and so) it is not admissible to say that the said white[3] horses are not horses. (If you grant that) white horses exist, how do you make out that they are not horses?

B. If you want to get a horse, a yellow horse or a black one will do perfectly well; but if you want to get a white horse, a yellow horse or a black one will not do. On the assumption that a white horse is a horse, what you are wanting to get is one thing, namely a white horse which is not different from a horse (generally). In that case, how is it that a yellow horse or a black one will do (from one point of view) and will not do (from another point of

1. I take it that *k'o* in this kind of connection both in this author and others of his age can only be rendered by an expression such as 'logically admissible,' though 'logically' of course must not be taken to have the same content as the modern Western philosopher's 'formal logic.'

2. 'Logically' is omitted here and later for the sake of brevity.

3. Emending *wu* to *pai.*

view)? If a thing both will do and will not do, its image (in the mind) is not clearly defined.[1] The fact is, yellow horses and black ones (represent) the one-ness of horse-ness and may (logically) be used as corroborative of the fact that horses exist: but they may not (logically) be used as corroborative of the fact that white horses exist. This proves that white horses are not horses.

A. You make out that a horse's having colour makes it not a horse; but in the world of experience [lit. heaven below] there are no horses which have not colour. Is it admissible then to say that there are no horses in the world?

B. To be sure horses have colour and therefore there are white horses in existence. Suppose, however, that horses did not have colour, there would without question still be horses, and it would be entirely beside the mark to cite white horses as instances. Therefore white horses are not horses. (Further) your 'white horse' is horse-ness plus white-ness. That being so, I therefore say a white horse is not a horse.

A. (Granted that) horse-ness does not require the addition of white-ness, and that white-ness does not require the addition of horse-ness to make white-ness; but we can make a harmony of horse-ness and white-ness with the double name 'white horse.' Whether the two qualities blend or not, the making of the name is admissible.[2] Therefore I say that it is not admissible to maintain that a white horse is not a horse.

B. To take the existence of white horses as equal to the existence of horses (generally) is to hold that the existence of white horses is equal to the existence of yellow horses. Is that admissible?

A. It is not admissible.

B. Then, to take the existence of horses (generally) as

1. Compare the 'undistributed middle' of modern formal logic.
2. Eliding *wei*.

different from the existence of yellow horses, this is differentiating yellow horses from horses (generally); and to do that is to regard yellow horses as not horses; and to do that and at the same time regard white horses as horses, this is equal to a flying creature going into a pond (like a fish), to an inner and outer coffin being in different places. It is an instance of speech which is universally recognized as self-contradictory, as a subversive statement.

A. My statement that if there are white horses it is inadmissible to say that there are no horses·in existence, this was made irrespective of the whiteness. Although[1] it is irrespective, there still are white horses and it is inadmissible to say there are no[2] horses. Therefore (my statement) is a means of getting at the existence of horses. It is nothing more than using horse-ness for getting at the existence of horses. It is not regarding white horses as horses (generally). Therefore with regard to your view of white[3] horses, it is inadmissible to say they are not horses.[4]

B. Whiteness does not determine what it whitens, so that it is admissible to disregard it. But the name 'white horse' equals saying that whiteness does determine what it whitens and determines the thing which is not whitened as not white. The name 'horse' does not take colour into account one way or the other, and for this reason yellow horses and black horses are admissible as representatives of it. The name 'white horse' (on the other hand) is in relation to the rejection and acceptance of colour; and, because yellow and black horses are all cases in which the colour concerned is rejected, therefore white horses are the only ones which are admissible as representatives. Not rejecting is the antithesis to rejecting. Therefore I say that white horses are not horses.

1. Emending *shih* to *sui* and *chieh* to *yi* or some such copula.
2. Emending *yu* to *wu*.
3. Emending *yu* to *pai*.
4. Emending the first *ma* to *fei*.

A. If one finds a white (element) in an object, it is not admissible to say that there is no whiteness there, and if one finds a hard (element) in an object, it is not admissible to say that there is no hardness there; so that with regard to the stone (which is both white and hard) surely there are three (affirmations).

B. Seeing does not find the hard (element) in the object, but does find the white (element) without the hard. Feeling with the hand does not find the white (element) in it, but does find the hard (element) without the white.

A. If there were no whiteness in the material world, it would be impossible to see the stone, and if there were no hardness it would be impossible to feel the stone. Since whiteness and stone are not mutually exclusive, is it admissible to make the three concepts unrelated to each other?[1]

B. They are of their nature unrelated, not made to be unrelated.

A. With its whiteness and its hardness the stone of necessity finds these (two qualities) complementary to each other. How, then, can they be unrelated?

B. The finding of the whiteness and the finding of the hardness in the stone involve a seeing and a not-seeing which are irrespective of each other. . . Since one and one are not complementary to each other, therefore they are irrespective of each other. Being irrespective equals being unrelated. (*Kung-sun Lung,* c. 5.)

Group 1.

Fire is not hot [i.e. the sensation of heat is in us and not in the fire].

Eyes do not see [i.e. it is the mind which perceives by means of the eye and light].

---

1. *Ts'ang,* lit. hidden. This character became a technical term for the Dialecticians, denoting a logical situation in which two or more concepts could not be related to each other.

T-squares are not square, and compasses cannot make circles [i.e. T-squares and compasses cannot be relied on to make the perfect square and the perfect circle as visualized by the mind].

The shadow of a flying bird never moves.

Group 2.

An egg has hair [? meaning that an egg produces a feathery, hairy creature].

A chicken has three legs [? meaning that the statement about it having two legs introduces a third element of leg-ness into the concept 'chicken'].

A dog can be a sheep [? meaning that since everything is in process of changing into something else, therefore a dog can become a sheep].

An orphan colt has never had a mother [? meaning that an orphan is a child which has no mother].

Han Fei Tzǔ

HAN FEI TZǓ (*c.* 280-233 B.C.). The greatest philosopher of law (*fa chia*) was the only nobleman among the major philosophers of the classical period. He was a prince of the royal family of the small state of Han, situated in central China. According to his biography in the *Shih Chi* (Records of History), written a century after his death, he studied under Hsun Tzǔ. Distressed by local conditions, he tried unsuccessfully to influence the ruler. Ironically, his advice was not heeded by the king of Han but by a rival, the king of Ch'in, who soon conquered all of China. In an age which prized eloquence, Han Fei Tzǔ (Han Fei-tse) stuttered. His difficulty in persuading others may have persuaded him to set his ideas down in writing. At any rate, he produced the final and most readable exposition of the theories of the legalist school of philosophy.

Sent as an envoy to Ch'in in 234 B.C., Han Fei Tzǔ was at first welcomed by the king. Later, at the urging of Li Ssu, a royal minister, he was thrown into prison, where he committed suicide. Fortunately, his writings have survived.

Sometimes referred to as mystical materialism, the doctrine of Han Fei Tzǔ shows a marked appreciation of Taoist principles but concentrates upon the problems of government, statecraft, authority, and public welfare. Less than half of the material in the book bearing his name can be attributed with certainty to him. The fifty-five chapters of his book offer a remarkable synthesis of previous Legalist theories, which stand as the Chinese counterpart to the political theories of postmedieval Europe. Han Fei Tzǔ's views were similar to those of Jeremy Bentham and other British utilitarians.

Six Contrarieties

From *The Complete Works of Han Fei Tzŭ*, translated by W. K. Liao, 2 vols., London, Probsthain, 1939 and 1959.

W HO fears death and shuns difficulty, is the type of citizen who would surrender or retreat, but the world reveres him by calling him "a life-valuing gentleman". Who studies the ways of the early kings and propounds theories of his own, is the type of citizen that would neglect the law, but the world reveres him by calling him "a cultured and learned gentleman". Who idles his time away and obtains big awards, is the type of citizen who would live on charities, but the world reveres him by calling him "a talented gentleman". Who twists his speeches and pretends to erudition, is the fraudulent and deceitful type of citizen, but the world reveres him by calling him "an eloquent and intelligent gentleman". Who brandishes his sword and attacks and kills, is the violent and savage type of citizen, but the world reveres him by calling him "a hardy and courageous gentleman". Who saves thieves and hides culprits, is the type of citizen that deserves the death penalty, but the world reveres him by calling him "a chivalrous and honorable gentleman". These six types of citizens are what the world praises.

Who would venture risks and die in the cause of loyalty, is the type of citizen that chooses death before infidelity, but the world despises him by calling him "a planless subject". Who learns little but obeys orders, is the law-abiding type of citizen, but the world despises him by calling him "a naive and rustic subject". Who works hard and earns his livelihood, is the productive type of citizen, but the world despises him by calling him "a small-talented subject". Who is frank, generous, pure, and genuine, is the right and good type of citizen, but the world despises him by calling him "a foolish and silly subject". Who esteems commands and reveres public affairs, is the superior-respecting type of citizen, but the world despises him by calling him "a cowardly and faint-hearted subject". Who suppresses thieves and oppresses culprits, is the superior-obeying type of citizen, but the world despises him by calling him "a flattering and slanderous subject". These six types of citizens are what the world blames.

Thus, the wicked, fraudulent, and useless citizens include six types, but the world praises them in those manners; so do the tilling, fighting, and useful citizens include six types, but the world blames them in these manners. These are called "six contrarieties".

If the hemp-clothed commoners in accordance with their private interests praise people, and if the lord of this age believing in bubble reputations respects them, then whoever is respected, will be accorded profits. If the hundred surnames on account of private feud with them slander them, and if the lord of this age, as misled by the beaten track of men, despises them, then whoever is despised, will suffer damage. Therefore, fame and rewards will go to selfish, vicious citizens deserving punishment; while blame and damages will befall public-spirited, upright gentlemen deserving reward. If so, then to strive for the wealth and strength of the state is impossible.

The ancients had a proverb saying: "To govern the people is like washing one's head. Though there are falling hairs, the washing must needs be done." Whoever regrets the waste of the falling hairs and forgets the gain of the growing hairs, does not know the doctrine of expediency.[1]

Indeed, opening boils causes pain; taking drugs causes

---

1. The doctrine of expediency is peculiarly utilitarian: The end justifies any means. It is what the Confucians abhorred most and the Legalists practised best.

bitter taste. Yet, if boils are not opened on account of pain and drugs not taken on account of bitterness, the person will not live and the disease will not stop.

Now the relationship between superior and inferior involves no affection of father and son, if anyone wishes to rule the inferiors by practising righteousness, the relationship will certainly have cracks. Besides, parents in relation to children, when males are born, congratulate each other, and, when females are born, lessen the care of them. Equally coming out from the bosoms and lapels of the parents, why should boys receive congratulations while girls are ill-treated? Because parents consider their future conveniences and calculate their permanent benefits. Thus, even parents in relation to children use the calculating mind in treating them, how much more should those who have no affection of parent and child?

The learned men of to-day, on counselling the lord of men, all persuade him to discard the profit-seeking mind and follow the way of mutual love. Thereby they demand more from the lord of men than from parents. Such is an immature view of human relationships: it is both deceitful and fallacious. Naturally the enlightened sovereign would not accept it. The sage, in governing the people, deliberates upon laws and prohibitions. When laws and prohibitions are clear and manifest, all officials will be in good order. He makes reward and punishment definite. When reward and punishment are never unjust, the people will attend to public duties. If the people attend to public duties and officials are in good order, then the state will become rich; if the state is rich, then the army will become strong. In consequence, hegemony will be attained. The enterprise of the Hegemonic Ruler is the highest goal of the lord of men. With this highest goal in view the lord of men attends to governmental affairs. Therefore, the officials he appoints to office must have the required abilities, and the rewards and punishments he enforces must involve no selfishness but manifest public justice to gentry and commoners. Whoever exerts his strength and risks his life, will be able to accomplish merits and attain rank and bounty. When rank and bounty have been attained, the enterprise of wealth and nobility will be accomplished. Now, wealth and nobility constitute the highest goal of the ministers. With this highest goal in view the ministers attend to their official duties. Therefore, they will work hard at the peril of their lives and never resent even the exhaustion of their energy. This amounts to the saying that if the ruler is not benevolent and the ministers are not loyal, hegemony cannot be attained.

Indeed, the culprits, if infallibly detected, would take precautions; if definitely censured, they would stop. If not detected, they would become dissolute; if not censured, they would become active. For illustration, when cheap articles are left at a deserted spot, even Tsêng Shan and Shih Ch'in can be suspected of stealing them; whereas when a hundred pieces of gold hang at the market-place, even the greatest robber dare not take them. Even Tsêng Shan and Shih Ch'in are liable to suspicion at a deserted spot if detection is unlikely; if sure to be found out, the greatest robber dare not touch the gold hanging at the market-place.

Therefore, the enlightened sovereign in governing the state would increase custodians and intensify penalties and make the people stop vices according to law but not owing to their own sense of integrity. For illustration, mothers love children twice as much as fathers do, but a father enforces orders among children ten times better than a mother does. Similarly, officials have no love for the people, but they enforce orders among the people ten thousand times better than their parents do. Parents heap up their love, but their orders come to naught; whereas officials exercise force and the people obey them. Thus, you can easily make the choice between severity and affection.

Furthermore, what parents desire of children is safety and prosperity in livelihood and innocence in conduct. What the ruler requires of his subjects, however, is to demand their lives in case of emergency and exhaust their energy in time of peace. Now, parents, who love their children and wish them safety and prosperity, are not listened to; whereas the ruler, who neither loves nor benefits his subjects but demands their death and toil, can enforce his orders. As the enlightened sovereign knows this principle, he does not cultivate the feeling of favour and love, but extends his influence of authority and severity. Mothers love sons with deep love, but most of the sons are spoilt, for their love is over-extended; fathers show their sons less love and teach them with light bamboos,[1] but most of the sons turn out well, for severity is applied.

If any family of to-day, in making property, share hunger and cold together and endure toil and pain with one another, it would be such a family that can enjoy warm clothes and nice food in time of warfare and famine. On the contrary, those who help one another with clothing and food and amuse one another with entertainments, would become such families that give wives in marriage and set children for sale in time of famine and during the year of drought. Thus, law as the way to order may cause gain at first, but will give gain in the long run; whereas benevolence as the way to order may give pleasure for the moment, but will become fruitless in the end. Measuring their relative weights and choosing the one for the greatest good, the sage would adopt the legal way of mutual perseverance and discard the benevolent way of mutual pity. The teachings of the learned men all say, "Mitigate penalties". This is the means of inviting turmoil and ruin. In general, the definiteness of reward and punishment is based on encouragement and prohibition. If rewards are liberal, it is easy to get what the superior wants; if punishments are heavy, it is easy to forbid what the superior hates. Indeed, whoever wants to benefit, hates injury, which is the opposite of benefit. Then how can there be no hatred for the opposite

1. Used in punishing criminals and mischievous children.

of the wanted? Similarly, whoever wants order, hates chaos, which is the opposite of order. For this reason, who wants order urgently, his rewards must be liberal; who hates chaos badly, his punishments must be heavy. Now, those who apply light penalties are neither serious in hating chaos nor serious in wanting order. Such people are both tactless and helpless. Therefore, the distinction between the worthy and the unworthy, between the stupid and the intelligent, depends on whether reward and punishment are light or heavy.

Moreover, heavy penalties are not for the sole purpose of punishing criminals. The law of the intelligent sovereign, in suppressing rebels, is not disciplining only those who are being suppressed, for to discipline only the suppressed is the same as to discipline dead men only; in penalizing robbers, it is not disciplining only those who are being penalized, for to discipline only the penalized is the same as to discipline convicts only. Hence the saying: "Take seriously one culprit's crime and suppress all wickednesses within the boundaries." This is the way to attain order. For the heavily punished are robbers, but the terrified and trembling are good people. Therefore, why should those who want order doubt the efficacy of heavy penalties?

Indeed, liberal rewards are meant not only to reward men of merit but also to encourage the whole state. The rewarded enjoy the benefits; those not as yet rewarded look forward to their future accomplishment. This is to requite one man for his merit and to encourage the whole populace within the boundaries. Therefore, why should those who want order doubt the efficacy of liberal rewards?

Now, those who do not know the right way to order all say: "Heavy penalties injure the people. Light penalties can suppress villainy. Then why should heavy penalties be necessary?" Such speakers are really not well versed in the principles of order. To be sure, what is stopped by heavy penalties is not necessarily stopped by light penalties; but what is stopped by light penalties is always stopped by

231

heavy penalties. For this reason, where the superior sets up heavy penalties, there all culprits disappear. If all culprits disappear, how can the application of heavy penalties be detrimental to the people?

In the light of the so-called "heavy penalties", what the culprits can gain, is slight, but what the superior inflicts, is great. As the people never venture a big penalty for the sake of a small gain, malefactions will eventually disappear. In the face of the so-called "light penalties", however, what the culprits gain, is great, but what the superior inflicts, is slight. As the people long for the profit and ignore the slight punishment, malefactions never will disappear. Thus, the early sages had a proverb, saying: "Nobody stumbles against a mountain, but everybody trips over an ant-hill." The mountain being large, everyone takes notice of it; the ant-hill being small, everyone disregards it. Now supposing penalties were light, people would disregard them. To let criminals go unpunished is to drive the whole state to the neglect of all penalties; to censure criminals properly is to set traps for the people. Thus, light punishment is an ant-hill to the people. For this reason, the policy of light punishment would either plunge the state into confusion or set traps for the people. Such a policy may thus be said to be detrimental to the people.

The learned men of to-day, one and all, cite the panegyrics in the classics, and, without observing closely the real facts, of the present age, say: "If the superior does not love the people and always levies exactions and taxations, then living expenses will become insufficient and the inferiors will hate the superior. Hence the chaos in the world." This means that if the superior lets the people have enough money to spend and loves them besides, then notwithstanding light punishment order can be attained. Such a saying is not true. Generally speaking, men incur heavy punishment only after they have had enough money. Therefore, though you let them have enough money to spend and love them dearly, yet light penalties cannot get them out of disorder.

Take, for example, the beloved sons of wealthy families, who are given sufficient money to spend. Having sufficient money to spend, they spend it freely. Spending money freely, they indulge in extravagance. The parents, loving them so much, cannot bear to restrict them. Not restricted, they become self-willed. Being extravagant, they impoverish their families. Being self-willed, they practise violence. Such is the calamity of deep love and light penalty, even though there is enough money to spend.

Men as a whole, while living, if they have enough money to spend, do not use energy; if the superior's rule is weak, they indulge in doing wrong. He who has enough money to spend and yet still exerts himself strenuously, can be nobody but Shên-nung. Those who cultivate their conduct though the superior's rule is weak, can be nobody but Tsêng Shan and Shih Ch'iu. Clearly enough, indeed, the masses of people cannot live up to the levels of Shên-nung, Tsêng Shan and Shih Ch'iu.

Lao Tan[1] said: "Who knows how to be content, gets no humiliation, who knows where to stop, risks no vitiation."[2] Indeed, who on account of vitiation and humiliation seeks nothing other than contentment, can be nobody but Lao Tan. Now, to think that by contenting the people order can be attained is to assume everybody to be like Lao Tan. For illustration, Chieh, having the dignity of the Son of Heaven, was not content with the honour; and, having the riches within the four seas, was not content with the treasures. The ruler of men, though able to content the people, cannot content all of them with the dignity of the Son of Heaven while men like Chieh would not necessarily be content with the dignity of the Son of Heaven. If so, even though the ruler might attempt to content the people, how could order

1. Lao Tzŭ's appellation.
2. Lao Tzŭ's *Tao Teh Ching*, Chap. XLIV.

be attained? Therefore, the intelligent sovereign, when governing the state, suits his policy to the time and the affairs so as to increase his financial resources, calculates taxes and tributes so as to equalize the poor and the rich, extends ranks and bounties for the people so as to exert their wisdom and ability, enlarges penal implements so as to forbid villainy and wickedness, and makes the people secure riches by virtue of their own efforts, receive punishments owing to their criminal offences, get rewards by performing meritorious services, and never think of any gift by beneficence and favour. Such is the course of imperial and kingly government.

If all men are asleep, no blind man will be noticed; if all men remain silent, no mute will be detected. Awake them and ask each one to see, or question them and ask each one to reply. Then both the blind and the mute will be at a loss. Likewise, unless their speeches be heeded, the tactless will not be known; unless appointed to office, the unworthy will not be known. Heed their speeches and seek their truth; appoint them to office and hold them responsible for the results of their work. Then both the tactless and the unworthy would be at a loss. Indeed, when you want to get wrestlers but merely listen to their own words, then you cannot distinguish between a mediocre man and Wu Huo. Given tripods and bowls, then both the weak and the strong come to the fore. Similarly, official posts are the tripods and bowls to able men. Entrusted with affairs, the stupid and the intelligent will be differentiated. As a result, the tactless will not be used; the unworthy will not be appointed to office.

Nowadays, those who find their words not adopted, pretend to eloquence by twisting their sentences; those who are not appointed to office, pretend to refinement by disguising themselves. Beguiled by their eloquence and deceived by their refinement, the sovereigns of this age honour and esteem them. This is to tell the bright without finding their sight and to tell the eloquent without finding their replies, wherefore the blind and the mute never will be detected. Contrary to this, the intelligent sovereign, whenever he listens to any speech, would hold it accountable for its utility, and when he observes any deed, would seek for its merit. If so, empty and obsolete learning cannot be discussed and praised and fraudulent action cannot be disguised.

Li Ssu

LI SSU (D. 208 B.C.) Both Han Fei Tzǔ and Li Ssu
were students of Hsün Tzǔ, the most important of the
Legalists. As an official under the Ch'in dynasty, Li Ssu
contrived to have his fellow student imprisoned, even
though he did not consider himself Han Fei Tzǔ's equal.
The latter died in prison.

It has been said that China was the first nation to
formulate the concept of egalitarianism. Confucius and
others taught the equality of all men. Any Chinese philosophy, to gain wide acceptance, had to subscribe to
the doctrine. Since those who preached the equality of
all men were generally scholars and sages, it was logical
for rulers who found the doctrine unpalatable to per-
secute philosophers and burn their books. Li Ssu has
the dubious distinction of having taken the leading role
in one of the most massive book-burning campaigns
ever undertaken. It was at his urging as Prime Minister
that Emperor Ch'in Shih Huang-ti ordered the burning
of all scholarly books. Fortunately, many of them were
simply hidden away until the political atmosphere
changed. Other measures advocated by the Prime Minister produced much-needed reforms: the abolition of all
feudal ranks and privileges, centralization of administrative procedures, standardization of weights, measures,
and writing script, and the construction of better roads.
The Chinese people soon achieved a new sense of national unity and national identity.

Memorials

From *Sources of Chinese Tradition*, Volume I, edited by William Theodore de Bary, New York, Columbia University Press, 1960.

MEMORIAL ON ANNEXATION OF FEUDAL STATES
[From *Shih chi*, 87:2a-b]

H E who waits on others misses his opportunities, while a man aiming at great achievements takes advantage of a critical juncture and relentlessly follows it through. Why is it that during all the years that Duke Mu of Ch'in [621-659 B.C.] was overlord (*pa*) among the feudal princes, he did not try to annex the Six States to the east? It was because the feudal lords were still numerous and the power of the imperial Chou had not yet decayed. Hence, as the Five Overlords succeeded one another, each in turn upheld the House of Chou. But since the time Duke Hsiao of Ch'in [361-338 B.C.] the House of Chou has been declining, the feudal states have been annexing one another, and east of the pass there remain only Six States.

Through military victories, the State of Ch'in has, in the time of the last six kings, brought the feudal lords into submission. And by now the feudal states yield obeisance to Ch'in as if they were its commanderies and prefectures. Now, with the might of Ch'in and the virtues of Your Highness, at one stroke, like sweeping off the dust from a kitchen stove, the feudal lords can be annihilated, imperial rule can be established, and unification of the world can be brought about. This is the one moment in ten thousand ages. If Your Highness allows it to slip away and does not press the advantage in haste, the feudal lords will revive their strength and organize themselves into an anti-Ch'in alliance. Then no one, even though he possessed the virtues of the Yellow Emperor, would be able to annex their territories.

MEMORIAL ON THE ABOLITION OF FEUDALISM
[From *Shih chi*, 6:12b]

Numerous were the sons, younger brothers, and other members of the royal family that were enfeoffed by King Wăn and King Wu at the founding of the Chou dynasty. But as time passed, these relatives became estranged and alienated one from another; they attacked each other as if they were enemies. Eventually the feudal lords started wars and sent punitive expeditions against one another, and the king could do nothing to stop them. Now, owing to the divine intelligence of Your Majesty, all the land within the seas is unified and it has been divided into commanderies and prefectures. The royal princes and the meritorious ministers have been granted titles and bountifully rewarded from the government treasury,[1] and it has proved sufficient. When the government institutions have been thus changed and there has been no contrary opinion in the empire, it is evidently the way to keep peace and quiet. To institute a feudal nobility again would not be advantageous.

MEMORIAL ON THE BURNING OF BOOKS
[From *Shih chi*, 87:6b-7a]

In earlier times the empire disintegrated and fell into disorder, and no one was capable of unifying it. Thereupon the various feudal lords rose to power. In their discourses they all praised the past in order to disparage the present and embellished empty words to confuse the truth. Everyone cherished his own favorite school of learning and criticized what had been instituted by the authorities. But at

---

1. That is, instead of being granted noble titles and income from a fief, they have received honorary ranks and salaries paid out of taxes.

present Your Majesty possesses a unified empire, has regulated the distinctions of black and white, and has firmly established for yourself a position of sole supremacy. And yet these independent schools, joining with each other, criticize the codes of laws and instructions. Hearing of the promulgation of a decree, they criticize it, each from the standpoint of his own school. At home they disapprove of it in their hearts; going out they criticize it in the thoroughfare. They seek a reputation by discrediting their sovereign; they appear superior by expressing contrary views, and they lead the lowly multitude in the spreading of slander. If such license is not prohibited, the sovereign power will decline above and partisan factions will form below. It would be well to prohibit this.

Your servant suggests that all books in the imperial archives, save the memoirs of Ch'in, be burned. All persons in the empire, except members of the Academy of Learned Scholars, in possession of the *Book of Odes*, the *Book of History*, and discourses of the hundred philosophers should take them to the local governors and have them indiscriminately burned. Those who dare to talk to each other about the *Book of Odes* and the *Book of History* should be executed and their bodies exposed in the market place. Anyone referring to the past to criticize the present should, together with all members of his family, be put to death. Officials who fail to report cases that have come under their attention are equally guilty.[1] After thirty days from the time of issuing the decree, those who have not destroyed their books are to be branded and sent to build the Great Wall. Books not to be destroyed will be those on medicine and pharmacy, divination by the tortoise and milfoil, and agriculture and arboriculture. People wishing to pursue learning should take the officials as their teachers.

1. The passage from the beginning of the paragraph to this point has been inserted from the fuller account given in *Shih chi*, 6:23b.

MEMORIAL ON EXERCISING HEAVY CENSURE
[From *Shih chi*, 87:15a-18a]

The worthy ruler should be one able to fulfill his kingly duties and employ the technique of censure.[1] Visited with censure, the ministers dare not but exert their ability to the utmost in devotion to their ruler. When the relative positions between minister and ruler are thus defined unmistakably, and the relative duties between superior and inferior are made clear, then none in the empire, whether worthy or unworthy, will dare do otherwise than exert his strength and fulfill his duties in devotion to the ruler. Thus the ruler will by himself control the empire, and will not be controlled by anyone. Then he can enjoy himself to the utmost. How can a talented and intelligent ruler afford not to pay attention to this point?

Hence, Shen Pu-hai[1] has said: "To possess the empire and yet not be able to indulge one's own desires is called making a shackles out of the empire." The reason is that a ruler who is unable to employ censure must instead labor himself for the welfare of the people as did Yao and Yü. Thus it may be said that he makes shackles for himself. Now, if a ruler will not practice the intelligent methods of Shen Pu-hai and Han Fei Tzŭ, or apply the system of censure in order to utilize the empire for his own pleasure, but on the contrary purposelessly tortures his body and wastes his mind in devotion to the people — then he becomes the slave of the common people instead of the domesticator of the empire. And what honor is there in that? When I can make others devote themselves to me, then I am honorable and they are humble; when I have to devote myself to others, then I am humble and they are honorable. Therefore he who devotes himself

1. Here is the central theme of this memorial. The Chinese term may be more literally translated as "inspection and punishment." To relieve the awkwardness from the repeated use of this cumbersome expression, we have adopted "censure" as a more convenient, though less exact, equivalent throughout the memorial.

to others is humble, and he to whom others devote themselves is honorable. From antiquity to the present, it has never been otherwise. When men of old considered anyone respectable and virtuous, it was because he was honorable; when they considered anyone despicable and unworthy, it was because he was humble. Now, if we should exalt Yao and Yü because they devoted themselves to the empire, then we would have missed entirely the reason for considering men respectable and virtuous. This may indeed be called a great misapprehension. Is it not fitting then to speak of it as one's shackles? It is a fault resulting from the failure to exercise censure.

Hence, Han Fei Tzǔ has said: "The affectionate mother has spoiled children, but the stern household has no overbearing servants." [ch. 50] And the purpose for saying so is to make certain that punishments are applied.

Hence, according to the laws of Lord Shang [Shang Yang], there was corporal punishment for the scattering of ashes in the streets. Now, the scattering of ashes is a small offense, whereas corporal punishment is a heavy penalty. Only the intelligent ruler is capable of applying heavy censure against a light offense. If a light offense is censured heavily, one can imagine what will be done against a serious offense! Thus the people will not dare to violate the laws. . . .

The fact that intelligent rulers and sage-kings were able for a long time to occupy the exalted position, hold great power, and monopolize the benefits of the empire is due to nothing other than their being able, on their own responsibility, to exercise censure without neglect and to apply severe punishments without fail. It was for this reason that none in the empire dared to be rebellious. If, now, a ruler does not busy himself with what prevents rebellion, but instead engages in the same practices by which the affectionate mother spoils her children, indeed he has not understood the principles of the sages. When one fails to practice the

1. A Legalist philosopher, d. 337 B.C.

statecraft of the sages, what else does he do except make himself the slave of the empire? Is this not a pity?

As a matter of fact, when men who uphold frugality and economy, humanity and righteousness, are installed in the court, then wild and unrestrained revels are cut short. When ministers given to remonstrating and lecturing are admitted to a ruler's side, then abandoned and reckless aims become curbed. When the deeds of patriots and martyrs are given prominence in the world, then all thought of indulgence and comfort has to be abandoned. Therefore the intelligent ruler is one able to keep out these three classes of men and to exercise alone the craft of the ruler, whereby he keeps his obedient ministers under control and his clear laws in effect. Therefore his person becomes exalted and his power great. All talented rulers should be able to oppose the world and suppress established usage, destroying what they hate and establishing what they desire. Thus they may occupy a position of honor and power while they live, and receive posthumous titles that bespeak their ability and intelligence after they die. So the intelligent ruler acts on his decisions by himself, and none of the authority lies with his ministers. Only thus can he obliterate the path of humanity and righteousness, close the mouths of irresponsible speakers, and keep in confinement the deeds of patriots. Stopping the avenues of hearing and sight, he sees and hears inwardly by himself. Then from without he cannot be moved by the deeds of humane and righteous men and patriots; from within he cannot be carried away by arguments of remonstrance and disputation. Therefore he is able to act according to his heart's desire, and no one dares oppose him.

Thus only may a ruler be said to have succeeded in understanding the craft of Shen Pu-hai and Han Fei Tzŭ, and in practicing the laws of Lord Shang. I have never heard of the empire falling into disorder while these laws were practiced and this craft understood. Hence, it is said that the way of the king is simple and easily mastered, yet only the intelligent ruler is able to carry it out.

Thus only may the exercise of censure be said to be real. [When the exercise of censure is real,] the ministers will be without depravity. When the ministers are without depravity, the empire will be at peace. When the empire is at peace, its ruler will be venerated and exalted. When the ruler is venerated and exalted, the exercise of censure will be without fail. When the exercise of censure is without fail, what is sought for will be obtained. When what is sought for is obtained, the state will be wealthy. When the state is wealthy, its ruler's pleasures will be abundant. Therefore, when the craft of exercising censure is instituted, then all that the ruler desires is forthcoming. The ministers and people will be so busy trying to remedy their faults that they will have no time to scheme for trouble.

Thus is the way of the emperor made complete, and thus may the ruler be said really to understand the craft between ruler and subject. Though Shen Pu-hai and Han Fei Tzŭ were to return to life, they would have nothing to add.

Huai-nan Tzŭ

HUAI-NAN TZŬ (*c.* 180-122 B.C.). The most prominent Tâoist philosopher between the ancient school of
the fourth century B.C. and the Neo-Tâoist school of
the third and fourth centuries A.D. was Liu An, Prince
of Huai-nan and grandson of the founder of the Han
dynasty. Born around the year 180 B.C., he plotted a
rebellion, failed to carry it off, and died by his own hand
in 122 B.C. to escape the humiliation of being punished
for his deeds.

The collection of twenty-one philosophical discussions
known today as the *Huai-nan Tzŭ* is one of a number
of works produced by his court. It is a joint product
of himself and some of the thousands of scholars who
enjoyed his patronage. The lengthy chapters deal with
government, military strategy, astronomy, physics, etc.
The ideas attributed to Huai-nan Tzŭ are not very original, but by restating and elaborating the views of Lao
Tzŭ and Chuang Tzŭ, he preserved the Tâoist tradition
at a time when Confucianism had assumed a dominant
role in government as well as in philosophy. He may
be said to have prepared the way, at least indirectly,
for the rationalistic critic, Wang Ch'ung (27-100?).

In the eleventh essay of the *Huai-nan Tzŭ*, from which
the following selections are taken, Tâoist theory is applied to the realm of human behavior. The author examines different practices and customs, and concludes
that value judgments must be suspended.

Placing Customs on a Par

From *The Huai-nan-tzŭ, Book Eleven: Behavior, Culture and the Cosmos*, by Benjamin E. Wallacker, (American Oriental Series, Volume 48), New Haven, American Oriental Society, 1962.

1. ACTING in [one's] Nature is called [acting in] the Way, obtaining one's heavenly Nature is called [obtaining] Virtue. Only after the Nature is lost do we ennoble Altruism; only after the Way is lost do we ennoble Propriety.

Therefore, Altruism and Propriety being established, the Way and the Virtue will move away. If Rites and Music are adorned, then the pure[-spun] and the Whole-wood will be dispersed. If right and wrong take form, then the Hundred Surnames will become bedazzled. If pearls and jade are honored, then all under heaven will compete.

All four of these are indeed products of deteriorating generations, usages of branch-tip generations [i.e. generations remote from the trunk-root or base].

2. Now Rites are the means to separate the honorable from the mean, to differentiate the noble from the base. Propriety is the means to bring about suitable conjunction between lord and minister, father and son, elder brother and younger brother, husband and wife, friend and friend. Those who perform Rites in the present generation display respect and esteem but are full of malice; those who perform Propriety indulge in largesse but are bent on obtaining [something]. If then there arises mutual defamation between lord and minister and mutual resentment between [those as closely related as] bone and flesh, they have lost the trunk-root of Rites and Propriety. Thus, in their complex

involvement they lay much onus on one another.

3. Now when water amasses, it produces fish eating other fish; when earth amasses, it produces beasts digging caves for themselves; and if Rites and Propriety are adorned, it produces deceitful and secretive scholars.

Now to blow on ashes and wish not to get cinders in the eye and to wade in water and wish not to get wet — these [wishes] may not be attained.

4. Anciently, the people were puerile and ignorant and did not know east from west. [A man's] visage did not exceed emotions, and words did not overflow practices. Their clothing was warm but lacked decorative pattern; their weapons were blunt but lacked edge. Their singing was gleeful but lacked warble; their weeping was grievous but lacked voice. Having drilled wells, they drank; having ploughed fields, they ate. They had no means to put forth their finery [in largesse], and they did not seek to obtain [anything]. Kith and kin did not revile or flatter one another; friend and friend did not display resentment or Virtue to one another.

Then with the birth of Rites and Propriety and the ennoblement of goods and wealth, fabrication and feigning sprouted and flourished. Both defamation and flattery flurried; resentment and Virtue were practiced together. . . .

6. Tzŭ-lu saved a drowning [man] and accepted an ox in thanks. Confucius said, "The country of Lu assuredly will be fond of rescuing people from distress."

Tzŭ-kung redeemed a man [from captivity in a foreign state] but did not accept [the customary reward of] money from the treasury. Confucius said, "The country of Lu shall never again redeem men."

Tzŭ-lu accepted and [thereby] encouraged Virtue; Tzŭ-kung declined and [thereby] arrested goodness. The enlightenment of Confucius, knowing the great from the small and knowing the far from the near, was to understand the natural relationship [of events].

Viewed in this light, punctiliousness has its place, but it should not be publicly practiced.

Thus, [prescribed] practices which are placed on a par with [prevailing] custom may be followed, and [prescribed] functions which are congruent to abilities are easily performed. Boastful feigning which would delude the generation and highflown practices which would set one apart from the multitude — these the sage man does not consider to be popular custom.

Wide mansions and broad houses, vestibules in rows and ante-rooms which lead off in many directions are places in which a man is secure; a bird entering them becomes anxious. High mountains and perilous precipices, deep woods and clumped brush are places in which the tiger and leopard take pleasure; a man entering them becomes fearful. River valleys and pervasive moors, amassed waters and deep springs are places in which the turtle and lizard find advantage; a man entering them dies. *Hsien-ch'ih* and *Ch'eng-yün*, *Chiu-shao* and *Liu-ying* are [songs] in which a man takes musical [pleasure]; a bird or beast hearing them is startled. Deep gorges and sheer cliffs, prominent trees and high stretching branches are places in which long-armed monkeys and long-tailed monkeys take pleasure; a man ascending them shudders.

The forms [of the environments] are distinctive, and the Natures [of the inhabitants] are divergent. That which gives pleasure becomes that which gives grief; that which gives security becomes that which gives peril.

Then when we come to all that is covered and sustained by heaven and earth and all that is shone upon and monitored by the sun and moon, let each be so deployed that it takes advantage within its Nature and is secure in its residence, and that it stays where it is fit to stay and performs within its abilities.

7. Truly, in the stupid there is an asset, and in the sagacious there is insufficiency. A pillar may not be used to pic

the teeth, and a hair-pin may not be used to hold up a house. A horse may not be used to pull what is heavy, and an ox may not be used to pursue what is swift. Lead may not be used to make a sword, and bronze may not be used to make a crossbow. Iron may not be used to make a boat, and wood may not be used to make a cooking-pot. We use each where it is best suited and apply it where if fits. . . .

8. Thus, the laws and registers of the prior kings were not instituted by them but served as a base for them, and their prohibitions and penal executions were not enacted by them but were preserved by them.

In all cases those who governed things did not use things but used concord; those who governed concord did not use concord but used men; those who governed men did not use men but lords; those who governed lords did not use lords but used desires; those who governed desires did not use desires but used Nature; those who governed Nature did not use Nature but used Virtue; those who governed Virtue did not use Virtue but used the Way.

9. In seeking the original [condition] of man's Nature one finds it to be weedridden and rank, and one does not get at the clear and light. Perhaps it is because things have dirtied it.

At birth the babies of the Ch'iang, Ti, Fu, and Ti [peoples] are all of the same voice. But when they reach maturity, even with many interpreters one is not able to understand their words, for they are distinctive in teachings and customs. Now if a three month old baby is removed from the country of his birth to another country, then he cannot know his native customs.

Viewed in this light, clothing and raiment, Rites and customs are not of the Nature of man but are received from without. . . .

10. Now when one is in doubt while sailing in a boat, he does not know east from west. Should he see the polestar, he is awakened. Now [one's] Nature for its part is man's

polestar. If one has the means to see the self, then one does not fall into error because of the emotional affect of things. But if one does not have the means to see the self, then one will move about and be in doubt and confusion. It may be compared to swimming in Lung-hsi. The more one thrashes about, the more he sinks.

Confucius said to Yen Hui, "While of my service to you there is [much which you have] forgotten, [I] also have forgotten [much] wherein you have been served by me. Although this be so, that you have forgotten [much] about me, there is still something which is not forgotten, something which is preserved." Thus, Confucius knew his trunk-root.

Now no move made when one has unleashed [his] desires and lost [his] Nature has ever been correct. If one govern the person thus, then there will be peril; if one govern the country thus, then there will be chaos; if one send in the army thus, then there will be crushing defeat.

11. Therefore, one who does not hear the Way lacks means to revert to [his] Nature. Indeed, the sage kings of old were able to obtain it [i.e. the Way] in the self, and indeed [their] orders were put into practice and [their] bans were effected. [Their]fame was handed down to later generations, and [their] Virtue extended to the four seas.

Therefore, whenever one is about to undertake an affair, one should certainly first calm the mind and clear the spirit. If the spirit is clear and the mind calm, then things may be corrected. It is like the impression of a seal put into clay. If [the seal is placed] correctly, [the impressions] will be correct. If [the seal is placed] crookedly, [the impression] will be crooked. . . .

12. Now one who is laden with grief hears the voices of singing and cries; one who is laden with glee sees someone weeping and laughs. Grief allows glee, and laughter allows grief — this is because of being laden.

Therefore, we ennoble voidness. Truly, if a river is dammed up, then waves swell; and if the breath is disordered, then knowledge is befuddled. Befuddled knowledge cannot be used to rule, and waved water cannot be used to level.

13. Thus, the sage king having grasped the unity, let him not lose it. Then the emotional affect of the myriad things shall be fathomed, and the four barbarians and the nine provinces shall submit. Now the unity is perfect nobility without match under heaven. The sage depends on the "without match," and thus popular mandate shall attach [to him].

14. Those who perform Altruism assuredly discourse upon it on the basis of grief and glee; those who perform Propriety assuredly cast light upon it on the basis of taking and giving. While their sight does not exceed ten *li*, they wish to shine universally on the people within the seas. They are not able to supply enough grief and glee. While they do not have the accumulated wealth of the empire, they wish to provide universally for the myriad people. They are wanting in [material] gain.

15. Moreover, in gladness and anger, grief and glee there is something which is spontaneous when affected. Indeed, weeping bursting from the mouth and tears emerging from the eyes are both stirred from within and given form without. It is just like the flowing down of water and stretching up of smoke. Now is there anyone who pushes them?

Truly, a man who forces [his] weeping may be sick, but he is not in grief; and a man who forces familiarity may be laughing, but he is not in harmony. Emotions burst from within, and the voice responds from without. . . .

Now when birds take flight, they form columns; and when beasts take up abode, they form groups. Was there anyone to teach them?

16. Thus, the country of Lu submitted to the Rites of the *u* and practiced the methods of Confucius. The territory was pared away, and the name [of Lu] was despised. [The

state] was unable to cause those near to act as kin or those distant to come.

King Kou-chien of Yüeh [was one who] sheared [his] hair and tattooed [his] body. He did not have the constraint of the skin cap and the inserted tablet or the postures of hook-like arching and square-like bending. Even though this was so, he was victorious over Fu-ch'ai at Wu Hu. He faced south [in the tradition of Chinese rulers] and hegemonized over the empire, and all twelve feudal lords from above the Ssu [river] came to court guiding the nine I [barbarians].

In the countries of the Hu, Mo, and Hsiung-nu they relaxed [their] bodies and drew out [their] hair; sat bent as winnow-baskets and talked back; but the countries did not perish. They were not necessarily without Rites.

King Chuang of Ch'u [was one who wore] ample clothes and full robes, yet his orders were practiced in the empire, and it followed that he hegemonized over the feudal lords.

Lord Wen of Chin [was one who wore] clothing of coarse linen and skins of the ewe [and] sheep and who belted his sword with leather, yet his authority was established within the seas.

Can it really be that the Rites of Tsou and Lu alone are called "Rites"?

17. Therefore, one who enters a country should follow its customs, and one who enters a house should avoid its tabus. If one enters [a place] not violating any prohibitions and advances [to a place] not opposing any countermands, one shall have no cause for trouble, even though he goes to the countries of the I and Ti and the bared and naked ones, and intertwines [chariot] ruts beyond the far quarters.

18. Rites are the [external] pattern for real substance and Altruism is the activation of grace. Indeed, Rites are based on human emotions and they provide a moderating pattern for them; but Altruism brings forth a blush which shows on the countenance. For Rites not to surpass the real

252

substance and Altruism not to overflow grace is the Way of a well-governed generation.

Now three years' mourning may force a man beyond what he can reach, and he uses play-acting to sustain his emotions. Yet three months' [mourning] constraint cuts grief short and coerces and presses [one's] Nature.

Now the *Ju* and the Mohists do not seek after the end and beginning of human emotion, but they endeavor to practice regulations which are the inverse of each other. . . .

20. Thus, the enlightened king prepares Rites and Propriety and [of them] makes clothing; divides moderation and practice and [of them] makes a belt. The clothing is sufficient to cover the form, to follow the "Canon and Mound," to lend humility to bowing and bending, to give advantage to the person and body, and to lend suitability to movements and steps. He does not venture into odd and pretty aspects nor into angled and biased trimmings. The belt is sufficient to knot at the tassel and take up the flaps, to bind [what should be] tight and connect [what should be] fast. He feels no urgency in making shoes with pattern and hook, distended and short.

Truly, he prepares Rites and Propriety and practices the perfect Virtue, but he is not narrowly bound by the *Ju* and the Mohists.

21. As for those whom we call enlightened, we do not mean to say that they see others; they simply see themselves. As for those whom we call perceptive, we do not mean to say that they hear others; they simply hear themselves. As for those whom we call intelligent, we do not mean to say that they know others; they simply know themselves.

Therefore, the personality is that upon which the Way depends. If the personality is obtained, then the Way shall be obtained. When the Way has been obtained, [one's] listening will be perceptive, [one's] practices will be followed.

Thus, the sage man's shaping and preparing of things is somewhat like the hewing, trimming, drilling, and pegging of the carpenter or the cutting, slicing, dividing, and separating of the butcher. The fit is obtained by bending, not by breaking or wounding.

If one is an inept craftsman, then this is not so. Big things stop up the hole and will not go in, and small things are slender and do not fill the space around. [Such work] is motivated by the heart and sent out to the hands [and there] it is exceedingly deformed.

Now when the sage man hews and trims a thing, he cuts it and halves it, parts it and disperses it. Having taken license and having erred, he then plans to unite [it] again. He no sooner leaves its root than he returns to its gate. Having sculptured and having carved, once more he reverts to the Whole-wood. In his joining he acts within the Way and Virtue; in his parting he acts on the prevailing standards. In turning about he enters the somber mystery; in his dispersing he responds to the formless [i.e. the source of all forms]. Rites and Propriety, moderation and practice – just how can these reach the trunk-root of perfect government?

22. Many of the [present] generation who are enlightened in [prescribed] functions depart from the trunk-root of the Way and Virtue and say, "Rites and Propriety suffice to govern the empire." These [people] are not worth speaking to about method. The so-called "Rites" and "Propriety" are the laws and registers, habits and customs of the [legendary] Five Emperors and Three Kings. They are merely the footprints of one generation. . . .

23. Therefore, [the sages] were not legally bound to already existing laws, but they legalized their means to enact laws. The means to enact laws is to introduce and repeal along with transformations [in conditions]. Now perfect nobility lies just in this ability to introduce and repeal along with the transformations.

Truly, the singing of Hu Liang may be followed, but his

254

means to sing may not be performed. The laws of the sage man may be viewed, but his means to incept laws may not be traced to its origin. The words of the argumentative scholar may be heard, but his means to talk may not be delineated in form. . . .

24. The ultimate greatness of the Whole-wood is such that it is without form or shape; the ultimate minuteness of the Way is such that it is without degree or weight. Indeed, one cannot put a compass to the roundness of heaven, and one cannot put a carpenter's square to the square of the earth. From antiquity to the present, we call that "time"; the four quarters, up and down, we call that "space." The Way lies in their midst, but no one knows its place [of origin]. Truly, we cannot talk about the great with those who do not see far; we cannot discuss the ultimate with those whose knowledge is not broad.

Long ago Feng I obtained the Way in order to lurk in the great river; Ch'ien Ch'ieh obtained the Way in order to live in the K'un-lun; Pien Ch'üeh in order to cure disease; Tsao Fu in order to drive horses; I used it to shoot; Chuei used it to hew. In each case what was performed was different, but what was taken as the Way was one [and the same].

Now those who are endowed with the Way and thereby understand [various] things have no grounds for defaming each other. It is just like those who join together to irrigate their fields — in receiving water they are equal. . . .

25. Truly, the laws and registers of the Three August Ones and the Five Emperors were distinct prescriptions, yet they were even in obtaining the people's heart. Thus, T'ang [founder of the Shang-Yin dynasty], on entering Hsia, used its laws; and King Wu [founder of Chou], on entering Yin, practiced its Rites. [Those institutions] by which Chieh and Chou [last rulers of Hsia and Yin] perished were the very ones by which T'ang and Wu did govern.

Indeed, even though engraving tool and gouge, trimmer and saw are laid out, if one is not a good craftsman, he will not be able to work the wood. Even though furnace and bellows and earthen mould are set out, if one is not a skillful smith, he will not be able to govern the metal.

T'an, the butcher of oxen, dissected nine oxen in one morning, yet [his] knife still could be used to shave hair; and Ting, the kitchen-man, used [his] knife for nineteen years, yet the edge was as if it were newly made and whetstoned. Why was this so? They swam [i.e. roamed freely] in the midst of the multitudinous voids.

Now it is like compass and square, hook and cord — these are the tools of skill, but they are not the means by which one becomes skillful. Thus, with an unstringed zither, though one be the [Music] Master Wen, one cannot make a tune. If it is strung, one still may not be able to evoke sorrow. Truly, strings are the tools of sorrow, but they are not the means by which one evokes sorrow.

26. Now it is like the carpenter's connecting triggers, revolving openings, covert closures, and dizzy inlays. He enters into the minuteness of deep chaos and the extremity of spiritual concord. He swims [i.e. roams freely] midst heart and hand, and there is no impinging on things. A father is not able to instruct [his] son [in this art].

The blind [music] master freed his mind to physiognomize things, and he copied spirits and excelled in dancing. [This art] took form in strings. An elder brother is not able to explain [the art to his] younger brother.

Now then, the water-level performs leveling, and the cord performs straightening. But it seems that their capacities do not lie within the cord and water level [themselves]. That [these tools] may be used to level and straighten is a method which cannot be shared.

Truly, upon striking [the note] *kung*, the *kung* [string on a musical instrument close by] will respond, and upon plucking [the note] *chüeh*, the *chüeh* [string on another instrument] will move. These are the responses of the same sounds to each other. [But if we pluck a note] which does not match any of the five sounds, all twenty-five strings will respond. This is a Way which is not handed down.

Thus, *hsiao-t'iao* is the lord of form, and *chi-mo* is the master of sound.

27. There are no grounds under heaven upon which right and wrong can be fixed. Each generation takes as right that which is taken as right by it, and takes as wrong that which is taken as wrong by it. That which is called "right" and "wrong" by each [generation] is different. All take themselves as right and take others as wrong.

Viewed in this light, things which combine with the self still do not possess rightness at the outset, and those which oppose the heart still do not possess wrongness at the outset. Truly, those who seek the right are not seeking the inner structure of the Way but are seeking a combining with the self. And those who push away the wrong do not smite the aberrant and deflected but push away an opposition to the heart. But opposition to the ego does not mean that a thing cannot combine with other [people], and combination with the ego does not mean that a thing is not in negation with custom. The right of perfect rightness is without wrongness, and the wrong of perfect wrongness is without rightness. These are the veritable right and wrong.

Now it is like those who are right in this but wrong in that, wrong in this but right in that. This is called "one right, one wrong." This one right and wrong is [but] a nook and angle; that one right and wrong is space and time.

Now I wish to select the right and reside in it, and to select the wrong and push it away. Yet I do not know what is called right and wrong by the generation. I do not know which is right and which is wrong.

257

28. Lao-tzŭ said, "Governing a great country is like cooking a small fresh fish."

Suppose a natural mother treats her son's bald scabby-head and the blood flow reaches his ears. Those who see it consider this as the perfection of her love. Yet if it be done by a step-mother, then those who pass consider it jealousy. The emotions of the affair are as one; the difference is in the point of view.

Looking at an ox from the top of a city-wall, it looks like a sheep; looking at a sheep, it looks like a young-pig. This is because one is high up.

If one observes [his] face in the water of a basin, then it is round; if in a cup, then it is oval. The form of the face does not in fact change. The rounding and ovalling is due to the difference in the place in which [the face] is observed.

Now, although I wish to correct my person and anticipate things, how can I know from whence the generation observes me? Suppose I should turn about trying to transform myself and strive to run along with the generation. It will be as though I were trying to escape the rain — there will be no place to go without getting wet.

If one is always wishing to be in the void, then he shall be unable to be void. Now suppose one does not [seek] voidness, but is spontaneously voided. This is [a case of an aim] which cannot be brought about through conscious effort.

29. Truly, one who is merged with the Way is like a chariot wheel-axle. It does not revolve of itself, but it is carried along with the hub a thousand *li*, turning about in the inexhaustible plains.

One who is not merged with the Way is like one meandering and in doubt. If he is given directions, he heeds [those directions] wherever he is, yet making one slight error he goes awry. Suddenly he no longer has his bearings, and once again he is meandering and in doubt. Truly, he ends his life being menial to others. He is just like a vane when it sees the wind — without the interval of a moment it is fixed.

Thus, the sage man embodies the Way and reverts to his Nature. If one does not transform in anticipation of transformations, then one shall be close to escape.

30. The duties of a well-governed generation are easy to keep; its functions are easy to perform; its Rites are easy to practice; and its debts are easy to repay.

Because of this, men do not hold two offices at once, and officers do not perform two functions at once. Scholar, farmer, craftsman, and merchant are [all of them, each] in his separate village and in his different province.

Therefore, farmer and farmer speak of strength; scholar and scholar speak of practices; craftsman and craftsman speak of arts; and merchant and merchant speak of calculation.

Because of this, among scholars there are no omitted practices; among farmers there are no neglected deeds; among crafts men there are no crude jobs; and among merchants there are no losses on goods. Each takes security in his Nature, none falls to parrying with another. . . .

31. Now foreknowledge and farsightedness, looking through a thousand *li* are the summits of human talent, and a well-governed generation does not require [such abilities] of the people. Broad hearing and strong memory, oral debate and lexical glibness are the excellence of human knowledge, and the enlightened master does not seek [such abilities] among the inferiors.

Disdaining the generation and taking things lightly, not sloshing about in customs are the highflown practices of scholars, and a well-governed generation does not consider them to be within the popular capacity. Spiritual triggers and covert closures, engraving and gouging without [leaving] traces are the refinements of human art, and a well-governed generation does not consider them to be popular industry. . . .

Lu Pan and Mo-tzǔ made a hawk of wood and flew it, for three days it did not roost, but they should not be used as [the standard for] craftsmen.

Truly, heights which cannot be reached should not be taken as man's measure, and practices which cannot be attained should not be taken as the country's customs.

32. Now [suppose a certain man] in testing the weight of the light and the heavy does not err even a *chu* or *liang*. The sage man will not use him but will weigh [things] on a weighing steelyard. [Suppose a certain man] in sighting the high and the low does not miss even a *ch'ih* or *ts'un*. The enlightened master will not rely on him but will seek [the height] in the tube water-level.

Why is this so? Human talent may not be used exclusively, but degrees and measures may be handed from generation to generation.

Thus, if a country is well-governed, it may be guarded even with stupidity; if an army is well-regulated, it may be used even with critical expedience. . . .

34. The discourse of the Way and Virtue is just like the sun and moon. South of the Chiang [Yangtze], north of the [Yellow] River one is not able to alter their pointing; even galloping and dashing a thousand *li*, one is not able to change their position.

[The alternatives involved in] action or non-action, Rites and customs, are like the location of a house. Eastern households call them western households, yet western households call them eastern households. Even if Kao Yao investigated the inner structure of it, he would not be able to fix its [true] place.

Truly, action and non-action are the same; defaming and flattering lie in custom. Thought and practice are uniform; failing and succeeding lie in season. . . .

35. In the present generation men of custom consider merit achieved to be worthiness; consider being equal to calamity to be knowledge; consider encountering difficulty to be stupidity; and consider dying for [one's] duty to be foolishness. I consider that each man simply puts forth that in which he can reach his limit. . . .

Action and non-action negate each other, concupiscence and desire are inverse to each other, but each man takes pleasure in his endeavor. Whom now shall we employ to correct them?

Tseng-tzǔ said, "If you slap the boat in the midst of water, the birds, on hearing it, will soar high; the fish, on hearing it, will hide in the deep." Thus, where each hurries will differ, but both get to the place where they find advantage.

Indeed, when Hui-tzǔ passed [the place] Meng-chu, his retinue of chariots numbered a hundred. When Chuang-tzǔ saw them, he threw away his extra fish, [wishing to have no more than he needed].

The pelican drinks several dippers of water, but that is not enough [for him]. The cicada has [water] enter its mouth like dew, but it is satisfied.

Chih Po had the Three Chin [states], but his desires were not filled. Lin Lei and Jung Chi-ch'i, whose clothes hung down like straw, were not dissatisfied in mind.

When we view it in this light, each is different in trend and practice. How thus, can there be mutual defamation?

Now those who [attach] importance to life do not harm themselves by profiting; those who stand by duty do not selfishly seek to aviod difficulties; those who covet emoluments see only profit and do not look back at the person; those who are fond of fame do not selfishly acquire it, if it not be [gained] through Propriety.

If we would make a comparison of these [differing attitudes], we would find them to be as far apart as ice and charcoal, the hook and the cord. When can they be brought together?

If we put a sage man in the middle [of these different

actions and attitudes], he will cover and possess [all of] them, and there will be nothing which is either "right" or "wrong."

Now the flying birds master nests, and foxes master caves. Those who [inhabit] nests, the nest being achieved, obtain a roost in it. Those who [inhabit] caves, the cave being achieved, obtain a lodging in it. Action and non-action, practices and Propriety are, for their part, the places roosted on and lodged in by man. Each takes pleasure where he is secure, and arrives where he would tread — we call them achieved men. Truly, one who uses the Way to discourse, takes up all [things] and places them on a par.

36. In the Way of a well-governed country the superior [authority] has no molesting orders, and the officials have no vexatious governing. The scholars have no feigned practices, and the craftsmen have no licentious arts. Its affairs are carried through to completion but are not entangled; its vessels are complete but are not adorned.

If it is a disordered generation, then it is not so. Those who perform [prescribed] practices hoist up each other with high-sounding [talk]; those who perform Rites display gravity to each other through feigning. Chariot beds are extreme in carving and sculpture, and vessel utensils are in contest in incision and chasing. Those who seek goods vie over those which are difficult to acquire — they consider them treasures. Those who criticize literature are content with petty carping — they consider it wit.

In competing they make strange debates. They stop only after a long time, but they do not come to conclusions and make no contribution to the government. In the craftsmanship they make odd vessels. They string out years [in the labor] and finally complete [them] — yet [the vessels] are not congruent with use. . . .

37. Further, if one is a rich man, the chariot bed is clothed in pictorial brocade; the horse adornments feature yak-tail and ivory. [There are] curtains and canopies, carpets and

262

mats, diagonal and embroidered stuffs, girdles and sashes, blue-green and yellow all mixed — it cannot be imagined.

If one is a poor man, in summer he wears rough wool and uses cord for a belt, swallows pulse-beans and drinks water to fill his intestines and to endure the heat and warmth. If it is winter, sheep skins in undone plates and smock-frock rough wool do not cover the form, and he warms himself at the mouth of the stove.

Truly, one cannot differentiate them — they are like a row of doors, people on a par. However, the divergence of the poor from the rich is like that between a lord of men and a captive slave — how can one illustrate it?

Now those who ride along on their odd skills and perform what is aberrant and awry are sufficient to themselves within one generation. Those who guard what is correct and go along with the inner structure and do not selfishly seek to acquire [things] are not [themselves] exempt from the calamities of famine and cold, but still they wish the people would give up the branch-tip and revert to the trunk-root. This is like trying to plug up the flow after it has burst from the fount. . . .

Now I have never heard, from ancient times to the present, of a situation in which famine and cold had arrived together, and one could still hope to be without those who violate laws and parry execution.

38. Truly, Altruism and provincialism are [matters] of season; they are not [matters] of practice. Profit and loss are [matters] of fate; they are not [matters] of knowledge.

Now among the soldiers of a defeated army, even the brave and martial will flee and run away, and the leader is not able to stop [them]. Yet in the ranks of a triumphant army, even terrified ones will march to the death, and fear is not able to make [them] run.

Indeed, if the Chiang or the [Yellow] River cut through and flow, father and son, elder brother and younger brother of one village leave each other behind and run. They

263

compete to ascend hillside and slope, to go up to a high hillock. The light-footed take priority and cannot look back at one another.

When a generation enjoys pleasure, and the will is calm, if [its people] see men of a neighboring country drowning, they grieve even for them. Then how much more [grief-stricken] would they be for kith and kin?

Truly, if [one's] person is secure, then [one's] grace reaches neighboring countries — [one's] will is burned out in their behalf. If [one's] person is in peril, then he forgets his own kith and kin, and Altruism cannot be released.

One who is swimming is not able to pull up a drowning man, for his own hands and feet are urgently needed. One who is being burned is not able to rescue [others] from the fire, for the person and body are in pain.

Now if the people have a surplus, then they yield; if they are insufficient, then they compete. If they yield, then Rites and Propriety are born; if they compete, then cruelty and disorder arise.

If one knocks on a gate seeking water or fire and there is not one who does not give it, it is because there is a sufficiency of plenty.

If in the woods they do not sell firewood and on the lakes they do not peddle fish, it is because that which is had is in surplus.

Truly, when things abound, desires decrease; when seeking is sated, competition stops.

At the time of the Ch'in [dynasty] kings some men pickled [their new-born] children, because material gain was not sufficient. When the Liu [Han dynasty royal] family took over the rule, childless goodmen gathered orphans, because there was a surplus of wealth.

Truly, if the generation is well-governed, then even petty men hold to correctness, and profit cannot tempt [them]. If the generation is in disorder, then even gentlemen become wanton, and laws cannot prohibit it.

Tung Chung-shu

TUNG CHUNG-SHU (177-104 B.C.). One of the most renowned Confucianists of his time, Tung Chung-shu served as chief minister to two feudal princes and as adviser to a Han emperor. He defended orthodox Confucianism against its rivals, Tâoism and Legalism, and succeeded in establishing it as the state doctrine and the basis of education. Combining the cosmology of the Yin Yang school and Confucian ethics, he formulated his famous system of correspondence between nature and man.

The official records indicate that he was a diligent student of the *Spring and Autumn Annals* ("so devoted that for three years he did not look at his own back garden"), a competent teacher with many disciples ("giving his lectures from behind a curtain, and exacting a strict attention to propriety"), and a wise counselor to Wu, whom he futilely urged "to the adoption of vigorous measures of reform." After a rival caused him to lose favor with the emperor, he "went back to his books and disciples, and spent the rest of his long life in studying, teaching, and writing."

It was in 213 B.C. that the Ch'in dictatorship, which lasted only fourteen years, sought to control thought by burning all books except those in the royal archives and works on agriculture, medicine, and divination. During its early years the Han dynasty (202 B.C. — 221 A.D.) first favored Legalism and Tâoism, but after hidden copies of the Confucian texts reappeared, rituals assumed more and more importance in official functions. Modified by Tung Chung-shu in such a way as to glorify the ruler,

Confucianism became the state cult (136 B.C.) and the basis of all education (124 B.C.).

A firm believer in retribution, Tung Chung-shu dealt severely with rival schools, strongly advocating the "science of catastrophes and anomalies" and the doctrines of the Five Agents and the Three Standards. He held that the cosmic order results from the harmony of the positive universal principle in nature (yang) and its negative counterpart (yin). Similarly, the moral order results from the harmony of yang and yin in man. The Five Agents through which the two principles operate (water, fire, wood, metal, and earth) have direct correspondence with the five senses, tastes, colors, tones, atmospheric conditions, virtues, ancient emperors, etc. According to the doctrine of the Three Standards, the ruler is the standard of the minister, the father of the son, and the husband of the wife; for the active or male cosmic principle corresponds to the ruler, father, and husband, while the passive or female cosmic principle corresponds to the minister, son, and wife. His system provided an explanation of human affairs and natural events in terms of a macrocrosm-macrocosm relationship. In setting forth his ideas, he drew from his knowledge of cosmology, political theory, history and ethics.

Luxuriant Gems of the
Spring and Autumn Annals

From *Sources of Chinese Tradition,* Volume I, edited by William Theodore de Bary, New York, Columbia University Press, 1960.

[From *Ch'un-ch'iu fan-lu,* Sec. 19, 6:7a-8a]

T HE ruler is the basis of the state. In administering the state, nothing is more effective for educating the people than reverence for the basis. If the basis is revered then the ruler may transform the people as though by supernatural power, but if the basis is not revered then the ruler will have nothing by which to lead his people. Then though he employ harsh penalties and severe punishments the people will not follow him. This is to drive the state to ruin, and there is no greater disaster. What do we mean by the basis? Heaven, earth, and man are the basis of all creatures. Heaven gives them birth, earth nourishes them, and man brings them to completion. Heaven provides them at birth with a sense of filial and brotherly love, earth nourishes them with clothing and food, and man completes them with rites and music. The three act together as hands and feet join to complete the body and none can be dispensed with. . . . If all three are lacking, then the people will become like deer, each person following his own desires, each family possessing its own ways. Fathers cannot employ their sons nor rulers their ministers, and though there be walls and battlements they will be called an "empty city." Then will the ruler lie down with a clod of earth or a pillow. No one menacing him, he will endanger himself; no one destroying him, he will destroy himself. This is called a spontaneous punishment, and when it descends, though he hide in halls of encircling stone or barricade himself behind steep defiles, he can never escape. But the enlightened and worthy ruler, being of good faith, is strictly attentive to the three bases. His sacrifices are conducted with utmost reverence; he makes offerings to and serves his ancestors; he advances brotherly affection and encourages filial conduct. In this way he serves the basis of Heaven. He personally grasps the plow handle and plows a furrow, plucks the mulberry himself and feeds the silkworms,[1] breaks new ground to increase the grain supply and opens the way for a sufficiency of clothing and food. In this way he serves the basis of earth. He sets up schools for the nobles and in the towns and villages to teach filial piety and brotherly affection, reverence and humility. He enlightens the people with education and moves them with rites and music. Thus he serves the basis of man. If he rightly serves these three, then the people will be like sons and brothers, not daring to be unsubmissive. They will regard their country as a father or a mother, not waiting for favors to love it nor for coercion to serve it, and though they dwell in fields and camp beneath the sky they will count themselves more fortunate than if they lived in palaces. Then will the ruler go to rest on a secure pillow. Though none aid him he will grow mighty of himself, though none pacify his kingdom peace will come of its own. This is called a spontaneous reward, and when it comes, though he relinquish his throne, give up his kingdom and depart, the people will take up their children on their backs, follow him, and keep him as their lord, so that he can never leave them.

HOW THE WAY OF THE KING JOINS THE TRINITY

[From *Ch'un-ch'iu fan-lu*, Sec. 43, 11:5a-b; Sec. 44, 11:6b-9b]

Those who in ancient times invented writing drew three lines and connected them through the middle, calling the

1. Symbolic acts. It is not suggested that the emperor should actually work in the fields.

character "king" [王]. The three lines are Heaven, earth, and man, and that which passes through the middle joins the principles of all three. Occupying the center of Heaven, earth, and man, passing through and joining all three — if he is not a king, who can do this?

Thus the king is but the executor of Heaven. He regulates its seasons and brings them to completion. He patterns his actions on its commands and causes the people to follow them. When he would begin some enterprise, he observes its numerical laws. He follows its ways in creating his laws, observes its will, and brings all to rest in humanity. The highest humanity rests with Heaven, for Heaven is humaneness itself. It shelters and sustains all creatures. It transforms them and brings them to birth. It nourishes and completes them. Its works never cease; they end and then begin again, and the fruits of all its labors it gives to the service of mankind. He who looks into the will of Heaven must perceive its endless and inexhaustible humaneness.

Since man receives his life from Heaven, he must also take from Heaven its humaneness and himself be humane. Therefore he reveres Heaven and knows the affections of father and son, brother and brother; he has a heart of trust and faithfulness, compassion and mercy; he is capable of acts of decorum and righteousness, modesty and humility; he can judge between right and wrong, between what accords with and what violates duty. His sense of moral order is brilliant and deep, his understanding great, encompassing all things.

Only the way of man can form a triad with Heaven. Heaven's will is constantly to love and benefit, its business to nourish and bring to age, and spring and autumn, winter and summer are all the instruments of its will. The will of the king likewise is to love and benefit the world, and his business to bring peace and joy to his time; and his love and hate, his joy and anger, are his instruments. The loves and hates, joys and angers of the king are no more than the spring and summer, autumn and winter, of Heaven. It is by mild or cool, hot or cold, weather that all things are transformed and brought to fruition. If Heaven puts forth these in the proper season, then the year will be a ripe one; but if the weather is unseasonable, the year will be lean. In the same way if the ruler of men exercises his love and hate, his joy and anger, in accordance with righteousness, then the age will be well governed; but if unrighteously, then the age will be in confusion. Thus we know that the art of governing well and bringing about a ripe year are the same; that the principle behind a chaotic age and a lean year is identical. So we see that the principles of mankind correspond to the way of Heaven. [Sec. 44, 11:6b-7b]

The cool and mild, the cold and hot seasons of Heaven are actually one and the same with man's emotions of contentment and anger, sorrow and joy. . . . These four temperaments are shared with Heaven and man alike, and are not something engendered by man alone. Therefore man can regulate his emotions, but he cannot extinguish them. If he regulates them, they will follow with what is right, but if he attempts to suppress them disorder will result. . . .

The spirit of spring is loving, of autumn, stern, of summer, joyous, and of winter, sad. . . . Therefore the breath of spring is mild, for Heaven is loving and begets life. The breath of summer is warm, and Heaven makes glad and nourishes. The breath of autumn is cool, and so Heaven is stern and brings all to fruition. The breath of winter is cold, and Heaven grieves and lays all to rest. Spring presides over birth, summer over growth, autumn over the gathering in, and winter over the storing away. [Sec. 43, 11:5a-b]

The ruler holds the position of life and death over men; together with Heaven he holds the power of change and transformation. There is no creature that does not respond to the changes of Heaven. The changes of Heaven and earth are like the four seasons. When the wind of their love blows, then the air will be mild and the world teem with life, but when the winds of their disfavor come forth, the air will be cold and all things die. When they are joyous the skies are warm and all things grow and flourish, but from their wrath comes the chill wind and all is frozen and shut up.

The ruler of men uses his love and hate, his joy and anger to change and reform the customs of men, as Heaven employs warm and cool, cold and hot weather to transform the grass and trees. If joy and anger are seasonably applied, then the year will be prosperous, but if they are used wrongly and out of season, the year will fail. Heaven, earth, and man are one, and therefore the passions of man are one with the seasons of Heaven. So the time and place for each must be considered. If Heaven produces heat in the time for cold, or cold in the season of heat, then the year must be bad, while if the ruler manifests anger when joy would be appropriate, or joy where anger is needed, then the age must fall into chaos.

Therefore the great concern of the ruler lies in diligently watching over and guarding his heart, that his loves and hates, his angers and joys may be displayed in accordance with right, as the mild and cool, the cold and hot weather come forth in proper season. If the ruler constantly practices this without error, then his emotions will never be at fault, as spring and autumn, winter and summer are never out of order. Then may he form a trinity with Heaven and earth. If he holds these four passions deep within him and does not allow them recklessly to come forth, then may he be called the equal of Heaven. [Sec. 44, 11:8b-9b]

HUMAN NATURE AND EDUCATION

[From *Ch'un-ch'iu fan-lu*, Sec. 35, 10:3a-5b]

For discovering the truth about things there is no better way than to begin with names. Names show up truth and falsehood as a measuringline shows up crooked and straight. If one inquires into the truth of a name and observes whether it is appropriate or not, then there will be no deception over the disposition of truth. Nowadays there is considerable ignorance on the question of human nature and theorists fail to agree. Why do they not try returning to the word "nature" itself? Does not the word "nature" (*hsing*) *mean* "birth" (*sheng*), that which one is born with?[1] The properties endowed spontaneously at birth are called the nature. The nature is the basic substance. Can the word "good," we inquire, be applied to the basic substance of the nature? No, it cannot. . . . Therefore the nature may be compared to growing rice, and goodness to refined rice. Refined rice is produced from raw rice, yet unrefined rice does not necessarily all become refined. Goodness comes from the nature of man, yet all natures do not necessarily become good. Goodness, like the refined rice, is the result of man's activities in continuing and completing Heaven's work; it is not actually existent in what Heaven itself has produced. Heaven acts to a certain degree and then ceases, and what has been created thus far is called the heavenly nature; beyond this point is called the work of man. This work lies outside of the nature, and yet by it the nature is inevitably brought to the practice of virtue. The word "people" (*min*) is taken from the word "sleep" (*ming*). . . .

The nature may be compared to the eyes. In sleep the eyes are shut and there is darkness; they must await the wakening before they can see. At this time it may be said that they have the potential disposition to see, but it cannot be said that they see. Now the nature of all people has this potential disposition, but is not yet awakened; it is as though it were asleep and awaiting the wakening. If it receives education, it may afterwards become good. In this condition of being not yet awakened, it can be said to have the potential disposition for goodness, but it cannot be said to be good. . . . Heaven begets the people; their nature is that of potential good, but has not yet become actual good. For this reason

1. Tung is using a favorite Chinese type of argument, that based upon the supposed affinities between characters of similar pronunciation. Such "puns," as we should call them, are intended to be taken in all seriousness.

it sets up the king to make real their goodness. This is the will of Heaven. From Heaven the people receive their potentially good nature, and from the king the education which completes it. It is the duty and function of the king to submit to the will of Heaven, and thus to bring to completion the nature of the people.

PRODUCTION AND SUCCESSION OF THE FIVE AGENTS

[From *Ch'un-ch'iu fan-lu*, 58, 59]

How the five agents produce each other

The vital forces of Heaven and earth join to form a unity, divide to become the yin and yang, separate into the four seasons, and range themselves into the five agents. "Agent" in this case means activity. Each of the activities is different, therefore we speak of them as the five activities. The five activities are the five agents. In the order of their succession they give birth to one another, while in a different order they overcome each other. Therefore in ruling, if one violates this order, there will be chaos, but if one follows it, all will be well governed. [59]

How the five agents overcome each other[1]

Wood is the agent of the Minister of Agriculture. If the Minister of Agriculture becomes corrupt, playing partisan politics and forming cliques, obscuring the wisdom of the ruler, forcing worthy men into retirement, exterminating the high officials, and teaching the people wild and prodigal ways, then the retainers of the lords will wander about and neglect the work of the fields, amusing themselves with gambling, cockfighting, dog racing, and horsemanship; old and young will be without respect, great and small will

---

1. The order of the sections has been rearranged in translation.

trespass upon each other; thieves and brigands will arise, perverse and evil men who destroy reason. It is then the duty of the Minister of the Interior to punish him. . . . Now wood is the agent of agriculture, and agriculture is the occupation of the people. If the people are not compliant but revolt, then the Minister of the Interior is ordered to punish the leaders of the rebellion and set things right. Therefore we say metal overcomes wood.

Metal is the agent of the Minister of the Interior. If the Minister of the Interior acts rebelliously, encroaching upon the ruler, taking a high hand with the military forces, seizing authority and usurping power, punishing and slaughtering the guiltless, invading and attacking with ruthlessness and violence, making war and snatching gain, disobeying orders, ignoring prohibitions, disrespecting the generals and leaders, and misusing the offices and troops, then the armies will be exhausted, the land lost, and the ruler suffer disgrace. . . . Metal is the agent of the Minister of the Interior. If he is weak and does not know to use the officers and men properly, then the Minister of War must punish him. Therefore we say fire overcomes metal.

Fire is the agent of the Minister of War. If the Minister of War gives himself up to rebellion and scornful talk, libeling and defaming people, then within the palace flesh and blood relatives will be set against each other, faithful ministers driven away, wise and sage men ruined, and the slander and evil will grow day by day. . . . Now fire is the agent of the courtier [i.e., Minister of War]. When he turns to evil and slander, deceiving the ruler, then he who administers the law shall carry out punishment. It is water that administers the law, therefore we say that water overcomes fire.

Water is the agent of the Minister of Justice. If the Minister of Justice turns to false ways, using extravagant respect and petty caution, crafty words and insinuating looks, taking bribes when he hears law suits, prejudiced and unfair, slow to issue orders but quick to punish, punishing and executing the guiltless, then the Minister of Works must correct him. Ying T'ang, Minister of Justice of Ch'i, is an example of this. T'ai Kung, who held a fief in Ch'i, once asked him what were the essentials of ruling a state. Ying T'ang replied: "Simply practice humanity and righteousness, that is all."

"What do you mean by humanity and righteousness?" T'ai Kung asked. Ying T'ang replied: "Humanity means loving men. Righteousness means respecting the aged."

"Loving men and respecting the aged," said T'ai Kung, "just what does that mean?"

"Loving men," said Ying T'ang, "means that, though you have sons, you do not accept any support from them. Respecting the aged means that if a man's wife is older than he, the husband submits to her."

T'ai Kung replied: "I wish to use humanity and righteousness to govern the state of Ch'i, and now you take this so-called humanity and righteousness of yours and throw the country into confusion. I must punish you and bring order to Ch'i again."

Ying T'ang's assertion violates the traditional ethic that a son always serves and supports his father, a wife her husband. The reason T'ai Kung is so outraged at Ying T'ang's statement is that, according to Confucian belief, the slightest violation of the proper order in the ethical, political, or natural worlds will inevitably throw all the others into disorder. This is why Confucianism insists so upon the minutest observance of order and propriety in all things and why it has been led at times into extreme conservatism.

Now it is water that administers the law. If the administrator is prejudiced and unfair, using the law only to punish people, then the Minister of Works must execute him. Therefore we say that earth overcomes water.

Earth is the agent of the servants of the ruler and their head is the Minister of Works. If he is very subtle, then whatever the prince does he will approve: whatever the prince says, he will reply. "Excellent!" Fawning upon the prince and complying with his desires, aiding and carrying out his private whims, he will busy himself with whatever pleases the prince in order to gladden his will, complying with the prince's faults and misdeeds and betraying him into unrighteousness. Great will be such a ruler's palaces and halls, many his terraces and pavilions, with carved ornaments, sculpted and inlaid and resplendent with five hues; but his taxes and levies will be without measure, plundering the people of their means, his expeditions and corvées many and burdensome, robbing the people of their time. He will think up endless projects to wear out the people's strength, and they will groan in oppression and revolt and abandon his land. King Ling of Ch'u was like this, raising the Terrace of the Heavenly Valley, and when after three years it was still not completed, the people were exhausted and spent and they rose up in revolt and killed him. Now earth is the agent of the king's servants. If the king is extravagant and wasteful, exceeding all bounds and forgetting propriety, then the people will rebel and when the people rebel, the ruler is lost. Therefore we say wood overcomes earth. [58]

Wang Ch'ung

WANG CH'UNG (C. 27-97 A.D.). In most Chinese works Wang Ch'ung is classed as a miscellaneous writer or as one of the Eclectics (Tsa Chia) who, though they do not belong to a single school, Confucianism, Moism, or Tâoism, combine the doctrines of various schools. Chinese critics, inclined to regard his disrespect toward his forefathers as wicked and perverse even while admitting that he was right in denouncing what is base and exposing falsehoods, conclude that he may be impugned by many but will always have admirers, Europeans generally concur with the admirer who spoke of him as "a philosopher, perhaps the most original and judicious among all the metaphysicians China has produced, . . . who handles mental and physical problems in a style and with a boldness unparalleled in Chinese literature."

Wang Ch'ung was a precocious child with a phenomenal memory and the ability to reduce complex issues to a few basic principles. He had an undistinguished public career as secretary of a district, his advancement limited, perhaps, by his independent spirit. Though he lived in a state of poverty, his spirit was unbroken. He was an avid student of ancient literature and had a great admiration for superior men. For years he tried in vain to gain the attention of the Emperor. Finally, told that Wang Ch'ung outshone both Mencius and Hsün Tzǔ, Emperor Chang Ti invited him to come to the royal court. Ill health forced him to decline the invitation.

His works differ markedly from those of his predecessors. Whereas the Analects and similar works are largely collections of detached aphorisms, each of his essays is

277

built around a single theme. A prolific writer, he completed a book on Macrobiotics, Censures on Morals, and Government, in addition to more than a hundred essays originally included in the *Lun-Hêng*.

The eighty-four essays that have survived, while they do not present a systematic digest of his thought, combine the satirical gifts of Lucian and the devastating wit of Voltaire, and they reveal the workings of one of the most ingenious minds of all time.

Wang Ch'ung recognized two principles, the Yang fluid and the Yin fluid, both of which were evolved from Chaos when the original fluid split into a finer substance and a coarser substance. The Yin forms the body of man, the Yang his vital spirit and mind. The Yang fluid adheres to the body during life but is dispersed by death and lost. He denied teleology, rejected traditional beliefs and dogma, and insisted that theories must stand the test of evidence. Thus he raised the pitch of skepticism to a new height and prepared the way for the growth of rationalism and naturalism in the Wei-Chin period (220-420).

Wrong Notions About
Happiness (Fu-hsü)

From *Lun-Heng. Philosophical Essays of Wang Ch'ung*, translated by Alfred Forke, London, Luzac, 1907.

PEOPLE universally believe that he who does good, meets with happiness, and that the evil-doers are visited with misfortune. That Heaven sends down happiness or misfortune in response to man's doings. That the rewards graciously given by the sovereigns to the virtuous, are visible, whereas the requital of Heaven and Earth is not always apparent. There is nobody, high or low, clever or imbecile, who would disagree with this view. Only because people see such deeds recorded in books, and witness that sometimes the good really become happy, they come to believe this, and take it as self-evident. Sometimes also sages and wise men, with a view to inducing people to do good, do not hesitate to assert that it must be so, thus showing that virtue gets its reward. Or those who hold this view, have themselves experienced that felicity arrived at a certain juncture. A thorough investigation, however, will convince us that happiness is not given by Heaven as a favour.

King *Hui* of *Ch'u*,[1] when eating salad, found a leech upon his plate, and forthwith swallowed it. He thereupon felt a pain in his stomach, and could eat nothing. On his premier asking him, how he had got this disease, he replied: — "Eating salad, I found a leech. I thought that, if I scolded those responsible for it, but did not punish them, I would

1. 487-430 B.C.

disregard the law, and not keep up my dignity. Therefore, I could not allow my subjects to get wind of the matter. Had I, on the other hand, reproved and chastised the defaulters, strict law would have required the death of all the cooks and butlers. To that I could not make up my mind. Fearing, lest my attendants should perceive the leech, I promptly swallowed it."

The premier rose from his seat, bowed twice, and congratulated the king, saying, "I have been told that Heaven is impartial, and that virtue alone is of any avail. You have benevolence and virtue, for which Heaven will reward you. Your sickness will do you no great harm."

The same evening, when the king withdrew, the leech came out, and an ailment of the heart and stomach of which he had been suffering for a long while, was cured at the same time. Could not this be considered an evidence of Heaven's partiality for virtue? — No. This is idle talk.

If King *Hui* swallowed the leech, he was far from being what a sovereign should be, and for unbecoming deeds Heaven does not give marks of its favour. King *Hui* could not bear to reproach the guilty with the leech for fear, lest his cooks and butlers should all have to suffer death according to law. A ruler of a State can mete out rewards and punishments at pleasure, and pardoning is a prerogative of his. Had King *Hui* reprimanded all for the leech found in his salad, the cooks and butlers would have had to submit to law, but afterwards the king was at liberty not to allow that the lives of men were taken merely for a culinary offence. Thus to forgive, and to remit the penalty, would have been an act of great mercy. If the cooks had received their punishment, but were not put to death, they would have completely changed for the future. The king condoning a small offence, and sparing the lives of the poor devils, would have felt all right, and not been sick. But he did nothing of that sort. He ate perforce something obnoxious to his health. Allowing his butlers to remain ignorant of their fault, he lost his royal dignity, because he did not repress their bad conduct. This was objectionable in the first place.

If cooks and butlers in preparing a dish do not make it sweet- or sour enough, or if an atom of dust no bigger than a louse, hardly perceptible or visible to the eye, falls into the salad, if in such a case a sovereign in fixing a penalty takes into consideration the mind of the offender, and therefore abstains from divulging his fault, one may well speak of clemency. Now, a leech is an inch or more long and $1/10$ of an inch or more broad. In a salad a one-eyed man must see it. The servants of the king showed an utter want of respect, taking no care to cleanse the salad. Theirs was a most serious offence. For King *Hui* not to reprimand them was a second mistake.

In a salad there must be no leech. If so, one does not eat it, but throws it to the ground. Provided one is anxious, lest the attendants should discover it, he may hide it in his bosom. Thus the leech can escape observation. Why must one eat it *coûte-que-coûte?* If something uneatable is by inadvertence in a salad so, that it can be concealed, to eat it by force is a third mistake.

If Heaven had rewarded an unbecoming act, an unworthy person would have been the recipient of Heaven's grace. The inability to reprove for the sake of a leech is, in the eyes of the world, something very excellent. Now, there is many an excellent man, whose deeds are similar to the swallowing of a leech. If for swallowing a leech Heaven grants liberation from sickness, excellent men must always be without ailings. The virtue of this kind of men is, however, small only and not to be compared with the perfect character of the true sages and their guileless demeanour. There are many sages who would push their kindness of heart so far as to put up with human faults. Yet the Emperor *Wu Wang* was of a weak health, and *Confucius* seriously ill. Why has Heaven been so inconsistent in the distribution of its favour?

It may be that after King *Hui* had swallowed the leech, it came out again in a natural way of itself. Whenever anybody eats a living thing, it will inevitably die. The stomach is hot inside. When the leech is gulped down, it does not die instantaneously, but owing to the high temperature of the stomach it begins to move. Hence the pain in the stomach. After a short while, the leech dies, and the pain in the stomach ceases also.

It is in the nature of leeches to suck blood. King *Hui's* heart and bowel complaint was probably nothing but a constipation of blood. Therefore this constipation was cured along with the death of the blood-sucking animal, just as a man suffering from the skin disease known as "rat" can be cured by eating a cat, because it is natural to cats to eat rats. The various things overcome one another. Remedies and antidotes are given on the same principle. Therefore it cannot be a matter for surprise that by eating a leech a disease should be removed. Living things, when eaten, will die. Dead, they invariably come out in a natural way. Consequently, the re-appearance of the leech cannot be an act of special grace.

The premier seeing the kindheartedness of King *Hui* and knowing that the leech after entering the stomach must come forth again, when dead, therefore bowed twice, and congratulated the king upon his not being injured by his disease. He thereby showed his power of forethought, and pleased his sovereign. His utterance is in the same style as that of *Tse Wei*,[2] who said that a star would shift its place,[3] and of the "Great Diviner," who asserted that the earth was going to move.

A family in *Sung* had for three generations never swerved from the path of virtue. Without any apparent reason a black cow belonging to this family dropped a white calf. *Confucius* was asked, and said that it was a lucky omen, and that the calf ought to be sacrificed to the spirits, which

1. Astrologer at the court of Duke *Ching* of *Sung* (515-451 B.C.) who venerated him like a god.
2. The planet Mars (cf. p. 127).
3. The "Great Diviner" of *Ch'i*, on whom vid. p. 112.

was done accordingly. After one year, the father of the family became blind without a reason. The cow then produced a white calf a second time. The father sent his son to ask *Confucius*, who replied that it was a propitious portent, and that the animal must be immolated, which was done again. After a year, the son lost his eye-sight, nobody knew why. Subsequently, *Ch'u* attacked *Sung*, and besieged its capital. At that time the besieged were in such a distress, that they exchanged their sons, and ate them, breaking their bones, which they used as firewood.[1] It was but for their blindness that father and son were not called upon to mount guard on the city wall. When the enemy's army raised the siege, father and son could see again. This is believed to be a proof of how the spirits requited great deserts, but it is idle talk: —

If father and son of that family in *Sung* did so much good, that the spirits rewarded them, why must they first make them blind, and afterwards restore their sight? Could they not protect them, if they had not been blind and always seeing? Being unable to help men, if not blind, the spirits would also be powerless to protect the blind.

Had the two commanders of *Sung* and *Ch'u* made such a furious onslaught, that the weapons were blunted, the dead bodies covered with blood, the warriors captivated, or killed never to come back, then blindness might have afforded an excuse for not going to the front, and that might have been construed as a divine protection. But before the armies of *Sung* and *Ch'u* came to blows, *Hua Yüan* and *Tse Fan*[4] made a covenant, and went back. The two forces returned home unscathed, and the blades of the swords, and the points of the arrows were not blunted by use. The duty

---

1. This fact is mentioned in the *Shi-chi* chap. 38, p. 14v. The siege took place from 595-594 B.C. The whole story seems to be a quotation from *Lieh Tse* VIII, 6v. or from *Huai Nan Tse* XVIII, 6 who narrate it with almost the same words.
2. *Hua Yüan* was the general of *Sung, Tse Fan* that of *Ch'u.* Both armies being equally exhausted by famine, the siege was raised.

of mounting the city wall did not entail death, consequently the two good men could not have obtained the divine protection, while this duty was being performed. In case they had not been blind at that time, they would not have died either. The blind and the not blind all got off. What benefit did those good men derive then from their blindness, for which the spirits were responsible?[1]

Were the families of the blind alone well off, when the State of *Sung* was short of provisions? All had to exchange their sons with the families which mounted guard on the wall, and they split their bones. If in such straits such good people alone were still blind and unable to see, the spirits in giving their aid have failed to discriminate justly between the good and the wicked.

Father and son had probably been blinded by exposure to cold wind, a mere chance. When the siege was over they owed their cure to chance also. The world knowing that they had done good works, that they had offered two white calves in sacrifice, that during the war between *Sung* and *Ch'u* they alone had not mounted the wall, and that after the siege they regained their sight, thought this to be the recompense of virtue, and the protection granted by the spirits.

When the minister of *Ch'u*, *Sun Shu Ao*[2] was a boy, he beheld a two-headed snake, which he killed and buried. He then went home, and cried before his mother. She asked him, what was the matter. He replied: — "I have heard say that he who sees a two-headed snake must die. Now, when I went out, I saw a two-headed snake. I am afraid that I must leave you and die, hence my tears." Upon his mother

---

1. According to *Lieh Tse* and *Huai Nan Tse* the two blind men were in fact, saved from death by their blindness. *Lieh Tse loc. cit.* adds that over half of the defenders of the city wall were killed, and *Huai Nan Tse* says that all except the two blind men were massacred by the besieger *Wang Ch'ung* follows the *Shi-chi* in his narrative of the salvation of the city.

2. 6th cent. B.C.

284

inquiring, where the snake was now, he rejoined: — "For fear lest others should see it later, I have killed it outright, and buried it."

The mother said: — "I have heard that Heaven will recompense hidden virtue. You are certainly not going to die, for Heaven must reward you." And, in fact, *Sun Shu Ao* did not die, but, later on, became prime minister of *Ch'u*. For interring one snake he received two favours. This makes it clear that Heaven rewards good actions.

No, it is idle talk. That he who sees a two-headed snake, must die, is a common superstition, and that Heaven gives happiness as a reward for hidden virtue, a common prejudice. *Sun Shu Ao*, convinced of the superstition, buried the snake, and his mother, addicted to the prejudice, firmly relied on the heavenly retaliation. This would amount to nothing else than that life and death were not depending on fate, but on the death of a snake.

T'ien Wên[1] of *Ch'i*, Prince of *Mêng Ch'ang*, was born on the 5th day of the 5th moon.[2] His father *T'ien Ying* expostulated with his mother saying, why do you rear him? She replied: — "Why do you not wish to rear a fifth month child?" *T'ien Ying* said: — "A fifth month son will become as high as a door, and kill both his father and mother." She rejoined: — "Does the human fate depend on Heaven or on doors? If on Heaven, you have nothing to complain of, if on a door, he must become as high as a door. Who ever attained to that?"[3]

Later on, *T'ien Wên* grew as high as a door, but *T'ien Ying* did not die. Thus the apprehension to rear a child in the fifth month proved unfounded. The disgust at the sight of a two-headed snake is like the repugnance to rear a child of the fifth month. Since the father of such a child did not

1. Died 279 B.C.
2. This day is still now regarded as very unlucky in many respects, although it be the Great Summer Festival or the Dragon Boat Festival. On the reasons cf. *De Groot, Les Fêtes annuelles à Émoui.* Vol. I, p. 320.
3. A quotation from the *Shi-chi*, chap. 75, p. 2v.

die, it follows that a two-headed snake cannot bring misfortune either.

From this point of view, he who sees a two-headed snake, does not die, as a matter of course, but not on account of having buried a snake. If for interring one snake one receives two favours, how many must one obtain for ten snakes? *Sun Shu Ao* by burying a snake, lest other persons should look at it, showed an excellent character. The works of excellent men do not merely consist in burying snakes. *Sun Shu Ao* may have accomplished many other meritorious acts, before he buried the snake. Endowed with a good nature by Heaven, people do good under all circumstances. Such well deserving persons ought to see propitious things, instead of that he unexpectedly falls in with a snake that kills man. Was perhaps *Sun Shu Ao* a wicked man, before he beheld the snake, and did Heaven intend to kill him, but condoned his guilt, and spared his life upon seeing him burying the snake?

A stone is hard from the time of its formation, a fragrant flower has its perfume from the time, when it came out. If it be said that *Sun Shu Ao's* virtue became manifest, when he buried the snake, then he would not have received it from Heaven at his birth.

The Confucianist *Tung Wu Hsin* and the Mêhist *Ch'an Tse*[1] met, and spoke about *Tâo*. *Ch'an Tse* extolled the Mêhist theory of the help of the spirits,[2] and as an instance adduced duke *Mu* of *Ch'in*. His excellent qualities were so brilliant that God granted him an age of ninety years.[3]

Ch'an Tse gets into trouble with *Yao* and *Shun*, who were not favoured with a long life and *Chieh* and *Chou*, who did not die young. *Yao, Shun, Chieh,* and *Chou* belong to re-

---

1. A scholar of the *Han* time.
2. Demons and spirits who reward the virtuous, and punish the perverse, play an important part in the doctrine of *Mê Ti*. (Cf. *Faber, Micius,* Elberfeld 1877, p. 91.)
3. The parallel passage in chap. XXVII speaks of nineteen extra years, with which the Duke was rewarded.

mote antiquity, but in modern times likewise duke *Mu* of *Ch'in*[1] and duke *Wên of Chin*[2] are difficult to account for.

The posthumous name expresses man's actions. What he has done during his life-time, appears in his posthumous title. *Mu* is an expression for error and disorder,[3] *Wên* means virtue and goodness. Did Heaven reward error and disorder with long years, and take the life of him who practised virtue and benevolence?

The reign of Duke *Mu* did not surpass that of Duke *Wên* of *Chin*, and the latter's posthumous title was better than that of Duke *Mu*. But Heaven did not extend *Wên* of *Chin's* life, he only granted longer years to Duke *Mu*.[4] Thus the retribution of Heaven would appear as capricious and perverse as Duke *Mu* himself was.

Under heaven the good men are few, and the bad ones many. The good follow right principles, the bad infringe Heaven's commands. Yet the lives of bad men are not short therefore, nor the years of the good ones prolonged. How is it that Heaven does not arrange that the virtuous always enjoy a life of a hundred years, and that the wicked die young, or through their guilt?

---

1. 658—619 B.C.

2. 634—626 B.C.

3. The *Mu* in the Duke of *Ch'in's* name signifies: — majestic, grand admirable.

4. The *Shi-chi* knows nothing of such a miracle. Duke *Mu* was a great warrior as was Duke *Wên*, but the latter's rule is described by *Sse Ma Ch'ien* as very enlightened and beneficial. Cf., on Duke *Mu*: — *Chavannes, Mém. Historique.* Vol. II, PP. 25-45, and on Duke *Wên*. Vol. IV, PP. 291-308.)

287

WRONG NOTIONS ON UNHAPPINESS

(Huo-hsü)

Since what the world calls happiness and divine grace is believed to be the outcome of moral conduct, it is also a common belief that the victims of misfortune and disgrace are thus visited because of their wickedness. Those sunk in sin, and steeped in iniquity Heaven and Earth punish, and the spirits retaliate upon them. These penalties, whether heavy or light, will be enforced, and the retributions of the spirits reach far and near.

Tse Hsia[1] is related to have lost his sight, while mourning for his son. *Tsêng Tse*[2] by way of condolence wept. *Tse Hsia* thereupon exclaimed "O Heaven, I was not guilty!" *Tsêng Tse* grew excited, and said "In what way are you innocent, *Shang*?"[3] I served our master with you between the *Chu*[4] and the *Sse*, but you retired to the region above the West River,[5] where you lived, until you grew old. You misled the people of the West River into the belief that you were equal to the master. That was your first fault. When mourning for your parents, you did nothing extraordinary, that people would talk about. That was your second fault. But in your grief over your son, you lost your eye-sight. That was your third fault. How dare you say that you are not guilty?"

Tse Hsia threw away his staff, went down on his knees and said, "I have failed, I have failed! I have left human society, and also led a solitary life for ever so long."[6]

---

1. A disciple of *Confucius*.
2. One of the most famous disciples of *Confucius*, whose name has been connected with the authorship of the Great Learning.
3. *Pu Shang* was the name of *Tse Hsia*. *Tse Hsia* is his style.
4. A small river in the province of *Shantung*, flowing into the *Sse*.
5. Presumably the western course of the Yellow River.
6. Quoted from the *Li-ki*, *T'an Kung I* (cf. *Legge's* translation, *Sacred Books* of the East Vol. XXVII, p. 135).

Thus *Tse Hsia* having lost his sight, *Tsêng Tse* reproved him for his faults. *Tse Hsia* threw away his stick, and bowed to *Tsêng Tse's* words. Because, as they say, Heaven really punishes the guilty, therefore evidently his eyes lost their sight. Having thus humbly acknowledged his guilt, he is reported to have regained his sight by degrees. Everybody says so, nevertheless a thorough investigation will show us that this belief is illusory.

Loss of sight is like loss of hearing. Loss of sight is blindness, and loss of hearing, deafness. He who suffers from deafness, is not believed to have faults, therefore it would be erroneous to speak of guilt, if a man becomes blind. Now the diseases of the ear and the eye are similar to those of the heart and the stomach. In case the ear and the eye lose their faculties, one speaks of guilt perhaps, but can any fault be inferred, when the heart or the stomach are sick?

Po Niu was ill. *Confucius* grasped his hand through the window saying "It will kill him, such is his fate! Such a man to get such a disease!"[1] Originally *Confucius* spoke of *Po Niu's* bad luck, and therefore pitied him. Had *Po Niu's* guilt been the cause of his sickness, then Heaven would have punished him for his wickedness, and he would have been on a level with *Tse Hsia*. In that case *Confucius* ought to have exposed his guilt, as *Tsêng Tse* did with *Tse Hsia*. But instead he spoke of fate. Fate is no fault.

Heaven inflicts its punishments on man, as a sovereign does on his subjects. If a man thus chastised, submits to the punishment, the ruler will often pardon him. *Tse Hsia* admitted his guilt, humiliated himself, and repented. Therefore Heaven in its extreme kindness ought to have cured his blindness, or, if *Tse Hsia's* loss of sight was not a retribution from Heaven, *Tse Hsia* cannot have been thrice guilty.

Is not leprosy much worse than blindness? If he who

---

1. Quotation of *Analects* VI, 8.

lost his sight, had three faults, was then the leper[1] ten times guilty?

Yen Yüan[2] died young and Tse Lu came to a premature end, being chopped into minced meat.[3] Thus to be butchered is the most horrid disaster. Judging from Tse Hsia's blindness, both Yen Yüan and Tse Lu must have been guilty of a hundred crimes. From this it becomes evident that the statement of Tsêng Tse was preposterous.

Tse Hsia lost his sight, while bewailing his son. The feelings for one's children are common to mankind, whereas thankfulness to one's parents is sometimes forced. When Tse Hsia was mourning for his father and mother, people did not notice it, but, when bewailing his son, he lost his sight. This shows that his devotion to his parents was rather weak, but that he passionately loved his son. Consequently he shed innumerable tears. Thus ceaselessly weeping, he exposed himself to the wind, and became blind.

Tsêng Tse following the common prejudice invented three faults for Tse Hsia. The latter likewise stuck to the popular belief. Because he had lost his sight, he humbly acknowledged his guilt. Neither Tsêng Tse nor Tse Hsia could get rid of these popular ideas. Therefore in arguing, they did not rank very high among Confucius' followers.

King Hsiang of Ch'in[4] sent a sword to Po Ch'i,[5] who thereupon was going to commit suicide, falling on the sword. "How have I offended Heaven?," quoth he. After a long while he rejoined: — "At all events I must die. At the battle of Ch'ang-p'ing[6] the army of Chao, several hundred thou-

---

1. Po Niu, who was suffering from leprosy.
2. The favourite disciple of Confucius, whose name was Yen Hui.
3. The Tso-chuan, Book XII Duke Ai 15th year, relates that Tse Lu was killed in a revolution in Wei, struck with spears, no mention being made of his having been hacked to pieces (cf. Legge, Ch'un Ch'iu Pt. II, p. 842). This is related, however, in the Li-ki, T'an-kung I (Legge Sacred Books Vol. XXVII, p. 123) and by Huai Nan Tse VII, 13v.
4. King Ch'ao Hsiang of Ch'in 305-249 B.C.
5. A famous general of the Ch'in State who by treachery annihilated the army of Chao Vid. p. 136.
6. In Shansi.

sand men, surrender, but I deceived them, and caused them to be buried alive. Therefore I deserve to die." Afterwards he made away with himself.[1]

Po Ch'i was well aware of his former crime, and acquiesced in the punishment consequent upon it. He knew, how he himself had failed, but not, why the soldiers of *Chao* were buried alive. If Heaven really had punished the guilty, what offence against Heaven had the soldiers of *Chao* committed, who surrendered? Had they been wounded and killed on the battle-field by the random blows of weapons, many out of the four hundred thousand would certainly have survived. Why were these also buried in spite of their goodness and innocence? Those soldiers being unable to obtain Heaven's protection through their virtue, why did *Po Ch'i* alone suffer the condign punishment for his crime from Heaven? We see from this that *Po Ch'i* was mistaken in what he said.

The *Ch'in* emperor *Erh Shih Huang-Ti*[2] sent an envoy to *Mêng T'ien*,[3] and commanded him to commit suicide. *Mêng T'ien* heaving a deep sigh said "How have I failed against Heaven? I die innocent." After a long while, he slowly began, "Yet I am guilty, therefore I am doomed to die. When I was constructing the Great Wall connecting *Liao-tung*[4] with *Lin-t'ao*,[5] ten thousand *Li* in a straight line, I could not avoid cutting the veins of the earth. That was my guilt." Upon this he swallowed a drug, and expired.[6]

The Grand Annalist *Sse Ma Ch'ien* finds fault with him. "When the *Ch'in* dynasty, he said, had exterminated the feudal princes, and peace was not yet restored to the em-

---

1. *Po Ch'i* had fallen into disfavour with his liege upon refusing to lead another campaign against *Chao*.
2. 209-207 B.C.
3. A general of *Erh Shih Huang-Ti's* father, *Ch'in Shih Huang-Ti*, who fought successfully against the *Hsiung-nu*, and constructed the Great Wall as a rampart of defence against their incursions.
4. The Manchurian province of *Fâng-t'ien*.
5. A city in *Wansu* at the western extremity of the Great Wall.
6. Quoted from the *Shi-chi* chap. 88, p. 5.

pire, nor the wounds healed, *Mêng T'ien*, a famous general at that time, did not care to strongly remonstrate with the emperor, or help people in their distress, feeding the old, befriending the orphans, or bringing about a general concord. He flattered those in power, and instigated them to great exploits. That was the fault of men of his type, who well deserved to be put to death. Why did he make the veins of the earth responsible?"[1]

If what *Mêng T'ien* said was wrong, the strictures of the Grand Annalist are not to the point either. How so? *Mêng T'ien* being guilty of having cut the veins of the earth, deserved death for this great crime. How did the earth, which nourishes all beings, wrong man? *Mêng T'ien*, who cut its veins, knew very well that by doing so he had committed a crime, but he did not know, why by lacerating the veins of the earth he had made himself guilty.[2] Therefore it is of no consequence, whether *Mêng T'ien* thus impeached himself, or not. The Grand Annalist blames *Mêng T'ien* for not having strongly protested, when he was a famous general, that therefore he met with this disaster, for those that do not speak, when they ought to remonstrate, will have to suffer a violent death.

Sse Ma Ch'ien himself had to suffer for *Li Ling* in the warm room.[3] According to the Grand Annalist's own view the misfortune suffered tells against a person. Consequently capital punishment takes place by Heaven's decree. If *Sse*

1. Remarks of *Sse Ma Ch'ien* to *Shi-chi* chap. 88, p. 5v.
2. The earth is here treated like an animated being, and its wounding by digging out ditches for the earth-works requisite for the Great Wall, and by piercing mountains, is considered a crime. But provided that *Mêng T'ien* suffered the punishment of his guilt, then another difficulty arises. Why did Heaven allow Earth to be thus maltreated, why did it punish innocent Earth? *Wang Ch'ung's* solution is very simple. Heaven neither rewards nor punishes. Its working is spontaneous, unpremeditated, and purposeless. *Mêng T'ien's* death is nothing but an unfelicitous accident.
3. For his intercession in favour of the defeated general *Li Ling* the emperor *Wu Ti* condemned *Sse Ma Ch'ien* to castration, which penalty was inflicted upon him in a warm room serving for that purpose. (Cf. *Chavannes, Mém. Historiques* Vol. I, p. XL.)

Ma Ch'ien censures *Mêng T'ien* for not having strongly remonstrated with his sovereign, wherefore he incurred his disaster, then there must have been something wrong about himself likewise, since he was put into the warm room. If he was not wrong, then his criticisms on *Mêng T'ien* are not just.

In his memoir on *Po Yi*[1] the Grand Annalist, giving examples of good and bad actions says, "Out of his seventy disciples *Confucius* only recommended *Yen Yüan* for his ardent love of learning. Yet *Yen Yüan* was often destitute. He lived on bran, of which he could not even eat his fill, and suddenly died in his prime. Does Heaven reward good men thus?"

"Robber *Chê* assassinated innocent people day after day, and ate their flesh. By his savageness and imposing haughtiness he attracted several thousand followers, with whom he scourged the empire. Yet he attained a very great age after all. Why was he so specially favoured?"

Yen Yüan ought not to have died so prematurely, and robber *Chê* should not have been kept alive so long. Not to wonder at *Yen Yüan's* premature death, but to say that *Mêng T'ien* deserved to die, is inconsistent.

The *Han* general *Li Kuang*[2] said in a conversation which he had with the diviner *Wang Shê*, "Ever since the *Han*[3] have fought the *Hsiung-nu*,[4] I was there. But several tens of officers of a lower rank than commander of a city gate, with scarcely moderate abilities, have won laurels in the

---

1. *Shi-chi* chap. 61, p. 3v. *Po Yi* (12th cent. B.C.) and his elder brother *Shu Ch'i* were sons of the Prince of *Ku-chu* in modern *Chili*. Their father wished to make the younger brother *Shu Ch'i* his heir, but he refused to deprive his elder brother of his birth-right, who, on his part, would not ascend the throne against his father's will. Both left their country to wander about in the mountains, where at last they died of cold and hunger. They are regarded as models of virtue.

2. Died 125 B.C.

3. The *Han* dynasty. The Former *Han* dynasty reigned from 206 B.C.-8 A.D. the Later *Han* dynasty from 25-220 A.D.

4. A Turkish tribe.

campaigns against the *Hu*[1] and marquisates withal. I do not yield the palm to these nobles, but how is it that I have not even acquired a square foot of land as a reward for my services, and much less been enfeoffed with a city? Are my looks not those of a marquis? Surely it is my fate."

Wang Shê asked him to think, whether there was anything which always gave him pangs of conscience. *Li Kuang* replied, "When I was magistrate of *Lung-hsi*,[2] the *Ch'iang*[3] continuously rebelled. I induced over eight hundred to submission, and, by a stratagem, had them all killed on the same day. This is the only thing for which I feel sorry up to now."

Wang Shê rejoined: — "There can be no greater crime than to murder those that have surrendered. That is the reason, why you, general, did not get a marquisate."[4]

Li Kuang agreed with him, and others who heard of it, believed this view to be true. Now, not to become a marquis is like not becoming an emperor. Must he who is not made a marquis, have anything to rue, and he who does not become emperor, have committed any wrong? *Confucius* was not made an emperor, but nobody will say of him that he had done any wrong, whereas, because *Li Kuang* did not became a marquis, *Wang Shê* said that he had something to repent of. But his reasoning is wrong.

Those who go into these questions, mostly hold that, whether a man will be invested with a marquisate or not, is predestined by Heaven, and that marks of Heaven's fate appear in his body. When the great general *Wei Ch'ing*[5] was in the *Chien-chang* palace, a deported criminal with an iron collar predicted his fate to the effect that he was so distinguished, that he would even be made a marquis. Later on, he in fact became a marquis over ten thou-

1. A general term for non-Chinese tribes in the north.
2. District in *Kansu*.
3. Tribes in the West of China.
4. A quotation from *Shi-chi* chap. 109, p. 6, the biography of General *Li*.
5. A favourite and a general of *Han Wu Ti*, died 106 B.C.

sand families, owing to his great services. Before *Wei Ch'ing* had performed his great achievements, the deported criminal saw those signs pointing to his future rank. Consequently, to be raised to the rank of a marquis depends on fate, and man cannot attain to it by his works. What the criminal said turned out true, as shown by the result, whereas *Wang Shê's* assertion is untenable and without proof. Very often people are perverse and selfish without becoming unhappy by it, and others who always follow the path of virtue, may lose their happiness. *Wang Shê's* opinion is of the same kind as the self-reproach of *Po Ch'i*, and the self-impeachment of *Mêng T'ien*.

In this flurried, bustling world it constantly happens that people rob and murder each other in their greed for wealth. Two merchants having travelled together in the same cart or the same boat a thousand Li, one kills the other, when they arrive at a far-off place, and takes away all his property. The dead body is left on the spot, uncared for, and the bones bleach in the sun unburied. In the water, the corpse is eaten up by fish and turtles, on land, ants and vermin feed upon it. The lazy fellows won't exert their strength in agriculture, but resort to commerce, and even that reluctanly, in order to amass grain and goods. When then in a year of scarcity they have not enough to still the hunger of their bellies, they knock down their fellow-citizens like beasts, cut them to pieces, and eat their flesh. No difference is made between good and bad men, they are all equally devoured. It is not generally known, and the officials do not hear of it. In communities of over a thousand men up to ten thousand only one man out of a hundred remains alive, and nine out of ten die.[1] This is the height of lawlessness and atrocity, yet all the murderers walk publicly about, become wealthy men, and lead a gay

---

1. A Chinese does not take exception to the incongruity of the equation: — 100:1=10:1. The meaning is plain: — a small percentage of survivors, and a great many dying.

and pleasant life, without Heaven punishing them for their utter want of sympathy and benevolence.

They kill one another, when they meet on the roads, not because they are so poor, that they cannot undertake anything, but only because they are passing through hard times, they feed on human flesh, thus bringing endless misery on their fellow-creatures, and compassing their premature deaths. How is it possible that they can make their guilt public, openly showing to the whole world the indelible proofs thereof? *Wang Shê's* opinion can certainly not be right.

The historians tell us that *Li Sse,*[1] envious that *Han Fei Tse*[2] equalled him in talent, had him assassinated in jail[3] in *Ch'in,* but that, afterwards, he was torn to pieces by carts,[4] furthermore that *Shang Yang,*[5] under pretence of his old friendship, captured *Ang,* prince of *Wei,* but that, subsequently, he had to suffer death. They wish to imply that those men had to endure these misfortunes as a punishment for their having destroyed a wise man, or broken an old friendship. For what cause had *Han Fei Tse* given, to be incarcerated by *Li Sse,* or what fault had prince *Ang* committed, to be taken prisoner by *Shang Yang?* How did the murder of a scholar, who died in prison, and the breaking

---

1. Prime Minister of *Ch'in Shih Huang-Ti* and a great scholar. He studied together with *Han Fei Tse* under the philosopher *Hsün Tse.*

2. A Taoist philosopher, son of a duke of the *Han* State.

3. By his intrigues *Li Sse* had induced the king of *Ch'in* to imprison *Han Fei Tse.* He then sent him poison, with which *Han Fei Tse* committed suicide. Vid. *Shi-chi* chap. 63, p. 11v., Biography of *Han Fei Tse.*

4. *Li Sse* fell a victim to the intrigues of the powerful eunuch *Chao Kao.* The *Shi-chi* chap. 87, p. 20v., Biography of *Li Sse,* relates that he was cut asunder at the waist on the market place. At all events he was executed in an atrocious way. The tearing to pieces by carts driven in opposite directions is a punishment several times mentioned in the *Ch'un-ch'iu.*

5. *Shang Yang* is *Wei Yang,* Prince of *Shang,* died 338 B.C. In the service of the *Ch'in* State he defeated an army of *Wei,* commanded by Prince *Ang,* whom he treacherously seized, and assassinated at a meeting, to which he had invited him as an old friend. According to the *Shi-chi,* chap. 68, p. 9, Biography of Prince *Shang,* he lost his life in battle against his former master, and his corpse was torn to pieces by carts like *Li Sse.*

of an old friendship resulting in the arrest of the prince, bring about the violent death of the culprit, torn to pieces by carts,[1] or the decapitation? If *Han Fei Tse* or prince *Ang* were wicked, and Heaven had placed retribution in the hands of *Li Sse* and *Shang Yang*, then the latter would have acted by Heaven's order, and be deserving of his reward, not of misfortune. Were *Han Fei Tse* and prince *Ang* blameless, and not punished by Heaven, then *Li Sse* and *Shang Yang* ought not to have imprisoned and captured them.

It will be argued that *Han Fei Tse* and Prince *Ang* had concealed their crimes, and hidden their faults so, that nobody heard about them, but Heaven alone knew, and therefore they suffered death and mishap. The guilt of men consists, either in outrages on the wise, or in attacks on the well-minded. If they commit outrages on the wise, what wrong have the victims of these outrages done? And if they attack the well-minded, what fault have the people thus attacked committed?[2]

When misery or prosperity, fortune or mishap are falling to man's share with greater intensity, it is fate, when less so, it is time. *T'ai Kung*[3] was in great distress, when he happened to be enfeoffed with a territory by the *Chou* king *Wên Wang*. *Ning Ch'i*[4] was living in obscurity and difficulties, when Duke *Huan* of *Ch'i* gave him an appointment. It cannot be said that these two men, when they were poor and miserable, had done wrong, but had reformed, when they obtained their investment or appointment. Calamity and prosperity have their time, and good or bad luck depend on fate.

1. The culprit being bound to the carts, which then were driven in different directions.
2. Why does Heaven punish the innocent through the guilty? If *Han Fei Tse* and *Ang* had sinned in secret, Heaven would have been unjust towards those they had wronged, and so on.
3. A high officer, who had gone into exile to avoid the tyrannous rule of *Chou Hsin* 1122 B.C., and subsequently joined *Wên Wang*.
4. *Ning Ch'n* lived in the 7th cent.B.C.

T'ai Kung and *Ning Ch'i* were worthies, but they may have had their faults. Sages, however, possess perfect virtue. Nevertheless *Shun* was several times almost done to death by the foul play of his father and brother. When he met with *Yao*, the latter yielded the throne to him, and raised him to the imperial dignity. It is evident that, when *Shun* had to endure these insidious attacks, he was not to blame, and that he did not behave well, when he was made emperor. First, his time had not yet come, afterwards, his fate was fulfilled, and his time came.

When princes and ministers in olden days were first distressed, and afterwards crowned with success, it was not, because they had at first been bad, and Heaven sent them calamities, or that subsequently they suddenly improved, and then were helped and protected by the spirits. The actions and doings of one individual from his youth to his death bear the same character from first to last. Yet one succeeds, the other fails, one gets on, the other falls off, one is penniless, the other well-to-do, one thriving, the other ruined. All this is the result of chance and luck, and the upshot of fate and time.

298

GAUTAMA BUDDHA

GAUTAMA BUDDHA (*c.* 563-483 B.C.). Although
Siddhartha Gautama, known as Buddha, the "Awakened,"
was not a Chinese philosopher, he was the historic founder of a religion which profoundly influenced Chinese
thinkers and continues to provide a common cultural
bond throughout central, northern and southern Asia.

Buddhism first arrived in China about the first century
A.D. via Central Asia. Translation of Buddhist scriptures
began in the middle of the second century, and by the
first quarter of the third century two Buddhist movements had been recorded: *dhyāna* (concentration) and
prajñā (wisdom). Buddhism made great strides during
the Epoch of the Three Kingdoms (220-280), when it
became an authorized religion, and during the Period
of the Six Dynasties (420-589). It became a complement of both Tâoism and Confucianism, exercising a
profound influence over Chinese life and politics, particularly during these two periods of disunity. Tâoist
concepts facilitated the assimilation of Buddhism, which
was a religion based on a philosophy of human nature,
in a land where interpretation by analogy was widely
practiced. The Tâo was equated with Tathata, *wu wei*
(nonaction, taking no action, withdrawal, etc.) with
Nirvâṇa, the Confucian golden mean with the Buddhist
middle path. One third-century Confucian called the
Chinese classics the flowers and Buddhism their fruit.
One tradition even asserts that Buddhism is a foreign
variant of Tâoism, Buddha having studied under Lao
Tzŭ.

The Chinese made Buddhism a system embracing both Tâoist and Confucian elements. Mencius' doctrine that everything is within mind agrees with the Buddhist idea that every object is mind only. The doctrine of the Tâo prepares the way for acceptance of the Buddhist concept of Nirvâna, viewed as the essential nature of the universe, according to which man must live without renouncing life. Seven schools developed during the early period of Buddhist infiltration into China, but they did not exert much influence on later schools. They generally fell into two groups, schools of non-being and schools of being. Chinese Buddhism was later divided into ten schools, of which the most important was the Meditation School, first propagated by Tao-sheng, then by Bodhidharma, who is traditionally credited with founding the doctrine of Zen Buddhism. Almost all of these schools taught that everyone could attain Buddhahood.

Gautama Buddha was the son of a ruler of ancient Northern India. The date of his birth is placed about 563 B.C. He was born a warrior prince, but at the age of twenty-nine, having married and had a son, he decided to renounce the world. Abandoning his family and possessions, he gave himself up to asceticism and concentration of thought, under the guidance of masters of these disciplines. After seven years, he concluded that this method failed to bring him nearer to the wisdom he sought as a means of escaping rebirth into a life which he had found not worth living — so, for a time, he tried starvation and self-torture. This too, was to no avail. But suddenly, while sitting under the sacred fig tree at Bodhi Gaya, he underwent a powerful illumination and beheld the great truths he had been seeking. Henceforth, he was Buddha.

Gautama's first aim had been merely his own salvation now, moved by pity for mankind, he resolved to bestow on others the Four Great Truths and the Eightfold Path. He began his ministry at Benares, where he at first converted five monks who had been his companions in asceticism, then many of the youth of the city, then a thousand Brahman priests.

He spent the remainder of his life wandering about and preaching his new creed, which spread with extraordinary rapidity. He died not far from his native region about the year 477 B.C.

The Attainment of Buddhahood

From the *Sacred Writings*, New York, P. F. Collier & Son Company.

THERE IS NO EGO

I. Translated from the Milindapañha (25[1])

THEN drew near Milinda the king to where the venerable Nagasena was; and having drawn near he greeted the venerable Nagasena; and having passed the compliments of friendship and civility, he sat down respectfully at one side. And the venerable Nāgasena returned the greeting; by which, verily, he won the heart of king Milinda.

And Milinda the king spoke to the venerable Nāgasena as follows:—

"How is your reverence called? Bhante, what is your name?"

"Your majesty, I am called Nāgasena; my fellow-priests, your majesty, address me as Nāgasena: but whether parents give one the name Nāgasena, or Sūrasena, or Virasena, or Sihasena, it is, nevertheless, your majesty, but a way of counting, a term, an appellation, a convenient designation, a mere name, this Nāgasena; for there is no Ego here to be found."

Then said Milinda the king,—

"Listen to me, my lords, ye five hundred Yonakas, and ye eighty thousand priests! Nagasena here says thus: 'There is no Ego here to be found.' Is it possible, pray, for me to assent to what he says?"

301

And Milinda the king spoke to the venerable Nāgasena as follows:—

"Bhante Nāgasena, if there is no Ego to be found, who is it then furnishes you priests with priestly requisites, — robes, food, bedding, and medicine, the reliance of the sick? who is it makes use of the same? who is it keeps the precepts? who is it applies himself to meditation? who is it realizes the Paths, the Fruits, and Nirvāṇa? who is it destroys life? who is it takes what is not given him? who is it commits immorality? who is it tells lies? who is it drinks intoxicating liquor? who is it commits the five crimes that constitute 'proximate karma?'[1] In that case, there is no merit; there is no demerit; there is no one who does or causes to be done meritorious or demeritorious deeds; neither good nor evil deeds can have any fruit or result. Bhante Nāgasena, neither is he a murderer who kills a priest, nor can you priests, bhante Nāgasena, have any teacher, preceptor, or ordination. When you say, 'My fellow-priests, your majesty, address me as Nāgasena, what then is this Nāgasena? Pray, bhante, is the hair of the head Nāgasena?"

"Nay, verily, your majesty."

"Is the hair of the body Nāgasena?"

"Nay, verily, your majesty."

"Are nails... teeth... skin... flesh... sinews... bones ... marrow of the bone ... kidneys ... heart ... liver ... pleura ... spleen ... lungs ... intestines ... mesentery ... stomach ... faeces ... bile ... phlegm ... pus ... blood ... sweat ... fat ... tears ... lymph ... saliva ...

1. Translated from the Sārasaṅgaha, as quoted in Trenckner's note to this passage:

"By *proximate karma* is meant karma that ripens in the next existence. To show what this is, I [the author of the Sārasaṅgaha] give the following passage from the Atthānasutta of the first book of the Aṅguttara-Nikāya: — 'It is an impossibility, O priests, the case can never occur, that an individual imbued with the correct doctrine should deprive his mother of life, should deprive his father of life, should deprive a saint of life, should in a revengeful spirit cause a bloody wound to a Tathāgata, should cause a schism in the church. This is an impossibility.' "

302

snot ... synovial fluid ... urine ... brain of the head Nāgasena?"

"Nay, verily, your majesty."

"Is now, bhante, form Nāgasena?"

"Nay, verily, your majesty."

"Is sensation Nāgasena?"

"Nay, verily, your majesty."

"Is perception Nāgasena?"

"Nay, verily, your majesty."

"Are the predispositions Nāgasena?"

"Nay, verily, your majesty."

"Is consciousness Nāgasena?"

"Nay, verily, your majesty."

"Are, then, bhante, form, sensation, perception, the predispositions, and consciousness unitedly Nāgasena?"

"Nay, verily, your majesty."

"Is it, then, bhante, something besides form, sensation, perception, the predispositions, and consciousness, which is Nāgasena?"

"Nay, verily, your majesty."

"Bhante, although I question you very closely; I fail to discover any Nāgasena. Verily, now, bhante, Nāgasena is a mere empty sound. What Nāgasena is there here? Bhante, you speak a falsehood, a lie: there is no Nāgasena."

Then the venerable Nāgasena spoke to Milinda the king as follows:—

"Your majesty, you are a delicate prince, an exceedingly delicate prince; and if, your majesty, you walk in the middle of the day on hot sandy ground, and you tread on rough grit, gravel, and sand, your feet become sore, your body tired, the mind is oppressed, and the body-consciousness suffers. Pray, did you come afoot, or riding?"

"Bhante, I do not go afoot: I came in a chariot."

"Your majesty, if you came in a chariot, declare to me the chariot. Pray, your majesty, is the pole the chariot?"

"Nay, verily, bhante."

303

"Is the axle the chariot?"

"Nay, verily, bhante."

"Are the wheels the chariot?"

"Nay, verily, bhante."

"Is the chariot-body the chariot?"

"Nay, verily, bhante."

"Is the banner-staff the chariot?"

"Nay, verily, bhante."

"Is the yoke the chariot?"

"Nay, verily, bhante."

"Are the reins the chariot?"

"Nay, verily, bhante."

"Is the goading-stick the chariot?"

"Nay, verily, bhante."

"Pray, your majesty, are pole, axle, wheels, chariot-body, banner-staff, yoke, reins, and goad unitedly the chariot?"

"Nay, verily, bhante."

"Is it, then, your majesty, something else besides pole, axle, wheels, chariot-body, banner-staff, yoke, reins and goad which is the chariot?"

"Nay, verily, bhante."

"Your majesty, although I question you very closely I fail to discover any chariot. Verily now, your majesty, the word chariot is a mere empty sound. What chariot is there here? Your majesty, you speak a falsehood, a lie: there is no chariot. Your majesty, you are the chief king in all the continent of India; of whom are you afraid that you speak a lie? Listen to me, my lords, ye five hundred Yonakas, and ye eighty thousand priests! Milinda the king here says thus: 'I came in a chariot;' and being requested, 'Your majesty, if you came in a chariot, declare to me the chariot,' he fails to produce any chariot. Is it possible, pray, for me to assent to what he says?"

When he had thus spoken, the five hundred Yonakas applauded the venerable Nāgasena and spoke to Milinda the king as follows:—

"Now, your majesty, answer, if you can."

Then Milinda the king spoke to the venerable Nāgasena as follows:—

"Bhante Nāgasena, I speak no lie: the word 'chariot' is but a way of counting, term, appellation, convenient designation, and name for pole, axle, wheels, chariot-body, and banner-staff."

"Thoroughly well, your majesty, do you understand a chariot. In exactly the same way, your majesty, in respect of me, Nāgasena is but a way of counting, term, appellation, convenient designation, mere name for the hair of my head, hair of my body . . . brain of the head, form, sensation, perception, the predispositions, and consciousness. But in the absolute sense there is no Ego here to be found. And the priestess Vajira, your majesty, said as follows in the presence of The Blessed One:—

"'Even as the word of "chariot" means
That members join to frame a whole;
So when the Groups appear to view,
We use the phrase, "A living being."[1]'"

"It is wonderful, bhante Nāgasena! It is marvellous, bhante Nāgasena! Brilliant and prompt is the wit of your replies. If The Buddha were alive, he would applaud. Well done, well done Nāgasena! Brilliant and prompt is the wit of your replies."

2. Translated from the Visuddhi-Magga (chap. XVIII).

Just as the word "chariot" is but a mode of expression for axle, wheels, chariot-body, pole, and other constituent members, placed in a certain relation to each other, but when we come to examine the members one by one, we discover that in the absolute sense there is no chariot; and just as the word "house" is but a mode of expression for wood and other constituents of a house, surrounding space in a certain relation, but in the absolute sense there is no

1. That is, "a living entity."

house; and just as the word "fist" is but a mode of expression for the fingers, the thumb, etc., in a certain relation; and the word "lute" for the body of the lute, strings, etc.; "army" for elephants, horses, etc.; "city" for fortifications, houses, gates, etc.; "tree" for trunk, branches, foliage, etc., in a certain relation, but when we come to examine the parts one by one, we discover that in the absolute sense there is no tree; in exactly the same way the words "living entity" and "Ego," are but a mode of expression for the presence of the five attachment groups, but when we come to examine the elements of being one by one, we discover that in the absolute sense there is no living entity there to form a basis for such figments as "I am," or "I"; in other words, that in the absolute sense there is only name and form. The insight of him who perceives this is called knowledge of the truth.

He, however, who abandons this knowledge of the truth and believes in a living entity must assume either that this living entity will perish or that it will not perish. If he assume that it will not perish, he falls into the heresy of the persistence of existences; or if he assume that it will perish, he falls into that of the annihilation of existences. And why do I say so? Because, just as sour cream has milk as its antecedent, so nothing here exists but what has its own antecedents. To say, "The living entity persists," is to fall short of the truth; to say, "It is annihilated," is to outrun the truth. Therefore has The Blessed One said:—

"There are two heresies, O priests, which possess both gods and men, by which some fall short of the truth, and some outrun the truth; but the intelligent know the truth.

"And how, O priests, do some fall short of the truth?

"O priests, gods and men delight in existence, take pleasure in existence, rejoice in existence, so that when the Doctrine for the cessation of existence is preached to them, their minds do not leap toward it, are not favorably disposed toward it, do not rest in it, do not adopt it.

"Thus, O priests, do some fall short of the truth."

"And how, O priests, do some outrun the truth?

"Some are distressed at, ashamed of, and loathe exist-ence, and welcome the thought of non-existence, saying, 'See here! When they say that on the dissolution of the body this Ego is annihilated, perishes, and does not exist after death, that is good, that is excellent, that is as it should be.'

"Thus, O priests, do some outrun the truth.

"And how, O priests, do the intelligent know the truth?

"We may have, O priests, a priest who knows things as they really are, and knowing things as they really are, he is on the road to aversion for things, to absence of passion for them, and to cessation from them.

"Thus, O priests, do the intelligent know the truth."

3. Translated from the Mahā-Nidāna-Sutta (256²¹) of the Digha-Nikāyā.

"In regard to the Ego, Ananda, what are the views held concerning it?

"In regard to the Ego, Ananda, either one holds the view that sensation is the Ego, saying, 'Sensation is my Ego;'

"Or, in regard to the Ego, Ananda, one holds the view, Verily, sensation is not my Ego; my Ego has no sensation;'

"Or, in regard to the Ego, Ananda, one holds the view, 'Verily, neither is sensation my Ego; nor does my Ego have no sensation. My Ego has sensation; my Ego possesses the faculty of sensation.' "

"In the above case, Ananda, where it is said, 'Sensation is my Ego,' reply should be made as follows: 'Brother, there are three sensations; the pleasant sensation, the unpleasant sensation, and the indifferent sensation. Which of these three sensations do you hold to be the Ego?'

"Whenever, Ananda, a person experiences a pleasant sen-sation, he does not at the same time experience an unpleasant sensation, nor does he experience an indifferent sensation; only the pleasant sensation does he then feel. Whenever, Ananda, a person experiences an unpleasant sensation, he does not at the same time experience a pleasant sensation, nor does he experience an indifferent sensation; only the unpleasant sensation does he then feel. Whenever, Ananda, a person experiences an indifferent sensation, he does not at the same time experience a pleasant sensation, nor does he experience an unpleasant sensation; only the indifferent sensation does he then feel.

"Now pleasant sensations, Ananda, are transitory, are due to causes, originate by dependence, and are subject to decay, disappearance, effacement, and cessation; and unpleasant sensations, Ananda, are transitory, are due to causes, originate by dependence, and are subject to decay, disappearance, effacement, and cessation; and indifferent sensations, Ananda, are transitory, are due to causes, originate by dependence, and are subject to decay, disappearance, effacement, and cessation. While this person is experiencing a pleasant sensation, he thinks, 'This is my Ego.' And after the cessation of this same pleasant sensation, he thinks, 'My Ego has passed away.' And while he is experiencing an indifferent sensation, he thinks, 'This is my Ego.' And after the cessation of this same indifferent sensation, he thinks, 'My Ego has passed away.' So that he who says, 'Sensation is my Ego,' holds the view that even during his lifetime his Ego is transitory, that it is pleasant, unpleasant, or mixed, and that it is subject to rise and disappearance.

"Accordingly, Ananda, it is not possible to hold the view, 'Sensation is my Ego.'

"In the above case, Ananda, where it is said, 'Verily sensation is not my Ego; my Ego has no sensation,' reply should be made as follows: 'But, brother, where there is no sensation, is there any "I am"?' "

"Nay, verily, Reverend Sir."

"Accordingly, Ananda, it is not possible to hold the view, 'Verily, sensation is not my Ego; my Ego has no sensation.'

"In the above case, Ananda, where it is said, 'Verily, neither is sensation my Ego, nor does my Ego have no sensation. My Ego has sensation; my Ego possesses the faculty of sensation,' reply should be made as follows: 'Suppose, brother, that utterly and completely, and without remainder, all sensation were to cease — if there were nowhere any sensation, pray, would there be anything, after the cessation of sensation, of which it could be said, "This am I"?' "

"Nay, verily, Reverend Sir."

"Accordingly, Ananda, it is not possible to hold the view, 'Verily, neither is sensation my Ego, nor does my Ego have no sensation. My Ego has sensation; my Ego possesses the faculty of sensation.'

"From the time Ananda, a priest no longer holds the view that sensation is the Ego, no longer holds the view that the Ego has no sensation, no longer holds the view that the Ego has sensation, possesses the faculty of sensation, he ceases to attach himself to anything in the world, and being free from attachment, he is never agitated, and being never agitated, he attains to Nirvāṇa in his own person; and he knows that rebirth is exhausted, that he has lived the holy life, that he has done what it behooved him to do, and that he is no more for this world.

"Now it is impossible, Ananda, that to a mind so freed a priest should attribute the heresy that the saint exists after death, or that the saint does not exist after death, or that the saint both exists and does not exist after death, or that the saint neither exists nor does not exist after death.

"And why do I say so?

"Because, Ananda, after a priest has been freed by a thorough comprehension of affirmation and affirmation's range, of predication and predication's range, of declaration and declaration's range, of knowledge and knowledge's field of action, of rebirth and what rebirth affects, it is impossible for him to attribute such a heretical lack of knowledge and perception to a priest similarly freed."

THE MIDDLE DOCTRINE
1. Translated from the Samyutta-Nikāya (XXII. 90[16])

The world, for the most part, O Kaccāna, holds either to a belief in being or to a belief in non-being. But for one who in the light of the highest knowledge, O Kaccāna, considers how the world arises, belief in the non-being of the world passes away. And for one who in the light of the highest knowledge, O Kaccāna, considers how the world ceases, belief in the being of the world passes away. The world, O Kaccāna, is for the most part bound up in a seeking, attachment, and proclivity [for the groups], but a priest does not sympathize with this seeking and attachment, nor with the mental affirmation, proclivity, and prejudice which affirms an Ego. He does not doubt or question that it is only evil that springs into existence, and only evil that ceases from existence, and his conviction of this fact is dependent on no one besides himself. This, O Kaccāna, is what constitutes Right Belief.

That things have being, O Kaccāna, constitutes one extreme of doctrine; that things have no being is the other extreme. These extremes, O Kaccāna, have been avoided by The Tathāgata, and it is a middle doctrine he teaches:—

On ignorance depends karma;

On karma depends consciousness;

On consciousness depend name and form;

On name and form depend the six organs of sense;

On the six organs of sense depends contact;

On contact depends sensation;

On sensation depends desire;

On desire depends attachment;

On attachment depends existence;

On existence depends birth;

On birth depend old age and death, sorrow, lamentation, misery, grief, and despair. Thus does this entire aggregation of misery arise.

But on the complete fading out and cessation of ignorance ceases Karma;

On the cessation of karma ceases consciousness;

On the cessation of consciousness cease name and form;

On the cessation of name and from cease the six organs of sense;

310

On the cessation of the six organs of sense ceases contact;
On the cessation of contact ceases sensation;
On the cessation of sensation ceases desire;
On the cessation of desire ceases attachment;
On the cessation of attachment ceases existence;
On the cessation of existence ceases birth;
On the cessation of birth cease old age and death, sorrow, lamentation, misery, grief and despair. Thus does this entire aggregation of misery cease.

2. Translated from the Samyutta-Nikāya (XII. 35[1])

Thus have I heard.

On a certain occasion The Blessed One was dwelling at Savatthi in Jetavana monastery in Anāthapindika's Park. And there The Blessed One addressed the priests.

"Priests," said he.

"Lord," said the priests to The Blessed One in reply.

And The Blessed One spoke as follows:

"O priests, on ignorance depends karma; . . . Thus does this entire aggregation of misery arise."

"Reverend Sir, what are old age and death? and what is it has old age and death?"

"The question is not rightly put," said The Blessed One. "O priest to say: 'What are old age and death? and what is it has old age and death?' and to say: 'Old age and death are one thing, but it is another thing which has old age and death,' is to say the same thing in different ways. If, O priest, the dogma obtain that the soul and the body are identical, then there is no religious life; or if, O priest, the dogma obtain that the soul is one thing and the body another, then also there is no religious life. Both these extremes, O priest, have been avoided by The Tathāgata, and it is a middle doctrine he teaches: 'On birth depend old age and death.'"

"Reverend Sir, what is birth? and what is it has birth?"

"The question is not rightly put," said The Blessed One.

"O priest, to say: 'What is birth? and what is it has birth?' and to say: 'Birth is one thing, but it is another thing which has birth,' is to say the same thing in different ways. If, O priest, the dogma obtain that the soul and the body are identical, then there is no religious life; or if, O priest, the dogma obtain that the soul is one thing and the body another, then also there is no religious life. Both these extremes, O priest, have been avoided by The Tathāgata, and it is a middle doctrine he teaches: 'On existence depends birth.'"

"Reverend Sir, what is existence? . . . attachment? . . . desire? . . . sensation? . . . contact? . . . the six organs of sense? . . . name and form? . . . consciousness? . . . karma? and what is it has karma?"

"The question is not rightly put," said The Blessed One. "O priest, to say: 'What is karma? and what is it has karma?' and to say: 'Karma is one thing, but is it another thing which has karma,' is to say the same thing in different ways. If, O priest, the dogma obtain that the soul and the body are identical, then there is no religious life; or if, O priest, the dogma obtain that the soul is one thing and the body another, then also there is no religious life. Both these extremes, O priest, have been avoided by The Tathāgata, and it is a middle doctrine he teaches: 'On ignorance depends karma.'

"But on the complete fading out and cessation of ignorance, O priest, all these refuges, puppet-shows, resorts, and writhings, — to wit: What are old age and death? and what is it has old age and death? or, old age and death are one thing, but it is another thing which has old age and death; or, the soul and the body are identical, or the soul is one thing, and the body another, — all such refuges of whatever kind are abandoned, uprooted, pulled out of the ground like a palmyra-tree, and become non-existent and not liable to spring up again in the future.

"But on the complete fading out and cessation of ignorance, O priest, all these refuges, puppet-shows, resorts, and writhings, — to wit: What is birth? . . . existence? . . . . attachment? . . . desire? . . . sensation? . . . contact? . . . the

six organs of sense? . . . name and form? . . . consciousness?
. . .karma? and what is it has karma? or, karma is one
thing, but it is another thing which has karma; or the soul
and the-body are identical, or the soul is one thing and the
body another, — all such refuges are abandoned, uprooted,
pulled out of the ground like a palmyra-tree, and become
non-existent and not liable to spring up again in the future."

3. Translated from the Visuddhi-Magga (chap. XVII.)

Inasmuch as it is dependently on each other and in unison
and simultaneouly that the factors which constitute dependence originate the elements of being, therefore did The Sage
call these factors Dependent Origination.

For the ignorance etc. which have been enumerated as
constituting dependence, when they originate any of the elements of being, namely, karma and the rest, can only do so
when dependent on each other and in case none of their
number is lacking. Therefore it is dependently on each other
and in unison and simultaneously that the factors which
constitute dependence originate the elements of being, not
by a part of their number nor by one succeeding the other.
Accordingly The Sage, skilful in the art of discovering the
signification of things, calls this dependence by the name of
Dependent Origination.

And in so doing, by the first of these two words is shown
the falsity of such heresies as that of the persistence of existences, and by the second word, a rejection of such heresies as
that existences cease to be, while by both together is shown
the truth.

By the first: — The word "Dependent," as exhibiting a full
complement of dependence and inasmuch as the elements of
being are subject to that full complement of dependence,
shows an avoidance of such heresies as that of the persistence of existences, the heresies, namely, of the persistence
of existences, of uncaused existences, of existences due to an
overruling power, of self-determining existences. For what

313

have persistent existences, uncaused existences, etc., to do with a full complement of dependence?

By the second word: — The word "Origination," as exhibiting an origination of the elements of being and inasmuch as the elements of being originate by means of a full complement of dependence, shows a rejection of such heresies as that of the annihilation of existences, the heresies, namely, of the annihilation of existences, of nihilism, of the inefficacy of karma. For if the elements of being are continually originating by means of an antecedent dependence, whence can we have annihilation of existence, nihilism, and an inefficacy of karma?

By both together: — By the complete phrase "Dependent Origination," inasmuch as such and such elements of being come into existence by means of an unbroken series of their full complement of dependence, the truth, or middle course, is shown. This rejects the heresy that he who experiences the fruit of the deed is the same as the one who performed the deed, and also rejects the converse one that he who experiences the fruit of a deed is different from the one who performed the deed, and leaning not to either of these popular hypotheses, holds fast by nominalism.

KARMA
Translated from the Visuddhi-Magga (chap. XVII.)

The kinds of karma are those already briefly mentioned as consisting of the triplet beginning with meritorious karma and the triplet beginning with bodily karma, making six in all.

To give them here in full, however, meritorious karma consists of the eight meritorious thoughts which belong to the realm of sensual pleasure and show themselves in almsgiving, keeping the precepts, etc., and of the five meritorious thoughts which belong to the realm of form and show themselves in ecstatic meditation, — making thirteen thoughts; demeritorious karma consists of the twelve demeritorious

314

thoughts which show themselves in the taking of life, etc.; and karma leading to immovability consists of the four meritorious thoughts which belong to the realm of formlessness and show themselves in ecstatic meditation. Accordingly these three karmas consist of twenty-nine thoughts.

As regards the other three, bodily karma consists of the thoughts of the body, vocal karma of the thoughts of the voice, mental karma of the thoughts of the mind. The object of this triplet is to show the avenues by which meritorious karma, etc., show themselves at the moment of the initiation of karma.

For bodily karma consists of an even score of thoughts, namely, of the eight meritorious thoughts which belong to the realm of sensual pleasure and the twelve demeritorious ones. These by exciting gestures show themselves through the avenue of the body.

Vocal karma is when these same thoughts by exciting speech show themselves through the avenue of the voice. The thoughts, however, which belong to the realm of form, are not included, as they do not form a dependence for subsequent consciousness. And the case is the same with the thoughts which belong to the realm of formlessness. Therefore they also are to be excluded from the dependence of consciousness. However, all depend on ignorance.

Mental karma, however, consists of all the twenty-nine thoughts, when they spring up in the mind without exciting either gesture or speech.

Thus, when it is said that ignorance is the dependence of the karma-triplet consisting of meritorious karma, etc., it is to be understood that the other triplet is also included.

But it may be asked, "How can we tell that these karmas are dependent on ignorance?" Because they exist when ignorance exists.

For, when a person has not abandoned the want of knowledge concerning misery, etc., which is called ignorance, then by that want knowledge concerning misery and concerning anteriority, etc., he seizes on the misery of the round of rebirth with the idea that it is happiness and hence begins to perform the threefold karma which is its cause; by that want of knowledge concerning the origin of misery and by being under the impression that thus happiness is secured, he begins to perform karma that ministers to desire, though such karma is really the cause of misery; and by that want of knowledge concerning cessation and the path and under the impression that some particular form of existence will prove to be the cessation of misery, although it really is not so, or that sacrifices, alarming the gods by the greatness of his austerities, and other like procedures are the way to cessation, although they are not such a way, he begins to perform the threefold karma.

Moreover, through this non-abandonment of ignorance in respect of the Four Truths, he does not know the fruition of meritorious karma to be the misery it really is, seeing that it is completely overwhelmed with the calamities, birth, old age, disease, death, etc.; and so to obtain it he begins to perform meritorious karma in its three divisions of bodily, vocal and mental karma, just as a man in love with a heavenly nymph will throw himself down a precipice. When he does not perceive that at the end of that meritorious fruition considered to be such happiness comes the agonizing misery of change and disappointment, he begins to perform the meritorious karma above described, just as a locust will fly into the flame of a lamp, or a man that is greedy after honey will lick the honey-smeared edge of a knife. When he fails to perceive the calamities due to sensual gratification and its fruition, and, being under the impression that sensuality is happiness, lives enthralled by his passions, he then begins to perform demeritorious karma through the three avenues, just as a child will play with filth, or one who wishes to die will eat poison. When he does not perceive the misery of the change that takes place in the constituents of being even in the realm of formlessness, but has a perverse belief in persistence, etc., he begins to perform mental karma that leads

316

to immovability, just as a man who has lost his way will go after a mirage.

As, therefore, karma exists when ignorance exists but not when it does not exist, it to be understood that this karma depends on ignorance. And it has been said as follows:

"O priests, the ignorant, uninstructed man performs meritorious karma, demeritorious karma, and karma leading to immovability. But whenever, O priests, he abandons his ignorance and acquires wisdom, he through the fading out of ignorance and the coming into being of wisdom does not even perform meritorious karma."

FRUITFUL AND BARREN KARMA
1. Translated from the Añguttara-Nikāya (III. 33[1])
[I. FRUITFUL KARMA]

There are three conditions, O priests, under which deeds are produced. And what are the three? Covetousness is a condition under which deeds are produced; hatred is a condition under which deeds are produced; infatuation is a condition under which deeds are produced.

When a man's deeds, O priests, are performed through covetousness, arise from covetousness, are occasioned by covetousness, originate in covetousness, wherever his personality may be, there those ripen, and wherever they ripen, there he experiences the fruition of those deeds, be it in the present life, or in some subsequent one.

When a man's deeds, O priests, are performed through hatred, . . . are performed through infatuation, arise from infatuation, are occasioned by infatuation, originate in infatuation, wherever his personality may be, there those deeds ripen, and wherever they ripen, there he experiences the fruition of those deeds, be it in the present life, or in some subsequent one.

It is like seed, O priests, that is uninjured, undecayed, unharmed by wind or heat, and is sound, and advantageously sown in a fertile field on well-prepared soil; if then rain

317

falls in due season, then, O priests, will that seed attain to growth, increase, and development. In exactly the same way, O priests, when a man's deeds are performed through covetousness, arise from covetousness, are occasioned by covetousness, originate in covetousness, wherever his personality may be, there those deeds ripen, and wherever they ripen, there he experiences the fruition of those deeds, be it in the present life, or in some subsequent one; when a man's deeds are performed through hatred, . . . are performed through infatuation, arise from infatuation, are occasioned by infatuation, originate in infatuation, wherever his personality may be, there those deeds ripen, and wherever they ripen, there he experiences the fruition of those deeds, be it in the present life, or in some subsequent one.

These, O priests, are three conditions under which deeds are produced.

[II. Barren Karma]

There are three conditions, O priests, under which deeds are produced. And what are the three? Freedom from covetousness is a condition under which deeds are produced; freedom from hatred is a condition under which deeds are produced; freedom from infatuation is a condition under which deeds are produced.

When a man's deeds, O priests, are performed without covetousness, arise without covetousness, are occasioned without covetousness, originate without covetousness, then, inasmuch as covetousness is gone, those deeds are abandoned, uprooted, pulled out of the ground like a palmyra-tree, and become non-existent and not liable to spring up again in the future.

When a man's deeds, O priests, are performed without hatred, . . . are performed without infatuation, arise without infatuation, are occasioned without infatuation, originate without infatuation, then, inasmuch as infatuation is gone, those deeds are abandoned, uprooted, pulled out of the

318

ground like a palmyra-tree, and become non-existent and not liable to spring up again in the future.

It is like seed, O priests, that is uninjured, undecayed, unharmed by wind or heat, and is sound, and advantageously sown; if some one then burn it with fire and reduce it to soot, and having reduced it to soot were then to scatter it to the winds, or throw it into a swift-flowing river, then, O priests, will that seed be abandoned, uprooted, pulled out of the ground like a palmyra-tree, and become non-existent and not liable to spring up again in the future. In exactly the same way, O priests, when a man's deeds are performed without covetousness, arise without covetousness, are occasioned without covetousness, originate without covetousness, then, inasmuch as covetousness is gone, those deeds are abandoned, uprooted, pulled out of the ground like a palmyra-tree, and become non-existent and not liable to spring up again in the future; when a man's deeds are performed without hatred, . . . without infatuation, arise without infatuation, are occasioned without infatuation, originate without infatuation, then, inasmuch as infatuation is gone, those deeds are abandoned, uprooted, pulled out of the ground like a palmyra-tree, and become non-existent and not liable to spring up again in the future.

These, O priests, are the three conditions under which deeds are produced.

> A wise priest knows he now must reap
> The fruits of deeds of former births.
> For be they many or but few.
> Deeds done in covetousness or hate,
> Or through infatuation's power,
> Must bear their needful consequence.
> Hence not to covetousness, nor hate,
> Nor to infatuation's power
> The wise priest yields, but knowledge seeks
> And leaves the way to punishment.

"O priests, if any one says that a man must reap accord ing to his deeds, in that case, O priests, there is no religiou life, nor is any opportunity afforded for the entire extinctio of misery. But if any one says, O priests, that the reward man reaps accords with his deeds, in that case, O priest there is a religious life, and opportunity is afforded for th entire extinction of misery.

"We may have the case, O priests, of an individual wh does some slight deed of wickedness which brings him t hell, or, again, O priests, we may have the case of anothe individual who does the same slight deed of wickednes and expiates it in the present life, though it may be in way which appears to him not slight but grievous.

"What kind of individual, O priests, is he whose sligh deed of wickedness brings him to hell? — Whenever, (priests, an individual is not proficient in the managemer of his body, not proficient in the precepts, is not proficie in concentration, is not proficient in wisdom, and is limite and bounded, and abides in what is finite and evil: such a individual, O priests, is he whose slight deed of wickednes brings him to hell.

"What kind of individual, O priests, is he who does th same slight deed of wickedness, and expiates it in the preser life, though it may be in a way which appears to him n slight but grievous? — Whenever, O priests, an individual proficient in the management of his body, is proficient in th precepts, is proficient in concentration, is proficient in wis dom, and is not limited, nor bounded, and abides in the un versal: such an individual, O priests, is he who does th same slight deed of wickedness, and expiates it in the preser life, though it may be in a way which appears to him n slight but grievous.

"It is as if, O Priests, a man were to put a lump of sa into a small cup of water. What think ye, O priests? Woul now the river Ganges be made salt and undrinkable by th lump of salt."

"Yes, Reverend Sir."

"And why?"

"Because, Reverend Sir, there was but a small amount of water in the cup, and so it was made salt and undrinkable by the lump of salt."

"It is as if, O priests, a man were to throw a lump of salt into the river Ganges. What think ye, O priests? Would now the river Ganges be made salt and undrinkable by the lump of salt?"

"Nay, verily, Reverend Sir."

"And why not?"

"Because, Reverend Sir, the mass of water in the river Ganges is great, and so is not made salt and undrinkable by the lump of salt."

"In exactly the same way, O priests, we may have the case of an individual who does some slight deed of wickedness which brings him to hell; or, again, O priests, we may have the case of another individual who does the same slight deed of wickedness, and expiates it in the present life, though it may be in a way which appears to him not slight but grievous.

[Repetition of paragraphs 3 and 4, above.]

"We may have, O priests, the case of one who is cast into prison for a half-penny, for a penny, or for a hundred pence; or, again, O priests, we may have the case of one who is not cast into prison for a half-penny, for a penny, or for a hundred pence.

"Who, O priests, is cast into prison for a half-penny, for a penny, or for a hundred pence?

"Whenever, O priests, any one is poor, needy, and indigent: he, O priests, is cast into prison for a half-penny, for a penny, or for a hundred pence.

"Who, O priests, is not cast into prison for a half-penny, for a penny, or for a hundred pence?

Whenever, O priests, any one is rich, wealthy, and affluent: he, O priests, is not cast into prison for a half-penny, for a penny, or for a hundred pence.

"In exactly the same way, O priests, we may have the case of an individual who does some slight deed of wickedness which brings him to hell; or, again, O priests, we may have the case of another individual who does the same slight deed of wickedness, and expiates it in the present life, though it may be in a way which appears to him not slight but grievous.

[Repetition of paragraphs 3 and 4, above.]

"Just as, O priests, a butcher and killer of rams will smite one man if he steal a ram, and will bind another who steals a ram, he will not attack, nor bind him, nor burn him, nor wreak his pleasure on him.

"Who is he, O priests, whom a butcher and killer of rams will smite if he steal a ram, and will bind him, and burn him, and wreak his pleasure on him?

"Whenever, O priests, the robber is poor, needy, and indigent: him, O priests, a butcher and killer of rams will smite if he steal a ram, and will bind him, and burn him, and wreak his pleasure on him.

"Who is he, O priests, whom a butcher and killer of rams will not smite if he steal a ram, nor bind him, nor burn him, nor wreak his pleasure on him?

"Whenever, O priests, the robber is rich, wealthy, and affluent, a king, or king's minister: him, O priests, a butcher and killer of rams will not smite if he steal a ram, nor bind him, nor burn him, nor wreak his pleasure on him. On the contrary, he will stretch out his joined palms, and make supplication, saying, 'Sir, give me the ram, or the price of the ram.'

"In exactly the same way, O priests, we may have the case of an individual who does some slight deed of wickedness which brings him to hell; or again, O priests, we may have the case of another individual who does the same slight deed of wickedness, and expiates it in the present life,

322

though it may be in a way which appears to him not slight but grievous.

[Repetition of paragraphs 3 and 4, above.]

"O priests, if any one were to say that a man must reap according to his deed, in that case, O priests, there is no religious life, nor is any opportunity afforded for the entire extinction of misery, But if any one says, O priests, that the reward a man reap accords with his deeds, in that case, O priests, there is a religious life, and opportunity is afforded for the entire extinction of misery."

THE WAY OF PURITY
Translated from the Visuddhi-Magga (chap. I.)

Therefore has The Blessed One said:
"What man his conduct guardeth, and hath wisdom,
And thoughts and wisdom traineth well,
The strenuous and the able priest,
He disentangles all this snarl."

When it is said *hath wisdom*, there is meant a wisdom for which he does not need to strive. For it comes to him through the power of his deeds in a former existence.

The strenuous and the able priest. Perseveringly by means of the above-mentioned heroism, and intelligently through the force of his wisdom, should he *guard* his *conduct*, and *train* himself in the quiescence and insight indicated by the words *thoughts* and *wisdom*.

Thus does The Blessed One reveal the Way of Purity under the heads of conduct, concentration, and wisdom. Thus does he indicate the three disciplines, a thrice noble religion, the advent of the threefold knowledge, etc., the avoidance of the two extremes and the adoption of the middle course of conduct, the means of escape from the lower and other states of existence, the threefold abandonment of the corruptions, the three hostilities, the purification from the three corruptions, and the attainment of conversion and of the other degrees of sanctification.

And how?

By conduct is indicated the discipline in elevated conduct; by concentration, the discipline in elevated thoughts; and by wisdom, the discipline in elevated wisdom.

By conduct, again, is indicated the nobleness of this religion in its beginning. The fact that conduct is the beginning of this religion appears from the passage, "What is the first of the meritorious qualities? Purity of conduct." And again from that other, which begins by saying, "It is the non-performance of any wickedness." And it is noble because it entails no remorse or other like evils.

By concentration is indicated its nobleness in the middle. The fact that concentration is the middle of this religion appears from the passage which begins by saying, "It is richness in merit." It is noble because it brings one into the possession of the magical powers and other blessings.

By wisdom is indicated its nobleness at the end. The fact that wisdom is the end of this religion appears from the passage,

"To cleanse and purify the thoughts,
'T is this the holy Buddhas teach,"

and from the fact that there is nothing higher than wisdom. It is noble because it brings about imperturbability whether in respect of things pleasant or unpleasant. As it is said:

"Even as the dense and solid rock
Cannot be stirred by wind and storm;
Even so the wise cannot be moved
By voice of blame or voice of praise."

By conduct, again, is indicated the abandonment of the knowledge. For by virtuous conduct one acquires the threefold knowledge, but gets no further. By concentration is indicated the advent of the Six High Powers. For by concentration one acquires the Six High Powers, but gets no further. By wisdom is indicated the advent of the four analytical sciences. For by wisdom one acquires the four analytical sciences, and in no other way.

By conduct, again, is indicated the avoidance of the extreme called sensual gratification; by concentration, the avoidance of the extreme called self-torture. By wisdom is indicated the adoption of the middle course of conduct.

By conduct, again, is indicated the means of escape from the lower states of existence; by concentration, the means of escape from the realm of sensual pleasure; by wisdom, the means of escape from every form of existence.

By conduct, again, is indicated the abandonment of the corruptions through the cultivation of their opposing virtues; by concentration, the abandonment of the corruptions through their avoidance; by wisdom, the abandonment of the corruptions through their extirpation.

By conduct, again, is indicated the hostility to corrupt acts; by concentration, the hostility to corrupt feelings; by wisdom, the hostility to corrupt propensities.

By conduct, again, is indicated the purification from the corruption of bad practices; by concentration, the purification from the corruption of desire; by wisdom, the purification from the corruption of heresy.

And by conduct, again, is indicated the attainment of conversion, and of once returning; by concentration, the attainment of never returning; by wisdom, the attainment of saintship. For the converted are described as "Perfect in the precepts," as likewise the once returning; but the never returning as "Perfect in concentration," and the saint as "Perfect in wisdom."

Thus are indicated the three disciplines, a thrice noble religion, the advent of the threefold knowledge, etc., the avoidance of the two extremes and the adoption of the middle course of conduct, the means of escape from the lower and other states of existence, the threefold abandonment of the corruptions, the three hostilities, the purification from the three corruptions, and the attainment of conversion and of the other degrees of sanctification; and not only these nine triplets, but also similar ones.

Now although this *Way of Purity* was thus taught under the heads of conduct, concentration, and wisdom, and of the many good qualities comprised in them, yet this with excessive conciseness; and as, consequently, many would fail to be benefited, we here give its exposition in detail.

CONCENTRATION

1. Translated from the Visuddhi-Magga (chap. III.)

What is concentration? Concentration is manifold and various, and an answer which attempted to be exhaustive would both fail of its purpose and tend to still greater confusion. Therefore we will confine ourselves to the meaning here intended, and say — Concentration is an intentness of meritorious thoughts.

2. Translated from the Añguttara-Nikāya (III. 88)

And what, O priests, is the discipline in elevated concentration?

Whenever, O priests, a priest, having isolated himself from sensual pleasures, having isolated himself from demeritorious traits, and still exercising reasoning, still exercising reflection, enters upon the first trance, which is produced by isolation and characterized by joy and happiness; when, through the subsidence of reasoning and reflection, and still retaining joy and happiness, he enters upon the second trance, which is an interior tranquilization and intentness of thoughts, and is produced by concentration; when, through the paling of joy, indifferent, contemplative, conscious, and in the experience of bodily happiness — that state which eminent men describe when they say, "Indifferent, contemplative, and living happily" — he enters upon the third trance; when through the abandonment of happiness, through the abandonment of misery, through the disappearance of all antecedent gladness and grief, he enters upon the fourth trance, which has neither misery nor happiness, but is

326

contemplation as refined by indifference, this, O priests, is called the discipline in elevated concentration.

3. Translated from the Aṅgutara-Nikāya (II. 3¹⁰)

What advantage, O priests, is gained by training in quiescence? The thoughts are trained. And what advantage is gained by the training of the thoughts? Passion is abandoned.

Ko Hung

KO HUNG (*c.* 268-334 A.D.). Yang Hsiung divested Confucianism of the whimsical interpretations contributed to it under the influence of Yin Yang philosophy and opened the way for its fusion with Tâoism. The amalgamation of Confucianism and Tâoism was facilitated by the confusion and suffering resulting from wars waged among the Six Dynasties during the Wei (220-265) and Chin (265-419) eras. Hsiang Hsiu (221-300) and Kuo Hsiang (d. 312) were the important philosophers of the rationalist wing of Neo-Tâoism. The other subschool of Neo-Tâoism, sometimes referred to as the Sentimentalists, was represented by men like Chih-tun (314-366) and Wang Hui-chih (died *c.* 388). Both groups stressed the precept that life has to be lived according to one's internal nature, but the Rationalists identified internal nature with reason while the Sentimentalists interpreted it as a kind of impulse.

Ko Hung, also called Pao-p'u Tzŭ ("the philosopher who embraces simplicity"), mingled Taoist philosophy and Confucian ethics. His stress on alchemy, particularly internal alchemy, raised the practice of breath control, diet, meditation, etc. to a prominent position in Tâoism. Ko Hung and his predecessor Wei Po-yang provided Tâoism with a theoretical foundation and an elaborate system of practice. Later, in the fifth century, K'ou Ch'ien-chih established the rituals and codes of the cult, its deities, and its theology. Tâoism became the state religion in 440 A.D., while Buddhism was still being persecuted.

The Philosopher Who
Embraces Simplicity

THE BELIEF IN IMMORTALS

From *Sources of Chinese Tradition*, Volume I, edited by William Theodore de Bary, New York, Columbia University Press, 1960.

[From *Pao-p'u Tzŭ*, 2:1a-4a; 12a]

SOMEONE asked: Is it really possible that spiritual beings and immortals (*hsien*) do not die?

Pao-p'u Tzŭ said: Even if we had the greatest power of vision, we could not see all the things that have corporeal form. Even if we were endowed with the sharpest sense of hearing, we could not hear all the sounds there are. Even if we had the feet of Ta-chang and Hsu-hai [expert runners], what we had already trod upon would not be so much as what we have not. And even if we had the knowledge of [the sages] Yü, I, and Ch'i-hsieh, what we know would not be so much as what we do not know. The myriad things flourish. What is there that could not exist? Why not the immortals, whose accounts fill the historical records? Why should there not be a way to immortality?

Thereupon the questioner laughed heartily and said: Whatever has a beginning necessarily has an end, and whatever lives must eventually die. . . . I have only heard that some plants dry up and wither before frost, fade in color during the summer, bud but do not flower, or wither and are stripped of leaves before bearing fruit. But I never heard of anyone who enjoys a life span of ten thousand years.

and an everlasting existence without end. Therefore people of antiquity did not aspire to be immortals in their pursuit of knowledge, and did not talk of strange things in their conversation. They cast aside perverse doctrines and adhered to what is natural. They set aside the tortoise and the crane [symbols of immortality] as creatures of a different species, and looked upon life and death as morning and evening. . . .

Pao-p'u Tzŭ answered: . . . Life and death, beginning and end, are indeed the great laws of the universe. Yet the similarities and differences of things are not uniform. Some are this way and some are that. Tens of thousands of varieties are in constant change and transformation, strange and without any definite pattern. Whether things are this way or that, and whether they are regular or irregular in their essential and subsidiary aspects, cannot be reduced to uniformity. There are many who say that whatever has a beginning must have an end. But is it not in accord with the principle [of existence] to muddle things together and try to make them all the same. People say that things are bound to grow in the summer, and yet the shepherd's-purse and the water chestnut wilt. People say that plants are bound to wither in the winter, and yet the bamboo and the cypress flourish. People say whatever has a beginning will have an end, and yet Heaven and earth are unending. People say whatever is born will die, and yet the tortoise and the crane live forever. When the yang is at its height, it should be hot, and yet the summer is not without cool days. When the yin reaches its limit, it should be cold, and yet even a severe winter is not without brief warm periods. . . .

Among creatures none surpasses man in intelligence. As creatures of such superior nature, men should be equal and uniform. And yet they differ in being virtuous or stupid, in being perverse or upright, in being fair or ugly, tall or short, pure or impure, chaste or lewd, patient or impatient, slow or quick. What they pursue or avoid in their interests and what their eyes and ears desire are as different as Heaven and

331

earth, and as incompatible as ice and coals. Why should you only wonder at the fact that immortals are different and do not die like ordinary people? . . . But people with superficial knowledge are bound by what is ordinary and adhere to what is common. They all say that immortals are not seen in the world, and therefore they say forthwith that there cannot be immortals. [2:1a-4a]

Among men some are wise and some are stupid, but they all know that in their bodies they have a heavenly component (*hun*) and an earthly component (*p'o*) of the soul. If these are partly gone, man becomes sick. If they are completely gone, man dies. If they are partially separated from the body, the occult expert has means to retain and restrict them. If they are entirely separated, there are principles in the established rites to recall them. These components of the soul as entities are extremely close to us. And yet although we are born with them and live with them throughout life, we never see or hear them. Should one say that they do not exist simply because we have not seen or heard them? [2:12a]

ALCHEMY

[From *Pao-p'u Tzǔ*, 2:3b-4a; 3:1a, 5a; 4:1a-3a; 6:4a]

The immortals nourish their bodies with drugs and prolong their lives with the application of occult science, so that internal illness shall not arise and external ailment shall not enter. Although they enjoy everlasting existence and do not die, their old bodies do not change. If one knows the way to immortality, it is not to be considered so difficult. [2:3b-4a]

Among the creatures of nature, man is the most intelligent. Therefore those who understand [creation] slightly can employ the myriad things, and those who get to its depth can enjoy [what is called in the *Lao Tzǔ*] "long life and everlasting existence" [Ch. 59]. As we know that the best medicine can prolong life, let us take it to obtain immortality, and as we know that the tortoise and the crane have longevity, let us imitate their activities to increase our span of life. . . . Those who have obtained Tâo are able to lift themselves into the clouds and the heavens above and to dive and swim in the rivers and seas below. [3:1a, 5a]

Pao-p'u Tzŭ said: I have investigated and read books on the nourishment of human nature and collected formulas for everlasting existence. Those I have perused number thousands of volumes. They all consider reconverted cinnabar [after it has been turned into mercury] and gold fluid to be the most important. Thus these two things represent the acme of the way to immortality. . . . The transformations of the two substances are the more wonderful the more they are heated. Yellow gold does not disintegrate even after having been smelted a hundred times in fire, and does not rot even if buried in the ground until the end of the world. If these two medicines are eaten, they will strengthen our bodies and therefore enable us not to grow old nor to die. This is of course seeking assistance from external substances to strengthen ourselves. It is like feeding fat to the lamp so it will not die out. If we smear copperas on our feet, they will not deteriorate even if they remain in water. This is to borrow the strength of the copper to protect our flesh. Gold fluid and reconverted cinnabar, however, upon entering our body, permeate our whole system of blood and energy and are not like copperas which helps only on the outside. [4:1a-3a]

It is hoped that those who nourish life will learn extensively and comprehend the essential, gather whatever there is to see and choose the best. It is not sufficient to depend on cultivating only one thing. It is also dangerous for people who love life to rely on their own specialty. Those who know the techniques of the *Classic of the Mysterious Lady* and the *Classic of the Plain Lady* [books on sexual regimen no longer extant] will say that only the "art of the chamber" will lead to salvation. Those who understand the method of breathing exercises will say that only the permeation of the vital power can prolong life. Those who know the method of stretching and bending will say that only physical exercise can prevent old age. And those who know the formulas of herbs will say that only medicine will make life unending. They fail in their pursuit of Tâo because they are so one-sided. People of superficial knowledge think they have enough when they happen to know of only one way and do not realize that the true seeker will search unceasingly even after he has acquired some good formulas. [6:4a]

THE MERIT SYSTEM
[From *Pao-P'u Tzŭ*, 3:7b-10b; 6:5b-7a]

Furthermore, as Heaven and Earth are the greatest of things, it is natural, from the point of view of universal principles, that they have spiritual power. Having spiritual power it is proper that they reward good and punish evil. Nevertheless their expanse is great and their net is widemeshed.[1] There is not necessarily an immediate response [result] as soon as this net is set in operation. As we glance over the Tâoist books of discipline, however, all are unanimous in saying that those who seek immortality must set their minds to the accumulation of merits and the accomplishment of good work. Their hearts must be kind to all things. They must treat others as they treat themselves, and extend their humaneness (*jen*) even to insects. They must rejoice in the fortune of men and pity their suffering, relieve the destitute and save the poor. Their hands must never injure life, and their mouths must never encourage evil. They must consider the success and failure of others as their own. They must not regard themselves highly, nor praise themselves. They must not envy those superior to them, nor flatter dangerous and evil-minded people. In this way they may become virtuous and blessed by Heaven; they may be successful in whatever they do, and may hope to become immortal.

1. The net of Heaven which eventually catches all evildoers in its meshes, a very old concept in Chinese thought.

If, on the other hand, they hate good and love evil; if their words do not agree with their thoughts; if they say one thing in people's presence and the opposite behind their backs; if they twist the truth; if they are cruel to subordinates or deceive their superiors; if they betray their task and are ungrateful for kindness received; if they manipulate the law and accept bribes; if they tolerate injustice but suppress justice; if they destroy the public good for their selfish ends; if they punish the innocent, wreck people's homes, pocket their treasures, injure their bodies, or seize their positions; if they overthrow virtuous rulers or massacre those who have surrendered to them; if they slander saints and sages or hurt Tâoist priests; if they shoot birds in flight or kill the unborn in womb or egg; if in spring or summer hunts they burn the forests or drive out the game; if they curse spiritual beings; if they teach others to do evil or conceal their good deeds or endanger others for their own security; if they claim the work of others as their own; if they spoil people's happy affairs or take away what others love; if they cause division in people's families or disgrace others in order to win; if they overcharge or underpay; if they set fire or inundate; if they injure people with trickery or coerce the weak; if they repay good with evil; if they take things by force or accumulate wealth through robbery and plunder; if they are unfair or unjust, licentious, indulgent, or perverted; if they oppress orphans or mistreat widows; if they squander inheritance and accept charity; if they cheat or deceive; if they love to gossip about people's private affairs or criticize them for their defects; if they drag Heaven and Earth into their affairs and rail at people in order to seek vindication; if they fail to repay debts or play fair in the exchange of goods; if they seek to gratify their desires without end; if they hate and resist the faithful and sincere; if they disobey orders from above or do not respect their teachers; if they ridicule others for doing good; if they destroy people's crops or harm their tools so as to nullify their utility, and do not feed people with clean food; if they

cheat in weights or measures; if they mix spurious article
with genuine; if they take dishonorable advantage; if the
tempt others to steal; if they meddle in the affairs of othei
or go beyond their position in life; if they leap over wells o
hearths [which provide water and fire for food]; if they sin
in the last day of the month [when the end should be sen
off with sorrow] or cry in the first day of the month [whe:
the beginning should be welcomed with joy]; if they com
mit any of these evil deeds; it is a sin.

The Arbiter of Human Destiny will reduce their terms c
life by units of three days or three hundred days in proportio
to the gravity of the evil. When all days are deducted the
will die. Those who have the intention to do evil but hav
not carried it out will have three-day units taken just as i
they had acted with injury to others. If they die before a
their evil deeds are punished, their posterity will suffer fc
them. [6:5b-7a]

Someone asked: Is it true he who cultivates the way [t
become an immortal] should first accomplish good deeds

Pao-p'u Tzŭ answered: Yes, it is true. The middle sectio
of the *Yu-ch'ien ching* says: "The most important thing is t
accomplish good works. The next is the removal of fault
For him who cultivates the way, the highest accomplishmer
of good work is to save people from danger so they ma
escape from calamity, and to preserve people from sicknes
so that they may not die unjustly. Those who aspire to b
immortals should regard loyalty, filial piety, harmony, obe
dience, love, and good faith as their essential principles c
conduct. If they do not cultivate moral conduct but merel
devote themselves to occult science, they will never attai
everlasting life. If they do evil, the Arbiter of Human Destin
will take off units of three hundred days from their allotte
life if the evil is great, or units of three days if the evil
small. Since [the punishment] depends on the degree of evi
the reduction in the span of life is in some cases great and i
others small. When a man is endowed with life and give
a life span, he has his own definite number of days. If h

number is large, the units of three hundred days and of three days are not easily exhausted and therefore he dies later. On the other hand, if one's allotted number is small and offences are many, then the units are soon exhausted and he dies early."

The book also says: "Those who aspire to be terrestrial immortals should accomplish three hundred good deeds and those who aspire to be celestial immortals should accomplish 1,200. If the 1,199th good deed is followed by an evil one, they will lose all their accumulation and have to start all over. It does not matter whether the good deeds are great or the evil deed is small. Even if they do no evil but talk about their good deeds and demand reward for their charities, they will nullify the goodness of these deeds although the other good deeds are not affected." The book further says: "If good deeds are not sufficiently accumulated, taking the elixir of immortality will be of no help." [3:7b-8a, 10a-b]

TÁOISM IN RELATION TO OTHER SCHOOLS
[From *Pao-p'u Tzŭ*, 10:1a-b; 12: 1a-b]

Someone said: If it were certain that one could become an immortal, the sages would have trained themselves to be such. But neither Duke Chou nor Confucius did so. It is clear that there is no such possibility.

Pao-p'u Tzŭ answered: A sage need not be an immortal and an immortal need not be a sage. The sage receives a mandate [from Heaven], not to attend to the way of everlasting life, but to remove tyrants and eliminate robbers, to turn danger into security and violence into peace, to institute ceremonies and create musical systems, to propagate laws and give education, to correct improper manners and reform degenerate customs, to assist rulers who are in danger of downfall and to support those states that are about to collapse. . . . What the ordinary people call sages are all sages who regulate the world but not sages who attain Táo. The

Yellow Emperor and Lao Tzŭ were sages who attained Tâo, while Duke Chou and Confucius were sages who regulated the world [12:1a-b]

Someone asked: Which is first and which is last, Confucianism or Tâoism?

Pao-p'u Tzŭ answered: Tâoism is the essence of Confucianism and Confucianism is an appendage to Tâoism. First of all[1] there was the "teaching of the yin-yang school which had many taboos that made people constrained and afraid." "The Confucianists had extensive learning but little that was essential; they worked hard but achieved little." "Mo-ism emphasized thrift but was difficult to follow," and could not be practiced exclusively. "The Legalists were severe and showed little kindness"; they destroyed humanity and righteousness. "The teachings of the Taoist school alone enable men's spirits to be concentrated and united and their action to be in harmony with the formless. . . . Tâoism embraces the good points of both Confucianism and Mo-ism and combines the essentials of the Legalists and Logicians. It changes with the times and responds to the transformations of things. . . . Its precepts are simple and easy to understand; its works are few but its achievements many." It is devoted to the simplicity that preserves the Great Heritage and adheres to the true and correct source. [10:1a-b]

1. Most of the following is quoted from the essay on the six philosophical schools by the Han historian Ssu-ma T'an (d. 110 B.C.).

Kuo Hsiang

KUO HSIANG (d. 312 A.D.). A revival of Tâoism occurred during the "Period of Disunity" (220-620) that followed Wang Ch'ung. Neo-Tâoism took the form of a revolt against static Confucian morals. For Hsiang Hsiu (*c.* 221-300) "taking no action" meant "embracing the Tâo, cherishing simplicity, and giving free scope to the inevitable." The Perfect Man is responsive to the outside world but is not "ensnared by things." In practical agreement with Hsiang Hsiu was his contemporary, Kuo Hsiang, who collaborated with him in writing a commentary on the *Chuang Tzŭ*.

Kuo Hsiang emphasized the Tâoist principles of spontaneous self-transformation, harmony, interdependence of all things, and the necessity of responding positively to the universal flux. By shifting Tâoism's stress on the contemplative, solitary life to a positive concern for the realm of human affairs. he and his collaborator brought Neo-Tâoism closer to the orthodox Confucian position. Like other Neo-Tâoists who admired the *Lao Tzŭ* and *Chuang Tzŭ*, his aim was to give new meaning to Confucian texts. In their commentaries men like Hsiang Hsiu, Kuo Hsiang, Wang Pi (226-249), and Ho Yen (d. 249 A.D.) used Tâoist terms and concepts, reinterpreting them in the context of the moral and social philosophy of Confucianism. Kuo Hsiang's central themes — in his commentary on the *Chuang Tzŭ*, based on the notes of Hsiang Hsiu — are self-transformation and contentment, with equal emphasis on the inner and the outer life.

Commentary on the Chuang Tzǔ

From *Sources of Chinese Tradition*, Volume I, edited by William Theodore de Bary, New York, Columbia University Press, 1960.

NATURE AND NONEXISTENCE

[From Commentary on *Chuang Tzǔ*, Sec. 1, 1:8b; Sec. 2, 1:21a-23a; Sec. 22, 7:54b-55b]

THE music of nature is not an entity existing outside of things. The different apertures, the pipes and flutes and the like, in combination with all living beings, together constitute nature. Since nonexistence is nonbeing, it cannot produce being. Before being itself is produced, it cannot produce other beings. Then by whom are things produced? They spontaneously produce themselves, that is all. By this is not meant that there is an "I" to produce. The "I" cannot produce things and things cannot produce the "I." The "I" is self-existent. Because it is so by itself, we call it natural. Everything is what it is by nature, not through taking any action. Therefore [Chuang Tzǔ] speaks in terms of nature. The term nature [literally Heaven] is used to explain that things are what they are spontaneously, and not to mean the blue sky. But someone says that the music of nature makes all things serve or obey it. Now, nature cannot even possess itself. How can it possess things? Nature is the general name for all things. [Sec. 2, 1:21a]

Not only is it impossible for nonbeing to be changed into being. It is also impossible for being to become nonbeing. Therefore, although being as a substance undergoes infinite changes and transformations, it cannot in any instance become nonbeing. . . . What came into existence before there were things? If I say yin and yang came first, then since yin and yang are themselves entities, what came before them? Suppose I say nature came first. But nature is only things being themselves. Suppose I say perfect Tâo came first. But perfect Tâo is perfect nonbeing. Since it is nonbeing, how can it come before anything else? Then what came before it? There must be another thing, and so on *ad infinitum*. We must understand that things are what they are spontaneously and not caused by something else. [Sec. 22, 7:54b-55b]

Everything is natural and does not know why it is so. The more things differ in corporeal form, the more they are alike in being natural. . . . Heaven and earth and the myriad things change and transform into something new every day and so proceed with time. What causes them? They do so spontaneously. . . . What we call things are all that they are by themselves; they did not cause each other to become so. Let us leave them alone and the principle of being will be perfectly realized. The ten thousand things are in ten thousand different conditions, and move forward and backward differently, as though there were a True Lord to make them so. But if we search for evidences for such a True Lord, we fail to find any. We should understand that things are all natural and not caused by something else. [Sec. 2, 1:22b-23a]

The universe is the general name for all things. They are the reality of the universe while nature is their norm. Being natural means to exist spontaneously without having to take any action. Therefore the fabulous *p'eng* bird can soar high and the quail can fly low, the cedrela can live for a long time and the mushroom for a short time. They are capable of doing these not because of their taking any action but because of their being natural. [Sec. 1, 1:8b]

341

If we insist on the conditions under which things develop and search for the cause thereof, such search and insistence will never end, until we come to something that is unconditioned, and then principles of self transformation will become clear. . . . There are people who say that the penumbra is conditioned by the shadow, the shadow by the body, and the body by the Creator. But let us ask whether there is a Creator or not. If not, how can he create things? If there is, he is incapable of materializing all the forms. Therefore we can talk about creation, we must understand the fact that all forms materialize by themselves. If we go through the entire realm of existence, we shall see that there is nothing, not even the penumbra, that does not transform itself beyond the phenomenal world. Hence everything creates itself without the direction of any Creator. Since things create themselves, they are unconditioned. This is the norm of the universe. [Sec. 2, 2:46b-47a]

In the cutting of a tree the workman does not take any action; the only action he takes is in plying the ax. In the actual managing of affairs, the ruler does not take any action; the only action he takes is in employing his ministers. If the ministers can manage affairs, the ruler can employ ministers, the ax can cut the tree, and the workman can use the ax, each corresponding to his capacity, then the laws of nature will operate of themselves, not because someone takes action. If the ruler does the work of his ministers, he will no longer be the ruler, and if the ministers control the ruler's employment, they will no longer be ministers. Therefore when each attends to his own responsibility, both ruler and ruled will be contented and the principle of taking no action will be attained. [Sec. 13, 5:25a-b]

It is he who does no governing who can govern the empire. Therefore Yao governed by not governing; it was not because of his governing that his empire was governed. Now [the recluse] Hsü-yu only realized that since the empire was well-governed he should not replace Yao. He thought it was Yao who did the actual governing. Consequently he said to Yao: "You govern the empire." He should have forgotten such words and investigated into that condition of peace. Someone may say: "It was Yao who actually governed and put the empire in good order but it was Hsü-yu who enabled Yao to do so by refusing to govern himself." This is a great mistake. Yao was an adequate example of governing by not governing and acting by not acting. Why should we have to resort to Hsü-yu? Are we to insist that a man fold his arms and sit in silence in the middle of some mountain forest before we will say he is practicing "nonaction"? This is why the words of Lao Tzŭ and Chuang Tzŭ are rejected by responsible officials. This is why responsible officials insist on remaining in the realm of action without feeling any regret. [Sec. 1, 1:9b-10a]

By taking no action is not meant folding one's arms and closing one's mouth. If we simply let everything act by itself, it will be contented with its nature and destiny. To have no alternative but [to rule an empire] is not to be forced into doing so by power or punishment. If only Tâo is embraced and simplicity cherished, and what has to be is allowed to run its maximum course, then the world will naturally be contented with itself. [Sec. 11, 4:29a]

CONTENTMENT

[From Commentary on *Chuang Tzŭ*, Sec. 1, 1:14a Sec. 3, 2:1a-6b; Sec. 4, 3:28a; Sec. 9, 4:11b]

If a person is perfectly at ease with his spirit and physical power, whether he lifts something heavy or carries something light, it is due to the fact that he is using strength to a desired degree. If a person loves fame and is fond of supremacy and is not satisfied even when he has broken his

343

back in the attempt, it is due to the fact that human knowledge knows no limit. Therefore what is called knowledge is born of our losing our balance and will be eliminated when ultimate capacity is realized intuitively. Intuitively realizing ultimate capacity means allowing one's lot to reach its highest degree, and [in the case of lifting weights] not adding so much as an ounce beyond that. Therefore though a person carries ten thousand pounds, if it is equal to his capacity he will suddenly forget the weight upon his body. Though a person attends to ten thousand matters [if his capacity is equal to them] he will be utterly unaware that the affairs are upon him. These are the fundamentals for the cultivation of life. . . . If one attains the Mean and intuitively realizes the proper limit, everything can be done. The cultivation of life does not seek to exceed one's lot but to preserve the principle of things and to live out one's allotted span of life. [Sec. 3, 2:1a-2a]

Joy and sorrow are the results of gains and losses. A gentleman who profoundly penetrates all things and is in harmony with their transformations will be contented with whatever time may bring. He follows the course of nature in whatever situation he may be. He will be intuitively united with creation. He will be himself wherever he may be. Where does gain or loss, life or death, come in? Therefore, if one lets what he has received from nature take its own course, there will be no place for joy or sorrow. [Sec. 3, 2:6a-b]

Allow the foot to walk according to its capacity, and let the hand grasp according to its strength. Listen to what the ear hears and see what the eye sees. In knowing, stop at what cannot be known. In action, stop at what cannot be done. Employ [the faculties] as they would use themselves. Do things that would be done by themselves. Be unrestrained within one's lot but do not attempt the least outside of it. This is the easiest way of taking no [unnatural] action. There has never been a case of taking no action and yet of one's nature and life not being preserved, and I have never

344

heard of any principle according to which the preservation of nature and life is not a blessing. [Sec. 4, 3:28a]

The expert driver utilizes the natural capacity of horses to its limit. To use the capacity to its limit lies in letting it take its own course. If forced to run at a rapid pace, with the expectation that they can exceed their capacity, horses will be unable to bear it and many will die. On the other hand, if both worn-out and thoroughbred horses are allowed to use their proper strength and to adapt their pace to their given lot, even if they travel to the borders of the country, their nature will be fully preserved. But there are those who, upon hearing the doctrine of allowing the nature of horses to take its own course, will say: "Then set the horses free and do not ride on them"; and there are those who, upon hearing the doctrine of taking no action, will immediately say: "It is better to lie down than to walk." Why are so much off the track and unable to return? In this they have missed Chuang Tzǔ's ideas to a very high degree. [Sec. 9, 4:11b]

If one is contented wherever he goes, he will be at ease wherever he may be. Even life and death cannot affect him, much less flood or fire. The perfect man is not besieged by calamities, not because he escapes from them but because he advances the principles of things and goes forward and naturally comes into union with good fortune. [Sec. 1, 1:14a]

SOCIETY AND GOVERNMENT

[From Commentary on *Chuang Tzǔ*, Sec. 1, 1:11b, 14b; Sec. 4, 2:7a-25a; Sec. 6, 3:19a; Sec. 13, 5:35a; Sec. 14, 5:42a, 44b]

Man in society cannot get away from his fellow beings. The changes in society vary from generation to generation according to different standards. Only those who have no minds of their own and do not use their own judgment can adapt themselves to changes and not be burdened by them. [Sec. 4, 2:7a]

Events that took place in the past have disappeared with

345

the past. Some may be transmitted to us [in writing], but can this make the past exist in the present? The past is not in the present and even every present is soon changed. Therefore only when one abandons the pursuit of knowledge, lets nature take its own course, and changes with the times, can he be perfect. [Sec. 13, 5:35a]

Humanity and righteousness are principles of human nature. Human nature undergoes changes and is different past and present. If one takes a temporary abode in a thing and then moves on, he will intuit [the reality of things]. If, however, he stops and is confined to one place, he will develop prejudices. Prejudices will result in hypocrisy, and hypocrisy will result in many reproaches. [Sec. 14, 5:44b]

To cry as people cry is a manifestation of the mundane world. To identify life and death, forget joy and sorrow, and be able to sing in the presence of the corpse is the perfection of transcendental existence. . . . Therefore the principles of things have their ultimates, and internal and external reality are to be intuited by means of each other. There has never been a person who has roamed over the entire realm of external reality and yet has not intuited internal reality, nor has there been anyone who could intuit internal reality and yet did not roam over the realm of external reality. [Sec. 6, 3:19a]

Although the sage is in the midst of government, his mind seems to be in the mountain forest. . . . His abode is in the myriad things, but it does not mean that he does not wander freely. [Sec. 1, 11b, 14b]

When a thousand people gather together with no one as their leader, they will be either unruly or disorganized. Therefore when there are many virtuous people, there should not be many rulers, but when there is no virtuous person, there should be a ruler. This is the principle of Heaven and man and the most proper thing to do. [Sec. 4, 2:16b]

The ceremonies of ancient kings were intended to meet the needs of the time. When the time has past and the ceremonies are still not cast away, they will become an evil influence to the people and serve to hasten the start of affectations and imitation. [Sec. 14, 5:42a]

When the king does not make himself useful in the various offices, the various officials will manage their own affairs. Those with clear vision will do the seeing, those with sharp ears will do the listening, the wise will do the planning, and the strong will provide protection. What need is there to take any action? Only profound silence, that is all. [Sec. 4, 2:25a]

Hui-yüan

HUI-YÜAN (*c.* 334-416). By the fourth century A.D.,
many different Buddhist scriptures had been translated
into Chinese and assimilated by Tâoists and Confucianists
alike. Hui-yüan, a Tâoist monk of Shansi Province,
actively promoted a new religious philosophy based on
certain scriptures that extolled the power of Amitabha
to save all mortals. After he settled in the Lu-Feng
Monastery in Hupeh, noted for its ponds of white lotus
blossoms, he attracted many disciples. They conferred
on his school the name of "White Lotus Religion." Inspired by the teaching of Tâo-an, he stressed piety and
salvation by faith in the grace of Amitâbha, who has
the power to save all mortals in his glorious "Pure Land"
in the Western Quarter of the heavens. After death,
according to his doctrine, all faithful believers will be
transported over the sea of death and reborn in the Pure
Land of Bliss. Much later, in the fourteenth century, a
secret political society adopted the name of "White Lotus," causing Hui-yüan's followers to change their name
to Pure Land School.

The founder of the Pure Land School taught that
nirvana and the nature of dharmas (elements) are unchangeable, urged repetition of Buddha's name as an aid
to meditation, and stressed the indestructibility of the
spirit. The Ultimate, he said, is above life and death,
being and nonbeing.

The early Buddhist clerics in China knelt in their religious ceremonies but displayed no signs of respect to
laymen of authority. During the Eastern Chin period,
the practice was brought under discussion at court. No

settlement was reached, however, until Huan Shuan (369-404) referred the problem to Hui-yüan for decision. The latter replied, setting forth his views in a letter. The high minister accepted the argument that monks need not bow down before the emperor. Shortly thereafter Hui-yüan composed his treatise entitled "A Monk Does Not Bow Down Before a King."

A Monk Does Not Bow Down Before a King

From *Sources of Chinese Tradition*, Volume I, edited by William Theodore de Bary, New York, Columbia University Press, 1960.

BUDDHISM IN THE HOUSEHOLD

[From *Hung-ming chi*, in *Taishō daizōkyō*, LII, 29-32]

IF one examines the broad essentials of what the teachings of Buddha preach, one will see that they distinguish between those who leave the household life and those who remain in it. Those who remain within the household life and those who leave it are, in all, of four kinds. In propagating the doctrine and reaching the beings their achievement is equal to that of emperors and kings, their transfiguring effect greater than that of the way of government. When it comes to affecting members and enlightening the times, there is no age that is without them. But, as chance has it, they sometimes function and sometimes conceal themselves, retiring or making their appearance as the faith diminishes or prospers. What can be discussed in words I beg to state in brief.

Those who revere the Buddhist laws but remain in their homes are subjects who are obedient to the transforming powers [of temporal rulers]. Their feelings have not changed from the customary, and their course of conduct conforms to the secular world. Therefore this way of life includes the affection of natural kinship and the proprieties of obedience to authority. Decorum and reverence have their basis herein, and thus they form the basis of the doctrine. That on which they are based has its merit in the past. Thus, on the basis of intimacy it teaches love, and causes the people to appreciate natural kindness; on the basis of austerity it teaches veneration, and causes the people to understand natural respect. The achievement of these two effects derives from an invisible cause. Since the cause is not in the present, one must trace it to its source. Therefore the doctrine makes a punishment of sinful karma, causing one to be fearful and thus circumspect; it makes a reward of the heavenly palaces, causing one to be joyous and then to act. These are the retributions that follow like shadows and echoes, and that are clearly stated in the doctrine. Thus obedience is made the common rule, and the natural way is not changed. . . .

Hence one may not benefit by [the ruler's] virtue and neglect propriety, bask in his kindness and cast aside due respect. Therefore they who rejoice in the way of Shakya invariably first serve their parents and respect their lords. They who change their way of life and throw away their hair ornaments must always await [their parents'] command, then act accordingly. If their lords and parents have doubts, then they retire, inquire of their wishes and wait until [the lords and parents] are enlightened. This, then, is how the teaching of Buddha honors life-giving and assists kingly transformation in the way of government.

BUDDHISM OUTSIDE THE HOUSEHOLD

This second part sets forth the core of Hui-yüan's argument as to why the monk should not make a display of respect for worldly potentates. The monk, so the argument goes, is not a disrespectful, much less an impious, person, but he stands completely outside of the framework of lay life, hence he should not abide by its regulations insofar as merely polite accomplishments are concerned.

He who has left the household life is a lodger beyond the earthly [secular] world, and his ways are cut off from those of other beings. The doctrine by which he lives enables him to understand that woes and impediments come from having a body, and that by not maintaining the body one terminates woe. . . .

If the termination of woe does not depend on the maintenance of the body, then he does not treasure the benefits that foster life. This is something in which the principle runs counter to physical form and the Way is opposed to common practice. Such men as these commence the fulfillment of their vows with the putting away of ornaments of the head [shaving the head], and realize the achievement of their ideal with the changing of their garb. . . . Since they have changed their way of life, their garb and distinguishing marks cannot conform to the secular pattern. . . . Afar they reach to the ford of the Three Vehicles,[1] broadly they open up the Way of Heaven and man. If but one of them be allowed to fulfill his virtue, then the Way spreads to the six relations and beneficence flows out to the whole world. Although they do not occupy the positions of kings and princes, yet, fully in harmony with the imperial ultimate, they let the people be. Therefore, though inwardly they may run counter to the gravity of natural relationships, yet they do not violate filial piety; though outwardly they lack respect in serving the sovereign, yet they do not lose hold of reverence.

HE WHO SEEKS THE FIRST PRINCIPLE IS NOT OBEDIENT TO CHANGE

Question: If we examine Lao Tzǔ's meaning, we see that for him Heaven and earth are great because of their attainment of the One, kings and princes are honored because they embody obedience.[2] [Heaven and earth] have attained the

1. That is, postponing enlightenment in order to bring closer to salvation, attaining enlightenment by personal exertions in an age in which there is no Buddha, and attaining enlightenment by hearing the Buddha's preaching.
2. A reference to *Lao Tzǔ*, 39.

One, therefore they are the source of the myriad changes; [kings and princes] embody obedience, therefore they have the power of moving others [to obey]. Thus the clarification of the First Principle must of necessity reside in the embodiment of the Ultimate, and the embodiment of the Ultimate must of necessity depend upon obedience to change. Therefore the wise men of yore made this the subject of noble discourses, and from this the opinion of the multitude may not differ. If one differs with the opinion of the multitude, one's principles have nothing worth accepting. And yet you speak of not obeying change. Why?

Answer: In general, those who reside within the limits [of ordinary existence] receive life from the Great Change. Although the numerous varieties of things have a myriad of differences and subtle and gross are of different lineage, if one reduces them to their ultimate, there are only the soulful and the soulless. The soulful have a feeling toward change. The soulless have no feeling toward change. If there is no feeling toward change, when change ends, life is finished. Their life does not depend upon feeling. Therefore the form decays and change ceases. If there is feeling toward change, [the feeling being] reacts to things and moves. Motion must depend upon feeling, therefore the life does not cease. If the life does not cease, the change is ever more far reaching and the physical forms pile up more and more. The feelings are more of a handicap and the encumbrances more weighty. The woes are indescribable. Therefore the scriptures say that Nirvana is changeless, making the cessation of change its home, while the three worlds[1] are in flux, making sin and pain their place. When change is exhausted, then causes and conditions cease forever; when there is flux, then the suffering of pain has no limit. How can we prove that this is so? Life is fettered by physical form, and life depends upon change. When there is change

1. The world of desire, form and no form, a feature of Indian cosmology adopted by the Buddhists.

354

and the feelings react, then the spirit is barred from its source and the intellect is blinded to its own illumination. If one is thus shut up as in a hard shell, then what is preserved is only the self, and what is traversed is only the state of flux. Thereupon the bridle of the spirit loses its driver, and the road to rebirth is reopened daily. One pursues lust in the long stream of time; is one affected thus only once? Therefore he who returns to the source and seeks the First Principle does not encumber his spirit with life. He who breaks out of the grimy shell does not encumber his life with feelings. If one does not encumber one's spirit with life, then one's spirit can be made subtle. The subtle spirit transcending sense-objects — this is what is meant by Nirvana. The name Nirvāṇa, can it possibly be an empty appellation? I beg leave to extend this argument and so prove its truth. Heaven and earth, though they are great because they give life to living beings, cannot cause a living being not to die. Kings and princes, though they have the power of preserving existence, cannot cause a preserved creature to be without woe. Therefore in our previous discussion we have said, "[He who has left the household life] understands that woes and impediments come from having a body, and that by not maintaining the body one terminates woe. He knows that continued life comes from undergoing change, and by not obeying this change he seeks the First Principle." Herein lay our meaning, herein lay our meaning. This is why the monk refuses homage to the Lord of the Myriad Chariots [i.e., the emperor] and keeps his own works sublime, why he is not ranked with kings or princes and yet basks in their kindness.

WHEN THE PHYSICAL FORM IS EXHAUSTED THE SPIRIT DOES NOT PERISH

Early Buddhism in India, unlike the Upanishadic philosophy which asserted the identity of the individual soul with the world soul, denied the existence of the soul altogether.

Among the Chinese to whom Buddhism was first introduced, however, there was already a widespread belief in spirits. which strongly conditioned their understanding of the new faith. Upon them the Buddhist denial of the soul made less of an impression than other doctrines which seemed to confirm their own beliefs. In the first place, Buddhism preaches reincarnation, which to the Chinese seemed impossible without an individual soul. In the second place, those scriptures that preached the Storehouse of Consciousness and the presence of Buddhahood in all living beings seemed to be speaking of a soul in different language. But basically it seems to have been a belief already strongly held in the immortality of the soul that inclined the Chinese to interpret Buddhism in this fashion and to ignore the many denials of the soul in the canonical texts. Hui-yüan was one of the learned monks influenced by this belief, and no doubt it was shared by many lesser clerics.

Within the Chinese intellectual tradition, however, there were some who took an opposing view, including Confucian rationalists and naturalistic Tâoists. Thus, while deeply attached to the custom of ancestor worship as a family rite, the Confucianists tended to deny the survival of the individual soul after the death of the body. From another point of view Chuang Tzŭ accepted death as a natural and welcome release from life, there being for him no further problem of continued reincarnation or a need to escape it. It is on this basis that Hui-Yüan's fictitious opponent in this final dialogue challenges the Buddhist doctrine of karma and transmigration.

Question: . . . The receipt of spirit is limited to one life. When the life is exhausted, the breath evaporates, and it is the same as nothing. The spirit, though it is more subtle than matter, is still a transformed manifestation of the yin and the yang. When they have been transformed there is life; when they are transformed again there is death. When they come together there is a beginning; when they disperse there is an end. If one reasons from this, one must know that the spirit and the body are transformed together, and that originally they are of the same line. The subtle and the gross are one breath, and from beginning to end they have the same abode. While the abode is whole, the breath comes together and there is a spirit; when the abode crumbles, the breath disperses and the light goes out. When it disperses, it returns what it has received to the Great Origin. When it has perished, it returns to a state of nothingness. Return and termination are natural destinies. Who could create them? . . . Also, the spirit resides in the body as fire is in the wood. While [the body] lives [the spirit] exists, but when [the body] crumbles [the spirit] must perish. When the body departs the soul disperses and has no dwelling. When the tree rots the fire dies out and has nothing to attach to. That is the principle. Even if the matter of sameness and difference were obscure and difficult to clarify, the doctrine of being and nonbeing must rest in coming together and dispersion. Coming together and dispersion is the general term for the change of the breath; it is the birth-and-death of the myriad changes.

[In his reply Hui-yüan explains the principle of reincarnation in terms of individual lives or destinies. The key Chinese word here is *shu*, literally "number," which refers to the individual life-span or allotted destiny. At the same time, however, it has Buddhist overtones suggesting the process of multiple causation (karma) which determines the individual lot in life, and thus, in its most general sense, the world of multiplicity subject to endless change and transmigration.]

Answer: What is the spirit? It is subtlety that has reached the extreme and become immaterial. The extreme of subtlety cannot be charted by the trigrams and explanations [of the *Book of Changes*]. Therefore the sage calls it "more subtle than matter" and so names it. . . .

The spirit is in perfect accord and has no creator; it is subtle to the extreme and has no name. In response to beings it moves; borrowing an individual lot [i.e, the life of an individual person] it acts. It responds to things but is not a thing; therefore though the things may change it does not perish. It borrows a lot [in life] but it is not itself that lot; therefore though the lot be run out, it does not end. Having feelings, it can respond to things; having intelligence, it can be found [embodied] in allotted destinies. There are subtle and gross destinies and therefore the nature of each is different. There are bright and dull intellects and therefore their understanding is not always the same. If one reasons from this, then one knows that change is felt by the feelings, and that the spirit is transmitted through change. Feelings are the mother of change, and the spirit is the root of the feelings. The feelings have a way of uniting with physical things, and the spirit has the power of moving imperceptibly. But a person of penetrating perception returns to the Source, while one who is lost in the principle merely runs after physical things.[1] . . .

Feelings and things possessing a destined lot and the changes they occasion have no bounds. Causes and conditions closely interlock, and imperceptibly transmit and transfer. Were it not for those of penetrating vision, who would know of their transformations and who would know of their coming together? I beg leave to prove it for your sake, my worthy opponent, by recourse to fact. The passage of fire to firewood is like the passage of the soul to the body. The passage of fire to different firewood is like the passage of the soul to a new body. If the former firewood is not the latter firewood, then we know that the way in which the finger exhausts its duty is past comprehension.[2] If the former body

1. That is, the enlightened person attains nirvāna (which for Hui-yüan means that the soul returns to its point of origin), while the victim of error suffers endless reincarnation.
2. This is an allusion to the closing sentence of the *Chuang Tzŭ*, ch. 3, which reads (according to the traditional interpretation), "If the finger fulfills its duty in adding firewood, then the transmission of the fire knows no exhaustion." Hui-yüan interprets this to mean that, just as the fire moves from the old firewood to the new, so the soul moves from the old body to the new. For him this is very important, since in his view it is a corroboration from a secular Chinese source of the Buddhist theory of reincarnation.

is not the latter body, then one understands that the inter-action of the feelings and the individual destiny is profound. The person in error, seeing the body wither in one life, thinks that the spirit and the feelings perish with it. It is as if one were to see the fire die out in one piece of wood, and say that all fire had been exhausted for all time.

T'an-luan

T'AN-LUAN (476-542). The *Wei-shih* (Consciousness Only) school represented one of the major developments of Mahāyāna or Great Vehicle philosophy in India. It was originally called Yogācāra (Way of Yoga) and stressed the attainment of mystical enlightenment through metaphysical reflections. Vasubandhu (*c.* 420-500), the younger brother of Asanga, the founder of the school, elaborated its philosophical basis. Together with the Middle Doctrine school founded in India by Nāgārjuna (*c.* 100-200 A.D.) and transmitted in China through Seng-chao (384-414), the Wei-shih school dominated the intellectual life of China from the fifth to the seventh century.

By the fourth century A.D., many different Buddhist scriptures had been translated into Chinese. Hui-yüan (*c.* 334-416) actively promoted a new religious philosophy based on certain scriptures which had been placed in his hands. These sacred writings described the glorious "Pure Land" in the western quarters of Heaven, where all those who had faith in the saving grace of Amitābha might dwell eternally. An essay ascribed to Vasubandhu sets forth the essence of the *Pure Land Scripture*. T'an-luan, a famous patriarch of the Pure Land School, based his commentary on a Chinese translation of the Sanskrit essay.

Commentary to Vasubandhu's Essay on Rebirth

From *Sources of Chinese Tradition*, Volume I, edited by William Theodore de Bary, New York, Columbia University Press, 1960.

[From *Wang-sheng lun chu*, in *Taishō daizōkyō*, XL, 827-36]

Behold the phenomena of yon sphere,
How they surpass the paths of the three worlds!

THE reason that the [Amita] Buddha brings forth the pure merit of these adornments of his sphere is that He sees the phenomena of the three worlds as false, ceaselessly changing in a cycle, and without end, going round like a cankerworm imprisoned like a silkworm in its own cocoon. Alas for the sentient beings, bound to these three worlds, perverse and impure! He wishes to put the beings in a place that is not false, not ceaselessly changing in a cycle, not without end that they may find a great, pure place supremely happy For this reason He brings forth the pure merit of these adornments. What is meant by "perfection"? The meaning is that this purity is incorruptible, that it is incontaminable It is not like the phenomena of the three worlds, which are both contaminable and corruptible.

"Behold" means "observe." "Yon" means "that happy land." "The phenomena of yon sphere" means "the pure character of that happy sphere". . . . "It surpasses the paths of the three worlds." "Path" means "passageway." By such and-such a cause one obtains such-and-such an effect. With such-and-such an effect one requites such-and-such a cause

Through the passageway of the cause one reaches the effect. Through the passageway of the effect one requites the cause. Hence "paths". . . . These three worlds, in sum, are the dark house in which the common man, subject to life and death, drifts and goes in a cycle. Though pain and pleasure may differ slightly, though long and short may vary for a time, if one looks at these common men in their totality, there is none without defilement. Holding one another up, leaning on one another, they go in a cycle without end. . . . Now as cause, now as effect, vanity and falsehood succeed each to the other. But happiness is born of the bodhisattva's merciful right view, it is founded on the original vow of the Thus-Come-One's divine power. Those born of womb, eggs, and moisture, as a result of them rise above themselves; the long rope with which karma binds is, by them, forever cut. . . . "It surpasses the Three Worlds," — truly these are words near to the understanding.

> It is completely like the atmosphere,
> Extensive and great and without limit.

These two verses refer to the perfection of the merit of the quantity of the adornments of this sphere. The reason that the Buddha brings forth this merit of the quantity of these adornments is that He sees the three worlds as narrow and small, in ruins and with gaping holes and bumps. Their shrines and temples are cramped, or their lands and fields are restricting. The road of ambition is short, or the mountains and rivers are insurmountable. Or else countries are divided by boundaries. Such are the various impediments there. For this reason the bodhisattva raised the prayer concerning the merit of the quantity of adornments: "I pray that my land may be like the atmosphere, extensive and great without limits." "Like the atmosphere" means that, though those who come to be reborn therein may be numerous, yet they shall be as if they were nought. "Extensive and great without limits" completes the above meaning of being like the atmosphere. Why like the atmosphere? Because it is extensive and great without limits. "Perfection" means that, though the beings of the ten directions that go to be reborn there, whether those already reborn, those now being reborn, or those going to be reborn, are incalculable and unlimited, basically the place shall ever be like the atmosphere, extensive and great and without limits, never at any time full. Therefore he says, "It is completely like the atmosphere, extensive and great without limit." [pp. 827-28]

Question: Vasubandhu . . . says: "All together with the sentient beings shall go to be reborn in the Happy Land." To which "beings" does this refer?

Answer: If we examine the *Scripture of the Buddha of Limitless Life,* preached at Rajagriha city, we see that the Buddha announced to Ananda: "The Buddhas, the Thus-Come-Ones of the ten directions, as numerous as the sands of the Ganges, shall all together praise the incalculable awesome divinity and merit of the Buddha of Limitless Life. Then all of the beings that are, if, hearing his name, they shall with a believing heart rejoice for but a single moment of consciousness and with minds intent on being reborn in His land, shall be immediately enabled to go there and be reborn and stay there without return. There shall be excepted only those who commit the Five Violations[1] and malign the True Law." From this we see that even the commonest of men may go thither to be reborn. . . .

Question: The *Scripture of the Buddha of Limitless Life* says: "Those who pray to go thither to be reborn can all go thither to be reborn. Only those who commit the Five Violations and malign the True Law are excepted." The *Scripture of the Contemplation of the Buddha of Limitless Life* says: "They who perpetrate the Five Violations and the Evils,[2] indeed, they who do all manner of evil, may also

1. These are parricide, matricide, murder of an arhant, introduction of disharmony into the monastic community, and striking a Buddha so as to cause him to bleed.

2. These are killing, stealing, adultery, lying, duplicity, slander, obscene language, lust, anger, and false views.

364

go thither to be reborn." How are these two scriptures to be reconciled?

Answer: The one scripture specifies two kinds of grave sin. One is the Five Violations, the other is the maligning of the True Law. By virtue of both of these two kinds of grave sin one is unable to go thither to be reborn. The other scripture merely speaks of perpetrating the sins of the Ten Evils and the Five Violations, but says nothing of maligning the True Law. Since one does not malign the True Law, therefore one is able to be reborn there.

Question: Even if a man is completely guilty of the Five Violations, as long as he does not malign the True Law, the scripture allows that he can be reborn there. On the other hand, if there is a man who merely maligns the True Law but is not guilty of the sins of the Five Violations, if he prays to go thither to be reborn, can he be reborn there or not?

Answer: If he merely maligns the True Law, though he might have no other sins, he most certainly cannot be reborn there. Why do I say this? The scriptures say: "Those guilty of the Five Violations descend into the midst of the Hell of Uninterrupted Suffering and there suffer fully one cosmic period of grave punishment. Those who malign the True Law descend into the midst of the Hell of Uninterrupted Suffering, and, when this period is exhausted, turn about and go into the midst of another Hell of Uninterrupted Suffering. In this way they go through hundreds and thousands of such hells." The Buddha records no time at which they are able to leave, because the sin of maligning the True Law is extremely grave. Also, the "True Law" is the Law of Buddha. Once these foolish men have given expression to such calumny, how can they possibly pray for rebirth in Buddha's Land? Even if they were to pray for rebirth there out of a sole desire for the comforts and pleasures of that Land, it would still be like seeking waterless ice or smokeless fire. How could there be any way of obtaining it? [p. 834]

But there are some who call upon His name and bear it in mind, but whose ignorance persists and whose wishes remain unfulfilled. Why? Because they do not practice truly, nor in keeping with His name and its meaning. What is meant by "not practicing truly, nor in keeping with His name and its meaning"? The meaning is ignorance of the fact that the Thus-Come-One is the Body of True Character, the Body that acts for the sake of the beings. Also, "not in keeping" is of three kinds. First is impure faith, since it seems to exist and yet seems not to exist. Second is the lack of unity of faith, since it is not firm. Third is the discontinuity of faith, since it is interrupted by other thoughts. [p. 835]

How does one give rise to a prayerful heart? One always prays, with the whole heart single-mindedly thinking of being ultimately reborn in the Happy Land, because one wishes truly to practice *samatha* [concentration]. . . .

Samatha is rendered *chih* [stop] in three senses. First, one thinks single-mindedly of Amita Buddha and prays for rebirth in His Land. This Buddha's name and that Land's name can stop all evil. Second, that Happy Land exceeds the paths of the three worlds. If a man is born in that Land, he automatically puts an end to the evils of body, mouth, and mind. Third, Amita Buddha's power of enlightenment and persistent tenacity can naturally arrest the mind that seeks after lower stages of the Vehicles. These three kinds of *chih* arise from Buddha's real merit. Therefore it is said that "one wishes truly to practice *Samatha*" [concentration].

How does one observe? With wisdom one observes. With right mindfulness one observes Him, because one wishes truly to practice *vipasyana* [insight]. . . .

Vipasyana is translated *kuan* [insight] in two senses. First, while yet in this world, one conceives a thought and views the merit of the above mentioned three kinds of adornments. This merit is real, hence the practitioner also gains real merit. "Real merit" is the ability to be reborn with certainty in that Land. Second, once one has achieved rebirth in that Pure Land one immediately sees Amita Buddha. The pure-hearted bodhisattva who has not yet fully perceived is now able to perceive fully the Law Body that is above differences and, together with the pure-hearted bodhisattvas and the bodhisattvas of the uppermost station, to attain fully to the same quiescent equality. Therefore it is said that "one wishes truly to practice *vipasyana*." [pp. 835-36]

How does one apply [one's own merit] to and not reject all suffering beings? By ever making the vow to put such application first, in order to obtain a perfect heart of great compassion.

"Application" has two aspects. The first is the going aspect, the second is the returning aspect. What is the "going aspect"? One takes one's own merit and diverts it to all the beings, praying that all together may go to be reborn in Amita Buddha's Happy Land. What is the "returning aspect"? When one has already been reborn in that Land and attained to the perfection of concentration and insight, and the power of saving others through convenient means, one returns and enters the withered forest of life and death, and teaches all beings to turn together to the Path of the Buddha. [p. 836]

Chih K'ai

CHIH K'AI (538-597). The Lotus Sutra (*Scripture of the Lotus of the Wonderful Law*) was one of the favorite sutras of Chih K'ai (or Chih-i), third patriarch of the T'ien-T'ai School of Buddhism. Written by an unknown Indian Buddhist, the Lotus Sūtra was translated from the Sanskrit by Dharmaraksa about 310 A.D. More than any other Buddhist scripture, it contains the Mahāyanist teachings that make Buddhism "The Religion of Infinite Compassion." It explains in dramatic form the One Great Vehicle that gives all men access to salvation by becoming Bodhisattvas and finally Buddhas.

Chih K'ai believed that all sects had a place in the Buddhist system. The first patriarch of the T'ien-T'ai School was Hui Wen (*c.* 550), and the second was Hui Wen Ssu (515-577), but Chih K'ai is recognized as the real founder of the school. It derives its name from the mountains in Chekiang ("Heavenly Terrace") where he settled and taught. Because the Lotus Sutra was its basic text, the school is also referred to as the Fa-hua or Lotus School. Thirty-two of Chih K'ai's disciples spread its teachings throughout China.

The T'ien-T'ai doctrine centers around the principle of the Perfectly Harmonious Threefold Truth: (1) all things are void because they are produced by causation; (2) nevertheless, all things have temporary existence; and (3) Emptiness and Temporariness characterize all things and are the Mean. Thus three is one and one is three.

The selections from the commentary presented here are preceded by a selection from the Lotus Sutra offering the message of salvation for all.

The Scripture of the Lotus of the Wonderful Law

From *Sources of Chinese Tradition*, Volume I, edited by William Theodore de Bary, New York, Columbia University Press, 1960.

[From *Taishō daizōkyō*, IX, 8-9, 15]

THE Buddha appears in the world
Only for this One Reality.
Both the Shravaka Vehicle and the Pratyeka-buddha Vehicle
  are not real.
For never by the Small Vehicle
Would the Buddhas save all beings.
The Buddha himself abides in the Great Vehicle,
And in accordance with the Law he has attained,
By meditation and wisdom and the effort and ornament of
  virtue,
He saves all beings.
I have realized the Supreme Way.
The Law of the Great Vehicle applies to all beings.
If I converted by the Small Vehicle
Even one single human being,
I should fall into stinginess and greed.
Such a thing cannot be done.
If men turn in faith to the Buddha,
The Tathagata[1] will not deceive them.
O, Shariputra! you should know that
From the very start I made a vow,
With the desire to enable all beings

---

1. The Thus-Come-One, a name for the Buddha.

To be the same as we are,
To convert all beings
And enable them all to enter the Path of the Buddha.
Although I preach Nirvaṇa,
It is not real extinction.
All dharmas from the beginning
Are always tranquil in themselves and are devoid of appearance.
When the Budda-son fulfills his course,
He becomes a Buddha in his next life.
Because of my adaptability [to use very suitable means for salvation]
I reveal the Law of Three Vehicles.
Any among the living beings,
Who have come into contact with former Buddhas,
Have learned the Law and practiced charity,
Or have undergone discipline and endured forbearance and humiliation,
Or have made serious efforts at concentration and understanding, etc.,
And cultivated various kinds of blessing and wisdom—
All of these people,
Have reached the level of Buddhahood.

. . . .

Those people who, for the sake of the Buddha,
Installed images,
Or have had them carved,
Have reached the level of Buddhahood.

. . . .

Those who with a happy frame of mind
Have sung the glory of the Buddha,
Even with a very small sound,

. . . .

Or have worshiped,
Or have merely folded their hands,

. . . .

Or have uttered one "Namo" [Praise be . . .],

371

All have reached the level of Buddhahood.
About the Buddhas of the past—
After they passed away from this world,
They heard the Law,
And all reached the level of Buddhahood.
As to the Buddhas of the future,
Their number will be infinite.
All these Tathāgatas
Will preach the Law by all suitable means,
All these Buddhas,
With an infinite number of suitable means,
Will save all living beings,
And enable them to dwell in the Pure Wisdom of the
    Buddha.
Among those who have heard the Law,
None will fail to become Buddha.
All Buddhas have taken the vow:
"The Buddha-way which I walk,
I desire to enable all living beings
To attain the same way with me."
Although Buddhas in future ages
Preach hundreds and thousands and tens of thousands
Of methods, beyond number,
In reality there is only the One Vehicle.
All the Buddhas, past and future,
Know that dharmas have no [self-] nature,
And Buddha-seeds [all beings and defilements] are pro-
    duced by causation.
Therefore they preach the One Vehicle. [pp. 8-9]
All the Shrāvakas
And Pratyeka-buddhas
Cannot by their powers
Penetrate this scripture.
You, Shāriputra,
Can, into this scripture,
Enter only by faith. [p. 15]

THE PROFOUND MEANING OF THE SCRIPTURE
OF THE LOTUS OF THE WONDERFUL LAW

[From *Fu-hua hsüan-i*, in *Taishō daizōkyō*, XXXIII, 693]

THE Master of Nan-yüeh [Hui-ssu] cites three kinds of dharmas, namely, the dharma of the sentient beings, the Buddha-dharma, and the Mind-dharma. The scripture says: "In order to cause the beings to open to view and enter perceptively into the Buddha's knowledge-and-insight". . . . If the beings did not possess the Buddha's knowledge-and-insight, what need to speak of "opening"? It should be known from this that the Buddha's knowledge-and-insight is stored up in the beings. The scripture also says: "With the mere eyes engendered by one's father and mother [eyes of flesh] one can see through the inner and outer Mount Meru [eyes of gods], see deeply into all matter and remain uncontaminated by attachment to any of it [eyes of wisdom], and see matter without error [dharma-eyes]. Though one has not yet attained freedom from defilement, yet one's-sense shall be as pure as this, one eye embodying the functions of all eyes [Buddha-eyes]." The above is a passage from this scripture explaining the "subtlety" of the dharma of the beings. The *Mahāparinirvāṇa Scripture* says: "Though one who has learned the Great Vehicle has eyes of flesh, one calls them Buddha-eyes." The other five senses, beginning with those of the ear and nose, by the same token are also thus. The *Angulimaliya Scripture* says: "The so-called eye-sense is ever present in the Buddhas, complete and fully functioning, seeing clearly and distinctly. All the other senses, up to and including the mind-sense, are also thus." The *Prajñāpāramita Scripture* says: "[The six senses are] six self-mastering kings, for by nature they are pure." It also says: "All dharmas are contained in the eye. They are contained in it and do not exceed it. Even the eye is unattainable [having no substantial existence]. How much the less its containing or not containing! The same is true of all the other senses, up to and including the mind-sense, which in the same way contain all the dharmas." This means that the scriptures declare the "subtlety" of the dharma of the beings.

The subtlety of the Buddha-dharma is as the scripture says: "Cease, cease! No need to speak. My dharma is subtle and difficult to conceive. (The Buddha-dharma does not exceed the tentative and the ultimate.) This dharma is extremely, profoundly subtle, hard to see and hard to understand. Of all the varieties of beings there is none that can know the Buddha. (This refers to the subtlety of His transcendental wisdom.) When it comes to the other dharmas apart from the Buddha, there is also none that can fathom them. (This refers to the subtlety of His immanent wisdom.) As for these two dharmas, only the Buddhas can exhaust the reality of the dharmas. This is called 'the subtlety of the Buddha-dharma.' "

The subtlety of the Mind-dharma is as when in the performance of the four comfortable activities one keeps the mind under control and perceiving all dharmas, neither falters nor retreats, but experiences joy in a single instant, etc. The *Scripture of the View of Samantabhadra* says: "My mind is of itself empty, sin and grace have no subject. When one looks at the mind there is no mind, dharmas are not enduring dharma. Also, the mind is pure dharma." The *Vimalakirtinirdesa* says: "To look at the body, it is reality, and the same is true of looking at the Buddha. The release of the Buddhas is to be sought in the mental activities of the beings." The *Flower Garland Scripture* says: "The Mind, the Buddha, and the beings — these three are without distinction. To destroy the fine impurities of the mind is better than all the rolls of scripture." This is called "the subtlety of the Mind-dharma."

Now, on the basis of these three dharmas, we shall make distinctions of even greater detail.

To detail the dharma of the beings is to discuss the whole range of cause and effect, as all the dharmas. To detail the Buddha-dharma is to take the standpoint of effect. To detail the Mind-dharma is to take the standpoint of cause.

374

The dharma of the beings consists of two parts, the former a statement of the number of dharmas, the latter an interpretation of the appearance of these dharmas.

As for the number, the scriptures sometimes declare that one dharma comprises all dharmas, meaning that the Mind is the three worlds and that there is no dharma apart from it, everything else being merely the creation of the single Mind. They sometimes declare that two dharmas comprise all dharmas, to wit, name and form. In all the worlds there are only name and form. They sometimes declare that three dharmas comprise all dharmas, namely, life, consciousness, and warmth.[1] In this way the number is increased by one at a time until it reaches a hundred thousand. The present scripture uses ten dharmas to comprise all dharmas, namely, the such-like character, such-like nature, such-like substance, such-like power, such-like activity, such-like causes, such-like conditions, such-like effects, such-like retributions, such-like beginning-and-end-ultimate, and the like of the dharmas. The Master of Nan-yüeh reads these phrases with the word "like" at the end of each, calling them the "ten likes." The Master of T'ien-t'ai says that, if they are to be read for meaning, there are in all three different ways of reading them. The first is "this character's suchness, this nature's suchness, . . . this retribution's suchness." The second is "such-like character, such-like nature, . . . such-like retribution." The third is "their character is like this, their nature is like this, . . . retribution is like this." Since all readings contain the word "like," the word "like" is common to all of them.

The first reading gives the passage the meaning of Emptiness. If one reads "such-like character, such-like nature, etc.," enumerating the character, nature, etc., of Emptiness, assigning names and titles in a differentiated series, such a reading gives the passage the meaning of Temporariness.

1. The Sarvāstivāda school posits the existence of a life element which transmits the consciousness and bodily warmth of each being from incarnation to incarnation.

If one reads "character is like this, etc.," then one is equating the ten dharmas to the "this" of the reality of the Middle Way. Such a reading gives the passage the meaning of the Mean [of Emptiness and Temporariness]. Distinction makes it easier to undertand, hence we specify Emptiness, Temporariness, and the Mean. But if one is to speak from the standpoint of meaning, Emptiness is identical with Temporariness and the Mean. If one explains Emptiness in terms of suchness, then one Emptiness equals all Emptiness. If one details the aspects of suchness into character, etc., then one Temporariness equals all Temporariness. If one discusses the Mean in terms of "this," then one Mean equals all Means. They are not one, two, three, and yet they are one, two, three. They are neither horizontal nor vertical. This is called the true character. Only the Buddhas can exhaust these dharmas. These ten dharmas comprise all dharmas. If one is depending upon meaning, then one may interpret the passage in three senses. If one is depending upon rhythm, then one must read according to the verses, "The meaning of such-like great effect and retribution and of sundry natures and characters."

. . . .

All "dharma-spheres" are so-called in three senses. The number ten depends entirely on the dharma-spheres. Outside of the dharma-spheres there is no other dharma. That which depends and that upon which it depends are joined together in the appellation, hence we speak of the "ten dharma-spheres." Secondly, of these ten kinds of dharmas, each has a different lot. Their several causes and effects are separate from one another, and the common and saintly states have their differences. Therefore the word "sphere" is added to their name. Thirdly, of these ten, each and every dharma-sphere in and of itself comprises all dharma-spheres. For example, all dharmas are contained in hell. This state, without exceeding itself, is substantially identical with Truth, and requires no other point of reliance. Therefore the name "dharma-sphere." The same is true of all other dharma-spheres, up to and including that of the Buddha. If the number ten depends on the dharma-spheres, then that which depends, accompanying that upon which it depends, enters directly into the sphere of Emptiness. To say that the ten spheres are delimited one from another refers to the sphere of the temporary. To say that the number ten is all the dharma-spheres refers to the sphere of the Mean. Wishing to make this easy to understand we distinguish in this way. If we were to speak from the standpoint of meaning, then Emptiness is identical with Temporariness and the Mean. There is no one, two, three, as we have said before.

This one dharma-sphere contains the ten "such-likes." Ten dharma-spheres contain one hundred "such-likes." Also, since one dharma-sphere contains the other nine dharma-spheres as well, there are thus a hundred dharma-spheres and a thousand "such-likes." One may unite them under five distinctions, the first being evil, the second good, the third the Two Vehicles, the fourth the bodhisattva, and the fifth the Buddha. One may then divide these into two dharmas, the first four being the tentative dharma, the last one being the ultimate dharma. To treat them in detail, each of them comprises both the tentative and the ultimate. We observe this dichotomy only as a practical expedient. But this tentative-and-ultimate, this inconceivable, is the object of the twofold wisdom of the Buddhas of the three periods [past, present, and future]. If one takes this as an object, what dharma is not contained therein? If this object impels wisdom, what wisdom is not impelled thereby? Therefore the scripture says "dharmas." "Dharmas" means that the object understood is broad. "Only the Buddhas can exhaust [them]" means that the wisdom that understands it is deep, reaching its limit, and scouring its bottom.

Hsüan-tsang

HSÜAN-TSANG (596-664). The founder of the Idealistic School of Buddhism in China was also the most
important figure in the Mahayana development in the
Far East. Hsüan-tsang (or Hsüan-chuang) entered a monastery of the Pure Land School and was ordained at
the age of thirteen. He traveled extensively to study under different masters. Still in search of the true doctrine,
he left China secretly in 629, accompanied by a small
group, and finally arrived at the cradle of Buddhism. For
sixteen years he studied and debated with the most eminent Indian scholars. He returned to his homeland in
645, bringing with him 657 Buddhist works. With numerous assistants, he devoted the next twenty years to the
largest translation project in Chinese history and succeeded in translating seventy-five of the Buddhist texts.
His return had been the occasion of a warm Imperial
welcome and marked a new stage in the history of Buddhism. When he died, after almost twenty years of teaching and working out new trends of Buddhist thought, the
emperor respectfully suspended audiences for three days.

The essentials of the Idealistic School (also called the
Consciousness-Only, Wei-Shih, Fa-Hsiang, or Dharma-
Character School) which he founded are summed up in
Vasubandhu's *Treatise on Achieving Pure Consciousness*
and its shorter counterpart, *The Treatise in Twenty
Stanzas on Representation Only.* The central doctrine of
the school is that there are eight consciousnesses (the five
sense-consciousnesses, a sense-center consciousness, a
thought-center consciousness, and the storehouse con-

sciousness), all of them changing perpetually. The school aimed to show that man's belief in his own existence and that of the objects around him is entirely illusory, that nothing is real but consciousness, and that salvation is to be achieved by reducing the store of consciousness to pure being, identical with Thusness (Tathatā). Ten Indian philosophers elaborated on the meaning of Vasubandhu's shorter treatise. Hsüan-tsang selected, summarized, and systematized their interpretations. The result was the most important philosophical work of the school, his treatise on the *Confirmation of the Consciousness-Only System*.

Hsüan-tsang's school began to decline in the ninth century and finally disappeared, perhaps because its philosophy was too abstracted and subtle. Twentieth-century scholars have evidenced a new interest in the ancient school, and a few Buddhists have tried to revive its teachings.

Confirmation of the Consciousness-Only System

From *Sources of Chinese Tradition*, Volume I, edited by William Theodore de Bary, New York, Columbia University Press, 1960.

[From the *Ch'eng-wei-shih lun*, in *Taishō daizōkyō*, XXXI, 7, 10, 22, 25, 37, 38]

THE verse [by Vasubandhu] says:

First of all, the storehouse [ālaya] consciousness,
Which brings into fruition the seeds [effects of good and evil deeds].
[In its state of pure consciousness] it is not conscious of its clinging and impressions.
In both its objective and subjective functions it is always associated with touch,
Volition, feeling, sensation, thought, and cognition.
But it is always indifferent to its associations. . . .

The Treatise says:
The first transformation of consciousness is called alaya in both the Mahāyāna and Hīnayāna. . . . Why are the seeds so-called? It means that in consciousness itself fruitions, functions, and differentiations spontaneously arise. These are neither the same nor different from the consciousness or from what they produce. . . .

In this way the other consciousnesses which "perfume" [affect] it and the consciousness which is perfumed arise and perish together, and the concept of perfuming is thus established. To enable the seeds that lie within what is perfumed [storehouse consciousness] to grow, as the hemp plant is perfumed, is called perfuming. As soon as the seeds are produced, the consciousnesses which can perfume become in their turn causes which perfume and produce seeds. The three dharmas [the seeds, the manifestations, and perfuming] turn on and on, simultaneously acting as cause and effect. . . .

The verse says:
The second transformation
Is called the mind-consciousness
Which, while it depends on that transformation, in turn conditions it.
It has the nature and character of intellection.
It is always accompanied by the four evil defilements,
Namely, self-delusion, self-view,
Self-conceit, and self-love,
And by touch, etc. [volition, feeling, sensation, thought, and cognition]. . . .
The Treatise says:

"That transformation" refers to the first transformation, because according to the sacred teaching, this consciousness depends on the storehouse consciousness. . . . "It" refers to the consciousness on which this transformation depends, because according to the sacred teaching, this consciousness conditions the storehouse consciousness.

Spontaneously this mind perpetually conditions the storehouse consciousness and corresponds to the four basic defilements. What are the four? They are self-delusion, self-view, and also self-conceit and self-love. These are the four different names. Self-delusion means ignorance, lack of understanding of the character of the self, and being unenlightened about the principle of the non-self. Therefore it is called self-delusion. Self-view means clinging to the view that the self exists, erroneously imagining to be the self certain dharmas that are not the self. Therefore it is called self-view. Self-conceit means pride. On the strength of what is clung to as the self, it causes the mind to feel superior and lofty. It is therefore called self-conceit.

The verse says:
Next comes the third transformation
Which consists of the last categories of discrimination
With subject and object as the nature and character.
They are neither good nor evil.

The Treatise says:
This consciousness is divided into six categories, in accordance with the six different sense organs and the six sense objects. They refer to the consciousness of sight and so on [hearing, smell, taste] in the sense-center consciousness. . . .

The verse says:
Based on the root-consciousness [ālaya]
The five consciousnesses [of the senses] manifest themselves in accordance with the conditioning factors.
Sometimes [the senses manifest themselves] together and sometimes not,
Just as waves [manifest themselves] depending on water conditions.
The sense-center consciousness always arises and manifests itself,
Except when born in the realm of the absence of thought,
In the state of unconsciousness, in the two forms of concentration,
In sleep, and in that state where the spirit is depressed or absent.

The Treatise says:
The root consciousness is the storehouse consciousness because it is the root from which all pure and impure consciousnesses grow. . . . By "conditioning factors" are meant the mental activities, the sense organs, and sense objects. It means that five consciousnesses are dependent internally upon the root consciousness and externally follow

the combination of the conditions of the mental activities, the five sense organs, and sense objects. They [the senses] manifest themselves together and sometimes separately. This is so because the external conditions may come to be combined suddenly or gradually. . . .

The verse says:
Thus the various consciousnesses are but transformations
That which discriminates and that which is discriminated
Are, because of this, both unreal.
For this reason, everything is mind only.

The Treatise says:
"The various consciousnesses" refer to the three transformations of consciousness previously discussed and their mental qualities. They are all capable of transforming into two seeming portions, the perceiving portion and the perceived portion. The term "transformation" is thus employed. The perceiving portion that has been transformed is called "discrimination" because it can apprehend the perceived portion [as the object of perception]. The perceived portion that has been transformed is called the "object of discrimination" because it is apprehended by the perceiving portion. According to this correct principle, aside from what is transformed in consciousness, the self and dharmas are both definitely nonexistent, because apart from what apprehends and what is apprehended, there is nothing else, and because there are no real things apart from the two portions.

Therefore everything created [by conditions] and noncreated, everything seemingly real or unreal, is all inseparable from consciousness.

Fa-tsang

FA-TSANG (643-712). The Hua-yen philosophy is opposed at many points to the idealistic doctrines of Hsüan-tsang. The nominal founder of the Hua-Yen (Flowery Splendor) or Wreath School, known in Japan as the Kegon sect, was Tu-shun. He wrote and lectured on the *Hua-yen ching* (Flowery Splendor Scripture), from which this highly syncretic school derives its name. But the real founder of the school was Fa-tsang. Using the simple ideas of the *Hua-yen ching*, or *Avatamsaka Sutra*, as framework, he elaborated a complete philosophical system. The Sanskrit sutra is said to have been Buddha's first discourse, delivered only two weeks after his enlightenment. Buddha is reputed to have preached it only to Bodhisattvas because mere mortals could not comprehend it. The sutra was first translated in 420 A.D. but attracted little attention until the time of Tu-shun (557-640). Fa-tsang devoted his most important works to the exposition of its teachings.

Empress Wu (r. 684-705) favored Fa-tsang and asked him to lecture on the *Hua-yen ching* in 699. While attempting to explain his abstruse philosophy to her, he used the figure of a golden lion. The scripture is supposed to outline the whole development of Buddhist thought from its primitive stages up to the system of Mahayana. The metaphysical ideas of the Hua-Yen School are explained by Fa-tsang in his treatise called the *Golden Lion*. They constitute a system of objective idealism in which a universal, immutable mind is the ground of all phenomenal manifestations.

The Golden Lion

From *Sources of Chinese Tradition*, Volume I, edited by William Theodore de Bary, New York, Columbia University Press, 1960.

[From *Chin-shih-tzu chang*, in *Taishō daizōkyō*, XLV, 663-67]

1. Clarification of Dependent Origination

Gold has no self-nature. Through the agency of a skilled craftsman there is at length the coming-into-being of his phenomenon of the lion. But since this coming-into-being is dependent, therefore it is called "dependent origination."

2. Distinction of Matter and Emptiness

The character [phenomenon] of the lion is empty [of substantial reality]; there is nothing but gold. The lion is not existent, but the substance of gold is not nonexistent. Therefore they are called separately Emptiness. Also, Emptiness, having no self-character and manifesting itself through matter, does not prevent illusory existence. Therefore they are separately called matter and Emptiness.

3. Relation to Three Natures

The Yogāchāra school, whose philosophy influenced the Hua-yen, posited a triad of natures. The first of these is the world of phenomena, that which is "ubiquitously construed and clung to." The second nature is "dependent on something else," that is, the product of causes and conditions. The third nature is "perfect." It refers to the identity of everything with the Absolute.

The lion comes into existence because of our senses. This is called "ubiquitously construed." The golden lion has apparent existence. This is called "dependent on something else." The nature of the gold [of which the lion is made] is unaltered. This is called "roundly perfected."

4. Manifestation of Characterlessness

Since the gold comprises the whole lion, and since there is no lion-character to be found apart from the gold, therefore it is called "characterlessness."

5. Explanation of Not-Coming-into-Being

If one rightly looks at the lion at the time of its coming into being, it is only gold that comes into being. Apart from the gold there is nothing. Although the lion has [the characteristics of] coming into being and extinction, the gold-substance at bottom neither increases nor decreases. Therefore we say that there is no coming-into-being.

6. Treatment of the Five Doctrines

This golden lion is nothing but dharmas of cause and condition, coming into being and perishing every moment. There is in reality no lion-character to be found. This is called the Doctrine of the Shravaka Ignorant of the Dharmas. Secondly, these dharmas, born of conditions, are each without self-nature. It is absolutely only Emptiness. This is called the Initial Doctrine of the Great Vehicle. Thirdly, although there is absolutely only Emptiness, this does not prevent the illusory dharmas from remaining as they are. The two/phenomena of conditioned origination and temporary or transitory existence subsist side by side. This is called the Final Doctrine of the Vehicle. Fourthly, since these two aspects cancel each other out, they both perish, and neither [the result of] our senses nor false existence exists. Neither of the two aspects has any potential power and both Emptiness and existence perish. Then the way of names and words [which gives rise to phenomena] is terminated, and the mind [that contemplates them] has nought to attach itself to. This is called the Sudden Doctrine of the Great Vehicle. Fifthly, when the erroneous consciousness has been annihilated and true substance revealed, all becomes a single mass. Vigorously then does function arise, and on each occasion perfect reality obtains. The myriad forms, in disarray, mix and yet are not confused. The all is one, both alike having no "nature." [At the same time] the one is the all, for cause and effect clearly follow each other. The [potential] power and the [actual] function involve each other, the folding and unfolding are unhampered. This is called the Rounded Doctrine of the Single Vehicle.

7. Mastering the Ten Profound Theories

The gold and the lion come into being at the same time, full and complete. This is called the Theory of Simultaneous Completeness and Mutual Correspondence. Secondly, the gold and the lion come into being each being compatible with the other, the one and the many each having no obstruction for the other. In this situation the principle [one] and fact [many] are different. Whether the one or the many, each occupies its own position. This is called the Theory of the Mutual Compatibility and Difference of the One and the Many. Thirdly, if one contemplates the lion, then it is only a lion, and there is no gold about it. In this case the gold is hidden and the lion manifested. If one contemplates the gold, then it is only gold, and there is no lion about it. In this case the gold is manifested and the lion is hidden. If one contemplates both, then both are manifested and both hidden. Being hidden, they are concealed and secret. Being manifested, they are evident and revealed. This is called the Theory of the Mutual Completion of the Hidden and the Manifested. Fourthly, the lion's eyes, ears, limbs, joints, and every single pore completely contain the golden lion. In each pore the lion simultaneously and all at once enters into a single strand of hair. Each and every strand of hair contains unlimited lions. Each [of these lions] in turn has hairs each and every one of which contains unlimited lions, all of which in turn enter into a single strand of hair. In this way the progression is infinite, like the celestial jewels on the net of Indra. This is called the Theory of the Realm of Indra's Net. Fifthly, since this lion's eye completely contains the lion, the whole lion is pure eye. If the ear completely contains the lion, then the whole lion is pure ear. If all the sense organs simultaneously contain it, then all are complete, each of them pure and each of them mixed [with the others]. Also, each one of them is a full storehouse. This we call the Theory of the Full Possession by the Storehouse of the Faculties of Purity and Mixture. Sixthly, since the lion's several organs each and every hair involve the whole lion, each of them pervading the whole, the lion's ear is its eye, its eye is its ear, its ear is its nose, its nose is its tongue, its tongue is its body. Each freely maintains its existence without conflict or obstruction. This is called the Theory of the Dharmas Mutually Identified While Self-existent. Seventhly, the gold and lion may be hidden or manifest, one or many, definitely pure or definitely mixed, powerful or powerless, this or that. The principle and the comparison illuminate each other. Fact and principle are both revealed. They are completely compatible with each other, and do not obstruct each other's peaceful existence. When the most minute are thus established and distinguished this is called the Theory of the Small and Minute Being Compatible Along with Peaceful Existence. Eighthly, this lion is a created dharma, coming into being and perishing every instant, dividing into three periods of time, past, present, and future, without a moment's interval. Of these three periods of time each contains within itself past, present, and future. By uniting three triads of degrees one has nine periods, which again in turn may be united to form a single dharma. Although they are nine periods, they each have their differences of coalescence and separation. Yet they exist in mutual dependence, fading one into the other without obstruction, and all together constituting a single moment of thought. This is called the Theory of the Distinct Existence of Separate Dharmas in the Ten Periods.[1] Ninthly, this lion and this gold may be hidden or manifested, one or many, thus having no self-nature, being evolved out of the Mind. Yet whether spoken of as fact or principle, they are completed

1. The nine periods separately, plus all of them as one period.

389

Skillful Completion Through the Evolution of the Mind—and they have existence. This is called the Theory of the Only. Tenthly, this lion is spoken of in order to demonstrate ignorance, while the reality of the gold is spoken of in order to manifest the True Nature. These two, principle and fact, explained in conjunction and likened to storehouse consciousness, cause right understanding to be born. This is called the Theory of the Manifestation of the Doctrine with Reference to Facts and the Fostering of Understanding Thereby.

8. Binding Together the Six Characters

The lion is the character of universality. The five sense-organs, being various and different, are the characters of speciality. Since they arise out of a single condition, they are the characters of similarity. The fact that its eyes, etc. do not overlap is the character of diversity. Since the lion is made of the combination of these sense organs, this is the character of integration. The several organs each occupying its own position is the character of disintegration.

9. Achievement of Bodhi

"Bodhi" means the Way, it means enlightenment. When the eye beholds the lion, it sees that all created dharmas, even before disintegration, are from the very beginning quiescent and extinct. By avoiding both attachment and renunciation, one, along this very road, flows into the sea of perfect knowledge. Therefore it is called "the Way." One understands that all of the misconstructions perpetrated since time without beginning have not a single real substance to them. Therefore one calls this "enlightenment." Ultimately, it contains within itself the wisdom that comprises all kinds. This is called "the achievement of bodhi."

10. Entry into Nirvāṇa

When one sees this lion and this gold, the two characters are both annihilated, the passions do not come into being, and although beauty and ugliness are displayed before the eye, the mind is as calm as the sea. False thoughts vanish completely, there are no pressures. One issues forth from one's bonds and separates oneself from hindrances, and cuts off forever the foundations of suffering. This is called "entering Nirvāṇa."

Hui-neng

HUI-NENG (658-713). The basic classic of Zen Buddhism, *The Platform Scripture*, is traditionally believed to represent a lecture given by Hui-neng, the Sixth Patriarch, in the Ta-fan Temple in Shao-chou, and recorded by his pupil Fa-hai. The origins of Zen(*dhyāna* in Sanskrit, pronounced *ch'an* in Chinese and *zen* in Japanese) can be traced to India and the teachings of Gautama Buddha. At first the stress was on meditation (the original meaning of the word *dhyāna*) but the doctrine was transformed after it was introduced into China, completely divested of meditation, and made into a way of life that became dominant and had a strong influence on Chinese philosophy and art from the ninth through the fourteenth century. Recently it has been introduced to the Western world through Japan. Zen teaches that the elements of existence (dharma) are products of the human mind, which is identical with the one, inexpressible, inconceivable, universal Reality or Void. These teachings, together with the stress placed on alertness and the use of unique techniques to shock the mind, make it a revolutionary and unconventional doctrine.

Though Indian Zen techniques were introduced into China as early as the second century B.C., Bodhidharma, the First Patriarch of the Zen School, is traditionally credited with founding the new doctrine. He arrived in Canton toward the end of the fifth century A.D. and taught his beliefs in north China for half a century. He urged his many followers to discard all Buddhist scriptures except one, the *Scripture about the Buddha Enter-*

ing into Lanka, which teaches that the True State or Nirvāṇa is total Emptiness and that emancipation follows intuition of this highest truth. The so-called Lanka doctrine of Bodhidharma was transmitted through several generations to Hui-neng, a man of humble origin, revolutionary ideas, and enduring influence.

Born in Fan-yang, southwest of Peking, he lost his father when he was still very young and had to move to a district which included the city of Canton. At the age of twenty-four, while he was peddling firewood in the city, he heard a customer recite the *Diamond Scripture.* Struck by the strange ideas expressed by Gautama Buddha, the illiterate peddler made inquiries which eventually led him to Hupei, where he listened to the teachings of the Fifth Patriarch Hung-jen, became a Buddhist priest and, in 676, gave his first formal lecture in the Fa-hsing Temple. He propagated the Law of the Buddha for thirty-seven years, attracting the most famous Zen Masters of his age, including the forty-three "heirs of the law" who spread his teachings all over China.

The Platform Scripture

From *The Platform Scripture,* translated by Wing-tsit Chan, New York, St. John's University Press, 1963.

GREAT Master Hui-neng ascended the high seat in the lecture hall of the Ta-fan Temple to preach the Law of the Perfection of Great Wisdom and to give the discipline that frees one from the attachment to differentiated characters. There were present more than ten thousand monks, nuns, disciples who had renounced their families, and laymen. The prefect of Shao-chou, Wei-ch'ü, more than thirty government officials, and over thirty Confucian scholars jointly requested the Great Master to preach the Law of the Perfection of Great Wisdom. Thereupon the prefect ordered the disciple, Monk Fa-hai, to record the lecture so that it would prevail in future generations. It was to enable seekers of the Way to have something to rely on and to follow when they in turn transmitted and taught the Law according to this fundamental doctrine, that this *Platform Scripture* was spoken.

2. Great Master Hui-neng said: Good and learned friends, think of the Law of the Perfection of Great Wisdom with a pure mind.

Then the Great Master remained silent, concentrated in mind and tranquil in spirit. After a long while he said: Good and learned friends, listen quietly. My deeply loving father was originally a native of Fan-yang. After his demotion from office, he was banished to Ling-nan and became a citizen of Hsin-chou. My father passed away when I was very young. My aged mother and I, an orphan, moved to Nan-hai. We were poor and life was hard. I peddled firewood in the city. Once a customer bought some fuel and led me to a government store. The customer took the fuel-wood and I received the money. As I withdrew toward the door, I suddenly saw a customer reading the *Diamond Scripture*. As soon as I heard it, I understood and was immediately enlightened. Thereupon I asked the customer, "From what place did you bring this scripture?"

The customer answered, "I paid reverence to priest Hung-jen, the Fifth Patriarch, in the Feng-mu Mountain in the eastern part of Huang-mei district in Ch'i-chou. I found there more than a thousand disciples. There I heard the Great Master exhort both disciples who have renounced their families and laymen, saying that if they would only hold on to this one book, the *Diamond Scripture*, they would be able to see their own nature and immediately would be enlightened and become Buddhas." After I heard what he said and due to causes operating in my previous lives I begged leave of my mother and went to Feng-mu Mountain in Huang-mei to pay reverence to priest Hung-jen, the Fifth Patriarch.

3. Priest Hung-jen asked me, "Whence have you come to this mountain to pay reverence to me? What do you wish from me?"

I answered, "Your disciple is a native of Ling-nan, a citizen of Hsin-chou. I have purposely come a great distance to pay you reverence. I seek nothing other than to practice the Law of the Buddha."

The Great Master reproved me, saying, "You are from Ling-nan, and furthermore, you are a barbarian. How can you become a Buddha?"

I answered, "Although people are distinguished as northerners and southerners, there is neither north nor south in the Buddha-nature. The physical body of the barbarian and [that of] the monk are different. But what difference is there in their Buddha-nature?"

The Great Master intended to argue with me further, but, seeing people around, said nothing more. He ordered me to attend to duties, among the rest. Then a lay attendant ordered me to the rice-pounding area to pound rice. This I did for more than eight months.

4. One day the Fifth Patriarch suddenly called his disciples to come to him. When we had already assembled, he said, "Let me say this to you: Life and death are serious matters. You disciples are engaged all day in making offerings, going after fields of blessings only, and you make no effort to achieve freedom from the bitter sea of life and death. If you are deluded in your own nature, how can blessings save you? Go to your rooms, all of you, and think for yourselves. Those who possess wisdom use the wisdom *(prajñā)* inherent in their own nature. Each of you must write a verse and present it to me. After I see the verses, I will give the robe and the Law to the one who understands the basic idea and will appoint him to be the Sixth Patriarch. Hurry, hurry!"

5. After the disciples had received these instructions, they each retired to their own rooms. They said to each other, "There is no need to calm our minds and devote our attention to composing verses to present to the priest. Head Monk Shen-hsiu is an instructor of rituals. When he acquires the Law, we can of course follow and stay with him. We do not have to write verses." They were satisfied. None dared present a verse.

At that time there were three corridors in front of the hall of the Great Master. Offerings were made there. It was planned to paint there on the walls as records the pictures of the transfiguration of the assembly depicted in the *Scripture about the Buddha Entering into Lanka* and also pictures of the five Patriarchs transmitting the robe and the Law so that these stories might prevail in future generations. The artist Lu Chen had examined the wall. He was to begin work the next day.

6. Head Monk Shen-hsiu thought, "These people would not present verses to show their minds because I am an instructor. If I do not present a verse to show my mind, how

can the Fifth Patriarch see whether my understanding is shallow or deep? I shall present the verse of my heart to the Fifth Patriarch to show my ideas. It is good to seek the Law, but not good to seek the patriarchate. It would be similar to that of the ordinary people and I would be usurping the holy rank. If I do not present a verse to manifest my mind, I shall never acquire the Law." He thought for a long time but found it an extremely difficult matter. He then waited until midnight, and without allowing anyone to see him, went to the wall in the middle of the southern corridor and wrote a verse to manifest what was in his mind, thus wishing to seek the Law. "If the Fifth Patriarch sees the words of this verse — the words of this verse . . . If they are not acceptable, it is of course because the obstruction of my past deeds is so heavy that I am not qualified to obtain the Law. The Patriarch's holy opinion is difficult to guess but I shall be satisfied in my mind."

At midnight Head Monk Shen-hsiu, holding a candle, wrote a verse on the wall of the south corridor, without anyone knowing about it, which said:

> The body is the tree of perfect wisdom (bodhi).
> The mind is the stand of a bright mirror.
> At all times diligently wipe it.
> Do not allow it to become dusty.

7. After Head Monk Shen-hsiu had finished writing the verse, he returned to his room to retire without anyone seeing him. The next morning the Fifth Patriarch called court artist Lu to come to the south corridor to paint the pictures of the scripture about the Buddha entering into Lanka. Suddenly the Fifth Patriarch saw the verse. After reading it, he said to the court artist, "I will give you thirty thousand cash and will be much obliged to you for your coming from afar. But we will not paint the transfigurations. The *Diamond Scripture* says, 'All characters are unreal and imaginary. It is better to keep this verse and let deluded people read it. If People practice according to it,

they will not fall into the Three Evil Stages. People who practice according to the Law will enjoy great benefits."

Thereupon the Great Master called all the disciples to come and burn incense before the verse so that everyone would see it and a sense of reverence would arise in all of them. "All of you read this. Only those who understand this verse will be able to see their own nature. Those who practice according to it will not fall."

The disciples all read the verse and a sense of reverence was aroused in them. They said, 'Wonderful!'

Thereupon the Fifth Patriarch called Head Monk Shen-hsiu into the hall and asked, "Was this verse written by you? If you wrote it, you should receive my Law."

Head Monk Shen-hsiu said, "Please pardon me. In fact, I did write it. Yet I dare not seek the position of the patriarch. I hope Your Holiness will be compassionate and see if your disciple possesses a small amount of wisdom and understands the basic idea."

The Fifth Patriarch said, "The verse you wrote shows some but not complete understanding. You have arrived at the front door but you have not yet entered it. Ordinary people, by practicing in accordance with your verse, will not fail. But it is futile to seek the supreme perfect wisdom while holding to such a view. One must enter the door and see his own nature. Go away and come back after thinking a day or two. Write another verse and present it to me. If then you have entered the door and have seen your own nature, I will give you the robe and the Law." Head Monk Shen-hsiu went away and for several days could not produce another verse.

8. A boy was reciting this verse while passing by the rice-pounding area. As soon as I heard it, I knew that the author had not seen his own nature or understood the basic idea. I asked the boy, "What verse were you reciting a little while ago?" The boy answered, "Do you know that the Great Master said life and death are important matters? He wishes to transmit the robe and the Law to someone. He told the

disciples to write and present a verse for him to see. He who understood the basic idea would be given the robe and the Law as testimony of making him the Sixth Patriarch. The head monk by the name of Shen-hsiu wrote in the south corridor a verse that frees one from the attachment to differentiated characters. The Fifth Patriarch told all the disciples to read it. Whoever understood this verse would immediately see his own nature, and those who practiced according to it would be emancipated."

I replied, "I have been pounding rice here for more than eight months and have not been to the front of the hall. Will you, sir, lead me to the south corridor so that I might see this verse and pay reverence to it. I also wish to recite it and to fulfill the conditions for birth in the Buddha-land in my next life."

As the boy led me to the south corridor, I immediately paid reverence to the verse. As I did not know how to read, I asked someone to read it to me. After I heard it, I immediately understood the basic idea. I also composed a verse and asked a person who could read to write it on the wall of the western corridor to manifest what was in my own mind. It is useless to study the Law if one does not understand his own mind. Once a person understands his own mind and sees his own nature, he will immediately understand the basic idea.

My verse says:

> Fundamentally perfect wisdom has no tree.
> Nor has the bright mirror any stand.
> Buddha-nature is forever clear and pure.
> Where is there any dust?

Another verse says:

> The mind is the tree of perfect wisdom.
> The body is the stand of a bright mirror.
> The bright mirror is originally clear and pure.
> Where has it been defiled by any dust?

Monks in the hall were all surprised at these verses. I, however, went back to the rice-pounding area. The Fifth Patriarch suddenly realized that I alone had the good knowledge and understanding of the basic idea but he was afraid lest the rest learn it. He therefore told them, "He does not understand perfectly after all."

9. The Fifth Patriarch waited till midnight, called me to come to the hall, and expounded the *Diamond Scripture*. As soon as I heard this, I understood. That night the Law was imparted to me without anyone knowing it, and thus the method of sudden enlightenment and the robe were transmitted to me. "You are now the Sixth Patriarch. This robe is the testimony of transmission from generation to generation. As to the Law, it is to be transmitted from mind to mind. Let people achieve enlightenment through their own effort."

The Fifth Patriarch said, "Hui-neng, from the very beginning, in the transmission of the Law one's life is as delicate as hanging by a thread. If you remain here, someone might harm you. You must leave quickly."

10. After I received the robe and the Law, I left at midnight. The Fifth Patriarch personally saw me off at the courier's station at Chiu-chiang. I then understood the instructions of the Patriarch. "Go and work hard. Carry the Law to the south. Do not preach for three years, for it is not easy for this Law to flourish. Later when you spread the Law and convert people, when you skillfully guide deluded people and open up their minds, you will not be different from me."

Having said goodbye, I started south.

11. In two months I reached the Ta-yü Mountain. I did not realize that there were several hundred people coming after me. They wanted to follow me and to snatch the robe and the Law. But half way they all withdrew, except one monk whose family name was Ch'en and whose private name was Hui-shun. He was formerly a general of the third rank. His nature and disposition were crude and evil. He

got straightly to the peak, rushed forward and grabbed me. I immediately gave the robe of the Law to him but he refused to take it. "I purposely came this long way to seek the Law; I do not need the robe." Thereupon I transmitted the Law to him on the peak. As he heard what I said, his mind was opened. I told him to go to the north to convert the people there immediately.

12. Then I came and stayed in this place and associated with government officials, disciples who have renounced their families, and lay folk. This, after all, was due to causes operating over many long periods of time. The doctrine has been handed down from past sages; it is not my own wisdom. Those who wish to hear the teachings of past sages must purify their hearts. Having heard them, they must vow to rid themselves of delusions and thereby to become enlightened, as the former sages. (This is the method described below.)

Great Master Hui-neng declared: Good and learned friends, perfect wisdom is inherent in all people. It is only because they are deluded in their minds that they cannot attain enlightenment by themselves. They must seek the help of good and learned friends of high standing to show them the way to see their own nature. Good and learned friends, as soon as one is enlightened, he attains wisdom.

13. Good and learned friends, calmness and wisdom are the foundations of my method. First of all, do not be deceived into thinking that the two are different. They are one substance and not two. Calmness is the substance of wisdom and wisdom is the function of calmness. Whenever wisdom is at work, calmness is within it. Whenever calmness is at work, wisdom is within it. Good and learned friends, the meaning here is that [calmness and] wisdom are identified. Seekers of the Way, arouse your minds. Do not say that wisdom follows calmness or vice versa, or that the two are different. To hold such a view would imply that the dharmas possess two different characters. In the case of those whose words are good but whose hearts are not good,

402

wisdom and calmness are not identified. But in the case of those whose hearts and words are both good and in whom the internal and the external are one, calmness and wisdom are identified. Self-enlightenment and practice do not consist in argument. If one is concerned about which comes first, he is a [deluded] person. If he is not freed from the consideration of victory or defeat, he will produce the dharmas and the self. He cannot become free from the Four Characters.

14. Calmness in which one realizes that all dharmas are the same means to practice [attaining] a straightforward mind at all times, whether walking, standing, sitting, or reclining. The *Scripture Spoken by Vimalakirti* says, "The straightforward mind is the holy place. The straightforward mind is the Pure Land." Do not be crooked in the activities of your mind and merely talk about straightforwardness. One who merely talks about calmness in which one realizes that all dharmas are one and does not practice a straightforward mind is not a disciple of the Buddha. To practice a straightforward mind only and to be unattached to any dharma is called calmness in which one realizes that all dharmas are the same. Deluded people attached to the characters of dharmas hold that calmness, in which one realizes that all dharmas are the same, means simply to sit unperturbed and to remove erroneous thoughts without allowing others to arise in the mind; that to them is calmness in which one realizes that all dharmas are the same. If this were the case, this Law would [render us] equivalent to insentient beings and would be a cause of hindrance to the Way. The Way must be in operation. Why should it be impeded instead? When the mind is not attached to dharmas, then the Way is in operation. When it is attached then it is in bondage. If it were correct to sit without motion, Vimalakirti would not have reprimanded Sariputra for sitting silently in the forest.

Good and learned friends, I also know some who teach people to sit and look into the mind as well as to look at purity, so that the mind will not be perturbed and nothing will arise from it. Devoting their efforts to this, deluded people fail to become enlightened; consequently they are so attached to this method as to become insane. There have been several hundred such cases. Therefore I know that to teach people this way is a great mistake.

15. Good and learned friends, in what way are calmness and wisdom the same? They are like the lamp and its light. With the lamp there is light. Without the lamp there is no light. The lamp is the substance of the light while the light is the function of the lamp. In name they are two but in substance they are not different. It is the same with calmness and wisdom.

16. Good and learned friends, in method there is no distinction between sudden enlightenment and gradual enlightenment. Among men, however, some are intelligent and others are stupid. Those who are deluded understand gradually, while the enlightened achieve understanding suddenly. But when they know their own minds, then they see their own nature, and there is no difference in their enlightenment. Without enlightenment, they remain forever bound in transmigration.

Shen-hui

SHEN-HUI (670-762). A disciple of Hui-neng, Shen-hui had a large following, enjoyed the support of the aristocratic element of society, and was a prime mover in the campaign to discredit the Northern School of Zen. His dates, usually given as 668-760, have recently been revised in the light of modern scholarship. Before becoming a Buddhist priest, he studied both Confucianism and Tâoism. In 734, after he had accepted the radically new doctrines of Hui-neng (658-713), the illiterate woodpeddler to whom *The Platform Scripture* the basic classic of Zen Buddhism, is attributed, he openly attacked the teachings of Shen-hsieu. The latter was the leader of the sect later known as the Northern School of Zen, and his prestige and influence had caused his teachings to dominate the religious and intellectual scene. The freshness and vigor of the challenging doctrines promulgated by Hui-neng and Shen-hui soon attracted many adherents to the new sect, later known as the Southern School, which eventually overshadowed its rival and remained dominant thereafter. The Southern School advocates sudden enlightenment, while the Northern School stresses gradual enlightenment.

Shen-hui, like the other disciples of Hui-neng, insisted that Nirvāṇa is identical with the original substance, that all men can become Buddhas, and that all of the activities of the mind are functions of the ultimate principle, and that "the absence of thought" can lead one to the Buddha-mind, or return to the original state of tranquility. Toward the end of his life, he was banished to Kiangsi, accused of "gathering large crowds with harmful motives."

405

Conversations

From *Buddhist Texts through the Ages*, translated and edited by Edward Conze (in collaboration with I. B. Horner, D. Snellgrove, and A. Waley), Oxford, England, Bruno Cassirer, 1954.

THE Master Shen-tsu asked Shen-hui: "You say that our Original Nature has the characteristics of the Absolute. In that case it has no colour, blue, yellow or the like, that the eye can see. How then can one perceive one's Original Nature?" Shen-hui answered, "Our Original Nature is void and still. If we have not experienced Enlightenment, erroneous ideas arise. But if we awaken to the erroneous nature of these ideas, both the Awakening and the wrong idea simultaneously vanish. That is what I mean by 'perceiving one's Original Nature'." Shen-tsu again asked: "Despite the light that comes from the Awakening, one is still on the plane of Birth and Destruction. Tell me by what method one can get clear of Birth and Destruction?" Shen-hui answered, "It is only because you put into play the ideas of Birth and Destruction that Birth and Destruction arise. Rid yourself of these ideas, and there will be no substance to which you can even distantly apply these names. When the light that comes from the Awakening is quenched, we pass automatically into Non-being, and there is no question of Birth or Destruction." (1)

* * *

"The passions (klesa)," said the disciple Wu-hsing, "are boundless and innumerable. Buddhas and Bodhisattvas pass through aeons of austerity before achieving success. How was it that the dragon's daughter was instantaneously converted and forthwith achieved Complete Enlightenment?"

406

"Conversion," said Shen-hui, "can be either sudden or gradual; both delusion and the Awakening can come to pass slowly or swiftly. That delusion can go on for aeon after aeon and the Awakening can come in a single moment is an idea that is difficult to understand. I want first of all to illustrate the point by a comparison; I think it will help you to understand what I mean. A single bundle of thread is made up of innumerable separate strands; but if you join

1. See Saddharma Pundarika, Ch. IV. (Tak. IX, 35).

them together into a rope and put it on a plank, you can easily cut through all these threads with one stroke of a sharp knife. Many though the threads may be, they cannot resist that one blade. With those who are converted to the way of the Bodhisattvas, it is just the same. If they meet with a true Good Friend who by skilful means brings them to immediate perception of the Absolute, with Diamond Wisdom they cut through the passions that belong to all the stages of Bodhisattvahood. They suddenly understand and are awakened, and see for themselves that the True Nature of the dharmas is empty and still. Their intelligence is so sharpened and brightened that it can penetrate unimpeded. When this happens to them, all the myriad entanglements of Causation are cut away, and erroneous thoughts many as the sands of the Ganges in one moment suddenly cease. Limitless virtues are theirs, ready and complete. The Diamond Wisdom is at work, and failure now impossible."(2)

* * *

"What is the Void?" asked the Master of the Law Ch'ung-yüan. "If you tell me that it exists, then you are surely implying that it is solid and resistant. If on the other hand you say it is something that does not exist, in that case why go to it for help?" "One talks of the Void," replied Shen-hui, "for the benefit of those who have not seen their own Buddha-natures. For those who have seen their Buddha-natures the Void does not exist. It is this view about the Void that I call 'going to it for help'." (3)

* * *

407

"You must not take it amiss," said Shen-hui to the Master of the Law Ch'ung-yüan and some others, "if I tell you the following story. Nowadays such a lot of people are giving instruction in Dhyana that students are becoming completely bewildered. I am afraid that among these instructors there may well be some that are bent upon leading students of religion astray and destroying the True Law — such teachers being in fact Heretics in disguise, or even the Evil One Mara himself. That is the reason why I tell you this story. Well, it was in the period Chiu-shih (700 A.D.). The Empress Wu Hou summoned the monk Shen-hsiu[1] to serve in the Palace and when he was about to leave his monastery . . . his followers, both laymen and monks, asked him how they were to carry on their spiritual exercises in his absence, and where they were to turn for guidance. 'You will have to go to Shao-chou,' said Shen-hsiu. 'You will find there a great Good Friend.[2] It was to him that the great Master Hung-jen handed on the succession. That is the place to go to for Buddha's Law. They have it all there. If there is anything that you cannot decide about for yourselves, go there and you will be astonished! That Master really does understand the true principles of Buddhism.' Accordingly in . . . the third year of Ching-lung (709) Shen-hsiu's disciple Kuang-chi (affecting to carry out this advice) went to Hui-neng's monastery at Shao-chou and after spending about ten days there he went at midnight to the Master's cell and stole the Mantle of Succession. Hui-neng screamed and his disciples Hui-yüan and Hsüan-wu hearing him scream went to see what was wrong. Just outside Hui-neng's cell they met Kuang-chi, who grasped Hsüan-wu's hand and warned him not to make any noise (as the Master was asleep). However, the two disciples thought they had better go and see if Hui-neng was all right. 'Some one has been in my cell,' said Hui-neng when they

1. Leader of the Northern School of Dhyana.
2. Hui-neng, leader of the Southern School.

408

came to him. 'He grabbed at the Mantle and carried it off.' Presently a number of monks and some laymen too, both southerners resident at the monastery and visitors from the north, came to Hui-neng's cell and questioned him about the intruder. 'Was he a monk or a layman?' they asked. 'I could not see,' said Hui-neng. 'Someone certainly came in, but whether he was a monk or a layman I can't say.' They also asked whether the man was a northerner or a southerner. As a matter of fact Hui-neng knew who the man was; but he was afraid that, if he mentioned his name, his own disciples might do Kuang-chi some injury. That was why he answered as he did. 'This is not the first time,' Hui-neng went on. 'It was stolen three times from my master Hung-jen, and Hung-jen told me that it was also stolen once from his master Tao-hsin. . . . This mantle is destined to bring to a head the quarrel between the monks and laymen of the South and those of the North. They will never meet save with sword or cudgel in hand.'" (4)

Han Yü

HAN YÜ (768-824). The impact of Buddhist philosophy on the Chinese mind was strongest during the period that stretched from the middle T'ang (*c.* 750) to the late Sung (*c.* 1250). Han Yü and his pupil Li Ao (d. 844) rose to defend Confucianism against the subtle infiltration of the alien, other-worldly philosophy of Buddhism. They were not only forerunners of the Neo-Confucianism that flourished in the eleventh century; they had an important role in determining its direction.

Han Yü had a stormy career as a public official. Convinced of the importance of his mission as a defender of Confucianism, he criticized the Tâoists and the Buddhists with equal vigor and maintained that the true meaning of *Tâo* and *Te* was to be sought in the Confucian classics. Famous as a literary stylist, he still stands high in the estimation of Chinese scholars. His eloquence is most moving when he extols Confucianism as the source of all that is best in Chinese civilization and censures Tâoism and Buddhism as causes of steady degeneration from the society created by the ancient sages.

What is the True Way (Yüan Tâo)

From *Sources of Chinese Tradition,* Volume I, edited by William Theodore de Bary, New York, Columbia University Press, 1960.

[From *Ch'ang-li hsien-sheng wen-chi,* SPTK ed., 11:1a-3b]

TO love universally is called humanity (*jen*); to apply this in a proper manner is called righteousness (*i*). The operation of these is the Way (*Tâo*), and its inner power (*te*) is that it is self-sufficient, requiring nothing from outside itself. Humanity and righteousness are fixed principles, but the Way and its inner power are speculative concepts. Thus we have the way of the gentleman and the way of the small man, and both good and evil power. Lao Tzǔ made light of humanity and righteousness, but he did not thereby abolish them. His view was narrow like that of a man who sits at the bottom of a well and looks up at the sky, saying, "The sky is small." This does not mean that the sky is really small. Lao Tzǔ understood humanity and righteousness in only a very limited sense, and therefore it is natural that he belittled them. What he called the Way was only the Way as he saw it, and not what I call the Way; what he called inner power was only power as he saw it, and not what I call inner power. What I call the Way and power are a combination of humanity and righteousness and this is the definition accepted by the world at large. But what Lao Tzǔ called the Way and power are stripped of humanity and righteousness, and represent only the private view of one individual.

After the decline of the Chou and the death of Confucius, in the time of Ch'in's book burnings, the Tâoism of the

Han, and the Buddhism of the Wei, the Chin, the Liang, and the Sui, when men spoke of the Way and power, of humanity and righteousness, they were approaching them either as followers of Yang Chu or of Mo Tzŭ, of Lao Tzŭ or of Buddha. Being followers of these doctrines, they naturally rejected Confucianism. Acknowledging these men as their master, they made of Confucius an outcast, adhering to new teaching and vilifying the old. Alas, though men of later ages long to know of humanity and righteousness, the Way and inner power, from whom may they hear of them? . . .

In ancient times there were only four classes of people, but now there are six.[1] There was only one teaching, where now there are three.[2] For each family growing grain, there are now six consuming it; for each family producing utensils, there are now six using them; for one family engaged in trade, six others take their profits. Is it surprising then that the people are reduced to poverty and driven to theft?

In ancient times men faced many perils, but sages arose who taught them how to protect and nourish their lives, acting as their rulers and teachers. They drove away the harmful insects and reptiles, birds and beasts, and led men to settle in the center of the earth. The people were cold and they made them clothes, hungry and they gave them food. Because men had dwelt in danger in the tops of trees or grown sick sleeping on the ground, they built them halls and dwellings. They taught them handicrafts that they might have utensils to use, trades so that they could supply their wants, medicine to save them from early death, proper burial and sacrifices to enhance their sense of love and gratitude, rites to order the rules of precedence, music to express their repressed feelings, government to lead the indolent, and punishments to suppress the overbearing.

1. The four classes of traditional Chinese society — official, farmer, artisan, and merchant — to which were added the Tâoist and the Buddhist clergy.
2. Confucianism, to which was added Tâoism and Buddhism.

Because men cheated each other, they made tallies and seals, measures and scales to insure confidence; because men plundered they made walls and fortifications, armor and weapons to protect them. Thus they taught men how to prepare against danger and prevent injury to their lives.

Now the Taoists tell us that "until the sages die off, robbers will never disappear," or that "if we destroy our measures and break our scales then the people will cease their contention."[1] Alas, how thoughtless are such sayings! If there had been no sages in ancient times, then mankind would have perished, for men have no feathers or fur, no scales or shells to protect them from cold and heat, no claws and teeth to contend for food. Therefore those who are rulers give commands which are carried out by their officials and made known to the people, and the people produce grain, rice, hemp, and silk, make utensils and exchange commodities for the support of the superiors. If the ruler fails to issue commands, then he ceases to be a ruler, while if his subordinates do not carry them out and extend them to the people, and if the people do not produce goods for the support of their superiors, they must be punished. Yet the Way [of the Tâoists and Buddhists] teaches men to reject the ideas of ruler and subject and of father and son, to cease from activities which sustain life and seek for some so-called purity and Nirvana. Alas, it is fortunate for such doctrines that they appeared only after the time of the Three Reigns and thus escaped suppression at the hands of Yü and T'ang, kings Wen and Wu, the Duke of Chou and Confucius, but unfortunate for us that they did not appear before the Three Reigns so that they could have been rectified by those sages. . . .

The *Book of Rites* says: "The ancients who wished to illustrate illustrious virtue throughout the kingdom first ordered well their own states. Wishing to order well their states, they first regulated their families. Wishing to regu-

1. *Chuang Tzǔ*, Sec. 10.

late their families, they first cultivated their persons. Wishing to cultivate their persons, they first rectified their hearts. Wishing to rectify their hearts, they first sought to be sincere in their thoughts" [*Great Learning*, I]. Thus when the ancients spoke of rectifying the heart and being sincere in their thoughts, they had this purpose in mind. But now [the Taoists and Buddhists] seek to govern their hearts by escaping from the world, the state and the family. They violate the natural law, so that the son does not regard his father as a father, the subject does not look upon his ruler as a ruler, and the people do not serve those whom they must serve.

When Confucius wrote in the *Spring and Autumn Annals*, he treated as barbarians those feudal lords who observed customs, and as Chinese those who had advanced to the use of Chinese ways. The *Analects* [III, 5] says: "The barbarians with rulers are not the equal of the Chinese without rulers." The *Book of Odes* [Odes of Lu, 4] says: "Fight against the barbarians of the west and north, punish those of Ching and Shu." Yet now [the Buddhists] come with their barbarian ways and put them ahead of the teachings of our ancient kings. Are they not become practically barbarians themselves?

What were these teachings of our ancient kings? To love universally, which is called humanity; to apply this in the proper manner, which is called righteousness; to proceed from these to the Way and to be self-sufficient without seeking anything outside, which is called [inner] power. The *Odes* and the *History*, the *Changes* and the *Spring and Autumn Annals*, are their writings; rites and music, punishments and government, their methods. Their people were the four classes of officials, farmers, artisans, and merchants; their relationships were those of sovereign and subject, father and son, teacher and friend, guest and host, elder and younger brother, and husband and wife. Their clothing was hemp and silk; their dwelling halls and houses; their food grain and rice, fruit and vegetables, fish and meat. Their ways were easy to understand; their teachings simple

415

to follow. Applied to oneself, they brought harmony and blessing; applied to others, love and fairness. To the mind they gave peace; to the state and the family all that was just and fitting. Thus in life men were able to satisfy their emotions, and at death the obligations due them were fulfilled. Men sacrificed to Heaven and the gods were pleased; to the spirits of their ancestors and the ancestors received their offerings. What Way is this? It is what *I* call the Way, and not what the Tâoists and Buddhists call the Way. Yao taught it to Shun, Shun to Yü, Yü to T'ang, and T'ang to kings Wen and Wu and the Duke of Chou. These men taught it to Confucius and Confucius to Mencius, but when Mencius died it was no longer handed down. Hsün Tzŭ and Yang Hsiung understood elements of it, but their understanding lacked depth; they spoke of it but incompletely. In the days before the Duke of Chou, the sages were rulers and so they could put the Way into practice, but after the time of the Duke of Chou they were only officials and so they wrote at length about the Way.

What should be done now? I say that unless [Tâoism and Buddhism] are suppressed, the Way will not prevail; unless these men are stopped, the Way will not be practiced. Let their priests be turned into ordinary men again, let their books be burned and their temples converted into homes. Let the Way of our former kings be made clear to lead them, and let the widower and the widow, the orphan and the lonely, the crippled and the sick be nourished. Then all will be well.

Hui Hai

HUI HAI (fl. *c.* 780). Born in Yüeh Chou around the middle of the Tang dynasty (618-907), Hui Hai studied under two eminent Zen masters and set down in dialogue form his insights into "the essential gateway to truth by means of instantaneous awakening."

Known at first by the surname of Chu, a word which is identical in sound with the Chinese word meaning pearl, he entered the Great Cloud Monastery in his native city, studied under the Venerable Tâo Chih, and received the religious name of Hui Hai (Ocean of Wisdom). Later, attracted perhaps by the fame of Ma Tsu, he journeyed to Kiangsi and entered the monastery of Ma Tsu. Enlightenment came to him while he was engaged in a dialogue with Ma Tsu (d. 788), the famous Zen master who caused him to be known affectionately as the "Great Pearl." Hui Hai returned, after spending six years in Kiangsi, to Yüeh Chou. There he cared for Tâo Chih, his aging master, and wrote the book for which he is remembered.

On reading the completed manuscript, Ma Tsu remarked, "In Yüeh Chou there is now a great pearl." The name by which Hui Hai is widely remembered today recalls both his lay surname and the richly deserved compliment paid him by his former teacher. In his treatise he employs the dialogue system, popular in his period and particularly forceful since it gives the impression of a direct encounter between master and disciple, and treats systematically the various tenets common to

417

the Mahāyāna heritage as well as those peculiar to the different sects. Throughout his exposition, he stresses deliverance from the round of endless births and deaths, and the attainment of Buddhahood.

On Sudden Illumination

From *The Zen Teaching of Hui Hai on Sudden Illumination,* translated by John Blofeld. Published by Rider & Company, London. Copyright 1962 by John Blofeld. Used by permission of the Hutchinson Publishing Group, London.

1. Humbly I prostrate myself before the Buddhas of the Ten Quarters[1] and the Excellent Company of Bodhisattvas. In setting forth this treatise, I am apprehensive that I may fail correctly to interpret the Sacred Mind. If so, may I be given a chance for repentance and reform. However, if I do succeed in imparting the Sacred Truth, I dedicate the resultant merit to all living beings in the hope that each of them will attain Buddhahood in his next life.

* * *

2. Q: What method must we practise in order to attain deliverance?[2]

A: It can be attained only through a sudden Illumination.[3]

Q: What is a sudden Illumination?

A: Sudden means ridding yourselves of deluded thoughts[4] instantaneously. Illumination means the realization that Illumination is not something to be attained.

1. The zenith, nadir and eight compass points.
2. Deliverance from Samsāra, the round of endless births and deaths, by entrance into Nirvāna. However, the higher Mahāyāna teaching, as will be seen from this book, indicates that Nirvāna and Samsāra are one and that the Illumined man sees them thus.
3. The Chinese words are 'tun wu', of which the former means 'sudden' and the latter is identical with the Japanese word 'satori'.
4. Deluded thoughts are thoughts involving the dualism of opposites such as love and hatred, distinctions between self and other, and all the countless thinking processes which proceed from unillumined minds.

419

Q: From where do we start this practice?
A: You must start from the very root.
Q: And what is that?
A: MIND is the root.
Q: How can this be known?
A: The Laṅkāvatara Sūtra says: 'When mental processes (hsin) arise, then do all dharmas (phenomena) spring forth; and when mental processes cease, then do all dharmas cease likewise.' The Vimalakirti Sūtra says: 'Those desiring to attain the Pure Land[1] must first purify their own minds, for the purification of mind IS the purity of the Buddha-Land.' The Sūtra of the Doctrine Bequeathed by the Buddha says: 'Just by mind-control, all things become possible to us.' In another sūtra it says: 'Sages seek from mind, not from the Buddha; fools seek from the Buddha instead of seeking from mind. Wise men regulate their minds rather than their persons; fools regulate their persons rather than their minds.' The Sūtra of the Names of the Buddha states: 'Evil springs forth from the mind, and by the mind is evil overcome.' Thus we may know that all good and evil proceed from our minds and that mind is therefore the root. If you desire deliverance, you must first know all about the root. Unless you can penetrate to this truth, all your efforts will be in vain; for, while you are still seeking something from forms external to yourselves, you will never attain. The

1. The Pure Land (Sukhāvatī) is the immediate goal of countless Chinese, Japanese, Korean and Vietnamese Buddhists, who conceive of it as a Buddha-Land formed as a result of Amida Buddha's compassionate vow to save all sentient beings who put their faith in him. In that land, beings not yet ready for Nirvāṇa are prepared by the Buddha for that ultimate stage. There are other Buddhists for whom the Pure Land is a symbol of the Dharmakāya, of purified mind and so on. Though some Western Buddhists have written scornfully of the Pure Land form of Buddhism, there is ample evidence that its methods often lead to Illumination. The symbols it employs stand for the same truths as those taught by the Zen School and offer an easier approach for certain kinds of people. The constant repetition of Amida Buddha's name, accompanied by the right mental practices, is just another way of attaining full concentration and entering into samādhi. Dr. D. T. Suzuki and other eminent Zen authorities have testified to this.

Dhyānapāramitā Sūtra says: 'For as long as you direct your search to the forms around you, you will not attain your goal even after aeon upon aeon; whereas, by contemplating your inner awareness, you can achieve Buddhahood in a single flash of thought.'

Q: By what means is the root-practice to be performed?

A: Only by sitting in meditation, for it is accomplished by dhyāna (ch'an) and samādhi (ting). The Dhyānapāramita Sutra says: 'Dhyana and samadhi are essential to the search for the sacred knowledge of the Buddhas; for, without these, the thoughts remain in tumult and the roots of goodness suffer damage.'

Q: Please describe dhyana and samadhi.

A: When wrong thinking ceases, that is dhyana; when you sit contemplating your original nature,[1] that is samādhi, for indeed that original nature is your eternal mind. By samādhi, you withdraw your minds from their surroundings, thereby making them impervious to the eight winds, that is to say, impervious to gain and loss, calumny and eulogy, praise and blame, sorrow and joy. By concentrating in this way, even ordinary people may enter the state of Buddhahood. How can that be so? The Sūtra of the Bodhisattva-Precepts says: 'All beings who observe the Buddha-Precept thereby enter Buddhahood.' Other names for this are deliverance, gaining the further shore, transcending the six states of mortal being,[2] o'erleaping the three worlds,[3]

1. Original nature, self-nature, own-nature (pên hsing and tzǔ hsing) all have the same meaning. The Chinese omission of such words as 'your', 'its' and so on makes it easier for the reader to keep in mind that the self-nature of all sentient beings is one and the same.

2. The six states of mortal being or six realms are birth in the heavens, birth as asuras, as humans, as animals, as pretas, or in the hells. All alike are temporary conditions, though of varying duration, and none of them is a proper goal for Buddhists since even the denizens of the highest heavens are in danger of being brought low again by the turning of Samsāra's Wheels.

3. Samsāra is said to be composed of three kinds of worlds — worlds of desire, such as this one; worlds of form without desire; and worlds of formlessness.

421

3. Q: Whereon should the mind settle and dwell?

A: It should settle upon non-dwelling and there dwell.

Q: What is this non-dwelling?

A: It means not allowing the mind to dwell upon anything whatsoever.

Q: And what is the meaning of that?

A: Dwelling upon nothing means that the mind is not fixed upon good or evil, being or non-being, inside or outside or somewhere between the two, void or non-void, concentration or distraction. This dwelling upon nothing is the or becoming a mighty Bodhisattva, an omnipotent Sage, a Conqueror!

* * *

state in which it should dwell; those who attain to it are said to have non-dwelling minds — in other words, they have Buddha-Minds!

Q: What does mind resemble?

A: Mind has no colour, such as green or yellow, red or white; it is not long or short; it does not vanish or appear; it is free from purity and impurity alike; and its duration is eternal. It is utter stillness. Such, then, is the form and shape of our original mind, which is also our original body — the Buddhakaya![1]

Q: By what means do this body or mind perceive? Can they perceive with the eyes, ears, nose, sense of touch and consciousness?

A: No, there are not several means of perception like that.

Q: Then, what sort of perception is involved, since it is unlike any of those already mentioned?

A: It is perception by means of your own nature (svabhava). How so? Because your own nature being essentially pure and utterly still, its immaterial and motionless 'substance' is capable of this perception.[2]

1. The Buddhakāya (Buddha-Body) is another term for the Dharmakāya — the undifferentiated 'Body' in which the Buddhas and all other beings are conceived of as one with the Absolute. All of us possess this 'Body' but, prior to Illumination, are not aware of it.

2. The act of perceiving, being a function of everyone's own-nature, continues independently of there being objects to perceive.

Q: Yet, since that pure 'substance' cannot be found, where does such perception come from?

A: We may liken it to a bright mirror which, though it contains no forms, can nevertheless 'perceive' all forms. Why? Just because it is free from mental activity. If you students of the Way had minds unstained,[1] they would not give rise to falsehood and their attachments to the subjective ego and to objective externals would vanish; then purity would arise of itself and you would thereby be capable of such perception. The Dharmapada Sutra says: 'To establish ourselves amid perfect voidness in a single flash is excellent wisdom indeed!'

* * *

4. Q: According to the Vajra-Body Chapter of the Mahā-parinirvāṇa Sūtra, 'the (indestructible) diamond-body[2] is imperceptible, yet it clearly perceives; it is free from discerning and yet there is nothing which it does not comprehend'. What does this mean?

A: It is imperceptible because its own nature is a formless 'substance' which is intangible; hence it is called imperceptible; and, since it is intangible, this 'substance' is observed to be profoundly still and neither vanishing nor appearing. Though not apart from our world, it cannot be influenced by the worldly stream; it is self-possessed and sovereign, which is the reason why it clearly perceives. It is free from discerning in that its own nature is formless and basically undifferentiated. Its comprehending everything means that the undifferentiated 'substance' is endowed with functions as countless as the sands of the Ganges; and, if all

1. 'Wu jan' may be translated as pure, undefiled, unstained, etc. I prefer the more literal and picturesque term 'unstained', because it fits in so well with the analogy of the surface of a mirror. A mirror can reflect every kind of form and yet remain spotless, for it is entirely indifferent to what it reflects. Our minds when purified will become similarly impervious to stain. It must be added that, from a Buddhist point of view, a stain is a stain whether it results from something we call good or something we call evil.

2. The Diamond Body is another term for the Buddhakāya — that 'Body' which symbolizes the oneness of everyone's own-nature.

423

phenomena were to be discerned simultaneously, it would comprehend all of them without exception. In the Prajña Gatha it is written:

> Prajñā, unknowing, knoweth all;
> Prajñā, unseeing, seeth all.

* * *

5. Q: There is a sūtra which says that not to perceive anything in terms of being or non-being is true deliverance. What does it mean?

A: When we attain to purity of mind, that is something which can be said to exist. When this happens, our remaining free from any thought of achievement is called not perceiving anything as existent; while reaching the state in which no thoughts arise or persist, yet without being conscious of their absence, is called not perceiving anything as non-existent. So it is written: 'Not to perceive anything in terms of being and non-being', etc. The Surangama Sūtra says: 'Perceptions employed as a base for building up positive concepts are the origin of all ignorance (avidyā),[1] perception that there is nothing to perceive — that is Nirvāṇa, also known as deliverance.'

* * *

6. Q: What is the meaning of 'nothing to perceive'?

A: Being able to behold men, women and all the various sorts of appearances while remaining as free from love or aversion as if they were actually not seen at all — that is what is meant by 'nothing to perceive'.

Q: That which occurs when we are confronted by all sorts of shapes and forms is called perception. Can we speak of perception taking place when nothing confronts us?

A: Yes.

---

1. This means primordial ignorance, the cause of all our wanderings in Samsāra's round, in that it obscures from us the fact of our Buddha-Nature and leads us into the dualism of love and hatred, good and bad, existence and non-existence, and so on. Illumination means dispersal of the darkness of this ignorance.

Q: When something confronts us, it follows that we perceive it, but how can there be perception when we are confronted by nothing at all?

A: We are now talking of that perception which is independent of there being an object or not. How can that be? The nature of perception being eternal, we go on perceiving whether objects are present or not.[1] Thereby we come to understand that, whereas objects naturally appear and dissappear, the nature of perception does neither of those things; and it is the same with all your other senses.

Q: When we are looking at something, does the thing looked at exist objectively within the sphere of perception or not?

A: No, it does not.

Q: When we (look around and) do not see anything, is there an absence of something objective within the sphere of perception?

A: No, there is not.

*   *   *

7. Q: When there are sounds, hearing occurs. When there are no sounds, does hearing persist or not?

A: It does.

Q: When there are sounds, it follows that we hear them, but how can hearing take place during the absence of sound?

A: We are now talking of that hearing which is independent of there being any sound or not. How can that be? The nature of hearing being eternal, we continue to hear whether sounds are present or not.

Q: If that is so, who or what is the hearer?

1. See note 10.

A: It is your own nature which hears and it is the inner cognizer who knows.[1]

Q: As to the gateway of sudden Illumination, what are its doctrine, its aim, its substance and its function?[2]

A: To refrain from thinking (nien) is its doctrine; not to allow wrong thoughts to arise is its aim; purity is its substance and wisdom is its function.

Q: We have said that its doctrine is to refrain from thinking, but we have not yet examined the meaning of this term. What is it that we must refrain from thinking about?

A: It means that we must refrain from wrong thinking, but not from right thinking.

Q: What are wrong thinking and right thinking?

A: Thinking in terms of being and non-being is called wrong thinking, while not thinking in those terms is called

right thinking. Similarly, thinking in terms of good and evil is wrong; not to think so is right thinking. The same applies to all the other categories of opposites — sorrow and joy, beginning and end, acceptance and rejection, dislikes and likes, aversion and love, all of which are called wrong thinking, while to abstain from thinking in those categories is called right thinking.

Q: Please define right thinking (more positively).

A: It means thinking solely of Bodhi (Enlightenment).

Q: Is Bodhi something tangible?

A: It is not.

1. The inner cognizer is the highest part of our consciousness — that which knows and is fully aware of everything but which does not discriminate between one thing and another.

2. The words 't'i' and 'yung' ('substance' and 'function') are briefly defined in the list of Chinese words offering special difficulties which appears after these notes. These two words are of the greatest importance to our understanding of Ch'an (Zen). 'Substance' is often likened to a lamp and 'function' to its light. The former would be useless unless capable of functioning by producing light; the latter would be non-existent without the former. As already explained, the meaning of 'substance' is the intangible and indefinable reality which is the true nature of everyone, and 'function' denotes its infinite capacity to produce every sort of energy, form and so on.

Q: But how can we think solely of Bodhi if it is intangible?

A: It is as though Bodhi were a mere name applied to something which, in fact, is intangible, something which never has been or ever will be attained. Being intangible, it cannot be thought about, and it is just this not thinking about it which is called rightly thinking of Bodhi as something not to be thought about — for this implies that your mind dwells upon nothing whatsoever. The term 'not to be thought about' is like the various kinds of not-thinking mentioned earlier, all of which are but names convenient for use in certain circumstances — all are of the one substance in which no differences or diversities exist. Simply to be conscious of mind as resting upon nothing whatsoever is to be without thought; and whoever reaches this state is naturally delivered.

* * *

8. Q: What is the meaning of to act as the Buddhas do?

A: It menas total abstention from action,[1] which is also termed right or holy action. It is very similar to what we were talking about before, for it means not acting as if things really are or are not, and not acting from motives of aversion, love and all the rest. The Great Canon of Monastic Rules says: 'The Sages do not act like other beings; nor do other beings act like the Sages.'

* * *

9. Q: What does right perception mean?

A: It means perceiving that there is nothing to perceive.

1. As will be seen from what follows, 'total abstention form action' is a phrase not to be taken literally by turning ourselves into blocks of wood or stone. It means abstention from action dictated by impure motives involving love, hatred and all other pairs of opposites, but not from the actions necessary for responding to the needs of the moment. This conception of non-action is close to the Tâoistic conception of 'wu wei'. In response to hunger, we eat, but this should be done without gluttony, fastidiousness, etc. Similarly, in these days, most people, especially those with families to support, have to work; but each job should be done for its own sake without dwelling upon the profit or loss likely to accrue, and without zest or aversion for particular aspects of the work.

Q: And what does that mean?

A: It means beholding all sorts of forms, but without being stained by them as no thoughts of love or aversion arise in the mind. Reaching this state is called obtaining the Buddha-Eye, which really means just that and nothing else. Whereas, if the spectacle of various forms produces love or aversion in you, that is called perceiving them as though they had objective existence, which implies having the eye of an ordinary person, for indeed ordinary people have no other sort of eye. It is the same with all the other organs of perception.

* * *

10. Q: When you said that wisdom is the function, what did you mean by wisdom?

A: The knowledge that by realizing the voidness of all opposites deliverance is assured and that, without this realization, you will never gain deliverance. This is what we call wisdom or knowing wrong from right. Another name for it is knowing the function of the 'substance'. Concerning the unreality of opposites, it is the wisdom inherent in the 'substance' which makes it known that to realize their voidness means liberation and that there can be no more doubt about it. This is what we mean by function. In speaking thus of the unreality of opposites, we refer to the non-existence of relativities such as 'is' and 'is not', good and evil, love and aversion, and so on.

Q: By what means can the gateway of our school be entered?

A: By means of the dānapāramitā.

Q: According to the Buddha, the Bodhisattva-Path comprises six paramitas. Why, then, have you mentioned only the one? Please explain why this one alone provides a sufficient means for us to enter.

A: Deluded people fail to understand that the other five all proceed from the danaparamita and that by its practice all the others are fulfilled.

Q: Why is it called the dānapāramitā?

428

A: Dana means relinquishment.

Q: Relinquishment of what?

A: Relinquishment of the dualism of opposites.

Q: Which means?

A: It means total relinquishment of ideas as to the dual nature of good and bad, being and non-being, love and aversion, void and non-void, concentration and distraction, pure and impure. By giving all of them up, we attain to a state in which all opposites are seen as void. The real practice of the danaparamita entails achieving this state without any thought of 'Now I see that opposites are void' or 'Now I have relinquished all of them.' We may also call it the simultaneous cutting off of the myriad types of concurrent causes; for it is when these are cut off that the whole Dharma-Nature becomes void; and this voidness of the Dharma-Nature means the non-dwelling of the mind upon anything whatsoever. Once that state is achieved, not a single form can be discerned. Why? Because our self-nature is immaterial and does not contain a single thing (foreign to itself). That which contains no single thing is true Reality, the marvellous form of the Tathagata. It is said in the Diamond Sutra: 'Those who relinquish all forms are called Buddhas (Enlightened Ones).'

Q: However, the Buddha did speak of six paramitas, so why do you now say they can all be fulfilled in that one? Please give your reason for this.

A: The Sūtra of the Questions of Brahma says: 'Jāla-vidya, the Elder, spoke unto Brahma and said: "Bodhisattvas by relinquishing all defilements (klesa) may be said to have fulfilled the dānapāramitā, also known as total relinquishment; being beguiled by nothing, they may be said to have fulfilled the sīlapāramitā, also known as observing the precepts; being hurt by nothing, they may be ˙said to have fulfilled the ksāntipāramitā, also known as exercising forbearance; clinging to nothing, they may be said to have fulfilled the vīryapāramita, also known as exercising zeal; dwelling on nothing, they may be said to have fulfilled the

429

dhyānaparāmitā, also known as practising dhyāna and samādhi; speaking lightly of nothing, they may be said to have fulfilled the prajñaparamita, also known as exercising wisdom. Together, they are named the six methods."'

Now I am going to speak about those six methods in a way which means precisely the same — the first entails relinquishment; the second, no arising (of perception, sensation, etc., etc., etc.); the third, no thinking; the fourth, remaining apart from forms; the fifth, nonabiding (of the mind); and the sixth, no indulgence in light speech. We give different names to these six methods only for convenience in dealing with passing needs; for, when we come to the marvellous principle involved in them all, we find no differences at all. So you have only to understand that, by a single act of relinquishment, EVERYTHING is relinquished; and that no arising means no arising of anything whatsoever. Those who have lost their way have no intuitive understanding of this; that is why they speak of the methods as though they differed from one another. Fools bogged down in a multiplicity of methods revolve endlessly from life-span to life-span. I exhort you students to practise the way of relinquishment and nothing else, for it brings to perfection not only the other five paramitas but also myriads of dharmas (methods).

* * *

11. Q: What are the 'three methods of training (to be performed) at the same level' and what is meant by performing them on the same level?

A: They are discipline (vinaya), concentration (dhyāna) and wisdom (prajña).[1]

Q: Please explain them one by one.

A: Discipline involves stainless purity.[2] Concentration in-

1. Elsewhere in this text I have sometimes translated 'ting' as 'samādhi', but the trio 'chieh ting hui' is generally translated 'discipline, concentration and wisdom'.

2. Purity means something much more than the moral purity normally implied by this term in English; it means freedom from ALL attachment and discrimination whatsoever; it would be marred by attachment to good as much as by attachment to bad.

volves the stilling of your minds so that you remain wholly unmoved by surrounding phenomena. Wisdom means that your stillness of mind is not disturbed by your giving any thought to that stillness, that your purity is unmarred by your entertaining any thought of purity and that, in the midst of all such pairs of opposites as good and evil, you are able to distinguish between them without being stained by them and, in this way, to reach the state of being perfectly at ease and free of all dependence. Furthermore, if you realize that discipline, concentration and wisdom are all alike in that their substance is intangible and that, hence, they are undivided and therefore one — that is what is meant by three methods of training performed at the same level.

* * *

12. Q: When the mind rests in a state of purity, will that not give rise to some attachment to purity?

A: If, on reaching the state of purity, you refrain from thinking 'now my mind is resting in purity', there will be no such attachment.

Q: When the mind rests in a state of void, will that not entail some attachment to void?

A: If you think of your mind as resting in a state of void, then there will be such an attachment.

Q: When the mind reaches the state of not dwelling upon anything, and continues in that state, will there not be some attachment to its not dwelling upon anything?

A: So long as your mind is fixed solely on void, there is nothing to which you can attach yourself. If you want to understand the non-dwelling mind very clearly, while you are actually sitting in meditation, you must be cognizant only of the mind and not permit yourself to make judgements — that is, you must avoid evaluations in terms of good, evil or anything else. Whatever is past is past, so do not sit in judgement upon it; for, when minding about the past ceases of itself, it can be said that there is no longer any past. Whatever is in the future is not here yet, so do not

431

direct your hopes and longings towards it; for, when minding about the future ceases of itself, it can be said that there is no future.[1] Whatever is present is now at hand; just be conscious of your non-attachment to everything — non-attachment in the sense of not allowing any love or aversion for anything to enter your mind; for, when minding the present ceases of itself, we may say that there is no present. When there is no clinging to any of those three periods, they may be said not to exist.

Should your mind wander away, do not follow it, whereupon your wandering mind will stop wandering of its own accord. Should your mind desire to linger somewhere, do not follow it and do not dwell there, whereupon your mind's questing for a dwelling-place will cease of its own accord. Thereby, you will come to possess a non-dwelling mind — a mind which remains in the state of non-dwelling. If you are fully aware in yourself of a non-dwelling mind, you will discover that there is just the fact of dwelling, with nothing to dwell upon or not to dwell upon. This full awareness in yourself of a mind dwelling upon nothing is known as having a clear perception of your own mind or, in other words, as having a clear perception of your own nature. A mind which dwells upon nothing is the Buddha-Mind, the mind of one already delivered, Bodhi-Mind, Uncreate Mind; it is also called realization that the nature of all appearances is unreal. It is this which the sutras call 'patient realization of the Uncreate'.[2] If you have not realized it yet, you must strive and strive, you must in-

1. When memory and reverie are cut off, past and future cease to exist. The present does, of course, exist in a firmer sense than either of the others, but it is not PRESENT except when thought of in relation to past and future. The state of mind of an Illumined man is independent of time-relationships.

2. Literally, 'realization of "the patient endurance of the Uncreate" (anutpattikadharmakṣānti)'. The meaning of this Sanskrit Mahāyāna term is 'the patient endurance entailed in resting in the imperturbable Reality beyond birth and death'. The prajñāpāramitā Sāstra defines it as imperturbably abiding with unflinching faith in the Bhūtatathatā which is free from relativity and subject neither to creation nor destruction'.

crease your exertions. Then, when your efforts are crowned with success, you will have attained to understanding from within yourself — an understanding stemming from a mind that abides nowhere, by which we mean a mind free from delusion and reality alike. A mind disturbed by love and aversion is deluded; a mind free from both of them is real; and a mind thus free reaches the state in which opposites are seen as void, whereby freedom and deliverance are obtained.

Huang Po

HUANG PO (died *c.* 850). Much of what is known
of the life and teachings of Huang Po (Hsi Yün, T'uan
Chi, or Obaku) comes from amanuensis, P'ei Hsiu,
who recorded "only about a fifth" of the teachings that
had been transmitted to him directly. The Zen master was
known by several names during his lifetime, and the
name by which he is now known was taken from that of
the mountain where he lived for many years. P'ei Shieu
states in his preface to the recorded teachings of the
great Zen master (written in 858) that the latter came
to Chung Lin in 843 and to Wan Ling in 849. P'ei Shieu
questioned the Zen master on both occasions, set down
what he had learned and considered to be a direct
transmission of the Wordless Doctrine, and entrusted
his manuscript to two monks with instructions for them
to return to Mount Huang Po and find out whether the
recorded teachings agreed with what the elder monks
who resided there had heard in the past. Huang Po
seems to have died around the middle of the ninth
century, after transmitting the Wordless Doctrine to I
Hsüan, founder of the Lin Chi (Rinzai) sect, which
still flourishes in China and Japan.

Huang Po is thought to have been the third in descent from Hui Nêng, the Sixth and last of the Chinese
Patriarchs who continued the mystical transmission of
the wordless doctrine, or "with Mind transmitted Mind,"
after it had been passed on from Gautama Buddha
through a long line of Indian Patriarchs of the Dhyana
branch of the great Mahàyàna School of Buddhism,
which claims to have preserved the highest teachings of

435

Gautama Buddha. By the time Hui Nêng received the Wordless Doctrine, the Dhyāna, or Zen, branch had split into two fractions, one teaching that the process of Enlightenment is gradual, the other that it is sudden. Huang Po taught the doctrine of Sudden Enlightenment through intuitive knowledge or direct perception of truth, making use of sermons, anecdotes, dialogues, and above all, parables. Thousands came to look up to him as to a mountain, to listen to his teachings, and to receive intuitive knowledge which could not be communicated by words. By a single phrase or paradox, he could destroy an idol of the mind, it was said, and precipitate Sudden Enlightenment or set a disciple on the right path.

Sermons and Dialogues

From *The Zen Teachings of Huang Po on the Transmission of Mind*, translated by John Blofeld. Published by Grove Press, Inc., New York. Copyright 1958 by John Blofeld. Used by permission.

1. THE Master said to me: All the Buddhas and all sentient beings are nothing but the One Mind, beside which nothing exists. This Mind, which is without beginning, is unborn[1] and indestructible. It is not green or yellow, and has neither form nor appearance. It does not belong to the categories of things which exist or do not exist, nor can it be thought of in terms of new or old. It is neither long nor short, big nor small, for it transcends all limits, measures, names, traces and comparisons. It is that which you see before you — begin to reason about it and you at once fall into error. It is like the boundless void which cannot be fathomed or measured. The One Mind alone is the Buddha, and there is no distinction between the Buddha and sentient things, but that sentient beings are attached to forms and so seek externally for Buddhahood. By their very seeking they lose it, for that is using the Buddha to seek for the Buddha and using mind to grasp Mind. Even though they do their utmost for a full aeon, they will not be able to attain to it. They do not know that, if they put a stop to conceptual thought and forget their anxiety, the Buddha will appear before them, for this Mind is the Buddha and the Buddha is all living beings. It is not the less for being mani-

1. Unborn, not in the sense of eternity, for this allows contrast with its opposite; but unborn in the sense that it belongs to no categories admitting of alteration or antithesis.

fested in ordinary beings, nor is it greater for being manifested in the Buddhas.

* * *

2. As to performing the six paramitas[1] and vast numbers of similar practices, or gaining merits as countless as the sands of the Ganges, since you are fundamentally complete in every respect, you should not try to supplement that perfection by such meaningless practices. When there is occasion for them perform them; and, when the occasion is passed, remain quiescent. If you are not absolutely convinced that the Mind is the Buddha, and if you are attached to forms, practices and meritorious performances, your way of thinking is false and quite incompatible with the Way. The Mind is the Buddha, nor are there any other Buddhas or any other mind. It is bright and spotless as the the Mind of the Buddha and of sentient beings. If you void, having no form or appearance whatever. To make use of your minds to think conceptually is to leave the substance and attach yourselves to form. The Ever-Existent Buddha is not a Buddha of form or attachment. To practise the six paramitas and a myriad similar practices with the intention of becoming a Buddha thereby is to advance by stages, but the Ever-Existent Buddha is not a Buddha of stages. Only awake to the One Mind, and there is nothing whatsoever to be attained. This is the REAL Buddha. The Buddha and all sentient beings are the One Mind and nothing else.

* * *

3. Mind is like the void in which there is no confusion or evil, as when the sun wheels through it shining upon the four corners of the world. For, when the sun rises and illuminates the whole earth, the void gains not in brilliance; and, when the sun sets, the void does not darken. The phenomena of light and dark alternate with each other,

1. Charity, morality, patience under affliction, zealous application, right control of mind and the application of the highest wisdom.

438

but the nature of the void remains unchanged. So it is with look upon the Buddha as presenting a pure, bright or Enlightened appearance, or upon sentient beings as presenting a foul, dark or mortal-seeming appearance, these conceptions resulting from attachment to form will keep you from supreme knowledge, even after the passing of as many aeons as there are sands in the Ganges. There is only the One Mind and not a particle of anything else on which to lay hold, for this Mind is the Buddha. If you students of the Way do not awake to this Mind substance, you will overlay Mind with conceptual thought, you will seek the Buddha outside yourselves, and you will remain attached to forms, pious practices and so on, all of which are harmful and not at all the way to supreme knowledge.

* * *

4. Making offerings to all the Buddhas of the universe is not equal to making offerings to one follower of the Way who has eliminated conceptual thought. Why? Because such a one forms no concepts whatever. The substance of the Absolute is inwardly like wood or stone, in that it is motionless, and outwardly like the void, in that it is without bounds or obstructions. It is neither subjective nor objective, has no specific location, is formless, and cannot vanish. Those who hasten towards it dare not enter, fearing to hurtle down through the void with nothing to cling to or to stay their fall. So they look to the brink and retreat. This refers to all those who seek such a goal through cognition. Thus, those who seek the goal through cognition are like the fur (*many*), while those who obtain intuitive knowledge of the Way are like the horns (*few*).[1]

* * *

5. Mañjusri represents fundamental law and Samantabhadra, activity. By the former is meant the law of the real and unbounded void, and by the latter the inexhaustible

1. Compare this with Professor Suzuki's: 'That which is known as mind in discursive reasoning is no-mind, though without this Mind cannot be reached.'

439

activities beyond the sphere of form. Avalokiteśvara represents boundless compassion; Mahāsthāma, great wisdom, and Vimalakīrti, spotless name.[1] Spotless refers to the real nature of things, while name means form; yet form is really one with real nature, hence the combined term 'spotless name'.[2] All the qualities typified by the great Bodhisattvas are inherent in men and are not to be separated from the One Mind. Awake to it, and it is there. You students of the Way who do not awake to this in your own minds, and who are attached to appearances or who seek for something objective outside your own minds, have all turned your backs on the Way. The sands of the Ganges! The Buddha said of these sands: 'If all the Buddhas and Bodhisattvas with Indra and all the gods walk across them, the sands do not rejoice; and, if oxen, sheep, reptiles and insects tread upon them, the sands are not angered. For jewels and perfumes they have no longing, and for the stinking filth of manure and urine they have no loathing.'

❊   ❊   ❊

6. This Mind is no mind of conceptual thought and it is completely detached from form. So Buddhas and sentient beings do not differ at all. If you can only rid yourselves of conceptual thought, you will have accomplished everything. But if you students of the Way do not rid yourselves of conceptual thought in a flash, even though you strive for aeon after aeon, you will never accomplish it. Enmeshed in the meritorious practices of the Three Vehicles, you will be unable to attain Enlightenment. Nevertheless, the realization of the One Mind may come after a shorter or a longer period. There are those who, upon hearing this

1. This abstract notion of the Bodhisattvas, regarded by some sects as individual spiritual entities, is shared by some Buddhists outside the Zen Sect.
2. Zen teaches that, though the phenomenal world based on sensory experience has only relative existence, it is wrong to regard it as something separate from the One Mind. It is the One Mind wrongly apprehended. As the Hridaya Sūtra says: 'Form is not different from void, void from form; form is void and void is form.'

teaching, rid themselves of conceptual thought in a flash. There are others who do this after following through the Ten Beliefs, the Ten Stages, the Ten Activities and the Ten Bestowals of Merit. Yet others accomplish it after passing through the Ten Stages of a Bodhisattva's Progress.[1] But whether they transcend conceptual thought by a longer or a shorter way, the result is a state of BEING: there is no pious practising and no action of realizing. That there is nothing which can be attained is not idle talk; it is the truth. Moreover, whether you accomplish your aim in a single flash of thought or after going through the Ten Stages of a Bodhisattva's Progress, the achievement will be the same; for this state of being admits of no degrees, so the latter method merely entails aeons of unnecessary suffering and oil.[2]

* * *

7. The building up of good and evil both involve attachment to from.[3] Those who, being attached to form, do evil have to undergo various incarnations unnecessarily; while those who, being attached to form, do good, subject themselves to toil and privation equally to no purpose. In either case it is better to achieve sudden self-realization and to grasp the fundamental Dharma. This Dharma is Mind, beyond which there is no Dharma; and this Mind is the Dharma, beyond which there is no mind. Mind in itself is no mind, yet neither is it no-mind. To say that mind is no-mind implies something existent.[4] Let there be a silent

1. These various categories of ten are all part of the doctrine as taught by certain other sects. Huang Po wishes to make it clear that, though these may be useful in preparing the ground, the mind must in any case take a sudden leap, and that having passed through these stages in nowise constitutes partial Enlightenment.

2. Merit, however excellent in itself, has nothing to do with Enlightenment.

3. According to Zen, virtuous actions should be performed by adepts, but not with a view to accumulating merit and not as a means to Enlightenment. The door should remain perfectly unattached to the actions and to their results.

4. In other words, Mind is an arbitrary term for something that cannot properly be expressed in words.

441

understanding and no more. Away with all thinking and explaining. Then we may say that the Way of Words has been cut off and movements of the mind eliminated. This Mind is the pure Buddha-Source inherent in all men. All wriggling beings possessed of sentient life and all the Buddhas and Bodhisattvas are of this one substance and do not differ. Differences arise from wrong-thinking only and lead to the creation of all kinds of karma.[1]

* * *

8. Our original Buddha-Nature is, in highest truth, devoid of any atom of objectivity. It is void, omnipresent, silent pure; it is glorious and mysterious peaceful joy — and that is all. Enter deeply into it by awaking to it yourself. That which is before you is it, in all its fullness, utterly complete There is naught beside. Even if you go through all the stages of a Bodhisattva's progress towards Buddhahood, one by one; when at last, in a single flash, you attain to full realization, you will only be realizing the Buddha-Nature which has been with you all the time; and by all the fore going stages you will have added to it nothing at all.[2] You will come to look upon those aeons of work and achieve ment as no better than unreal actions performed in a dream That is why the Tathagata said: 'I truly attained nothing from complete, unexcelled Enlightenment. Had there been anything attained, Dipamkara Buddha would not have made the prophecy concerning me.'[3] He also said: 'Thi

1. Karma, even good karma, leads to rebirth and prolongs the wanderings of the supposedly individual entity; for when good karma has worked itself out in consequent enjoyment, the 'individual' is as far from understanding the One Mind as ever.
2. Enlightenment must come in a flash whether you have passed through the preliminary stages or not, so the latter can well be dispensed with except that, for reasons unconnected with Enlightenment, Zen requires of adepts an attitude of kindness and helpfulness towards all living creature
3. This quotation refers to the Diamond either directly or indirectly. Dipamkara Buddha, during a former life of Gautama Buddha, prophesied that he would one day attain to Buddhahood. Huang Po means that the prophecy would not have been made if Dipamkara Buddha had supposed that Gautama Buddha's Enlighten ment would lead to the actual attainment of something he had not a ready *been* from the very first; for then Enlightenment would not have led to Buddhahood, which implies a voidness of all distinctions such as attainer, attained, non-attainer and non-attained.

442

Dharma is absolutely without distinctions, neither high nor low, and its name is Bodhi.' It is pure Mind, which is the source of everything and which, whether appearing as sentient beings or as Buddhas, as the rivers and mountains of the world which has form, as that which is formless, or as penetrating the whole universe, is absolutely without distinctions, there being no such entities as selfness and otherness.

* * *

9. This pure Mind, the source of everything, shines forever and on all with the brilliance of its own perfection. But the people of the world do not awake to it, regarding only that which sees, hears, feels and knows as mind. Blinded by their own sight, hearing, feeling and knowing, they do not perceive the spiritual brilliance of the source-substance. If they would only eliminate all conceptual thought in a flash, that source-substance would manifest itself like the sun ascending through the void and illuminating the whole universe without hindrance or bounds. Therefore, if you students of the Way seek to progress through seeing, hearing, feeling and knowing, when you are deprived of your perceptions, your way to Mind will be cut off and you will find nowhere to enter. Only realize that, though real Mind is expressed in these perceptions, it neither forms part of them or is separate from them. You should not start REASONING from these perceptions, nor allow them to give rise to conceptual thought; yet nor should you seek the One Mind apart from them or abandon them in your pursuit of the Dharma. Do not keep them or abandon them or dwell in them or cleave to them. Above, below and around you, all is spontaneously existing, for there is nowhere which is outside the Buddha-Mind.

* * *

10. When the people of the world hear it said that the Buddhas transmit the Doctrine of the Mind, they suppose that there is something to be attained or realized apart from Mind, and thereupon they use Mind to seek the Dharma, not knowing that Mind and the object of their

443

search are one. Mind cannot be used to seek something from Mind; for then, after the passing of millions of aeons, the day of success will still not have dawned. Such a method is not to be compared with suddenly eliminating conceptual thought, which is the fundamental Dharma. Suppose a warrior, forgetting that he was already wearing his pearl on his forehead, were to seek for it elsewhere, he could travel the whole world without finding it. But if someone who knew what was wrong were to point it out to him, the warrior would immediately realize that the pearl had been there all the time. So, if you students of the Way are mistaken about your own real Mind, not recognizing that it is the Buddha, you will consequently look for him elsewhere, indulging in various achievements and practices and expecting to attain realization by such graduated practices. But, even after aeons of diligent searching, you will not be able to attain to the Way. These methods cannot be compared to the sudden elimination of conceptual thought, in the certain knowledge that there is nothing at all which has absolute existence, nothing on which to lay hold, nothing on which to rely, nothing in which to abide, nothing subjective or objective. It is by preventing the rise of conceptual thought that you will realize Bodhi; and, when you do, you will just be realizing the Buddha who has always existed in your own Mind! Aeons of striving will prove to be so much wasted effort; just as, when the warrior found his pearl, he merely discovered what had been hanging on his forehead all the time; and just as his finding of it had nothing to do with his efforts to discover it elsewhere. Therefore the Buddha said: 'I truly attained nothing from complete, unexcelled Enlightenment.' It was for fear that people would not believe this that he drew upon what is seen with the five sorts of vision and spoken with the five kinds of speech. So this quotation is by no means empty talk, but expresses the highest truth.

SHAO YUNG

SHAO YUNG (1011-1077). Profoundly affected by
Tâoism, Shao Yung (Shao K'ang-chieh or Shao Yao-fu)
tried to fashion from *I Ching (Book of Changes)*
a distinctive philosophy of human nature and society,
using the symbolism of the ancient book of divination
to represent the annual succession of seasons in their
recurrent functioning under *Yin* (Earth) and *Yang*
(Heaven). In his distinctive theory of number as the
key to an understanding of human nature and society,
man is seen as the product of the creative activity of the
Supreme Ultimate, working through Yin and Yang.
Though man is no longer the center of the universe, he
is the most important element in the vast process of
the evolution of natural phenomena, and he has an
almost unlimited capacity for perfectibility. Evolution
begins with the Great Ultimate (*Li* or *Tâo*), proceeds
through Yin and Yang, spirit, number, form, and finally
reaches materiality. Like other Neo-Confucianists, he
held that all things contain principles and that supreme
principles govern the universe. He went beyond the other
Neo-Confucianists, however, in holding that these principles can be reduced to numbers and that man, like
all other things, is governed by numbers. Thus he followed the common practice of tracing the pattern of
cosmic evolution from the Great Ultimate through the
negative and positive forces of the universe to the
multiplicity of things, but he attributed the universal
operation, or Change, to spirit, and he added the concept of number.

Shao Yung served his government in a few minor capa-

445

cities but his life in general was one of quietude and poverty. Highly esteemed during his lifetime for his integrity and scholarship, he merited the epithet of K'ang-chie ("calm, possessing self-control"), which was given to him after he died and which became his usual designation in literature. In 1235 he was admitted to the Confucian Temple, and in 1267 he was ennobled. His greatest and best known work is the *Huang-chi ching-shih shu* (Supreme Principles Governing the World), in which he attempted to view all things objectively and to discover number or principle which is inherent in them.

The Supreme Principles Governing the World

From *Sources of Chinese Tradition*, Volume I, edited by William Theodore de Bary, New York, Columbia University Press, 1960.

[From *Huang-chi ching-shih shu*, SPPY ed., 7A:24b-8b:23a]

As the Great Ultimate becomes differentiated, the two primary modes appear. The yang descends and interacts with the yin, and yin rises to interact with yang, and consequently the four secondary forms are constituted. Yin and yang interact and generate the four secondary forms of Heaven; the element of weakness and the element of strength interact and generate the four secondary forms of earth; and consequently the eight trigrams are completed. The eight trigrams intermingle and generate the myriad things. Therefore the One is differentiated into two, two into four, four into eight, eight into sixteen, sixteen into thirty-two, and thirty-two into sixty-four. Thus "in the successive division of yin and yang and the mutual operation of strength and weakness, the six positions [of the lines in each hexagram] in the *Book of Changes* form an orderly pattern."[1] Ten is divided into 100, 1,000, and 10,000. This is similar to the fact that the root engenders the trunk; the trunk, branches; and the branches, leaves. The greater the division, the smaller the result, and the finer the division, the more complex. Taken as a unit, it is One. Taken as diffused development, it is the many. Hence the heavenly principle divides, the earthly principle unites; the *chen* hexagram [symbol of development] augments, and the *sun* hexagram [symbol

1. *Book of Changes*, Shuo-kua 2.

of bending] diminishes. Augmentation leads to division, division leads to diminution, and diminution leads to unity. [7A:24b]

The Great Ultimate is One. It produces the two [yin and yang] without engaging in activity. The two constitute spirit. Spirit engenders number, number engenders form, and form engenders material objects. [8B:23a]

Forms and numbers in the universe can be calculated, but their wonderful operations cannot be fathomed. The universe can be fully investigated through principles but not through corporeal forms. How can it be fully investigated through external observation? [8A:16b]

HISTORY

[From *Huang-chi ching-shih shu,* SPPY ed., 5:15a-b]

Therefore from the times of old in the administration of their empires rulers have had four kinds of Mandates: Correct Mandate, Accepted Mandate, Modified Mandate, and Substituted Mandate. Correct Mandate is that which is completely followed. Accepted Mandate is that which is followed with certain changes. Modified Mandate is mostly changed but partly followed. Substituted Mandate is that which is changed completely. That which is followed completely is continued completely. That which is followed with certain changes is continued with some deletions. That which is mostly changed but partly followed has [a great deal of] deletion followed by continuation. That which is changed completely is deleted completely. That which is changed completely is work meant for one generation. That which is mostly changed but partly followed is work meant for a hundred generations. That which is followed completely is work meant for a thousand generations. That which follows what ought to be followed and changes what ought to be changed is work meant for countless generations. Work meant for one generation, is this not the way of the Five Overlords? Work meant for ten generations, is this not the way of the Three Kings? Work meant for a hundred generations, is this not the way of the Five Emperors? Work meant for a thousand generations, is this not the way of the Three August Sovereigns? Work meant for countless generations, is this not the way of Confucius? Thus we know that the overlords, kings, emperors, and sovereigns had what were called Mandates for a limited number of generations. But the Mandate of Confucius transcends generations.

MAN

[From *Huang-chi ching-shih shu*, SPPY ed., 7A:4a-8B:26a]

The origin of Heaven and earth is based on the principle of the Mean [centrality]. Thus the heavenly and earthly principles never deviate from this central principle of existence although they are engaged in incessant transformation. Man is central in the universe, and the mind is central in man. The sun is most glorious and the moon is full when they are in the central position. Therefore, the gentleman highly values the principle of centrality. [7B:4a]

Our nature views things as they are, but our passion causes us to see things subjectively and egoistically. Our nature is impartial and enlightened, but our passions are partial and deceived. When the material endowment in man is characterized by the Mean and harmony, the elements of strength and weakness in him will be balanced. If yang predominates, he will be off balance toward strength, and if yin predominates, he will be off balance toward weakness. As knowledge directed toward the nature of man increases, the knowledge directed toward things will decrease.

Man occupies the most honored position in the scheme of things because he combines in him the principles of all species. If he honors his own position and enhances his honor, he can make all species serve him.

The nature of all things is complete in the human species.

The spirit of man is the same as the spirit of Heaven and earth. Therefore, when he deceives himself, he is deceiving Heaven and earth. Let him beware!

Spirit is nowhere and yet everywhere. The perfect man can penetrate the minds of others because he is based on the One. Spirit is perforce called the One and the Way (Tâo). It is best to call it spirit. [8B:16a-17b]

The mind is the Great Ultimate. The human mind should be as calm as still water. Being calm, it will be tranquil. Being tranquil, it will be enlightened.

In the pursuit of prior existence [spiritual culture] sincerity is basic. Perfect sincerity can penetrate all spirits. Without sincerity, the Way cannot be attained.

Our substance and nature come from Heaven, but learning lies with man. Substance and nature develop from within, while learning enters into us from without. "It is due to our nature that intelligence results from sincerity,"[2] but it is due to learning that sincerity results from intelligence.

The learning of a gentleman aims precisely at enriching his personality. The rest, such as governing people and handling things, is all secondary.

Without sincerity, one cannot investigate principle to the utmost.

Sincerity is the controlling factor in one's nature. It is beyond space and time.

He who acts in accordance with the principle of Heaven will have the entire process of creation in his grip. When the principle of Heaven is achieved, not only his personality, but also his mind, are enriched. And not only his mind but also his nature and destiny are enriched. To be in accordance with principle is normal, but to deviate from principle is abnormal. [8B:25a-26a]

OBSERVATION OF THINGS

[From *Huang-chi ching-shih shu*, SPPY ed., 6:26a-8B:27b]

When the mind retains its unity and is not disturbed, it can act on, and react to, all things harmoniously. Thus the mind of the gentleman is "empty" [absolutely pure and peaceful] and is not disturbed. [8B:29a]

1. *Mean*, 21.

450

By viewing things is not meant viewing them with one's physical eyes but with one's mind. Nay, not with one's mind but with the principle inherent in things. There is nothing in the universe without its principle, nature, and destiny. These can be known only when principle has been investigated to the utmost, when the nature is completely developed, and when destiny is fulfilled. The knowledge of these three is true knowledge. Even the sage cannot go beyond it. Whoever goes beyond it cannot be called a sage.

A mirror reflects because it does not obscure the corporeal form of things. But water [with its purity] does even better because it reveals the universal character of the corporeal form of things as they really are. And the sage does still better because he reflects the universal character of the feelings of all things. The sage can do so because he views things as things view themselves; that is, not subjectively but from the viewpoint of things. Since he is able to do this, how can there be anything between him and things? [6:26a-b]

When one can be happy or sad with things as though he were the things themselves, one's feelings may be said to have been aroused and to have acted to the proper degree. [8B:26a]

We can understand things as they are if we do not impose our ego on them. The sage gives things every benefit and forgets his own ego.

To let the ego be unrestrained is to give rein to passion; to give rein to passion is to be deluded; and to be deluded is to be ignorant. To follow the natural principles of things, on the other hand, is to grasp their nature; to grasp their nature is to be in possession of spiritual power; and to possess spiritual power is to achieve enlightenment. [8B:27b]

Chou Tun-i

CHOU TUN-I (1017-1073). Generally referred to as the pioneer of Neo-Confucianism, Chou Tun-i (Chou Lien-ch'i or Chou Lien-hsi) outlined its metaphysics in two short treatises. In the *T'ai-chi-t'u (An Explanation of the Diagram of the Great Ultimate)* and the *T'ung-shu (Comprehensive Unity)* he assimilated the Tâoist concept of non-being to Confucianism but restored Chinese philosophy to a healthier state by ridding it of Tâoist fantasy and mysticism. He based his entire philosophy on *I Ching (Book of Changes)*, causing the ancient work on divination and its commentaries to assume unusual importance in Neo-Confucianism.

As prefect of Nan K'ang in Kiangsi, he built a retreat on Lu Shan, which he named the Lien-Hsi Studio. He was known afterwards as "The Master of Lien-hsi." For him sagehood derives from *jen* (humanity, human-heartedness, love, etc.) and *i* (righteousness), both rooted in the creative power of Ultimate Reason. Progress toward sagehood is marked by a slow return to original sincerity through elimination of desire and righteous conduct into complete universality of spirit, the ultimate goal. Chou Tun-i initiated the use of *li* (immaterial principle) and *ch'i* (material essence). These concepts were later elaborated by the Ch'eng Brothers and by Chu Hsi. The first major Sung scholar to attempt to redefine Confucian metaphysics and cosmology used the contents of *I Ching* to illustrate his theory.

An Explanation of the Diagram of the Great Ultimate

From *Sources of Chinese Tradition*, Volume I, edited by William Theodore de Bary, New York, Columbia University Press, 1960.

[From *T'ai-chi-t'u shuo*, in *Chou Lien-ch'i chi*, 1:2a-b]

THE Non-ultimate! And also the Great Ultimate (*T'ai-chi*). The Great Ultimate through movement generates the yang. When its activity reaches its limit, it becomes tranquil. Through tranquillity the Great Ultimate generates the yin. When tranquillity reaches its limit, activity begins again. Thus movement and tranquillity alternate and become the root of each other, giving rise to the distinction of yin and yang, and these two modes are thus established.

By the transformation of yang and its union with yin, the five agents of water, fire, wood, metal, and earth arise. When these five material-forces (*ch'i*)[1] are distributed in harmonious order, the four seasons run their course.

The five agents constitute one system of yin and yang, and yin and yang constitute one Great Ultimate. The Great Ultimate is fundamentally the Non-ultimate. The five agents arise, each with its specific nature.

When the reality of the Non-ultimate and the essence of yin and yang and the five agents come into mysterious union, integration ensues. The heavenly principle (*ch'ien*) con-

---

1. Rendered "vital force(s)" as it appears in earlier sources, *ch'i* is modified to "material-force" in this chapter where its role as the basic matter or stuff of the universe is stressed. Other widely used translations for *ch'i* are "ether" and "matter-energy."

stitutes the male element, and the earthly principle (*k'un*) constitutes the female element. The interaction of these two material forces engenders and transforms the myriad things. The myriad things produce and reproduce resulting in an unending transformation.

It is man alone who receives [the material forces] in their highest excellence, and therefore he is most intelligent. His corporeal form appears, and his spirit develops consciousness. The five moral principles of his nature (humanity, righteousness, decorum, wisdom, and good faith) are aroused by, and react to, the external world and engage in activity; good and evil are distinguished and human affairs take place.

The sage orders these affairs by the principles of the Mean, correctness, humanity, and righteousness, considering tranquillity to be the ruling factor. Thus he establishes himself as the ultimate standard for man. Hence the character of the sages is "identical with that of Heaven and earth; his brilliance is identical with that of the sun and moon; his order is identical with that of the four seasons; and his good and evil fortunes are identical with those of heavenly and earthly spirits."[1] The gentleman cultivates these moral qualities and enjoys good fortune, whereas the inferior man violates them and suffers evil fortune.

Therefore it is said: "The yin and the yang are established as the way of heaven; the elements of strength and weakness as the way of earth; and humanity and righteousness as the way of man."[2] It is also said there: "If we investigate into the cycle of things, we shall understand the concepts of life and death."[3] Great is the *Book of Changes!* Herein lies its excellence!

1. *Book of Changes*, hexagram 1.
2. *Book of Changes*, Shuo-kua 2.
3. *Book of Changes*, Hsi Tz'ŭ 1.

SELECTIONS FROM AN INTERPRETATION
OF THE BOOK OF CHANGES

[From *T'ung shu, in Chou Lien-ch'i chi*, 5:1a-b, 17b-19a, 38b]

CHAPTER 1: SINCERITY

Sincerity *(ch'eng)*[1] is the essence of sagehood. "Great is the heavenly principle, the Originator. All things obtain their beginning from it."[2] It is the source of sincerity. "The Way of the heavenly principle is to change and transform, so that everything obtains its correct nature and destiny."[3] In this way sincerity is established. It is pure and perfectly good. Therefore, "The successive movement of the yin and the yang constitutes the Way. What issues from the Way is good and that which realizes it is the individual nature."[4] Origination and development characterize the penetration of sincerity, and adaptation and correctness are its completion [or recovery]. Great is the *Changes*, the source of nature and destiny! [5:1a-3b]

CHAPTER 4: SAGEHOOD

"The state of absolute quiet and inactivity" is sincerity. The spirit is that which, "When acted on, immediately penetrates all things."[5] And the state of subtle emergence is the undifferentiated state between existence and nonexistence when activity has started but has not manifested itself in corporeal form. Sincerity is infinitely pure and hence evident. The spirit is responsive and hence works wonders. And emergence is subtle and hence abstruse. The sage is the one who is in the state of sincerity, spirit, and subtle emergence. [5:17b-19a]

---

1. A fundamental concept in the *Mean*, where it represents not only sincerity but also absolute genuineness or realness.
2. *Book of Changes*, hexagram 1.
3. *Book of Changes*, hexagram 1.
4. *Book of Changes*, Hsi tz'ǔ 1.
5. *Book of Changes*, Hsi-tz'ǔ 1.

Can one become a sage through learning?

Yes. . . . The essential way is to attain oneness [of mind]. By oneness is meant having no desire. Having no desire one is "empty" [absolutely pure and peaceful] while tranquil, and straightforward while in action. Being "empty" while tranquil, one becomes intelligent and hence penetrating. Being straightforward while active, one becomes impartial and hence all-embracing. Being intelligent, penetrating, impartial, and all-embracing, one is almost a sage. [5:38b]

Chang Tsai

CHANG TSAI (1020-1077). Indispensable to the study of Neo-Confucianism, the works of Chang Tsai (Chang Heng-ch'u or Chang Tzǔ-hou) exerted a strong influence over later Chinese philosophers. Like Chou Tun-i and Shao Yung, he drew his inspiration mainly from *I Ching*. But whereas Chou Tun-i held that evolution proceeds from the Great Ultimate through the Yin and Yang and the Five Agents to the multiplicity of things, and whereas Shao Yung made evolution proceed from the Great Ultimate through Yin and Yang and other stages to concrete things, Chang Tsai discarded the Five Agents as well as the Yin and Yang, and made material force (*ch'i*) identical with the Great Ultimate itself. His fundamental concept, that the universe is one but its manifestations are many, had a lasting impact on his contemporaries and successors.

Chang Tsai was a typical Confucian government official and teacher. Under the direction of a prominent scholar, he studied the *Chung Yung (Golden Mean)* and went on to Tâoist and Buddhist works. When he finally returned to Confucian works, he discussed them with the Ch'eng, his nephews, the Ch'eng brothers. He is traditionally assigned the role of the second major thinker in the line of Neo-Confucian succession, after Chou Tun-i. His most importance important works are the *Cheng-meng (Correcting Youthful Ignorance)* and the *Hsi-ming (Western Inscription)*. The latter, which explores the idea that the man of love identifies himself with all men and with the universe, is one of the most celebrated essays in Neo-Confucian literature.

459

Great Harmony

From *Sources of Chinese Tradition*, Volume I, edited by William Theodore de Bary, New York, Columbia University Press, 1960.

[From *Cheng-meng*, I, in *Chang Heng-ch'ü chi*, 2:3b-10b]

ALTHOUGH material-force in the universe integrates and disintegrates, and attracts and repulses in a hundred ways, nevertheless the principle (*li*) according to which it operates has an order and is unerring.

The Great Vacuity of necessity consists of material-force. Material-force of necessity integrates to become the myriad things. Things of necessity disintegrate and return to the Great Vacuity. Appearance and disappearance following this cycle are all a matter of necessity. When, in the midst [of this universal operation] the sage fulfills the Way to the utmost, and identifies himself [with the universal processes of appearance and disappearance] without partiality, his spirit is preserved in the highest degree. Those [the Buddhists] who believe in annihilation expect departure without returning, and those [the Tâoists] who cling to everlasting life and are attached to existence expect things not to change. While they differ, they are the same in failing to understand the Way. Whether integrated or disintegrated, my body remains the same. One is qualified to discuss the nature of man when one realizes that death is not annihilation.

When it is understood that Vacuity, Emptiness, is nothing but material-force, then existence and nonexistence, the hidden and the manifest, spirit and external transformation, and human nature and destiny, are all one and not a duality.

He who apprehends integration and disintegration, appearance and disappearance, form and absence of form, and can trace them to their source, penetrates the secret of change.

If it is argued that material-force is produced from Vacuity, then because the two are completely different, Vacuity being infinite while material-force is finite, the one being substance and the other function, such an argument would fall into the naturalism of Lao Tzŭ who claimed that existence comes from nonexistence and failed to understand the eternal principle of the undifferentiated unity of existence and nonexistence. If it is argued that the countless phenomena are but things perceived in the Great Vacuity, then since things and the Vacuity would not be mutually conditioned, since the form and nature of things would be self-contanied, and since these, as well as Heaven and man, would not be interdependent, such an argument would fall into the doctrine of the Buddha who taught that mountains, rivers, and the whole earth are all subjective illusions. This principle of unity is not understood because ignorant people know superficially that the substance of the nature of things is Vacuity, Emptiness, but do not know that function is based on the way of Heaven [law of nature]. Instead, they try to explain the universe with limited human knowledge. Since the undertaking is not thorough, they falsely assert that the universal operation of the principles of Heaven and earth is but illusory. They do not know the essentials of the hidden and the manifest, and jump to erroneous conclusions. They do not understand that the successive movements of the yin and the yang cover the entire universe, penetrate day and night, and form the standards of Heaven, earth, and man. Consequently they confuse Confucianism with Buddhism and Tâoism. When they discuss the problems of the nature [of man and things] and their destiny or the way of Heaven, they either fall into the trap of illusionism or are determined that existence comes from nonexistence, and regard these doctrines as the summit of philosophical insight as well as the way to enter

461

into virtue. They do not know to choose the proper method but instead seek excessive views. Thus they are blinded by onesided doctrines and fall into error.

As the Great Vacuity, material-force is extensive and vague. Yet it ascends, descends, and moves in all ways without ever ceasing....That which floats upward is the yang that is clear, while that which sinks to the bottom is the yin that is turbid. As a result of their contact and influence and of their integration and disintegration, winds and rains, snow and frost, come into being. Whether it be the countless variety of things in their changing configurations or the mountains and rivers in their fixed forms, the dregs of wine or the ashes of fire, there is nothing [in which the principle] is not revealed.

If material-force integrates, its visibility becomes effective and corporeal form appears. If material-force does not integrate, its visibility is not effective and there is no corporeal form. While material-force is integrated, how can one not say that it is temporary? While it is disintegrated, how can one hastily say that it is nonexistent? For this reason, the sage, having observed and examined above and below, only claims to know the causes of what is hidden and what is manifest but does not claim to know the causes of existence and nonexistence.

Material-force moves and flows in all directions and in all manners. Its two elements unite and give rise to concrete stuff. Thus the great variety of things and human beings is produced. In their ceaseless successions the two elements of yin and yang constitute the great principles of the universe.

[The *Book of Changes*] says: "The sun and moon push each other in their course and thus light appears. Winter and summer push each other and thus the year is completed."[1] Spirit is not conditioned by space and change does not assume any physical form. "The successive movement

1. Hsi Tz'ŭ, II, 5.

of yin and yang," "unfathomable is the movement of yin and yang"[1] – These describe the Way that penetrates day and night.

No two of the products of creation are alike. From this we know that although the number of things is infinite, at bottom there is nothing without yin or yang [which differentiates them]. From this we know also that the transformations and changes in the universe are due to these two fundamental forces.

THE "WESTERN INSCRIPTION" (HSI-MING)

[From *Chang Heng-ch'ü chi*, 1:1a-5b]

Heaven is my father and earth is my mother, and even such a small creature as I find an intimate place in their midst.

Therefore that which extends throughout the universe I regard as my body and that which directs the universe I consider as my nature.

All people are my brothers and sisters, and all things are my companions.

The great ruler [the emperor] is the eldest son of my parents [Heaven and earth], and the great ministers are his stewards. Respect the aged – this is the way to treat them as elders should be treated. Show affection toward the orphaned and the weak – this is the way to treat them as the young should be treated. The sage identifies his character with that of Heaven and earth, and the virtuous man is the best [among the children of Heaven and earth]. Even those who are tired and infirm, crippled or sick, those who have no brothers or children, wives or husbands, are all my brothers who are in distress and have no one to turn to.

When the time comes, to keep himself from harm – this is the care of a son. To rejoice in Heaven and have no anxiety – this is filial piety at its purest.

He who disobeys [the principle of Heaven] violates virtue. He who destroys humanity (*jen*) is a robber. He who

1. Hsi Tz'ŭ, I, 4-5.

promotes evil lacks [moral] capacity. But he who puts his moral nature into practice and brings his physical existence to complete fulfillment can match [Heaven and earth].

He who knows the principles of transformation will skillfully carry forward the undertakings [of Heaven and earth], and he who penetrates spirit to the highest degree will skillfully carry out their will.

Do nothing shameful even in the recesses of your own house and thus bring no dishonor to them. Preserve the mind and nourish the nature and thus [serve them] with untiring effort.

The great Yü hated pleasant wine but attended to the protection and support of his parents. Border Warden Ying cared for the young and thus extended his love to his own kind.

Emperor Shun's merit lay in delighting his parents with unceasing effort, and Shen-sheng's reverence was demonstrated when he awaited punishment without making an attempt to escape.

Tseng Ts'an received his body from his parents and reverently kept it intact throughout life, while [Yin] Po-ch'i vigorously obeyed his father's command.

Wealth, honor, blessing, and benefit are meant for the enrichment of my life, while poverty, humble station, care, and sorrow will be my helpmates to fulfillment.

In life I follow and serve [Heaven and earth]. In death I will be at peace.

Ch'eng Hao

CH'ENG HAO (1032-1086). After Chang Tsai, Neo-Confucianism divided into two schools founded by two brothers. Ch'eng Hao (Ch'eng Ming-tao, Ch'eng Hou, or Ch'eng Po-tun) is looked upon as the forerunner of the idealistic school later developed by Chu Hsi. The younger brother, Ch'eng I, is considered to be the forerunner of the rationalistic school headed by Lu Hsiang-shan (1139-1193).

Ch'eng Hao served as a government official and had an excellent record in social and educational achievements. He studied Tâoism and Buddhism for decades before repudiating both and becoming the greatest Confucian since Mencius. He reinterpreted *jen* (humanity) in a metaphysical way, making the practice of *jen* depend on realizing the oneness of oneself with the universe. He is said to have practiced his philosophy of composure so well that he could remain imperturbable under the most provocative conditions.

Many of the writings of the two brothers are assigned to both, and scholars rarely agree on attributing a particular work to either one of them. The memorial presented here was presented by Ch'eng Hao to Emperor Shen-tsung (r. 1068-85). Reflecting the view that improper government is in some way responsible for all human evils, the memorial calls attention to situations that require bold action and stresses the Confucian principles on which the moral reformation of mankind must be based.

Ten Matters Calling for Reform

From *Sources of Chinese Tradition,* Volume I, edited by William Theo dore de Bary, New York, Columbia University Press, 1960.

[From *Ming-tao wen-chi,* SPPY ed., 2:6a-7b; *Sung-Yüan hsüeh-an* 14:332]

YOUR servant considers that the laws established by the sage-kings were all based on human feelings and in keeping with the order of things. In the great reigns of the Two Emperors and Three Kings, how could these laws not but change according to the times and be embodied in systems which suited the conditions obtaining in each? However, in regard to the underlying basis of government, to the teachings by which the people may be shepherded, to the principles which remain forever unalterable in the order of things, and to that upon which the people depend for their very existence, on such points there has been no divergence but rather common agreement among the sages of all times, early or late. Only if the way of sustaining life itself should fail, could laws of the sage-kings ever be changed. Therefore in later times those who practiced the Way [of the sage-kings] to the fullest achieved perfect order, while those who practiced only a part achieved limited success. This is the clear and manifest lesson of past ages. . . .

But it may be objected that human nature today is no longer the same as in ancient times, and that what has come down to us from the early kings cannot possibly be restored in the present. . . . Now in ancient times all people, from the Son of Heaven down to the commoners, had to have teachers and friends in order to perfect their virtue. Therefore even the sages — Shun, Yü, [King] Wǎn, and [King] Wu — had those from whom they learned. Nowadays the function of the teacher and preceptor is unfulfilled and the ideal of the "friend-minister" is not made manifest. Therefore the attitude of respect for virtue and enjoyment in doing good has not been developed in the empire. There is no difference between the past and the present in this matter.

A sage-king must follow Heaven in establishing the offices of government. Thus the functions relating to Heaven, earth, and the four seasons did not change throughout the reigns of the Two Emperors and the Three Kings, and for this reason all the regulations were carried out and everything was well ordered. In the T'ang dynasty these institutions were still preserved in attenuated form, and in its [initial] period of peace and order, the government and regulations of the T'ang had some semblance of correctness. Today, however, the offices and ranks have been thrown into great confusion, and duties and functions have not been performed. This is the reason why the ideal of peace and order has not been achieved. There is no difference between the past and present in this matter.

Heaven created men and raised up a ruler to govern and to guide them. Things had to be so regulated as to provide them with settled property as the means to a flourishing livelihood. Therefore the boundaries of the land had to be defined correctly, and the well-fields had to be equally distributed — these are the great fundamentals of government. The T'ang dynasty still maintained a system of land distribution based on the size of the family.[1] Now nothing is left, and there is no such system. The lands of the rich extend on and on, from this prefecture to that subprefecture, and there is nothing to stop them. Day by day the poor scatter and die from starvation, and there is no one to take pity on them. Although many people are more fortunate,

1. Under the equal land system of the T'ang, each adult was entitled to hold 30 *mu* of hereditary land and 80 *mu* on assignment from the state.

still there are countless persons without sufficient food and clothing. The population grows day by day, and if nothing is done to control the situation, food and clothing will become more and more scarce, and more people will scatter and die. This is the key to order and disorder. How can we not devise some way to control it? In this matter, too, there is no difference between past and present.

In ancient times, government and education began with the local villages. The system worked up from [the local units of] *pi, lü, tsu, tang, chou, hsiang, tsan,* and *sui.*[1] Each village and town was linked to the next higher unit and governed by them in sequence. Thus the people were at peace, and friendly toward one another. They seldom violated the criminal law, and it was easy to appeal to their sense of shame. This is in accord with the natural bent of human feelings and, therefore, when practiced, it works. In this matter, too, there is no difference between past and present.

Education in local schools was the means by which the ancient kings made clear the moral obligations of human relationships and achieved the ethical transformation of all under Heaven. Now true teaching and learning have been abandoned, and there is no moral standard. Civic ceremonies have ceased to be held in the local community and propriety and righteousness are not upheld. Appointments to office are not based upon the recommendation of the village communities, and the conduct [of appointees to high office] not proven by performance. The best talents are not nurtured in the schools, and the abilities of men are mostly wasted. These are matters clearly evident, and there is in them no difference between the past and the present.

In ancient times, government clerks and runners were paid by the state, and there was no distinction between soldiers and farmers. Now the arrogant display of military power has exhausted national resources to the limit. Your

1. Units of local administration in ascending order as described in the classic *Rites of Chou.*

servant considers that if the soldiery, with the exception of the Imperial Guards, is not gradually reconverted to a peasant militia, the matter will be of great concern. The services of government clerks and runners have inflicted harm all over the empire; if this system is not changed, a great disaster is inevitable. This is also a truth which is most evident, and there is no difference between the past and the present.

In ancient times, the people had to have [a reserve of] nine years' food supply. A state was not considered a state if it did not have a reserve of at least three years' food. Your servant observes that there are few in the land who grow food and many who consume it. The productivity of the earth is not fully utilized and human labor is not fully employed. Even the rich and powerful families rarely have a surplus; how much worse off are the poor and weak! If in one locality their luck is bad and crops fail just one year, banditry becomes uncontrollable and the roads are full of the faint and starving. If, then, we should be so unfortunate as to have a disaster affecting an area of two or three thousand square *li*, or bad harvests over a number of years in succession, how is the government going to deal with it? The distress then will be beyond description. How can we say, "But it is a long, long time since anything like that has happened," and on this ground trust to luck in the future? Certainly we should gradually return to the ancient system — with the land distributed equally so as to encourage agriculture, and with steps taken by both individuals and the government to store up grain so as to provide against any contingency. In this, too, there is no difference between past and present.

In ancient times, the four classes of people each had its settled occupation, and eight or nine out of ten people were farmers. Therefore food and clothing were provided without difficulty and people were spared suffering and distress. But now in the capital region there are thousands upon thousands of men without settled occupations — idlers

469

and beggars who cannot earn a living. Seeing that they are distressed, toilsome, lonesome, poor, and ill, or resort to guile and craftiness in order to survive and yet usually cannot make a living, what can we expect the consequence to be after this has gone on for days and years? Their poverty being so extreme, unless a sage is able to change things and solve the problem, there will be no way to avoid complete disaster. How can we say, "There is nothing that can be done about it"? This calls for consideration of the ancient [system] in order to reform the present [system], a sharing by those who have much so as to relieve those who possess little, thus enabling them to gain the means of livelihood by which to save their lives. In this, too, there is no difference between the past and the present.

The way the sages followed the will of Heaven and put things in order was through the administration of the six resources.[1] The responsibility for the administration of the six resources was in the hands of the Five Offices. There were fixed prohibitions covering the resources of hills, woodlands, and streams. Thus the various things were in abundance and there was no deficiency in the supply. Today the duties of the Five Offices are not performed and the six resources are not controlled. The use of these things is immoderate and the taking of them is not in due time and season. It is not merely that the nature of things has been violated, but that the mountains from which forests and woods grow have all been laid bare by indiscriminate cutting and burning. As these depredations still go uncurbed, the fish of the stream and the beasts of the field are cut short in their abundance and the things of nature [Heaven] are becoming wasted and exhausted. What then can be done about it? These dire abuses have now reached the extreme, and only by restoring the ancient system of official control over hills and streams, so as to preserve and develop them, can the trend be halted, a change made, and a per-

1. That is, fire, metal, wood, earth, and grain.

manent supply be assured. Here, too, there is no difference between the past and the present.

In ancient times, there were different ranks and distinctions observed in official capping ceremonies, weddings, funerals, sacrifices, carriages, garments, and utensils, and no one dared to exceed what he was entitled to. Therefore expenses were easily met and people kept their equanimity of mind. Now the system of rites is not maintained in practice, and people compete with each other in ostentation and extravagance. The families of officials are unable to maintain themselves in proper style, whereas members of the merchant class sometimes surpass the ceremonial display of kings and dukes. The system of rites is unable to regulate the human feelings, and the titles and quantities[1] are unable to preserve the distinction between the noble and the mean. Since there have been no fixed distinctions and proportions, people have become crafty, deceitful, and grasping; each seeks to gratify his desires and does not stop until they are gratified. But how can there be an end to it? This is the way leading to strife and disorder. How, then, can we not look into the measures of the ancient kings and adapt them to our need? Here, too, there is no difference between the past and the present.

The above ten points are but the primary ones. Your servant discusses these main points merely to provide evidence for his belief that the laws and institutions of the Three Dynasties can definitely be put into practice. As to the detailed plans and procedures for their enactment, it is essential that they conform to the instructions contained in the Classics and be applied with due regard for human feelings. These are fixed and definite principles, clearly apparent to all. How can they be compared with vague and impractical theories? May your sage intelligence deign to consider them.

1. As stated in the classic *Tso Chuan* there was to be a proportionate relation between one's rank and the quantity of goods one might devote to social display within the limits of good form (SPPY ed. 9:8b; Legge I, 97).

Ch'eng I

CH'ENG I (1033-1107). The fame of Ch'eng I (Ch'eng I-chüan or Ch'eng-cheng-shu) as a classical scholar and commentator is greater than that of his brother. The Confucian Tablets note that, whereas Ch'eng Hao had genius, a taste for poetry, and a loving heart, Ch'eng I had "industry, a desire to be right, and a self-sustained spirit." Though honest and upright in all his ways, "he had no grace of manner or tenderness of heart." His independent thinking led him to make a sharp distinction between *li* (principle) and *ch'i* (matter), and to affirm four precepts: creative evolution continuously generates new forms; the principle of a particular thing is the principle of all things; one who understands the principle of a single thing understands the principle of the self; and one who understands the principle of the self achieves humanity.

On many points the two brothers agreed. Both believed that human nature is essentially good, and both made *jen*, a term signifying to them complete unity with the universe, the fundamental ground of ethics. Though critics have found fault with their interpretation of the Classics, they are acknowledged to have given a stimulus to the serious study of these ancient works.

Ch'eng I and Ch'eng Hao foreshadowed the two major directions Neo-Confucianism was to take, the idealistic and the rational, under Chu Hsi and Lu Hsiang-shan.

Philosophy of Human Nature

From *Sources of Chinese Tradition*, Volume I, edited by William Theodore de Bary, New York, Columbia University Press, 1960.

[From *Erh Ch'eng ts'ui-yen*, 3:4a; *Erh Ch'eng i-shu*, 18:17a-b; 19:4b]

THE nature cannot be spoken of as internal or external. [*Ts'ui-yen*, 3:4a]

The mind in itself is originally good. As it expresses itself in thoughts and ideas, it is sometimes good and sometimes evil. When the mind has been aroused, it should be described in terms of feelings, and not as the mind itself. For instance, water is water. But as it flows, some to the east and some to the west, it is called streams and branches. [*I-shu*, 18:17a]

The nature comes from Heaven, whereas capacity comes from material-force. When material-force is clear, capacity is clear. On the other hand, when material-force is turbid, capacity is turbid. Take, for instance, wood. Whether it is straight or crooked is due to its nature. But whether it can be used as a beam or as a truss is determined by its capacity. Capacity may be good or evil, but the nature [of man and things] is always good. [19:4b]

Question: Do joy and anger come from our nature?

Answer: Yes. As soon as there is consciousness, there is our nature. As there is our nature, there must be feelings. Without nature, how can there be feelings?

Further Question: Suppose you said that joy and anger come from the outside?

Answer: Joy and anger do not come from the outside.

They are due to external influence, but they arise from within.

Question: Are joy and anger to man's nature as waves are to water?

Answer: Yes. It is the nature of water to be clear, still, and smooth like a mirror, but when it strikes sand and stone, or when the ground underlying it is not level, it immediately begins to move violently. Or when wind blows over it, it develops waves and currents. But are these the nature of water? In man's nature there are only the four beginnings [of humanity, righteousness, decorum, and wisdom], and not the various forms of evil. But as without water there cannot be waves, so without nature there cannot be feelings. [18:17b]

Question: Since man's nature is originally enlightened, why is it sometimes obscured?

Answer: This must be investigated and understood. Mencius was correct in saying that man's nature is good. Even Hsün Tzu and Yang Hsiung failed to understand human nature, and Mencius was superior to other Confucianists in that he understood this. Man's nature is universally good. In cases where there is evil it is because of one's capacity. The nature is the same as principle, and principle is the same whether in the sage-emperors Yao and Shun or in the common man in the street. Material-force, which may be either clear or turbid, is the source of capacity. Men endowed with clear material-force are wise, while those endowed with turbid material-force are stupid.

Further Question: Can stupidity be changed?

Answer: Yes. Confucius said: "The most intelligent and the most stupid cannot be changed."[1] But in principle they can. Only those who ruin themselves and cast themselves away cannot be changed.

Question: Is it due to their capacity that the most stupid ruin and throw themselves away?

1. *Analects*, XVII, 3.

475

Answer: Certainly. But it cannot be said that capacity cannot be changed. Since all have the same basic nature, who cannot be changed? Because they ruin and cast themselves away and are not willing to learn, people are unable to change. In principle, if they were willing to learn, they could change. [18:17b]

SERIOUSNESS AND HUMANITY

[From *Erh Ch'eng i-shu*, 2A:13b; 15:1a, 8b, 9a; 18:3a, 5b, 6b; and *Erh Ch'eng ts'ui-yen*, 1:1b, 7b]

As to the meaning of the principle of Heaven: To be sincere is to be sincere to this principle, and to be serious [or reverent] is to be serious about this principle. It is not that there is something called sincerity or seriousness by itself. [*I-shu*, 2A:13b]

For moral cultivation, one must practise seriousness; for the advancement of learning, one must extend his knowledge to the utmost. [18:5b]

Question: What about people who devote all their effort to seriousness in order to straighten the internal life, but make no effort to square the external life?

Answer: What one has inside will necessarily be shown outside. Only worry that the internal life is not straightened. If it is straightened, then the external life will necessarily be squared. [18:3a]

If one makes singleness of mind the ruling factor with absolute stead-fastness and exercises [what the *Book of Changes calls*] 'seriousness to straighten the internal life,'[1] he will possess great natural power. [15:1a]

Someone asked whether the will is necessary for seriousness.

Answer: In the initial stage, how can the will be dispensed with? Without the will, nothing can ensue [from consciousness].

Further Question: Is seriousness not tranquillity?

1. Hexagram 2.

Answer: As soon as you speak of tranquillity, you fall into the doctrine of Buddhism. Only the word "seriousness" should be used but never the word "tranquillity." As soon as you use the word "tranquillity," you imply that seriousness is forgetfulness [or unconsciousness]. Mencius said: "There must be endeavor, but let there be no anxious expectation. Let the mind not forget its objective, but let there be no artificial effort to help it grow."[1] "There muts be endeavor" means that the mind is active. Not to forget but to have no anxious expectation means not to try to make it grow. [18:6b]

"When you go abroad, behave to everyone as if you were receiving a great guest. Employ the people as if you were assisting at a great sacrifice."[2] [When Confucious said that], he meant nothing other than seriousness [or reverence]. Seriousness means unselfishness. As soon as one lacks seriousness, thousands of selfish desires arise to injure his humanity. [15:9a]

The Master said: Those who are sincere are always serious. Those who have not yet reached the state of sincerity must be serious before they become sincere. [*Ts'ui-yen,* 1:1b]

The Master said: The humane man regards Heaven and earth and all things as one body. There is nothing which is not part of his self. Knowing that, where is the limit [of his humanity]? If one does not possess [humanity as part of] himself, he will be thousands of miles away from Heaven and earth and the myriad things. [1:7b]

Essentially speaking, the way of humanity may be expressed in one word, namely, impartiality. However, impartiality is but the principle of humanity; it should not be equated with humanity itself. When man puts impartiality into practice, that is humanity. Because of impartiality, one can accommodate both others and himself. Therefore a

1. *Mencius,* IIA, 2.
2. *Analects,* XII, 2.

477

humane man is a man of both altruism and love. Altruism is the application of humanity while love is its function. [*I-shu*, 15:8b]

INVESTIGATION OF THINGS

[From *Erh Ch'eng i-shu*, 2A:22b; 15:1a, 11a; 18-5b, 8b-9a]

To investigate things in order to understand principle to the utmost does not require the investigation of all things in the world. One has only to investigate the principle in one event exhaustively and the principle in other things or events can then be inferred. For example, when we talk about filial piety, we must find out what constitutes filial piety. If principle cannot be exhaustively understood in one event, investigate another. One may begin with either the easiest or the most difficult, depending on one's capacity. There are thousands of tracks and paths to the capital, yet one can enter if he has found just one way. Principle can be exhaustively understood in this way because all things share the same principle. Even the most insignificant of things and events have principle. [15:11a]

Someone asked what the first step was in the art of moral cultivation.

Answer: The first thing is to rectify the heart and make the will sincere. The sincerity of the will depends upon the extension of knowledge and the extension of knowledge depends upon the investigation of things. The word *ko* (investigate) means to arrive, as in saying: "The spirits of impercial progenitors have arrived."[1] There is principle in everything, and one must investigate principle to the utmost. There are many ways of doing this. One way is to read about and discuss truth and principles. Another way is to talk about people and events of the past and present, and to distinguish which are right and which wrong. Still another way is to handle affairs and settle them in the proper way. All these are ways to investigate the principle of things exhaustively. [18:5b]

1. *Book of History*, I chi.

To investigate principle to the utmost does not mean that it is necessary to investigate the principle of all things to the utmost or that principle can be understood merely by investigating one particular principle. It means that if one investigates more and more, one will naturally come to understand principle. [2A:22b]

Question: Do observation of things and self-examination mean returning to the self to seek [principles] after principles have been discovered in things?

Answer: You do not have to say that. Things and the self are governed by the same principle. If you understand one you understand the other, for the truth within and the truth without are identical. In its magnitude it reaches the height of heaven and the depth of earth, but in its refinement it constitutes the reason for being of every single thing. The student should appreciate both.

Further Question: In the extension of knowledge, how about seeking first of all in the four beginnings [of humanity, righteousness, decorum and wisdom]?

Answer: To seek in our own nature and feeling is indeed to be concerned with our moral life. But every blade of grass and every tree possesses a principle which should be examined. [18:8b-9a]

A thing is an event. If the principles underlying all events are investigated to the utmost, there is nothing that cannot be understood.

If one extends knowledge to the utmost, one will have wisdom. Having wisdom, one can then make choices. [15:1a]

The investigation of principle to the utmost, the complete development of human nature, and the fulfillment of destiny are one and only one. As principle is exhaustively investigated, our nature is completely developed, and as our nature is completely developed, our destiny is fulfilled.[18:9a]

CRITICISM OF BUDDHISM AND TÂOISM

[From *Erh Ch'eng i-shu*, 15:5b, 7b; 18:10b]

The doctrines of Buddhism are not worthy of matching the

479

doctrines of our sage. One need only compare them, and having observed that they are different, leave Buddhism well enough alone. If one tries to investigate all its theories, it is probably an impossible task, for before one has done that, the preoccupation will already have transformed him into a Buddhist. But let us take a look at Buddhism from its practice. In deserting his father and leaving his family, the Buddha severed all human relationships. It was merely for himself that he lived alone in the forest. Such a person should not be allowed in any community. Generally speaking, he did to others what he himself despised. Such is not the mind of the sage, nor is it the mind of a gentleman. The Buddhists themselves will not abide by the principles of the relationship between ruler and minister, between father and son, and between husband and wife, and criticize others for not doing as they do. They leave these human relationships to others and have nothing to do with them, setting themselves apart as a special class. If this is the way to lead the people, it will be the end of the human race. As to their discourse on principle and the nature of things, it is primarily in terms of life and death. Their feelings are based on love of life and fear of death. This is selfishness. [15:5b]

You cannot say that the teachings of the Buddhists are ignorant, for actually they are quite profound. But essentially speaking, they can finally be reduced to a pattern of selfishness. Why do we say this? In the world there cannot be birth without death or joy without sorrow. But wherever the Buddhists go, they always want to pervert this truth and preach the elimination of birth and death and the neutralization of joy and sorrow. In the final analysis this is nothing but self-interest. The teachings of the Tâoists even carry with them an element of treachery, as evidenced in their sayings that the purpose of giving is to take away and the purpose of opening is to close.[1] Furthermore, their general intention is to fool the people and to be wise themselves.

1. *Lao Tzŭ*, 26.

When [the First Emperor] of Ch'in fooled his people, his tricks probably were derived from the Tâoists. [15:7b]

The Buddhists advocate the renunciation of the family and the world. Fundamentally the family cannot be renounced. Let us say that it can, however, when the Buddhists refuse to recognize their parents as parents and run away. But how can a person escape from the world? Only when a person no longer stands under heaven or upon the earth is he able to forsake the world. But while he continues to drink when thirsty and eat when hungry, he still stands under heaven and sets his feet on earth. [18:10b]

Yüan-wu Ko-chin

YÜAN-WU KO-CHIN (1063-1135). The *Pi-Yen-Lu*
"Records (of the Abbot's Office) of the Emerald Rock,"
printed in China around 1300, represents the work of
an eminent Chinese Ch'an (Zen) master, Yüan-wu
Ko-chin, with wit and wisdom enlarged upon the hundred "Examples" or, "Master Biographies with Anecdotes," collected, annotated and embellished with poems
by Hsüe-tou (980-1052) early in the 11th century. It
explains the methods, imagery, and meaning of the
doings and teachings of most famous masters of the
art of *Dhyǎna* or deep concentration, the last requirement of the Buddha's Noble Eightfold Path, which
leads to complete and blissful freedom, known as *Nir-
vǎṇa*. The massive work, used extensively by all serious
Zennists in the Far East as an indispensable source book,
initiates the reader with unrivaled lucidity into a
technique that may seem strange to the matter-of-fact
thinking of Westerners, but is considered panacean and
essential as a harbinger of peace of mind, heart and
soul to all Orientals who believe that words alone do
not hold the key to the true values, locked deep in
one's self.

Fa-Yen Answers Hui-Chao Regarding the Buddha Question

The three "Examples" presented here were translated by Kurt F. Lei decker from Wilhelm Gundert's German edition of the *Pi-Yen-Lu* Gundert's explanatory remarks are enclosed in brackets.

Reference

THE *one* little sentence which precedes the voice, — that all the thousand holy ones cannot pass on to you. So long as you have not heard it in private audience it is as if thousands of worlds separated you from it.

Even if someone had gotten an intellectual knowledge regarding that which precedes the voice which would enable him to cut short the cleverest man in the world, he still would not be a sound and solid fellow.

Therefore it is said: Heaven cannot vault it, earth cannot bear it, universal space cannot hold it, sun and moon cannot illumine it. Only where, in solitude and without Buddha, one calls himself exalted, in such a case it is passable to an extent.

However, even that may not be it. But if you see it shine through at the tip of every little hair and see it emitting tremendous brilliancy, then you can take seven paces straight ahead and eight sideways, can dispose of all things freely, being your own master, can take what the hand seizes, and there is nothing that contains a No.

Answer me for once: What kind of a thing is it which, in order to acquire it, brings about such miracles? And again

I say: All you that are here are you comprehending it, then?

> The steeds of long ago, sweat-covered,
> Who knows of them today?
> The deeds, the glory of all times,
> Praise of them is never sufficient.

However, let what I am saying here be what it may. But what about the task which Hsüa-tou submits here for solution? Take a look at what was written.

Example

We submit

A monk put the question to Fa-yen in the following words: Hui chao has to discuss something with the Venerable: What about the Buddha?

Fa-yen replied: You are Hui-chao.

Subsidiary Remarks on the Example

"A monk put the question to Fa-yen in the following words." — What is his intention? He is already carrying his sentence on the wooden collar of his neck. [The very fact that he is approaching with a question shows that there is something the matter with him. Who is reconciled with himself doesn't need to ask any more.]

"Hui-chao has to discuss something with the Venerable: What about the Buddha?" — What is he saying here? — His eyeballs protrude from his forehead.

"Fa-yen replied: You are Hui-chao." — That just drops from his mouth full-fledged. — An iron ball of rice and sugar! — If you take one of my men I take one of yours. [If you approach me with a question relating to the Buddha, then I meet you with the question relating to Hui-chao.]

Explanation of the Example

The Zen-master Fa-yen [Dharma-eye] had a special insight into the simultaneity of filing and pecking and mastered this art in practice. It was just on that account that he was able to give such an answer which, as one is wont to say, goes way beyond wording and gesture. It gives testimony to the possession of a regal freedom which, depending on the time and the circumstances, now releases and now gathers to itself, which can take life or give it entirely according to one's own decision. That in itself is something very prodigious.

However, now and then there are quite a few who make this statement the object of calculating reasoning and not rarely fall into erroneous interpretations because of a limited understanding. They do not know the manner of these ancients who always give forth only with a word or half a short sentence and carry on like one who, at night, with the aid of a spark struck from the flint or during the flashing of lightning are able to illuminate the right road in its entire stretch and show it to another person. Those that came after merely start with the wording and declare: Hui-chao himself is a Buddha, that is the meaning of Fa-yen's answer. Others say this Hui-chao is exactly like the peasant who in search of his buffalo is riding around on the very same buffalo. Others again say that the question itself is the correct thing. [The Buddha is already contained in it.] What has that to do with the matter on hand? With interpretations of this sort one does harm not only to oneself but, in addition, drags the ancients into the dust.

If you want to correctly appraise what is going on inside this master, then you ought not to think at all otherwise than that you are confronted with a man who, even though you strike him with a stick, does not turn his head, who has teeth like planted swords and a mouth like a cup full of blood, a man who goes straight to the heart of the matter which lies beyond words and knows precisely what the end result will be. Not until you approach him with presuppositions such as these will you do him justice at least a little bit. If each one of you brings only such embarrassing explanations to the problem, then he belongs to those people who in the whole wide world are about to exterminate the trunk of the Indian barbarians [the Sangha of the Buddha]. Also the sequel to that discussion which is to the effect that upon Fa-yen's answer the Zen guest Hui-chao left him with a glow in his heart, is to be explained only in this way that he had made visits to the masters and made self-perfection his main daily task. Thus only could it happen that immediately upon a single word by Fa-yen he experienced it as if the bottom had been knocked out of the barrel.

It was simply exactly as in the case of the superintendent of the monastery Tze who belonged to Fa-yen's order, except for his never having sought the master in regard to any question whatsoever. One day Fa-yen asked him: Superintendent Tze, why don't you ever come to me in my room? Tze replied: Does not the Venerable Sir know that I have already stuck my head into the Monastery of the Great Summit? Fa-yen pleaded: Please tell me about that! And Tze related: To the master there I put this question: What is it about the Buddha? And he answered me: The boys Ping and Ting come running and ask for fire. Fa-yen said: A good answer; I only fear that you misunderstood it. Please explain it to me a little more clearly! Tze replied: Now, to be sure, Ping and Ting are connected with fire; thus, people are looking for fire who themselves possess fire within them! Thereupon Fa-yen said: Didn't I tell you, Superintendent? You have in truth misunderstood. Upon that Superintendent Tze got up, sorely offended, took his leave and left crossing the Yangtze Kiang. Afterwards Fa-yen said to his disciples: If ever this man returns he can be saved; if he is not coming back he is finished. On the way, however, Tze became pensive and said to himself: A master like this who is over 500 monks surely would not want to hold me up to ridicule. He turned around and went a second time into the presence of Fa-yen. This one said: Go and ask; I shall answer you. Tze, then, asked him: What is it about the Buddha? And Fa-yen made this answer: The brothers Ping and Ting come running and ask for fire. Upon these words the great light momentarily dawned on the Superintendent Tze.

Today there are people who simply stare at one with wide open eyes and explain the way in which they understand it: The Superintendent Tze was quite right in his question and the answer also doesn't intend to dispute it. But whoever has sat at the master's feet for long needs to be told the story only once and he will immediately understand what is meant. In Fa-yen's school one is wont to say in such a case: "The arrows meet head-on with their tips." In this school one does not make use of the five steps [of master Liang-chie of Tung-shan] or of the four categories [of master Lin-chi], but simply concentrates on "the arrows meeting head-on with their tips." This is common usage with Fa-yen. A word is dropped and already one gets the salient point. One encounters a clearing and already can see fully to the end. If you throw out questions on the occasion of an utterance and permit yourself reflections, you rush headlong into darkness and grope here and everywhere helplessly with your hands.

Since his public appearance as a master Fa-yen had an audience of 50 disciples with the result that at that period the teachings of the Buddha experienced a great upswing. At that time Te-shao [afterwards] Country Chief [on Tientai-shan] had persuaded himself after a long stay with Su-shan that he had understood his meaning, had copied Su-shan's daily utterances, collected portraits of him and now was travelling [a master in his own right, as it were] with a following of travelling scholars throughout the land. Thus he also came into the company of Fa-yen. And here, likewise, he did not seek out the master, as we would expect, in his room, but had the disciples whom he had brought along walk behind those belonging to the order of the master. Now, one day when Fa-yen had seated himself in his professorial chair a monk broke ranks and asked: What about a drop of water from the well of Tzao? Fa-yen answered him: It is a drop of water from the well of Tzao.

488

Visibly disappointed and dejected the monk went back to his place. Te-shao, on the contrary, who was sitting among those gathered and heard Fa-yen's answer momentarily saw the great light dawn on himself. Te-shao afterwards appeared publicly as master and professed to be a pupil of Fa-yen's. He dedicated a poem to Fa-yen; it runs as follows.

> Tung-hsüan — this summit's height
> Is not a place for human beings.
> Heart seizes all, nothing is shut out,
> Eye is replete with mountains blue.

Fa-yen put his seal to this poem in that he answered him: This one verse only and nothing besides is needed to keep up our school. Some day kings and princes will honor you. I do not come up to you.

Behold, thus did the ancients achieve enlightenment. Now according to what order of reasoning did this happen? You ought not simply have a Monk of the Mountain [myself, Yüan-wu] explain that to you. Everyone must pursue this problem twice every twelve hours of the day by practicing the finest discrimination in things spiritual. If he, afterwards, in this manner makes the matter of that vision his own, then one day it will no longer be difficult for him to offer his assistance at the crossroads of the country for the benefit of mankind.

This is the reason why Fa-yen replies to his question as to what the Buddha is: You are Hui-chao. How could one have offended the other in this case? The question is in order, without wrong. And exactly so is the answer, without malice. Just look into what Yün-men says: "If a person does not search himself upon a word by the master, then question and answer miss one another. If you put emphasis on reflecting and pondering, in what eternity do you hope to find enlightenment still?" Now, on the next page, you find the poem of Hsüa-tou. He clears it up magnificently.

Poem

In the country bordering on the river the vernal
  wind will and will not blow.
A quail calls out deep in the hiding place where
  flowering shrubs grow.
A fish jumped up at the three-tiered waterfall,
  rose in the air and became a dragon.
Now you can still see fools by night dipping out
  water at the weir.

Interspersed Remarks on the Poem

"In the country bordering on the river the vernal wind
will and will not blow." — Where in all the world did he
get that from? [This really has nothing to do with the
example!] — Still one already sees the glow of spring! [One
notices that a light is dawning in the monk Hui-chao.]

"A quail calls out deep in the hiding place where flowering shrubs grow." What for this *"nan-nan?"* [What for this
call of the quail? Even without it one knows that spring is
here.] — "Already the winds waft other melodies to me."
[First it was said spring would not come; now it is a different
song] — What do you mean, there is no such thing! [The
pupil is not supposed to cling to these pictures. They are
unimportant.]

"A fish jumped up at the three-tiered waterfall, rose in
the air and became a dragon." — He should not impose upon
a congregation of serious monks! [Are we not people of
the same ilk as Hui-chao? It is unrefined to sound high-
falutingly with dragons and the like.] — You crush such a
dragon by stepping on its head. Otherwise he becomes
dangerous.

"Now you can still see fools by night dipping water at
the weir." — They hold onto the railing; they feel their way
along the wall. — They push the gate open, they stand in
front of the door to the house [in order to waylay the master
of the house who hasn't been home for ever so long]. — This

490

sort of carrying on is not meant for robed monks. — That means waiting for the rabbit at the tree trunk.

Explanation of the Poem

The expertness of Hsüa-tou with which he molded a poem from the opaque, knotty, angular, incoherent talk of the ancients which is hard to get your teeth in, hard to chew, hard to illumine, which opens the eyes of people for this sort of thing, is in itself something extraordinary. He knows Fa-yen's twist by which to push the bolt open. He understands where the shoe pinches Hui-chao and on top of it all is concerned that later generations might arrive at wrong interpretations of Fa-yen's words. These are the presuppositions for this poem.

The monk puts this question as the example reports it, and Fa-yen retorts. That is the topic of which Hsüa-tou speaks in the first two verses: "In the country bordering on the river the vernal wind will and will not blow. A quail calls out deep in the hiding place where flowering shrubs grow." These two are [mark well] a single verse [they form the same unity as the rasping of the matured chicklet in the interior of the egg and the pecking thrusts of the hen's bill which picks the egg open from the outside]. Now, tell me, please: What does Hsüa-tou wish to indicate with these verses? Most people, be it to the west of the river, be it to the south, understand the matter as having two sides and maintain that the first verse has reference to Fa-yen's answer: You are Hui-chao. They have to announce nothing further. Therefore, not even the vernal wind dares to blow [against the grandeur of Fa-yen's words which put everything to silence]. The second verse, however, "A quail calls out deep in the hiding place where flowering shrubs grow" is supposed to have reference to the fact that everywhere people vigorously discuss this word of Fa-yen's; that is said to be like the calls of quails in the hiding place of the flowering bushes. Now, really, what would this also have to do with the whole matter! These people don't notice at all that

491

these two verses of Hsüa-tou's are one only. Here we should have neither seam nor crack. I state it plainly: Words, too, hit the meaning; speech, likewise, hits the meaning. This covers heaven and earth. That person asks: What is it about the Buddha? Fa-yen says: You are Hui-chao. And Hsüa-tou replies: "In the country bordering on the river the vernal wind will and will not blow. A quail calls out deep in the hiding place where flowering shrubs grow." If you pocket everything [as a gambler in a game of luck would pick up his take], then you are walking in the red glow of the morning sky. But if you put an interpretation with a prejudiced mind, then you have three more lives coming to you, if not even sixty cycles [kalpas].

In the third and fourth verses Hsüa-tou now openly states, because he is so charitable with others [hinted in his first two verses, but only in disguise], that the great light dawned upon the Zen master Hui-chao on the spot when he heard Fa-yen's answer, and he clothes it in a simile: "A fish jumped up at the three-tiered waterfall, rose in the air and became a dragon. Now you can still see fools by night dipping out water at the weir." The three-tiered cascade at the Yü-men or Yü Gate, also called the Dragongate, came about in that [according to very ancient tradition] King Yü had the mountain tunnelled at that place and [for the purpose of damming the tremendous fall and constructing irrigation canals] built three steps [that is, weirs]. If, now on the third day of the third month the peaches are in bloom, the sensation passes through heaven and earth and brings it about that a few fishes [they are very powerful carps, to be sure] hurl themselves upward at the waterfalls and push through this Dragongate. If a fish has succeeded in doing this, horns grow on its head, its tail spreads in the shape of a horse's mane, it reaches for the clouds and flies off. If a fish is unsuccessful in its jump he must return with injured cranium.

Now if fools merely chew on these words [that is, Hui-chao's question and Fa-yen's answer] then it is exactly as if they "were dipping out water by night" in search of the fish. They don't understand at all that it had long ago changed into a dragon. The old master Shou-tuan composed a poem in reference to this which reads:

> He pulled out a large and shining dime
> And bought himself an oil cake with it,
> Enjoyed it, sent it to his stomach.
> No longer does one hear of his having suffered
> hunger.

This poem is excellent; only, it is terribly clumsy. Hsüa-tou's, however, is all the more refined; it is not jagged at the cutting edge, hence no one can injure his hand. The librarian Ching at that time showed a special preference for this poem of Hsüa-tou's and enjoyed asking his pupils: What do you make of that verse: "A fish jumped up at the three-tiered waterfall, rose in the air and became a dragon?" I for my person do not think this question absolutely necessary. I merely ask you: Where does it occur nowadays that a fish changes into a dragon and flies off?

Example the Twenty-First

CHI-MEN'S LOTUS FLOWER AND LOTUS LEAVES

Reference

The banner of the *Dharma* planted, the meaning of our faith proclaimed — in this manner one scatters flowers on brocaded ground.

The feed basket untied, the burden lifted — thus there is great time of peace.

Perhaps someone is capable of recognizing a word in its uniqueness which follows no rule. Then he could, by one corner, make himself intelligible the other three. Perhaps no one has achieved that yet. Then let him be as before and, being all ear, listen to the solution.

493

Example

We submit:

A monk asked Chi-men[1]: What is the lotus flower so long as it has not grown out of the water?
Chi-men said: Lotus flower.
The monk asked: But what afterwards when it has emerged from the water?
Chi-men said: Lotus leaves.

Subsidiary Remarks on the Example

A monk asked Chi-men: "What is the lotus flower so long as it has not grown out of the water?" — He fishes on ground where nothing is to be presumed [that is, he asks where nothing is to be asked]. — He washes a lump of dirt in dirty water [thus the clot becomes still dirtier; by questioning, the unfathomable becomes only more difficult to fathom]. — How did he happen to get into this game of question and answer?

"Chi-men said: Lotus flower." — One, two, three, four, five, six, seven (thus smoothly and matter-of-factly does this answer come forth). — He throws everybody in deadly doubt.

"The monk asked: But what afterwards when it has emerged from the water?" — Would that he desisted from preparing for himself an existence in the death-cave of hungry ghosts. [If the monk continues to ask like this he will perish spiritually.] — Again he does it! [First, he is concerned about the condition of the lotus flower under water. Instead of regaining his wits when the master answers, he continues to vacillate between these two poles.]

"Chi-men said: Lotus leaves." — In a pinch Yu-chou might yet do; the bitterest is the Southern Region. [What is meant is that the first answer of Chi-men's might yet do, but the second one is insupportable.] — Two heads with three

1. Chi-men Kuang-tzŭ.

494

faces [Chi-men's words lead to inconceivable ideas.] — He makes everybody a laughing-stock.

Explanation of the Example

In so far as Chi-men admits the intellectual capability of the questioner and occupies himself with the material on hand we do not have too much difficulty with the intelligibility of his answer. However, in the manner in which he cuts off the flow of ordinary thinking he goes miles beyond all understanding.

Tell me, if you will: This lotus flower, if it has grown above the water and so long as it has not grown out of it, is it one and the same thing or is it two different things? If you are able to see it correctly as it is in fact, I acknowledge that you have gained entrance into these things.

But even so the matter remains difficult enough. For if you maintain that it is one and the same thing then you present Buddhahood as a shaky matter and vulgarize the whole matter. However, if you say it is two things you are still caught up in contrasting inner and outer. But if you embark on the downward course of analytical explanation and continue in it you will never arrive at a point of rest and terminus.

Tell me, if you will, what does the old master really have in mind? In the last analysis he is not concerned with so many questions. Therefore, Tou-tzi says: "By no means remain caught up in names, words, numbers, and proverbs! If once you are through with all that sort of thing you will naturally no longer cling to details. Then you no longer concern yourself with such and such ranks and inequalities. Then it is you who takes up into himself all these things and all things together no longer can take you up into themselves. Basically and fundamentally one cannot win anything nor can one lose anything; there is no dream, no illusion, there are not so and so many names and categories. For this intrinsic reality one should not wish to determine at all costs names and ideograms. You would not

495

allow yourself to be intimidated with empty phrases, would you? Only because you are asking questions do we have words. If you do not ask me what, then, should I be able to say to you that is useful? The entire discussion, — all that you are bringing on; with yourself this has nothing to do whatever."

One of the ancients [it was Pai-chang] says: "Where it is a matter of somebody's reaching out for knowledge of the Buddha-nature, there it is necessary to pay attention to the time and the hour, to cause and motive."

Look here what Yün-men has to lay before us. A monk asked master Ling-yün: What was the Buddha before he appeared in the world? Ling-yün raised his yak-tail. The monk continued to ask: What was he after his appearance? Again Ling-yün raised his yak-tail. Concerning this behavior of master Ling-yün, Yün-men remarked: "In the first instance Ling-yün hit the mark; the second time he missed it." Yün-men says, furthermore: "If Ling-yün does not react at all to the difference in the condition of the Buddha after and before his appearance, what has become of the time and the hour which the monk is trying to find out by his question?"

The ancients went by this rule: One question, one answer. Without much ado they complied with the time and the hour. If you ask for words, hunt for proverbs, ultimately you do not reach any agreement. Not until you arrive at the position of advancing toward and releasing the word contained in the word, the meaning contained in the meaning, the motive contained in the motive, until you are free and composed, will you perceive the place which Chi-men's answer is pointing out.

Yün-men says: "From time immemorial up to the present it has always been a matter of a single tiny jolt. It is not a matter of yes and no, not one of profit or loss, nor whether anything is to be produced or not to be produced."

The ancients have left us a feasible road in this matter which leads out and in. [That is to say, the intercourse with

he master in question and answer. For, one who is inexperienced needs the guiding hand not only so long as he is
ensnared in the delusion of being and possessing, but also
when he begins to dissociate and lose himself in empty
nothingness. But even if he has overcome the first diseases
of childhood he still has a very long road in front of him.]
If a person has not established himself in himself he holds
on to the bamboo fence and gropes along the wall, reaches
for straws and fumbles for trees. Should one, then, advise
him to let go of everything he stumbles into the thicket,
into empty space, in all sorts of desolate places. If someone
has achieved it he will "at none of the twelve hours in a
day cling to anything whatsoever or support himself by
it." But even if he doesn't cling to anything or rely on
anything, it is still a question of how he will behave if one
bares in front of him an inner emotion or an external cir-
cumstance [as in the case of this example], and how he then
tackles and investigates it.

This monk is asking: What, then, is the lotus flower so
long as it has not grown out of the water? Chi-men replies:
Lotus flower. Thus an answer which simply cuts off the
question neatly. This is highly peculiar. People in general
call that a paradox, a statement which turns things upside
down. Where, in this case, tell me, would there be anything
placed upside down? Just take a look once what Yen-tou
[who lived 828-887] says: "Whenever you listen to a master
talk you must always reverently pay attention to what he
was thinking about even before he opens his mouth. Then
we might tolerably be in a position to understand." If the
ancients once lay bare how they react within they have
already sprung a leak and are disjoined [that is to say, they
allow themselves to drop from the highest level to the second
one, are concerned with words, with individual objects and
questions, thus quitting their immersion in the emptiness
which includes within itself everything for the world of individual things and their opposites.]

But the scholars of today no longer pay attention to the

meaning and opinion of the ancients. They simply come along and carry on their theoretical discussions concerning the relationship between 'out of the water' and 'not yet out of it.' What has that to do with the real matter on hand?

Now look here. A monk asks Chi-men: Wherein does the essence of wisdom consist? Men replied: The Venus shell carries the luminous moon within itself. The monk further asked: And wherein does the effect of wisdom consist? Chi-men said: In that the female hare is pregnant from the moonbeam. Observe the manner in which he is answering questions. But in the whole wide world people do not even get the feel of the pulse beat of his words. [According to the popular conception in the China of that time the pearls in the flesh of the Venus muscle originate after having been fertilized by the moon in the night of the full moon of the eighth month. In the same night also the female hares become impregnated by the moonbeam. Both of them are similes for eternal wisdom which permeates all. According to the old categories of Chinese thinking the monk enquired first after the essence then after the effects of wisdom. Chi-men's answers simply pass over this distinction; they only prevent the mind from laying itself bare to wisdom.]

Assume someone would ask me, Chia-shan: What is the lotus flower so long as it has not grown out of the water? I would answer him simply: This post here, the lantern there. Please tell me: Now, would that be the same as the lotus flower or something else? [Post and lantern in Yüan-wu's surrounding are constituents of the Vihāra and perhaps of the garden, objects and symbols of the district in which people who renounce themselves and the world strive for the highest ultimate truth.]

And what if the lotus has grown out of the water? To this I would reply: On the ends of my walking stick on my neck I carry sun and moon; below, my feet are wading deep in the worst mud. [In contrast to the direction pointing beyond as the metaphor of post and lantern present it, this is the direction pointing downward which deals with all the badness and all the sorrows of the world.]

Tell me, if you please: Now, is this correct or isn't it? Take care, however, that you do not by mistake pay attention to the starlet on the beam of a pair of scales instead of to the stone weight! Hsüa-tou in his boundless goodness and charity beats with his poem all interpretations to smithereens which people make on an emotional basis.

Poem

Lotus flower, lotus leaves — suggest it to you.
Above the water exactly as below — how can that
    be true?
Depart from the river south and north, inquire of
    the old Wang!
If a fox has doubted sufficiently it is the next one's
    turn.

"Lotus flower, lotus leaves — suggest it to you." — He [Hsüa-tou] means it well and thoughtfully like an old grandmother. — A public notice, ready and visible to all! — But the manner in which he says it is, however, already too delicate and elegant.

"Above the water exactly as below — how can that be true?" — He is washing a lump of earth in the muddy water. — He also could have treated the two conditions [above the water and under the water] separately, which would have been quite in order. It really is not proper to be so negligent as to grossify this matter and then to act as if it had been settled.

"Go from the river south and north, inquire of the old Wang!" — But where in the world is the hero of the novel? [It surely is not a matter of any Mr. Wang or Chang; as always it is a matter concerning only yourself.] — What is to be gained from your applying to this old Wang? — You only wear out your sandals.

"If a fox has doubted sufficiently it is the next one's turn." — Let's bury them all in the same pit! — From yourself your doubts arise! — By no manner or means will they become allayed. — Now a blow with the stick! Do you comprehend?

Explanation of the Poem

Chi-men came originally from Chekiang. He knew what he wanted, set out for the distant Si-chuan and went for guidance to Hsiang-lin. After he had already penetrated he turned around and settled down in the monastery 'Gate of Wisdom,' Chi-men, in the district city of Sui-chou. Hsüa-tou is [figuratively speaking] his first-born son. He saw him, experienced him and has been thoroughly initiated into the secret of his depths. Out of this personal experience he begins his poem straight away with the words: "Lotus flower, lotus leaves — suggest it to you."

"Above the water exactly as below — how can that be true?" A saying such as this one we can grasp and understand as it was pronounced only on the spot. The monk from the mountain [that is, I, Yüan-wu] has already said: "What is the lotus flower so long as it is still under water? The post here, the lantern there. And what about it when it has grown above the water? On the ends of my walking stick on my neck I carry sun and moon; below, my feet are wading deep in the worst mud. Take care, however, that you do not by mistake pay attention to the starlet on the beam of a pair of scales instead of to the stone weight!" Today, all people can do is to chew on the words of such masters, never to be done with it. Please tell me: What is the time at which the lotus flower has emerged from the water? And what is the time at which it has not yet emerged? If you have won the right perspective for these two problems then we gladly permit you to have a very personal confrontation with the master Chi-men.

Hsüa-tou says, moreover: If you absolutely cannot see it, then "go from the river south and north, enquire of the old Wang!" He intends to say: Go ahead, visit all recognized masters south of the Yangtze Kiang and to the north of it

500

ask them concerning 'above the water' and concerning 'below the water,' next arrange their two different answers to both questions neatly together south of the river, then put the one heap of proverbs on the other and let the whole whirl in a circle to bring forth doubts! Only tell me now: When will you reach the stage of having no more doubts? You behave exactly like the field fox when it goes on ice. Full of doubts and hesitations he stops after every little step and listens whether he won't hear water, and only when there is no noise to be heard he dares to cross the river. And: "If a fox has doubted sufficiently, it is the next one's turn." If you who have have put your trust in the guidance of a master behave like the fox with his doubts and hesitations, — when, indeed, will you find your rest, your peace?

Example the Twenty-Sixth

PAI-CHANG ON HERO MOUNTAIN

Example

We submit:

A monk asked Pai-chang[1]: What is there that is extraordinary? Pai-chang replied: To sit alone here on Hero Mountain.
The monk bowed reverently.
Thereupon Pai-chang struck him.

Subsidiary Remarks on the Example

"A monk asked Pai-chang: What is there that is extraordinary?" — There is a ring in these words. — He has something up his sleeves. — He bewilders us, as it were. — Eyes he has and he has not seen anything yet.

"Pai-chang retorted: To sit alone here on Hero Mountain." — A word replete with dignity which makes the four times hundred provinces in the realm tremble. — Now, for him

1. Pai-chang Huai-hai, 749(?)-814.

who sits here, as for him who stands here, the battle is lost.

"The monk bowed reverently." — Cunning fellows of a robed brother! — With adversaries of this kind the disputation must be accordingly.

"Thereupon Pai-chang struck him." — The perfect master! — Why is he not more liberal with his speech? — A sentence is not passed for nothing.

Explanation of the Example

To be equipped at the right moment with eyes and not pay attention to danger and impending disaster! Therefore it has been said: How will he who does not penetrate into the tiger's lair intend to catch the tiger's young?

Pai-chang's habit it was to sit there like a tiger with his paws spread. The monk, too, does not dodge in this case where it is a matter of life and death. He is pert enough to stroke the tiger's whiskers. Thus he enquired: "What is there that is extraordinary?" He too was equipped with eyes. Thus, Pai-chang took the load off his shoulders and put it on his own in that he gave him this answer: "To sit alone here on Hero Mountain." Thereupon the monk bowed reverently. It belongs to a monk wearing the robe and a master that, even before anyone asks him, he already distinguishes his sense and meaning clearly; thus only he will find the one correct answer. That the monk thereupon bows reverently differs from what one would ordinarily do. He too must have eyes; then only will he be right. Never allow your habitual psychic stance to be altered with a view to others! To know and understand one another yet remain like strangers!

This monk simply asked: "What is there that is extraordinary?" Pai-chang replied: "To sit alone here on Hero Mountain." The monk bows reverently, and Pai-chang strikes him. Look here how they do it. If it's a question of giving the other free reins they do it mutually. If it's a matter of calling a halt and putting an end to it they neatly part without leaving a trace behind. [It is as if in spite of their opposition between them there existed a secret understanding.]

Tell me please: What does the monk mean when he bows reverently to Pai-chang? If you say he did well, why and for what reason, then, does Pai-chang strike him? Contrariwise, if you say that it wasn't the correct thing to do, what, then, was the fault in the reverent bow? In order to clearly recognize here the difference between weal and woe, black and white, one must already stand on an eminence from where one sees oneself confronted by a thousand peaks. In bowing reverently to Pai-chang the monk, as it were, strokes the tiger's whiskers. He is now merely concerned with tacking freely. But it is not for nothing that Pai-chang has a third eye between the parting of the hair and bears on his arm, above the wrist, the imprint of a seal. His glance penetrates the four regions of the world, pierces down deeply and distinguishes sharply from where the winds blow. And it is for this that he administered blows to that monk in exchange for the bow. Another one probably would not know so easily how to shift in such a case. For the monk replies exchanging move for move, idea for idea and fights the master's perception with his own. Therefore his reverent bow.

It is a similar process as in the case of Nan-chüan. This one said one day: "Yesterday, about the third watch of the night, the Bodhisattvas Mañjusri and Samantabhadra appeared to me. They theorized about buddhadharma. I administered each one of them twenty blows with my stick and banned them to the mountains of the two iron rings [which surround the world mountain Sumeru, thus to the extreme end of the world]." Thereupon, Chao-chou the future master, broke ranks from among the listeners and said: "Venerable Sir, who gets to feel your stick with this hint?" Nan-chüan replied: "What didn't the old master Wang [that is to say, Nan-chüan] do right?" Chao-chou bowed reverently.

If a teacher of our faith becomes listless it may be that

he does not appraise correctly how the questioner takes his answer. However, as soon as he hits upon the meaning which the questioner attributes to his words and moves him, then he has established contact with him and can continue to help him effectively. My one-time teacher from the Mountain of the Fifth Patriarch used to say: "The task of the master to answer the pupil's questions required the same attention and caution as when one spars with an opponent in front of horses' hoops. In order to understand this Pai-chang [and his masterly technique] correctly you must resolutely dissociate yourself from all impressions of seeing and hearing, of voice and gestures, sitting quietly, must grasp firmly the meaning of the question put and master it yourself; only then will you succeed." And now tell me, if you will: How would it be to again let go after one has grasped? Look here how Hsüa-tou presents this dialogue in his poem.

Poem

Colt of heavenly steed disports himself on parental
    meadows,
Converter who uniquely opened here, closed there.
And should, when lightning strikes and sparks fly,
    the mind remain steadfast,
The weather clears: Someone arrived and stroked the
    tiger's whiskers.

Interspersed Remarks on the Poem

"Colt of heavenly steed disports himself on parental meadows." — Such a one is born at best one in five hundred years. — Among a thousand and ten thousand, perhaps, one or half a one. — Sons continue their father's occupation.

"Converter who uniquely opened here, closed there." — For a long time past this needed no explanation. — That is the man who has gained freedom. — That is the right man and master for a case of this nature.

"And should, when lightning strikes and sparks fly, the

504

mind remain steadfast" — There, blow follows blow. — To the left, to the right! — Don't you also see how Pai-chang withal only wants to help that other person? Or don't you notice this?

"The weather clears: Someone arrived and stroked the tiger's whiskers." — Thirty blows with the stick are his [the monk's] for this [as mark of recognition]! — Manly courage from strict discipline. — Relentlessly surrendering body and life is in order. — Let us give him a free move in the game.

Explanation of the Poem

Hsüa-tou has insight into the connection, therefore he highlights it in his poem. One day the colts of heavenly steeds ran for a thousand Li hither and thither in a mad gallop as if they were flying; hence one gave them this name. Hsüa-tou praises in this poem master Pai-chang as he covers the realm of the patriarchs from east to west and from west to east, once to, once fro, seven times straight ahead, eight times crosswise, completely without restraint, just like such a colt of heaven which, though dashing about madly in estafette gait, nevertheless constantly perceives where the road is clear. This is simply due to the fact that he [Pai-chang] inherited from his own master the Patriarch Ma, his great spiritual liveliness and mighty dynamism.

Here is an example! A monk asked Patriarch Ma: What, in brief, is the meaning of the Buddhadharma? The master struck him and retorted: had I not struck you I would live to see the day when the whole wide realm makes a laughing stock of me.

Again, someone else asked: What is the meaning of the arrival of our Patriarch Bodhidharma out of the West? The master replied: Come closer to me and I will tell you! The monk came closer. Thereupon Ma took him by the ear, struck him and said: Six ears together do not mastermind a plot.

Look what superior freedom this master is capable of! That is what happens in a school where men are transformed.

There one either rolls up and ties his scroll [something the other does not understand] or one unrolls and spreads it out. One time one lays oneself bare without any restraint whatever. The next time one curls up without granting the least insight. Still another time one does neither this nor that. Just as it is said: On the same track the wagon trails still differ.

In the first two verses, thus, Hsüa-tou praises the virtuosity of Pai-chang. If he continues, however, by saying: "In lightning and flying sparks the mind remains steadfast," then his praise is for the monk who, at any rate, demonstrates a little agility and presence of mind in this lightning-like dispute.

Yen-tou once said: "To ward off something is esteemed noble, to pursue something base. In a verbal dispute each one is on his own while on his private turntable."

And Hsüa-tou says [in his poem apropos another example]:

Originally the mind's wheel stands still.
If it spins, then always to either side only.

Should the wheel not be able to turn, what practical value would that have? Whoever wants to be a real fellow should have knowledge about a little agility and presence of mind; only in this way will he be successful. However, today people always try to oblige the master, but then they must suffer that he will drill a hole in their noses [and take them in tow]. How will they ever get through in this way? This monk, however, still preserves the agility of his mind "when lightning strikes and sparks fly," and bows reverently to the master.

Thus, says Hsüa-tou at the end, "the weather clears: Someone arrived and stroked the tiger's whiskers." Pai-chang, to be sure, resembles somewhat such a great sneaking animal. And it is a laughing matter if this monk now approaches him and strokes his whiskers.

Chu Hsi

CHU HSI (1130-1200). Generally ranked as the greatest of the Neo-Confucianists, equaled only by Confucius and Mencius in historical importance, Chu Hsi (Chu Hui-an, Chu Yüan-hui, Chu Chung-hui) distinguished himself early in life as a patriot-scholar and continued through his influence to dominate Chinese life for several centuries. His feat of syncretism is comparable to that of St. Thomas Aquinas. He invested the Classics with an eclectic cosmology and metaphysics, interpreting the basic texts of Confucianism in the light of accumulated knowledge and filling the gaps in the ancient system. He stressed logic, consistency, and conscientious observance of classical authority. His analytical commentaries on the classics and his conservative ethic shaped Chinese scholarship and mores until modern times.

To explain the existence of ignorance and evil among human beings who are supposed to be essentially good, he made a distinction between man's original nature and his actual nature as it is embodied in material force (*ch'i*), which gives being its substance and form. He held that the Great Ultimate "is identical with the principle (*li*) of the universe," that "there is a Great Ultimate in each thing," and that "the Great Ultimate is nothing but the principle of ultimate goodness." It was in his famous debate with Lu Hsiang-shan over the Supreme Ultimate that the dualism of Chu Hsi, in contrast to the monism of his opponent, became most obvious.

Chu Hsi, a native of Anhui, studied first under his

father, then under Li T'ung, whose teachings were in the tradition of Ch'eng Hao and Ch'eng I. Time after time he petitioned the emperor to resist the invading enemy, to impeach inept officials, and to practice the Confucian principles of "investigation of things" and "extension of knowledge." He declined official posts repeatedly, preferring the peace and quiet he could enjoy as guardian of a temple. His official life, apart from the guardianship, was intermittent and turbulent, for he criticized incompetency wherever he detected it. His lectures at the White Deer Grotto in present Kiangsi attracted many prominent scholars. His teachings, too radical for the officials to accept, were prohibited in 1196. Yet the four Confucian texts established by the great Sung scholar (*The Great Learning, The Mean, Analects,* and *Mencius*) served as the basis of the civil service examinations required of candidates for government posts for a period of six centuries (1313-1905). His influence spread to Japan where a school of Neo-Confucianism, the Shushi School, was named after him.

The Doctrine of the Mean

From *A Source Book in Chinese Philosophy*, translated and compiled by Wing-tsit Chan, Princeton, New Jersey, Princeton University Press, 1963.

CHU Hsi's Remark: "Master Ch'eng I (Ch'eng I-ch'uan, 1033-1107) said, 'By *chung* (central) is meant what is not one-sided, and by *yung* (ordinary) is meant what is unchangeable. *Chung* is the correct path of the world and *yung* is the definite principle of the world.' 'This work represents the central way[2] in which the doctrines of the Confucian school have been transmitted.' Fearing that in

1. Originally a chapter in the *Li chi* (*Book of Rites*), evidently it existed in the early Han dynasty (206 B.C.-A.D. 220) independently. Moreover, commentaries in the Han and Liang (502-557) times were written on it as an independent work, although these commentaries are no longer extant. As in the case of the *Great Learning*, great interest in it arose in the Sung period (960-1279). Both Ssu-ma Kuang (1019-1086) and Ch'eng Hao (Ch'eng Ming-tao, 1032-1085) wrote commentaries on it. But it was Chu Hsi who brought it into prominence. He redivided the old text, the one used in Cheng Hsüan's (127-200) commentary, the *Li chi cheng-i* or Correct Meaning of the *Book of Rites* (in the Thirteen Classics Series), into thirty-three sections without altering the order of the text. Thus the text became much clearer. He accepted the account in Ssu-ma Ch'ien's *Shih-chi* (Records of the Historian), ch. 47 (see French translation by Chavannes, *es mémoires historiques*, vol. 5, p. 431), that Confucius' grandson Tzu-su (492-431 B.C.) was the author. Many modern scholars refuse to accept the theory; some have dated it around 200 B.C. The work is not consistent either in style or in thought. It may be a work of more than one person over a considerable period in the fifth or fourth century B.C. English translations by Legge, "The Doctrine of the Mean," and Ku Hung-ming, "Central Harmony," follow Chu Hsi's sectioning, while Hughes, "The Mean-in-Action," follows the Cheng Hsüan text. In our translation, Chu Hsi's arrangement is followed.

2. The term *hsin-fa* is Buddhist, meaning transmission from mind to mind without the use of words. Ch'eng borrowed the term but used it an entirely different sense, taking *hsin* (mind) to mean "central," and emphasizing the use of words.

time errors should arise, Tzŭ-ssu wrote it down and transmitted it to Mencius. The book 'first speaks of one principle, next it spreads out to cover the ten thousand things, and finally returns and gathers them all under the one principle.' Unroll it, and it reaches in all directions. Roll it up, and it withdraws and lies hidden in minuteness. 'Its meaning and interest are inexhaustible.'[1] The whoe of is solid learning. If the skillful reader will explore and brood over it and apprehend it, he may apply it throughout his life, and will find it inexhaustible."

1. What Heaven (*T'ien, Nature*) imparts to man is called human nature. To follow[2] our nature is called the Way (Tâo). Cultivating the Way is called education. The Way cannot be separated from us for a moment. What can be separated from us is not the Way. Therefore the superior man is cautious over what he does not see and apprehensive over what he does not hear. There is nothing more visible than what is hidden and nothing more manifest than what is subtle. Therefore the superior man is watchful over himself when he is alone.

Before the feelings of pleasure, anger, sorrow, and joy are aroused it is called equilibrium (*chung*, centrality, mean). When these feelings are aroused and each and all attain due measure and degree, it is called harmony. Equilibrium is the great foundation of the world, and harmony its universal path. When equilibrium and harmony are realized to the highest degree, heaven and earth will attain their proper order and all things will flourish.

> *Chu Hsi's Remark.* "In the above first chapter, Tzŭ-ssu relates the ideas which had been transmitted to him, as the basis of discourse. First, it shows clearly that the origin of the Way is traced to Heaven and is un-

1. *I-shu* (Surviving Works), 7:3b, 14:1a, 18:30a; *Wai-shu* (Additiona Works), 11:1b, both in ECCS.
2. Interpretation according to Cheng Hsüan, *Chung-yung chu* (Commentary on the *Doctrine of the* Mean).

changeable, while its concrete substance is complete in ourselves and may not be departed from. Next, it speaks of the essentials of preserving, nourishing, and examining the mind. Finally, it speaks of the meritorious achievements and transforming influence of the sage and the spirit man in their highest degree. Tzŭ ssu's hope was that the student should hereby return to search within himself to find these truths, so that he might remove his selfish desires aroused by external temptations, and realize in full measure the goodness which is natural to him. This is what scholar Yang meant when he said that this chapter is the quintessence of the whole work.[5] In the following ten chapters, Tzŭ-ssu quotes Confucius in order fully to develop the meaning of this chapter."

2. Chung-ni (Confucius) said, "The superior man [exemplifies] the Mean (chung-yung).[2] The inferior man acts contrary to the Mean. The superior man [exemplifies] the Mean because, as a superior man, he can maintain the Mean at any time. The inferior man [acts contrary to][3] the Mean because, as an inferior man, he has no caution."

1. Although none of the commentators in the Chung-yung Chang-chü (Commentary on the Doctrine of the Mean) in the Ssu-shu ta-ch'üan (Great Collection of Commentaries on the Four Books) mentioned the name of the man, this refers to Yang Shih (Yang Kuei-shan, 1053-1135). In his Chung-yung huo-wen (Questions and Answers on the Doctrine of the Mean), Chu Hsi repeatedly commented on Yang's theories. The particular remark in question, however, is not found in the Yang Kuei-shan chi (Collected Works of Yang Shih). It was probably transmitted orally and was well known to scholars.

2. The term chum-yung, literally "centrality and universality," has been translated as moderation, the Mean, mean-in-action, normality, universal moral order, etc. According to Cheng Hsüan, yung means the ordinary and chung-yung means using the Mean as the ordinary way. According to Chu Hsi, it means neither one-sided nor extreme but the ordinary principle of the Mean. The Mean is the same as equilibrium and harmony in ch. 1.

3. Following Wang Su's (195-256) text.

3. Confucius said, "Perfect is the Mean. For a long time few people have been able to follow it."[1]

4. Confucius said, "I know why the Way is not pursued. The intelligent go beyond it and the stupid do not come up to it. I know why the Way is not understood.[2] The worthy go beyond it and the unworthy do not come up to it. There is no one who does not eat and drink, but there are few who can really know flavor."

5. Confucius said, "Alas! How is the Way not being pursued!"

6. Confucius said, "Shun[3] was indeed a man of great wisdom! He loved to question others and to examine their words, however ordinary. He concealed what was bad in them and displayed what was good. He took hold of their two extremes, took the mean between them, and applied it in his dealing with the people. This was how he became Shun (the sage-emperor)."

7. Confucius said, "Men all say, 'I am wise'; but when driven forward and taken in a net, a trap, or a pitfall, none knows how to escape. Men all say, 'I am wise'; but should they choose the course of the Mean, they are not able to keep it for a round month."

8. Confucius said, "Hui[4] was a man who chose the course of the Mean, and when he got hold of one thing that was good, he clasped it firmly as if wearing it on his breast and never lost it."

9. Confucius said, "The empire, the states, and the families can be put in order. Ranks and emolument can be declined. A bare, naked weapon can be tramped upon. But the Mean cannot [easily] be attained."

1. A similar saying is found in *Aanalects*, 6:27.
2. Some eleventh-century scholars thought that the word "pursued" and "understood" should be interchanged, for intelligence and stupidity pertain to understanding while worthiness and unworthiness pertain to action.
3. Legendary sage-emperor (3rd millennium B.C.).
11. Name of Confucius' favorite pupil, Yen Yüan (521-490 B.C.).

10. Tzu-lu[1] asked about strength. Confucius said, "Do you mean the strength of the South, the strength of the North, or the strength you should cultivate yourself? To be genial and gentle in teaching others and not to revenge unreasonable conduct — this is the strength of the people of the South. The superior man lives by it. To lie under arms and meet death without regret — this is the strength of the people of the North. The strong man lives by it. Therefore the superior man maintains harmony (in his nature and conduct] and does not waver. How unflinching is his strength! He stands in the middle position and does not lean to one side. How unflinching is his strength! When the Way prevails in the state, [if he enters public life], he does not change from what he was in private life. How unflinching is his strength! When the Way does not prevail in the state, he does not change even unto death. How unflinching is his strength!"

11. "There are men who seek for the abstruse, and practice wonders. Future generations may mention them. But that is what I will not do. There are superior men who act in accordance with the Way, but give up when they have gone half way. But I can never give up. There are superior men who are in accord with the Mean, retire from the world and are unknown to their age, but do not regret. It is only a sage who can do this."

12. "The Way of the superior man functions everywhere and yet is hidden. Men and women of simple intelligence can share its knowledge; and yet in its utmost reaches, there is something which even the sage does not know. Men and women of simple intelligence can put it into practice; and yet in its utmost reaches there is something which even the sage is not able to put into practice. Great as heaven and earth are, men still find something in them with which to be dissatisfied. Thus with [the Way of] the

1. Confucius' pupil, whose family name was Chung and private name Yu (542-480 B.C.).

superior man, if one speaks of its greatness, nothing in the world can contain it, and if one speaks of its smallness, nothing in the world can split it. The *Book of Odes* says, 'The hawk flies up to heaven; the fishes leap in the deep.'[1] This means that [the Way] is clearly seen above and below. The Way of the superior man has its simple beginnings in the relation between man and woman, but in its utmost reaches, it is clearly seen in heaven and on earth."

> *Chu Hsi's Remark.* "The above twelfth chapter contains the words of Tzŭ-ssu, which are meant to clarify and elaborate on the idea of chapter 1 that the Way cannot be departed from. In the following eight chapters, he quotes Confucius here and there to clarify it."

13. Confucius said, "The Way is not far from man. When a man pursues the Way and yet remains away from man, his course cannot be considered the Way. The *Book of Odes* says, 'In hewing an axe handle, in hewing an axe handle, the pattern is not far off.'[2] If we take an axe

handle to hew another axe handle and look askance from the one to the other, we may still think the pattern is far away. Therefore the superior man governs men as men, in accordance with human nature, and as soon as they change [what is wrong], he stops. Conscientiousness (*chung*) and altruism (*shu*) are not far from the Way. What you do not wish others to do to you, do not do to them.

"There are four things in the Way of the superior man, none of which I have been able to do. To serve my father as I would expect my son to serve me: that I have not been able to do. To serve my ruler as I would expect my ministers to serve me: that I have not been able to do.

1. Ode no. 239.
2. Ode no. 158.

514

To serve my elder brothers as I would expect my younger brothers to serve me: that I have not been able to do. To be the first to treat friends as I would expect them to treat me: that I have not been able to do. In practicing the ordinary virtues and in the exercise of care in ordinary conversation, when there is deficiency, the superior man never fails to make further effort, and when there is excess, never dares to go to the limit. His words correspond to his actions and his actions correspond to his words.[1] Isn't the superior man earnest and genuine?"

> Comment. It is often said that Confucianism teaches only the "negative golden rule," not to do to others what one does not want them to do to him. However, the golden rule is here positively stated, that is, do to others what one expects others to do to him. There is no question about the positive character of the Confucian doctrine which is clearly stated in terms of conscientiousness and altruism.[2]

14. The superior man does what is proper to his position and does not want to go beyond this. If he is in a noble station, he does what is proper to a position of wealth and honorable station. If he is in a humble station, he does what is proper to a position of poverty and humble station. If he is in the midst of barbarian tribes, he does what is proper in the midst of barbarian tribes. In a position of difficulty and danger, he does what is proper to a position of difficulty and danger. He can find himself in no situation in which he is not at ease with himself. In a high position he does not treat his inferiors with contempt. In a low position he does not court the favor of his superiors. He rectifies himself and seeks nothing from others, hence he has no complaint to make. He does not complain against

1. See above, ch. 2, comment on *Analects*, 2:18.
2. *ibid.*, comment on *Analects*, 4:15. For a discussion on *chung-shu*, see Appendix.

Heaven above or blame men below.[1] Thus it is that the superior man lives peacefully and at ease and waits for his destiny (*ming*, Mandate of Heaven, fate),[2] while the inferior man takes to dangerous courses and hopes for good luck. Confucius said, "In archery we have something resembling the Way of the superior man. When the archer misses the center of the target, he turns around and seeks for the cause of failure within himself."

15. The Way of the superior man may be compared to traveling to a distant place: one must start from the nearest point. It may be compared to ascending a height: one must start from below. The *Book of Odes* says, "Happy union with wife and children is like the music of lutes and harps. When brothers live in concord and at peace, the harmony is sweet and delightful. Let your family live in concord, and enjoy your wife and children."[3] Confucius said, "How happy will parents be!"

16. Confucius said, "How abundant is the display of power of spiritual beings! We look for them but do not see them. We listen to them but do not hear them. They form the substance of all things[4] and nothing can be without them. They cause all people in the world to fast and purify themselves and put on the richest dresses to perform sacrifices to them. Like the spread of overflowing water they seem to be above and to be on the left and the right. The *Book of Odes* says, 'The coming of spiritual beings cannot be surmised. How much less can we get tired of them.'[5] Such is the manifestation of the subtle. Such is the impossibility of hiding the real (*ch'eng*)."

1. A similar saying is found in *Analects*, 14:37.
2. On the doctrine of waiting for destiny, see above ch. 3, comment on *Mencius*, Additional Selections, 7A:1.
3. Ode no. 164.
4. This is Chu Hsi's interpretation of *t'i-wu* in his *Chung-yung chang-ch'ü*. See also below, ch. 30, n.83.
5. Ode no. 256.

17. Confucius said, "Shun was indeed greatly filial! In virtue he was a sage; in honor he was the Son of Heaven (emperor); and in wealth he owned all within the four seas (China). Temple sacrifices were made to him, and his descendants preserved the sacrifices to him. Thus it is that he who possesses great virtue will certainly attain to corresponding position, to corresponding wealth, to corresponding fame, and to corresponding long life. For Heaven, in the production of things, is sure to be bountiful to them, according to their natural capacity. Hence the tree that is well taken care of is nourished and that which is about to fall is overthrown. The *Book of Odes* says, 'The admirable, amiable prince displayed conspicuously his excellent virtue. He put his people and his officers in concord. And he received his emolument from Heaven. It protected him, assisted him, and appointed him king. And Heaven's blessing came again and again.'[1] Therefore he who possesses great virtue will surely receive the appointment of Heaven."

18. Confucius said, "King Wăn was indeed the only one without sorrow! He had King Chi for father and King Wu[2] for son. His father laid the foundation of [the great work of the Chou dynasty] and his son carried it on. King Wu continued the enterprise of King T'ai,[3] King Chi, and King Wăn. Once he buckled on his armor [and revolted against wicked King Chou of Shang], the world came into his possession, and did not personally lose his great reputation through the empire. In honor he was the Son of Heaven, and in wealth he owned all within the four seas. Temple sacrifices were made to him, and his descendants preserved the sacrifices to him.

"King Wu received Heaven's Mandate to rule in his old age. Duke Chou[4] carried to completion the virtue of

1. Ode no. 249.
2. King Wen (r. 1171-1122 B.C.) was the founder of the Chou dynasty. King Wu (r. 1121-1116 B.C.) was his successor.
3. King Chi's father.
4. King Wu's brother (d. 1094 B.C.)

King Wăn and King Wu. He honored T'ai and Chi with the posthumous title of king. He sacrificed to the past reigning dukes of the house with imperial rites. These rites were extended to the feudal lords, great officers, officers, and the common people. If the father was a great officer, and the son a minor officer, when the father died, he was buried with the rite of a great officer but afterward sacrificed to with the rite of a minor officer. If the father was a minor officer and the son was a great officer, then the father was buried with the rite of a minor officer but afterward sacrificed to with the rite of a great officer The rule for one year of mourning for relatives was extended upward to include great officers, but the rule for three years of mourning was extended upward to include the Son of Heaven. In mourning for parents, there was no difference for the noble or the commoner. The practice was the same."

19. Confucius said, "King Wu and Duke Chou were indeed eminently filial. Men of filial piety are those who skillfully carry out the wishes of their forefathers and skillfully carry forward their undertakings. In spring and autumn they repaired their ancestral temple, displayed their ancestral vessels and exhibited the ancestral robes, and presented the appropriate offerings of the season. The ritual of the ancestral temple is in order to place the kindred on the left or on the right according to the order of descent. This order in rank meant to distinguish the more honorable or humbler stations. Services in the temple are arranged in order so as to give distinction to the worthy [according to their ability for those services]. In the pledging rite inferiors present their cups to their superior, so that people of humble stations may have something to do. In the concluding feast, honored places were given people with white hair, so as to follow the order of seniority. To occupy places of their forefathers, to practice their rites, to perform their music, to reverence those whom they honored, to love those who were dear to them, to serve the dead as they were served while alive, and to serve the departed as they were

served while still with us: this is the height of filial piety.

"The ceremonies of sacrifices to Heaven and Earth are meant for the services of the Lord on High, and the ceremonies performed in the ancestral temple are meant for the services of ancestors. If one understands the ceremonies of the sacrifices to Heaven and Earth and the meaning of the grand sacrifice and the autumn sacrifice to ancestors, it would be as easy to govern a kingdom as to look at one's palm."

20. Duke Ai[1] asked about government. Confucius said, "The governmental measures of King Wăn and King Wu are spread out in the records. With their kind of men, government will flourish. When their kind of men are gone, their government will come to an end. When the right principles of man operate, the growth of good government is rapid, and when the right principles of soil operate, the growth of vegetables is rapid. Indeed, government is comparable to a fast-growing plant.[2] Therefore the conduct of government depends upon the men. The right men are obtained by the ruler's personal character. The cultivation of the person is to be done through the Way, and the cultivation of the Way is to be done through humanity. Humanity (*jen*) is [the distinguishing characteristic of] man,[3] and the greatest application of it is in being affectionate toward relatives. Righteousness (*i*) is the principle of setting things right and proper, and the greatest application of it is in honoring the worthy. The relative degree of affection we ought to feel for our relatives and the relative grades in the honoring of the worthy give rise to the rules of propriety. [If those in inferior positions do not have the confidence of their superiors, they will not be able to govern the people].[4]

1. Ruler of Lu (r. 494-465 B.C.).
2. Some say that Confucius' words stop here, the rest being Tzŭ-ssu's elaboration.
3. Cf. *Mencius*, 7B:16.
4. Cheng Hsüan correctly pointed out in his commentary that this sentence is duplicated near the end of the chapter and is therefore superfluous.

Comment. The sentence "Humanity is [the distinguishing characteristic of] man" is perhaps the most often quoted on the subject of humanity (*jen*). In Chinese it is "*jen* is *jen*," the first *jen* meaning humanity and the second referring to man. It is not just a pun, but an important definition of the basic Confucian concept of humanity, for to Confucianists, the virtue of humanity is meaningless unless it is involved in actual human relationships. This is the reason Cheng Hsüan defined it as "people living together," the definition to which scholars of the Ch'ing dynasty (1644-1912) returned in their revolt against the Neo-Confucianists of the Sung dynasty who interpreted *jen* as a state of mind.[1]

"Therefore the ruler must not fail to cultivate his personal life. Wishing to cultivate his personal life, he must not fail to serve his parents. Wishing to serve his parents, he must not fail to know man. Wishing to know man, he must not fail to know Heaven.

"There are five universal ways [in human relations], and the way by which they are practiced is three. The five are those governing the relationship between ruler and minister, between father and son, between husband and wife, between elder and younger brothers, and those in the intercourse between friends. These five are universal paths in the world.[2] Wisdom, humanity, and courage, these three are the universal virtues. The way by which they are practiced is one.

"Some are born with the knowledge [of these virtues]. Some learn it through study. Some learn it through hard work. But when the knowledge is acquired, it comes to the same thing. Some practice them naturally and easily. Some practice them for their advantage. Some practice them

1. See Chan, "The Evolution of the Confucian Concept *Jen*," *Philosophy East and West*, 4 (1955), 295-319.
2. See above, ch. 3, comment on *Mencius*, Additional Selections, 3A:4.

with effort and difficulty. But when the achievement is made, it comes to the same thing."

Confucius said, "Love of learning is akin to wisdom. To practice with vigor is akin to humanity. To know how to be shameful is akin to courage. He who knows these three things knows how to cultivate his personal life. Knowing how to cultivate his personal life, he knows how to govern other men. And knowing how to govern other men, he knows how to govern the empire, its states, and the families.

"There are nine standards by which to administer the empire, its states, and the families. They are: cultivating the personal life, honoring the worthy, being affectionate to relatives, being respectful toward the great ministers, identifying oneself with the welfare of the whole body of officers, treating the common people as one's own children, attracting the various artisans, showing tenderness to strangers from far countries, and extending kindly and awesome influence on the feudal lords. If the ruler cultivates his personal life, the Way will be established. If he honors the worthy, he will not be perplexed. If he is affectionate to his relatives, there will be no grumbling among his uncles and brothers. If he respects the great ministers, he will not be deceived. If he identifies himself with the welfare of the whole body of officers, then the officers will repay him heavily for his courtesies. If he treats the common people as his own children, then the masses will exhort one another [to do good]. If he attracts the various artisans, there will be sufficiency of wealth and resources in the country. If he shows tenderness to strangers from far countries, people from all quarters of the world will flock to him. And if he extends kindly and awesome influence over the feudal lords, then the world will stand in awe of him.

"To fast, to purify, and to be correct in dress [at the time of solemn sacrifice], and not to make any movement contrary to the rules of propriety — this is the way to cultivate the personal life. To avoid slanderers, keep away seductive beauties, regard wealth lightly, and honor virtue — this is the way to encourage the worthy. To give them honorable position, to bestow on them ample emoluments, and to share their likes and dislikes — this is the way to encourage affection for relatives. To allow them many officers to carry out their functions — this is the way to encourage the great ministers. To deal with them loyally and faithfully and to give them ample emoluments — this is the way to encourage the body of officers. To require them for service only at the proper time [without interfering with their farm work] and to tax them lightly — this is the way to encourage the common masses. To inspect them daily and examine them monthly and to reward them according to the degree of their workmanship — this is the way to encourage the various artisans. To welcome them when they come and send them off when they go and to commend the good among them and show compassion to the incompetent — this is the way to show tenderness to strangers from far countries. To restore lines of broken succession, to revive states that have been extinguished, to bring order to chaotic states, to support those states that are in danger, to have fixed times for their attendance at court, and to present them with generous gifts while expecting little when they come — this is the way to extend kindly and awesome influence on the feudal lords.

"There are nine standards by which to govern the empire, its states, and the families, but the way by which they are followed is one. In all matters if there is preparation they will succeed; if there is no preparation, they will fail. If what is to be said is determined beforehand, there will be no stumbling. If the business to be done is determined beforehand, there will be no difficulty. If action to be taken is determined beforehand, there will be no trouble. And if the way to be pursued is determined beforehand, there will be no difficulties.[1] If those in inferior positions do not have the confidence of their superiors, they will not be able to govern the people. There is a way to have the confidence

1. According to K'ung Ying-ta (574-648; see *Li chi cheng-i*): There will be no limit to its possibility.

of the superiors: If one is not trusted by his friends, he will not have the confidence of his superiors. There is a way to be trusted by one's friends: If one is not obedient to his parents, he will not be trusted by his friends. There is a way to obey one's parents: If one examines himself and finds himself to be insincere, he will not be obedient to his parents. There is a way to be sincere with oneself: If one does not understand what is good, he will not be sincere with himself. Sincerity is the Way of Heaven. To think how to be sincere is the way of man. He who is sincere is one who hits upon what is right without effort and apprehends without thinking. He is naturally and easily in harmony with the Way. Such a man is a sage. He who tries to be sincere is one who chooses the good and holds fast to it.

"Study it (the way to be sincere) extensively, inquire into it accurately, think over it carefully, sift it clearly, and practice it earnestly. When there is anything not yet studied, or studied but not yet understood, do not give up. When there is any question not yet asked, or asked but its answer not yet known, do not give up. When there is anything not yet thought over, or thought over but not yet apprehended, do not give up. When there is anything not yet sifted, or sifted but not yet clear, do not give up. When there is anything not yet practiced, or practiced but not yet earnestly, do not give up.[1] If another man succeed by one effort, you will use a hundred efforts. If another man succeed by ten efforts, you will use a thousand efforts. If one really follows this course, though stupid, he will surely become intelligent, and though weak, will surely become strong."

Comment. The five steps of study, inquiry, thinking, sifting, and practice could have come from John Dewey.

21. It is due to our nature that enlightenment results from sincerity. It is due to education that sincerity results

1. Chu Hsi's interpretation: Either do not study at all, or do not give up until what you studied is all understood, etc.

from enlightenment. Given sincerity, there will be enlightenment, and given enlightenment, there will be sincerity.

> *Chu Hsi's Remark.* "In the above twenty-first chapter, Tzŭ-ssu continues Confucius' idea in the preceding chapter of the Way of Heaven and the way of man as a basis for discussion. In the following twelve chapters, Tzŭ-ssu reiterates and elaborates the idea of this chapter."

22. Only those who are absolutely sincere can fully develop their nature. If they can fully develop their nature, they can then fully develop the nature of others. If they can fully develop the nature of others, they can then fully develop the nature of things. If they can fully develop the nature of things, they can then assist in the transforming and nourishing process of Heaven and Earth. If they can assist in the transforming and nourishing process of Heaven and Earth, they can thus form a trinity with Heaven and Earth.

> *Comment.* Whether this chapter refers to rulers, as Cheng Hsüan and other Han dynasty scholars contended, or to the sage, as Chu Hsi and other Sung scholars thought, is immaterial. The important point is the ultimate trinity with Heaven and Earth. It is of course another way of saying the unity of man and Heaven or Nature, a doctrine which eventually assumed the greatest importance in Neo-Confucianism.[1]

23. The next in order are those who cultivate to the utmost a particular goodness. Having done this, they can attain to the possession of sincerity. As there is sincerity, there will be its expression. As it is expressed, it will become conspicuous, it will become clear. As it becomes clear, it will

1. See below, pp. 524, 666, 752.

move others. As it moves others, it changes them. As it changes them, it transforms them. Only those who are absolutely sincere can transform others.

24. It is characteristic of absolute sincerity to be able to foreknow. When a nation or family is about to flourish, there are sure to be lucky omens. When a nation or family is about to perish, there are sure to be unlucky omens. These omens are revealed in divination and in the movements of the four limbs. When calamity or blessing is about to come, it can surely know beforehand if it is good, and it can also surely know beforehand if it is evil. Therefore he who has absolute sincerity is like a spirit.

25. Sincerity means the completion of the self, and the Way is self-directing. Sincerity is the beginning and end of things. Without sincerity there would be nothing. Therefore the superior man values sincerity. Sincerity is not only the completion of one's own self, it is that by which all things are completed. The completion of the self means humanity. The completion of all things means wisdom. These are the character of the nature, and they are the Way in which the internal[1] and the external are united. Therefore whenever it is employed, everything done is right.

Comment. In no other Confucian work is the Way (Tâo) given such a central position. This self-directing Way seems to be the same as the Tâo in Tâoism. But the difference is great. As Ch'ien Mu has pointed out, when the Tâoists talk about Tâo as being natural, it means that Tâo is void and empty, whereas when Confucianists talk about Tâo as being natural, they describe it as sincerity. This, according to him, is a great contribution of the *Doctrine of the Mean.*[2] It should also be pointed out that with Confucianists, "The Way is

---

1. It is not clear whether this refers to sincerity, the character of the nature, or the Way.
2. *Ssu-chu shih-i* (Explanation of Meanings of the Four Books), 1953.

not far from man."[1] Contrary to the Tâo of Tâoism, the Confucian Tâo is strongly humanistic.

26. Therefore absolute sincerity is ceaseless. Being ceaseless, it is lasting. Being lasting, it is evident. Being evident, it is infinite. Being infinite, it is extensive and deep. Being extensive and deep, it is high and brilliant. It is because it is extensive and deep that it contains all things. It is because it is high and brilliant that it overshadows all things. It is because it is infinite and lasting that it can complete all things. In being extensive and deep, it is a counterpart of Earth. In being high and brilliant, it is a counterpart of Heaven. In being infinite and lasting, it is unlimited. Such being its nature, it becomes prominent without any display, produces changes without motion, and accomplishes its ends without action.[2]

The Way of heaven and Earth may be completely described in one sentence: They are without any doubleness and so they produce things in an unfathomable way. The Way of Heaven and Earth is extensive, deep, high, brilliant, infinite, and lasting. The heaven now before us is only this bright, shining mass; but when viewed in its unlimited extent, the sun, moon, stars, and constellations are suspended in it and things are covered by it. The earth before us is but a handful of soil; but in its breadth and depth, it sustains mountains like Hua and Yüeh without feeling their weight, contains the rivers and seas without letting them leak away, and sustains all things. The mountain before us is only a fistful of straw; but in all the vastness of its size, grass and trees grow upon it, birds and beasts dwell on it, and stores of precious things (minerals) are discovered in it. The water before us is but a spoonful of liquid, but in all its unfathomable depth, the monsters, dragons, fishes, and

1. See above, *The Mean*, ch. 13.
2. Perhaps this is a step further than described in *The Mean*, ch. 23 and the translation should be "becomes prominent without any display, can change others without moving them, and complete [the self and all things, as in *The Mean*, ch. 25] without any action."

526

unceasing."[1] This is to say, this is what makes Heaven to be Heaven. Again, it says, "How shining is it, the purity of King Wen's virtue!"[2] This is to say, this is what makes King Wen what he was. Purity likewise is unceasing.

27. Great is the Way of the sage! Overflowing, it produces and nourishes all things and rises up to the height of heaven. How exceedingly great! [It embraces] the three hundred rules of ceremonies and the three thousand rules of conduct. It waits for the proper man before it can be put into practice. Therefore it is said, "Unless there is perfect virtue, the perfect Way cannot be materialized." Therefore the superior man honors the moral nature and follows the path of study and inquiry. He achieves breadth and greatness and pursues the refined and subtle to the limit. He seeks to reach the greatest height and brilliancy and follows the path of the Mean. He goes over the old so as to find out what is new.[3] He is earnest and deep and highly respects all propriety. Therefore when occupying a high position, he is not proud, and when serving in a low position, he is not insubordinate. When the Way prevails in the country, he can rise to official position through his words. When the turtles are produced in them, and wealth becomes abundant because of it [as a result of transportation]. The *Book of Odes* says, "The Mandate of Heaven, how beautiful and Way does not prevail in the country, he can preserve himself through silence. The *Book of Odes* says, "Intelligent and wise, he protects his person."[4] This is the meaning.

> *Comment.* The two different approaches through "honoring the moral nature" and "following the path of study and inquiry" represent the two tendencies between the rationalistic Neo-Confucianism of Ch'eng I and Chu Hsi on the one hand and the idealistic Neo-Con-

1. Ode no. 267.
2. *ibid.*
3. The same saying appears in *Analects*, 2:11.
4. Ode no. 260.

fucianism of Lu Hsiang-shan (Lu Chiu-yüan, 1139-1193) and Wang Yang-ming (Wang Shou-jen, 1472-1529) on the other. They were the issue between Chu and Lu in their famous debate in 1175.[1]

28. Confucius said, "To be stupid and like to use his own judgment, to be in a humble station and like to dictate, to live in the present world and go back to the ways of antiquity — people of this sort bring calamity on themselves. Unless one is the Son of Heaven, he does not decide on ceremonies [of social order], make regulations, or investigate (determine) the form and pronunciation of characters. In the world today, all carriages have wheels of the same size, all writing is done with the same characters,[2] and all conduct is governed by the same social relations. Although a man occupies the throne, if he has not the corresponding virtue, he may not dare to institute systems of music and ceremony. Although a man has the virtue, if he does not occupy the throne, he may not dare to institute systems of music and ceremony either."

Confucius said, "I have talked about the ceremonies of the Hsia dynasty (2183-1752 B.C.?). but what remains in the present state of Ch'i (descendant of Hsia) does not provide sufficient evidence. I have studied the ceremonies of the Shang dynasty (1751-1112 B.C.). They are still preserved in the present state of Sung (descendant of Shang). I have studied the ceremonies of the [Western] Chou dynasty (1111-770 B.C.). They are in use today. I follow the Chou."[3]

29. If he who attains to the sovereignty of the world has three important things [ceremonies, regulations, and the form and pronunciation of characters], he will make few

1. See below, ch. 33, sec. 31, and comment on it.
2. Many modern writers have pointed out that these were not conditions of the fourth century B.C. but of the Ch'in dynasty (221-206 B.C.) when writing and measurements were unified.
3. Sf. *Analects*, 3:9.

mistakes. However excellent may have been the regulations of former times, there is no evidence for them. Without evidence, they cannot command credence, and not being credited, the people would not follow them. However excellent might be the regulations made by one in a low position, his position is not an honored one. The position not being honored does not command credence, and not being credited, the people would not follow them. Therefore the Way of the true ruler is rooted in his own personal life and has its evidence [in the following] of the common people. It is tested by the experience of the Three Kings[1] and found without error, applied before Heaven and Earth and found to be without contradiction in their operation, laid before spiritual beings without question or fear, and can wait a hundred generations for a sage [to confirm it] without a doubt. Since it can be laid before spiritual beings without question or fear, it shows that he knows [the Principle of] Heaven. Since it can wait for a hundred generations for a sage without a doubt, it shows that he knows [the principles of] man. Therefore every move he makes becomes the way of the world, every act of his becomes the model of the world, and every word he utters becomes the pattern of the world. Those who are far away look longingly for him, and those who are near do not get weary of him. The *Book of Odes* says, "There they do not dislike him, here they do not get tired of him. Thus from day to day and night, they will perpetuate their praise."[2] There has never been a ruler who did not answer this description and yet could obtain early renown throughout the world.

30. Chung-ni (Confucius) transmitted the ancient traditions of Yao and Shun, and he modeled after and made brilliant the systems of King Wăn and King Wu. He conformed with the natural order governing the revolution of the seasons in heaven above, and followed the principles governing

1. Founders of the Hsia, Shang, and Chou dynasties.
2. Ode no. 278.

land and water below. He may be compared to earth in its supporting and containing all things, and to heaven in its overshadowing and embracing all things. He may be compared to the four seasons in their succession, and to the sun and moon in their alternate shining. All things are produced and developed without injuring one another. The courses of the seasons, the sun, and moon are pursued without conflict. The lesser forces flow continuously like river currents, while the great forces go silently and deeply in their mighty transformations. It is this that makes heaven and earth so great.

31. Only the perfect sage in the world has quickness of apprehension, intelligence, insight, and wisdom, which enable him to rule all men; magnanimity, generosity, benignity, and tenderness, which enable him to embrace all men; vigor, strength, firmness, and resolution, which enable him to maintain a firm hold; orderliness, seriousness, adherence to the Mean, and correctness, which enable him to be reverent; pattern, order, refinement, and penetration, which enable him to excercise discrimination. All embracing and extensive, and deep and unceasingly springing, these virtues come forth at all times. All embracing and extensive as heaven and deep and unceasingly springing as an abyss! He appears and all people respect him, speaks and all people believe him, acts and all people are pleased with him. Consequently his fame spreads overflowingly over the Middle Kingdom (China, the civilized world), and extends to barbarous tribes. Wherever ships and carriages reach, wherever the labor of man penetrates, wherever the heavens overshadow and the earth sustains, wherever the sun and moon shine, and wherever frosts and dew fall, all who have blood and breath honor and love him. Therefore we say that he is a counterpart of Heaven.

32. Only those who are absolutely sincere can order and adjust the great relations of mankind, establish the great foundations of humanity, and know the transforming and nourishing operations of heaven and earth. Does he depend

on anything else? How earnest and sincere — he is humanity! How deep and unfathomable — he is abyss! How vast and great — he is heaven! Who can know him except he who really has quickness of apprehension, intelligence, sageliness, and wisdom, and understands the character of Heaven?

33. The *Book of Odes* says, "Over her brocaded robe, she wore a plain and simple dress,"[1] for she disliked the loudness of its color and patterns. Thus the way of the superior man is hidden but becomes more prominent every day,[2] whereas the way of the inferior man is conspicuous but gradually disappears. It is characteristic of the superior man to be plain, and yet people do not get tired of him. He is simple and yet rich in cultural adornment. He is amiable and yet systematically methodical. He knows what is distant begins with what is near. He knows where the winds (moral influence) come from. And he knows the subtle will be manifested. Such a man can enter into virtue.

The *Book of Odes* says, "Although the fish dive and lie at the bottom, it is still quite clearly seen."[3] Therefore the superior man examines his own heart and sees that there is nothing wrong there, and that he is not dissatisfied with himself. The superior man is unequaled in the fact that he [is cautious] in those things which people do not see. The *Book of Odes* says, "Though the ceiling looks down upon you, be free from shame even in the recesses of your own house."[4] Therefore the superior man is reverent without any movement and truthful without any words. The *Book of Odes* says, "Throughout the sacrifice not a word is spoken, and yet [the worshipers are influenced and transformed] without the slightest ocntention."[5] Therefore the superior man does not resort to rewards and the people are encouraged to virtue. He does not resort to anger and the people are awed. The *Book of Odes* says, "He does not display his

1. Ode no. 57, actually a paraphrase.
2. Cf. *Lao Tzu*, ch. 24.
3. Ode no. 192.
4. Ode no. 256.
5. Ode no. 302.

virtue, and yet all the princes follow him."[1] Therefore when the superior man is sincere and reverent, the world will be in order and at peace. The *Book of Odes* says, "I cherish your brilliant virtue, which makes no great display in sound or appearance."[2] Confucius said, "In influencing people, the use of sound or appearance is of secondary importance." The *Book of Odes* says, "His virtue is as light as hair."[3] Still, a hair is comparable..[4] "The operations of Heaven have neither sound nor smell."[5]

Chu Hsi's Remark. In the above thirty-third chapter, Tzŭ-ssu returns to the ideas of "carrying out to the limit" and "exhausting the most refined" (discussed in previous chapters) to search for their source. Furthermore, he extends the discussion to include the effort of the learner who, for his own sake, learns to be careful while alone — an effort which, through earnestness and reverence, culminates in the glory of world peace. Then he further praises the wonder of all this, and does not stop until he describes it as being without sound or smell. What he does is to pick out the essence of the whole work and talk about it in simple terms. He felt deeply and most earnestly as he instructed people by going over the points again and again. Should the student not apply his mind to the utmost [in studying this work]?

1. Ode no. 269.
2. Ode no. 241.
3. Ode no. 260. Both Chu Hsi and Cheng Hsüan believed that this sentence was uttered by Confucius.
4. Chu Hsi considered this sentence and the rest to be by Tzŭ-ssu. Cheng Hsüan and K'ung Ying-ta, however, considered them to be by Confucius.
5. Ode no. 235.

Lu Hsiang-shan

LU HSIANG-SHAN (1139-1192). One of the most significant events in the history of Chinese philosophy was the dispute between Chu Hsi (1130-1200), the great syncretist whose achievement is compared to that of St. Thomas Aquinas, and his most eloquent contemporary over the nature of the Supreme Ultimate, conceived as the source of all being and the root of moral conduct. Lu Hsiang-shan (Lu Wang, Lu Chiu-yüan, styled Tzǔ-ching and given two literary names in later life, Ts'un-chai and Hsiang-shan) wrote little but exerted a lasting influence through his teaching. In the course of one of his lectures on moral principles, he is said to have moved his audience to tears. He recognized no duality between principle or natural law (*li*) and material force (*ch'i*), posited by Chu Hsi as the two aspects of the universe, and insisted that mind *is* principle. Mind is not the function of man's nature but is identical with the universe. The mind is the embodiment of reason and can be trained by "tranquil repose" leading to direct perception of the essences of truth and goodness and the individual's union with the universe.

Though Chu Hsi represents the final culmination of the Ch'eng-Chu school of Neo-Confucianism in the third period of the Sung philosophy (960-1269), Lu Hsiang-shan, who died eight years before him, represents the initial stage of a doctrine that belongs to the fourth and last period. His views, though anticipated to some extent by Ch'eng Hao, were continued and elaborated by his successors, particularly Wang Yang-ming,

533

who brought the doctrine of Mind to full flowering three centuries later.

Born in Chinhou in present Kiangsi, he was from a prominent family with a good literary reputation. He had a successful career as an official of the government and a professor of the national university. Once he was asked for a formula for ridding the government of corruption. He replied that four things can heal a nation: "To employ the worthy, to appoint the capable, to reward the meritorious, and to punish the sinful." He was canonized as Wen-an, and his tablet was placed in the Confucian temple in 1530. His literary remains were collected by his eldest son, published by Yüan Hsi in 1212, and republished in 1521 by Wang Yang-ming. His philosophy was revived by Liang Sou-ming, whose book *The Civilization and Philosophy of the East and the West* (1912) was a great sensation in China.

Law, Mind and Nature

From *Lu Hsiang-sh m, A Twelfth Century Chinese Idealist Philosopher,*
by Siu-chi Huang (American Oriental Series, Volume 27), New Haven,
Connecticut, American Oriental Society, 1944.

I. LAW

IT has already been mentioned that, according to the Neo-
Confucianists, Law (*li*) is a metaphysical concept lying
beyond time and space; it is the guiding and directing principle of the entire cosmos. That is to say, there exists one
universal Law that makes the universe as a whole operate
as it does according to a certain pattern; at the same time,
each individual thing or object has its own Law or principle
of existence, which is part of the one universal Law. Examples are the Law of light, which is manifested on a bright
sunny day, the Law of darkness in night, the Law of vision
in the eyes, the Law of triangularity in triangles, and the
Law of Beauty in beautiful things.

But Law or *Li* means much more than simply a cosmic
order of the universe or a rule of existence inherent in each
individual thing. It is, too, an ethical principle, and hence
identical with Moral Order or Truth (*tâo*). Thus in man this
universal Law is manifested in its various aspects under
the form of the fundamental virtues of Human-heartedness
(*jen*), Righteousness (*i*), Propriety (*li*), and Wisdom (*chih*).
In other words, there is one universal Law which is perfectly
good and pure; it is therefore an ethical standard for man.

Lu Hsiang-shan adopts the traditional interpretation of
Law as developed by the Sung Neo-Confucianists: (a) that
it is the orderly principle underlying the universe as well as

each individual thing, and (b) that it is a purely moral criterion for human conduct. Unlike Chu Hsi, however, he is not greatly interested in meaning (a), but greatly stresses meaning (b). He therefore unhesitatingly declares that the so-called "investigation of things," originally cited in the *Great Learning* as the starting point for virtue, and emphasized by the Ch'eng-Chu school, is in reality, not fundamental.[1] A conversation between Lu Hsiang-shan and his pupil, Li Po-min, touches on this point:

"Po-min asked: 'How is one to investigate things (*ko wu*)?'

"The teacher [Lu Hsiang-shan] said: 'Investigate the Law of things.'[2]

"Po-min said: 'The ten thousand things (*wan wu*) under Heaven are extremely multitudinous; how, then, can we investigate all of them exhaustively?'

"The teacher replied: 'The ten thousand things are already complete in us.[3] It is only necessary to apprehend their Law'" (*Conversations*, 35.287-8).

Evidently the assertion of the Neo-realists of Western philosophy that there is a world independent of the knowing conscious self would not interest Lu Hsiang-shan. What primarily concerns him is the single proposition that there exists one Law which is perfectly good and hence is to be regarded as the purely ethical standard for all men throughout all ages.

"This Law fills the universe. Even Heaven and Earth, or ghosts and spirits, cannot diverge from it; how much less, then, can men? If one genuinely understands this Law, there can be no partiality as between the other person and myself. The good that lies in others likewise lies in me. Therefore,

---

1. The phrase, "investigation of things" (*ko wu*), has reference to the famous passage in the *Great Learning*, Intro. 2-4 (Legge's tr., pp. 411-2).

2. *Wu li*, i.e., the underlying principles of things.

3. A famous passage from *Mencius*, VIIa, 4 (Legge's tr., p. 326). It exemplifies the mystical view of Mencius that men can become one with the universe. Cf. Fung Yu-lan, *History of Chinese Philosophy* (Bodde's tr., pp. 129-30, 375).

the good which others possess is a good that *I* also possess" (Letter to Wu Tzŭ-ssu, 11.104).

In another passage Lu Hsiang-shan says: "To investigate things is to investigate this [Law]. Fu Hsi[1] looked up [to contemplate the brilliant] forms [exhibited in Heaven], and looked down [to survey] the patterns [shown on Earth].[2] He was, indeed, the first to exert his effort in [thus apprehending] this [Law]. If it were not so, what is called the 'investigation of things' (*ko wu*) would be an insignificant matter" (*Conversations*, 35.311).

The above passages show that Lu Hsiang-shan implicitly takes the apprehension of Law as the foundation for any "investigation of things," which, according to the *Great Learning*, will in its turn lead to the extension of knowledge, sincerity of thought, rectification of the Mind, regulation of the family, and good order in the state.

Though a wide knowledge of things is no doubt useful, yet, for Lu Hsiang-shan, it may lead to confusion and error if it is not placed in its proper position, secondary to an understanding of the universal Law that underlies all phenomenal things.

"Fundamentally, this is what Heaven has bestowed upon us, and is not infused into us from wthout.[3] To comprehend this Law is to become lord [over oneself]. He who can truly thus become lord cannot then be moved by external things, or influenced by depraved talk.

"What troubles you, my friend, is precisely that you do not apprehend this Law, are not lord over yourself, and have already become entangled in superficial doctrines and empty theories. The livelong day you rely only on external opinions to be your 'lord,' whereas what Heaven has bestowed on us you make your 'guest' [i.e., secondary], thus reversing

1. Fu Hsi is traditionally said to have lived 2953-2838 B.C., and to have invented the Eight Trigrams, which are the basis of the *Book of Changes*.
2. See *Book of Changes*, "Great Appendix" (Legge's., pp. 382-3).
3. See *Mencius*, VIa, 6 (Legge's tr., pp. 278-9).

the positions of what should be lord and what guest. You are led astray, thus being unable to return, and are deceived, thus being unable to gain a clarification. Simple and clear is this Law, so that it may be understood [even] by women and children when they hear it. And yet the industrious pedants become lost and deceived by [their misapprehension of] it; they create for themselves irrelevant theories, in which they wrap themselves" (Letter to Tseng Chai-chih, 1.17).

The argument that an understanding of Law is fundamental, and a knowledge of external things is secondary, is based on two assumptions.

First, only through an understanding of Law can we know the external world, for all things are embodied in Law. In other words, a true knowledge of things implies an understanding of Law; but Law exists quite apart from the casual type of knowledge which consists merely in knowing things. This first assumption is brought out in the following passages:

"The ten thousand things are profusely contained within a square inch of space [i.e., the Mind]. Filling the Mind, and, pouring forth, filling the entire universe, there is nothing that is not this law" (*Conversations*, 34.276).

"It is extremely difficult for man to learn. All things which are covered by Heaven, supported by Earth, born in spring, grown in summer, reaped in autumn, and stored in winter, are embodied in this Law. Man, who lives in the midst of them, must keenly understand this Law and know how to explain it" (*Conversations*, 35.294).

"In the knowledge of the Superior Man (*chün tzŭ*) of ancient times, it is its extensiveness that has been highly esteemed. And yet to know exhaustively all the things under Heaven merely means [to know] this Law. To have an extensive and wide view [of things] means merely to attach value to fine subtleties. Knowledge or non-knowledge [of this sort] fundamentally adds or subtracts nothing from this Law" (*Conversations*, 35.295).

The second assumption is that we should seek to apprehend this Law, because it lies within ourselves, and thus gives us the key to our own understanding.

"How can this Law not exist in us? If we cause our Will (*chih*) not to waver [in its pursuit of Law], then it [Law] will daily become clearer and brighter, like a stream which daily grows more luxuriant. If one seeks to infuse it [this Law into oneself] from without, this is to choke oneself off from its source and cut oneself off from its origin" (Letter to Chao Jan-tao, 12.111-2).

Lu Hsiang-shan repeatedly insists that Law is universal. It is therefore incorrect to regard him as a solipsist, maintaining that the external world and other selves have no independent existence apart from the self.

"The Law which I apprehend is the correct, real, eternal and universal Law of the world. This is the meaning [of the passage]:[1] '[The Truth or Way (*tâo*)] is rooted in his own person, and sufficient attestation of it is given by the masses of the people. He examines it by comparison with that of the Three Kings,[2] and finds it wthout mistake. He sets it up before Heaven and Earth, and there is nothing in it that is contradictory. He presents himself with it before the ghosts and spirits, and no doubts about it arise. He is prepared to wait for the appearance of a sage a hundred ages after, and has no misgivings.' Scholars truly must exhaust this Law, and apprehend this Law" (Letter to T'âo Tsan-chung, 15.132).

The passage which Lu Hsiang-shan quotes refers to the political administration of a state by a well qualified ruler, who understands the supernatural forces of the universe as well as men. Lu Hsiang-shan quotes it to illustrate that

---

1. See *Doctrine of the Mean*, II, 49 (Legge's tr., p. 325).
2. The Three Kings are, according to tradition, the founders of the first three Chinese dynasties, namely: Yü (2205?-2197? B.C.), founder of the Hsia dynasty (2205?-1766? B.C.); T'ang (1766?-1753? B.C.), founder of the Shang dynasty (1766-1122? B.C.); and Kings Wăn (1184?-1157? B.C.) and Wu (1156?-1116? B.C.), co-founders of the Chou dynasty (1122?-256 B.C.), who are counted as one.

Law is universal and transcends the restrictions of time and space. Therefore, he says, he who apprehends this Law will find himself in harmony with the supernatural forces of the universe and also with men in all ages.

The following passages likewise show Lu Hsiang-shan's emphasis upon the universality of Law:

"Beyond the Truth (*tâo*) no thing exists; outside of things no Truth exists" (*Conversations*, 34.258).

"The true Law under Heaven does not admit of duality. If one apprehends this Law, [one will find that] Heaven and Earth cannot differ from it, the sages and worthies of a thousand ages cannot differ from it. But if one does not apprehend this Law, one's own private standards will be heterodox standards" (Letter to T'âo Tsan-chung, 15.133).

"In all affairs, one should only observe what their Law is; one should not observe who the man concerned with them is" (*Conversations*, 35.305).

Before leaving the subject of Law, the question might be raised: How are we to apprehend this Law? The answer is to be found in Lu's doctrine of Mind which is the topic of the following section.

2. MIND AND LAW

Mind (*hsin*) is Lu Hsiang-shan's primary interest; for the chief objective of his philosophy is to teach men to develop the Original Mind (*pen hsin*) and to restore it if it has been lost. This concept of Mind is, to be sure, not new, for in it he largely follows the ideas of Mencius, who said: "The way to acquire learning is none other than to seek for one's lost Mind."[1] Lu's original contribution, however, lies in the fact that through his stress on the concept he created an entirely new philosophic school, that of the Mind, or literally, the "Learning of the Mind" (*hsin hsüeh*). Except for Chinese Buddhism, which had originated in

1. *Mencius*, VIa, 11 (Legge's tr., p. 290).

540

India, this was the first appearance of a specific school of Mind in Chinese philosophy. According to the Buddhist theory of "Mind Only" (*wei shih*), all things except Mind are empty and illusory, and apart from Mind nothing is real.[1] Although Lu Hsiang-shan, in his stress on Mind, is plainly indebted to Buddhism, his concept of Mind nevertheless differs from that of Buddhism.

What is Mind? What is its relation to the external world? What is the relationship between Mind and Law? And what is the relation of Mind to Nature (*hsing*)?

Although Mind is his central concept, Lu Hsiang-shan does not give a systematic treatment of it, nor even a definition. It seems, however, that he, in part, agrees with the other Neo-Confucianists that Mind is that which thinks, feels and reflects. Chu Hsi was once asked: "Is [man's] intellectual faculty the Mind or is it the Nature (*hsing*)?" To this he replied: "The intellectual faculty is the Mind alone and not the Nature."[2] Whereas Mind, for Chu Hsi, is a purely intellectual faculty, Nature, he says, is a common possession of men, animals, and inanimate objects alike. For example, even a stone has its own particular and innate Nature, but it does not have a Mind.[3] Every man, on the contrary, no matter who he may be, is also possessed of a Mind. Lu Hsiang-shan's theory of the relation between Mind and Nature will be discussed later, but it should be noted here that he expounds a similar view of Mind as being the mental constitution possessed by man.

"Men are not trees or stones; how, then, can they be without Mind? It is the noblest and the greatest among the five senses. It is said in the 'Great Plan' that 'the virtue of thinking is perspicacity, which becomes manifest in sagacity.'[4]

1. See Fung Yu-lan, *Chung-kuo Che-hsüeh Shih* (History of Chinese Philosophy), Shanghai, 1935, Vol. 2, pp. 705-7.
2. See Fung Yu-lan, "The Philosophy of Chu Hsi" (Bodde's tr., p. 34).
3. See Fung Yu-lan, *Chung-kuo Che-hsüeh Shih* (History of Chinese Philosophy), Vol. 2, pp. 940-1.
4. See *Book of History*, V, 4, vi (Legge's tr., pp. 326-7).

Mencius also said: 'To the Mind belongs the office of thinking. By thinking it gets the right views of things; by neglecting to think, it fails to do this.'[1] . . . Again he said: 'It is not only men of distinguished talents who have this Mind. All men have it; but such men of distinguished talents are not to lose it' "[2] (Letter to Li Tsai, 11.105-6).

The above passage indicates that, for Lu Hsiang-shan, Mind is man's peculiar possession; its activities of reflecting, thinking and apprehending distinguish man as a sentient, conscious and intellectual being, who is able to embrace and understand all things. The following striking statement was made when he was still in his teens:

"The things that lie within the universe are those that lie within myself; the things that lie within myself are those that lie within the universe. Thus, the universe is my Mind and my Mind is the universe.

"If in the Eastern Sea there were to appear a sage, he would have this same Mind and this same Law. If in the Western Sea there were to appear a sage, he would have this same Mind and this same Law. If in the Southern or Northern Seas there were to appear sages, they [too] would have this same Mind and this same Law. If a hundred or a thousand generations ago, or a hundred or a thousand generations hence, sages were to appear, they [likewise] would have this same Mind and this same Law" (*Annals*, 36.314).

This last passage clearly indicates that what Lu Hsiang-shan means by Mind is something more than a subjective, finite mind, possessed by each individual man, who is thereby endowed with the capacity of knowing and thinking. Lu Hsiang-shan at this point diverges from the Ch'eng-Chu school inasmuch as he identifies Mind with the universal Law. Hence his concept of Mind implies not only the subjective mind of a conscious, sentient and thinking being,

1. *Mencius*, VIa, 15 (Legge's tr., p. 294).
2. *Mencius*, VIa, 10 (Legge's tr., p. 288).

542

but also an objective universal Mind. Here then arise the questions: What is this universal Mind? What is the relationship between this objective and universal Mind, i.e., the non-ego, and the subjective and finite mind, i.e., the ego? Can the subjective mind or the objective Mind or both be identical with Law? The following statements will help us to understand the answers Lu Hsiang-shan would give to the above questions:

"Mencius said: 'He who has developed completely all his Mind knows his Nature. Knowing his Nature, he knows Heaven.'[1] Mind is only one Mind. The Mind of any given person, or that of my friend, or that of a sage of a thousand generations ago, or again, that of a sage of a thousand generations hence — their Minds are all only [one] like this. The extent of the Mind is very great. If I can develop completely my Mind, I thereby become identified with Heaven. To acquire learning consists of nothing more than to apprehend this" (*Conversations*, 35.290).

Lu Hsiang-shan's insistence on the unity of Law and Mind appears in the following statements:

"All men have this Mind, and all Minds are endowed with Law; [hence,] Mind is the same as Law. It is therefore said: 'Law and Righteousness (*i*) are agreeable to the Mind, just as the flesh of grass and grain-fed animals is agreeable to my mouth.'[2] What is to be valued in the scholar is his desire to plumb to the utmost this Law and to develop completely this Mind" (Letter to Li Tsai, 11.105-6).

"If the sages and worthies of a thousand ages of antiquity were to be assembled at the same table, there would certainly be no [single] Law on which they would be wholly in agreement. And yet this Mind and this Law are one in principle throughout 'ten thousand ages'" (*Conversations*, 34.264).

---

1. *Mencius*, VIIa, 1 (Legge's tr., p. 324).
2. *Mencius*, VIa, 7 (Legge's tr., pp. 282-3).

Lu Hsiang-shan's doctrine of the unity of Law and Mind may be summarized as follows: The objective Mind is universal. It can be known and apprehended by the subjective finite minds, which are, conversely, expressions of this all-comprehending Mind. It is this universal Mind with which Law is identified. This Law, the governing principle of the universe, constitutes the unity, coherence, sequence and, above all, goodness of the world, which each individual Mind has the capacity of understanding, and with which man should live in accord. Here Lu Hsiang-shan expresses himself as an ardent idealist, whose idealism "means, in name and in truth, the freedom in this universe of the thinker, the unlimited right of Idea in a world where nothing that is is ultimately irrational."[1] For him, Mind is all-embracing; it is the embodiment of Law: "This Law is exceedingly clear, and is endowed with man's mind."[2] Hence, the finite minds, like the "windowless" monads of Leibniz, can be in harmony with the universal Mind, or the whole; there is no division between the ego and the non-ego, the external and internal, and no dualism.

Consistently with his monistic position, Lu Hsiang-shan further diverges from the other Neo-Confucianists when they maintain the doctrine that Mind is actually to be classified into two categories: the Mind of Man (*jen hsin*) and the Mind of Spirit (*tâo hsin*).[3] His attack on this dualistic concept is clearly expounded in the following passage:

"What is said about [the difference between] Heavenly Law (*t'ien li*) and Human Desire (*jen yü*) is not best doctrine. For if Heaven [alone] is [possessed of] Law, while man is [possessed only of] Desire, then Heaven and man are different in category. This theory [of distinguishing between

1. See Hocking, William E., *The Meaning of God in Human Experience*, New Haven and London, 1912, p. xii.
2. See Letter to Tseng Chai-chih, 1.19.
3. See above, p. 28.

544

Heaven and man] originated with Lao Tzu.[1] . . . It is said in the *Book of History*: 'The Mind of Man is unstable; the Mind of Spirit is but a spark.'[2] Interpreters have frequently explained the Mind of Man as being equivalent to Human Desire, and the Mind of Spirit as being equivalent to Heavenly Law. This explanation is incorrect, for Mind is one; how, then, can man have two Minds?" (*Conversations,* 34.258).

The above statement shows Lu Hsiang-shan's monistic view and his consequent opposition to the dualism that would describe the Mind of Man in terms of Human Desire and the Mind of Spirit in terms of Heavenly Law. He, for his part, insists emphatically that there is only one Mind, with which all individual finite minds should be in accord; furthermore, this one Mind (like the one Law) transcends time and space.

"In all affairs and all things under Heaven there is only one Law; there are not two Laws" (*Conversations,* 35.306).

"Law is the universal Law of all under Heaven; Mind is the common Mind of all under Heaven" (Letter to T'ang Ssu-fa, 15.134).

"Mind is one Mind, and Law is one Law. Oneness (*i*) pertains to them throughout, and even in their most subtle meaning they contain no duality (*erh*). [In other words,] this Mind and this Law truly do not admit of any dualism" (Letter to Tseng Chai-chih, 1.17).

This last passage, if read by itself, would be somewhat obscure. When connected with the foregoing passages, however, its meaning is clear: Lu Hsiang-shan maintains

1. Lao Tzŭ seems to have distinguished between two Ways or *Tǎo*: the Way of Man (*jen tǎo*), which as such is fallible, and the Way of Heaven (*t'ien tǎo*) (cf. Heracleitus' "Logos"), which is eternal and constitutes a universal order. Man should therefore strive for a higher life under the guidance of the Heavenly Way or Truth (*t'ien tǎo*). See *Lao-tzŭ*, ch. 77 (Waley's tr., p. 237). It is from this passage that the Ch'eng-Chu school derived its idea of a dualistic distinction between two kinds of Mind.

2. See *Book of History*, II, 2, ii (Legges's tr., pp. 61-2).

that all Minds are one with the one universal Mind, and all Laws are one with the one universal Law; furthermore, that this one Mind is the same as this one Law.

3. MIND AND NATURE

The question to be solved now is: Since Lu Hsiang-shan identifies Law with Mind, what, then, is the relationship between Mind and another key term of the Neo-Confucianists, Nature (*hsing*)? The differentiation of Mind and Nature made by Chang Tsai is: "The Mind unites the Nature and the Feelings (*ch'ing*)."[1] Ch'eng I's illustration of this distinction reads: "The Mind is like the seed-corn; the principle of life contained in it is the Nature; the putting of life on the part of the positive Ether (*yang ch'i*) is Feeling."[2] Chu Hsi supports the view of Chang Tsai and Ch'eng I by saying: "The Nature is the Law of the Mind; Feelings are the activities of the Mind; Capacity (*ts'ai*) is what gives to the Feelings their ability to act in a certain way."[3]

In short, according to the Ch'eng-Chu school, Nature is a possession common to men, animals, and inanimate objects alike, and as such is simply another name for Law as found particularized in individual things. Nature is Law, and Mind is consciousness, hence Mind and Nature are not the same. Chu Hsi's doctrine of Nature was influenced by the Buddhist conception that human Nature and the external Nature of the universe are not to be separated; hence, for him, Nature has a cosmological significance.

Lu Hsiang-shan differs from the Ch'eng-Chu school, inasmuch as he seems to accept the thesis of Mencius that it is the possession of Nature that makes man differ from the lower animals.[4] The term Nature is highly ambiguous. Lu

1. The statement is quoted by Bruce, *Chu Hsi and His Masters*, p. 236.
2. See *The Philosophy of Human Nature* (Bruce's tr., p. 235).
3. See Fung Yu-lan, "The Philosophy of Chu Hsi" (Bodde's tr., p. 35).
4. See *Mencius*, IVb, 19 (Legge's tr., p. 201).

Hsiang-shan, unfortunately, seems to have taken it so much for granted that nowhere does he bother to attempt a clear definition. Nevertheless, it may be suggested that his concept seems to be similar to the following definition, which has been selected from a list of sixty-six possible meanings of "Nature," as compiled by Lovejoy: "Good 'by nature' for the individual is that internal order or organization of the soul in which the part ('reason' or 'conscience') whose nature it is to rule controls the other parts."[1]

Lu Hsiang-shan, following the general premise of Mencius, accepts the idea that Mind and Nature are synonymous. He would agree with Chu Hsi's first premise that Nature is Law, yet at the same time, he adds his own idea: "Mind is the same as Law."[2] Hence for him Nature and Mind are one. The following passage shows his disagreement with the Ch'eng-Chu school:

"As to the Feelings (*ch'ing*), Nature (*hsing*), Mind (*hsin*) and Capacity (*ts'ai*), these are all the same thing; it is only in their use of words that people differentiate between then. . . . If we must needs speak thus, [we may say that] what pertains to Heaven is Nature, and what pertains to Man is Mind. Such [differentiation] follows my friend's way of speaking; yet in actual fact, one does not have to thus" (*Conversations*, 35.290).

Lu Hsiang-shan's central interest is in the ethical rather than the metaphysical aspect of Mind. Therefore the question that concerns him primarily is how to develop the human Mind, which is endowed with the capacity of knowing and in its original state is in harmony with the universal Mind or Law. In connection with this point, he accepts the doctrine that man has been endowed with a Nature essentially good, and about this Lu has much to say.

1. See Lovejoy, A. O., and Boas G., *Primitivism and Related Ideas in Antiquity*, Baltimore, 1935, "Appendix on some Meanings of Nature," No. 51, p. 453.
2. See Letter to Li Tsai, 11.106.

4. THE GOODNESS OF HUMAN NATURE

Lu Hsiang-shan's ethical ideas are quite similar to those of the English intuitionists, and particularly the Cambridge Platonists. In agreement with Cudworth,[1] Lu Hsiang-shan would pay no attention to the language of the juridical intuitionists, who regard conscience as the voice of a supernatural being, and posit God as the Law Giver. Nor would he sympathize with Hobbesian legal relativism and make morality depend on the absolute power of civil authority. For Lu Hsiang-shan holds that it is the Nature of the human Mind to apprehend immediately and directly the Truth or Moral Order (*tâo*), which is the objective standard of moral life: "The Truth (*tâo*) fills the universe, nowhere being concealed"; again: "It [i.e., *Tâo*] lies directly before one's eyes."[2]

It has already been said that, for the Neo-Confucianists, Law (*li*) is the ethical standard for man; in the virtues of Human-heartedness, Righteousness, Propriety and Wisdom are all included; and these four cardinal virtues are inherent in the Nature of man. The question may now be raised: Are there any distictions between these four principles? It seems that the three separate faculties, Intellect, Feeling and Volition, are all included in them. Yet it is to be noted that, though distinct from each other, they do not form four separate "watertight" compartments. The feeling of commiseration, the will to refrain from wrong things, the sense of modesty and humility, and the knowledge of rightness and wrongness, are each the whole Mind or Nature. In other words, these four moral principles are not separate faculties of the Mind, but the whole Mind viewed from different aspects.

1. Cudworth, R., *Treatise Concerning Eternal and Immutable Morality.* See extract in Selby-Bigge, L. A., *British Moralists*, Oxford, 1897, Vol. 2, pp. 247-66; also Sidgwick, H., *Outlines of the History of Ethics*, London, 1925, pp. 170-1.

2. Letter to Chao Chien, 1.20.

Lu Hsiang-shan, like the other Sung philosophers, eagerly accepts the doctrine of the goodness of human Nature, as expounded by Mencius, and rejects the theory of Hsün Tzŭ, Mencius' great opponent, that the Nature of man is evil. The goodness of human Nature, Mencius had said, is as inevitable and natural as the tendency of water to flow downward.[1] The following passages illustrate how closely Lu Hsiang-shan follows Mencius on this point:

"Mankind has been allotted an intermediate position between Heaven and Earth in which to live. [Holding this favored position,] there are no [men] whose Original Minds (*pen hsin*) are not good" (Letter to Wang Shun-po, 11.108).

"The four fundamental principles are all innately possessed by men; they are complete without any increase being made to them"[2] (*Conversations*, 35.296).

The doctrine that human Nature is perfectly good is connected with the view that the Nature of man has spontaneous and intuitive moral knowledge. This view of intuitive knowledge is shared by all the Neo-Confucianists, though it is particularly emphasized by Lu Hsiang-shan, and by his later exponent, Wang Yang-ming. For Lu Hsiang-shan and the other Neo-Confucianists, intuition is a simple and concrete manifestation of the original human Mind. In other words, it is a natural moral response of man. A familiar illustration cited by Mencius and frequently used by the Neo-Confucianists is that anyone who sees a child about to fall into a well will naturally have a sense or a feeling of alarm, and will spontaneously try to rescue the child. This he will do quite irrespective of any selfish motive that may arise later on second thought, such as, for example, a desire to make a public display of this heroic deed. Intuition is therefore quite different from intellect or reason, which, if

---

1. See *Mencius*, VIa, 2 (Legge's tr., pp. 271-2).
2. The four fundamental principles (*ssu tuan*) are, according to Mencius, the roots out of which spring the four major virtues. Thus the feeling of commiseration is the root of Human-heartedness, etc.

allowed to operate, may cause the man to rescue the child merely out of motives of self interest, or may even conceivably cause him to refrain entirely from rescuing the child, should he, on second thought, realize that that child's father is his own enemy.[1]

Lu Hsiang-shan's own theory of the Mind's intuitive knowledge is clear and definite, and in it he equates this intuitive knowledge with Law.

"Mencius said: 'The Way of Heaven (t'ien tâo) is one, and only one.'[2] Again he said:[3] There are but two courses (tâo) [which can be pursued], that of Human-heartedness (jen) and its opposite.'[4] What is right is Human-heartedness; what is opposed to the right is the opposite to Human-heartedness. Human-heartedness is identical with this Mind and this Law. He who seeks will find it; and what he finds will be this Law. He who has foreknowledge knows this Law; he who has foreunderstanding understands this Law. To love one's parents is this Law; to respect one's elder brother also is this Law. To see a child about to fall into a well, and then to have a Mind [that experiences feelings] of alarm and commiseration, is this Law. To feel shame for what is shameful and hate what is hateful, is this Law. To know that what is right is right, and what is wrong is wrong, is this Law. To be modest when it is proper to be modest, and to be humble when it is proper to be humble, is this Law. Reverence (ching) is this Law, and so is Righteousness (i). What is internal is this Law, and so too what is external. . . .

"Mencius said: 'To know without any cognition is intuitive knowledge (liang chih). To be capable of knowing without the exercise of study is intuitive capacity (liang neng).'[5]

1. See *Mencius*, IIa, 6 (Legge's tr., p. 78).
2. See *Mencius*, IIIa, 1 (Legge's tr., p. 110).
3. Lu Hsiang-shan wrongly attributes this quotation to Mencius. According to the original text, it is a saying attributed by Mencius to Confucius.
4. *Mencius*, IVa, 2 (Legge's tr., p. 169).
5. *Mencius*, VIIa, 15 (Legge's tr., p. 332).

These are given to us by Heaven; they are innate (*ku yu*), and not infused into us from without.[1] It is therefore said: 'All things are complete within us. There is no greater joy than to find Sincerity (*ch'eng*) when one examines oneself.'[2] Such is my Original Mind (*pen hsin*)" (Letter to Tseng Chai-chih, 1.18).

The dictinction made by the other Neo-Confucianists between the Mind of Man and the Mind of Spirit is rejected by Lu Hsiang-shan, and replaced by his doctrine of the Original Mind (*pen hsin*). Lu Hsiang-shan is the only Sung philosopher who repeatedly and emphatically uses the term, in order thus to avoid the dualistic tendency of the Ch'eng-Chu school. The Original Mind, he says, is the innate possession of man.

"Our Original Mind is not infused into us from without. At the present time, [in its original state,] is it not peaceful and harmonious, and furthermore, without impediment? If we do not follow it with care and guard over it with stern attention, wicked influences and bad habits may take advantage of our negligence to assault us, and will thus destroy our Original Mind" (Letter to Chu-ko Ch'eng, 4.47).

What is the Original Mind? An interesting conversation on the subject between Lu Hsiang-shan and his pupil Yang Chien reads as follows:

"[The question was asked:][3] 'What is the Original Mind?' The teacher [Lu Hsiang-shan] replied: 'The feeling of commiseration is the basis of Human-heartedness. The feeling of shame and dislike is the basis of Righteousness. The feeling of modesty and complaisance is the basis of Propriety. The feeling of right and wrong is the basis of Wisdom. All these are the Original Mind.'[4]

1. Although Lu Hsiang-shan uses his own wording here, the ideas are derived from Mencius. See *Mencius*, VIa, 6 (Legge's tr., pp. 278-9).
2. *Mencius*, VIIa, 4 (Legge's tr., pp. 326-7).
3. By Yang Chien (1141-1226), styled Ching-chung, a pupil of Lu Hsiang-shan. He was a poet and official, and later was appointed magistrate at Lo-p'ing.
4. Here Lu Hsiang-shan quotes Mencius' statement.

551

"[Yang Chien] continued: 'I already understood this in my childhood; but what, precisely, is my Original Mind?' This question was repeatedly asked, but the teacher never changed his explanation; Ching-chung [i.e., Yang Chien], too, never came to understand [the true answer].

"It happened that a fan-vendor brought a lawsuit to court. Ching-chung, after having settled the rightness and wrongness of the case, asked the same question as before.

"The teacher said: 'I hear you have just settled the case of the fan-vendor. [Evidently,] you know that what is right is right and what is wrong is wrong. This [knowledge], then, is your Original Mind.' . . . Suddenly, Ching-chung understood it entirely. . . . He all at once realized that this Mind has no beginning nor end, and that it permeates everywhere" (*Annals*, 36.317).

Inasmuch as the Original Mind of man is innate, what one should do is to acquire the unflinching determination to develop it to its full capabilities.

"The teacher [Lu Hsiang-shan] said: 'Even if one really has Will (*chih*), one still has to differentiate between the two paths of power and wealth [on the one hand] Truth (*tâo*) and Righteousness (*i*) [on the other]. What I have been talking about is all something that you, my friend, [already] possess innately. Even so as regards the transmitted teachings of the sages and worthies: these too are innately possessed by man. How, indeed, could they be something that is seized from without [i.e., is not innately possessed], and thus is presented to us? If we but succeed in fully developing that which Heaven has bestowed on us, so rich and so noble, then we will not fail to possess that whereby a man is a man!'

"[Li] Po-min asked: 'In one's everyday common actions, wherefrom does one begin one's effort?'

"The teacher replied: 'If one can apprehend what Heaven has bestowed upon us — supreme in nobility and supreme in richness — then one will automatically keep away from evil and depravity. One will adhere only to the upright, and

552

furthermore, will have understanding of that with which we have been innately endowed.'

"Po-min said: 'Evil and depravity are things that I have never dared to commit.'

"The teacher said: 'It is only because of rigid control in this respect. But there are some [things] which cannot be controlled, and such will in future also require effort. That is why one must gain apprehension of what Heaven has bestowed upon us'" (*Conversations*, 35.287).

To sum up: Like all the Neo-Confucianists, Lu Hsiang-shan's primary objective is the concept of Mind, though he lays even greater stress on it than the others. For him, Mind is that which is characterized by its capacity of knowing, thinking and reflecting; through it man can really know the Truth or *Tâo*. And yet, Lu Hsiang-shan is not a subjective idealist as a modern writer thinks he is.[1] For he never forgets that beyond the finite minds there exists the one universal Mind, identified with the one universal Law, which permeates the entire universe, and is apprehensible and knowable; hence the universe is the macrocosm, and the individual Mind is the microcosm.

But this is not all. What is more important, this universal Law consists of the ethical principles of Human-heartedness, Righteousness, Propriety and Wisdom, and is the purely moral standard of man; it is therefore man's duty to live in conformity and harmony with the perfect goodness of the Law. Furthermore, the Original Mind of man is endowed with a Nature essentially good; the original goodness of human Nature enables man to experience spontaneously and intuitively the feelings of commiseration, of shame and dislike, of modesty and complaisance, and of right and wrong, which are, in turn, the very basis of the four cardinal virtues.

Lu Hsiang-shan's ethics is indeed laid on a sound foundation by postulating the existence of a universal Law or

1. See Hsiang Lin-ping, *Chung-kuo Che-hsüeh Shih Kang-yao* (An Outline History of Chinese Philosophy), Shanghai, 1939, pp. 454-64.

Mind, which is real, infinite, eternal and good, and in the bosom of which the finite individual minds can permanently be conserved. Hence the double aspect of the subjective and objective Mind, the ego and the non-ego, the internal and external, are harmoniously combined into one unique unity.

The doctrine of the goodness of human Nature, however, is now forced to deal with two sorts of difficult questions.

First, is it always the case that man's first response is spontaneously good? Can the simple case of rescuing a child from danger be a sufficient basis for asserting that the Nature of man is originally good? This view was first attacked by Hsün Tzŭ, the great opponent of Mencius, who criticized the doctrine of the original goodness of human Nature as a partial truth only. For it is not infrequently true that man's selfish desire springs out of the very first immediate response. Hsün Tzŭ then cites an illustration of two brothers dividing an inheritance: if the first response, he argues, is always good, then neither of the brothers would have any desire to obtain more than his just share of the property for himself.[1] But in many cases, a man on first thought merely desires his own gain and satisfaction. Instances of this sort show that the doctrine of the goodness of human Nature requires more convincing proof.

Secondly, if the human Nature is originally good, intuitive and spontaneous, how do we account for moral temptation and conflict? And how does it happen that the Mind becomes lost? The reply to these questions is given in Lu Hsiang-shan's doctrine of evil, an important topic which will be considered next.

1. For Hsün Tzŭ, see *The Works of Hsüntze* (Dubs' tr., London, 1928), and *Hsüntze, the Moulder of Ancient Confucianism*, by Dubs, H. H., London, 1927. For the illustration in question, see *The Works of Hsüntze*, p. 304.

5. THE DOCTRINE OF EVIL

Lu Hsiang-shan, in his doctrine of evil, as in his doctrine of the goodness of human Nature, largely follows Mencius, though he seems to lay more emphasis on it than Mencius does. The following passage from Mencius illustrates his recognition of the influence of the environment upon human conduct: "In good years the children of the people are most of them good, while in bad years most of them abandon themselves to evil." To this he adds: "It is not owing to their natural powers conferred by Heaven that they are thus different. The abandonment is owing to the circumstances through which they allow their Minds to be ensnared and submerged in evil."[1]

Like Mencius, Lu Hsiang-shan admits the existence of evil, and like him too, he says that it results only from the influence of external things upon the originally good Nature.

"Human Nature is originally good. Any evil in it results from the changes made upon it by [external] things. He who knows the injury caused by [those external] things and who can revert to himself [i.e., can return to his original condition], can then know that goodness is the innate possession of our Nature" (*Conversations*, 34.272).

The following passages exemplify the power of such external influence:

"Mencius spoke of the goodness of [human] Nature; therefore he said that there are no men who are not good. But now if you [deliberately] say that a man is not good, that man will, [as a result,] of his own accord do what is not good, and will furthermore regard you as [likewise] not being good" (*Conversations*, 34.268).

"Mind should not be contaminated with anything; it should stand alone and independent. In its original state,

---

1. See *Mencius*, VIa, 7 (Legge's tr., p. 280). Cf. also Hu Shih, *Chung-kuo Che-hsüeh Shih Ta-kang* (An Outline History of Chinese Philosophy), Shanghai, 15th edition, 1930, pp. 293-6.

the Mind of Man contains no disorder, [but gradually and] confusedly it is led astray by [external] things. If one has the proper spirit, he will immediately rise [above things], and will [attain the original] good. But if one continuously moves away [from the Original Mind], he will then become corrupted" (*Conversations*, 35.296).

The question now arises: Is evil, then, merely relative? This question will be discussed presently. At this point it should simply be noted that although Lu Hsiang-shan admits the existence of evil when expounding the goodness of human Nature, nevertheless, for him, goodness is something prior and innate, while evil is always posterior and acquired.

"Where there is good there must be evil. [The transition from one to the other] is truly [like] the turning over of one's hand. Goodness, however, is so from the very beginning, whereas evil comes into existence only as a result of such a 'turning over'" (*Conversations*, 34.261).

It has been suggested earlier that the Ch'eng-Chu school connected the problem of evil with the doctrine of Matter or Ether (*ch'i*). Its theory of evil, however, is somewhat ambiguous, particularly when it maintains its belief in the goodness of the Nature at the same time that it speaks about the physical *Ch'i*. Thus Chu Hsi says: "The Nature of all men is good and yet there are those who are good from their birth and those who are evil from their birth. This is because of the inequality of the ethereal endowment (*ch'i*)."[1] Again: "'Given the existence of Law, there follows the existence of Ether. Given the Ether, there must be Law. . . . Those whose ethereal endowment is clear are the sages and worthies in whom the Nature is like a pearl lying in clear and cold water. Those whose ethereal endowment is turbid are the foolish and degenerate, in whom the Nature is like a pearl lying in muddy water."[2] Matter or Ether is

---

1. See *The Philosophy of Human Nature* (Bruce's tr., p. 85).
2. *Ibid.* (Bruce's tr., pp. 90-91).

thus, simply because it is material; it is considered to be bad and to corrupt the good Nature. But herein lies the paradox of the doctrine. For since everything possesses Law, and Law is an ethical principle, therefore everything must be good. But, on the other hand, since everything in this world is also made up of Matter or *Ch'i*, therefore if this *Ch'i* is bad, then everything that it comprises is likewise bad.

This dualism made by the Ch'eng-Chu school between Law and Matter, in which it linked the former with goodness and the latter with evil, was later severely attacked by the somewhat materialistic school that developed in the Ch'ing dynasty (1644-1911) as a reaction against Neo-Confucianism. The two philosophers, Yen Hsi-chai (1635-1704) and Tai Tung-yüan (1723-1777), in particular, argued that the dualistic distinction made by the Ch'eng-Chu school between a metaphysical Law and physical Matter is erroneous; the two are merely differing aspects of the same thing. Thus Matter is simply the basic stuff out of which any thing is made, while Law simply constitutes the characteristic principle or pattern that is to be found always in that thing. (To give an explanatory example of our own: The tendency of water to flow downward, or to freeze when cold, may both be said to constitute the principles or Laws characteristic of water. But these Laws or principles are not for that reason to be regarded as more "metaphysical" or less "physical" than is the water itself in which they are always to be found.) Hence to impute good to Law and evil to Matter is absurd. How, for example, can it be seriously argued that the eye, simply because it consists of Matter, is therefore bad, whereas the capacity for vision possessed by that eye, which constitutes its Law or underlying principle, is for that reason good?[1]

Lu Hsiang-shan's lack of interest in the material *Ch'i* frees him from this paradoxical difficulty which the Ch'eng-

1. See Fung Yu-lan, *Chung-kuo Che-hsüeh Shih* (History of Chinese Philosophy), Vol. 2, p. 985; also Hsü, P. C., *Ethical Realism in Neo-Confucian Thought*, Peiping, 1933, pp. 93-106.

Chu school was compelled to face. Instead of discussing the doctrine of evil in its metaphysical aspects, Lu Hsiang-shan centers his attention upon Material Desire (*wu yü*), which he regards as the main source of evil. Human Desire is also recognized by Chu Hsi as a cause of evil; for example, he was once asked: "Are those in whom the Ether is clear therefore free from Material Desire (*wu yü*)?" To this he replied: "That cannot be asserted. The Desire for food and drink and the Desire for musical sounds are common to all. Even though the Ether (*ch'i*) with which he is endowed is clear, a man will drift into Desire at the least relaxation of watchfulness and self-control."[1]

Lu Hsiang-shan, for his part, denies that it is the physical *Ch'i* that causes men to be bad. Men, he says, are simply led astray through their indulgence in Material Desire. Thus their Original Mind becomes lost. That is to say, originally there is no moral inequality among men; what makes one man superior in moral quality to another is solely his ability to overcome the temptation created by Desire.

"What is it that will injure your Mind? It is Desire (*yü*). When Desires are many, what we can preserve of our [Original] Mind is inevitably little; and [conversely], when the Desires are few, what we can preserve of our [Original] Mind is inevitably much.[2] Therefore, the Superior Man does not worry that his Mind is not preserved, but rather worries that his Desires are not made few. For if the Desires were eliminated, the Mind would automatically be preserved. Thus, then, does not the preserving of what is good in our Mind depend upon the elimination of what does it injury?" (*Collected Literary Remains*, 32.247-8).

"Common men and vulgarians are submerged [either] by poverty or wealth, or by high or low position, or by benefit or injury, or by profit or loss, or by sounds and colors,

1. See *The Philosophy of Human Nature* (Bruce's tr., pp. 106-7).
2. For the title of this passage, Lu Hsiang-shan uses a quotation from Mencius: "To nourish the Mind there is nothing better than to make the Desires few." See *Mencius*, VIIb, 35 (Legge's tr., p. 373).

or by sensuality and Desire (*yü*). They [thus] destroy their 'virtuous Mind' (*liang hsin*),[1] and have no regard for Righteousness (*i*) and Law (*li*). How very lamentable it is!

"If scholars of today could only concentrate their attention on Truth (*tâo*) and Law (*li*) — in every affair being observant of the right, and refusing to follow the Passions (*ch'ing*) and Desires — then, even though their understanding were not wholly complete and clear, and their conduct were not entirely according to the mean and moderate, yet they would not fail to be the successors of good men and correct scholars [i.e., of the sages and worthies of ancient times]" (Letter to Fu Fu-chung, 4.52).

"There is not one who does not love his parents and respect his elder brother. But when one is blind by profit and Desire, then it is otherwise" (*Conversations*, 35.296).

What, then, is the origin of Material Desire, if as Lu Hsiang-shan seems to believe, it is not a product of Matter (*ch'i*)? To this, unfortunately, he gives no clear reply. The foregoing statements show that he is evidently not attracted by the metaphysical interpretation of the physical *Ch'i*, pronounced by the Ch'eng-Chu school to be an essential source of evil. Nor would he agree with Hsün Tzu's psychology that Desire is instinctive, nor again would he accept the Christian Doctrine of the Fall; for he insists on the perfectness of human Nature. The only answer that he seems to suggest is that Desire is acquired. Although the original Nature of man is perfectly good, and material things as such are not bad, yet man's Mind, instead of being developed to its fullest capacity, sometimes becomes lost by its indulgence in Material Desire.

The second source of evil, says Lu Hsiang-shan, lies in ignorance or superficial opinion. Such ignorance and superficiality, he believes, are by no means confined to the uneducated. They are also to be found among those in-

---

1. The term "virtuous Mind" (*liang hsin*) is from Mencius. See *Mencius*, VIa, 8 (Legge's tr., p. 284).

tellectual pedants who, while they consider themselves to have acquired wide knowledge, have done so in a stupid or superficial way, and are actually just as deficient, morally, as are ordinary people. On this point he writes as follows:

"Those who follow Material Desires (*wu yü*) gallop [after them] without knowing [where] to stop. Those who follow [superficial] opinions also gallop [after them] without knowing [where] to stop. Therefore, 'although the Way (*tao*) is near, yet they seek for it afar; although a thing is easy [to deal with], yet they seek for it in its difficult [aspects].'[1] But is the Truth [really] remote or the things [really] difficult? [It is because] their opinions are unsound, that they make difficulties for themselves. If one fully realizes one's error, then one's becloudings and doubts will be dissipated and one will reach the place in which to stop" (Letter to Chao Chien, 1.21).

"The Way (*tâo*) fills the universe, nowhere being concealed. It is, in Heaven, called the Negative and Positive principles (*yin* and *yang*); in Earth it is called Softness and Hardness; and in man it is called Human-heartedness (*jen*) and Righteousness (i).[2] Thus, then, Human-heartedness and Righteousness are man's Original Mind. . . .

"The foolish and unworthy, being deficient, are blinded by Material Desire, and thus lose their Original Mind. Whereas the Worthy and intelligent, going too far, are also blinded

1. Here Lu Hsiang-shan quotes Mencius. See *Mencius*, IVa, 11 (Legge's tr., p. 178).

2. The idea of this sentence is derived from the *Book of Changes*, "Great Appendix" (Legge's tr., pp. 423-4): "Anciently, when the sages made the *Changes*, it was with the design that [its figures] should be in conformity with the principles underlying the Nature [of men and things], and the ordinances [for them] appointed by [by Heaven]. With this view they exhibited [in them] the Way of Heaven, calling [the lines] *Yin* and *Yang;* the Way of Earth, calling [them] Softness and Hardness; and the Way of Man under the names of Human-heartedness and Righteousness."

by their [superficial] views, and [likewise] lose their Original Mind"[1] (Letter to Chao Chien, 1.20-1).

"The foolish and unworthy, being deficient, have never attained the proper [mean or standard]; the worthy and intelligent, going too far, have likewise never attained the proper [mean]. Having a weakness for music, color, wealth and material profit ([i.e., for luxuries of all kinds], they become accustomed to cunning and evil doings, become fettered by trivial and insignificant matters, and fall [a victim] to high sounding theories and superficial doctrines.

"Although the wise and the foolish, the worthies and the unworthies, differ from each other, yet inasmuch as their Minds have never attained the proper [mean], and they have been blinded by selfishness, so that the Truth (*tâo*) is not understood or practised [by them], they suffer from an identical defect" (Letter to Li Tsai, 11.106).

"They who lived in the prosperous, well-governed days of old, and who enjoyed the favor of the early sage-kings, were surely without this fault [i.e., misapprehension of Truth or *Tâo*]. But now, because they live in later generations, when the doctrines [of the early sages] have been interrupted, when the Truth (*tâo*) has been destroyed, and when strange theories and depraved doctrines expand and spread [everywhere], [even] resolute scholars come to grief and disaster. Thus they, as well as those ordinary men of the world who give rein to their Passions (*ch'ing*) and indulge their Desires, all are drowned" (Letter to Tseng Chai-chih, 1.17).

The above passages clearly indicate that, for Lu Hsiang-

1. This passage refers to the idea of "going too far" (*kuo*) and "falling short" (*pu chi*), which originates in the *Doctrines of the Mean*, I, 9 (Legge's tr., p. 302): "The Master [i.e., Confucius] said, 'I know how it is that the Path of the Mean is not walked in. The knowing go beyond it, and the stupid do not come up to it. The worthy go beyond it, and the unworthy do not come up to it.'"

To go too far is as wrong as to fall short, for both depart from the standard, i.e., the Golden Mean (*chung yung*) — an important moral concept of Chinese thought. To live in accord with the Golden Mean is to be without excess or deficiency.

shan, evil is not something innate or *a priori;* it is acquired and *a posteriori,* and comes into being as a result of giving in to Material Desire and superficial opinions. But why does he say that "where there is good there must be evil?" (*Conversations,* 34.261). Does evil, then, exist after all as something parallel and co-existent with good? The following passages further illustrate the relativity of the two concepts:

"The Superior Man truly wishes men to be good, yet in the world there cannot but be some negation of goodness, which thus does injury to our [original] goodness. He [likewise] wishes men to have Human-heartedness, yet in the world there cannot but be some negation of Human-heartedness, which thus does injury to our [original] Human-heartedness.

"Since there exist the negations of goodness and of Human-heartedness, which do injury to us, if we do not have the means to halt, control and rid ourselves of them, goodness cannot be extended nor can Human-heartedness be made to progress. For this reason, to rid ourselves of the negation of Human-heartedness is the way to become human-hearted, and to rid ourselves of the negation of goodness is the way to become good" (Letter to Hsin Yu-an, 5.59).

Lu Hsiang-shan, like Mencius, takes for granted the doctrine of the original goodness of human Nature. Yet it seems that he goes a step beyond Mencius by postulating the necessary existence of evil, in order thereby to make the concept of goodness assume meaning. For the statement that "where there is good there must be evil" seems to suggest more than a mere psychological observation on how easily original goodness may be changed to badness; it is also a logical recognition of the fact that the term "good" has no meaning in itself, but can exist only in relation to the term "bad". On this particular point, Lu Hsiang-shan must have agreed with Chu Hsi's statement: "Apart from its contrast with evil, good cannot be predicated of anything."[1] And yet, since he explicitly discards Chu Hsi's differentiation between the Mind of Man and the Mind of Spirit, it follows that he would not accept Chu Hsi's postulate that evil is a concept that exists only in correspondence with the concept of Matter (*ch'i*).

But how to explain the logical necessity of evil if evil is acquired and comes into existence only as result of man's indulgence in Desire? To this contradictory question Lu Hsiang-shan gives no reply. His only statement is that evil is an inescapable fact and a practical experience. It occurs even in Heaven. He writes:

"To say that the Mind of Man (*jen hsin*) is Human Artifice[2] and the Mind of Spirit (*tâo shin*) is Heavenly Law (*t'ien li*), is incorrect. The [term] Mind of Man is only talk [with no validity behind it]. . . . To speak of human Desire [in contrast to] Heavenly Law is incorrect. [For] there are both good and evil in Heaven.[3] How can all goodness be ascribed only to Heaven and all evil only to man?" (*Conversations*, 35.301).

According to Lu Hsiang-shan Heaven is essentially good, yet when the eclipses of the sun or the moon occur, it is bad. Likewise, human Nature is originally good, yet it is a fact that men are prone to do evil. Evil is therefore always potential, but at the same time something incidental and temporary; whereas the original goodness of human Nature is a universal truth and an eternal ideal of moral conduct.

Furthermore, Lu Hsiang-shan believes that man is himself responsible for his evil doings. He has it within his own

1. *Jen wei*, something man-made and therefore inferior.
2. See *The Philosophy of Human Nature* (Bruce's tr., p. 41).
3. The bad elements in Heaven cited by Lu Hsiang-shan himself, according to a note on this passage, are eclipses of the sun and the moon, and the evil stars. The belief in evil stars dates back at least to the T'ang dynasty (618-906), and probably earlier. Two malignant stars, for example, whose baleful influences have to be carefully watched, are known as *Ku*, "the Orphan," and *Hsü*, "the Void." See Doré, Henri, *Researches into Chinese Superstitions* (Kennelly's tr., Shanghai, 1914-1934, Vol. 4, pp. 386-7, 398-9).

power either to allow himself to become bad or to revert to the original state of goodness.

"The universe (*yü chou*) has never limited and separated itself from man, but it is man who limits and separates himself from the universe" (*Annals*, 36.314).

"The Truth (*tâo*) permeates all under Heaven; there is not even the smallest space [where it does not permeate]. The four 'fundamental principles' (*ssu tuan*)[1] and 'ten thousand virtues' (*wan shan*) are all conferred upon us by Heaven. They do not impose upon men the labor of adding any adornment.[2] But it is men themselves who have vices, and [therefore] separate themselves [from them]" (*Conversations*, 35.293).

"If Mind is not blinded by Material Desire, then Righteousness and Law are its innate possession" (Letter to Fu Ch'i-hsien, 14.127).

"The virtuous Mind (*liang hsin*) and correct Nature (*cheng hsing*) are possessed by all men. Who, if he does not lose this Mind, or oppose this Nature, will not be an upright man? But even if he does, on occasion, permit himself to fall away from them, how will he be far removed from them? For him not to do so [i.e., to cling to his good Nature], is to blind his own Mind and his own body" (Letter to Kuo Pang-jui, 13.120).

"[This] Law lies directly before one's eyes; it is only by man himself that it becomes obscured" (*Conversations*, 35.295).

The foregoing discussion shows that Lu Hsiang-shan recognizes evil as an inescapable experience of man. He accepts Mencius' view that evil is due to the influence of environment. Yet he seems to go beyond Mencius in emphasizing Material Desire as the main source of evil. But here arise the questions: How can one be influenced by the temptations of environment if the original Nature of man

---

1. See above, p. 42, note 4.
2. I.e., they exist perfect in themselves, quite independent of any human efforts to make them beautiful.

is perfectly good? How can and where-from does Material Desire arise if the Mind of man is good, intuitive and spontaneous? Both Chang Tsai and Ch'eng I, realizing the inadequacy of Mencius' doctrine of human Nature in connection with the problem of evil, turned toward the concept of Matter (*ch'i*) as the main source of evil. This explanation received strong support and development from Chu Hsi. In this way they were quite satisfied that Mencius' theory of the goodness of human Nature was safeguarded and made into a consistent system. As has already been said, Lu Hsiang-shan's lack of interest in the metaphysical interpretation of the problem of evil exonerates him from the criticisms made by the Ch'ing scholars, who were strongly opposed to the dualistic tendency of the Ch'eng-Chu school. And yet, he in his turn seems to be unaware of the incompleteness of Mencius' doctrine of human Nature, and thus falls into the mistake of neglecting to give an adequate explanation of Desire, which he considers to be the chief cause of evil.

Wang Yang-ming

WANG YANG-MING (1472-1528). It was around the middle of the Ming dynasty (1368-1644) that Mencius' doctrine of innate knowledge was revived in China and the Neo-Confucian school of Mind found a formidable champion. The statesman-general Wang Yang-ming (Wang Shou-jen or Wang Po-an) formulated a system of dynamic idealism which dominated Chinese life for a century and a half after his death. He refuted Chu Shi's interpretation of Confucianism, accepted as the orthodox one since 1313, and stressed four major concepts: *jen* (humanity) unites the sage with the universe; principle and the human mind which contains all things are one and are identical with the universe; self-perfection can be achieved without recourse to investigation into the principle of external things; and knowledge and action are one: knowledge is the beginning of action, action the completion of knowledge.

A native of Yüeh in Chekiang, he is said to have traveled widely at the age of fifteen, then prepared for the official examinations by setting up a study in a mountain cave, where he also read "in the literatures of Buddhism and Taôism." His early record of service in the government was unblemished until he offended a eunuch and was banished to modern Kueichow. There he took an interest in improving the conditions under which the rude tribesmen were living. It was there also that he began to work out his system of philosophy. Readmitted into royal favor in 1510, he served the state as a capable administrator, a cabinet member, and a general credited with many successful campaigns. Several years after his death, in 1567, he was given the honorific title of Wen-ch'eng (Completion of Culture). In 1584 he received the highest honor for a scholar when the emperor decreed that he be offered sacrifice in the Confucian temple.

Lu Hsiang-shan (1139-1193) had opposed Chu Hsi's philosophy, holding that there is no distinction between principle and material force, and that to investigate things means to investigate the mind. Wang Yang-ming continued and elaborated this line of thought. As the original mind is manifested, for example, in filial piety, the principle of filial piety becomes evident. It follows that all men have native knowledge of the good and the ability to do good, and that they are obligated to put their innate knowledge into practice. Love in the broadest sense is the ultimate extension to "form one body with Heaven and Earth."

Although his admirers called attention to the clarity, simplicity, and precision of his charming style, conflicting interpretations of his ideas soon sprang up. His contention that the mind has an inborn faculty for knowing sublime truths lent itself to two interpretations. Some of his successors viewed innate knowledge as conscience, others as mystical insight. It was the latter view that caused one group of his followers to be labeled the "Wildcat Ch'an School."

Instructions for Practical Life

The Highest Virtues are Innate

From *The Philosophy of Wang Yang-ming*, translated by Frederick Good-rich Henke, Chicago, Open Court Publishing Company, 1916.

I made inquiry regarding the saying from the Great Learning, "Knowing where to rest, the object of pursuit is determined."[1] "The philosopher Chu," I said, "held that all affairs and all things have definite principles. This appears to be out of harmony with your sayings."

The Teacher said: "To seek the highest virtue in affairs and things is only the objective side of the principles of righteousness. The highest virtues are innate to the mind. They are realized when the manifesting of lofty virtue has reached perfection. Nevertheless, one does not leave the physical realm out of consideration. The original notes say that the individual must exhaust heaven-given principles to the utmost and that no one with any of the prejudices of human passions will attain to the highest virtue."

I made inquiry saying, "Though the highest virtue be sought within the mind only, that may not enable the individual to investigate thoroughly the laws of the physical realm."

The Teacher said: "The mind itself is the embodiment of natural law. Is there anything in the universe that exists independent of the mind? Is there any law apart from the mind?"

I replied: "In filial obedience in serving one's parents,

1. Great Learning, Introduction, para. 2.

or faithfulness in serving one's prince, or sincerity in intercourse with friends, or benevolence in governing the people, there are many principles which I fear must be examined."

The Teacher, sighing, said: "This is an old evasion. Can it be fully explained in one word? Following your order of questions I will make reply. For instance, in the matter of serving one's father, one cannot seek for the principle of filial obedience in one's parent, or in serving one's prince one cannot seek for the principle of faithfulness in the prince, or in making friends or governing the people one cannot seek for the principle of sincerity and benevolence in the friend or the people. They are all in the mind, for the mind is itself the embodiment of principles. When the mind is free from the obscuration of selfish aims, it is the embodiment of the principles of Heaven. It is not necessary to add one whit from without. When service of parents emerges from the mind characterized by pure heaven-given principles, we have filial obedience; when service of prince emerges, faithfulness; when the making of friends or the governing of the people emerge, sincerity and benevolence. It is only necessary to expel human passions and devote one's energies to the eternal principles."

I said, "Hearing you speak thus, I realize that I understand you in a measure, but the old sayings trouble me, for they have not been completely disposed of. In the matter of serving one's parents, the filial son is to care for their comfort both in winter and summer, and inquire after their health every evening and every morning. These things involve many details. I do not know whether these details are to be investigated in the mind or not."

The Teacher said: "Why not investigate them? Yet in this investigation there is a point of departure; namely, to pay attention to the mind in getting rid of selfish aims and to foster the eternal principles. To understand the providing of warmth for one's parents in winter, is merely a matter of exhausting the filial piety of one's mind and of fearing lest a trifle of selfishness remain to intervene. To talk about providing refreshing conditions for one's parents during the summer, is again a matter of exhausting the filial piety of the mind and of fearing lest perhaps selfish aims be inter-mingled with one's efforts. But this implies that one must seek to acquire this attitude of mind for one's self. If the mind has no selfish aims, is perfectly under the control of heaven-given principles (natural law), and is sincerely de-voted to filial piety, it will naturally think of and provide for the comfort of parents in winter and summer. These are all things that emanate from a mind which truly honors the parents; but it is necessary to have a mind that truly honors the parents before these things can emanate from it. Com-pare it to a tree. The truly filial mind constitutes the roots; the many details are the branches and leaves. The roots must first be there, and then later there may be branches and leaves. One does not first seek for the branches and leaves and afterwards cultivate the roots.

"The Book of Rites says: 'The filial son who sincerely loves surely has a peaceful temper. Having a peaceful tem-per, he surely has a happy appearance. Having a happy appearance he surely has a pleasant, mild countenance.' It is because he has a profound love as the root that he is naturally like this."

The Unitary Character of Knowledge and Practice

Because I did not understand the admonition of the Teacher regarding the unitary character of knowledge and practice, Tsung-hsien, Wei-hsien and I discussed it back and forth without coming to any conclusion. Therefore I made inquiry of the Teacher regarding it. He said: "Make a suggestion and see." I said: "All men know that filial piety is due parents, and that the elder brother should be treated with respect; and yet they are unable to carry this out in practice. This implies that knowledge and practice really are two separate things."

The Teacher replied: "This separation is due to selfishness and does not represent the original character of knowledge and practice. No one who really has knowledge fails to practice it. Knowledge without practice should be interpreted as lack of knowledge. Sages and virtuous men teach men to know how to act, because they wish them to return to nature. They do not tell them merely to reflect and let this suffice. The Great Learning exhibits true knowledge and practice, that men may understand this. . . .

I said: "The ancients said that knowledge and practice are two different things. Men should also understand this clearly. One section treats of knowledge, another of practice. Thus may one acquire a starting-point for one's task."

The Teacher said: "But thereby you have lost the meaning of the ancients. I have said that knowledge is the purpose to act, and that practice implies carrying out knowledge. Knowledge is the beginning of practice; doing is the completion of knowing. If when one knows how to attain the desired end, one speaks only of knowing, the doing is already naturally included; or if he speaks of acting, the knowing is already included. That the ancients after having spoken of knowledge also speak of doing, is due to the fact that there is a class of people on earth who foolishly do as they wish and fail to understand how to deliberate and investigate. They act ignorantly and recklessly. It is necessary to discuss knowledge so that they can act correctly. There is another class of people who vaguely and vainly philosophize but are unwilling to carry it out in practice. This also is merely an instance of estimating shadows and echoes. The ancients of necessity discussed doing, for only then can such people truly understand. The language of the ancients is of necessity directed toward rectifying prejudices and reforming abuses. When one comprehends this idea, a word is sufficient. Men of the present, however, make knowledge and action two different things and go forth to practice, because they hold that one must first have knowledge before one is able to practice. Each one says, 'I proceed to investigate and discuss knowledge; I wait until knowledge is perfect and then go forth to practice it.' Those who to the very end of life fail to practice also fail to understand. This is not a small error, nor one that came in a day. By saying that knowledge and practice are a unit, I am herewith offering a remedy for the disease. I am not dealing in abstractions, nor imposing my own ideas, for the nature of knowledge and practice is originally as I describe it. In case you comprehend the purport, no harm is done if you say they are two, for they are in reality a unit. In case you do not comprehend the purport thereof and say they are one, what does it profit? It is only idle talk." . . .

The Philosopher Chu's Mistaken Interpretation of "Investigation of Things"

I made inquiry saying: "Yesterday I heard the Teacher's instructions about resting in the highest virtue. I realize that I am beginning to get a grasp of this task. Nevertheless, I think that your point of view cannot be reconciled with the philosopher Chu's instruction with reference to the investigation of things."

The Teacher said: "Investigation of things is what is meant by resting in the highest excellence. He who has knowledge of the highest excellence also understands the investigation of things."

I said: "Using the instruction of the Teacher, I yesterday pushed forward in the investigation of things, and it seemed as though I comprehended it in general; and yet the instruction of the philosopher Chu is all substantiated in what is called 'a state of discrimination and undividedness' by the Book of History, 'extensive studying and the keeping of one's self under restraint' by the Confucian Analects, and 'the exhausting of one's mental constitution in knowing one's nature' by Mencius. As a result, I am unable to understand fully."

The Teacher said: "Tzŭ-hsia was earnest in his belief in

the sages, while Tseng-tzŭ sought within himself for help. To be earnest in belief surely is correct, but not as much so genuineness in application. Since you cannot grasp this, why should you cling to the sayings of the ancients and thereby fail to apply yourself to what you ought to learn? The philosopher Chu believed the philosopher Ch'en, and yet when he reached places in which he did not understand him, did he ever suddenly and thoughtlessly accept his point of view? Discrimination, undividedness, 'extensive studying,' 'keeping one's self under restraint,' and 'exhausting one's mental constitution' are *ab initio* harmoniously blended with my sayings. But you have never thought about this. The philosophic teaching of Chu cannot but be related to and adapted from the views of others. It does not express the original meaning of the sages. Devotion to the essence implies a united task; extensive studying implies keeping one's self in restraint. I say that the virtuous man already knows that knowledge and practice are a unity. The mere saying of this is enough to show it. 'To exhaust one's mental constitution in order to understand one's nature and know heaven,' implies that the individual is born with knowledge of the duties and carries them out with ease. Preserving one's mental constitution and nourishing one's nature so as to serve heaven,[1] implies that the individual acquires knowledge of them by study and practices them from a desire for advantage. The saying, 'Neither a premature death nor a long life causes a man any double-mindedness,'[2] implies that the individual acquires knowledge of them after a painful feeling of his ignorance and practices them by strenuous effort. The philosopher Chu made a mistake in his teaching regarding the investigation of things because he inverted this idea, using 'the exhausting of one's mental constitution in knowing one's nature' as 'investigation of things for the purpose of extending knowledge to the utmost.'

1. Mencius, Book VII, Pt. I, Ch. 1, para. 2.
2. *Ibid.*, Book VII, Pt. I, Ch. 1, para. 3.

574

He wanted those who were learning for the first time to act as though they had been born with knowledge of duties and carried them out with natural ease. How can that be done?" . . .

Interpretation of a "Thing"

I said, "Yesterday when I heard your teaching I clearly realized that the task is as you describe it: having heard your words today, I am still less in doubt. Last night I came to the conclusion that the word 'thing' of 'investigating things' is to be identified with the word 'affair.' Both have reference to the mind."

The Teacher said: "Yes. The controlling power of the body is the mind. The mind originates the idea, and the nature of the idea is knowledge. Wherever the idea is, we have a thing. For instance, when the idea rests on serving one's parents, then serving one's parents is a 'thing'; when it is on serving one's prince, then serving one's prince is a 'thing'; when it is occupied with being benevolent to the people and kind to creatures, then benevolence to the people and kindness to creatures are 'things'; when it is occupied with seeing, hearing, speaking, moving, then each of these becomes a 'thing.' I say there are no principles but those of the mind, and nothing exists apart from the mind. The Doctrine of the Mean says: 'Without sincerity there would be nothing.'[1] The Great Learning makes clear that the illustrating of illustrious virtue consists merely in making one's purpose sincere, and that this latter has reference to investigating things."

The Teacher spoke again saying: "The 'examine' of 'examining into the nature of things', just as the 'rectify' of 'the great man can rectify the mind of the prince', of Mencius,[2] has reference to the fact that the mind is not right.

1. Doctrine of the Mean, Ch. 25, para. 2.
2. Works of Mencius, Book IV, Part I, Ch. 20.

Its object is to reinstate the original rightness. But the idea conveyed is that one must cast out the wrong in order to complete the right, and that there should be no time or place in which one does not harbor heaven-given principles. This includes a most thorough investigation of heaven-given principles.[1] Heaven-given principles are illustrious virtue; they include the manifesting of illustrious virtue."

Innate Knowledge

Again he said: "Knowledge is native to the mind; the mind naturally is able to know. When it perceives the parents it naturally knows what filial piety is; when it perceives the elder brother it naturally knows what respectfulness is: when it sees a child fall into a well it naturally knows what commiseration is. This is intuitive knowledge of good, and is not attained through external investigation. If the thing manifested emanates from the intuitive faculty, it is the more free from the obscuration of selfish purpose. This is what is meant by saying that the mind is filled with com-miseration, and that love cannot be exhausted. How-ever, the ordinary man is subject to the obscuration of private aims, so that it is necessary to develop the intuitive faculty to the utmost through investigation of things in order to overcome selfishness and reinstate the rule of natural law. Then the intuitive faculty of the mind will not be subject to obscuration, but having been satiated will func-tion normally. Thus we have a condition in which there is an extension of knowledge. Knowledge having been ex-tended to the utmost, the purpose is sincere."

Propriety in Its Relation to Principles

I made inquiry of the Teacher saying, "Though I ponder deeply I am unable to understand the use of 'extensive study

7. Used here and hereafter largely in the sense of natural law.

of all learning' in the task of keeping one's self under the restraint of the rules of propriety.[1] Will you kindly explain it somewhat?"

The Teacher said: "The word 'propriety' carries with it the connotation of the word 'principles.' When principles become manifest in action, they can be seen and are then called propriety. When propriety is abstruse and cannot be seen, it is called principles. Nevertheless, they are one thing. In order to keep one's self under the restraint of the rules of propriety it is merely necessary to have a mind completely under the influence of natural law (heaven-given principles). If a person desires to have his mind completely dominated by natural law, he must use effort at the point where principles are manifested. For instance, if they are to be manifested in the matter of serving one's parents, one should learn to harbor these principles in the serving of one's parents. If they are to be manifested in the matter of serving one's prince, one should learn to harbor them in the service of one's prince. If they are to be manifested in the changing fortunes of life, whether of wealth and position, or of poverty and lowliness, one should learn to harbor them whether in wealth and position, or in poverty and lowliness. If they are to be manifested when one meets sorrow and difficulty, or is living among barbarous tribes, one should learn to harbor them in sorrow and difficulty, or when one is among barbarous tribes. Whether working or resting, speaking or silent, under no conditions should it be different. No matter where they are manifested, one should forthwith learn to harbor them. This is what is meant by studying them extensively in all learning, and includes the keeping of one's self under the restraint of the rules of propriety. 'Extensive study of all learning' thus implies devotion to the best (discrimination). 'To keep one's self under the restraint of the rules of propriety' implies devoting one's self to a single purpose (undividedness)."

1. Confucian Analects, Book VI, Ch. 25.

The Mind is a Unity

I made inquiry saying: "An upright (righteous) mind is master of the body, while a selfish mind is always subject to the decrees (of the body). Using your instruction regarding discrimination and undividedness, this saying appears to be mistaken."

The Teacher said: "The mind is one. In case it has not been corrupted by the passions of men, it is called an upright mind. If corrupted by human aims and passions, it is called a selfish mind. When a selfish mind is rectified it is an upright mind; and when an upright mind loses its rightness it becomes a selfish mind. Originally there were not two minds. The philosopher Ch'eng said, 'A selfish mind is due to selfish desire; an upright mind is natural law (is true to nature).' Even though his discourse separates them, his thought comprehends the situation correctly. Now, you say that if the upright mind is master and the selfish mind is subject to decrees, there are two minds, and that heaven-given principles and selfishness can not co-exist. How can natural law be master, while selfishness follows and is subject to decrees?" .

Confucius Revised the Six Classics

I said, "Confucius revised the Six Classics in order to shed light on the doctrine."

The Teacher said: "Yes. But in interpreting the classics does one not follow Confucius?"

I said: "The writing of comments implies that there is something to be made clear in the doctrine. Interpreting the classics refers only to judging their effect and may not add anything to the doctrine itself."

The Teacher said: "Sir, do you consider him who understands the doctrine as thereby returning to honesty, reverting to sincerity, and perceiving the genuine method of conduct? Or do you think that he improves his composition, but merely for the sake of being able to dispute? The great confusion in the Empire is due to the victory of false learning and the decay of genuine conduct. It is not necessary to publish the Six Classics in order to cause the doctrine to be understood. Confucius revised them because that was the only thing feasible. From the time when Fu Hsi drew the eight diagrams up to the time of Wăn Wang and Chou Kung, portions of the Book of Changes, such as Lienshan and Kueits'ang, were discussed, often in a noisy, disorderly way.[1] I do not know how many scholars discussed them, but the doctrine of the Book of Changes was greatly perverted. Because the custom of admiring literary style daily increased within the Empire, Confucius, realizing that the discussions about the Book of Changes would be endless, chose the interpretation of Wen Wang and Chou Kung and eulogized it as being the only one that grasped the underlying idea. Thereupon the confused interpretations were entirely discarded and a unanimity of opinion was reached among expositors. The same situation prevailed in the case of the Book of History, the Book of Poetry, the Book of Rites and the Annals of Spring and Autumn. In the Book of History from the Tienmo on, and in the Book of Poetry from the Erhnan on — as, for example, in the Chiuch'iu and the Paso — all expressions of lewd wantonness and licentious excess, including I know not how many hundreds or thousands of leaves, were rejected, expunged, or revised by Confucius. Moreover, he did the same with the names of distinguished persons, things, and measures without limit. This was the first time that such sayings were discarded.

"Where did Confucius add a single sentence to the Books of History, Poetry, or Rites? The many present-day interpretations of the Book of Rites have all been agreed upon

1. The eight diagrams consist of eight combinations of a line and a divided line. They are said to have been copied from the back of a tortoise by the legendary monarch Fu Hsi. They were used in philosophizing and in speculating about nature.

and adopted by later scholars, and are not the interpretation of Confucius. Though the Annals of Spring and Autumn are attributed to Confucius, in actual fact they are an ancient record of the history of Lu Kuo. The one said to have written it wrote about ancient things; he who corrected it expunged much, abbreviating without making any additions. When Confucius transcribed the Six Classics, he was afraid that multitudinous characters would confuse the Empire. He decided to abridge them in order that the scholars of the Empire might get rid of the mere literary learning of the classics, and, seeking for what was genuine about them, no longer teach merely by using the literary style. After the revision of the Annals of Spring and Autumn, the more the multitude of characters increased, the more confused the Empire became.

The Work of Confucius Has Been Partly Undone

"(Ch'in) Shih Huang mistakenly burned the books from private motives, though he had no justification for doing so. If his purpose at that time was to exhibit the doctrine, he should have known enough to collect and burn all the sayings that were opposed to the classics and violated moral principles. That would have been in accord with the idea of revision. From the time of the Ch'in and Han dynasties, literary productions again daily increased in number. Though anyone should desire to dispose of them entirely, it would be utterly impossible. One should adopt the plan of Confucius: record that which is approximately correct, and publish it. All superstitious and perverse sayings should, of course, gradually be dropped. I do not know what interpretation of the classics prevailed contemporaneously with Wen Chung-tzŭ. As I look the matter over privately, I believe that a sage had arisen but was unable to effect a change. The misrule of the Empire was due to the fact that literary productions were abundant, but sincerity had decayed. Men, following their own opinions, sought for new mysteries that they might increase their fame. Ostentatious for the sake of becoming prominent, they confused the wise of the Empire, dulled the ears and eyes of the people, and caused them to dispute extravagantly. They assiduously corrected literary style in order to seek notoriety before the world, but did not understand the practice which is generously original and nobly true, and which returns to honesty and reverts to sincerity. All commentators use their literary productions to promote this."

I said: "Among commentators there are some that are indispensable. The classic called the Annals of Spring and Autumn would probably be difficult to understand if it were not for the Tso Chuan."[1]

The Teacher said: "You say that the interpretation of the Annals of Spring and Autumn depends upon the Tso Chuan and can be understood only after the latter has been read. The Annals of Spring and Autumn consists of abridged sayings. Why should the sage devote himself strenuously to profound, abstruse phraseology? The Tso Chuan consists mostly of the ancient history of Lu Kuo. If the Annals of Spring and Autumn can really be understood only after the reading of the Tso Chuan, why did Confucius revise it?"

I said: "The philosopher Ch'eng also said that the Tso Chuan is the case (Speaking from a legal standpoint) and the Spring and Autumn Annals are the judgment. For example, a certain book gives an account of the murder of a prince or the devastation of a state by war. But if the individual lacks knowledge of the particular affair it is difficult for him to pass judgment." . . .

Wang Discusses the Revision of the Classics

I said: "When the sages wrote the classics their aim

1. The famous commentary of Tso Ch'iu-ming upon the Spring and Autumn Annals.

was to get rid of the passions of men and harbor natural law. They preferred not to give to others a minute explanation of the events which occurred after the five rulers of the sixth century. That was right. But why is it that the affairs of the period prior to Yao and Shun were still less fully discussed?"

The Teacher said: "In the time of Hsi and Huang, important events occurred rarely and those who transmitted them were few in number. From this one may conclude that at that time all was well ordered, unpretentious, and without special elegance. The methods of government of the most ancient times were of that nature. Later generations have not been able to reproduce them."

I said: "Inasmuch as the records of the first three rulers had been handed down did Confucius revise them?"

The Teacher said: "Granting that there were those who transmitted them, yet in a changing world they gradually proved inadequate. The attitude of the community was increasingly disclosed and literary taste increased daily until we reach the end of the Chou dynasty. At that time they desired to adopt the manners and customs of the Hsia and Shan dynasties, but it was even then impossible to do so. How much less would they have been able to adopt those of the T'ang and Yü dynasties, or those of the time of Hsi and Huang! However, the path of duty was the same, though their methods of government had changed. Confucius recorded the doctrine of Yao and Shun as if they had been his ancestors, and elegantly exhibited the regulations of Wăn and Wu, which were really the principles of Yao and Shun.[1] But the methods of proper government were different, and thus it was not feasible to introduce the professions of the Hsia and Shan dynasties into the Chou dynasty. It was for this reason that the Duke of Chou desired to exhibit the virtues of the three emperors in his own person. When, however, he saw anything in them not

1. Doctrine of the Mean, Ch. 30, para. 1.

suitable to the time, he hesitated and pondered on it from daylight to night. How much less would it be possible to restore the government of the most ancient times! This the sages surely could abridge."

Speaking again, the Teacher said: "To devote one's self to an affair without effecting anything and without being able, as were the three emperors, to govern according to the times; and to desire to carry out the manners and customs of the ancients, these must be considered as devices of the Buddhists and Taoists. To desire to govern according to the times, and yet not to find the source thereof in the path of duty as did the three emperors; and to rule with a mind seeking honor and wealth, this is an occupation lower than that of a tyrant. Though numerous later scholars discussed back and forth, they merely discussed violent, audacious moral conduct." . . .

The Moral Purpose of the Sages

I said: "Leaving foot-prints in order to exhibit precepts also implies cherishing and defending the source of moral principles. Does not correcting the corresponding evils in order to prevent wickedness keep the passions of men from shooting forth?"

The Teacher said: "Surely the sage wrote the classics with this in mind. But one need not dote on literary expressions."

I again made inquiry saying: "The evil may serve as a warning signal. If one heeds the warning and corrects the evils, it may serve to prevent wickedness. Since they are only in the Book of Poetry, why not expunge Chen and Wei (two odes)? Is the assertion of former scholars true, that the evils may serve to regulate the easy-going habits of men?"

The Teacher said: "The Book of Poetry is not the original book of the Confucianists. Confucius said, 'Banish the songs of Cheng. The songs of Cheng are licentious.'[1] He also said, 'I hate the way in which the songs of Chen confound the music of Ya.'[2] That the songs of Chen and Wei are the sounds of a decaying state is according to the domestic discipline of the Confucianists. The three hundred sections which Confucius chose are all called the music of Ya.[3] All may be played in the temple of Heaven or for a village clan. All, therefore, were played pleasantly and harmoniously and greatly promoted virtuous disposition and changed evil usages. Why were the songs of Chen and Wei omitted? Because they fostered the growth of licentiousness and led to adultery. They doubtless were again adopted by ordinary scholars after the burning of the books by Emperor Ch'in, for the sake of making up full three hundred sections. They are expressions of debauchery such as are frequently gladly transmitted by ordinary vulgar people. The alleys of today are full of that sort of conversation. That wicked men may serve as a warning to the easygoing tendency of men, is a manner of approach which seeks verbal form without getting any real advantage, while at the same time it engages in apologizing discussions."

Because of interest in the loss of the original sayings of the ancients, I at first listened to the instruction of the Teacher, but was really fearful, doubtful, and without any point of contact. After I had heard the Teacher's instruction for a long time, I gradually realized that I must face about and rectify my steps. After that I first began to have faith that the learning of the Teacher had come direct from Confucius, and that the remaining discussions were all bypaths. Such discussions intercept the stream. He says that the investigating of things consists in making the purpose sincere; the understanding of virtue, in cultivating one's

1. Analects, Book XV, Ch. 10, para. 6.
2. Ibid., Book XVII, Ch. 18.
3. Refined, elegant music. Professor Alexander Y. Lee prefers to call it civil music.

self; the investigation of heaven-given principles, in exhausting one's disposition; the maintaining of constant inquiry and study, in honoring one's virtuous nature; the extending of learning, in keeping one's self under the restraint of the rules of propriety; being discriminating, in being undivided; and other like sayings. At first these are hard to harmonize, but after one has thought about them for a long time one spontaneously gesticulates with hands and feet.

Practical Ethical Instruction[1]

The Teacher said: "Seize hold of a good resolution as if the mind were distressed. Will there be any time to engage in idle talk or to care for idle affairs, if the mind is fully occupied with its distress?"

I, Lu Ch'eng, made inquiry saying: "There is the matter of mastering one's mind. If in studying one is engaged entirely with study, or in receiving guests one is completely engaged in receiving guests, may these be considered as examples of being undivided?"

The Teacher said: "If in being fond of women one gives one's self completely to salaciousness, or in desiring wealth one devotes one's self entirely to covetousness, may these be considered as instances of mastering one's mind? This is what is called urging things and should not be considered as mastering the mind. To master one's mind implies mastering moral principles."[1]

I made inquiry regarding the fixing of one's determination. The Teacher said: "It is simply a question of keeping heaven-given principles in mind; for this in itself is what is meant by fixing one's determination. If one is able to remember this, it will obviously become gradually fixed in the mind. It may be compared to the Taoists' saying, 'a matrix which brings forth the virtues of the sage.' One who

---

1. "Moral principles" here as elsewhere may also be translated "heaven-given principles" or "natural law."

585

constantly harbors a regard for natural law little by little becomes a beautiful, great sage and spirit-man. But it is also necessary, in obedience to this thought, to nurture and practice these principles."

The Teacher said: "If during the day one feels that work is becoming annoying, one should sit and rest. One should study though one feels an aversion to it. This is also giving a remedy for disease. In having intercourse with friends, mutually strive to be humble; for then you will derive benefit from your friendship. In case you strive for superiority you will be injured."

Later Scholars Wrote to Show Their Own Skill

I made inquiry saying, "There have been many commentators in the past. It is possible that some of them have brought confusion into right learning."

The Teacher replied: "The mind of man completely embraces natural law. The books written by sages and virtuous men, just as the artist's work that gives a life-like expression, show men the general outline so that they may earnestly seek the truth in them. The mental energy of the sages, as well as their bearing, their sayings, their joys, their actions, and their behavior, assuredly are things that could not be transmitted. When later generations wrote commentaries they took the things the sages had outlined, and transcribed them according to the pattern. But they did more than this; for they also falsely separated them and interpolated them so that they might thereby show their own skill. In doing so they have strayed far from the truth."

The Sage Lives True to Nature

I made inquiry saying, "Does the unlimited adaptability of the sage not also first have to be acquired?"

The Teacher said: "How can so much be acquired? The mind of the sage is like a bright mirror. There is only bright-

586

ness there, and thus the response will be true to the influence brought to bear upon it. It will reflect everything truly. Past forms do not linger there; nor does it need to prepare for those which it has not reflected. If according to the expositions of later generations it is necessary that preparation be made, it is quite contrary to the learning of the sages. Chou Kung regulated the rites of propriety and provided music in order to educate the Empire; and this all sages are able to accomplish. But why did not Yao and Shun accomplish it? Why was it delayed until the time of Chou Kung? Confucius revised the Six Classics in order to instruct all later generations. This, too, all sages are able to do. Why did not Chou Kung first accomplish it? Why was it delayed until the time of Confucius? One may know from these situations that when the sage meets with definite conditions, he does a definite work to meet the specific conditions. The only fear one need entertain is lest the mirror be clouded. One need not fear that when the thing comes before it, it will fail to reflect. Investigation of the change of events must also be carried on in accordance with the times. Naturally the student must first complete the task of brightening up the mirror. He should be grieved if his mind cannot become like a bright mirror, and should not grieve because things are continually changing."

I said, "Surely what you have said is of no immediate concern to me, for I have already made preparation for all sorts of imaginable circumstances. What do you think of such a reply?"

He said, "That way of talking is originally good. But if you do not carefully consider it, it brings distress."

The Principles of Righteousness Are Inexhaustible

The Teacher said: "The principles of righteousness have no fixed abode and are inexhaustible. I say unto you, Do not because of having acquired some virtue say, I will cease acquiring." He said again, "In ten years, twenty years,

587

fifty years, do not cease." At another time he spoke again, saying, "Sageness is like the evil of Chien and Chou.[1] Truly after their time evil was inexhaustible. If Chieh and Chou had not died, would evil have ceased? If virtue may be exhausted, why did King Wen look toward the right path as if he could not see it?"[2]

I made inquiry saying: "When I am tranquil I am conscious of good ideas, but when I meet with events (am subject to stimulation) the situation is different. How do you account for this?"

The Teacher said: "This shows that you know how to cultivate tranquility but do not understand how to control yourself. For this reason you are prostrate whenever you meet with a difficulty. When one has experience in affairs, he is able to stand firmly. Whether at rest or occupied, his purpose is fixed." . . .

Tranquility of Mind Explained

I made inquiry saying, "May the time in which one is in a tranquil state of mind be said to be a state of equilibrium?"

The Teacher said: "Men of today stay their minds only by controlling their passion nature, and thus when they are in a state of tranquility the passion nature alone is tranquil. This cannot be considered as the state of equilibrium in which there are no stirrings of feeling."

I said: "Though they are not in the state of equilibrium, are they not striving for it?"

He said: "The individual must expel passion and cherish natural law before he really engages in the task. When in a state of tranquility, one should constantly meditate how to get rid of passion and how to cherish natural law; and when at work one should also strive for the same end.

1. The Emperor Chieh ruled about 1818 B.C. He was detested for his cruelty. The Emperor Chou was the last ruler of the Shang dynasty. His crimes caused the overthrow of the dynasty at about 1154 B.C.
2. Mencius, Book IV, Pt. II, Ch. 20, para. 3.

It makes no difference whether one be in a state of tranquility or not. If one depends upon the state of tranquility, the fault of loving tranquility and despising activity gradually develops, and in connection therewith a great many other faults that are hidden away in the mind and will never be dislodged. As soon as conditions are favorable, they flourish as of old. In case action according to principles is the motivating purpose, how can there fail to be tranquility? But if tranquility itself is made the purpose, there will certainly be no compliance with principles."

The Harm of Foregone Conclusions

I made inquiry saying, "The disciples of Confucius discussed their wishes. Yu (Tzǔ-lu) and Ch'iu (Jan-yu) wished to be entrusted with a government position; Kung-hsi Chih wished to be responsible for ceremony and music. All these are very useful. But when one reaches the words of Tseng Hsi (Tseng Tien), only play is mentioned. Yet the sage favored him.[1] How is this to be interpreted?"

The Teacher said: "The three disciples had foregone conclusions and arbitrary predeterminations. Having these, they certainly would be turned aside from their purpose. In case they were able to carry out their desires, they would not be able to do the other important thing. Tseng Tien's wish, on the other hand, was without preconceived ideas and arbitrary predeterminations, and implied doing what is in accord with one's station and not desiring to go beyond this. Such a viewpoint means that when situated among barbarous tribes one does what is proper among barbarous tribes; that in sorrow and difficulty one adapts one's self to a position of sorrow and difficulty; and that there is no situation in which one is not self-possessed.

1. *Ibid.*, Book XI, Ch. 25, para. 3-7.

According to the language of the three disciples, the individual is merely a tool. Tseng Tien's wish implied that the individual is not to be a tool. Since each of the three disciples wished to perfect his ability with majesty, they were not like the ordinary man who speaks vainly and lacks genuineness. For these reasons the master also favored their desires."

How to Make Progress in Knowledge

I made inquiry saying, "What shall the individual do when he finds that he is making no progress in knowledge?"

The Teacher said: "In devoting one's self to study, one must have a point of departure. One should work from the starting-point forward, and advance by gradually completing each branch of study. The immortals have a good simile when speaking of small children; 'The child in its mother's womb consists only of pure vital force.' What knowledge can it have? After birth it is first able to cry; a little later, to laugh; still later, to recognize its parents and brothers; and after that it is able to stand, walk, grasp, and carry. This is universally true. It implies that mental and physical energy increases, that strength becomes more vigorous, and intelligence more ample as the days pass. These capacities are not acquired through direct endeavor or through a series of investigations after birth. This shows that there is a source. That the sage (Confucius) assumed regal sway over heaven and earth and nourished all things, is merely the result of progressive development from the equilibrium in which there is no stirring of pleasure, anger, sorrow, or joy. Later scholars do not understand what is meant by 'the investigation of things.' They see that the sage was omniscient and omnipotent, and thereupon desire at the very beginning to complete their quest. Is that in harmony with natural law?"

He spoke further saying: "In fixing the determination

590

one must work as though he were cultivating a tree. When the young tree has the first rootlets it does not yet have a trunk, and when the trunk appears it does not yet have branches. After the branches come the leaves, and after the leaves, the flowers and the fruit. When you first cultivate the roots you need only care for them by watering them. You should not think of cultivating branches, leaves, flowers, and fruit. What advantage is there in being anxious? But you should not forget to care for the tree and water it, lest perchance there be no branches, leaves, flowers, or fruit."

I said: "What shall be done when one studies and is unable to understand?"

The Teacher said: "It shows that the quest is confined to the meaning of the individual characters, and that therefore one does not understand the thought of what is read. This is not equal to the method of those who devoted themselves to education in ancient times, for they read much and were able to explain it. But the unfortunate thing was that though they were able to expound very clearly, they did not really gain any advantage. It is necessary to work on the base of native endowment. Whosoever is unable to understand or unable to practice should return in his work to his original mind. Then he should be able to comprehend. The Four Books and the Five Classics discuss the original nature of the mind. The original nature of the mind is to be identified with the path of duty (truth). He who understands the original nature of his mind thereby understands the path of duty, for the two cannot be distinguished. This is the point of departure in studying."

Some one inquired about the philosopher Chu, saying, "In case a man devotes himself to study, he need pay attention only to mind and principles. How is this to be interpreted?"

The Teacher said, "Mind is nature, and nature includes law and order. The character *yü* (and) after 'mind' perhaps makes it inevitable that they be considered as two. It will depend upon the way the student uses his good judgment with reference to this."

A Tentative Explanation of Evil

Some one said, "All men have natural endowment (mind), and the mind is the embodiment of heaven-given principles (natural law). Why then do some devote themselves to virtue and others to vice?"

The Teacher said, "The mind of the evil man has lost its original nature."

I made inquiry saying: "Analyze heaven-given principles and you will find them extremely pure and not in the least confused; unite them again and you will have exhausted their greatness and there will be nothing left. How is this to be understood?"

The Teacher replied: "Perhaps they will not be exhausted. Is it really possible that natural laws will admit of being analyzed, and how can they be reassembled? When one attains what the sages call the state of being discriminating and undivided, they have then been exhausted."

The Teacher said: "Self-investigation should be nurtured when one is busy with the affairs of life; the nurture of self should be investigated when one is not thus occupied."

The Great Problems of Life

I frequently made inquiry about Hsiang-shan's sayings regarding the way in which one should expend his energy with reference to human feelings and passions, as well as with reference to the vicissitudes of life.

The Teacher said: "There are no crises and problems beyond those of passion and change. Are not pleasure, anger, sorrow, and joy passions of men? Seeing, hearing, talking, working, wealth and honor, poverty and lowliness, sorrow and difficulty, death and life, all are vicissitudes of life. All are included in the passions and feelings of men. These need only to be in a state of perfect equilibrium and harmony, which, in turn, depends upon being watchful over one's self."

I made inquiry saying, "Is it true that we have the names benevolence, righteousness (duty to one's neighbor), propriety, and wisdom because we ourselves have manifested them?" The Teacher said, "Yes."

The Connotation of the Word "Nature"

On another day I said, "Are the feelings of commiseration, shame, dislike, modesty, complaisance, approval, and disapproval to be considered as nature manifesting virtue?"

The Teacher said: "Benevolence, justice, propriety, and wisdom are nature manifesting virtue. There is only one nature and no other. Referring to its substance, it is called heaven; considered as ruler or lord, it is called Shang-ti (God); viewed as functioning, it is called fate; as given to men it is called disposition; as controlling the body, it is called mind. Manifested by the mind, when one meets parents, it is called filial piety; when one meets the prince, it is called loyalty. Proceeding from this on the category is inexhaustible, but it is all one nature, even as there is but one man (generic sense). As compared with his father, man is called son; as compared with his son, he is called father. Proceeding from this one may go on indefinitely, yet there is but one man and no more. Man should use his energy on his nature. If he is able to understand clearly the connotation of the word nature, he will be able to distinguish ten thousand principles."

The Great Learning and the Doctrine of the Mean Compared

I made inquiry as to whether the Great Learning and the Doctrine of the Mean were alike or different in doctrine. The Teacher said: "Tzŭ-ssu incorporated the fundamental idea of the Great Learning in the first chapter of the Doctrine of the Mean."

How Confucius Adjusted Mutual Relationships

I made inquiry saying: "Confucius corrected the mutual relationships of the people. Former scholars said: 'Upward one tells the emperor, downward one tells the financial commissioner, that Chê has been cast aside and Ying established.' What do you hold of this?"

The Teacher said: "It is perhaps as described. Can it be that a man who with the utmost respect exhausts propriety in waiting for me to take up official business would be the first discarded by me? Would this be reasonable and right? Since Confucius was willing to give the government to Chê, Chê certainly had thoroughly repented, restored the state to his father and obeyed the sage. Confucius, a man of staunch virtue and complete sincerity, had certainly brought Chê of the state of Wei to a realization that he who has no father cannot be counted a man, and that he must go and welcome his father speedily with tears. The love of father and son is in accordance with nature. In case Chê truly and thoroughly repented in this manner, could K'uai Wai fail to be influenced and satisfied? When K'uai-Wai had returned, Chê would give him the state and ask to be executed. Since Wai would then have been influenced by his son, and the master, a man of complete sincerity, would have used his influence for peace in this matter, the father in turn would be unwilling to receive the state and would order Chê to rule. The body of ministers and the people would then also desire Chê to act as ruler. Chê, on the other hand, would confess his crime, request the emperor and tell the financial commissioner and all the noblemen that he wished to give the state to his father. Wai, the body of ministers, and the people would then publish the excellence of Chê's new awakening and unselfish filial piety, and would request the emperor and tell the financial commissioner and noblemen that they truly desired Chê to be the prince. Thereby the requests would center on Chê to cause him again to be the prince of the State of Wei. Chê would have no recourse except to do as in the story of a later emperor's father; that is, command the ministers and people to honor Wai as father of the duke, prepare the things necessary for the comfort of his father, and not till then step back and take up his position. In that way the prince would have carried out the doctrine of the prince, the minister that of the minister, the father that of the father, the son that of the son. The mutual relations would have been corrected, and conversation become filial. When once Chê had promoted this, he would be able to govern the Empire. The adjustment which Confucius made of the mutual relationships was perhaps of this kind."

Sorrow as a Test of True Learning

While I was the official in charge of the granaries of the Court of Ceremonies, I unexpectedly received a letter from home saying that my son was dangerously ill. My mind was filled with unendurable sorrow.

The Teacher said: "At this time you certainly should apply yourself to the truth (path of duty). If you allow this opportunity to slip by, of what advantage will it be for you to expound learning when you are in prosperity? You should gain experience now. The love of a father for his son is by nature the highest type of affection; but in accordance with natural law there is a state of equilibrium and harmony, which when exceeded leads to selfishness.

If at this point men understand that the carrying out of natural law means love, then they will not realize that former sorrows and afflictions are examples of the saying, 'If the mind be under the influence of sorrow and distress, a man will be incorrect in his conduct.' The influence of the seven passions is in most people excessive; in a few only does it fail to reach its proper proportion. When it is excessive, it is not in accordance with the original nature of the mind. It must be adjusted to reach the mean, for then first is it right. For instance, at the death of parents, is it not true that the son desires to mourn unto death because in that way his mind is put at rest? But it is nevertheless said, 'The collapse should not injure the natural disposition.' This does not imply that the sage is trying to quell it by force, but that nature has its limits which cannot be exceeded, and that everyone should recognize the nature of the mind. Nothing should be either added to or subtracted from this."

Many Fail to Reach the Ideal of the Classics

"Do not say that the equilibrium in which the passions are not manifested is kept by all men, that nature and its use have a common source, and that having nature, you also have its use. If one keeps the equilibrium in which the seven passions have been suppressed, one also is in the state of harmony in which they are manifested in proper degree. The present generation has been unable to acquire this harmony. From this one must know that the equilibrium in which they are suppressed cannot have been completely acquired.

"The restorative influence of the night is spoken of with reference to ordinary men; but the student, if he works diligently, may in the daytime, whether at work or at leisure, be the focus of the gathering and development of this restorative influence. It is not necessary to speak of the influence of night with reference to the sage." . . .

Adaptability is Indispensable

Wei Ch'ien made inquiry regarding the saying of Mencius, "By holding the medium without leaving room for the exigency of circumstances, it becomes like their holding their one point."[1]

The Teacher said: "The medium is merely natural law. And yet at any time it may change? How then can it be held? It certainly means that it must be suitably regulated in accordance with the occasion, and for that reason it would be difficult to establish a rule in advance. It would be as though later scholars through their expositions·undertook to determine a pattern without leaving a loophole for any change. That would carry with it the idea of holding."

T'ang Hsü made inquiry saying: "Is it true that in fixing the determination one should constantly cherish good thoughts, do good, and expel evil?"

The Teacher said: "The cherishing of good thoughts is in accordance with natural law. Such thoughts are themselves virtue. What other virtue shall one deliberate upon? They are not evil. What evil shall one expel? Thoughts are like the roots and rootlets of a tree. He who is fixing his determination need only fix his thoughts for a long time. When one is able to follow the desire of the heart without overstepping propriety, one's determination has become habitual.[2]

"It is of first importance that mental and animal energy, virtue, words, and acts should for the most part be controlled (gathered together). That they will lack unity at times is inevitable. Heaven and earth, man and things, are all alike in this.". . .

1. *Ibid.*, Book VII, Pt. I, Ch. 26, para. 3.
2. Analects, Book II, Ch. 4, para. 6.

Selfishness is a Root of Evil

The Teacher said: "Pleasure, anger, sorrow, and joy are in their natural condition in the state of equilibrium and harmony. As soon as the individual adds a little of his own ideas, he oversteps and fails to maintain the state of equilibrium and harmony. This implies selfishness.

"In subduing one's self, one must clear out selfish desire completely, so that not a bit is left. If a little is left, all sorts of evil will be induced to make their entrance.". . .

The Mind May Be Compared to a Mirror

Yueh-jen said: "The mind may be compared to a mirror. The mind of the sage is like a bright mirror, the mind of the ordinary man like a dull mirror. The saying of more recent natural philosophy may be compared to using it as a mirror to reflect things. If effort is expended in causing the mirror to reflect while the glass is still dull, how can one succeed? The natural philosophy of the Teacher is like a polished and brightened mirror. When after having been polished the mirror is bright, the power of reflecting has not been lost."

He asked regarding the general plan and the details (fineness and coarseness) of the doctrine.[1] The Teacher said: "The doctrine has neither general plan nor detailed structure. What men consider the general plan and the details may be made clear in examining a house. When one first enters it, one sees only the general plan. After a while one sees the supports and walls. Later still such things as the ornamental duckweed upon the supports become apparent. But all this is only a part of the same house."

---

1. Translated literally. May perhaps be freely translated "minutiae."

Lack of Effort Involves Selfishness and Hinders Progress

The Teacher said: "Sirs, how is it that recently when you approach me you have so few questions to ask regarding the things about which you are in doubt? When a man fails to put forth effort, he invariably believes that he well knows how to devote himself to study, and that all that is necessary is to follow the order and act (*i.e.* study). He certainly does not know that selfish desire increases every day like the dust of the earth. If one neglects to sweep for a day, another layer is added. If one really works with determination one realizes that the doctrine is inexhaustible. The more one searches, the profounder it becomes, until its essence and purity are fully comprehended."

Some one made inquiry saying: "After knowledge has been completed one can say that the thoughts are sincere. At present neither moral law nor the passions of men are throughly understood.[1] Under such circumstances how is anyone in a position to begin to subdue himself?"

The Teacher said: "If a person unceasingly applies himself truly and earnestly, he will daily better comprehend the subtle essence of the moral principles of the mind, as well as the subtlety of selfish desires. If he does not use his efforts in controlling himself, he will continually talk and yet never comprehend the meaning of moral principles or of selfish desire. The situation may be likened to a man traveling. When (by walking) he has covered a stage, he understands that stage. When he reaches a fork in the road and is in doubt he makes inquiry, and having made inquiry he again proceeds. In this way he gradually reaches his destination. Men of today are unwilling to abide by the moral principles which they already know, and to expel the passions they have already recognized; but are

1. Moral lay is its psychological aspects. May be translated "natural law."

599

downcast because they are unable to understand completely. They merely indulge in idle discussions. Of what advantage is this? They should wait until in the process of subduing and controlling themselves there are no more selfish motives to subdue, for then it would not be too late to sorrow because of their inability to understand fully.". . .

The Development of the Original Nature of the Mind is of First Importance

He made inquiry saying: "Is it necessary first to investigate the mutual human relationships, the things of nature, measures, and numbers?"

The Teacher said: "It is necessary to develop the original nature of the mind; then its use will include the state of equilibrium. In case one nourishes the original nature of the mind and attains to the equilibrium in which there is no stirring of feelings, there surely is present the state of harmony which results when the feelings are stirred and act in due degree. Of course it must be exhibited. If mind is lacking, the mutual human relationships, the things of nature, as well as measures and numbers, would have no relation to the self, though one explain them first; but would simply imply pretension and superficiality. When at times the feelings are displayed, the individual naturally does not maintain the equilibrium. I do not wish to say that the mutual relationships, the things of nature, measures, and numbers should be entirely left out of consideration. If the individual knows what is first and what is last, he will be near the truth."

He spoke again saying: "Man must develop in accordance with his capacity. Capacity constitutes his ability to accomplish things. For instance, the music of K'uei and the agriculture of Chi were noteworthy because they were

600

in harmony with their natural endowment.[1] He who would complete himself need only preserve the nature of his mind guileless in natural law. When the occasions on which he acts all take their origin from nature itself, he may be said to have ability. When a person reaches the state in which he is completely in accord with natural law, he is no longer a mere utensil. Had K'uei and Chi been ordered to exchange professions and engage in them successfully, they would have been able to do so."

Again he said: "In a position of wealth and honor to do what is proper to a position of wealth and honor, in a position of sorrow and difficulty to do what is proper to a position of sorrow and difficulty, implies that one is not a mere machine.[2] This an be accomplished only by the man who cultivates an upright mind."

The Teacher said: "To dig a pond several hundred *mu*[3] in size, but without a spring, is not equal to digging a well a few feet deep with a spring in it that runs without ceasing." The Teacher said this as he sat at the side of a pool near which there was a well. Subsequently he used this figure in elucidating learning.

The Mind Should Rule the Senses

He made inquiry saying, "In what way may the mind devote itself to things?"

The Teacher said: "When the people's prince is upright, reverent, and majestic, and the six boards distinguish their respective official duties, the Empire is well governed. In the same way the mind should govern the five senses. In our day when the eye wishes to see, the mind applies itself to color, and when the ear wishes to

1. K'uei was an officer who acted as director of music at the request of Emperor Shun. Chi was Emperor Shun's minister of agriculture.
2. The Doctrine of the Mean, Ch. 14, para. 2.
3. Yang and Yin are the two primeval forces.

hear, the mind devotes itself to sound. It is as though the people's prince were himself to take a seat on the Board of Civil Offices, when he wishes to choose an official, or on the Board of War, when he wishes to move the troops. In this way the original character of the prince would be sacrificed and in addition the six boards also would be unable to perform their official duties.". . .

A Virtuous Man Does Not Exalt Himself

I made inquiry saying: "Former scholars said: 'The truths expressed by the sage show him forth as lowly and humble. The words of a virtuous man exhibit and exalt his personality.' Do you consider that true?"

The Teacher said: "No. A statement such as that is false. The sage may be compared to heaven. There is no place where heaven is not present. Above the sun, moon and stars heaven is found, and below the nine divisions it is also found. How can heaven descend and make itself lowly? The implications here are greatness and the exercise of a transforming influence. The good man may be compared to a lofty mountain peak, maintaining his lofty height. Nevertheless, one a thousand feet high cannot stretch and become ten thousand feet high, and one ten thousand feet high cannot stretch and become a hundred thousand feet high. The good man does not exhibit and exalt himself. It is false to say, 'exhibits and exalts himself.' "

Nature is the Highest Good

The Teacher said: "Nature is the highest good. Nature is in its original condition devoid of all evil, and for this reason is called the highest good. To rest in the highest good implies returning to one's natural condition."

He (Shang-ch'ien) made inquiry saying, "Knowledge of the highest good is characteristic of my nature, and my nature is to be identified with my mind. My mind, however, is the place in which the highest good rests. In that case I should not, as of old, seek for the highest good confusedly in external things, but should fix my determination. When the determination has been fixed, it will not give trouble. Confusion will give place to quietude; quietude and absence of disorderly activity will usher in peace. When there is peace, both mind and will are interested in this alone. If in all planning and thinking I earnestly seek, I will surely get this highest good; but it can be acquired only after one is able to take serious thought for it. Is this manner of expounding the situation correct or not?"

The Teacher replied, "In general, it is."

Benevolence is the Principle of Continuous Creation and Growth

Shang-ch'ien made inquiry saying: "The philosopher Ch'eng said, 'The benevolent person considers heaven, earth, and all nature as an all-pervading unity.' How, then, does it come that the philosopher Mo, who loved all things, said nothing about benevolence?"

The Teacher said: "It is very hard to give an adequate reason for this. You yourselves, Sirs, will need by means of introspection to investigate this thoroughly up to the point where you understand it, for then first will you get satisfaction. Benevolence is the fundamental principle of continuous creating and growth. Though these are boundless in extent and everywhere present, their progress and manifestation proceed gradually. For instance, at the winter solstice one Yang is brought forth, and from this one Yang later six other Yangs are gradually developed[12] Were it not for the development of this one Yang, how could the six Yangs be generated? And the same holds true of the Yin. Because it is gradual in its operation, there is a beginning; and because there is a beginning, there is a bringing forth. Because it continues to bring forth, there is no ceasing. The tree begins by developing a bud. This is the point at which the tree's purpose to grow starts. After the bud has developed the trunk appears, and then the branches and leaves; and from that time it grows continually. If it has no bud, how can it have trunk, branches, and leaves? Its ability to develop a bud surely depends upon the root underneath; for if there is a root there can be growth, and without the root it must die. From what shall the buds develop if there is no root? The love of father and son, elder brother and younger brother, is the point at which the purpose of man's mind to develop begins. Just as in the tree the buds shoot forth, thus from this love toward the people and love of things trunk, branches, and leaves develop. The man named Mo loved all things without difference of degree. He looked upon his own father, his own son, his own elder brother, and his own younger brother even as he did upon the stranger; and for that reason he lacked a point from which he might start to develop. Where there is no ability to grow a bud, there are no roots, and consequently no continuous development. How can such a condition be called benevolence? Filial piety and respectfulness toward the elder brother are the beginning of benevolence; benevolence, however, must be manifested from within."

Action According to Moral Principles is Unselfish

Shang-ch'ien made inquiry saying: "Yen P'ing said, 'He who acts in accordance with moral principles does not have a selfish mind.' In what way should I distinguish between moral principles and unselfishness?"

The Teacher said: "The mind is to be identified with moral principles. When one's mind is freed from selfishness, acting in accordance with moral principles is a necessary accompaniment. If one does not act in accordance with moral principles, his mind is selfish. Perhaps it would be better not to distinguish between mind and moral principles in expounding this."

He made further inquiry saying: "The Buddhists are not infected by any of the selfishness of lust, and thus appear to have a mind free from selfishness. On the other hand, they outwardly disregard human relationships, and thus do not appear to be acting in accordance with moral principles."

The Teacher said: "This belongs to the same class of things. They all carry out the mind of a selfish personality."

Huang Tsung-hsi

HUANG TSUNG-HSI (1610-1695). Strongly motivated by the spirit of nationalism, Huang Tsung-hsi became involved in politics early in his youth. After the Manchus had succeeded in overthrowing the Ming Dynasty (1644), he withdrew from active participation in the political life of China and devoted his remaining years to pure scholarship. His treatise on political science (*Ming-I Tai-Fang Lu*), completed in 1662 and published in 1673, strongly influenced revolutionaries at the end of the Ch'ing dynasty. It is probably the most concise and most important critique of Chinese imperial institutions ever made from the Confucian viewpoint. His *History of Sung and Yüan Thinkers* and *Lives and Works of Ming Scholars* (1676) are generally considered to be the first important history of Chinese philosophy.

The selection presented here is from his famous treatise on political science. The treatise contains some surprisingly modern ideas on education, land reform, taxation, civil service examinations, etc. Huang Tsung-hsi's importance lies not in his originality, however, but in his ability to fuse the broad scholarship characteristic of the Chu Hsi school with an active interest in contemporary issues.

Kingship

From *Translations from the Chinese (The Importance of Understanding)*, by Lin Yutang, Cleveland and New York, The World Publishing Company, 1960.

IN prehistoric times, every man labored for himself and for his private interests, and there was no one to think of the public good or fight a common evil of society. Then the kings arose who worked for the public good and not the good of their own selves. They fought what was evil to the community as a whole and neglected what might not be good for their own selves. Thus kings were people who worked a thousand times harder than the people, without benefit to themselves. This as hardly an enviable position. Therefore, there were those who worked for the public benefit and never wanted to be called kings, like Shuyu and Wukuang, and other rulers who worked for the public benefit as kings and then handed over their power to others, like Yao and Shun; again others who were made kings and were forced to remain kings, like Yu. It was human nature, whether ancient or modern, not to relish such a position.

The kings of later times were different. They concentrated the power of government in themselves, and having done so, thought it even allowable to take all the profits of the land for themselves and throw all that was disagreeable and onerous upon others, so that the people were not able to work for their own benefits or their own good, while the profits of the land became the private property of one family. At first, the kings felt embarrassed, but later they lost such embarrassment. The land and the people then belonged to one ruling house, the exclusive right and privilege to be handed down to their children and their children's children. The First Emperor of Han betrayed this way of thinking when he said to a scholar, "Do you think my success at my *profession* is greater or lesser than yours?" Being a king *was* a profession, like all others carried on for benefit.

The difference lies in this: in ancient times, the people were the masters, and the kings the guests, and the object of the kings' labors was the people. Now it is the kings who are the masters and the people the guests, and there is not one corner of the earth where the people can live peacefully their own lives, all because of the rulers. Therefore, when someone aspires to be a king, he does not mind sacrificing the lives of millions and taking away children from their parents in order to work for his "private property." Without the slightest qualm of conscience, he says to himself, "I am building up this ruling house for my children." And when he has attained to kingship, he does not mind grinding out the bones and marrow of the people and breaking up families to labor and to serve that he alone may enjoy all the luxury and amusements of an easy living. Without a qualm of conscience, he says again to himself, "I am entitled to the earnings of my property, am I not?"

Kings have thus become the great enemy of the people. For if there were no kings, people would be able to work for their own benefit and their own living. Alas! is this the purpose for which kings exist?

In ancient times, the people loved their kings like their father and compared them to Heaven. That was well deserved. Now the people regard their kings as their enemy and call them "That lonely person." That is well deserved, too. There are narrow-minded scholars who still say that the cardinal relationship between king and subject is eternal, to the extent they doubt the propriety of Tang and

609

Wu in overthrowing their overlord tyrants Chieh and Chou, and are inclined to discredit the story of those patriots like Poyi and Shuchi who refused to serve a conqueror. It would seem to them that the lacerated flesh and bones of the millions of people were worth less than the mouse's head of a foreigner. Could it be that they truly believe that the whole world exists for the particular benefit of one person and one family in the heart of the Creator?

Therefore King Wu [who rose to overthrow a tyrant] was a sage. Mencius [who regarded it as right under certain circumstances for the people to regard their ruler as enemy] spoke the words of a sage. The kings of later times wish to wrap up kingship in the sacred cloak of a phrase "like father and like Heaven" behind which the people are not allowed to peer. Such rulers hold the views of Mencius as most inconvenient to themselves and would like to dethrone Mencius[1] from his place of worship. The narrow-minded scholars are to blame for leading them to think this way.

However, if it was possible for a king to maintain his private property forever and ever, one could understand the selfish motive which prompted such action. Since the king thought of the land as his own property, it was equally natural for some other people to desire to gain control of that same piece of property. The king could place all his property in an iron safe and have it heavily padlocked. But after all, there was only one man or family that wished to guard it, and many who wanted to get at it. In a few generations, and sometimes within the king's own lifetime, the blood of the king's own children flowed! People used to wish that they might never be born in a royal family, and the king Yitsung said once to his young princess, "Why were you doomed to be born in my family?" What a bitter

---

1. Mencius has always been regarded as cofounder of Confucianism with Confucius. One always speaks of Kung-Meng (or Confucius-Mencius).

confession of remorse! Is this not enough to cool off the ambition of someone who starts out to found a dynasty?

Therefore, if the functions of king and ministers are clearly understood, no one would want to occupy the position of power, as in the case of Shuyu and Wukuang in ancient times. If the functions of king and subject are not clearly understood, everybody would have the right to wish the throne. It may be difficult to understand the proper functions of king and subject, but it should not be difficult to weigh the advantages and disadvantages between temporary glory and a lasting disaster.

Ku Yen-wu

KU YEN-WU (1613-1682). The Ming dynasty came to an end with the fall of Peking to the Manchus in 1644. The advent of the Ch'ing dynasty (1644-1911) brought a shift in thinking and resulted in the rise of what is now known as Han Learning. Believing that Neo-Confucianists of the Sung (960-1279) and Ming (1368-1644) dynasties had been corrupted by the ideas of Buddhism and Tâoism, the followers of the new movement urged a return to the classical commentaries of the Han period (206 B.C.-265 A.D.).

Ku Yen-wu was born in the last days of the Ming dynasty. The chaotic conditions of his time drew his interest to economics, government, and other practical subjects. Determined to discover why the Ming dynasty had fallen and how a repetition of its mistakes could be avoided, he devoted his energies to intensive research. He ridiculed the intuitionism of the Wang Yang-ming school and insisted that scholars must study practical subjects and return to the ethical teachings of early Confucianism.

He is credited with perfecting the inductive method of research used with remarkable success by textual critics of the Ch'ing period. Thus he opened the way for a great movement that culminated in the adoption of the highest standards of research and evaluation by the group known as the New Text School.

True Learning: Broad Knowledge, and a Sense of Shame

From *Sources of Chinese Tradition*, Volume II, edited by William Theodore de Bary, New York, Columbia University Press, 1960.

[From "A Letter to a Friend Discussing the Pursuit of Learning," *T'ing-lin shih-wen chi*, 3:1a-2b]

I T is a matter of great regret to me that for the past hundred odd years, scholars have devoted so much discussion to the mind and human nature, all of it vague and quite incomprehensible. We know from the *Analects* that "fate and humanity (*jen*) were things which Confucius seldom spoke of" (IX, 1) and that Tzŭ-kung "had never heard him speak on man's nature and the way of Heaven" (V, 12). Though he mentioned the principle of human nature and fate in the appendices to the *Book of Changes*, he never discussed them with others. When asked about the qualities of a gentleman, Confucius said: "In his conduct he must have a sense of shame" (XIII, 20), while with regard to learning he spoke of a "love of antiquity" and "diligent seeking," discussing and praising Yao and Shun and transmitting their tales to his disciples. But he never said so much as a word about the so-called theory of "the precariousness [of the human mind] and the subtlety [of the mind of the Tao] and of the [need for keeping one's mind] refined and undivided,"[1] but only said "sincerely hold fast to the Mean — if within the four seas there be distress and poverty, your Heaven-conferred revenues will come to a perpetual end."[2] Ah, this is the reason for the learning of

1. Referring to the *Book of History*, Counsels of Great Yü II, a passage much quoted by Neo-Confucianists.
2. *Book of History*, Counsels of Great Yü II.

the sage. How simple, how easy to follow! . . . But gentlemen of today are not like this. They gather a hundred or so followers and disciples about them in their studies, and though as individuals they may be as different as grass and trees, they discourse with all of them on mind and nature. They set aside broad knowledge and concentrate upon the search for a single, all-inclusive method; they say not a word about the distress and poverty of the world within the four seas, but spend all their days lecturing on theories of "the weak and subtle," "the refined and the undivided." I can only conclude that their doctrine is more lofty than that of Confucius and their disciples wiser than Tzŭ-kung, and that while they pay honor to the school of Eastern Lu (Confucius) they derive their teaching on the mind directly from the two sage emperors Yao and Shun. . . .

What then do I consider to be the way of the sage? I would say "extensively studying all learning"[1] and "in your conduct having a sense of shame."[2] Everything from your own body up to the whole nation should be a matter of study. In everything from your personal position as a son, a subject, a brother, and a friend to all your comings and goings, your giving and taking, you should have things of which you would be ashamed. This sense of shame before others is a vital matter. It does not mean being ashamed of your clothing or the food you eat, but ashamed that there should be a single humble man or woman who does not enjoy the blessings that are his due. This is why Mencius said that "all things are complete in me" if I "examine myself and find sincerity."[3] Alas, if a scholar does not first define this sense of shame, he will have no basis as a person, and if he does not love antiquity and acquire broad knowledge, his learning will be vain and hollow. These baseless men with their hollow learning day after day pursue the affairs of the sage, and yet I perceive that with each day they only depart further from them.

1. *Analects,* VI, 255.
2. *Analects,* XIII, 20.
3. *Mencius,* VII A, 4.

Wang Fu-chih

WANG FU-CHIH (1619-1693). Born during the final years of the Ming dynasty (1368-1644), Wang Fu-chih tried to support what proved to be a lost cause. Realizing that his efforts to support the Ming cause had failed, he retired to his homeland and devoted his remaining years to scholarly pursuits. He wrote many works on the classics, history, literature, and philosophy. He also set forth his own anti-Manchu political ideas, but his works remained unpublished until two centuries after his death.

It is only recently that his philosophy has been widely appreciated. He attacked both the rationalist Neo-Confucianism of the Sung period (960-1279) and the idealistic tendency of the Ming. In this sense he anticipated Chinese thought of the next two centuries and inaugurated the modern period of Chinese philosophy. His materialistic teachings have caused him to be praised in Communist China as one of the greatest thinkers of all time. His philosophy is similar to that of the great eleventh-century Neo-Confucianist, Chang Tsai.

Man's Nature and Destiny

From *Sources of Chinese Tradition*, Volume I, edited by William Theodore de Bary, New York, Columbia University Press, 1960.

[From *Ch'uan-shan i-shu; Chou-i wai-chuan*, 5:25a-b]

THE whole world is nothing more than an instrument. One cannot say that an instrument is an instrument of the Way, for what is called the Way is simply the way of using an instrument. We know from human experience that if there is no use for an instrument, then the instrument does not exist; conversely, if an instrument actually exists, we need not worry about whether or not it has a use. . . . If there is no instrument, then there is no Way — this statement is seldom made and yet it is absolutely true. . . . Bows and arrows have never existed without the way of shooting them; carriages and carriage horses have never existed without the way of driving them; sacrificial animals and wine, badges and offerings, or bells and chimes, flutes and strings, have never existed without the ways of ritual and music. Therefore the existence of sons demands the existence of the way of a father, or the existence of brothers that of the way of a brother. (There are, however, many "ways" that potentially could exist but actually do not.) Therefore it is quite correct to say that no way exists independent of its instrument.

Many people simply fail to consider the matter carefully enough. Thus the sages of antiquity were able to make use of instruments, but they were not able to make use of the Way, for what is called the "way" *is* the use of instruments. . . . In using them men speak about them and so names come to be fixed to them. These names are fixed to the things from above, as it were, but they also exist among things. One cannot distinguish between a realm of names existing above and one existing among things. So above physical forms there is no so-called realm of the formless. . . . If one tried to set aside instruments and seek for that which existed before the instruments, one might span all the evolutions of past and present, exhaust Heaven, earth, man, and things, and one would not be able to find anything bearing even a name, much less reality. Thus Lao Tzǔ was deluded when he said that the Way exists in emptiness, for emptiness must be empty of instruments also, and Buddha was likewise mistaken when he declared that the Way exists in nothingness, for nothingness must be a nothingness of instruments. One may propound such wild theories endlessly, but one can never escape from instruments, and if one insists upon pronouncing names that are separated from instruments as though one were some god, whom could one hope to deceive?

ON THE INAPPLICABILITY OF ANCIENT INSTITUTIONS TO MODERN TIMES

[From *Tu T'ung-chien lun*, "Hsü-lun," 5b-6b]

The most effective way of governing is to examine the *Book of History* and temper its pronouncements with the words of Confucius. Surely nothing could be better than this. But the crucial point is whether the ruler's heart is reverent or dissolute, and whether his statutes are too lax or too harsh. Those who fall short are lazy, those who go too far do so from a desire to proceed too rapidly. The principal function of government is to make use of worthy men and promote moral instruction, and in dealing with the people to bestow on them the greatest humanity and love. All governments, from those of Yao and Shun, the Three Dynasties, the Ch'in or the Han down to the present must proceed upon this principle. Examining and selecting men according to principles, apportioning taxes and corvées with fairness, keeping order with arms, restraining with punishments, bringing order with statutes and precedents – these are the means by which all governments have achieved success.

But when it comes to setting up detailed regulations or making up directives, then the authors of the *Book of History* or Confucius offer no guidance. Is this because they ignored reality and paid no attention to details? The ancient institutions were designed to govern the ancient world, and cannot be applied to the present day. Therefore the wise man does not try to set up detailed systems. One uses what is right for today to govern the world of today, but this does not mean that it will be right for a later day. Therefore the wise man does not try to hand down laws to posterity. Thus neither the *History* nor Confucius describe feudalism, the well-field system, the triennial and sexennial meetings of feudal lords, the system for punitive expeditions, the establishment of offices or the awarding of benefices. How then should someone who is not the equal in virtue of the emperors Shun and Yü or Confucius still presume on the basis of his reading to lay down a system of laws for all time? It is quite true that the "Documents of Hsia" contains a section called "The Tribute of Yü." But the system described therein pertains only to the Hsia dynasty; the laws of the Hsia kings were by no means followed in the succeeding Shang and Chou periods. The "Documents of Chou" does in fact contain a section called "Institutes of Chou," but here again these apply only to the Chou. They formed the model for the Chou dynasty and were not carried over from the earlier dynasties of Shang and Hsia. . . .

Times change, conditions are different. How then can a government go along with these changes and keep its people from growing idle? There are crises of the moment to be met in each age, but the expedients used to meet them are not necessarily worthy of constituting a whole theory of government. Before the prefectural system was put into effect the people were supposedly following the principles and practices of the ancient kings, and yet these practices were different from what we read of in the *History* and Confucius. It is not necessary that one consult all the ages of the past and try to follow all their usages. In my writings I have sought the source of success and failure in government and tried to bring my ideas into accord with the fundamental principles of the governments of the sages. But when it comes to questions of particular incidents and laws, then one must follow the times and try to determine what is fitting in each case. Every age has its different points of laxity and strictness [in application]; every affair has its contingent circumstances. It is better therefore to have no inflexible rules, lest one use the letter of the law to do violence to its spirit. Everyone makes mistakes at times, so that one should not try to force the world to follow his own arbitrary views. . . . If these people who try to upset all the established ways of the world and throw everything into panic by putting into effect some private theory derived from their reading are allowed to go on having their way, I cannot say how things will end.

ON THE USE OF LAWS . . .

[From *Tu T'ung-chien lun*, 30:13b-15b]

The nation cannot be governed by laws. Yet if all laws disappear, then the people have no way to maintain their livelihood and rulers no way to guard the people. Therefore if the nation is to be governed, there must first be a leader who will set up laws and institutions to make the people understand that there is a Son of Heaven over them and officials in their midst, and that they are assured of protection so that they may plan for their own livelihood. These laws and institutions that are first set up can never be completely good, and if later ages observe them to the letter, they will bring suffering to the people and incite disorder. In this first and tentative stage, the lawmakers, in an effort to correct evil, may be excessively severe or, following the will of the vulgar, may err in the direction of laxity. They can only make a rough beginning and wait for those who come after to refine and finish. For this reason, the Ch'in laws were not uniformly bad chaotic days at the end of the Six States and opened up the way for a new rule by impressing upon the people the fact that laws existed. Then when the Han followed with for the people. Ch'in came to power in the confused and its broad and tolerant regime, it was able to simplify the laws and abolish those which were oppressive, bringing order to the world. . . .

Therefore I have said that if the nation is to be governed, there must first be a leader to set up laws and institutions. Although they may not be the best, they will be better than no laws at all. Han inherited the laws of Ch'in and reformed them; therefore it could not model its system upon that of the Three Dynasties. T'ang took over the laws of the T'o-pa and Yü-wen dynasties and reformed them, and so its system differed from that of the Former and Latter Han. Sung inherited and reformed the laws of the Kuo and Ch'ai regimes and so could not practice the same ways as the T'ang at its height. When bad laws have once been put into effect and the people have grown accustomed to them over a long period, they will inevitably be intent only upon following these laws. If one can only suppress the evil aspects of these laws and gradually improve them, then the world will eventually attain peace. But if the world is continually in a state of confusion, heir only to the dregs of corrupt government of the preceding dynasty, hastening onward in the decline, completely destroying what was good in the old system, the dissolute attacking each other, military upstarts and petty bureaucrats spreading evil in high positions, and if no one appears to correct or change the laws, then even the wisest of sovereigns will have difficulty in bringing about a speedy reform.

Kang Yu-wei

K'ANG YU-WEI (1858-1927). One of modern China's most eminent scholars and statesmen, K'ang Yu-wei, attempted to put into practice the teachings of Confucianism, which he advocated as the state religion. The last great Confucian, he tried in his lectures and writings to picture Confucius as a reformer rather than a conservative, and he succeeded in changing the traditional concepts of Confucius as well as of the Confucian Classics and certain basic Confucian doctrines. Believing that the Western nations owed their strength to their organized religions and their specialization in studies, he insisted that China must import specialized learning and adopt the religion of Confucianism.

A native of the Nan-hai district of Kwangtung (his honorary title was "Master Nan-hai"), he demonstrated his intellectual capacities at an early age. He studied diligently until the age of twenty-one, when he had a mystical experience ("While sitting in meditation . . . I received great enlightenment . . . and believed I was a sage") that caused him to give up instruction under his teacher and retreat to a mountain cave. There he spent his time in studying Taoist and Buddhist writings. Subsequently he traveled, became interested in practical studies, and organized an Anti-Footbinding Society. His unrelenting attempts to encourage reform seemed to have reached the point of fruition in 1898, when he met with the emperor for two hours and discussed reform measures. Many edicts were soon issued and might have brought about wholesale reform if the

Empress Dowager had not intervened, causing him to flee to Hong Kong. He remained abroad until the Republic of China was established in 1912. After he returned to his homeland, he tried twice to restore the monarchy, and failed both times. Finally, he had to leave the capital under the protection of American officials and return to Kwangtung. Shortly before his death, on the occasion of his seventieth birthday, his former pupils and followers gathered to pay him tribute. Liang Ch'i-ch'ao eulogized his teacher as the man who had initiated a new era in the history of China.

The *Ta T'ung Shu,* written in its earliest form when the author was twenty-seven, outlines a utopian conception of the world of the future. It is a world in which the sufferings of mankind have been ended by the establishment of the Universal Society. Revised over the years and given its final form in 1902, the work originally entitled *Universal Principles of Mankind* was too daring and too advanced for the times, according to "Sage K'ang." The first third of the work was published in 1913, but the complete book was not published until 1935, eight years after his death. The first utopian treatise in the long history of Chinese literature is also one of the most realistic in its proposed solutions to the great problems of mankind.

Entering the World and Seeing Universal Suffering

From *The One-World Philosophy of K'ang Yu-wei*, translated by Laurence G. Thompson, London, George Allen & Unwin Ltd., 1958.

THUS we see that the whole world is but a world of grief and misery, all the people of the whole world are but grieving and miserable people, and all the living beings of the whole world are but murdered beings. The azure Heaven and the round Earth are nothing but a great slaughter-yard, a great prison.

The sages have loved [suffering humanity]. They have gone into the sickrooms and jails, scratched a light and illuminated them. They have cooked rice and fed them. They have brought medicines and doctored them. We call them persons of *jen*. They help for the moment. But how can [this] compensate for [all] the suffering? . . .

The all-embracing Primal *Ch'i* created Heaven and Earth. 'Heaven' is [composed of] a single soul-substance; 'Man' is likewise [composed of] a single soul-substance. Although [individual] forms may differ in size, still, they are [all but] parts of the all-embracing *ch'i* of the ultimate beginnings [of the universe]. Ladle out every drop from the great ocean, and there will be nothing different. Confucius said, 'The earth began from spiritual *ch'i;* the spiritual *ch'i* was wind and thunder; the wind and thunder flowed [into] form, and all things came forth to birth.' Spirit is lightning which has awareness. There is nothing into which the lightning-flash cannot penetrate; [similarly], there is nothing which the spiritual *ch'i* cannot affect. Spirit [in] demons, spirit [in] emperors; giving birth to Heaven, giving birth to Earth; whole spirit, divided spirit; only [spirit] in the Beginnings, only [spirit] in man. How minute, how subtle, this stimulatingness of spirit! No creatures are without 'lightning', no creatures are without spirit.

Now spirit is aware-*ch'i*, the 'awareness' of the soul (*hun-chih*), vitality (*ching-shuang*), intelligence, shining virtue (*ming-te*). These several are differing names, but the same actuality. If there is perception and awareness, then there is attraction. Thus is it with the lodestone; how much more is it with man! Compassion is attraction (here we may call it empathy) in action. Therefore, of *jen* (i.e. compassion-attraction-empathy) and knowledge (i.e. awareness), both are harboured within [us], but knowledge (i.e. awareness) is prior [in experience]. *Jen* and knowledge (i.e. intellectual knowledge, this time) are both used [in action], but *jen* is nobler.

Master K'ang says, being that I am a man, I would be uncompassionate to flee from men, and not to share their griefs and miseries. And being that I was born into a family, and [by virtue of] receiving the nurture of others was able to have this life, I then have the responsibilities of a family member. Should I flee from this [responsibility] and abandon this family, my behaviour would be false. How could I bear to be so ungrateful? And why would it not be the same with the public debt we owe to one country and the world? Being that we are born into one country, have received the civilization of one country, and thereby have its knowledge, then we have the responsibilities of a citizen. If we flee from this [responsibility] and abandon this country, this country will perish and its people will be annihilated, and then civilization will be destroyed. This responsibility is [thus] likewise very great.

Being that I was born on the earth, then mankind in the ten thousand countries of the earth are all my brothers (literally, of the same womb) of different bodily types. Being that I have knowledge of them, then I have love (*ch'in*) for them. All that is finest and best of the former

626

wisdom of India, Greece, Persia, Rome, and of present-day England, France, Germany, and America, I have lapped up and drunk, rested on, pillowed on; and my soul in dreams has fathomed it. With the most ancient and noted savants, famous scholars, and great men, I have likewise often joined hands, to sit on mats side by side, sleeves touching, sharing our soup; and I have come to love them. The values and beauties of the dwellings, clothing, food, boats, vehicles, utensils, government, education, arts, and music of the ten thousand countries of the world I have daily received and utilized. Thereby my mind's eye and my soul-*ch'i* have been stimulated. Do they progress? — then I progress with them; do they retrogress? — then I retrogress with them; are they happy? — then I am happy with them; do they suffer? — then I suffer with them. Verily, it is like there being nothing which the lightning (or electricity) does not penetrate, like there being nothing which the *ch'i* does not encompass.

Then extending it to the [other beings] produced by the earth — the savages, the grasses and trees, the scaly fish, the insects, the birds and beasts; all the ten thousand forms and the thousand classes of womb-born, moisture-born, egg-born, transformation-born — with all, likewise, have my ears and eyes met, [into] all has my soul-awareness penetrated, [to] all has my love-attraction (or empathy) been drawn. And how could I be indifferent [to them]? Be their appearance pleasing, I enjoy them; be they well-favoured, I delight in them; be their appearance distressing, be they ill-favoured, I likewise have [feelings of] distress and misery activated within me.

The jungle of the world: I shall also flee from it; I shall practise the Brahmins' [Way] of immuring oneself in a snowy cave so as to purify the soul (*ching-hun*). But if all men abandoned their families and immured themselves, then it would not be [more than] several decades before the civilizations of the whole earth would revert to a world overgrown by grasses and trees and [dominated by] the birds and beasts. Still less could I bear to bring [such a state] to pass! . . .

Master K'ang was not born in another heaven, but in this heaven; he was not born on another earth, but on this earth. Therefore he has an affinity with the human beings of this earth, and is intimate with [them] when he encounters [them]. He was not born as a furred or feathered, scaly or finny creature, but as a man. Therefore he is more intimate with the 'round-headed and square-footed,' who are the same in appearance and nature. He is not a beyond-the-pale, cave [-dwelling] savage, but a man of a country with several thousand years of civilization; he is not a herd-boy or kitchenmaid, serf or illiterate, but a gentleman from a family with a tradition of literary studies for thirteen generations. Daily reading the writings of the ancients of several thousand years, he is thus intimate with the ancients. Because he looks at the several tens of nations of the earth, he thus is intimate with the people of the whole earth. Being able to think profoundly and look to the future, he thus is intimate with the people of the countless generations to come. To all that his perception and knowledge extends, he is unable to shut his eyes and keep it [from his concern], to cover his ears and stop them [from hearing about it].

Whereupon Master K'ang commenced first to examine antiquity, and then to study the present. Near at hand he observed China; far away he looked over the whole earth. [And he saw that] of the honoured, extending to emperors, of the base, extending to criminals; of the long-lived, extending to Chien P'eng, of the short-lived, like those who die in childhood; of the withdrawn [from life], like the bonzes and Taoist [recluses]; of the gregarious like the birds: under all heaven, on all the earth, among all men, [among] all the creatures, there are none which are not grieved and distressed. Though it be shallow or deep, large or small, yet grief and distress will oppress them — thick and heavy, murky and evil. There are none who can escape it in the slightest.

All the former philosophers have sorrowfully, anxiously thought if there be a way to deliver them, to ferry them all across [the sea of suffering]. Each has exhausted the thinking of his mind in devising methods to help them. But with the unexpected, all-engulfing torrents [of troubles], men are never able to recover from the diseases in which they are sunk. [The methods of the philosophers] may be able to effect a little improvement, [but] there are none which completely cure. They may prop up the east, but the west falls down; or [if] they support the head, the feet will ail. Can it be that the principles of medicine are not yet refined [sufficiently]? Or that the methods of medicine are not yet adequate? I deplore [this lack of a remedy]. Or is it [merely] that the time has not yet arrived [when the world can be saved]? . . .

To enjoy being in groups, and to hate solitude, to muman's nature. Therefore the mutual intimacy, mutual love, tually assist and mutually help, is what gives pleasure to mutual hospital, and mutual succouring of fathers and sons, husbands and wives, elder and younger brothers — which is not altered by considerations of profit or loss, or of difficulties — are what give pleasure to man. Those who have no father or son, husband or wife, elder or younger brother, then have no one to be intimate with them, to love them, to take them in, or to succour them. If at times they have friends, then through considerations of profit or loss, or of difficulties, [their friends] will change their minds, and cannot be relied upon. We call them orphans and widows, widowers and childless. We term them 'impoverished,' we pity them as 'defenceless.' This is the utmost pain of men. The sages, because of what gave pleasure to man's nature, and to accord with what is natural in matters human, then made the family law to control them. They said the father is merciful, the son filial; the elder brother is friendly, the younger brother respectful; the husband is upright, the wife complaisant. This is likewise [what] best accords with man's nature. This method is simply [for the purpose of] enabling man to increase his happiness, and nothing else.

To form factions and compete for mastery, to follow the strong (or, through force) to protect oneself, cannot be avoided by human nature. Therefore we have the divisions of tribes and states, and the laws of government by rulers and ministers, so as to protect the happiness of men's homes and property. Were tribes non-existent, were states not relied upon [for protection], were there no rulers and ministers, and no governments, were [men] unsettled like the wild deer, then it would come to pass that men would be captured and enslaved, and would not be able to preserve their homes and property. Thus they would be sunk in limitless suffering, and there would be no way [for them] to find happiness. The sages, because of what man's nature cannot avoid, and to accord with what is natural in matters human and in the conditions of the times, on their behalf established states, tribes, rulers, ministers, and laws of government. This method is simply [for the purpose of] enabling man to avoid suffering, and nothing else.

Man, his knowledge great and his thinking profound, [able] to anticipate the future and to plan a long time [ahead], already having experienced happiness in life before, still more seeks eternal happiness after death; already having experienced pleasure in his bodily soul, still more seeks eternal pleasure in his spiritual soul. The sages, because of what man's nature enjoys and what gives pleasure to it, therefore devised the [Buddhist] Law of abandoning the world, the [Taoist] Way of purifying the spirit and nourishing the soul, and the methods for [attaining] immortality. Thereby [men] seek to be [re-] born into Heaven and to attain enlightenment, to escape the Wheel of Life (i.e. the Buddhist cycle of birth-life-death-rebirth), and [to arrive at] the limitless realm where their happiness will be exceedingly great and lasting — very much more so than the several decades of man's [mortal] existence.

In such cases men are following their [own] desires in carrying out painful actions. They abandon their beloved homes, cut themselves off from the honours and luxuries of human society, enter the mountains and sit with their face to the wall [in meditation], naked and barefooted beg their food, perhaps eating once a day, perhaps eating nine times in thirty days, plaiting grass [for clothing], tasting dung, sleeping in the snow, staring at the sun, food for tigers, food for hawks. They do not walk in this path [for the reason that they desire] to attain suffering. They have weighed the [relative] duration and intensity of pains and pleasures, and therefore willingly carry out [actions which produce] the lesser pain and the shorter pain, so as to gain the longer pleasure and the greater pleasure. Regarding birth, old age, sickness, and death as painful, they therefore will seek for what is not painful and for what is most pleasurable. This is to a still greater degree the seeking of happiness and the seeking to escape suffering.

Filial sons and loyal ministers, upright husbands and chaste wives, brave generals and morally disciplined scholars, have walked in the paths of danger and hardship, have followed the ways of peril and difficulty. They have eaten suffering as if it were sweetmeats. They have 'given up their lives without changing [their convictions]'. They have 'died in defence of the Good Way.' . . . Thus, although [men] carry out painful actions, [they do so because] glory and fame lie therein, respect and recognition [are gained] thereby, and what gives them pleasure [is the result] of them. In this way, what causes them to suffer is changed into what makes them happy. . . .

Having been born in the Age of Disorder, my eyes have been struck by the way of suffering [of this Age], and I have thought if there be a way to save it. 'Bewildered, I have pondered.' [The solution lies] only in following the Way of One World of Complete Peace-and-Equality. If

631

we look at all the ways of saving the world through the ages, to discard the Way of One World and yet to hope to save men from suffering and to gain their greatest happiness, is next to impossible. The Way of One World is [the attainment of] utmost peace-and-equality, utmost justice, utmost *jen*, and the most perfect government. Even though there be [other] Ways, none can add to this. . . .

All these many [kinds] are the sufferings of human life; while the sufferings of the feathered and furred, the scaly and finny [creatures] cannot be described. But if we look at the miseries of life, [we see that] the sources of all suffering lie only in nine boundaries. What are the nine boundaries?

The first is called nation-boundaries: [this is] division by territorial frontiers and by tribes.

The second is called class-boundaries: [this is] division by noble and base, by pure and impure.

The third is called race-boundaries: [this is] division by yellow, white, brown, and black [skin types].

The fourth is called sex- (literally, form) boundaries: [this is] division by male and female.

The fifth is called family-boundaries: [this is] the private relationships of father and son, husband and wife, elder and younger brother.

The sixth is called occupation-boundaries: [this is] the private ownership of agriculture, industry, and commerce.

The seventh is called disorder-boundaries: [this is] the existence of unequal, unthorough, dissimilar, and unjust laws.

The eighth is called kind-boundaries: [this is] the existence of a separation between man, and the birds, beasts, insects, and fish.

The ninth is called suffering-boundaries: [this means], by suffering, giving rise to suffering. The perpetuation [of suffering] is inexhaustible and endless — beyond conception.

(The remedy for suffering lies, therefore, in abolishing these nine boundaries. The following nine parts of the book thus deal in detail with each of the boundaries, with the abolishment of each, and with the substitution of the One World of Complete Peace-and-Equality in their place.)

ABOLISHING BOUNDARIES OF KIND, AND LOVING ALL LIVING [THINGS]

After mankind have become equal, great *jen* will abound. However, the birth of the ten thousand creatures originates in the original ether; man is merely one species of creatures within [this] original ether. In remote antiquity, at the beginnings of human beings, [men] knew only to cleave to their own kind and preserve them. If not of their kind, then they would kill them. Therefore love of [one's own] kind was considered to be the great principle. Those who were said throughout the world to be loving of [their own] kind were called *jen;* those who did not love [their own] kind were called not-*jen*. Should [a man] kill [a one] of a different kind, then, taking it [that thereby] injury was avoided and harm prevented, [the killer] was likewise called *jen*. . . .

Confucius took the ancestors as the root of the [human] kind. Therefore father, mother, sons, and daughters are the root of love-of-kind; elder and younger brothers and kinsmen are the extension of love-of-kind; husband and wife are the 'intercoursing' of love-of-kind – if there is intercourse with an animal, then [the human being] does not love that [animal]. Extending it from this, [then] love of friends [exists] because they are the same kind in sound of voice; love of prince and minister [exists] because they are [engaged in] the same kind of affairs; love of neighbours [exists] because they are the kind who reside in the same place. We love the people of our city, our country, or the world, more or less, according as they are of the kind who dwell nearer to or farther from [us]. We take the one kind of form (i.e. the human kind) as the limit [to our love], and on this basis we deal with them (i.e. our own human kind), civilize them, govern them. Hence he who kills a man dies; he who saves a man is rewarded; he who succours men is praised. [But] he who kills another [kind of] creature sins not; he who succours another [kind of] creature [gains] no merit. . . . The main rule to be followed in the treatment of the birds and beasts is that those harmful to man will be exterminated, while those which cannot harm man will be preserved.

Therefore, the refraining from killing of [animals] will start with the kine, dogs, and horses, because they are intelligent and useful. It will next [be extended to include] fowl, swine, geese, and ducks, because they will *not* be useful [as food, in that age]. It will finally be extended [to include] fish, because their intelligence is slight [and yet they do have intelligence]. Thus, the [stage in which there is still] eating of flesh and killing of living [creatures] is One World's Age of Disorder; [the stage in which] electrical machines [are used] to slaughter animals is One World's Age of Increasing Peace-and-Equality; [the stage in which] killing is prohibited and the desire [to kill and eat animals] is ended is One World's Age of Complete Peace-and-Equality. [This] is a gradual progress. . . .

Buddha said to abstain from killing; and yet he daily killed countless living [beings]. Buddha told Ananda to fetch water in his bowl. Ananda said that water contains microbes, [and so] we ought not to take and drink it. Buddha said that what we cannot see, we may drink. Now Buddha referred to all living beings. But he should have [based his] discussion [on whether] a thing was animate or inanimate, not [on whether] it was visible or invisible. Should we effect that man would be invisible, then we could also kill men! At the same time, it is in fact impossible to carry out that we do not drink water. Therefore

Buddha's reply was evasive. Or, even if we knew that Buddha did not drink water, yet he could not help but breathe air. When the air is exhaled and inhaled, then living [beings] are killed. Since I cannot retire outside of the atmosphere and not inhale them, then how can I be *jen* to living creatures and not kill them? *Jen! Jen!* We shall never be able to perfect [it]. Thus [it was that] Confucius [said]: '[The Gentleman] stays far away from the kitchen.' Life! Life! Eternally there must be killing. Therefore Buddha limited [the proscription against killing to exclude] invisible [creatures]. Alas, alas! The production of life is inexhaustible; the Way is likewise inexhaustible (i.e. imperfectible). However, [given] this imperfectibility, [we should] bring [the Way] to [the highest possible] perfection and perfect it.

Therefore, the Way is based on [doing what] can be done, and that is all. What cannot be done, even though we wish to do it, cannot but be thwarted. There is that which limits my *jen*. There is that which thwarts my love. Alas, alas! And even though the [kind of] *jen* [which will prevail in] One World, and the [kind of] love [which will then bring about] abstinence from killing were to be established in all the heavens; yet, so far as being [true or perfect] *jen* is concerned, it would only be a drop in the great ocean! However, within all the heavens, or without all the heavens, so far as *jen* is concerned, neither can we add to this [imperfect and limited development of it].

ABOLISHING BOUNDARIES OF SUFFERING AND ATTAINING UTMOST HAPPINESS

In the beginnings of man he suffered because of hunger, and so he sought the fruit of the grasses and trees, and the flesh of birds and beasts to fill himself. If he could no get flesh and fruit, then he suffered. If he got and ate them, filled up on them, satiated [himself] with them, then he was happy. He suffered because the wind and rain and mist attacked his body, and so he wrapped [himself in the bark of] grasses and trees, and wove hemp and *ko* [into garments] to cover his body. If he could not get them, then he suffered. If he got and wore them, then he was happy. He suffered because he did not obtain [satisfaction of] his human (i.e. sexual) desire, and so he sought a mate to embrace. If he could not get [a mate], then he suffered. If he got one, then he was happy. Later, there were wise ones who 'in pursuing affairs added refinements' to the old ways. [Taking] food, they cooked it, roasted it, mixed it, and so increased [men's] happiness. [Taking] clothing, they [used] silk [material], made it gay with the 'five colours and the six hues', [devised] gowns, caps, and sandals, and so increased [men's] happiness. (Similarly with dwellings, and with gratification of sexual desire.) The increase of happiness is [caused by] that which more suits and better accords with man's spiritual soul and bodily soul, which heightens and expands [man's] enjoyment and pleasure. The inability to attain this happiness is suffering. [Suffering] is the spirit knotted-up, the body wounded, [the soul] melancholy and downcast. [The capacity for] increased happiness is limitless; [the capacity for] increased suffering is also limitless. The two are related faculties. Daily to bend our thoughts more earnestly to means of seeking happiness and avoiding suffering: this is to progress.

(This is what all the sages have had as their purpose, with all their material inventions and social techniques. We may judge them by the one criterion of the extent to which they have increased human happiness and decreased human suffering. Their methods must also be judged as valuable or not, according to the times and the environment.

(In One World everyone will live in public housing. Outside of their regular rooms at their place of work, everywhere they will find great hotels, whose beautiful and pleasant accommodations defy description. They will be of several grades, according to the money the guest wishes to spend. There will be four better kinds: 'movable rooms' [i.e. electrically powered cars that run on tracks], 'flying rooms,' or, 'flying ships', and [marine] ships. The people of this age will love to travel.) The grasses and trees are the most stupid, and therefore flourish but do not move about. The sheep and swine are not so stupid as the grass and trees, and are able to move about, but cannot go far. As for the great *p'eng*-bird and the yellow *ku*-bird, [they fly] a thousand *li* with a single movement [of their wings]. In antiquity, [men] aged and died without leaving their native village; [thus] they were like the grass and trees. In the Middle Age, [men] travel about like sheep and swine (i.e. only short distances). In the Age of Complete Peace-and-Equality, then they will be like the great *p'eng*-bird and the yellow *ku*-bird.

(All public and private residences will have to pass the inspection of the health authorities. Public hotels will be equipped with air-conditioning, electrical heating, massaging machines. There will be fast, electrically propelled ships on the water, equipped with every comfort and pleasure — even to gardens — and many people will live on these ships. On land there will be automobiles. These will be developed to the point that they will seat perhaps several hundred persons, and will go at great speeds. Perhaps they will be electrically powered; or it may be that they will be powered by some new fuel. Horse-drawn carriages will be used only for hauling short distances, or they may be entirely replaced by the electrical vehicles.) Therefore, at the beginning of One World, [people] will live on mountain tops; at the middle [period of that age], they will live on the sea; later, they will live in the air.

(There being no private homes, everyone will dine together, like a great convention. There will be no slaves or servants, but their functions will be performed by machines, shaped like birds and beasts. One will order by telephone, and food will be conveyed by mechanical devices — possibly a table will rise up from the kitchen below, through a hole in the floor. On the four walls will be lifelike, 'protruding paintings'; music will be playing, and there will be dancing. All this will stimulate the appetite. In all these things there will be refinement and moral uplift.

(At this time, people will eat their food in a liquid form — the essences extracted from solid matter. These essential juices will be more easily absorbed by the body than are the solids. There will be vapours which will be inhaled to give a joyful intoxication, but without harm to the body. By imbibing only the essences of foods, man's life will be prolonged.

(There follows a short section repeating the discussion [see above, Part IX] regarding non-killing of animals. There will be three stages within the Age of Complete Peace-and-Equality itself: The Age of Disorder, in which meat will still be eaten; the Age of Increasing Peace-and-Equality, in which the flesh of birds and animals will no longer be eaten; the Age of Complete Peace-and-Equality, in which even insects and fish will no longer be eaten, and in which all forms of life possessed of cognition will be equal. Equality will not extend to the vegetable kingdom, for man must eat to preserve himself, and because these forms of life are not possessed of the cognitive faculty, and hence are not to be included in the domain of *jen*.

(Clothing in this time will be made of materials and patterns suitable to weather conditions and to working comfort. They will have great variety and beauty, but will indicate no distinctions between people, except for the badges of honours for *jen* or knowledge. There will be constant progress in the use of all kinds of implements to advance civilization. Music will play a great part in all phases of human life. People will shave off all hair except for that in the nose [which fulfils the function of straining dust and impurities from the air]. This is on the ground that the nearer we are to the beasts, the hairier; the more civilized we become, the less hirsute. Furthermore, lack of hair contributes to cleanliness. Men and women will bathe several times daily, in water which will leave them fragrantly scented. This is not a matter of perfuming in the present manner, so that a woman will be more attractive as a sexual plaything. Rather it is like the matter of hair: thereby humans are farther elevated above the filthy, foul-smelling beasts. 'The beauties of the present age will still not equal the ugly of the Age of Complete Peace-and-Equality.' Even the toilet facilities of that time will be made pleasant with music and fragrant odours and mechanical contrivances for flushing away the filth.) For the time when people go to the toilet is the time when they are most tranquil and withdrawn from the hubbub [of the world]. If there is that whereby to lift their thoughts above this world (literally, move their thoughts of abandoning the world), to [inspire] their imaginations beyond the mundane (literally, ideas of discarding forms), then their souls will of themselves [rise] far [above] the worldly level.

(Everyone will receive a daily medical check-up. All phases of life will be under the supervision of the medical authorities. Contagious diseases will be eradicated. The whole earth will be made clean and healthful. About the only ailments remaining will be external ones, easily treated with medicines. Thus, although there will be public hospitals, they will be almost empty; the sick will comprise only those who are about to die [of old age]. In the case of the latter, should their sufferings be acute, and the doctors agree that there is no hope of improvement, then they may be mercifully put out of their agony by electrocution. . . . People of this time will attain to longevity of from a hundred or two hundred, to over a thousand years, due to progress in medical science, clothing, and diet.

(The search for longevity, for the art of becoming a spirit or immortal [shen-hsien], may be carried on only by those who have returned with twenty years of service the twenty years of support and education received from the public. Those who wish to retire from the world to carry

639

on these [Tâoistic] or Buddhistic practices may, therefore, do so after the age of forty. These capabilities will be the highest attainment of One World. But they may not interfere with the public service owed by everyone, or else the work of the world might be neglected, and civilization retrogress.)

Christianity takes reverence for God (*shen*) and love for men as its teaching of the Good; it takes repentance of sin and judgment after death as its [means of making people] frightened of [doing] evil. In the Age of Complete Peace-and-Equality, [people] will naturally love others, will naturally be without sin. Comprehending the natural workings of evolution, they will therefore not reverence God. Comprehending the impossibility (literally, difficulty) of limitless numbers of souls occupying the space [of 'Heaven'], they therefore will not believe in a Day of Judgment. The religion of Jesus will therefore, when we have attained One World, be extinct.

Islam speaks of the bonds of states, rulers, subjects, husbands, and wives. By the time we have entered [the Age of] One World, it will thus [already] be extinct. Although possessed of a soul, [yet for man] always to adduce God [in support of his] actions: such [a Way] is crude and superficial, and lacks sufficient substantiation. One World of Complete Peace-and-Equality is then the ideal of Confucius. Having arrived at this time, Confucius' theory of the Three Ages will have been completely fulfilled. However, the *I* [*Ching*] speaks of the alternations (literally, dispersing and gathering, or dissipating and growing) of *yin* and *yang;* [this theory] may be propagated, but [its workings] will not be apparent. For, the sickness being over, there is no need to use medicines; the shore having been reached, the raft [of Buddha's teachings] may likewise be discarded.

Therefore in the Age of One World only the studies of [the art of becoming] a spirit or immortal, and of [becoming] a buddha, will be widely practised. For One World is the ultimate Law of this world; but the study of immortality, of longevity without death, is even an extension of the ultimate Law of this world. The study of buddhahood, [a state] without birth or death, [implies] not [merely] a setting apart from the world, but [an actual] going out of this world; still more, it is a going out of One World. If we go this far, then we abandon the human sphere and enter the sphere of immortals and buddhas. Hereupon, the study of immortality and buddhahood then begins. [Comparing the two], the study of immortality is too crude, its subtle words and profound principles are not many, and its [ability] to intoxicate men's minds is limited. As for the universality and subtlety of the study of buddhahood, it extends to the point where the speaking of words is discontinued, and the activities of the mind are terminated. Although having sage-wisdom, not to move a hand (i.e. to remain quiescent): such [self-] containment is yet more profound. And further, there are also the mysterious arts of the Five Vanquishings and the Three Brilliants; the application of [their] supernatural powers is still more singular.

Therefore after One World there will first be the study of immortality. After [that] there will be the study of buddhahood. The inferior knowledge is the study of immortality; the superior knowledge is the study of buddhahood. After [the studies of] immortality and buddhahood will come the study of roaming through the heavens. I have another book [on that subject].

Sun Yat-sen

SUN YAT-SEN (1864-1925). The political philosophy of Sun Yat-sen was inspired by K'ang Yu-wei's book, *Ta T'ung Shu (Book of the Great Unity*, translated as *The One-World Philosophy of K'ang Yu-wei).* The great "Apostle of the Revolution" was baptized a Christian. After his death he became the canonized patron of the National People's Party *(Kuo-Min-Tang)* and ultimately of republican China. For his revolutionary campaign, he seized upon the teachings of the Lu-Wang School, which stressed self-Consciousness and provided a psychological basis for the revolution of 1911-12 and that of 1926-28.

Sun Yat-sen held that the ability to know must be supplemented by the ability to do, and that all modern progress is an expression of the basic unity of knowledge and action. He argued that the revolution must be accomplished first; then people could talk about learning to improve upon their accomplishment. He stressed the thrill of constructive action rather than its moralistic side, promoted by Wang Yang-ming. After the revolution of 1911, he allowed his secret revolutionary society to become an open political party. Lack of substantial progress caused him to accept Soviet help and to restructure the Kuomintang along Communist lines even though he continued to repudiate Marxism as such. The *Three People's Principles,* given its final form in a series of lectures to party members in 1924, served as the basic document of the Nationalist movement.

General Theory of Knowledge and Action

From *Sources of Chinese Tradition,* Volume I, edited by William Theodore de Bary, New York, Columbia University Press, 1960.

[From *Chung-shan ch'üan-shu,* Vol. II, *Chien-kuo fang-lüeh,* Part I (also entitled *Sun Wen hsüeh-shuo*), Ch. 5, pp. 31-33, 36-37]

THE doctrine of Wang Yang-ming, who taught the unity of knowledge and action, was intended to encourage men to do good. It may be inferred that Wang also considered it not difficult to know but difficult to act. . . . His efforts at encouraging people to do good are indeed admirable, but his teaching is incompatible with truth. What is difficult he considered easy, and what is easy, difficult. To encourage one to attempt the difficult is tantamount to asking one to act against human nature. . . .

It is said that the renovation of Japan was entirely inspired by the teaching of Wang Yang-ming. The Japanese them-selves believe this and pay high tribute to Wang. It should be noted, however, that Japan was still in the feudalistic stage before the [Meiji] Renovation.[1] The people were not yet removed from the tradition of the past and the spirit of initiative and enterprise was not extinct. In the face of foreign aggression, while the official classes were flounder-ing, patriotic citizens felt stirred to action. They advocated support of the emperor in order to resist the foreigners. . . . And when the Japanese failed to expel the foreigners, they immediately changed their course and turned to imitate the

1. The term Sun uses corresponds to the Japanese *ishin,* often rendered "Restoration." Sun has in mind, not the restoration of imperial rule, but the basic meaning of the term, renovation or reform.

way of the foreigners. The Renovation owed its success to their learning from the foreigners. Thus the Japanese effected their reforms without knowing the principle involved. This obviously had nothing to do with Wang's doctrine of the unity of action and knowledge. . . .

While Japan carried out her reforms without seeking to know about them, China would not undertake reform measures until she understood them, and even so she hesitated to act for fear of difficulty. The Chinese have been misled by the teaching that to act is even more difficult than to know. Reformation or change of institutions is a great national event. It is not always possible to comprehend the various measures in advance. Their significance is understood only after they have been carried out. The enterprising and adventurous spirit was mainly responsible for the success of the Japanese Renovation. They did not know what reformation was until they had accomplished it. It was then that they called it the Renovation.

In the case of China, however, she first sought a comprehension of the reform and then made attempts to carry it out. As such knowledge could never be acquired, action was indefinitely postponed. Thus, while the philosophy of Wang Yang-ming failed to discourage enterprising Japan, it did not do anything toward encouraging her. But when such a teaching was advocated in lethargic China, it only did her harm.

In an age of scientific discoveries, Wang's doctrine of the unity of knowledge and action is sound when applied to a particular period or a particular undertaking, but when it is applied to an individual, it is certainly erroneous. With the growth of modern science one's knowledge and one's action are more and more set apart. One who knows does not have to act, and not only that, but one who acts does not have to know. . . .

I have spared no efforts in writing page after page with a view to proving that it is easy to act but difficult to know. It is my strong conviction that this is the necessary course through which China is to be saved. The accumulating weakness and the dying state of the country are due to the misleading effect of the theory that to know is not difficult but to act is difficult. . . . Thus the Chinese shun what is [actually] easy and take to the difficult. At first they seek to know before acting. Then finding that this cannot be accomplished, they feel helpless and give up all thoughts of attempting. Some, imbued with an undaunted spirit, devote their life-long effort to acquiring the knowledge of a certain undertaking. They may have acquired the knowledge and yet hesitate to apply it, being obsessed with the thought that to act is even more difficult. Hence those who do not have the knowledge, of course, fail to act, but even those who have acquired it do not dare to act. It develops that there is nothing that can be attempted in the world. . . .

The advance of civilization is achieved by three groups of persons: first, those who see and perceive ahead, discoverers; second, those who see and perceive later, or promoters; and third, those who do not see or perceive, or practical workers. From this point of view, China does not lack practical workers, for the great masses of the people are of this kind. Some of my comrades, however, have the habit of saying that so-and-so is [merely] a theoretician, while so-and-so is a practical man. It is a grave fallacy indeed to entertain the idea that a few practical men could reform the nation.

Look at the huge factories, busy boulevards, and imposing buildings of the foreigners in Shanghai. The men of action who performed the work of construction were the Chinese workmen, while the foreigners were the thinkers or planners, who never personally undertook the construction. Hence in the construction of a country it is not the practical workers but the idealists and planners that are difficult to find. . . .

This is the reason for the lack of progress in our national reconstruction after the revolution. I therefore feel the necessity for this thorough refutation, hoping that those who see and perceive late can eventually awake from their

646

error and change their course. In this way they will no longer mislead the world with a theory seemingly right but actually wrong, and no longer hinder the great multitude of practical workers. Herein lies the great hope for the future of our reconstruction.

THE THREE PEOPLE'S PRINCIPLES

[From *Chung-shan ch'üan-shu*, I, 4-5, 15-16, 28-29, 51-52]

[*China as a Heap of Loose Sand*]. For the most part the four hundred million people of China can be spoken of as completely Han Chinese. With common customs and habits, we are completely of one race. But in the world what position do we occupy? Compared to the other peoples of the world we have the greatest population and our civilization is four thousand years old; we should therefore be advancing in the front rank with the nations of Europe and America. But the Chinese people have only family and clan solidarity; they do not have national spirit. Therefore even though we have four hundred million people gathered together in one China, in reality they are just a heap of loose sand. Today we are the poorest and weakest nation in the world, and occupy the lowest position in international affairs. Other men are the carving knife and serving dish; we are the fish and the meat. Our position at this time is most perilous. If we do not earnestly espouse nationalism and weld together our four hundred million people into a strong nation, there is danger of China's being lost and our people being destroyed. If we wish to avert this catastrophe, we must espouse nationalism and bring this national spirit to the salvation of the country. [pp. 4-5, Lecture 1]

[*China as a "Hypo-colony"*]. Since the Chinese Revolution, the foreign powers have found that it was much less easy to use political force in carving up China. A people who had experienced Manchu oppression and learned to overthrow

647

it, would now, if the powers used political force to oppress it, be certain to resist, and thus make things difficult for them. For this reason they are letting up in their efforts to control China by political force and instead are using economic pressure to keep us down. . . . As regards political oppression people are readily aware of their suffering, but when it comes to economic oppression most often they are hardly conscious of it. China has already experienced several decades of economic oppression by the foreign powers, and so far the nation has for the most part shown no sense of irritation. As a consequence China is being transformed everywhere into a colony of the foreign powers.

Our people keep thinking that China is only a "semi-colony" — a term by which they seek to comfort themselves. Yet in reality the economic oppression we have endured is not just that of a "semi-colony" but greater even than that of a full colony. . . . Of what nation then is China a colony? It is the colony of every nation with which it has concluded treaties; each of them is China's master. Therefore China is not just the colony of one country; it is the colony of many countries. We are not just the slaves of one country, but the slaves of many countries. In the event of natural disasters like flood and drought, a nation which is sole master appropriates funds for relief and distributes them, thinking this its own duty; and the people who are its slaves regard this relief work as something to which their masters are obligated. But when North China suffered drought several years ago, the foreign powers did not regard it as their responsibility to appropriate funds and distribute relief; only those foreigners resident in China raised funds for the drought victims, whereupon Chinese observers remarked on the great generosity of the foreigners who bore no responsibility to help. . . .

From this we can see that China is not so well off as Annam [under the French] and Korea [under the Japanese]. Being the slaves of one country represents a far higher status than being the slaves of many, and is far more advantageous.

Therefore, to call China a "semi-colony" is quite incorrect. If I may coin a phrase, we should be called a "hypo-colony." This is a term that comes from chemistry, as in "hypo-phosphite." Among chemicals there are some belonging to the class of phosphorous compounds but of lower grade, which are called phosphites. Still another grade lower, and they are called hypo-phosphites. . . . The Chinese people, believing they were a semi-colony, thought it shame enough; they did not realize that they were lower even than Annam or Korea. Therefore we cannot call ourselves a "semi-colony" but only a "hypo-colony." [pp. 15-16, Lecture 2]

[*Nationalism and Cosmopolitanism*]. A new idea is emerging in England and Russia, proposed by the intellectuals, which opposes nationalism on the ground that it is narrow and illiberal. This is simply a doctrine of cosmopolitanism. England now and formerly Germany and Russia, together with the Chinese youth of today who preach the new civilization, support this doctrine and oppose nationalism. Often I hear young people say: "The Three Principles of the People do not fit in with the present world's new tendencies; the latest and best doctrine in the world is cosmopolitanism." But is cosmopolitanism really good or not? If that doctrine is good, why is it that as soon as China was conquered, her nationalism was destroyed? Cosmopolitanism is the same thing as China's theory of world empire two thousand years ago. Let us now examine that doctrine and see whether in fact it is good or not. Theoretically, we cannot say it is no good. Yet it is because formerly the Chinese intellectual class had cosmopolitan ideas that, when the Manchus crossed China's frontier, the whole country was lost to them. . . .

We cannot decide whether an idea is good or not without seeing it in practice. If the idea is of practical value to us, it is good; if it is impractical, it is bad. If it is useful to the world, it is good; if it is not, it is no good. The nations which are employing imperialism to conquer others and which are trying to retain their privileged positions as sovereign lords are advocating cosmopolitanism and want the whole world to follow them. [pp. 28-29, Lecture 3]

[*Nationalism and Traditional Morality*]. If today we want to restore the standing of our people, we must first restore our national spirit. . . . If in the past our people have survived despite the fall of the state [to foreign conquerors], and not only survived themselves but been able to assimilate these foreign conquerors, it is because of the high level of our traditional morality. Therefore, if we go to the root of the matter, besides arousing a sense of national solidarity uniting all our people, we must recover and restore our characteristic, traditional morality. Only thus can we hope to attain again the distinctive position of our people.

This characteristic morality the Chinese people today have still not forgotten. First comes loyalty and filial piety, then humanity and love, faithfulness and duty, harmony and peace. Of these traditional virtues, the Chinese people still speak, but now, under foreign oppression, we have been invaded by a new culture, the force which is felt all across the nation. Men wholly intoxicated by this new culture have thus begun to attack the traditional morality, saying that with the adoption of the new culture, we no longer have need of the old morality. . . . They say that when we formerly spoke of loyalty, it was loyalty to princes, but now in our democracy there are no princes, so loyalty is unnecessary and can be dispensed with. This kind of reasoning is certainly mistaken. In our country princes can be dispensed with, but not loyalty. If they say loyalty can be dispensed with, then I ask: "Do we, or do we not, have a nation? Can we, or can we not, make loyalty serve the nation? If indeed we can no longer speak of loyalty to princes, can we not, however, speak of loyalty to our people?" [pp. 51-52, Lecture 6]

T'an Ssu-t'ung

T'AN SSU-T'UNG (1865-1898). The New Text School made great strides during the later part of the Ch'ing dynasty. The followers of Ku Yen-wu (1613-1682) insisted that the Han scholars were nearer to the teachings of Confucius than Sung scholars. They tried to revive Confucianism in its purity, not only as a philosophy but also as a religion to check the spread of Christianity. The most important political reformer of the later period was K'ang Yu-wei (1858-1927). His pupil, T'an Ssu-t'ung, was also a leading spirit in the reform movement. The nonconformist son of a high official, he studied Christianity, Buddhism, and Taoism as well as Confucianism. He found that they all shared the hope that man could attain the perfect life. He participated in the Hundred Days of Reform, risked death in an attempt to rescue Kuang-hsü emperor, and died a martyr at the age of thirty-three. His extremism made him a hero to the new generation of Chinese.

According to T'an Ssu-t'ung, the diversity of phenomena is explained by the infinite number of combinations of chemical elements in the varied forms of matter. His interpretation of *jen* as the unifying factor in all things reflects the influence of Western science on his thought. Like Chu Hsi, Wang Yang-ming, and K'ang Yu-wei, he interpreted *jen* as a universal spirit uniting people of all races, classes, and sexes into one harmonious whole. To bring about the Great Unity "when all men would be sublimely perfect," he committed himself to a revolutionary cause, and he met death at the execution-block calmly, a willing martyr to the cause of human freedom.

651

On the Study of Humanity

From *Sources of Chinese Tradition*, Volume II, edited by William Theodore de Bary, New York, Columbia University Press, 1960.

[From *T'an Liu-yang ch'üan-chi, Jen-hsüeh,* A:37a-b, B:1a-10a]

WHEN Confucius first set forth his teachings, he discarded the ancient learning, reformed existing institutions, rejected monarchism, advocated republicanism, and transformed inequality into equality. He indeed applied himself to many changes. Unfortunately, the scholars who followed Hsün Tzŭ forgot entirely the true meaning of Confucius' teaching, but clung to its superficial form. They allowed the ruler supreme, unlimited powers, and enabled him to make use of Confucianism in controlling the country. The school of Hsün Tzŭ insisted that duties based on human relationships were the essence of Confucianism, not knowing that this was a system applicable only to the Age of Disorder. Even for the Age of Disorder, any discussion of the human relationships[1] without reference to Heaven would be prejudicial and incomplete, and the evil consequences would be immeasurable. How much worse, then, for them recklessly to have added the three bonds,[2] thus openly creating a system of inequality with its unnatural dictinctions between high and low, and making men, the children of Heaven and earth, suffer a miserable life. . . .

For the past two thousand years the ruler-minister rela-

1. The relationships between ruler and minister, father and son, husband and wife, elder brother and younger brother, and friends.
2. Binding the minister to the ruler, the son to the father, the wife to the husband.

tionship has been especially dark and inhuman, and it has become worse in recent times. The ruler is not physically different or intellectually superior to man: on what does he rely to oppress 400 million people? He relies on the formulation long ago of the three bonds and five human relationships, so that, controlling men's bodies, he can also control their minds. As Chuang Tzŭ said "He who steals a sickle gets executed; he who steals a state becomes the prince." When T'ien Ch'eng-tzŭ stole the state of Ch'i, he also stole the [Confucian] system of humanity, righteousness and sage wisdom. When the thieves were Chinese and Confucianists, it was bad enough; but how could we have allowed the unworthy tribes of Mongolia and Manchuria, who knew nothing of China or Confucianism, to steal China by means of their barbarism and brutality! After stealing China, they controlled the Chinese by means of the system they had stolen, and shamelessly made use of Confucianism, with which they had been unfamiliar, to oppress China, to which they had been strangers. But China worshiped them as Heaven, and did not realize their guilt. Instead of burning the books in order to keep the people ignorant [as did the Ch'in], they more cleverly used the books to keep the people under control. Compared with them, the tyrannical emperor of the Ch'in dynasty was but a fool! [A:37a-38a]

At the beginning of the human race, there were no princes and subjects, for all were just people. As the people were unable to govern each other and did not have time to rule, they joined in raising up someone to be the prince. Now "joined in raising up" means, not that the prince selected the people [as for civil service],[1] but that the people selected the prince; it means that the prince was not far above the people, but rather on the same level with them. Again, by "joined in raising up" the prince, it means that there must be people before there can be a prince: the prince is therefore the "branch" [secondary] while the people are the

1. The term "raised up" or "recommended" had been applied to candidates selected for office.

"root" [primary]. Since there is no such thing in the world as sacrificing the root for the branch, how can we sacrifice the people for the prince? When it is said that they "joined in raising up" the prince, it necessarily means that they could also dismiss him. The prince serves the people; the ministers assist the ruler to serve the people. Taxes are levied to provide the means for managing the public affairs of the people. If public affairs are not well managed, it is a universal principle that the ruler should be replaced. . . .

The ruler is also one of the people; in fact, he is of secondary importance as compared to ordinary people. If there is no reason for people to die for one another, there is certainly less reason for those of primary importance to die for one of secondary importance. Then, should those who died for the ruler in ancient times not have done so? Not necessarily. But I can say positively that there is reason only to die for a cause, definitely not reason to die for a prince. [B:1a-b]

In ancient times loyalty meant actually being loyal. If the subordinate actually serves his superior faithfully, why should not the superior actually wait upon his subordinate also? Loyalty signifies mutuality, the utmost fulfillment of a mutual relationship. How can we maintain that only ministers and subjects should live up to it? Confucius said: "The prince should behave as a prince, the minister as a minister." He also said: "The father should behave as a father, the son as a son, the elder brother as an elder brother, the younger brother as a younger brother, the husband as a husband, the wife as a wife." The founder of Confucianism never preached inequality. [B:2b]

As the evils of the ruler-minister relationship reached their highest development, it was considered natural that the relationships between father and son and between husband and wife should also be brought within the control of categorical morality.[1] This is all damage done by the categorizing

1. Under the influence of Buddhism and perhaps utilitarianism, T'an viewed the traditional moral values as mere "names" or empty concepts (*ming*) in contrast to reality or actuality (*shih*).

of the three bonds. Whenever you have categorical obligations, not only are the mouths of the people sealed so that they are afraid to speak up, but their minds are also shackled so that they are afraid to think. Thus the favorite method for controlling the people is to multiply the categorical obligations. [B:7b-8a]

As to the husband-wife relationship, on what basis does the husband extend his power and oppress the other party? Again it is the theory of the three bonds which is the source of the trouble. When the husband considers himself the master, he will not treat his wife as an equal human being. In ancient China the wife could ask for a divorce, and she therefore did not lose the right to be her own master. Since the inscription of the tyrannical law [against remarriage] on the tablet at K'uai-chi during the Ch'in dynasty, and particularly since its zealous propagation by the Confucianists of the Sung dynasty — who cooked up the absurd statement that "To die in starvation is a minor matter, but to lose one's chastity [by remarrying] is a serious matter" — the cruel system of the Legalists has been applied to the home, and the ladies' chambers have become locked-up prisons. [B:7-8]

Among the five human relationships, the one between friends is the most beneficial and least harmful to life. It yields tranquil happiness and causes not a trace of pain — so long as friends are made with the right persons. Why is this? Because the relationship between friends is founded on equality, liberty, and mutual feelings. In short, it is simply because friendship involves no loss of the right to be one's own master. Next comes the relationship between brothers, which is somewhat like the relationship between friends. The rest of the five relationships which have been darkened by three bonds are like hell. [B:9a]

The world, misled by the conception of blood relations, makes erroneous distinctions between the nearly related and the remotely related, and relegates the relationship between friends to the end of the line. The relationship between friends, however, not only is superior to the other four relationships, but should be the model for them all. When these four relationships have been brought together and infused with the spirit of friendship, they can well be abolished. . . .

People in China and abroad are now talking of reforms, but no fundamental principles and systems can be introduced if the five relationships remain unchanged, let alone the three bonds. [B:9b-10a]

Hu Shih

HU SHIH (1891-1962). Chinese philosophers of the New Text School had little or no knowledge of Western thought. K'ang Yu-wei and T'an Ssu-tung knew something of science, mathematics, and Christianity as taught by the missionaries, but still they believed in the superiority of their own culture. Yen Fu (1853-1920), who was sent to England to study naval science, was the first person to introduce Western philosophy into China. Wang Kuo-wei (1877-1927) also studied Western philosophy. The lectures given by John Dewey and Bertrand Russell at the University of Peiping in 1919 interested a number of Chinese scholars in further studies. Yet the strong hold which tradition had on educated men was not easily broken, and it remained for Hu Shih, the leading Chinese disciple of John Dewey, to prepare the way for Westernization in thought and scholarship by advocating a new written language and a complete re-evaluation of the Chinese heritage.

Hu Shih studied agriculture at Cornell and Philosophy at Columbia, where John Dewey was his teacher. Even before he returned to his homeland, he began to advocate change. In a period of rising nationalism and expanding education, he knew that progress would depend largely on the adoption of a written language, simpler than the official language and flexible enough to accommodate new concepts from the West. As one of the leaders of the New Culture Movement he urged a sweeping re-examination of the classical tradition. His revolutionary program was backed by Ch'en Tu-hsiu, who was head of the department of literature at the University of Peiping and publisher of *The New Youth*. Instead of dwelling on the mistakes of the past, Hu Shih offered constructive proposals for the future, stressing the vernacular as a means of communication and stimulating literary activity along entirely new lines. During a long period of fermentation and transition in the cultural life of China, he remained a staunch proponent to the Western philosophy of pragmatism.

Pragmatism

From *Sources of Chinese Tradition,* Volume II, edited by William Theodore de Bary, Columbia University Press, 1960.

[From *Shih-yen chu-i,* in *Hu Shih wen-ts'un.* Collection I, ch. 2, pp. 291-320; originally published in *Hsin ch'ing-nien,* Vol. VI, No. 4 (April 1919), pp. 342-58]

THERE are two fundamental changes in basic scientific concepts which have had the most important bearings on pragmatism. The first is the change of the scientific attitude toward scientific laws. Hitherto worshipers of science generally had a superstition that scientific laws were unalterable universal principles. They thought that there was an eternal, unchanging "natural law" immanent in all things in the universe and that when this law was discovered, it became scientific law. However, this attitude toward the universal principle has gradually changed in the last several decades. Scientists have come to feel that such a superstitious attitude toward a universal principle could hinder scientific progress. Furthermore, in studying the history of science they have learned that many discoveries in science are the results of hypotheses. Consequently, they have gradually realized that the scientific laws of today are no more than the hypotheses which are the most applicable, most convenient, and most generally accepted as explanations of natural phenomena. . . . Such changes of attitude involve three ideas: 1) Scientific laws are formulated by men; 2) They are hypotheses — whether they can be determined to be applicable or not entirely depends on whether they can satisfactorily explain facts; 3) They are not the eternal, unchanging natural law. There may be such a natural law in the universe, but we cannot say that our hypothecated principles are this law. They are no more than a shorthand to record the natural changes known to us. [pp. 291-94]

Besides this, there was in the nineteenth century another important change which also had an extremely important bearing on pragmatism. This is Darwin's theory of evolution. . . . When it came to Darwin, he boldly declared that the species were not immutable but all had their origins and developed into the present species only after many changes. From the present onward, there can still be changes in species, such as the grafting of trees and crossing of fowls, whereby special species can be obtained. Not only do the species change, but truth also changes. The change of species is the result of adaptation to environment and truth is but an instrument with which to deal with environment. As the environment changes, so does truth accordingly. The concept of loyalty to the emperor during the Hsüant'ung era [1909-1911] was no longer the concept of loyalty to the emperor during the Yung-cheng and Ch'ien-lung eras [1723-1795]. Since the founding of the republic, such concepts have been completely cast aside and are useless. Only when we realize that there is no eternal, unchanging truth or absolute truth can we arouse in ourselves a sense of intellectual responsibility. The knowledge that mankind needs is not the way or principle which has an absolute existence but the particular truths for here and now and for particular individuals. Absolute truth is imaginary, abstract, vague, without evidence, and cannot be demonstrated. [pp. 294-95]

THE PRAGMATISM OF JAMES

What we call truth is actually no more than an instrument, comparable to this piece of paper in my hand, this chalk, this blackboard, or this teapot. They are all our instruments.

Because this concept produced results, people in the past therefore called it truth and because its utility still remains, we therefore still call it truth. If by any chance some event takes place for which the old concept is not applicable, it will no longer be truth. We will search for a new truth to take its place. . . .

Truth is recognized to be truth because it has helped us ferry the river or make a match. If the ferry is broken down, build another one. If the sailboat is too slow, replace it with a steam launch. If this marriage broker won't do, give him a good punch, chase him out, and ask a dependable friend to make a match.

This is the theory of truth in pragmatism. [pp. 309-10]

THE FUNDAMENTAL CONCEPTS OF DEWEY'S PHILOSOPHY

Dewey is a great revolutionist in the history of philosophy. . . . He said that the basic error of modern philosophy is that modern philosophers do not understand what experience really is. All quarrels between rationalists and empiricists and between idealists and realists are due to their ignorance of what experience is. [p. 316]

Dewey was greatly influenced by the modern theory of biological evolution. Consequently, his philosophy is completely colored by bio-evolutionism. He said that "experiencing means living; and that living goes on in and because of an environing medium, not in a vacuum. . . . The human being has upon his hands the problem of responding to what is going on around him so that these changes will take one turn rather than another, namely, that required by his own further functioning. . . . He is obliged to struggle — that is to say, to employ the direct support given by the environment in order indirectly to effect changes that would not otherwise occur. In this sense, life goes on by means of controlling the environment. Its activities must change the changes going on around it; they must neutralize hostile occurrences; they must transform neutral events into cooperative factors or into an efflorescence of new features."

This is what Dewey explained as experience. [p. 318]

The foregoing are the basic concepts of Dewey's philosophy. Summarized, they are: 1) Experience is life and life is dealing with environment; 2) In the act of dealing with environment, the function of thought is the most important. All conscious actions involve the function of thought. Thought is an instrument to deal with environment; 3) True philosophy must throw overboard the previous toying with "philosophers' problems" and turn itself into a method for solving human problems.

What is the philosophical method for solving human problems? It goes without saying that it must enable people to have creative intelligence, must enable them to envisage a bright future on the basis of present needs, and must be able to create new methods and tools to realize that future. [p. 320]

Mao Tse-tung

MAO TSE-TUNG (1893-   ). The founder and leader of the Chinese Communist state was born into a moderately prosperous peasant family of Shao Shan, in Hunan Province, on November 19, 1893. After receiving his degree from the Hunan Normal School in 1918, Mao Tse-tung worked briefly in the library of Peking University and as a teacher in Hunan. Converted by his own studies of Marx and Engels, he devoted his energies to organizing the Chinese Communist Party (1921), and by 1923 his local success had earned him a place in the national leadership of the party. In 1928 he helped to organize the Chinese Red Fourth Army, and six years later, as chairman of the Soviet Republic of China, he set up headquarters and prepared the foundations of the new Communist state. Reverses proved only temporary, and by 1949 his forces had won control of continental China. His influence throughout the Communist world increased considerably after the death of Stalin in 1953. By the time he gave up the title of Chairman of the People's Republic of China in 1959, he had gone far toward making China a Communist state. He has kept his title of Chairman of the Central Committee of the Communist Party of China and continues to act as spokesman for one-fourth of the human race.

His two basic theoretical works, reproduced here in their entirety, are *On Practice* (July 1937) and *On Contradiction* (August 1937). The first essay stresses the inseparability of theory and practice and demonstrates the importance which he attaches to the preservation of ideological unity. The second essay is of a more general nature but also has the object of overcoming the serious error of dogmatic thinking to be found in the Party in the early Yenan period. Originally delivered as lectures at the Anti-Japanese Military and Political College in Yenan, it was revised by Mao on its inclusion in his *Selected Works*.

On Practice*

From *The Selected Works of Mao Tse-tung*, published by the People's Publishing House, Peking, April, 1960.

ON THE RELATION BETWEEN KNOWLEDGE AND PRACTICE, BETWEEN KNOWING AND DOING

BEFORE Marx, materialism examined the problem of knowledge apart from the social nature of man and apart from his historical development, and was therefore incapable of understanding the dependence of knowledge on social practice, that is, the dependence of knowledge on production and the class struggle.

Above all, Marxists regard man's activity in production

---

* There used to be a number of comrades in our Party who were dogmatists and who for a long period rejected the experience of the Chinese revolution, denying the truth that "Marxism is not a dogma but a guide to action" and overawing people with words and phrases from Marxist works, torn out of context. There were also a number of comrades who were empiricists and who for a long period restricted themselves to their own fragmentary experience and did not understand the importance of theory for revolutionary practice or see the revolution as a whole, but worked blindly though industriously. The erroneous ideas of these two types of comrades, and particularly of the dogmatists, caused enormous losses to the Chinese revolution during 1931-34, and yet the dogmatists, cloaking themselves as Marxists, confused a great many comrades. "On Practice" was written in order to expose the subjectivist errors of dogmatism and empiricism in the Party, and especially the error of dogmatism, from the standpoint of the Marxist theory of knowledge. It was entitled "On Practice" because its stress was on exposing the dogmatist kind of subjectivism, which belittles practice. The ideas contained in this essay were presented by Comrade Mao Tse-tung in a lecture at the Anti-Japanese Military and Political College in Yenan.

as the most fundamental practical activity, the determinant of all his other activities. Man's knowledge depends mainly on his activity in material production, through which he comes gradually to understand the phenomena, the properties and the laws of nature, and the relations between himself and nature; and through his activity in production he also gradually comes to understand, in varying degrees, certain relations that exist between man and man. None of this knowledge can be acquired apart from activity in production. In a classless society every person, as a member of society, joins in common effort with the other members, enters into definite relations of production with them and engages in production to meet man's material needs. In all class societies, the members of the different social classes also enter, in different ways, into definite relations of production and engage in production to meet their material needs. This is the primary source from which human knowledge develops.

Man's social practice is not confined to activity in production, but takes many other forms — class struggle, political life, scientific and artistic pursuits; in short, as a social being, man participates in all spheres of the practical life of society. Thus man, in varying degrees, comes to know the different relations between man and man, not only through his material life but also through his political and cultural life (both of which are intimately bound up with material life). Of these other types of social practice, class struggle in particular, in all its various forms, exerts a profound influence on the development of man's knowledge. In class society everyone lives as a member of a particular class, and every kind of thinking, without exception, is stamped with the brand of a class.

Marxists hold that in human society activity in production develops step by step from a lower to a higher level and that consequently man's knowledge, whether of nature or of society, also develops step by step from a lower to a higher level, that is, from the shallower to the deeper, from the one-sided to the many-sided. For a very long period in history, men were necessarily confined to a one-sided understanding of the history of society because, for one thing, the bias of the exploiting classes always distorted history and, for another, the small scale of production limited man's outlook. It was not until the modern proletariat emerged along with immense forces of production (large scale industry) that man was able to acquire a comprehensive, historical understanding of the development of society and turn this knowledge into a science, the science of Marxism.

Marxists hold that man's social practice alone is the criterion of the truth of his knowledge of the external world. What actually happens is that man's knowledge is verified only when he achieves the anticipated results in the process of social practice (material production, class struggle or scientific experiment). If a man wants to succeed in his work, that is, to achieve the anticipated results, he must bring his ideas into correspondence with the laws of the objective external world; if they do not correspond, he will fail in his practice. After he fails, he draws his lessons, corrects his ideas to make them correspond to the laws of the external world, and can thus turn failure into success; this is what is meant by "failure is the mother of success" and "a fall into the pit, a gain in your wit". The dialectical-materialist theory of knowledge places practice in the primary position, holding that human knowledge can in no way be separated from practice and repudiating all the erroneous theories which deny the importance of practice or separate knowledge from practice. Thus Lenin said, *Practice is higher than (theoretical) knowledge, for it has not only the dignity of universality, but also of immediate actuality.*"[1] The Marxist philosophy of dialectical materialism has two out-

1. V. I. Lenin, "Conspectus of Hegel's *The Science of Logic*", Collected Works, Russ. ed., Moscow, 1958, Vol. XXXVIII, p. 205.

standing characteristics. One is its class nature: it openly avows that dialectical materialism is in the service of the proletariat. The other is its practicality: it emphasizes the dependence of theory on practice, emphasizes that theory is based on practice and in turn serves practice. The truth of any knowledge or theory is determined not by subjective feelings, but by objective results in social practice. Only social practice can be the criterion of truth. The standpoint of practice is the primary and basic standpoint in the dialectical-materialist theory of knowledge.[2]

But how then does human knowledge arise from practice and in turn serve practice? This will become clear if we look at the process of development of knowledge.

In the process of practice, man at first sees only the phenomenal side, the separate aspects, the external relations of things. For instance, some people from outside come to Yenan on a tour of observation. In the first day or two, they see its topography, streets and houses; they meet many people, attend banquets, evening parties and mass meetings, hear talk of various kinds and read various documents, all these being the phenomena, the separate aspects and the external relations of things. This is called the perceptual stage of cognition, namely, the stage of sense perceptions and impressions. That is, these particular things in Yenan act on the sense organs of the members of the observation group, evoke sense perceptions and give rise in their brains to many impressions together with a rough sketch of the external relations among these impressions: this is the first stage of cognition. At this stage, man cannot as yet form concepts, which are deeper, or draw logical conclusions.

As social practice continues, things that give rise to man's sense perceptions and impressions in the course of his practice are repeated many times; then a sudden change (leap)

2. See Karl Marx, "Theses on Feuerbach", Karl Marx and Frederick Engels, *Selected Works*, in two volumes, Eng. ed., FLPH, Moscow, 1958, Vol. II, p. 403, and V. I. Lenin, *Materialism and Empirio-Criticism*, Eng. ed., FLPH, Moscow, 1952, pp. 136-42.

takes place in the brain in the process of cognition, and concepts are formed. Concepts are no longer the phenomena, the separate aspects and the external relations of things; they grasp the essence, the totality and the internal relations of things. Between concepts and sense perceptions there is not only a quantitative but also a qualitative difference. Proceeding further, by means of judgement and inference one is able to draw logical conclusions. The expression in *San Kuo Yen Yi*,[1] "knit the brows and a stratagem comes to mind", or in everyday language, "let me think it over", refers to man's use of concepts in the brain to form judgements and inferences. This is the second stage of cognition. When the members of the observation group have collected various data and, what is more, have "thought them over", they are able to arrive at the judgement that "the Communist Party's policy of the National United Front Against Japan is thorough, sincere and genuine". Having made this judgement, they can, if they too are genuine about uniting to save the nation, go a step further and draw the following conclusion, "The National United Front Against Japan can succeed." This stage of conception, judgement and inference is the more important stage in the entire process of knowing a thing; it is the stage of rational knowledge. The real task of knowing is, through perception, to arrive at thought, to arrive step by step at the comprehension of the internal contradictions of objective things, of their laws and of the internal relations between one process and another, that is, to arrive at logical knowledge. To repeat, logical knowledge differs from perceptual knowledge in that perceptual knowledge pertains to the separate aspects, the phenomena and the external relations of things, whereas logical knowledge takes a big stride forward to reach the totality, the essence and the internal relations of things and discloses the inner

1. *San Kuo Yen Yi (Tales of the Three Kingdoms)* is a famous Chinese historical novel by Lo Kuan-chung (late 14th and early 15th century).

contradictions in the surrounding world. Therefore, logical knowledge is capable of grasping the development of the surrounding world in its totality, in the internal relations of all its aspects.

This dialectical-materialist theory of the process of development of knowledge, basing itself on practice and proceeding from the shallower to the deeper, was never worked out by anybody before the rise of Marxism. Marxist materialism solved this problem correctly for the first time, pointing out both materialistically and dialectically the deepening movement of cognition, the movement by which man in society progresses from perceptual knowledge to logical knowledge in his complex, constantly recurring practice of production and class struggle. Lenin said, "The abstraction of *matter*, of a *law* of nature, the abstraction of *value*, etc., in short, *all* scientific (correct, serious, not absurd) abstractions reflect nature more deeply, truly and *completely*."[4] Marxism-Leninism holds that each of the two stages in the process of cognition has its own characteristics, with knowledge manifesting itself as perceptual at the lower stage and logical at the higher stage, but that both are stages in an integrated process of cognition. The perceptual and the rational are qualitatively different, but are not divorced from each other; they are unified on the basis of practice. Our practice proves that what is perceived cannot at once be comprehended and that only what is comprehended can be more deeply perceived. Perception only solves the problem of phenomena; theory alone can solve the problem of essence. The solving of both these problems is not separable in the slightest degree from practice. Whoever wants to know a thing has no way of doing so except by coming into contact with it, that is, by living (practising) in its environment. In feudal society it was impossible to know the laws of capitalist society in advance because capi-

4. V. I. Lenin, "Conspectus of Hegel's *The Science of Logic*", *Collected Works*, Russ. ed., Moscow, 1958, Vol. XXXVIII, p. 161.

talism had not yet emerged, the relevant practice was lacking. Marxism could be the product only of capitalist society. Marx, in the era of laissez-faire capitalism, could not concretely know certain laws peculiar to the era of imperialism beforehand, because imperialism, the last stage of capitalism, had not yet emerged and the relevant practice was lacking; only Lenin and Stalin could undertake this task. Leaving aside their genius, the reason why Marx, Engels, Lenin and Stalin could work out their theories was mainly that they personally took part in the practice of the class struggle and the scientific experimentation of their time; lacking this condition, no genius could have succeeded. The saying, "without stepping outside his gate the scholar knows all the wide world's affairs", was mere empty talk in past times when technology was undeveloped. Even though this saying can be valid in the present age of developed technology, the people with real personal knowledge are those engaged in practice the wide world over. And it is only when these people have come to "know" through their practice and when their knowledge has reached him through writing and technical media that the "scholar" can indirectly "know" all the wide world's affairs". If you want to know a certain thing or a certain class of things directly, you must personally participate in the practical struggle to change reality, to change that thing or class of things, for only thus can you come into contact with them as phenomena; only through personal participation in the practical struggle to change reality can you uncover the essence of that thing or class of things and comprehend them. This is the path to knowledge which every man actually travels, though some people, deliberately distorting matters, argue to the contrary. The most ridiculous person in the world is the "know all" who picks up a smattering of hearsay knowledge and proclaims himself "the world's Number One authority"; this merely shows that he has not taken a proper measure of himself. Knowledge is a matter of science, and no dishonesty or conceit whatsoever is permissible. What is required is definitely the reverse — honesty and modesty. If you want knowledge, you must take part in the practice of changing reality. If you want to know the taste of a pear, you must change the pear by eating it yourself. If you want to know the structure and properties of the atom, you must make physical and chemical experiments to change the state of the atom. If you want to know the theory and methods of revolution, you must take part in revolution. All genuine knowledge originates in direct experience. But one cannot have direct experience of everything; as a matter of fact, most of our knowledge comes from indirect experience, for example, all knowledge from past times and foreign lands. To our ancestors and to foreigners, such knowledge was — or is — a matter of direct experience, and this knowledge is reliable if in the course of their direct experience the requirement of "scientific abstraction", spoken of by Lenin, was — or is — fulfilled and objective reality scientifically reflected, otherwise it is not reliable. Hence a man's knowledge consists only of two parts, that which comes from direct experience and that which comes from indirect experience. Moreover, what is indirect experience for me is direct experience for other people. Consequently, considered as a whole, knowledge of any kind is inseparable from direct experience. All knowledge originates in perception of the objective external world through man's physical sense organs. Anyone who denies such perception, denies direct experience, or denies personal participation in the practice that changes reality, is not a materialist. That is why the "know-all" is ridiculous. There is an old Chinese saying, "How can you catch tiger cubs without entering the tiger's lair?" This saying holds true for man's practice and it also holds true for the theory of knowledge. There can be no knowledge apart from practice.

To make clear the dialectical-materialist movement of cognition arising on the basis of the practice which changes reality — to make clear the gradually deepening movement of cognition – a few additional concrete examples are given below.

In its knowledge of capitalist society, the proletariat was only in the perceptual stage of cognition in the first period of its practice, the period of machine-smashing and spontaneous struggle; it knew only some of the aspects and the external relations of the phenomena of capitalism. The proletariat was then still a "class-in-itself". But when it reached the second period of its practice, the period of conscious and organized economic and political struggles, the proletariat was able to comprehend the essence of capitalist society, the relations of exploitation between social classes and its own historical task; and it was able to do so because of its own practice and because of its experience of prolonged struggle, which Marx and Engels scientifically summed up in all its variety to create the theory of Marxism for the education of the proletariat. It was then that the proletariat became a "class-for-itself".

Similarly with the Chinese people's knowledge of imperialism. The first stage was one of superficial, perceptual knowledge, as shown in the indiscriminate anti-foreign struggles of the Movement of the Taiping Heavenly Kingdom, the Yi Ho Tuan Movement, and so on. It was only in the second stage that the Chinese people reached the stage of rational knowledge, saw the internal and external contradictions of imperialism and saw the essential truth that imperialism had allied itself with China's comprador and feudal classes to oppress and exploit the great masses of the Chinese people. This knowledge began about the time of the May 4th Movement of 1919.

Next, let us consider war. If those who lead a war lack experience of war, then at the initial stage they will not understand the profound laws pertaining to the directing of a specific war (such as our Agrarian Revolutionary War of the past decade). At the initial stage they will merely experience a good deal of fighting and, what is more, suffer many defeats. But this experience (the experience of battles won and especially of battles lost) enables them to comprehend the inner thread of the whole war, namely, the laws of that specific war, to understand its strategy and tactics, and consequently to direct the war with confidence. If, at such a moment, the command is turned over to an inexperienced person, then he too will have to suffer a number of defeats (gain experience) before he can comprehend the true laws of the war.

"I am not sure I can handle it." We often hear this remark when a comrade hesitates to accept an assignment. Why is he unsure of himself? Because he has no systematic understanding of the content and circumstances of the assignment, or because he has had little or no contact with such work, and so the laws governing it are beyond him. After a detailed analysis of the nature and circumstances of the assignment, he will feel more sure of himself and do it willingly. If he spends some time at the job and gains experience and if he is a person who is willing to look into matters with an open mind and not one who approaches problems subjectively, one-sidedly and superficially, then he can draw conclusions for himself as to how to go about the job and do it with much more courage. Only those who are subjective, one-sided and superficial in their approach to problems will smugly issue orders or directives the moment they arrive on the scene, without considering the circumstances, without viewing things in their totality (their history and their present state as a whole) and without getting to the essence of things (their nature and the internal relations between one thing and another). Such people are bound to trip and fall.

Thus it can be seen that the first step in the process of cognition is contact with the objects of the external world; this belongs to the stage of perception. The second step is to synthesize the data of perception by arranging and reconstructing them; this belongs to the stage of conception, judgment and inference. It is only when the data of perception are very rich (not fragmentary) and correspond

674

to reality (are not illusory) that they can be the basis for forming correct concepts and theories.

Here two important points must be emphasized. The first, which has been stated before but should be repeated here, is the dependence of rational knowledge upon perceptual knowledge. Anyone who thinks that rational knowledge need not be derived from perceptual knowledge is an idealist. In the history of philosophy there is the "rationalist" school that admits the reality only of reason and not of experience, believing that reason alone is reliable while perceptual experience is not; this school errs by turning things upside down. The rational is reliable precisely because it has its source in sense perceptions, otherwise it would be like water without a source, a tree without roots, subjective, self-engendered and unreliable. As to the sequence in the process of cognition, perceptual experience comes first; we stress the significance of social practice in the process of cognition precisely because social practice alone can give rise to human knowledge and it alone can start man on the acquisition of perceptual experience from the objective world. For a person who shuts his eyes, stops his ears and totally cuts himself off from the objective world there can be no such thing as knowledge. Knowledge begins with experience — this is the materialism of the theory of knowledge.

The second point is that knowledge needs to be deepened, that the perceptual stage of knowledge needs to be developed to the rational stage — this is the dialectics of the theory of knowledge.[1] To think that knowledge can stop at the lower, perceptual stage and that perceptual knowledge alone is reliable while rational knowledge is not, would be to repeat the historical error of "empiricism". This theory errs in failing to understand that, although the data of perception reflect certain realities in the objective world (I am not speaking here of idealist empiricism which con-

1. "In order to understand, it is necessary empirically to begin understanding, study, to rise from empiricism to the universal." (*Ibid.*, p. 197.)

675

fines experience to so-called introspection), they are merely one-sided and superficial, reflecting things incompletely and not reflecting their essence. Fully to reflect a thing in its totality, to reflect its essence, to reflect its inherent laws, it is necessary through the exercise of thought to reconstruct the rich data of sense perception, discarding the dross and selecting the essential, eliminating the false and retaining the true, proceeding from the one to the other and from the outside to the inside, in order to form a system of concepts and theories — it is necessary to make a leap from perceptual to rational knowledge. Such reconstructed knowledge is not more empty or more unreliable; on the contrary, whatever has been scientifically reconstructed in the process of cognition, on the basis of practice, reflects objective reality, as Lenin said, more deeply, more truly, more fully. As against this, vulgar "practical men" respect experience but despise theory, and therefore cannot have a comprehensive view of an entire objective process, lack clear direction and long-range perspective, and are complacent over occasional successes and glimpses of the truth. If such persons direct a revolution, they will lead it up a blind alley.

Rational knowledge depends upon perceptual knowledge and perceptual knowledge remains to be developed into rational knowledge — this is the dialectical-materialist theory of knowledge. In philosophy, neither "rationalism" nor "empiricism" understands the historical or the dialectical nature of knowledge, and although each of these schools contains one aspect of the truth (here I am referring to materialist, not to idealist, rationalism and empiricism), both are wrong on the theory of knowledge as a whole. The dialectical-materialist movement of knowledge from the perceptual to the rational holds true for a minor process of cognition (for instance, knowing a single thing or task) as well as for a major process of cognition (for instance, knowing a whole society or a revolution).

But the movement of knowledge does not end here. If the dialectical-materialist movement of knowledge were to stop at rational knowledge, only half the problem would be dealt with. And as far as Marxist philosophy is concerned, only the less important half at that. Marxist philosophy holds that the most important problem does not lie in understanding the laws of the objective world and thus being able to explain it, but in applying the knowledge of these laws actively to change the world. From the Marxist viewpoint, theory is important, and its importance is fully expressed in Lenin's statement, "Without revolutionary theory there can be no revolutionary movement."[1] But Marxism emphasizes the importance of theory precisely and only because it can guide action. If we have a correct theory but merely prate about it, pigeonhole it and do not put it into practice, then that theory, however good, is of no significance. Knowledge begins with practice, and theoretical knowledge is acquired through practice and must then return to practice. The active function of knowledge manifests itself not only in the active leap from perceptual to rational knowledge, but — and this is more important — it must manifest itself in the leap from rational knowledge to revolutionary practice. The knowledge which grasps the laws of the world, must be redirected to the practice of changing the world, must be applied anew in the practice of production, in the practice of revolutionary class struggle and revolutionary national struggle and in the practice of scientific experiment. This is the process of testing and developing theory, the continuation of the whole process of cognition. The problem of whether theory corresponds to objective reality is not, and cannot be, completely solved in the movement of knowledge from the perceptual to the rational, mentioned above. The only way to solve this problem completely is to redirect rational knowledge to social practice, apply theory to practice and see whether it can achieve the objectives one has in mind. Many theories

1. V. I. Lenin, "What Is to Be Done?", *Collected Works*, Eng. ed., FLPH, Moscow, 1961, Vol. V, p. 369.

of natural science are held to be true not only because they were so considered when natural scientists originated them, but because they have been verified in subsequent scientific practice. Similarly, Marxism-Leninism is held to be true not only because it was so considered when it was scientifically formulated by Marx, Engels, Lenin and Stalin but because it has been verified in the subsequent practice of revolutionary class struggle and revolutionary national struggle. Dialectical materialism is universally true because it is impossible for anyone to escape from its domain in his practice. The history of human knowledge tells us that the truth of many theories is incomplete and that this incompleteness is remedied through the test of practice. Many theories are erroneous and it is through the test of practice that their errors are corrected. That is why practice is the criterion of truth and why "the standpoint of life, of practice, should be first and fundamental in the theory of knowledge."[1] Stalin has well said, "Theory becomes purposeless if it is not connected with revolutionary practice, just as practice gropes in the dark if its path is not illumined by revolutionary theory."[2]

When we get to this point, is the movement of knowledge completed? Our answer is: it is and yet it is not. When men in society throw themselves into the practice of changing a certain objective process (whether natural or social) at a certain stage of its development, they can, as a result of the reflection of the objective process in their brains and the exercise of their subjective activity, advance their knowledge from the perceptual to the rational, and create ideas, theories, plans or programmes which correspond in general to the laws of that objective process. They then apply these ideas, theories, plans or programmes in practice in the same objective process. And if they can realize the aims they

1. V. I. Lenin, *Materialism and Empirio-Criticism*, Eng. ed., FLPH, Moscow, 1952, p. 141.
2. J. V. Stalin, "The Foundations of Leninism", *Problems of Leninism*, Eng. ed., FLPH, Moscow, 1954, p. 31.

have in mind, that is, if in that same process of practice they can translate, or on the whole translate, those previously formulated ideas, theories, plans or programmes into fact, then the movement of knowledge may be considered completed with regard to this particular process. In the process of changing nature, take for example the fulfilment of an engineering plan, the verification of a scientific hypothesis, the manufacture of an implement or the reaping of a crop; or in the process of changing society, take for example the victory of a strike, victory in a war or the fulfilment of an educational plan. All these may be considered the realization of aims one has in mind. But generally speaking, whether in the practice of changing nature or of changing society, men's original ideas, theories, plans or programmes are seldom realized without any alteration. This is because people engaged in changing reality are usually subject to numerous limitations; they are limited not only by existing scientific and technological conditions but also by the development of the objective process itself and the degree to which this process has become manifest (the aspects and the essence of the objective process have not yet been fully revealed). In such a situation, ideas, theories, plans or programmes are usually altered partially and sometimes even wholly, because of the discovery of unforeseen circumstances in the course of practice. That is to say, it does happen that the original ideas, theories, plans or programmes fail to correspond with reality either in whole or in part and are wholly or partially incorrect. In many instances, failures have to be repeated many times before errors in knowledge can be corrected and correspondence with the laws of the objective process achieved, and consequently before the subjective can be transformed into the objective, or in other words, before the anticipated results can be achieved in practice. But when that point is reached, no matter how, the movement of human knowledge regarding a certain objective process at a certain stage of its development may be considered completed.

However, so far as the progression of the process is concerned, the movement of human knowledge is not completed. Every process, whether in the realm of nature or of society, progresses and develops by reason of its internal contradiction and struggle, and the movement of human knowledge should also progress and develop along with it. As far as social movements are concerned, true revolutionary leaders must not only be good at correcting their ideas, theories, plans or programmes when errors are discovered, as has been indicated above; but when a certain objective process has already progressed and changed from one stage of development to another, they must also be good at making themselves and all their fellow-revolutionaries progress and change in their subjective knowledge along with it, that is to say, they must ensure that the proposed new revolutionary tasks and new working programmes correspond to the new changes in the situation. In a revolutionary period the situation changes very rapidly; if the knowledge of revolutionaries does not change rapidly in accordance with the changed situation, they will be unable to lead the revolution to victory.

It often happens, however, that thinking lags behind reality; this is because man's cognition is limited by numerous social conditions. We are opposed to die-hards in the revolutionary ranks whose thinking fails to advance with changing objective circumstances and has manifested itself historically as Right opportunism. These people fail to see that the struggle of opposites has already pushed the objective process forward while their knowledge has stopped at the old stage. This is characteristic of the thinking of all die-hards. Their thinking is divorced from social practice, and they cannot march ahead to guide the chariot of society; they simply trail behind, grumbling that it goes too fast and trying to drag it back or turn it in the opposite direction.

We are also opposed to "Left" phrase-mongering. The thinking of "Leftists" outstrips a given stage of development of the objective process; some regard their fantasies as truth, while others strain to realize in the present an ideal which can only be realized in the future. They alienate themselves from the current practice of the majority of the people and from the realities of the day, and show themselves adventurist in their actions.

Idealism and mechanical materialism, opportunism and adventurism, are all characterized by the breach between the subjective and the objective, by the separation of knowledge from practice. The Marxist-Leninist theory of knowledge, characterized as it is by scientific social practice, cannot but resolutely oppose these wrong ideologies. Marxists recognize that in the absolute and general process of development of the universe, the development of each particular process is relative, and that hence, in the endless flow of absolute truth, man's knowledge of a particular process at any given stage of development is only relative truth. The sum total of innumerable relative truths constitutes absolute truth.[1] The development of an objective process is full of contradictions and struggles, and so is the development of the movement of human knowledge. All the dialectical movements of the objective world can sooner or later be reflected in human knowledge. In social practice, the process of coming into being, developing and passing away is infinite, and so is the process of coming into being, developing and passing away in human knowledge. As man's practice which changes objective reality in accordance with given ideas, theories, plans or programmes, advances further and further, his knowledge of objective reality likewise becomes deeper and deeper. The movement of change in the world of objective reality is never-ending and so is man's cognition of truth through practice. Marxism-Leninism has in no way exhausted truth but ceaselessly opens up roads to the knowledge of truth in the course of practice. Our conclusion is the concrete,

1. See V. I. Lenin, *Materialism and Empirio-Criticism*, Eng. ed., FLPH, Moscow, 1952, pp. 129-36.

681

historical unity of the subjective and the objective, of theory and practice, of knowing and doing, and we are opposed to all erroneous ideologies, whether "Left" or Right, which depart from concrete history.

In the present epoch of the development of society, the responsibility of correctly knowing and changing the world has been placed by history upon the shoulders of the proletariat and its party. This process, the practice of changing the world, which is determined in accordance with scientific knowledge, has already reached historic moment in the world and in China, a great moment unprecedented in human history, that is, the moment for completely banishing darkness from the world and from China and for changing the world into a world of light such as never previously existed. The struggle of the proletariat and the revolutionary people to change the world comprises the fulfilment of the following tasks: to change the objective world and, at the same time, their own subjective world — to change their cognitive ability and change the relations between the subjective and the objective world. Such a change has already come about in one part of the globe, in the Soviet Union. There the people are pushing forward this process of change. The people of China and the rest of the world either are going through, or will go through, such a process. And the objective world which is to be changed also includes all the opponents of change, who, in order to be changed, must go through a stage of compulsion before they can enter the stage of voluntary, conscious change. The epoch of world communism will be reached when all mankind voluntarily and consciously changes itself and the world.

Discover the truth through practice, and again through practice verify and develop the truth. Start from perceptual knowledge and actively develop it into rational knowledge; then start from rational knowledge and actively guide revolutionary practice to change both the subjective and the objective world. Practice, knowledge, again practice, and again knowledge. This form repeats itself in endless cycles, and with each cycle the content of practice and knowledge rises to a higher level. Such is the whole of the dialectical-materialist theory of knowledge, and such is the dialectical-materialist theory of the unity of knowing and doing.

ON CONTRADICTION

THE law of contradiction in things, that is, the law of the unity of opposites, is the basic law of materialist dialectics. Lenin said, "Dialectics in the proper sense is the study of contradiction *in the very essence of objects*."[1] Lenin often called this law the essence of dialectics; he also called it the kernel of dialectics.[2] In studying this law, therefore, we cannot but touch upon a variety of questions, upon a number of philosophical problems. If we can become clear on all these problems, we shall arrive at a fundamental understanding of materialist dialectics. The problems are: the two world outlooks, the universality of contradiction, the particularity of contradiction, the principal contradiction and the principal aspect of a contradiction, the identity and struggle of the aspects of a contradiction, and the place of antagonism in contradiction.

The criticism to which the idealism of the Deborin school has been subjected in Soviet philosophical circles in recent years has aroused great interest among us. Deborin's idealism has exerted a very bad influence in the Chinese Communist Party, and it cannot be said that

1. V. I. Lenin, "Conspectus of Hegel's *Lectures on the History of Philosophy*", *Collected Works*, Russ. ed., Moscow, 1958, Vol. XXXVIII, p. 249.

2. In his essay "On the Question of Dialectics", Lenin said, "The splitting in two of a single whole and the cognition of its contradictory parts (see the quotation from Philo on Heraclitus at the beginning of Section 3 'On Cognition' in Lassalle's book on Heraclitus) is the *essence* (one of the 'essentials', one of the principal, if not the principal, characteristics or features) of dialectics." (*Collected Works*, Russ. ed., Moscow, 1958, Vol. XXXVIII, p. 357.) In his "Conspectus of Hegel's *The Science of Logic*", he said, "In brief, dialectics can be defined as the doctrine of the unity of opposites. This grasps the kernel of dialectics, but it requires explanations and development." (*Ibid.*, p. 215.)

the dogmatist thinking in our Party is unrelated to the approach of that school. Our present study of philosophy should therefore have the eradication of dogmatist thinking as its main objective.

I. THE TWO WORLD OUTLOOKS

Throughout the history of human knowledge, there have been two conceptions concerning the law of development of the universe, the metaphysical conception and the dialectical conception, which form two opposing world outlooks. Lenin said:

> The two basic (or two possible? or two historically observable?) conceptions of development (evolution) are: development as decrease and increase, as repetition, *and* development as a unity of opposites (the division of a unity into mutually exclusive opposites and their reciprocal relation).[1]

Here Lenin was referring to these two different world outlooks.

In China another name for metaphysics is *hsuan-hsueh*. For a long period in history whether in China or in Europe, this way of thinking, which is part and parcel of the idealist world outlook, occupied a dominant position in human thought. In Europe, the materialism of the bourgeoisie in its early days was also metaphysical. As the social economy of many European countries advanced to the stage of highly developed capitalism, as the forces of production, the class struggle and the sciences developed to a level unprecedented in history, and as the industrial proletariat became the greatest motive force in historical development, there arose the Marxist world

1. V. I. Lenin, "On the Question of Dialectics", *Collected Works*, Russ. ed., Moscow, 1958, Vol. XXXVIII, p. 358.

outlook of materialist dialectics. Then, in addition to open and barefaced reactionary idealism, vulgar evolutionism emerged among the bourgeoisie to oppose materialist dialectics.

The metaphysical or vulgar evolutionist world outlook sees things as isolated, static and one-sided. It regards all things in the universe, their forms and their species, as eternally isolated from one another and immutable. Such change as there is can only be an increase or decrease in quantity or a change of place. Moreover, the cause of such an increase or decrease or change of place is not inside things but outside them, that is, the motive force is external. Metaphysicians hold that all the different kinds of things in the universe and all their characteristics have been the same ever since they first came into being. All subsequent changes have simply been increases or decreases in quantity. They contend that a thing can only keep on repeating itself as the same kind of thing and cannot change into anything different. In their opinion, capitalist exploitation, capitalist competition, the individualist ideology of capitalist society, and so on, can all be found in ancient slave society, or even in primitive society, and will exist for ever unchanged. They ascribe the causes of social development to factors external to society, such as geography and climate. They search in an over-simplified way outside a thing for the causes of its development, and they deny the theory of materialist dialectics which holds that development arises from the contradictions inside a thing. Consequently they can explain neither the qualitative diversity of things, nor the phenomenon of one quality changing into another. In Europe, this mode of thinking existed as mechanical materialism in the 17th and 18th centuries and as vulgar evolutionism at the end of the 19th and the beginning of the 20th centuries. In China, there was the metaphysical thinking exemplified in the saying "Heaven changeth not, likewise the Tâo changeth not,"[1] and it was supported by the decadent feudal ruling classes for a long time. Mechanical materialism and vulgar evolutionism, which were imported from Europe in the last hundred years, are supported by the bourgeoisie.

As opposed to the metaphysical world outlook, the world outlook of materialist dialectics holds that in order to understand the development of a thing we should study it internally and in its relations with other things; in other words, the development of things should be seen as their internal and necessary self-movement, while each thing in its movement is interrelated with and interacts on the things around it. The fundamental cause of the development of a thing is not external but internal; it lies in the contradictoriness within the thing. There is internal contradiction in every single thing, hence its motion and development. Contradictoriness within a thing is the fundamental cause of its development, while its interrelations and interactions with other things are secondary causes. Thus materialist dialectics effectively combats the theory of external causes, or of an external motive force, advanced by metaphysical mechanical materialism and vulgar evolutionism. It is evident that purely external causes can only give rise to mechanical motion, that is, to changes in scale or quantity, but cannot explain why things differ qualitatively in thousands of ways and why one thing changes into another. As a matter of fact, even mechanical motion under external force occurs through the internal contradictoriness of things. Simple growth in plants and animals, their quantitative development, is likewise chiefly the result of their internal contradictions. Similarly, social development is due chiefly not to external but to internal causes. Countries with almost the same geographical and climatic conditions display great diversity and

1. A saying of Tung Chung-shu (179-104 B.C.), a well-known exponent of Confucianism in the Han Dynasty.

unevenness in their development. Moreover, great social changes may take place in one and the same country although its geography and climate remain unchanged. Imperialist Russia changed into the socialist Soviet Union, and feudal Japan, which had locked its doors against the world, changed into imperialist Japan, although no change occurred in the geography and climate of either country. Long dominated by feudalism, China has undergone great changes in the last hundred years and is now changing in the direction of a new China, liberated and free, and yet no change has occurred in her geography and climate. Changes do take place in the geography and climate of the earth as a whole and in every part of it, but they are insignificant when compared with changes in society; geographical and climatic changes manifest themselves in terms of tens of thousands of years, while social changes manifest themselves in thousands, hundreds or tens of years, and even in a few years or months in times of revolution. According to materialist dialectics, changes in nature are due chiefly to the development of the internal contradictions in nature. Changes in society are due chiefly to the development of the internal contradictions in society, that is, the contradiction between the productive forces and the relations of production, the contradiction between classes and the contradiction between the old and the new; it is the development of these contradictions that pushes society forward and gives the impetus for the supersession of the old society by the new. Does materialist dialectics exclude external causes? Not at all. It holds that external causes are the condition of change and internal causes are the basis of change, and that external causes become operative through internal causes. In a suitable temperature an egg changes into a chicken, but no temperature can change a stone into a chicken, because each has different basis. There is constant interaction between the peoples of different countries. In the era of capitalism, and especially in the era of imperialism and proletarian revolution, the interaction and mutual impact of different countries in the political, economic and cultural spheres are extremely great. The October Socialist Revolution ushered in a new epoch in world history as well as in Russian history. It exerted influence on internal changes in the other countries in the world and, similarly and in a particularly profound way, on internal changes in China. These changes, however, were effected through the inner laws of development of these countries, China included. In battle, one army is victorious and the other is defeated; both the victory and the defeat are determined by internal causes. The one is victorious either because it is strong or because of its competent generalship, the other is vanquished either because it is weak or because of its incompetent generalship; it is through internal causes that external causes become operative. In China in 1927, the defeat of the proletariat by the big bourgeoisie came about through the opportunism then to be found within the Chinese proletariat itself (inside the Chinese Communist Party). When we liquidated this opportunism, the Chinese revolution resumed its advance. Later, the Chinese revolution again suffered severe setbacks at the hands of the enemy, because adventurism had risen within our Party. When we liquidated this adventurism, our cause advanced once again. Thus it can be seen that to lead the revolution to victory, a political party must depend on the correctness of its own political line and the solidity of its own organization.

The dialectical world outlook emerged in ancient times both in China and in Europe. Ancient dialectics, however, had a somewhat spontaneous and naive character; in the social and historical conditions then prevailing, it was not yet able to form a theoretical system, hence it could not fully explain the world and was supplanted by metaphysics. The famous German philosopher Hegel, who lived in the late 18th and early 19th centuries, made most important contributions to dialectics, but his dialectics was idealist. It was not until Marx and Engels, the great protagonists of the proletarian movement, had synthesized the positive achievements in the history of human knowledge and, in particular, critically absorbed the rational elements of Hegelian dialectics and created the great theory of dialectical and historical materialism that an unprecedented revolution occurred in the history of human knowledge. This theory was further developed by Lenin and Stalin. As soon as it spread to China, it wrought tremendous changes in the world of Chinese thought.

This dialectical world outlook teaches us primarily how to observe and analyse the movement of opposites in different things and, on the basis of such analysis, to indicate the methods for resolving contradictions. It is therefore most important for us to understand the law of contradiction in things in a concrete way.

II. THE UNIVERSALITY OF CONTRADICTION

For convenience of exposition, I shall deal first with the universality of contradiction and then proceed to the particularity of contradiction. The reason is that the universality of contradiction can be explained more briefly, for it has been widely recognized ever since the materialist-dialectical world outlook was discovered and materialist dialectics applied with outstanding success to analysing many aspects of human history and natural history and to changing many aspects of society and nature (as in the Soviet Union) by the great creators and continuers of Marxism — Marx, Engels, Lenin and Stalin; whereas the particularity of contradiction is still not clearly understood by many comrades, and especially by the dogmatists. They do not understand that it is precisely in the particularity of contradiction that the universality of contradiction resides. Nor do they understand how important is the study of the particularity of contradiction in the concrete things confronting us for guiding the course of revolutionary practice. Therefore, it is necessary to stress the study of the particularity of contradiction and to explain it at adequate length. For this reason, in our analysis of the law of contradiction in things, we shall first analyse the universality of contradiction, then place special stress on analysing the particularity of contradiction, and finally return to the universality of contradiction.

The universality or absoluteness of contradiction has a twofold meaning. One is that contradiction exists in the process of development of all things, and the other ·is that in the process of development of each thing a movement of opposites exists from beginning to end.

Engels said, "Motion itself is a contradiction."[1] Lenin defined the law of the unity of opposites as "the recognition (discovery) of the contradictory, *mutually exclusive*, opposite tendencies *in all* phenomena and processes of nature *(including* mind and society)".[2] Are these ideas correct? Yes, they are. The interdependence of the contradictory aspects present in all things and the struggle between these aspects determine the life of all things and push their development forward. There is nothing that does not contain contradiction; without contradiction nothing would exist.

Contradiction is the basis of the simple forms of motion (for instance, mechanical motion) and still more so of the complex forms of motion.

Engels explained the universality of contradiction as follows:

If simple mechanical change of place contains a contradiction, this is even more true of the higher forms of motion of matter, and especially of organic

1. Frederick Engels, "Dialectics. Quantity and Quality", *Anti-Dühring*, Eng. ed., FLPH, Moscow, 1959, p. 166.
2. V. I. Lenin, "On the Question of Dialectics", *Collected Works*, Russ. ed., Moscow, 1958, Vol. XXXVIII, pp. 357-58.

life and its development. . . . life consists precisely and primarily in this — that a being is at each moment itself and yet something else. Life is therefore also a contradiction which is present in things and processes themselves, and which constantly originates and resolves itself; and as soon as the contradiction ceases, life, too, comes to an end, and death steps in. We likewise saw that also in the sphere of thought we could not escape contradictions, and that for example the contradiction between man's inherently unlimited capacity for knowledge and its actual presence only in men who are externally limited and possess limited cognition finds its solution in what is — at least practically, for us — an endless succession of generations, in infinite progress.

. . . .one of the basic principles of higher mathematics is the contradiction that in certain circumstances straight lines and curves may be the same. . . .

But even lower mathematics teems with contradictions.[1]

Lenin illustrated the universality of contradiction as follows:

In mathematics: $+$ and $-$. Differential and integral.

In mechanics: action and reaction.

In physics: positive and negative electricity.

In chemistry: the combination and dissociation of atoms.

In social science: the class struggle.[2]

In war, offence and defence, advance and retreat, victory and defeat are all mutually contradictory phenomena. One cannot exist without the other. The two aspects are at once in conflict and in interdependence, and this constitutes the totality of a war, pushes its develop-

1. Frederick Engels, *op. cit.*, pp. 166-67.
2. V. I. Lenin, "On the Question of Dialectics", *Collected Works*, Russ. ed., Moscow, 1958, Vol. XXXVIII, p. 357.

ment forward and solves its problems.

Every difference in men's concepts should be regarded as reflecting an objective contradiction. Objective contradictions are reflected in subjective thinking, and this process constitutes the contradictory movement of concepts, pushes forward the development of thought, and ceaselessly solves problems in man's thinking.

Opposition and struggle between ideas of different kinds constantly occur within the Party; this is a reflection within the Party of contradictions between classes and between the new and the old in society. If there were no contradictions in the Party and no ideological struggles to resolve them, the Party's life would come to an end.

Thus it is already clear that contradiction exists universally and in all processes, whether in the simple or in the complex forms of motion, whether in objective phenomena or ideological phenomena. But does contradiction also exist at the initial stage of each process? Is there a movement of opposites from beginning to end in the process of development of every single thing?

As can be seen from the articles written by Soviet philosophers criticizing it, the Deborin school maintains that contradiction appears not at the inception of a process but only when it has developed to a certain stage. If this were the case, then the cause of the development of the process before that stage would be external and not internal. Deborin thus reverts to the metaphysical theories of external causality and of mechanism. Applying this view in the analysis of concrete problems, the Deborin school sees only differences but not contradictions between the kulaks and the peasants in general under existing conditions in the Soviet Union, thus entirely agreeing with Bukharin. In analysing the French Revolution, it holds that before the Revolution there were likewise only differences but not contradictions within the Third Estate, which was composed of the workers, the peasants and the bourgeoisie. These views of the Deborin school are anti-Marxist. This school does not understand that each and every difference already contains contradiction and that difference itself is contradiction. Labour and capital have been in contradiction ever since the two classes came into being, only at first the contradiction had not yet become intense. Even under the social conditions existing in the Soviet Union, there is a difference between workers and peasants and this very difference is a contradiction, although, unlike the contradiction between labour and capital, it will not became intensified into antagonism or assume the form of class struggle; the workers and the peasants have established a firm alliance in the course of socialist construction and are gradually resolving this contradiction in the course of the advance from socialism to communism. The question is one of different kinds of contradiction, not of the presence or absence of contradiction. Contradiction is universal and absolute, it is present in the process of development of all things and permeates every process from beginning to end.

What is meant by the emergence of a new process? The old unity with its constituent opposites yields to a new unity with its constituent opposites, whereupon a new process emerges to replace the old. The old process ends and the new one begins. The new process contains new contradictions and begins its own history of the development of contradictions.

As Lenin pointed out, Marx in his *Capital* gave a model analysis of this movement of opposites which runs through the process of development of things from beginning to end. This is the method that must be employed in studying the development of all things. Lenin, too, employed this method correctly and adhered to it in all his writings.

In his *Capital,* Marx first analyses the simplest, most ordinary and fundamental, most common and everyday *relation* of bourgeois (commodity) society, a relation

694

encountered billions of times, viz. the exchange of commodities. In this very simple phenomenon (in this "cell" bourgeois society) analysis reveals *all* the contradictions (or the germs of *all* the contradictions) of modern society. The subsequent exposition shows us the development (*both* growth *and* movement) of these contradictions and of this society in the Σ [summation] of its individual parts, from its beginning to its end.

Lenin added, "Such must also be the method of exposition (or study) of dialectics in general."[1]

Chinese Communists must learn this method; only then will they be able correctly to analyse the history and the present state of the Chinese revolution and infer its future.

III. THE PARTICULARITY OF CONTRADICTION

Contradiction is present in the process of development of all things; it permeates the process of development of each thing from beginning to end. This is the universality and absoluteness of contradiction which we have discussed above. Now let us discuss the particularity and relativity of contradiction.

This problem should be studied on several levels.

First, the contradiction in each form of motion of matter has its particularity. Man's knowledge of matter is knowledge of its forms of motion, because there is nothing in this world except matter in motion and this motion must assume certain forms. In considering each form of motion of matter, we must observe the points which it has in common with other forms of motion. But what is especially important and necessary, constituting as it does the foundation of our knowledge of a thing, is to observe what is particular to this form of motion of matter, namely, to observe the qualitative difference between this form of motion and other

1. *Ibid.*, pp. 358-59.

forms. Only when we have done so can we distinguish between things. Every form of motion contains within itself its own particular contradiction. This particular contradiction constitutes the particular essence which distinguishes one thing from another. It is the internal cause or, as it may be called, the basis for the immense variety of things in the world. There are many forms of motion in nature, mechanical motion, sound, light heat, electricity, dissociation, combination, and so on. All these forms are interdependent, but in its essence each is different from the others. The particular essence of each form of motion is determined by its own particular contradiction. This holds true not only for nature but also for social and ideological phenomena. Every form of society, every form of ideology, has its own particular contradiction and particular essence.

The sciences are differentiated precisely on the basis of the particular contradictions inherent in their respective objects of study. Thus the contradiction peculiar to a certain field of phenomena constitutes the object of study for a specific branch of science. For example, positive and negative numbers in mathematics; action and reaction in mechanics; positive and negative electricity in physics; dissociation and combination in chemistry; forces of production and relations of production, classes and class struggle, in social science; offence and defence in military science; idealism and materialism, the metaphysical outlook and the dialectical outlook, in philosophy; and so on — all these are the objects of study of different branches of science precisely because each branch has its own particular contradiction and particular essence. Of course, unless we understand the universality of contradiction, we have no way of discovering the universal cause or universal basis for the movement or development of things; however, unless we study the particularity of contradiction, we have no way of determining the particular essence of a thing which differentiates it from other things, no way of discovering the particular cause or particular basis for the movement or development of a thing, and no way of distinguishing one thing from another or of demarcating the fields of science.

As regards the sequence in the movement of man's knowledge, there is always a gradual growth from the knowledge of individual and particular things to the knowledge of things in general. Only after man knows the particular essence of many different things can he proceed to generalization and know the common essence of things. When man attains the knowledge of this common essence, he uses it as a guide and proceeds to study various concrete things which have not yet been studied, or studied thoroughly, and to discover the particular essence of each; only thus is he able to supplement, enrich and develop his knowledge of their common essence and prevent such knowledge from withering or petrifying. These are the two processes of cognition: one, from the particular to the general, and the other, from the general to the particular. Thus cognition always moves in cycles and (so long as scientific method is strictly adhered to) each cycle advances human knowledge a step higher and so makes it more and more profound. Where our dogmatists err on this question is that, on the one hand, they do not understand that we have to study the particularity of contradiction and know the particular essence of individual things before we can adequately know the universality of contradiction and the common essence of things, and that, on the other hand, they do not understand that after knowing the common essence of things, we must go further and study the concrete things that have not yet been thoroughly studied or have only just emerged. Our dogmatists are lazy-bones. They refuse to undertake any painstaking study of concrete things, they regard general truths as emerging out of the void, they turn them into purely abstract unfathomable formulas, and thereby completely deny and reverse the normal sequence by which man comes to know truth. Nor do they understand the interconnection of the

697

two processes in cognition – from the particular to the general and then from the general to the particular. They understand nothing of the Marxist theory of knowledge.

It is necessary not only to study the particular contradiction and the essence determined thereby of every great system of the forms of motion of matter, but also to study the particular contradiction and the essence of each process in the long course of development of each form of motion of matter. In every form of motion, each process of development which is real (and not imaginary) is qualitatively different. Our study must emphasize and start from this point.

Qualitatively different contradictions can only be resolved by qualitatively different methods. For instance, the contradiction berween the proletariat and the bourgeoisie is resolved by the method of socialist revolution; the contradiction between the great masses of the people and the feudal system is resolved by the method of democratic revolution; the contradiction between the colonies and imperialism is resolved by the method of national revolutionary war; the contradiction between the working class and the peasant class in socialist society is resolved by the method of collectivization and mechanization in agriculture; contradiction within the Communist Party is resolved by the method of criticism and self-criticism; the contradiction between society and nature is resolved by the method of developing the productive forces. Processes change, old processes and old contradictions disappear, new processes and new contradictions emerge, and the methods of resolving contradictions differ accordingly. In Russia, there was a fundamental difference between the contradiction resolved by the February Revolution and the contradiction resolved by the October Revolution, as well as between the methods used to resolve them. The principle of using different methods to resolve different contradictions is one which Marxist-Leninists must strictly observe. The dogmatists do not observe this principle; they do not understand that conditions differ in different kinds of revolution and so do not understand that different methods should be used to resolve different contradictions; on the contrary, they invariably adopt what they imagine to be an unalterable formula and arbitrarily apply it everywhere, which only causes setbacks to the revolution or makes a sorry mess of what was originally well done.

In order to reveal the particularity of the contradictions in any process in the development of a thing, in their totality or interconnections, that is, in order to reveal the essence of the process, it is necessary to reveal the particularity of the two aspects of each of the contradictions in that process; otherwise it will be impossible to discover the essence of the process. This likewise requires the utmost attention in our study.

There are many contradictions in the course of development of any major thing. For instance, in the course of China's bourgeois-democratic revolution, where the conditions are exceedingly complex, there exist the contradiction between all the oppressed classes in Chinese society and imperialism, the contradiction between the great masses of the people and feudalism, the contradiction between the proletariat and the bourgeoisie, the contradiction between the peasantry and the urban petty bourgeoisie on the one hand and the bourgeoisie on the other, the contradiction between the various reactionary ruling groups, and so on. These contradictions cannot be treated in the same way since each has its own particularity; moreover, the two aspects of each contradiction cannot be treated in the same way since each aspect has its own characteristics. We who are engaged in the Chinese revolution should not only understand the particularity of these contradictions in their totality, that is, in their interconnections, but should also study the two aspects of each contradiction as the only means of understanding the totality. When we speak of understanding each aspect of a contradiction, we mean understanding what specific position each aspect occupies, what concrete forms it assumes in its interdependence and in its contradiction with its opposite, and what concrete methods are employed in the struggle with its opposite, when the two are both interdependent and in contradiction, and also after the interdependence breaks down. It is of great importance to study these problems. Lenin meant just this when he said that the most essential thing in Marxism, the living soul of Marxism, is the concrete analysis of concrete conditions.[1] Our dogmatists have violated Lenin's teachings; they never use their brains to analyse anything concretely, and in their writings and speeches they always use stereotypes devoid of content, thereby creating a very bad style of work in our Party.

In studying a problem, we must shun subjectivity, one-sidedness and superficiality. To be subjective means not to look at problems objectively, that is, not to use the materialist viewpoint in looking at problems. I have discussed this in my essay "On Practice". To be onesided means not to look at problems all-sidedly, for example, to understand only China but not Japan, only the Communist Party but not the Kuomintang, only the proletariat but not the bourgeoisie, only the peasants but not the landlords, only the favourable conditions but not the difficult ones, only the past but not the future, only individual parts but not the whole, only the defects but not the achievements, only the plaintiff's case but not the defendant's, only underground revolutionary work but not open revolutionary work, and so on. In a word, it means not to understand the characteristics of both aspects of a contradiction. This is what we mean by looking at a problem one-sidedly. Or it may be called seeing the part but not the whole, seeing the trees but not the forest. That way it is impossible to find the method for resolving a contradiction, it is impossible to accomplish the tasks of the revolution, to carry out

1. See "Problems of Strategy in China's Revolutionary War".

assignments well or to develop inner-Party ideological struggle correctly. When Sun Wu Tzǔ said in discussing military science, "Know the enemy and know yourself, and you can fight a hundred battles with no danger of defeat",[1] he was referring to the two sides in a battle. Wei Cheng[2] of the Tang Dynasty also understood the error of one-sidedness when he said, "Listen to both sides and you will be enlightened, heed only one side and you will be benighted." But our comrades often look at problems one-sidedly, and so they often run into snags. In the novel Shui Hu Ch'uan, Sung Chiang thrice attacked Chu Village.[3] Twice he was defeated because he was ignorant of the local conditions and used the wrong method. Later he changed his method; first he investigated the situation, and he familiarized himself with the maze of roads, then he broke up the alliance between the Li, Hu and Chu Villages and sent his men in disguise into the enemy camp to lie in wait, using a stratagem similar to that of the Trojan Horse in the foreign story. And on the third occasion he won. There are many examples of materialist dialectics in Shui Hu Ch'uan, of which the episode of the three attacks on Chu Village is one of the best. Lenin said:

> ...in order really to know an object we must embrace, study, all its sides, all connections and "mediations". We shall never achieve this completely, but the demand for all-sidedness is a safeguard against mistakes and rigidity.[4]

1. See. ibid.
2. Wei Cheng (A.D. 580-643) was a statesman and historian of the Tang Dynasty.
3. Shui Hu Chuan (Heroes of the Marshes), a famous 14th century Chinese novel, describes a peasant war towards the end of the Northern Sung Dynasty. Chu Village was in the vicinity of Liangshanpo, where Sung Chiang, leader of the peasant uprising and hero of the novel, established his base. Chu Chao-feng, the head of this village, was a despotic landlord.
4. V. I. Lenin, "Once Again on the Trade Unions, the Present Situation and the Mistakes of Trotsky and Bukharin", Selected Works, Eng. ed., International Publishers, New York, 1943, Vol. IX, p. 66.

We should remember his words. To be superficial means to consider neither the characteristics of a contradiction in its totality nor the characteristics of each of its aspects; it means to deny the necessity for probing deeply into a thing and minutely studying the characteristics of its contradiction, but instead merely to look from afar and, after glimpsing the rough outline, immediately to try to resolve the contradiction (to answer a question, settle a dispute, handle work, or direct a military operation). This way of doing things is bound to lead to trouble. The reason the dogmatist and empiricist comrades in China have made mistakes lies precisely in their subjectivist, onesided and superficial way of looking at things. To be one-sided and superficial is at the same time to be subjective. For all objective things are actually interconnected and are governed by inner laws, but instead of undertaking the task of reflecting things as they really are some people only look at things one-sidedly or superficially and they know neither their interconnections nor their inner laws, and so their method is subjectivist.

Not only does the whole process of the movement of opposites in the development of a thing, both in their interconnections and in each of the aspects, have particular features to which we must give attention, but each stage in the process has its particular features to which we must give attention too.

The fundamental contradiction in the process of development of a thing and the essence of the process determined by this fundamental contradiction will not disappear until the process is completed; but in a lengthy process the conditions usually differ at each stage. The reason is that, although the nature of the fundamental contradiction in the process of development of a thing and the essence of the process remain unchanged, the fundamental contradiction becomes more and more intensified as it passes from one stage to another in the lengthy process. In addition, among the numerous major and minor contradictions which are determined or influenced by the fundamental contradictions, some become intensified, some are temporarily or partially resolved or mitigated, and some new ones emerge; hence the process is marked by stages. If people do not pay attention to the stages in the process of development of a thing, they cannot deal with its contradictions properly.

For instance, when the capitalism of the era of free competition developed into imperialism, there was no change in the class nature of the two classes in fundamental contradiction, namely, the proletariat and the bourgeoisie, or in the capitalist essence of society; however, the contradiction between these two classes became intensified, the contradiction between monopoly and non-monopoly capital emerged, the contradiction between the colonial powers and the colonies became intensified, the contradiction among the capitalist countries resulting from their uneven development manifested itself with particular sharpness, and thus there arose the special stage of capitalism, the stage of imperialism. Leninism is the Marxism of the era of imperialism and proletarian revolution precisely because Lenin and Stalin have correctly explained these contradictions and correctly formulated the theory and tactics of the proletarian revolution for their resolution.

Take the process of China's bourgeois-democratic revolution, which began with the Revolution of 1911; it, too, has several distinct stages. In particular, the revolution in its period of bourgeois leadership and the revolution in its period of proletarian leadership represent two vastly different historical stages. In other words, proletarian leadership has fundamentally changed the whole face of the revolution, has brought about a new alignment of classes, given rise to a tremendous upsurge in the peasant revolution, imparted thoroughness to the revolution against imperialism and feudalism, created the possibility of the transition from the democratic revolution to the socialist revolution, and so on. None of these was possible in the period

703

when the revolution was under bourgeois leadership. Although no change has taken place in the nature of the fundamental contradiction in the process as a whole, *i.e.*, in the anti-imperialist, anti-feudal, democratic-revolutionary nature of the process (the opposite of which is its semi-colonial and semi-feudal nature), nonetheless this process has passed through several stages of development in the course of more than twenty years; during this time many great events have taken place — the failure of the Revolution of 1911 and the establishment of the regime of the Northern warlords, the formation of the first national united front and the revolution of 1924-27, the break-up of the united front and the desertion of the bourgeoisie to the side of the counter-revolution, the wars among the new warlords, the Agrarian Revolutionary War, the establishment of the second national united front and the War of Resistance Against Japan. These stages are marked by particular features such as the intensification of certain contradictions (*e.g.*, the Agrarian Revolutionary War and the Japanese invasion of the four northeastern provinces), the partial or temporary resolution of other contradictions (*e.g.*, the destruction of the Northern warlords and our confiscation of the land of the landlords), and the emergence of yet other contradictions (*e.g.*, the conflicts among the new warlords, and the landlords' recapture of the land after the loss of our revolutionary base areas in the south).

In studying the particularities of the contradictions at each stage in the process of development of a thing, we must not only observe them in their interconnections or their totality, we must also examine the two aspects of each contradiction.

For instance, consider the Kuomintang and the Communist Party. Take one aspect, the Kuomintang. In the period of the first united front, the Kuomintang carried out Sun Yat-sen's Three Great Policies of alliance with Russia, co-operation with the Communist Party, and assistance to the peasants and workers; hence it was revolutionary and vigorous, it was an alliance of various classes for the democratic revolution. After 1927, however, the Kuomintang changed into its opposite and became a reactionary bloc of the landlords and big bourgeoisie. After the Sian Incident in December 1936, it began another change in the direction of ending the civil war and co-operating with the Communist Party for joint opposition to Japanese imperialism. Such have been the particular features of the Kuomintang in the three stages. Of course, these features have arisen from a variety of causes. Now take the other aspect, the Chinese Communist Party. In the period of the first united front, the Chinese Communist Party was in its infancy; it courageously led the revolution of 1924-27 but revealed its immaturity in its understanding of the character, the tasks and the methods of the revolution, and consequently it became possible for Chen Tu-hsiuism, which appeared during the latter part of this revolution, to assert itself and bring about the defeat of the revolution. After 1927, the Communist Party courageously led the Agrarian Revolutionary War and created the revolutionary army and revolutionary base areas; however, it committed adventurist errors which brought about very great losses both to the army and to the base areas. Since 1935 the Party has corrected these errors and has been leading the new united front for resistance to Japan; this great struggle is now developing. At the present stage, the Communist Party is a Party that has gone through the test of two revolutions and acquired a wealth of experience. Such have been the particular features of the Chinese Communist Party in the three stages. These features, too, have arisen from a variety of causes. Without studying both these sets of features we cannot understand the particular relations between the two parties during the various stages of their development, namely, the establishment of a united front, the break-up of the united front, and the establishment of another united front. What is even more fundamental for the study of the particular features of the two parties is the examination of the class basis of the two parties and the resultant contradictions which have arisen between each party and other forces at different periods. For instance, in the period of its first co-operation with the Communist Party, the Kuomintang stood in contradiction to foreign imperialism and was therefore anti-imperialist; on the other hand, it stood in contradiction to the great masses of the people within the country — although in words it promised many benefits to the working people, in fact it gave them little or nothing. In the period when it carried out the anti-Communist war, the Kuomintang collaborated with imperialism and feudalism against the great masses of the people and wiped out all the gains they had won in the revolution, and thereby intensified its contradictions with them. In the present period of the anti-Japanese war, the Kuomintang stands in contradiction to Japanese imperialism and wants co-operation with the Communist Party, without however relaxing its struggle against the Communist Party and the people or its oppression of them. As for the Communist Party, it has always, in every period, stood with the great masses of the people against imperialism and feudalism, but in the present period of the anti-Japanese war, it has adopted a moderate policy towards the Kuomintang and the domestic feudal forces because the Kuomintang has expressed itself in favour of resisting Japan. The above circumstances have resulted now in alliance between the two parties and now in struggle between them, and even during the periods of alliance there has been a complicated state of simultaneous alliance and struggle. If we do not study the particular features of both aspects of the contradiction, we shall fail to understand not only the relations of each party with the other forces, but also the relations between the two parties.

It can thus be seen that in studying the particularity of any kind of contradiction — the contradiction in each form of motion of matter, the contradiction in each of its processes of development, the two aspects of the contradiction in each process, the contradiction at each stage of a process, and the two aspects of the contradiction at each stage — in studying the particularity of all these contradictions, we must not be subjective and arbitrary but must analyse it concretely. Without concrete analysis there can be no knowledge of the particularity of any contradiction. We must always remember Lenin's words, the concrete analysis of concrete conditions.

Marx and Engels were the first to provide us with excellent models of such concrete analysis.

When Marx and Engels applied the law of contradiction in things to the study of the socio-historical process, they discovered the contradiction between the productive forces and the relations of production, they discovered the contradiction between the exploiting and exploited classes and also the resultant contradiction between the economic base and its superstructure (politics, ideology, etc.), and they discovered how these contradictions inevitably lead to different kinds of social revolution in different kinds of class society.

When Marx applied this law to the study of the economic structure of capitalist society, he discovered that the basic contradiction of this society is the contradiction between the social character of production and the private character of ownership. This contradiction manifests itself in the contradiction between the organized character of production in individual enterprises and the anarchic character of production in society as a whole. In terms of class relations, it manifests itself in the contradiction between the bourgeoisie and the proletariat.

Because the range of things is vast and there is no limit to their development, what is universal in one context becomes particular in another. Conversely, what is particular in one context becomes universal in another. The contradiction in the capitalist system between the social character of production and the private ownership of the means

707

of production is common to all countries where capitalism exists and develops; as far as capitalism is concerned, this constitutes the universality of contradiction. But this contradiction of capitalism belongs only to a certain historical stage in the general development of class society; as far as the contradiction between the productive forces and the relations of production in class society as a whole is concerned, it constitutes the particularity of contradiction. However, in the course of dissecting the particularity of all these contradictions in capitalist society, Marx gave a still more profound, more adequate and more complete elucidation of the universality of the contradiction between the productive forces and the relations of production in class society in general.

Since the particular is united with the universal and since the universality as well as the particularity of contradiction is inherent in everything, universality residing in particularity, we should, when studying an object, try to discover both the particular and the universal and their interconnection, to discover both particularity and universality and also their interconnection within the object itself, and to discover the interconnections of this object with the many objects outside it. When Stalin explained the historical roots of Leninism in his famous work, *The Foundations of Leninism,* he analysed the international situation in which Leninism arose, analysed those contradictions of capitalism which reached their culmination under imperialism, and showed how these contradictions made proletarian revolution a matter for immediate action and created favourable conditions for a direct onslaught on capitalism. What is more, he analysed the reasons why Russia became the cradle of Leninism, why tsarist Russia became the focus of all the contradictions of imperialism, and why it was possible for the Russian proletariat to become the vanguard of the international revolutionary proletariat. Thus, Stalin analysed the universality of contradiction in

708

imperialism, showing why Leninism is the Marxism of the era of imperialism and proletarian revolution, and at the same time analysed the particularity of tsarist Russian imperialism within this general contradiction, showing why Russia became the birthplace of the theory and tactics of proletarian revolution and how the universality of contradiction is contained in this particularity. Stalin's analysis provides us with a model for understanding the particularity and the universality of contradiction and their interconnection.

On the question of using dialectics in the study of objective phenomena, Marx and Engels, and likewise Lenin and Stalin, always enjoin people not to be in any way subjective and arbitrary but, from the concrete conditions in the actual objective movement of these phenomena, to discover their concrete contradictions, the concrete position of each aspect of every contradiction and the concrete interrelations of the contradictions. Our dogmatists do not have this attitude in study and therefore can never get anything right. We must take warning from their failure and learn to acquire this attitude, which is the only correct one in study.

The relationship between the universality and the particularity of contradiction is the relationship between the general character and the individual character of contradiction. By the former we mean that contradiction exists in and runs through all processes from beginning to end; motion, things, processes, thinking — all are contradictions. To deny contradiction is to deny everything. This is a universal truth for all times and all countries, which admits of no exception. Hence the general character, the absoluteness of contradiction. But this general character is contained in every individual character; without individual character there can be no general character. If all individual character were removed, what general character would remain? It is because each contradiction is particular that individual character arises. All individual character exists conditionally and temporarily, and hence is relative.

This truth concerning general and individual character, concerning absoluteness and relativity, is the quintessence of the problem of contradiction in things; failure to understand it is tantamount to abandoning dialectics.

IV. THE PRINCIPAL CONTRADICTION AND THE PRINCIPAL ASPECT OF A CONTRADICTION

There are still two points in the problem of the particularity of contradiction which must be singled out for analysis, namely, the principal contradiction and the principal aspect of a contradiction.

There are many contradictions in the process of development of a complex thing, and one of them is necessarily the principal contradiction whose existence and development determine or influence the existence and development of the other contradictions.

For instance, in capitalist society the two forces in contradiction, the proletariat and the bourgeoisie, form the principal contradiction. The other contradictions, such as those between the remnant feudal class and the bourgeoisie, between the peasant petty bourgeoisie and the bourgeoisie, between the proletariat and the peasant petty bourgeoisie, between the non-monopoly capitalists and the monopoly capitalists, between bourgeois democracy and bourgeois fascism, among the capitalist countries and between imperialism and the colonies, are all determined or influenced by this principal contradiction.

In a semi-colonial country such as China, the relationship between the principal contradiction and the non-principal contradictions presents a complicated picture.

When imperialism launches a war of aggression against such a country, all its various classes, except for some traitors, can temporarily unite in a national war against imperialism. At such a time, the contradiction between imperialism and the country concerned becomes the principal contradiction, while all the contradictions among the various classes within the country (including what was the principal contradiction, between the feudal system and the great masses of the people) are temporarily relegated to a secondary and subordinate position. So it was in China in the Opium War of 1840, the Sino-Japanese War of 1894 and the Yi Ho Tuan War of 1900, and so it is now in the present Sino-Japanese War.

But in another situation, the contradictions change position. When imperialism carries on its oppression not by war, but by milder means — political, economic and cultural — the ruling classes in semi-colonial countries capitulate to imperialism, and the two form an alliance for the joint oppression of the masses of the people. At such a time, the masses often resort to civil war against the alliance of imperialism and the feudal classes, while imperialism often employs indirect methods rather than direct action in helping the reactionaries in the semi-colonial countries to oppress the people, and thus the internal contradictions become particularly sharp. This is what happened in China in the Revolutionary War of 1911, the Revolutionary War of 1924-27, and the ten years of Agrarian Revolutionary War after 1927. Wars among the various reactionary ruling groups in the semi-colonial countries, e.g., the wars among the warlords in China, fall into the same category.

When a revolutionary civil war develops to the point of threatening the very existence of imperialism and its running dogs, the domestic reactionaries, imperialism often adopts other methods in order to maintain its rule; it either tries to split the revolutionary front from within or sends armed forces to help the domestic reactionaries directly. At such a time, foreign imperialism and domestic reaction stand quite openly at one pole while the masses of the people stand at the other pole, thus forming the principal contradiction which determines or influences the development of the other contradictions. The assistance given by various capitalist

711

countries to the Russian reactionaries after the October Revolution is an example of armed intervention. Chiang Kai-shek's betrayal in 1927 is an example of splitting the revolutionary front.

But whatever happens, there is no doubt at all that at every stage in the development of a process, there is only one principal contradiction which plays the leading role.

Hence, if in any process there are a number of contradictions, one of them must be the principal contradiction playing the leading and decisive role, while the rest occupy a secondary and subordinate position. Therefore, in studying any complex process in which there are two or more contradictions, we must devote every effort to finding its principal contradiction. Once this principal contradiction is grasped, all problems can be readily solved. This is the method Marx taught us in his study of capitalist society. Likewise Lenin and Stalin taught us this method when they studied imperialism and the general crisis of capitalism and when they studied the Soviet economy. There are thousands of scholars and men of action who do not understand it, and the result is that, lost in a fog, they are unable to get to the heart of a problem and naturally cannot find a way to resolve its contradictions.

As we have said, one must not treat all the contradictions in a a process as being equal but must distinguish betwen the principal and the secondary contradictions, and pay special attention to grasping the principal one. But, in any given contradiction, whether principal or secondary, should the two contradictory aspects be treated as equal? Again, no. In any contradiction the development of the contradictory aspects is uneven. Sometimes they seem to be in equilibrium, which is however only temporary and relative, while unevenness is basic. Of the two contradictory aspects, one must be principal and the other secondary. The principal aspect is the one playing the leading role in the contradiction. The nature of a thing is determined mainly by

712

the principal aspect of a contradiction, the aspect which has gained the dominant position.

But this situation is not static; the principal and the non-principal aspects of a contradiction transform themselves into each other and the nature of the thing changes accordingly. In a given process or at a given stage in the development of a contradiction, A is the principal aspect and B is the non-principal aspect; at another stage or in another process the roles are reversed — a change determined by the extent of the increase or decrease in the force of each aspect in its struggle against the other in the course of the development of a thing.

We often speak of "the new superseding the old". The supersession of the old by the new is a general, eternal and inviolable law of the universe. The transformation of one thing into another, through leaps of different forms in accordance with its essence and external conditions — this is the process of the new superseding the old. In each thing there is contradiction between its new and its old aspects, and this gives rise to a series of struggles with many twists and turns. As a result of these struggles, the new aspect changes from being minor to being major and rises to predominance, while the old aspect changes from being major to being minor and gradually dies out. And the moment the new aspect gains dominance over the old, the old thing changes qualitatively into a new thing. It can thus be seen that the nature of a thing is mainly determined by the principal aspect of the contradiction, the aspect which has gained predominance. When the principal aspect which has gained predominance changes, the nature of a thing changes accordingly.

In capitalist society, capitalism has changed its position from being a subordinate force in the old feudal era to being the dominant force, and the nature of society has accordingly changed from feudal to capitalist. In the new, capitalist era, the feudal forces changed from their former dominant position to a subordinate one, gradually dying out.

713

Such was the case, for example, in Britain and France. With the development of the productive forces, the bourgeoisie changes from being a new class playing a progressive role to being an old class playing a reactionary role, until it is finally overthrown by the proletariat and becomes a class deprived of privately owned means of production and stripped of power, when it, too, gradually dies out. The proletariat, which is much more numerous than the bourgeoisie and grows simultaneously with it but under its rule, is a new force which, initially subordinate to the bourgeoisie, gradually gains strength, becomes an independent class playing the leading role in history, and finally seizes political power and becomes the ruling class. Thereupon the nature of society changes and the old capitalist society becomes the new socialist society. This is the path already taken by the Soviet Union, a path that all other countries will inevitably take.

Look at China, for instance. Imperialism occupies the principal position in the contradicton in which China has been reduced to a semi-colony, it oppresses the Chinese people, and China has been changed from an independent country into a semi-colonial one. But this state of affairs will inevitably change; in the struggle between the two sides, the power of the Chinese people which is growing under the leadership of the proletariat will inevitably change China from a semi-colony into an independent country, whereas imperialism will be overthrown and old China will inevitably change into New China.

The change of old China into New China also involves a change in the relation between the old feudal forces and the new popular forces within the country. The old feudal landlord class will be overthrown, and from being the ruler it will change into being the ruled; and this class, too, will gradually die out. From being the ruled the people, led by the proletariat, will become the rulers. Thereupon, the nature of Chinese society will change and the old, semi-

714

colonial and semi-feudal society will change into a new democratic society.

Instances of such reciprocal transformation are found in our past experience. The Ching Dynasty which ruled China for nearly three hundred years was overthrown in the Revolution of 1911, and the revolutionary *Tung Meng Hui* under Sun Yat-sen's leadership was victorious for a time. In the Revolutionary War of 1924-27, the revolutionary forces of the Communist-Kuomintang alliance in the south changed from being weak to being strong and won victory in the Northern Expedition, while the Northern warlords who once ruled the roost were overthrown. In 1927, the people's forces led by the Communist Party were greatly reduced numerically under the attacks of Kuomintang reaction, but with the elimination of opportunism within their ranks they gradually grew again. In the revolutionary base areas under Communist leadership, the peasants have been transformed from being the ruled to being the rulers, while the landlords have undergone a reverse transformation. It is always so in the world, the new displacing the old being superseded by the new, the old being eliminated to make way for the new, and the new emerging out of the old.

At certain times in the revolutionary struggle, the difficulties outweigh the favourable conditions and so constitute the principal aspect of the contradiction and the favourable conditions constitute the secondary aspect. But through their efforts the revolutionaries can overcome the difficulties step by step and open up a favourable new situation; thus a difficult situation yields place to a favourable one. This is what happened after the failure of the revolution in China in 1927 and during the Long March of the Chinese Red Army. In the present Sino-Japanese War, China is again in a difficult position, but we can change this and fundamentally transform the situation as between China and Japan. Conversely, favourable conditions can be transformed into difficulty if the revolutionaries make mistakes. Thus the victory of the revolution of 1924-27 turned into defeat. The revolutionary base areas wich grew up in the southern provinces after 1927 had all suffered defeat by 1934.

When we engage in study, the same holds good for the contradiction in the passage from ignorance to knowledge. At the very beginning of our study of Marxism, our ignorance of or scanty acquaintance with Marxism stands in contradiction to knowledge of Marxism. But by assiduous study, ignorance can be transformed into knowledge, scanty knowledge into substantial knowledge, and blindness in the application of Marxism into mastery of its application.

Some people think that this is not true of certain contradictions. For instance, in the contradiction between the productive forces and the relations of production, the productive forces are the principal aspect; in the contradiction between theory and practice, practice is the principal aspect; in the contradiction between the economic base and the superstructure, the economic base is the principal aspect; and there is no change in their respective positions. This is the mechanical materialist conception, not the dialectical materialist conception. True, the productive forces, practice and the economic base generally play the principal and decisive role; whoever denies this is not a materialist. But it must also be admitted that in certain conditions, such aspects as the relations of production, theory and the superstructure in turn manifest themselves in the principal and decisive role. When it is impossible for the productive forces to develop without a change in the relations of production, then the change in the relations of production plays the principal and decisive role. The creation and advocacy of revolutionary theory plays the principal and decisive role in those times of which Lenin said, "Without revolutionary theory there can be no revolutionary movement."[1] When a task, no matter which, has to be performed, but there is as yet no guiding line, method, plan or policy, the principal and

1. V. I. Lenin, "What Is to Be Done?", *Collected Works*, Eng. ed., FLPH, Moscow, 1961, Vol. V, p. 369.

decisive thing is to decide on a guiding line, method, plan or policy. When the superstructure (politics, culture, etc.) obstructs the development of the economic base, political and cultural changes become principal and decisive. Are we going against materialism when we say this? No. The reason is that while we recognize that in the general development of history the material determines the mental and social being determines social consciousness, we also — and indeed must — recognize the reaction of mental on material thing, of social consciousness on social being and of the superstructure on the economic base. This does not go against materialism; on the contrary, it avoids mechanical materialism and firmly upholds dialectical materialism.

In studying the particularity of contradiction, unless we examine these two facets — the principal and the non-principal contradictions in a process, and the principal and the non-principal aspects of a contradiction — that is, unless we examine the distinctive character of these two facets of contradiction. we shall get bogged down in abstractions, be unable to understand contradiction concretely and consequently be unable to find the correct method of resolving it. The distinctive character or particularity of these two facets of contradiction represents the unevenness of the forces that are in contradiction. Nothing in this world develops absolutely evenly; we must oppose the theory of even development or the theory of equilibrium. Moreover, it is these concrete features of a contradiction and the changes in the principal and non-principal aspects of a contradiction in the course of its development that manifest the force of the new superseding the old. The study of the various states of unevenness in contradictions, of the principal and non-principal contradictions and of the principal and the non-principal aspects of a contradiction constitutes an essential method by which a revolutionary political party correctly determines its strategic and tactical policies both in political and in military affairs. All Communists must give it attention.

V. THE IDENTITY AND STRUGGLE OF THE ASPECTS OF A CONTRADICTION

When we understand the universality and the particularity of contradiction, we must proceed to study the problem of the identity and struggle of the aspects of a contradiction.

Identity, unity, coincidence, interpenetration, interpermeation, interdependence (or mutual dependence for existence), interconnection or mutual co-operation — all these different terms mean the same thing and refer to the following two points: first, the existence of each of the two aspects of a contradiction in the process of the development of a thing presupposes the existence of the other aspect, and both aspects coexist in a single entity; second, in given conditions, each of the two contradictory aspects transforms itself into its opposite. This is the meaning of identity.

Lenin said:

> *Dialectics* is the teaching which shows how *opposites* can be and how they happen to be (how they become) *identical* — under what conditions they are identical, transforming themselves into one another, — why the human mind should take these opposites not as dead, rigid, but as living, conditional, mobile, transforming themselves into one another.[1]

What does this passage mean?

The contradictory aspects in every process exclude each other, struggle with each other and are in opposition to each other. Without exception, they are contained in the process of development of all things and in all human thought. A simple process contains only a single pair of opposites, pairs of opposites are in contradiction to one another. That

1. V. I. Lenin, "Conspectus of Hegel's *The Science of Logic*", *Collected Works*, Russ. ed., Moscow, 1958, Vol. XXXVIII, pp. 97-98.

is how all things in the objective world and all human thought are constituted and how they are set in motion.

This being so, there is an utter lack of identity or unity. How then can one speak of identity or unity?

The fact is that no contradictory aspect can exist in isolation. Without its opposite aspect, each loses the condition for its existence. Just think, can any one contradictory aspect of a thing or of a concept in the human mind exist independently? Without life, there would be no death; without death, there would be no life. Without "above", there would be no "below"; without "below", there would be no "above". Without misfortune, there would be no good fortune; without good fortune, there would be no misfortune. Without facility, there would be no difficulty; without difficulty, there would be no facility. Without landlords, there would be no tenant-peasants; without tenant-peasants, there would be no landlords. Without the bourgeoisie, there would be no proletariat; without the proletariat, there would be no bourgeoisie. Without imperialist oppression of nations, there would be no colonies or semi-colonies; without colonies or semi-colonies, there would be no imperialist oppression of nations. It is so with all opposites; in given conditions, on the one hand they are opposed to each other, and on the other are interconnected, interpenetrating, interpermeating and interdependent, and this character is described as identity. In given conditions, all contradictory aspects possess the character of non-identity and hence are described as being in contradiction. But they also possess the character of identity and hence are interconnected. This is what Lenin means when he says that dialectics studies "how *opposites* can be . . . *identical*". How then can they be identical? Because each is the condition for the other's existence. This is the first meaning of identity.

But is it enough to say merely that each of the contradictory aspects is the condition for the other's existence, that there is identity between them and that consequently they can coexist in a single entity? No, it is not. The matter

719

does not end their dependence on each other for their existence; what is more important is their transformation into each other. That is to say, in given conditions, each of the contradictory aspects within a thing transforms itself into its opposite, changes its position to that of its opposite. This is the second meaning of the identity of contradiction.

Why is there identity here, too? You see, by means of revolution the proletariat, at one time the ruled, is transformed into the ruler, while the bourgeoisie, the erstwhile ruler, is transformed into the ruled and changes its position to that originally occupied by its opposite. This has already taken place in the Soviet Union, as it will take place throughout the world. If there were no interconnection and identity of opposites in given conditions, how could such a change take place?

The Kuomintang, which played a certain positive role at a certain stage in modern Chinese history, became a counter-revolutionary party after 1927 because of its inherent class nature and because of imperialist blandishments (these being the conditions); but it has been compelled to agree to resist Japan because of the sharpening of the contradiction between China and Japan and because of the Communist Party's policy of the united front (these being the conditions). Things in contradiction change into one another, and herein lies a definite identity.

Our agrarian revolution has been a process in which the landlord class owning the land is transformed into a class that has lost its land, while the peasants who once lost their land are transformed into small holders who have acquired land, and it will be such a process once again. In given conditions having and not having, acquiring and losing, are interconnected; there is identity of the two sides. Under socialism, private peasant ownership is transformed into the public ownership of socialist agriculture; this has already taken place in the Soviet Union, as it will take place everywhere else. There is a bridge leading from private property to public property, which in philosophy is called identity, or transformation into each other, or interpenetration.

To consolidate the dictatorship of the proletariat or the dictatorship of the people is in fact to prepare the conditions for abolishing this dictatorship and advancing to the higher stage when all state systems are eliminated. To establish and build the Communist Party is in fact to prepare the conditions for the elimination of the Communist Party and all political parties. To build a revolutionary army under the leadership of the Communist Party and to carry on revolutionary war is in fact to prepare the conditions for the permanent elimination of war. These opposites are at the same time complementary.

War and peace, as everybody knows, transform themselves into each other. War is transformed into peace; for instance, the First World War was transformed into the post-war peace, and the civil war in China has now stopped, giving place to internal peace. Peace is transformed into war; for instance, the Kuomintang-Communist co-operation was transformed into war in 1927, and today's situation of world peace may be transformed into a second world war. Why is this so? Because in class society such contradictory things as war and peace have an identity in given conditions.

All contradictory things are interconnected; not only do they coexist in a single entity in given conditions, but in other given conditions, they also transform themselves into each other. This is the full meaning of the identity of opposites. This is what Lenin meant when he discussed "how they happen to be (how they become) *identical* — under what conditions they are identical, transforming themselves into one another".

Why is it that "the human mind should take these opposites not as dead, rigid, but as living, conditional, mobile, transforming themselves into one another"? Because that is just how things are in objective reality. The fact is that the unity or identity of opposites in objective things is not dead or rigid, but is living, conditional, mobile, temporary and relative; in given conditons, every contradictory aspect transforms itself into its opposite. Reflected in man's thinking, this becomes the Marxist world outlook of materialist dialectics. It is only the reactionary ruling classes of the past and present and the metaphysicians in their service who regard opposites not as living, conditional, mobile and transforming themselves into one another, but as dead and rigid, and they propagate this fallacy everywhere to delude the masses of the people, thus seeking to perpetuate their rule. The task of Communists is to expose the fallacies of the reactionaries and metaphysicians, to propagate the dialectics inherent in things, and so accelerate the transformation of things and achieve the goal of revolution.

In speaking of the identity of opposites in given conditions, what we are referring to is real and concrete opposites and the real and concrete transformations of opposites into one another. There are innumerable transformations in mythology, for instance, Kua Fu's race with the sun in *Shan Hai Ching*,[1] Yi's shooting down of nine suns in *Huai Nan Tzu*,[2] the Monkey King's seventy-two metamorphoses in *Hsi Yu Chi*,[3] the numerous episodes of ghosts and foxes metamorphosed into human beings in the *Strange Tales of Liao Chai*,[4] etc. But these legendary transformations of

1. *Shan Hai Ching (Book of Mountains and Seas)* was written in the era of the Warring States (403-221 B.C.). In one of its fables Kua Fu, a superman, pursued and overtook the sun. But he died of thirst, whereupon his staff was transformed into the forest of Teng.
2. Yi is one of the legendary heroes of ancient China, famous for his archery. According to a legend in *Huai Nan Tzu*, compiled in the 2nd century B.C., there were ten suns in the sky in the days of Emperor Yao. To put an end to the damage to vegetation caused by these scorching suns, Emperor Yao ordered Yi to shoot them down. In another legend recorded by Wang Yi (2nd century A.D.), the archer is said to have shot down nine of the ten suns.
3. *Hsi Yu Chi (Pilgrimage to the West)* is a 16th century novel, the hero of which is the monkey god Sun Wu-kung. He could miraculously change at will into seventy-two different shapes, such as a bird, a tree and a stone.
4. The *Strange Tales of Liao Chai*, written by Pu Sung-ling in the 17th century, is a well-known collection of 431 tales, mostly about ghosts and fox spirits.

opposites are not concrete changes reflecting concrete contradictions. They are naive, imaginary, subjectively conceived transformations conjured up in men's minds by innumerable real and complex transformations of opposites into one another. Marx said, "All mythology masters and dominates and shapes the forces of nature in and through the imagination; hence it disappears as soon as man gains mastery over the forces of nature."[1] The myriads of changes in mythology (and also in nursery tales) delight people because they imaginatively picture man's conquest of the forces of nature, and the best myths possess "eternal charm", as Marx put it; but myths are not built out of the concrete contradictions existing in given conditions and therefore are not a scientific reflection of reality. That is to say, in myths or nursery tales the aspects constituting a contradiction have only an imaginary identity, not a concrete identity. The scientific reflection of the identity in real transformations is Marxist dialectics.

Why can an egg but not a stone be transformed into a chicken? Why is there identity between war and peace and none between war and a stone? Why can human beings give birth only to human beings and not to anything else? The sole reason is that the identity of opposites exists only in necessary given conditions. Without these necessary given conditions there can be no identity whatsoever.

Why is it that in Russia in 1917 the bourgeois-democratic February Revolution was directly linked with the proletarian socialist October Revolution, while in France the bourgeois revolution was not directly linked with a socialist revolution and the Paris Commune of 1871 ended in failure? Why is it, on the other hand, that the nomadic system of Mongolia and Central Asia has been directly linked with socialism? Why is it that the Chinese revolution can avoid a capitalist future and be directly linked with socialism with-

1. Karl Marx, "Introduction to the Critique of Political Economy". *A Contribution to the Critique of Political Economy*, Eng., ed., Chicago, 1904, pp. 310-11.

out taking the old historical road of the Western countries, without passing through a period of bourgeois dictatorship? The sole reason is the concrete conditions of the time. When certain necessary conditions are present, certain contradictions arise in the process of development of things and, moreover, the opposites contained in them are interdependent and become transformed into one another; otherwise none of this would be possible.

Such is the problem of identity. What then is struggle? And what is the relation between identity and struggle? Lenin said:

> The unity (coincidence, identity, equal action) of opposites is conditional, temporary, transitory, relative. The struggle of mutually exclusive opposites is absolute, just as development and motion are absolute.[1]

What does this passage mean?

All processes have a beginning and an end, all processes transform themselves into their opposites. The constancy of all processes is relative, but the mutability manifested in the transformation of one process into another is absolute.

There are two states of motion in all things, that of relative rest and that of conspicuous change. Both are caused by the struggle between the two contradictory elements contained in a thing. When the thing is in the first state of motion, it is undergoing only quantitative and not qualitative change and consequently presents the outward appearance of being at rest. When the thing is in the second state of motion, the quantitative change of the first state has already reached a culminating point and gives rise the dissolution of the thing as an entity and thereupon a qualitative change ensues, hence the appearance of a conspicuous change. Such unity, solidarity, combination, harmony, balance, stalemate, deadlock, rest, constancy, equilibrium, so-

1. V. I. Lenin, "On the Question of Dialectics", *Collected Works*, Russ. ed., Moscow, 1958, Vol. XXXVIII, p. 358.

lidity, attraction, etc., as we see in daily life, are all the appearances of things in the state of quantitative change. On the other hand, the dissolution of unity, that is, the destruction of this solidarity, combination, harmony, balance, stalemate, deadlock, rest, constancy, equilibrium, solidity and attraction, and the change of each into its opposite are all the appearances of things in the state of qualitative change, the transformation of one process into another. Things are constantly transforming themselves from the first into the second state of motion; the struggle of opposites goes on in both states but the contradiction is resolved through the second state. That is why we say that the unity of opposites is conditional, temporary and relative, while the struggle of mutually exclusive opposites is absolute.

When we said above that two opposite things can coexist in a single entity and can transform themselves into each other because there is identity between them, we were speaking of conditionality, that is to say, in given conditions two contradictory things can be united and can transform themselves into each other, but in the absence of these conditions, they cannot constitute a contradiction, cannot coexist in the same entity and cannot transform themselves into one another. It is because the identity of opposites obtains only in given conditions that we have said identity is conditional and relative. We may add that the struggle between opposites permeates a process from beginning to end and makes one process transform itself into another, that it is ubiquitous, and that struggle is therefore unconditional and absolute.

The combination of conditional, relative identity and unconditional, absolute struggle constitutes the movement of opposites in all things.

We Chinese often say, "Things that oppose each other also complement each other."[1] That is, things opposed to

1. The saying "Things that oppose each other also complement each other" first appeared in the *History of the Earlier Han Dynasty* by Pan Ku, a celebrated historian in the 1st century A.D. It has long been a popular saying.

each other have identity. This saying is dialectical and contrary to metaphysics. "Oppose each other" refers to the mutual exclusion or the struggle of two contradictory aspects. "Complement each other" means that in given conditions the two contradictory aspects unite and achieve identity. Yet struggle is inherent in identity and without struggle there can be no identity.

In identity there is struggle, in particularity there is universality, and in individuality there is generality. To quote Lenin, "... these *is* an absolute *in* the relative."[1]

VI. THE PLACE OF ANTAGONISM IN CONTRADICTION

The question of the struggle of opposites includes the question of what is antagonism. Our answer is that antagonism is one form, but not the only form, of the struggle of opposites.

In human history, antagonism between classes exists as a particular manifestation of the struggle of opposites. Consider the contradiction between the exploiting and the exploited classes. Such contradictory classes coexist for a long time in the same society, be it slave society, feudal society or capitalist society, and they struggle with each other; but it is not until the contradiction between the two classes develops to a certain stage that it assumes the form of open antagonism and develops into revolution. The same holds for the transformation of peace into war in class society.

Before it explodes, a bomb is a single entity in which opposites coexist in given conditions. The explosion takes place only when a new condition, ignition, is present. An analogous situation arises in all those natural phenomena

1. V. I. Lenin, "On the Question of Dialectics", *Collected Works*, Russ. ed., Moscow, 1958, Vol. XXXVIII, p. 358.

which finally assume the form of open conflict to resolve old contradictions and produce new things.

It is highly important to grasp this fact. It enables us to understand that revolutions and revolutionary wars are inevitable in class society and that without them, it is impossible to accomplish any leap in social development and to overthrow the reactionary ruling classes and therefore impossible for the people to win political power. Communists must expose the deceitful propaganda of the reactionaries, such as the assertion that social revolution is unnecessary and impossible. They must firmly uphold the Marxist-Leninist theory of social revolution and enable the people to understand that social revolution is not only entirely necessary but also entirely practicable, and that the whole history of mankind and the triumph of the Soviet Union have confirmed this scientific truth.

However, we must make a concrete study of the circumstances of each specific struggle of opposites and should not arbitrarily apply the formula discussed above to everything. Contradiction and struggle are universal and absolute, but the methods of resolving contradictions, that is, the forms of struggle, differ according to the differences in the nature of the contradictions. Some contradictions are characterized by open antagonism, others are not. In accordance with the concrete development of things, some contradictions which were originally non-antagonistic develop into anatagonistic ones, while others which were originally antagonistic develop into non-antagonistic ones.

As already mentioned, so long as classes exist, contradictions between correct and incorrect ideas in the Communist Party are reflections within the Party of class contradictions. At first, with regard to certain issues, such contradictions may not manifest themselves as antagonistic. But with the development of the class struggle, they may grow and become antagonistic. The history of the Communist Party of the Soviet Union shows us that the contradictions between the correct thinking of Lenin and Stalin and the fallacious thinking of Trotsky, Bukharin and others did not at first manifest themselves in an antagonistic form, but that later they did develop into antagonism. There are similar cases in the history of the Chinese Communist Party. At first the contradictions between the correct thinking of many of our Party comrades and the fallacious thinking of Chen Tu-hsiu, Chang Kuo-tao and others also did not manifest themselves in an antagonistic form, but later they did develop into antagonism. At present the contradiction between correct and incorrect thinking in our Party does not manifest itself in an antagonistic form, and if comrades who have committed mistakes can correct them, it will not develop into antagonism. Therefore, the Party must on the one hand wage a serious struggle against erroneous thinking, and on the other give the comrades who have committed errors ample opportunity to wake up. This being the case, excessive struggle is obviously inappropriate. But if the people who have committed errors persist in them and aggravate them, there is the possibility that this contradiction will develop into antagonism.

Economically, the contradiction between town and country is an extremely antagonistic one both in capitalist society, where under the rule of the bourgeoisie the towns ruthlessly plunder the countryside, and in the Kuomintang areas in China, where under the rule of foreign imperialism and the Chinese big comprador bourgeoisie the towns most rapaciously plunder the countryside. But in a socialist country and in our revolutionary base areas, this antagonistic contradiction has changed into one that is non-antagonistic; and when communist society is reached it will be abolished.

Lenin said, "Antagonism and contradiction are not at all one and the same. Under socialism, the first will disappear, the second will remain."[1] That is to say, antagonism is one

1. V. I. Lenin, "Remarks on N. I. Bukharin's *Economics of the Transitional Period*", *Selected Works*, Russ. ed., Moscow-Leningrad, 1931, Vol. XI, p. 357.

form, but not the only form, of the struggle of opposites; the formula of antagonism cannot be arbitrarily applied everywhere.

VII. CONCLUSION

We may now say a few words to sum up. The law of contradiction in things, that is, the law of the unity of opposites, is the fundamental law of nature and of society and therefore also the fundamental law of thought. It stands opposed to the metaphysical world outlook. It represents a great revolution in the history of human knowledge. According to dialectical materialism contradiction is present in all processes of objectively existing things and of subjective thought and permeates all these processes from beginning to end; this is the universality and absoluteness of contradiction. Each contradiction and each of its aspects have their respective characteristics; this is the particularity and relativity of contradiction. In given conditions, opposites possess identity, and consequently can coexist in a single entity and can transform themselves into each other; this again is the particularity and relativity of contradiction. But the struggle of opposites is ceaseless, it goes on both when the opposites are coexisting and when they are transforming themselves into each other, and becomes especially conspicuous when they are transforming themselves into one another; this again is the universality and absoluteness of contradiction. In studying the particularity and relativity of contradiction, we must give attention to the distinction between the principal contradiction and the non-principal contradictions and to the distinction between the principal aspect and the non-principal aspect of a contradiction; in studying the universality of contradiction and the struggle of opposites in contradiction, we must give attention to the distinction between the different forms of struggle. Otherwise we shall make mistakes. If, through study, we achieve a real understanding of the essentials explained above, we shall be able to demolish dogmatist ideas which are contrary to the basic principles of Marxism-Leninism and detrimental to our revolutionary cause, and our comrades with practical experience will be able to organize their experience into principles and avoid repeating empiricist errors. These are a few simple conclusions from our study of the law of contradiction.

Yu-lan Fung

YU-LAN FUNG (1895-   ). Professor Yu-lan Fung, the author of the standard *History of Chinese Philosophy* (1952-53) and *The New Rational Philosophy* (1939), is not only a historian of philosophy but a systematic philosopher whose way of thinking and conceiving reality shows striking analogies to George Santayana's views, though he is firmly rooted in the traditions of Confucianism. He has revived the rational philosophy of the brothers Ch'eng Ming-tâo and Ch'eng I Ch'uan (1032-1086 and 1033-1107, respectively) in order to "continue" but not to "follow" them. He distinguishes two realms, that of truth and that of actuality. Reason, according to him, belongs to the realm of truth. It is not in or above the world but rather it is a regulating principle of everything that appears in the actual world. The realm of actuality is not created by reason; it is self-existent. Since reason cannot create, it is a principle which is neither in reason nor in the actual world that brings things into real existence. This principle is called "the Vital Principle of the True Prime Unit." The essences of the realm of truth which are not the causes but the models of the real things can be known only by the objective and systematic studies, by means of inductive method and experimental logic. In this way, Fung has purified Neo-Confucianism from the Buddhist elements which had pervaded it in previous times. As early as 1939, he offered a materialistic interpretation of history. Recently he has stated that the Tâoist idea of reversion is dialectic, that the new rational philosophy is a twilight of Western philogophy, and that Marxism-Leninism is to modern medicine as traditional Chinese philosophy is to medieval medicine.

731

Philosophy of Contemporary China

From *Actes du Huitième Congrès Internationale de Philosophie,* 1934.

CHINA is now at a present that is not the natural growth of her past, but something forced upon her against her will. In the completely new situation that she has to face, she has been much bewildered. In order to make the situation more intelligible and to adapt to it more intelligently, she has to interpret sometimes the present in terms of the past and sometimes the past in terms of the present. In other words, she has to connect the new civilization that she has to face with the old that she already has and to make them not alien but intelligible to each other. Besides interpretation, there is also criticism. In interpreting the new civilization in terms of the old, or the old in terms of the new, she cannot help but to criticize sometimes the new in the light of the old, and sometimes the old in the light of the new. Thus the interpretation and criticism of civilizations is the natural product in China of the meeting of the West and the East and is what has interested the Chinese mind and has constituted the main current of Chinese thought during the last fifty years.

It may be noticed that the interpretation and criticism of the civilizations new and old, within the last fifty years, differ in different periods according to the degree of the knowledge or of the ignorance of the time regarding the new civilization that comes from outside. Generally speaking there have been three periods. The first period is marked with the ill-fated political reformation with the leadership of Kan Yu-wei under the Emperor Kuang-su in 1898.

Kan Yu-wei was a scholar of one of the Confucianist schools, known as the Kung Yang school. According to this school, Confucius was a teacher with divine personality. He devised a scheme that would cover all stages of human progress. There are mainly three stages. The first is the stage of disorder; the second, the stage of progressive peace; and the third, the stage of great peace. In the stage of disorder, every one is for one's own country. In the stage of progressive peace, all the civilized countries are united in one. In the stage of great peace, all men are civilized and humanity is united in one harmonious whole. Confucius knew beforehand all these that are to come. He devised accordingly three systems of social organization. According to Kan Yu-wei, the communication between the East and the West and the political and social reformations in Europe and America show that men are progressing from the stage of disorder to the higher stage, the stage of progressive peace. Most, if not all, of the political and social institutions of the West are already implied in the teaching of Confucius. Kan Yu-wei was the leader of the New Movement at his time. But in his opinion, what he was doing was not the adoption of the new civilization of the West, but rather the realization of the old teaching of Confucius. He wrote many Commentaries to the Confucian classics, reading into them his new ideas. Besides these he also wrote a book entitled *The Book on The Great Unity*, in which he gave a concrete picture of the utopia that will become a fact in the third stage of human progress according to the Confucianist scheme. Although the nature of this book is so bold and revolutionary that it will startle even most of the utopian writers, Kan Yu-wei himself was not an utopian. He insisted that the programme he set forth in his book cannot be put into practice except in the highest stage of human civilization, the last stage of human progress. In his practical political programme he insisted to have a constitutional monarchy.

One of the colleagues of Kan Yu-wei in the New Movement of that time was Tan Tse-tung, who was a more phil-

733

osophical thinker. He wrote a book entitled *On Benevolence* in which he also taught the Confucianist teaching of the three stages of human progress. According to him although Confucius set forth the general scheme of the three stages, most of the teaching of Confucius was for the stage of disorder. It is the reason why Confucius was often misunderstood as the champion of traditional institutions and conventional morality. The Christian teaching of universal love and the equality of men before God is quite near the Confucian teaching for the stage of progressive peace. The teaching that is near the Confucian teaching for the last stage of human progress is Buddhism which goes beyond all human distinctions and conventional morality.

The main spirit of this time is that the leaders were not antagonistic to the new civilization that came from the West, nor did they lack appreciation of its value. But they appreciated its value only in so far as it fits in the imaginary Confucian scheme. They interpreted the new in terms of, and criticized it in the light of, the old. It is to be noticed that the philosophical justification of the Revolution of 1911 with the result of the establishment of the Republic was mainly taken from Chinese philosophy. The saying of Mencius that "the people is first important, the country the second, the sovereign unimportant" was much quoted and interpreted. The teaching of the European revolutionary writers such as Rousseau also played its role, but people often thought that they are right because they agree with Mencius.

The second period is marked with the New Culture Movement which reached its climax in 1919. In this period the spirit of the time is the criticism of the old in the light of the new. Chen Tu-siu and Hui Shih were the leaders of the criticism. The latter philosopher wrote *An Outline of the History of Chinese Philosophy*, of which only the first part was published. It is in fact a criticism of Chinese philosophy rather than a history of it. The two most influential schools of Chinese philosophy, Confucianism and Taoism, were

734

much criticized and questioned from a utilitarian and pragmatic point of view. He is for individual liberty and development and therefore he found that Confucianism is wrong in the teaching of the subordination of the individual to his sovereign and his father, to his state and his family. He is for the spirit of struggle and conquering nature and therefore he found that Tāoism is wrong in the teaching of enjoying nature. In reading his book one cannot but feel that in his opinion the whole Chinese civilization is entirely on the wrong track.

In reaction there was a defender of the old civilization. Soon after the publication of Hui Shih's *History*, another philosopher, Lu Wang, published another book entitled *The Civilizations of the East and the West and their Philosophies*. In this book Liang Shu-ming maintained that every civilization represents a way of living. There are mainly three ways of living: the way of aiming at the satisfaction of desires, that at the limitation of desires and that at the negation of desires. If we choose the first way of living, we have the European civilization; if the second, the Chinese civilization; if the third, the Indian civilization. These three civilizations should represent three stages of human progress. Men should at first try their best to know and to conquer nature. After having secured sufficient ground for their place in nature, they should limit their desires and know how to be content. But there are certain inner contradictions in life that can not be settled within life. Therefore the last resort of humanity is the way of negating desires, negating life. The Chinese and the Indians are wrong not in the fact that they produced civilizations that seem to be useless. Their civilizations are of the first order and in them there are some things that humanity is bound to adopt. The Chinese and the Indians are wrong in the fact that they adopted the second and the third ways of living without living through the first. They are on the right track but at the wrong time. Thus the defender of the East also thought there must be something wrong in it.

His book therefore is also an expression of the spirit of his time.

The third period is marked with the Nationalist Movement of 1926 with the result of the establishment of the National Government. This movement was originally undertaken with the combined force of the Nationalists and the Communists. Sun Yat-sen, the leader of the Revolution of 1911 and of this movement, held the communistic society as the highest social ideal. But he was not a communist in that he was against the theory of class struggle and the dictatorship of the proletariat. He thought that the ideal society should be the product of love, not that of hatred. The Nationalists and the Communists soon split. With this movement the attitude of the Chinese towards the new civilization of the West takes a new turn. The new civilization of the West as represented in its political and economical organizations, once considered as the very perfection of human institutions, is now to be considered as but one stage of human progress. History is not closed; it is in the making. And what is now considered as the final goal that history is achieving, the peace of the world and the unity of man, looks more congenial to the old East than to the modern West. In fact, if we take the Marxian theory of human progress without its economical explanation of it, we see that between it and the teaching of the Kung Yang school as represented by Kan Yu-wei there is some similarity. Indeed Tan Tse-tung, in his book *On Benevolence,* knowing nothing about either Hegel or Marx, also pointed out what the Marxists may call the dialectical nature of human progress. He pointed out that there is some similarity between the future ideal society and the original primitive ones. But when we attain to the ideal, we are not returning to the primitive, we advance.

Is the spirit of this third period the same as that of the first? No, while the intellectual leaders of the first period were interested primarily in interpreting the new in terms of the old, we are now also interested in interpreting the old in terms of the new. While the intellectual leaders of the second period were interested in pointing out the difference between the East and the West, we are now interested in seeing what is common to them. We hold that if there is any difference between the East and the West, it is the product of different circumstances. In different circumstances men have different responses. If we see the response with the circumstances that produce it, we may probably say with Hegel that what is actual is also reasonable. Thus we are not interested now in criticizing one civilization in the light of the other, as the intellectual leaders of the first and the second periods did, but in illustrating the one with the other so that they may both be better understood. We are now interested in the mutual interpretation of the East and the West rather than their mutual criticism. They are seen to be the illustrations of the same tendency of human progress and the expressions of the same principle of human nature. Thus the East and the West are not only connected, they are united.

The same spirit is also seen in the work in technical philosophy. The Chinese and European philosophical ideas are compared and studied not with any intention of judging which is necessarily right and which is necessarily wrong, but simply with the interest of finding what the one is in terms of the other. It is expected that before long we will see that the European philosophical ideas will be supplemented with the Chinese intuition and experience, and the Chinese philosophical ideas will be clarified by the European logic and clear thinking.

These are what I consider to be characteristic of the spirit of time in the three periods within the last fifty years in Chinese history. If we are to apply the Hegelian dialectic, we may say that the first period is the thesis, the second the antithesis, and the third the synthesis.

737